# Taming the Tide of Capital Flows

# Taming the Tide of Capital Flows

## A Policy Guide

Atish R. Ghosh, Jonathan D. Ostry, and Mahvash S. Qureshi

The MIT Press
Cambridge, Massachusetts
London, England

This book was set in Palatino by Westchester Publishing Services. Printed and bound in the United States of America.

Library of Congress Cataloging-in-Publication Data
Names: Ghosh, Atish R., author. | Ostry, Jonathan David, 1962– author. | Qureshi, Mahvash Saeed, author.
Title: Taming the tide of capital flows : a policy guide / Atish R. Ghosh, Jonathan D. Ostry, and Mahvash S. Qureshi.
Description: Cambridge, MA : MIT Press, [2017] | Includes bibliographical references and index.
Identifiers: LCCN 2017018184 | ISBN 9780262037167 (hardcover : alk. paper)
Subjects: LCSH: Capital movements.
Classification: LCC HG3891 .G48 2017 | DDC 332/.0424—dc23
LC record available at https://lccn.loc.gov/2017018184

10  9  8  7  6  5  4  3  2  1

To our families

# Contents

# Preface

In mid-2009, even as the global financial crisis continued to ravage the world economy, capital flows to emerging market economies appeared to rebound, prompting us to think about how policy makers should respond to a possible resurgence of capital inflows. The issue seemed particularly pertinent given that several emerging markets, especially those in Eastern Europe, had recently experienced a capital flows–induced boom-bust cycle of epic proportions. When we embarked upon our research, we had no plans to write a book—let alone spend so much time over the next several years thinking about the issue. The further we delved into the topic, however, the more we realized that coming up with a coherent policy framework that took account of both the recipient country's interests, and respected multilateral considerations, was no mean task. Moreover, as the continued volatility of capital flows (the U.S. sovereign downgrade and taper tantrum episodes being prime examples) underscored, the question of how emerging markets should manage cross-border flows was likely to be relevant for many years to come.

We were well aware, of course, that we were not operating in a vacuum—the IMF has a long history with capital account management and capital controls (which we trace in this book)—but little could prepare us for how controversial the topic would turn out to be. The prevailing view in official circles (as well as much of academia) was that emerging markets should simply allow their currencies to appreciate in the face of capital inflows, and tighten fiscal policy if there was a risk of economic overheating. Foreign exchange intervention was recommended only to counter very short-term market volatility; as for capital controls, they were an anathema.

Our starting point was rather different. Policy makers have at their disposal potentially five tools: monetary and exchange rate policies, fiscal policy, macroprudential measures, and capital controls. There is no *a priori* reason to rule out the use of any of these instruments, or to impose a "moral hierarchy" among them. Despite this (what we considered to be) eminently reasonable approach, our first paper (an IMF Staff Position Note, titled, *Capital Inflows: The Role of Controls*) issued in January 2010 proved highly controversial, mainly because it recognized that capital controls on inflows might have a legitimate place within the policy maker's tool kit. While the paper also offered some preliminary evidence that emerging markets that had limited more risky inflows prior to the global financial crisis fared better during the crisis, it did little to satisfy the critics.

A second paper (*Managing Capital Inflows: What Tools to Use?*) issued in April 2011 was no less contentious (and amid concerns that the paper might be construed as representing the official "position" of the IMF staff, the title of the entire publication series was changed from "Staff Position Notes" to "Staff Discussion Notes"). The essential insight of that paper was that in open economies, many prudential measures—particularly those limiting foreign currency exposures—are economically equivalent to capital inflow controls. (For example, higher reserve requirements on banks' liabilities in foreign currency, while technically not a capital control because it applies equally to deposits of residents and nonresidents, could have the same impact on capital flows as an inflow control if most foreign currency liabilities of banks are to nonresidents.) This realization was important because in the post–global financial crisis landscape, macroprudential measures were all the rage. But if their effects on capital flows are largely equivalent to capital controls, then one cannot logically be in favor of macroprudential measures and against the use of capital inflow controls.

Following these two papers, we explored other dimensions of policies to manage capital flows including their effectiveness; the role of foreign exchange intervention to manage the exchange rate in inflation-targeting countries; and multilateral aspects of capital controls. As our research progressed, we realized that not only is it extremely important to carefully manage inflow surges if a crisis is to be avoided when flows ultimately recede, but also that there were deep-rooted misconceptions about certain policy tools—especially inflow controls—that often prevent their use in practice, even for prudential purposes. Existing policy advice thus tends to *pro*scribe more than it *pre*scribes. Moreover, a holistic framework that guides policy makers on when, how, and in what combination to use the various policy instruments to mitigate the untoward consequences of capital inflows was lacking. Furnishing policy makers with such a vade mecum is the purpose of this book.

Though the issues we cover here were often contentious, the debates vigorous, and the arguments heated, we have had enormous (intellectual) fun working on this book. We owe a debt of gratitude to the many friends and colleagues with whom we had numerous discussions, as well as to the participants in the many seminars and conferences around the world where we presented our work. Our special thanks to Olivier Blanchard who first encouraged us to work on this topic, and to Marcos Chamon, Anton Korinek, and Naotaka Sugawara—with whom we co-authored several research papers over the years on some of the topics covered in this book, and benefited enormously from their insights. It goes without saying that the views presented in this book are our own, and do not necessarily reflect those of our friends and colleagues, or of the IMF. We are also very grateful to Jane MacDonald and Emily Taber at the MIT Press, and to Chifundo Moya at the IMF for their diligent editorial support, without which this book would not have been possible. Finally, our immense thanks to our families for their endless support, patience, and encouragement as we endeavored to write this book.

# I Overview

# 1 Introduction

*The loans from the creditor country begin with a modest amount, then increase and proceed crescendo. They are likely to be made in exceptionally large amounts toward the culminating stage of a period of activity and speculative upswing, and during that stage become larger from month to month so long as the upswing continues. With the advent of crisis they are at once cut down sharply, even cease entirely.*

—Frank Taussig (1928, 130)

*Moreover, it may well be asked whether we can take it for granted that a return to freedom of exchanges is really a question of time. Even if the reply were in the affirmative, it is safe to assume that after a period of freedom the regime of control will be restored as a result of the next economic crisis.*

—Paul Einzig (1934, 8)

*Loose funds may sweep around the world, disorganizing all business. Nothing is more certain than that the movement of capital funds must be regulated—which, in itself, will involve far-reaching departures from laissez-faire arrangements.*

—John Maynard Keynes (1941)[1]

The global financial crisis has been a rude reminder of the volatility of capital flows to emerging market economies (EMEs). Flows to emerging markets, which had peaked at US$680 billion in 2007, turned sharply negative at the onset of the crisis in late 2008, throwing many of these countries into financial disarray and forcing massive external adjustment on them.[2] Exceptionally low interest rates and diminished growth prospects in advanced economies then fueled a resurgence of

---

1. "Post-War Currency Policy," cited in Johnson and Moggridge (1980, 31).
2. Data refer to a sample of fifty-three emerging market economies, listed in the data appendix. "Capital flows" here refers to net financial flows and excludes other investment liabilities of the general government (typically official loans) and reserve assets. Since it is traditional to refer to the financial side of the balance of payments as the capital

capital to EMEs in 2009, till the United States sovereign debt downgrade in 2011 spurred a flight to quality—ironically, into the US treasuries. A fresh surge of capital flows to EMEs began in 2012, until "taper talk" by the Federal Reserve sent capital scurrying back to advanced economies in mid-2013. Despite some differentiation across countries, several emerging markets experienced renewed inflows in 2014 that lasted until mid-2015, when the prospect of the US Federal Reserve's interest rate "liftoff" and the growth slowdown in China again weakened flows to EMEs significantly.

This dizzying experience makes one wonder whether emerging markets are necessarily at the mercy of global events or whether they can put in place policy measures—short of imposing financial autarky—during the inflow phase that will soften the blow when capital flows subsequently recede or reverse. Identifying such measures is the purpose of this book which, we believe, is the first to offer a modern and comprehensive vade mecum for emerging market policy makers contending with large and volatile capital flows.

The volatility of capital flows, especially to the emerging markets of the day, is not a new phenomenon—boom-bust cycles have been apparent since the earliest years of financial globalization. But particularly in the twentieth century, governments have not always taken a laissez-faire attitude to such flows. Indeed, both John Maynard Keynes and Harry Dexter White, the principal architects of Bretton Woods, envisaged the regulation of private cross-border capital flows (especially speculative hot-money flows) as a permanent feature of the post-war international financial landscape. And for the first thirty years or so after the war, this was largely the case: except in a handful of countries, governments often restricted their citizens' ability to either borrow or invest abroad. Following the collapse of Bretton Woods, however, capital account restrictions began to be lifted in advanced economies, and by the early-1980s, most had liberalized both inflows and outflows. In emerging market and developing countries, meanwhile, capital controls became increasingly discredited—largely because controls on capital *outflows* were frequently adopted as props for poor macroeconomic management, hence becoming associated with high inflation, financial repression, money-financed deficits, overvalued currencies, and generally weak economic performance.

account, throughout this book the terms "financial flows" and "capital flows" are used interchangeably.

While opening the capital account was never formally part of the package of policy reforms prescribed to emerging markets in the 1980s and 1990s (the package came to be known as the Washington Consensus), doing so was very much in the spirit of liberalization and deregulation that characterized the movement, as was the belief in subjecting government policies to the discipline of the international capital markets.[3] Thus, as emerging market governments succeeded in stabilizing their economies after the high-inflation 1970s and 1980s, they too started to liberalize their financial markets, both domestically and externally—often sweeping away capital *inflow* measures that had been imposed for prudential reasons, alongside outflow controls. The result, to borrow a phrase, was "Good-Bye Financial Repression, Hello Financial Crash" (Diaz-Alejandro 1985). Several emerging markets experienced massive capital inflows, consumption booms, and credit expansion in the late 1970s and early 1980s, followed by equally massive busts that imposed severe economic, social, and political costs.

Notwithstanding this experience, the trend toward capital account liberalization in emerging markets continued, albeit interrupted by the 1997 Asian crisis (arguably itself the result of premature liberalization), which put paid to the idea of giving the International Monetary Fund (IMF) jurisdiction over the capital account and the mandate to promote liberalization. As late as 2007, when EMEs were experiencing one of their periodic bouts of hot-money surges, the standard policy prescription called for them to maintain open capital accounts and respond with macroeconomic (mainly fiscal) adjustment, allowing their currencies to fluctuate in the process.[4]

Fast forward to 2010 and several countries that had previously liberalized their capital accounts (such as Brazil, Colombia, Indonesia, Peru, the Philippines, and Uruguay) were reimposing capital controls to stem inflows in the wake of the historically unprecedented accommodative monetary policies of the US Federal Reserve (later joined by the European Central Bank and the Bank of Japan). Capital controls, a long-forgotten subject in academia and a taboo among mainstream policy circles, were back in the limelight. By 2011, the Group of 20's *Coherent Conclusions for the Management of Capital Flows* recognized that

---

3. See Williamson (1990, 2009) for a discussion on the Washington Consensus.
4. See, for example, remarks made by the IMF's managing director, Rodrigo de Rato, "Capital Flows in an Interconnected World," at the SEACEN Governors Conference, Bangkok, Thailand, July 28, 2007 (https://www.imf.org/external/np/speeches/2007/072807.htm; last accessed on June 2, 2017).

"capital flow management may constitute part of a broader approach to protect economies from shocks," while a year later, the IMF's *The Liberalization and Management of Capital Flows: An Institutional View* (IMF 2012a) acknowledged that capital controls form a legitimate part of the policy toolkit.[5]

What had changed in the interim? Most fundamentally, the global financial crisis of 2008–2009 had been a vivid demonstration that not all borrowing and lending decisions are rational; that financial excesses and asset price bubbles are not only possible, they are probable in the face of large capital inflows; and that the private sector can—and often does—underestimate and misprice risk. After years of being lectured on how to run their economies, and on the virtues of unfettered markets and wholesale liberalization, it was perhaps not entirely without some schadenfreude that emerging markets took note that it was the advanced economies that were at the epicenter of the biggest economic crisis since the Great Depression. Buoyed by better growth prospects than advanced economies, it was thus with a sense of empowerment that the EMEs confronted the post–global financial crisis capital-inflow surge. In particular, they considered the surge to be a largely unwanted spillover of advanced economy monetary policies—a "monetary tsunami," and one that could, moreover, reverse just as suddenly once the extraordinary monetary stimulus was withdrawn, leaving them to deal with the consequences.[6] As Guido Mantega, the Brazilian finance minister, remarked in 2011: "Capital recipient countries are experiencing both commodity inflation and currency overvaluation related to capital inflows. Faced with these combined challenges they have to resort to capital controls . . . these measures of self-defense are a legitimate response to the effects of the monetary policies adopted by reserve currency issuing countries."[7]

---

5. G20, *Coherent Conclusions for the Management of Capital Flows Drawing on Country Experiences*, as endorsed by G20 finance ministers and central bank governors, October 15, 2011 (http://www.g20.utoronto.ca/2011/2011-finance-capital-flows-111015-en.pdf; last accessed on June 2, 2017).
6. The phrase "monetary tsunami" was coined by Brazil's president, Dilma Rousseff, in remarks made at the fourth BRICS Summit, March 29, 2012 (https://www.ft.com/content/a3b88472-7982-11e1-8fad-00144feab49a; last accessed on June 2, 2017).
7. Statement made (on behalf of the constituency comprising Brazil, Colombia, the Dominican Republic, Ecuador, Guyana, Haiti, Panama, Suriname, and Trinidad and Tobago) to the International Monetary and Financial Committee, Washington, DC, April 16, 2011 (https://www.imf.org/External/spring/2011/imfc/statement/eng/bra.pdf; last accessed on June 2, 2017).

The subsequent reversal of capital flows during the US sovereign debt rating downgrade in late 2011, and the "taper tantrum" in mid-2013, vindicated emerging market policy makers, and prompted them to call on advanced-economy central banks to take greater account of the financial spillovers from their highly accommodative monetary policies. Thus, in 2014, Raghuram Rajan, governor of the Reserve Bank of India, proposed that "large country central banks, both in advanced countries and emerging markets, internalize more of the spillovers from their policies in their mandate, and [be] forced by new conventions on the 'rules of the game' to avoid unconventional policies with large adverse spillovers and questionable domestic benefits."[8] Ben Bernanke, chairman of the Federal Reserve, countered such arguments vehemently, maintaining that the growth benefits of these policies outweighed any negative repercussions through capital flows, and left emerging markets better off in net terms.[9]

With source-country responsibilities for managing capital flows still very much under debate, there is a growing realization that it is up to emerging market policy makers to protect their economies from the vicissitudes of cross-border capital flows. But the question is how? What policy tools do they have at their disposal? When should these be deployed? Is there a natural mapping between instruments and objectives? How to choose between policies that seemingly serve the same purpose? The global financial crisis has spawned a huge literature on various policies such as monetary policy (especially in the context of advanced economies); the use of macroprudential measures; and, to a lesser degree, on the use and effectiveness of foreign exchange intervention and capital controls.[10] Still lacking, however, is a coherent, comprehensive treatment that ties these elements together and addresses specifically how emerging market countries should meet the particular challenges associated with volatile capital flows. That is the purpose of this book, which draws on both theory and empirics to help answer

---

8. Remarks entitled "Competitive Monetary Easing: Is It Yesterday Once More?" made at the Brookings Institution, Washington, DC, April 10, 2014 (https://www.rbi.org.in/scripts/BS_SpeechesView.aspx?Id=886; last accessed on June 2, 2017).
9. Remarks made by Ben Bernanke, chairman of the Federal Reserve, at the Brookings Institution, Washington, DC, April 10, 2014 (https://www.brookings.edu/events/global-monetary-policy-a-view-from-emerging-markets/; last accessed on June 2, 2017).
10. See, for example, Blanchard et al. (2012) and Akerlof et al. (2014). Jeanne, Subramanian, and Williamson (2012) revisit the experience of capital account liberalization in emerging market and developing economies, and discuss the desirable level of capital account liberalization.

these questions and provide practical advice to emerging market policy makers.

Our central thesis is simple: in principle, cross-border capital flows to emerging markets have the potential to bring several benefits; in practice, however, such flows are inherently risky—though some forms may be worse than others—potentially widening macroeconomic imbalances (economic overheating, currency appreciation and loss of competitiveness, excessive credit growth) and creating balance-sheet vulnerabilities (currency, maturity, and debt-equity mismatches). As such, capital flows require active policy management, which might mean mitigating their undesirable consequences using macroeconomic (monetary, fiscal, exchange rate) and macroprudential policies, or controlling their volume and composition directly using capital account restrictions, or both.[11] By the same token, if the inflow phase is successfully managed—through the use of structural measures to steer flows toward less risky types of liabilities, and the use of macroeconomic policies, prudential measures, and capital controls for abating the cyclical component of flows and their consequences—the economy is likely to benefit from foreign capital and to remain resilient when flows recede or reverse.

## 1.1   Capital Flows: A Snapshot

Before expanding on our thesis, it is useful to establish a few facts about capital flows to emerging markets. While chapter 2 delves into greater detail on the historical evolution of cross-border capital flows, figure 1.1 provides an initial snapshot of flows to fifty-three EMEs that form the core sample of countries in this book. During the course of forty years, net capital flows to these countries grew more than tenfold in real terms: from less than US$10 billion in 1970 to a peak of US$720 billion in 2010. But EMEs have also grown impressively over this period, so total flows have generally fluctuated between 2 and 4 percent of their aggregate GDP. While these aggregates give a sense of the total supply of capital to EMEs, of greater salience for countries trying to

---

11. As discussed in section 1.2, the distinction between capital controls and macroprudential policies is not always clear-cut: prudential measures, especially, those related to foreign currency transactions may also serve to limit capital flows. Moreover, managing the consequences of inflows might affect the inflows themselves; for instance, preventing currency appreciation through foreign exchange intervention might further perpetuate inflows, while lowering the policy interest rate may reduce inflows.

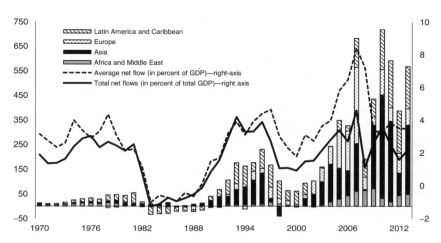

**Figure 1.1**
Net capital flows to EMEs, 1980–2013 (in billions of USD).
*Sources*: Authors' estimates based on IMF's International Financial Statistics and World Economic Outlook databases.
*Notes*: Net flows exclude other investment liabilities of the general government, and reserve asset flows. Sample comprises fifty-three emerging markets listed in the data appendix.

manage inflows is the volume of flows in percent of their *own* GDP. This statistic, which is the subject of most of our empirical analysis, shows much greater variation. The average fluctuates between a net *outflow* of 1 percent of GDP in 1983 and a net *inflow* of 8 percent of GDP in 2007.

Whether expressed in proportion of the aggregate, or the average of individual GDPs, the time series plot reveals three or four distinct peaks during the past forty years. The first peak occurs in the mid- to late 1970s, and corresponds to petrodollar recycling to developing countries to finance oil imports and ambitious public infrastructure projects (especially in Latin America). That cycle came to an abrupt end in the early 1980s, as US interest rates rose sharply in the context of the Volcker disinflation, which pushed the US economy into recession and depressed demand for developing-country exports and global commodity prices. What ensued was a lost decade for Latin America—which suffered persistent capital outflows on a net basis—until a fresh cycle of capital flows to EMEs began in the early 1990s.

During the 1990s episode, however, the predominant recipient of flows was Asia. Inflows to the region peaked in 1996, only to be followed by massive outflows during the 1997–1998 East Asian financial crisis. Flows recovered in the early 2000s; this time, the largest recipients were central and east European countries, though other regions also received substantial flows. This cycle ended with the onset of the global financial crisis in 2008, when net capital flows to EMEs switched from a peak of about US$180 billion in 2007Q2 to a net *outflow* of US$184 billion in 2008Q4. Nevertheless, flows to EMEs resumed rapidly, driven by exceptionally loose monetary policies and diminished growth prospects in advanced economies, reaching US$720 billion in 2010. Together with hiccups, such as the US sovereign downgrade, and the "taper tantrum," this most recent cycle appears to have largely ended in 2015 with the US Federal Reserve's liftoff and a general growth slowdown in emerging markets.

### 1.1.1 Dynamics of Capital Flows

The net capital inflows depicted in figure 1.1 consist of liability flows (nonresidents' acquisition of domestic assets) plus asset flows (residents' selling foreign assets and repatriating the proceeds).[12] Since these are recorded on a net basis, at any given moment either or both may be positive or negative. In the literature, liability flows and asset flows are commonly referred to as "gross inflows" and "gross outflows," respectively. We try to avoid this terminology as total inflows to an economy could equally come from nonresidents (which would show up as liability flows) or from residents (which would be recorded as asset flows). Likewise, total outflows from an economy could be driven by both nonresidents and residents. While there is considerable debate in the literature on whether it is net flows or gross flows that are important, our own sense is that, in general, net flows are associated with macroeconomic imbalances (overheating, currency appreciation, or credit growth), while gross flows—specifically, their accumulation into a *stock* of gross liabilities—are important for balance-sheet mismatches and vulnerabilities (see box 1.1 for a discussion).[13]

Traditionally, the balance of payments (BOP) of EMEs has been dominated by liability flows, though in recent years asset flows have gained importance as restrictions on residents' foreign investments (and their

---

12. This follows the IMF's *Balance of Payments Manual*, fifth edition (BPM5) convention, which is used throughout this book.

13. From a balance-sheet perspective, the stock of gross assets could equally be a cause of concern if such assets are highly risky (e.g., the subprime mortgage–backed assets held by European banks in the run-up to the global financial crisis). But from the perspective of emerging markets, it is the stock (and composition) of gross liabilities that is generally the main source of vulnerability.

**Box 1.1**
Net versus gross flows.

Traditionally, academic papers and policy debates in international economics have centered on current account imbalances and, correspondingly, on *net* capital flows.[1] Following the global financial crisis, however, several studies (e.g., Obstfeld 2010, 2012; Borio and Disyatat 2011; Borio, James, and Shin 2014; Avdjiev, McCauley, and Shin 2015) emphasize the importance of *gross* flows—indeed, a growing debate in the literature is whether it is net or gross capital flows that "matter." The answer, of course, is that both are important—albeit for different reasons. *Net flows* are relevant for macroeconomic imbalances (exchange rates; economic overheating), while *gross stocks* of liabilities (and hence gross flows from which they accumulate) matter for balance-sheet mismatches and financial vulnerabilities.[2]

We begin with some definitions. Net capital inflows are the sum of net liability flows (the purchase of domestic assets by nonresidents), and net asset flows (the sale of foreign assets and repatriation of the proceeds by residents). Because these are net, either or both may be positive or negative over any given interval of time (see box table 1.1). What are often called "gross inflows" in the literature are actually net liability flows; what are called "gross outflows" are the (negative of) net asset flows. We try to avoid the "gross flow" terminology as total inflows (or outflows) to an economy could equally come from nonresidents (which would show up as liability flows) or from residents (which would be recorded as asset flows).

**Box Table 1.1**
Net, asset, and liability flows.

| Net financial flows | Total inflows | Total outflows |
| --- | --- | --- |
| Asset flows | +(sale of foreign assets by domestic residents and repatriation of proceeds) | −(purchase of foreign assets by domestic residents) |
| Liability flows | +(purchase of domestic assets by nonresidents) | −(sale of domestic assets by nonresidents and repatriation of the proceeds) |

*Note*: The sign convention in the table follows the *Balance of Payments Manual* 5 methodology.

1. Obstfeld (2012) and Borio, James, and Shin (2014) note that the centrality of current account dates back to David Hume's view of the gold specie standard, under which current account balances were regarded as the source of cross-border (gold) flows.
2. A careful reading of some of the papers (e.g., Avdjiev, McCauley, and Shin 2015) that emphasize the importance of gross *flows* makes clear that the authors are, in fact, referring to the gross *stock* position.

**Box 1.1** (continued)

## Why Are Net Flows Relevant for Macroeconomic Imbalances?

The simple intuition is that a "dollar is a dollar." It makes no difference, in terms of the impact on the economy, whether it is a nonresident or a resident bringing it into the country. (Likewise, if the resident is bringing in a dollar, while the nonresident is taking a dollar out—or vice versa—there should be little or no impact on the economy.) Of course, if non-residents and residents put the funds to different *uses* (e.g., the nonresident chooses to finance foreign direct investment, while the resident deposits the funds in the domestic banking system or uses them to finance personal consumption), then the two flows may have a different impact. In fact, our empirical analysis in chapter 4 suggests that, while the form of the flow (FDI, portfolio debt and equity, other investment) *does* make (some) dif-ference, there is no necessary mapping between the form of the flow and its source (nonresident or resident). Accordingly, there is no statistically significant difference between the impact of nonresident (liability) and resident (asset) flows on macroeconomic variables—and it is only their sum, *net* flows, that matters for macroeconomic imbalances (overheating, currency appreciation, credit growth).

## Why Are Gross Liability Positions Relevant for Balance-Sheet Vulnerabilities?

The simple answer is that the entity that has the liabilities (the borrower) may not coincide with the entity that owns the assets. Hence, if there is a mismatch on one entity's balance sheet—for example, households have foreign currency–denominated mortgages but no source of FX income—then it is of cold comfort to them when currency depreciates that some-one else in the economy owns foreign currency assets. Consolidating balance sheets (e.g., to arrive at the country's net foreign asset position) can thus hide important vulnerabilities.

Consider South Korea, which was running current account surpluses in the run-up to the global financial crisis and had a positive net external asset position (with its stock of external assets exceeding the value of its stock of liabilities owed to nonresidents) in 2007. It was neverthe-less hit hard by the crisis because of the sectoral decomposition of its international investment position: the corporate and banking sector was a large net debtor—which affected the real economy and investor confidence—while the official sector had a positive net investment posi-tion, and made capital gains on its balance sheet (Avdjiev, McCauley, and Shin 2015).[3]

---

3. Another frequently cited example is that of cross-border bank flows and the US subprime mortgage crisis that triggered the global financial crisis. In the run-up to the crisis, European

**Box 1.1** (continued)

> When it comes to private sector's balance-sheet risks, therefore, it is the stock of gross liabilities (and their currency, maturity, debt-equity composition) that is important. Gross capital flows (i.e., asset flows and liability flows) then matter inasmuch as they measure the rate at which the respective stocks of assets and liabilities are changing (abstracting from valuation effects).
>
> ────────────────────────
>
> banks raised dollar funds by borrowing from US money-market funds, but this money flowed back to the US through purchases of securities backed by subprime mortgages. Although net flows between the US and Europe stayed small, the gross flows built vulnerabilities on the balance sheets of the European banks, hitting them hard with the collapse of the US subprime market (McGuire and von Peter 2012).

subsequent repatriation) have been liberalized (figure 1.2). Liability flows to EMEs comprise mostly foreign direct investment (FDI), which could be in the form of bonds or equity (figure 1.3[a]). Since the turn of the century, the category of "other liability flows"—which are usually cross-border bank flows or trade credits—has been of growing importance. The remainder consists of portfolio equity and portfolio bond flows, of which the latter has been dominant in recent years. On the asset side, the breakdown of flows corresponds to the foreign assets that domestic residents are buying or selling; while some emerging market corporations are undertaking greater FDI abroad, the bulk of the flows consist of "other asset flows" (i.e., bank deposits).

From figure 1.1, it is clear that EMEs periodically receive exceptionally large net inflows, or *surges*. In fact, the kernel-estimated density function of net capital flows to EMEs (in percent of their own GDP) has been shifting to the right over time, suggesting a greater occurrence of large inflow episodes over the last decade or so (figure 1.4 [a]). Moreover, the right tail of the density has also become thicker, implying that the number of EMEs experiencing large inflows has also risen. Underlying this shift toward larger net flows has been a rightward shift (larger inflows) of liabilities (figure 1.4[b]), whereas there has been a very slight leftward shift (larger outflows) of assets (figure 1.4[c]).

Liability flows and asset flows typically show a negative correlation (an increase in liability inflows is partly offset by an increase in asset outflows, and an increase in asset inflows is partly offset by an increase in liability outflows). During surges—which, for analytical purposes, we define here as net capital inflows (in percent of GDP) that lie in both

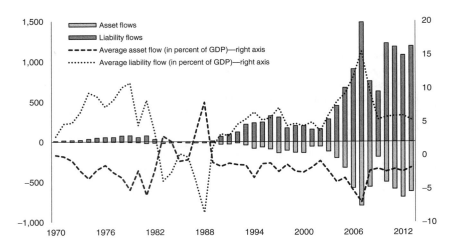

**Figure 1.2**
Asset and liability flows to EMEs, 1980–2013 (in billions of USD).
*Sources*: Authors' estimates based on IMF's International Financial Statistics and World
Economic Outlook databases.
*Notes*: Liability flows exclude other investment liabilities of the general government.
Asset flows exclude reserve assets.

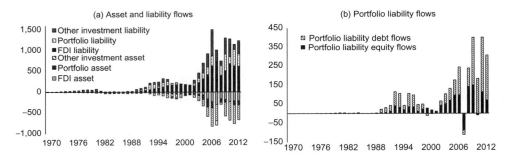

**Figure 1.3**
Flows by type to EMEs, 1980–2013 (in billions of USD).
*Sources*: Authors' estimates based on IMF's International Financial Statistics and World
Economic Outlook databases.

the country's own, and the EME sample's, top thirtieth percentile of
observations (see chapter 3)—however, the opposite is true. There is a
distinct rightward shift in the density functions of *both* asset and liability
flows, although this shift is more marked for the latter (figure 1.5). Thus,
consistent with figure 1.2, surges to emerging markets are mainly driven
by an uptick of liability flows, though the asset side could also play a role.

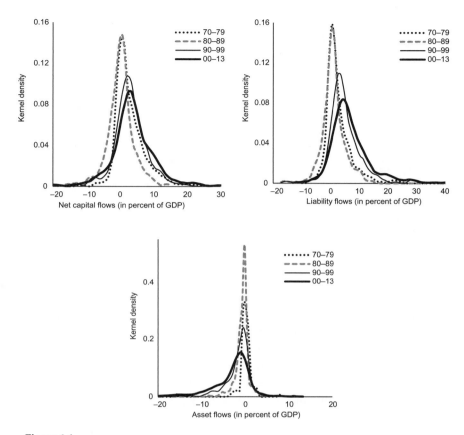

**Figure 1.4**
Distribution of capital flows to EMEs, 1970–2013 (in percent of GDP).
*Source*: Authors' estimates.
*Note*: x-axis truncated for graphical convenience.

What causes these surges? The synchronized rise and subsequent fall of flows to emerging markets in figure 1.1 suggests—and our formal analysis in chapter 3 tends to confirm—that some common global factors, such as advanced-economy (especially US) interest rates, global investors' risk aversion, and commodity prices are at play. It is also true, however, that during any given wave of capital flows to emerging markets, only about one-half of the countries in our sample receive inflow surges. Therefore, domestic factors that determine the attractiveness of the country as an investment destination must also be relevant.

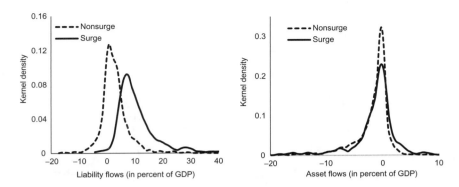

**Figure 1.5**
Distribution of flows in surges versus nonsurges, 1970–2013 (in percent of GDP).
*Source*: Authors' estimates.
*Note*: x-axis truncated for graphical convenience.

### 1.1.2  Consequences and Crashes

While capital flows can help finance much-needed investment or smooth consumption for credit-constrained individuals, they can also result in macroeconomic imbalances and balance-sheet vulnerabilities (these are explored in chapter 4). On the macroeconomic front, the main concerns are *economic overheating*: by boosting consumption and investment, inflows can stimulate aggregate demand beyond potential output, leading to positive output gaps and inflationary pressures; *currency appreciation*: as investors purchase domestic assets, they bid up the exchange rate and erode competitiveness, doing potentially lasting damage to the export sector; and domestic *credit booms*: as foreign funds are intermediated by the domestic banking system, they can lead to excessive credit growth, which in turn may fuel asset price bubbles and undermine financial stability.

As flows cumulate into stocks, moreover, they can also widen mismatches on domestic balance sheets. These may be *maturity* mismatches, whereby banks or end-borrowers (households and corporations) have long-term assets but short-term liabilities, exposing them to rollover/sudden-stop risk; *currency* mismatches, whereby the entity has foreign currency debt but repayment capacity (assets or income) in domestic currency, exposing it to the risk of currency depreciation or devaluation; or *debt-equity* mismatches, whereby the borrower's solvency may be jeopardized by a revaluation of his assets.

By widening these macroeconomic imbalances and balance-sheet mismatches, capital inflows—particularly debt flows—tend to increase the economy's vulnerability to crisis. Although this is true in general, it is especially the case following inflow surges. In fact, an EME is about three to five times more likely to suffer a currency and/or banking crisis after a surge than in more normal times. Yet not all surge episodes end in a crisis. The analysis conducted in chapter 4 suggests that global factors and domestic conditions, as well as the type of flow received over the episode, are important for determining how surges end. Specifically, surges in which macroeconomic imbalances and balance-sheet vulnerabilities are allowed to develop, and which are dominated by debt flows, are significantly more likely to end in crisis—underscoring the need to better manage the inflow phase, including in respect of the structural composition of flows that enter the economy.

## 1.2  Managing Capital Flows

National authorities have at their disposal potentially five tools to help manage capital inflows and mitigate their consequences: monetary (interest rate) policy, exchange rate (foreign exchange intervention) policy, fiscal policy, prudential measures, and capital controls. Yet the tenor of much of the policy advice given to EMEs over the years has been to continue the trend of liberalization (thus abjuring capital controls), to refrain from foreign exchange intervention (and allow the exchange rate to act as a shock absorber), and to tighten fiscal policy during inflow surges. Our philosophy, by contrast, is that policy makers should make full use of their available tool kit. In chapters 5–7, therefore, we discuss these policy tools in detail, and elaborate how—in our view—they fit together to address various macroeconomic and balance-sheet concerns.[14]

---

14. A potential sixth policy tool when contending with an inflow surge is the relaxation of controls on capital outflows—which could have an impact on the total volume of net flows and hence on the exchange rate and other macroeconomic variables. However, the direction of that impact is unclear. On the one hand, liberalizing capital outflows can reduce net inflows as some of the inflows are offset by outflows. On the other hand, greater assurance that capital can be repatriated may make the country a more attractive destination for nonresident and domestic investors. Moreover, since most EMEs have liberalized capital outflows, the scope for further policy action in this regard tends to be limited.

## 1.2.1   The Policy Tool Kit

The central bank's most commonly used instrument is the policy interest rate; and, with the exception of those with formal fixed exchange
rate regimes, most EME central banks have adopted inflation-targeting
(IT) frameworks. There is considerable debate about whether IT necessarily requires a freely floating exchange rate to maintain the central
bank's credibility. Early adopters of IT in advanced economies certainly
seemed to have thought so, but few EMEs can afford to be as indifferent
to exchange rate movements as advanced economies generally (though
not always) tend to be. Although we are sympathetic to the notion that
a central bank that does not communicate clearly its objectives and
policies will undermine its credibility, we would not agree with those
who argue that inflation-targeting central banks should not use sterilized intervention for fear of jeopardizing the credibility of their inflation target. Using a formal model, we show in chapter 6 that there is
no contradiction between IT and foreign exchange (FX) intervention—
on the contrary, willingness to intervene in the FX markets can actually
enhance the credibility of the central bank's IT framework. Hence, among
macroeconomic measures to respond to capital flows, the central bank
typically has both monetary policy and exchange rate (FX intervention)
policy at its disposal.

Tightening fiscal policy—in the sense of changing aggregate expenditure or taxation—is more problematic. Since discretionary measures
require legislative approval, there are typically long leads and lags; and
since fiscal policy is not under the control of the central bank, coordination with monetary policy is often difficult. In practice, therefore, except
for allowing automatic stabilizers to operate, the scope for quickly
implementing fiscal measures in the face of capital inflows is limited.
Perhaps that is why, despite being the most frequently given policy
advice to EMEs contending with capital inflows, fiscal policy is the
least-used instrument in practice (as documented in chapter 8). In this
book, therefore, fiscal policy is not our focus.

Among "unconventional" policies, we distinguish between capital
controls and prudential measures. Capital controls are commonly defined
as measures that limit the cross-border movement of capital by virtue of
the *residency* of parties to the transaction.[15] Typical measures applied on

---

15. There is no universally accepted legal definition of capital controls. In its Code of
Liberalisation of Capital Movements, the Organisation of Economic Co-operation and
Development (OECD) considers measures to be capital controls subject to liberalization
obligations if they discriminate between residents and nonresidents.

inflows include price-based restrictions (such as taxes or unremunerated reserve requirements on flows from nonresidents), or quantitative/ administrative restrictions (such as special licensing/reporting requirements, quantitative limits, or even outright bans). These controls may be economy-wide, or sector-specific (usually, the financial sector), or industry-specific (normally strategic industries such as defense or airlines). They may apply to all flows, or may differentiate by the flow's type (debt, equity, direct investment), duration (short-term vs. medium- and long-term), or currency denomination (domestic vs. foreign). A further distinction can be made between long-standing, *structural* capital controls that are part of the capital account regime and are not varied cyclically in response to the flows and ebbs of capital; and *cyclical* capital controls that are typically price-based restrictions whose rate is varied in response to the magnitude of flows.

Prudential measures generally apply to regulated financial institutions—mainly banks, but possibly also to other financial entities. These measures could be imposed for micro- or macroprudential reasons: microprudential measures seek to ensure the soundness of individual financial institutions; macroprudential measures aim to contain systemic risks and maintain the stability of the financial system as a whole.[16] The latter are thus the focus of attention here.[17]

Prudential measures can be distinguished according to whether they apply to the *liability* side of banks' balance sheets (such as reserve or liquidity requirements), or to the *asset* side (e.g., maximum loan-to-value [LTV] or debt-to-income [DTI] ratios, concentration limits, etc.). They can be further divided according to whether or not they discriminate on the basis of the currency denomination of the transaction:

• *Currency-based ("FX-related") prudential measures* discriminate based on the currency of the transaction (but not the residency of the parties to the transaction).[18] Typical examples of such measures are limits on

---

16. The actual measure—e.g., a maximum loan-to-value ratio on home mortgages—may be the same whether imposed for micro- or macroprudential reasons. In the former case, the intent would be to safeguard the balance sheet of the individual bank; in the latter case, more typically, the purpose would be to prevent overheating of the housing sector.

17. Traditionally, financial regulation took the form of microprudential policy, but the global financial crisis has underscored the importance of adopting a system-wide perspective that complements microprudential policies in order to prevent the build-up of macroeconomic vulnerabilities that could potentially destabilize several financial institutions simultaneously and threaten the financial system as a whole (IMF 2013a).

18. If a currency-based prudential measure also discriminates on the basis of residency, then it is treated as a capital control.

banks' open FX position (as a proportion of their capital); limits (or additional risk weights) on banks' investments in FX assets (e.g., loans to borrowers who lack a natural hedge); and higher reserve requirements (RRs) on FX liabilities.

• *Other (nondiscriminatory) prudential measures* are intended to reduce systemic risk generally—for example, by restraining the aggregate (or sector-specific) growth of lending by the domestic financial system—without discriminating on the basis of the residency of the parties or the currency denomination of the transaction. Typical measures include maximum LTV ratios, limits on domestic credit growth, asset classification and provision rules, sectoral (or borrower) limits on loan concentration, dynamic loan-loss provisions, and countercyclical capital requirements.

While capital controls are, by design, intended either to reduce the aggregate volume of capital inflows or to shift their composition toward less risky forms of liabilities (possibly, though not necessarily, affecting the total volume as well), prudential measures are designed to reduce financial vulnerabilities—including, but not exclusively, those associated with capital inflows. As a by-product, therefore, prudential measures, especially currency-based measures, might reduce the volume of (at least some types of) inflows, even if that is not their design intent.[19] In what follows, we often lump residency-based capital controls and currency-based prudential measures together, as both are likely to deter the cross-border movement of capital. We usually reserve the term "macroprudential" for measures that discriminate neither on the basis of residency nor on the basis of currency, and that are unlikely to have a direct impact on capital flows.

How prevalent are these various measures? Figure 1.6 shows the use of prudential measures in our sample as a whole, and by region. Among currency-based prudential measures, the most common is open FX position limits on banks, imposed by most emerging markets (the main exception being currency board countries, which often exempt exposures to the anchor currency). Prohibitions or limits in lending locally in FX are the next most common measure, employed by 70 percent of

---

19. It is for this reason that in recent policy discourse, capital controls and currency-based prudential measures that may limit capital flows have been collectively referred to as capital flow management measures, or CFMs (IMF 2012a). The classification of a particular measure as a CFM, however, requires an assessment of the country-specific circumstances and a "judgment as to whether the measure is, in fact, designed to limit capital flows"—which may not always be a straightforward task.

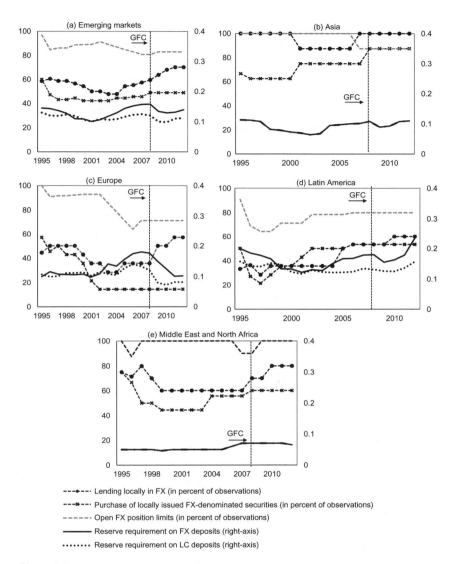

**Figure 1.6**
Prevalence of prudential measures in EMEs, 1995–2012.
*Sources*: Authors' estimates based on IMF's *Annual Report on Exchange Arrangements and Exchange Restrictions*, and Frederico, Vegh, and Vulletin (2014).
*Notes*: Values for reserve requirements (measures on the right-axis) are cross-country averages (depending on data availability). For Asia, and the Middle East and Africa, a single reserve requirement exists. For Asia, the drop in the percentage of countries with an open FX position limit in 2007 is the result of Malaysia's abolishing its net open-position limit on licensed onshore banks in April 2007. GFC = global financial crisis. LC = local currency.

the EMEs in our sample, with use increasing markedly since the global financial crisis. Cyclically varying reserve requirements are also widely used by emerging markets, and their average intensity across countries tends to correspond strongly with capital flows (increasing with inflows, and vice versa). In general, reserve requirements on both local and foreign currency deposits increased in the wake of the 2006–2007 surge and as flows rebounded to EMEs following the global financial crisis.

Virtually all countries in our sample impose some form of capital control on inflows (figure 1.7)—although, in a few instances, these are only restrictions on nonresidents (or foreigners) investing in certain strategic industries.[20] The average intensity of the inflow controls (measured on a crude scale from 0 to 1) diminished in the mid-2000s, rose during the 2006–2007 inflow surge to emerging markets, and then increased further with the post-2009 resumption of flows to EMEs. (The crudeness of the indices makes it difficult to distinguish between structural and cyclical measures for individual countries.) Regionally, Asian EMEs are the most likely to employ capital controls and prudential measures, followed by Latin America and then emerging Europe. Indeed, European emerging markets were the most aggressive in terms of liberalizing inflows and reducing prudential measures prior to the global financial crisis—they were also the hardest-hit in the crisis. Conversely, countries that had such measures in place in the run-up to the global financial crisis, fared significantly better during the crisis.[21]

### 1.2.2  Elements of the Policy Response

Armed with these various macroeconomic and unconventional policy tools, how should emerging markets manage capital inflows? At a conceptual level, there are two elements to the policy response. The first is *structural*: long-standing, acyclical measures to discourage highly volatile flows that are of little productive use to the economy, or to reduce especially risky transactions. As explained below, theory suggests, and empirics confirm, that certain types of flows—generally, short-term, foreign currency–denominated debt or debt-like instruments—have fewer benefits and pose greater risks to the recipient economy. To discourage such flows, capital controls (such as a tax on short-term borrowing, with exemptions for, e.g., trade finance) might usefully be applied. Similarly, higher capital charges or an outright ban on FX-denominated mortgages

---

20. Many advanced economies also limit foreign participation in strategic industries such as defense, airlines (or transportation), and banking.
21. See, for example, Chamon, Ghosh, and Kim (2012).

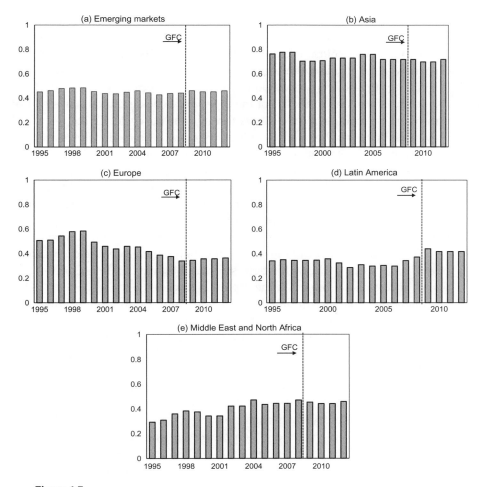

**Figure 1.7**
Prevalence of capital controls in EMEs, 1995–2012.
*Source*: Authors' estimates based on IMF's *Annual Report on Exchange Arrangements and Exchange Restrictions* (various issues).
*Notes*: Values are cross-country averages (depending on data availability). Capital inflow controls index ranges from 0 (no controls) to 1 (controls on all types of inflows). GFC = global financial crisis.

to households who cannot demonstrate earnings in foreign currency would be an example of a structural prudential measure intended to discourage or even eliminate a type of transaction that has proven to be especially risky in many emerging markets. Such structural measures (together with strong supervision of the financial sector) have a crucial role in enhancing the resilience of the economy to fickle capital flows by improving the composition of flows throughout the cycle. Of course, it may be difficult for the country to identify *ex ante* the riskier flows and to adopt narrowly targeted structural measures because the riskiness of the flow will depend on the circumstances facing the country, including the extent of its existing stock of risky liabilities. The authorities' tolerance for risk, moreover, might depend on the country's need for external financing. When there is a dearth of available funds, the country may be willing to accept even the more risky forms of liabilities; when there is a surfeit, there is less reason to do so. In general, therefore, the optimal policy framework will involve both structural and cyclical measures— that is, measures calibrated to the capital flow cycle.

This book considers in detail the *cyclical* response to large inflows. As noted above, capital inflows can widen macroeconomic imbalances: inflation and overheating of the economy, currency overvaluation, and excessive credit growth. Against these three imbalances—which are largely (though not completely) related to the total volume of capital inflows—policy makers also have three macroeconomic tools: the policy rate, sterilized intervention, and macroprudential measures (typically nondiscriminatory).[22] Our basic argument, laid out in chapters 5–6, is that all three tools should be employed, geared to their primary objectives (the interest rate for inflation, FX intervention for the exchange rate, macroprudential policies for domestic credit growth).[23] To the extent that their primary objectives are not jeopardized, they may also be used to address the other imbalances (for instance, if the economy is not overheating, then the policy interest rate could be lowered to bolster sterilized intervention in countering currency appreciation). With three possible imbalances and three instruments, there is a natural

22. The empirical evidence documented in chapter 4 shows that certain types of flows, particularly debt flows, are more prone to creating macroeconomic imbalances than, for example, FDI flows.

23. Interactions between the effects of these tools on their targets, together with their possible (positive or negative) impact on the volume of capital inflows, means that the various policy-making agencies (central bank, macroprudential regulator, ministry of finance) within the economy need to coordinate their actions carefully.

assignment or mapping between macroeconomic objectives and instruments. In this scheme, provided these macroeconomic tools are available and sufficiently effective to achieve their objectives at reasonable cost, there is little role for capital controls to manage the overall volume of flows. Instead capital controls can be reserved for altering the composition of inflows toward less risky types of liabilities. (In practice, however, capital controls may serve a dual role: to regulate the volume of flows as a backstop for macroeconomic tools when these are unavailable, ineffective, or too costly; and to alter the composition of flows away from the riskiest types of liabilities.)

What makes certain types of liabilities more risky? The riskiness of a liability is related to the magnitude of the real transfer the debtor must effect during times of stress, namely during output declines or sudden stops in capital flows. Thus, from the debtor's perspective, FX-denominated debt liabilities are the worst, and local currency equity-like liabilities are the best: the former maintain their value in the event of a sudden stop, while the latter decline in value. Moreover, because debt owed to nonresidents must be repaid in traded goods, whose marginal value will be high when there is a sudden stop or output shock, such liabilities are inherently more risky than those owed to residents, which in effect can be repaid in a combination of traded and nontraded goods (regardless of the denomination of the claim). In itself, even this would not suffice to justify government intervention in individual borrowing decisions because the riskiest forms of liabilities will also be the cheapest in which to borrow. Welfare-theoretic models, presented in chapter 7, however, suggest that—left to its own devices—the private sector will tend to overborrow, and to do so in excessively risky forms of liabilities relative to the social optimum. The government should therefore tax such borrowing to prevent the buildup of balance-sheet vulnerabilities, with the tax rate calibrated to the riskiness of the liability—taking into account its form (debt or equity), maturity, and currency mismatch relative to the borrower's income or assets, and whether it is owed to a resident or to a nonresident.

The measures to reduce balance-sheet vulnerabilities may be structural but will typically also need to entail a cyclical element. This is because the vulnerabilities are likely to be increasing as inflows surge and because the risk of a sudden stop is greatest during the inflow phase. If a sudden stop occurs, the measures should be removed given that there is a dearth of external financing. If flows recede more gradually, the measures may be removed as the vulnerabilities subside.

Broadly speaking, the analytical framework thus suggests that policy tools should be deployed to target specific risks. In practice, as chapter 8 shows, they will be combined and merged—for example, when applying capital controls as a backstop to macroeconomic policies, it may make sense to start with the riskiest forms of liabilities, thus addressing balance-sheet vulnerabilities as well. The effectiveness of tools in targeting the risks is an important consideration in determining the policy response; as documented in chapter 9, they may be effective on average, but that may not hold in all country settings. If they are effective, however, they may have spillover effects and raise multilateral concerns. Chapter 10 shows that such concerns do not proscribe the use of policies that are in a country's interest—though greater welfare gains could be achieved through policy cooperation (among the recipient countries, as well as between the source and recipient countries).

In determining the policy response, several pragmatic considerations also need to be taken into account. As we discuss in chapter 11, the availability of tools may depend on the country's institutional and supervisory capacities, as well as on political economy constraints. Multilateral considerations—specifically, the IMF's Article IV stricture against currency manipulation—may circumscribe elements of the policy response. There may be trade-offs in implementing policies as well—for example, narrowly targeted measures may be better on efficiency grounds, yet they may give greater scope for circumvention, including through relabeling of flows. Legal and institutional constraints on the availability and use of different policy instruments also matter. Membership in the OECD or the European Union (EU) or other treaty obligations, for instance, may preclude the use of capital controls.

Management of capital flows is thus more an art than a science. While theory can inform policy, real-world decision making is inherently more complicated, uncertain, and dynamic. The analysis in this book—comprising both theory and empirics—is intended to further our current state of knowledge, and to spur students and academic researchers to delve deeper into these topics. The policy prescriptions in this book, which build on the analysis, are intended to guide national authorities—always recognizing the practical difficulties in real-world decision making. We hope that graduate students, academics, and officials will find this book of use as they wrestle, in their own ways, with the age-old question of how countries can best manage—but still benefit from—cross-border capital flows.

## 1.3   The Book

In this book, we have sought to provide emerging market policy makers with a practical guide on how to manage capital inflows. Two issues that we do not explicitly discuss are (1) the optimal degree of capital account liberalization, and (2) what policy makers should do in the face of capital outflows. Regarding the former, countries have latitude to tailor how financially open they want to be even in the steady state, including through the use of structural capital controls and currency-based prudential measures against especially risky liabilities. Though we consider such structural measures in this book, our main focus is on cyclical measures that would be adopted in the face of inflow surges. It is indeed possible that emerging markets have liberalized too much or too fast, and that they should consider some rolling back of their financial openness. But these issues are beyond the scope of this book and are not taken up explicitly, except insofar as prescriptions on the use of capital controls to ameliorate the composition of flows and address financial-stability risks have implications for the extent of liberalization.

Regarding capital outflows, based on the evidence presented in this book, we believe that if countries have appropriate structural measures in place and manage the inflow phase through cyclical tools well, then the risk of a financial crisis (and the need for drastic policy measures as flows recede or reverse) would be considerably reduced. For cyclical measures taken in response to macroeconomic or balance-sheet imbalances, policy makers could unwind such measures during the bust phase, while retaining the structural measures to prevent the buildup of balance-sheet mismatches in the future.

This book is structured in four parts. Part I sets the stage by providing some basic facts and figures about capital flows to EMEs (chapter 1), and tracing in broad strokes the history—from the late nineteenth century to the present day—of cross-border capital flows and attempts at controlling them (chapter 2). It also reviews the formal literature on capital account liberalization and the use of capital controls. Part II—comprising chapters 3 and 4—explores the dynamics and drivers of large capital inflows (surges) in emerging markets, and examines the consequences of these inflows for macroeconomic imbalances and balance-sheet vulnerabilities. Part III lays out the analytical framework for discussing how various policies may be used to manage capital flows, and also looks at how emerging markets actually respond to such flows. Chapter 5 develops a simple model linking capital flows and policies to macroeconomic outcomes. Chapter 6 builds on this framework to take up the specific question of whether inflation-targeting central banks should also intervene in the foreign exchange market. Chapter 7 models balance-sheet vulnerabilities and derives the welfare-theoretic optimal government intervention to address them. Chapter 8 turns to policy implementation and documents how emerging markets typically respond to capital inflows in practice. Part IV discusses various pragmatic considerations in policy implementation. It begins, in chapter 9, by surveying evidence on the effectiveness of various policy tools. Chapter 10 discusses international spillovers, the multilateral impact of individual countries' policies, and the scope for international policy cooperation. Chapter 11 then draws together theory, empirics, and practical considerations to provide concrete policy advice for dealing with capital inflows. Chapter 12 concludes.

# 2 Regulating Capital Flows: A Historical Perspective

## 2.1 Introduction

Managing capital flows is scarcely a new idea: there is evidence, for example, of the use of exchange controls in ancient times.[1] Restrictions on the import and export of currency into and out of England are documented to have existed in the Middle Ages, as well as in the early modern period. In his 1758 treatise *L'Ami des hommes*, the Marquis de Mirabeau warns against relying on hot-money flows that may be fickle and subject to sudden repatriation.[2] Even during the latter half of the nineteenth century and the early decades of the twentieth—often considered the heyday of financial globalization—the leading capital exporters of the day (Britain, France, and Germany) sometimes limited foreign issuances on their markets, albeit more for political than for economic reasons. But prior to World War I, such measures were the exception rather than the rule, with little thought being given to controlling either the entry or exit of capital, despite the often massive volumes of flows. Over the subsequent century, however, there were several dramatic shifts in the thinking about—and practice of—restrictions on the movement of capital. Understanding when and why these came about is the subject of this chapter.

In tracing this history, it is useful to distinguish five key phases: pre–World War I (the classical gold standard), the interwar period (itself divisible into the reestablishment of the gold standard and its

---

1. Einzig (1970) documents the existence of exchange control policy in Sparta and Egypt under Ptolemaic and Roman rule.
2. England's restrictions in as early as 1299 noted by Lord Cromer, former governor of the Bank of England, in the 1966 Arthur K. Salomon Lecture "The International Capital Markets," delivered at New York University (cited in Bank of England 1967). Bloomfield (1938) cites the Marquis de Mirabeau; see also Brocard (1902).

subsequent demise), the Bretton Woods era, the adoption of generalized floating, and the aftermath of the 2008 global financial crisis. Over
this long span, the world underwent massive changes—political, economic, social, and technological—yet the narrative as regards capital
account management is relatively straightforward. Thinking in each
period was influenced by experience in the previous years, and practice
was determined by the relative ascendancy of two rival interests: national
governments and international bankers. The governments were increasingly expected to deliver steady growth and full employment policies,
while bankers remained more concerned with maintaining a liberal
international monetary and financial order in which they could profit
from cross-border intermediation (Helleiner 1994).[3]

Paralleling developments on the policy front have been advances in
economic theory. While the literature is vast, at its core the question
amounts to whether trade in financial securities should be on an equal
footing with trade in goods and services. Whereas free trade in the latter
is almost universally considered beneficial, a variety of theoretical models, together with a substantial body of empirical work, casts doubt on
whether the same can be said for asset flows. Broadly speaking, the
formal literature on the topic can thus be divided into two opposing
strands. The first seeks to establish, theoretically or empirically, the
growth and welfare benefits of allowing capital to flow from countries
where it earns a relatively low rate of return to those where it earns a
higher return. Accepting that open current and capital accounts are worthy long-term goals, a subbranch of this literature explores the optimal
sequencing of their liberalization.[4] The contrary strand stresses the macroeconomic challenges (including loss of policy autonomy) and financial-
stability risks engendered by unfettered capital flows; a subbranch of this
strand examines the efficacy of policy measures such as temporary capital controls and prudential measures in limiting either the flows themselves or their untoward consequences.

This chapter summarizes how thinking about capital flows and their
management has evolved in both policy-making and academic circles.
Section 2.2 traces—in broad strokes—major trends in cross-border capi-

---

3. This is akin to viewing the evolution of capital controls in the framework of the macroeconomic policy "trilemma" or the "impossible trinity" of fixed exchange rate regimes,
monetary policy autonomy, and full capital mobility—eloquently demonstrated by Fleming (1962) and Mundell (1963)—with one goal subordinated to the others at different
points of time.
4. It is perhaps surprising that few studies examine the possible trade-off between free
trade in goods and free movement of capital—an issue that historically has been central
to the policy debate; see Helleiner (1994).

tal flows, and the adoption of capital account regulations during the five phases mentioned above. Section 2.3 surveys the key theoretical and empirical literature on this topic. Section 2.4 concludes.

## 2.2   Capital Flows in the Long Run

### 2.2.1   The Golden Era of Financial Globalization
During the latter half of the nineteenth century and the early decades of the twentieth—the golden period of financial globalization— the major capital-exporting countries (Britain, France, and Germany) exported as much as 5 to 10 percent of GDP per year, mainly in long-term capital, to the developing and emerging market economies of the day (figure 2.1).

Foremost among the capital exporters was Great Britain, both in terms of the volume of lending and the diversity of countries to which she lent. Whereas Britain's lending in the first half of the nineteenth century had been mostly to European countries, by the latter part of the nineteenth century her portfolio was more heavily weighted to the Americas and to the British Empire and dominions, with Argentina, the United States, Canada, and India all notable recipients (table 2.1).[5] Boom-bust cycles in cross-border lending were already apparent (figure 2.1). After rising from less than 2 percent of GDP in 1860 to 8 percent of GDP in 1872, British long-term lending collapsed to about 1 percent of GDP during the Long Depression that followed the Panic of 1873— which itself was the result of overexpansion during the boom in the United States that followed the Civil War. A fresh cycle began in the 1880s, with Britain's capital exports increasing to more than 7 percent of GDP, only to collapse again to less than 2 percent of GDP in the aftermath of the Panic of 1893 (when half of the American railway companies went bankrupt, Argentina defaulted, Brazil and numerous other Latin American countries either defaulted or ran into severe debt-servicing difficulties, and Portugal and Greece unilaterally reduced their interest payments).

---

5. Hobson (1914) discusses how, in the eighteenth century, London gained supremacy over Amsterdam as an international financial center (Britain was probably a net debtor until after the end of Napoleonic Wars, but British financiers participated in foreign loans long before then), and the debate about whether Britain was exporting too much capital at that time, given its own industrialization and development needs. Viner (1928) notes that in fifteenth- and sixteenth-century French literature, the term *Anglais* had already been used as a derogatory term signifying "creditor." Hobson (1914), Feis (1965), and Simon (1968) discuss the geographical pattern of British lending in the late eighteenth century and early nineteenth century.

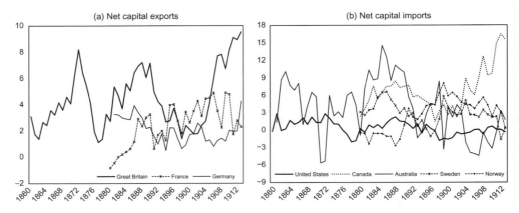

**Figure 2.1**
Net capital flows, 1860–1913 (in percent of GDP).
*Sources*: Bloomfield (1968), Mitchell (2013), and authors' estimates.

By the turn of the century, however, British lending had resumed as Argentina and Brazil restored their creditworthiness, American railways emerged from bankruptcy, and the establishment of the national gold standard boosted confidence in US investments. British alliances with Japan in 1902, and with Russia in 1907, increased lending to these sovereigns, while the Colonial Stocks Act of 1900, which made the securities of colonial governments eligible for inclusion in trust portfolios, further encouraged lending to the empire and dominions. By the eve of World War I, British national saving had reached 16 percent of GDP, of which more than half was being invested abroad, while her stock of foreign assets equaled US$18.5 billion—more than one and one-half times national income (or one-quarter of national wealth; table 2.1).

Underpinning these massive cross-border flows was both the gold standard, which provided long-term exchange rate stability and eliminated currency risk, and the absence of capital controls or other legal impediments to capital flows.[6] Britain was the most liberal in this regard. Despite the large volume of outflows, foreign investment faced little opposition from industry because it was often associated with increased orders for British exports of railway lines, rolling stock, and other capital equipment.[7] This liberal attitude was reflected in the laissez-faire official

6. The primary objective of central banks at that time was to maintain external stability. Cast in terms of the "trilemma," policy makers subordinated monetary policy to the goals of exchange rate stability and capital mobility.
7. Of the stock of British foreign investment, 40 percent was in the securities of railway companies and 12 percent in capital-intensive industries, while 30 percent consisted of

policy, which seldom restricted foreign issuances, except in a few cases where the political aims of the borrowing government ran contrary to British interests.[8]

France and Germany, the other major capital exporters (with stocks of foreign assets amounting to US$8.8 billion and US$5.5 billion, respectively, at end-1913), presented somewhat different situations. France's pattern of industrialization, with its greater emphasis on fine, artisanal products rather than mass-produced manufactures, meant that there were fewer domestic calls for savings (other than for railways and for French government bonds, *rentes*), which freed up funds for foreign investment. Nevertheless, by restricting listings on the Paris Bourse, French officials kept tight reins on the destination of foreign investments— directing them for political or commercial advantage.[9] In Germany, where the development of heavy industry and the needs of the state absorbed a substantial portion of domestic saving, the basic impetus for foreign investment was weaker, and the determination to ensure that domestic industry or the state benefited directly from the nation's foreign investments was correspondingly greater. Again, without imposing capital controls or exchange restrictions, but by limiting listings on the German stock exchange, and by determining which securities would be eligible for use as collateral for rediscounting at the central bank (Reichsbank), the state could exercise significant influence over lending to foreign companies or countries.[10]

loans to national or state governments—around one-half of which were associated with public infrastructure investments (Feis 1965, 27). Figures documented in Hobson (1914) suggest that over 1900–1909, British exports accounted for around one-half of rails, locomotives, and rolling stock imports by India and Argentina (the latter fell sharply in 1910–1911 as competition from Germany increased), and around one-quarter to one-third of imports by Australia and South Africa.

8. There was some "self-censorship" whereby respectable private banks that habitually handled sovereign issuances would not promote, and the public would not buy, the securities of foreign governments whose aims ran contrary to British interests. Overt intervention by the Foreign Office was therefore usually unnecessary, though at times the Office made its disapproval known and even took vigorous action to prevent participation by British financial institutions (Feis 1965, 91). Viner (1928) provides some examples of restrictions on capital exports exercised by the capital-exporting countries of that time.

9. For instance, the 1910 report of the board of directors of the Comptoire National d'Escompte notes: "In the selection of securities we offer to our clientele, we undertake, as a rule, not only to seek security of investment but also to take into account the view of our government and the economic and political advantages that may be obtained by France by the loans contracted by other countries" (Feis 1965, 123).

10. The promotion of German business interests was facilitated by the close connection between banks and industry, as evident from the testimony of a director of Friedrich

**Table 2.1**
Long-term publicly issued capital investment stock (1914, in millions).

| | Britain | | France | | Germany | |
|---|---|---|---|---|---|---|
| | US dollars | In percent of total | US dollars | In percent of total | US dollars | In percent of total |
| *Europe* | 535 | 2.9 | 2,538 | 28.7 | 2,104 | 37.9 |
| Austria | 39 | 0.2 | 433 | 4.9 | 709 | 12.8 |
| Balkan States | 84 | 0.5 | 492 | 5.6 | 402 | 7.2 |
| Italy | 62 | 0.3 | 256 | 2.9 | | |
| Portugal and Spain | 134 | 0.7 | 767 | 8.7 | 402 | 7.2 |
| Other Europe | 217 | 1.2 | 590 | 6.7 | 591 | 10.6 |
| Australia and New Zealand | 2,053 | 11.1 | | | | |
| *North America* | 6,258 | 33.7 | 394 | 4.4 | 875 | 15.7 |
| Canada | 2,538 | 13.7 | | | | |
| United States | 3,720 | 20.1 | | | | |
| *South America* | 3,730 | 20.1 | 1,181 | 13.3 | 898 | 16.2 |
| Argentina | 1,576 | 8.5 | | | | |
| Brazil | 730 | 3.9 | | | | |
| Mexico | 488 | 2.6 | | | | |
| Other Americas | 937 | 5.0 | | | | |
| *Asia* | 2,572 | 13.9 | 433 | 4.9 | 236 | 4.3 |
| India and Ceylon | 1,867 | 10.1 | | | | |
| China | 216 | 1.2 | | | | |
| Japan | 310 | 1.7 | | | | |
| Other Asia | 178 | 1.0 | | | | |
| *Africa* | 2,009 | 10.8 | | | 473 | 8.5 |
| South Africa | 1,825 | 9.8 | | | | |
| Other Africa | 184 | 1.0 | | | | |
| Egypt | 221 | 1.2 | 649 | 7.3 | | |
| Turkey | 118 | 0.6 | 649 | 7.3 | 426 | 7.7 |
| Russia | 542 | 2.9 | 2,223 | 25.1 | 426 | 7.7 |
| Other | 513 | 2.8 | 787 | 8.9 | 118 | 2.1 |
| Total | 18,552 | 100.0 | 8,854 | 100.0 | 5,555 | 100.0 |
| Total (percent of GDP) | | 160 | | 90.8 | | 44.8 |

*Source*: Feis 1965.

On the recipient-country end also, there were relatively few inflow restrictions, and those that did exist were mainly directed at limiting foreign control of important corporations and sectors of the economy (what, in Germany, came to be known as *ueberfremdung*—"alienation of control"—during the interwar period). More broadly, inflow restrictions at that time aimed at preventing political influence or subjugation by capital-exporting countries. Thus, a Russian decree of 1887 prohibited the ownership of land by foreigners along its frontiers with Asia and Poland, and a Prussian law of 1909—intended to limit French control over German coalfields—made acquisition of mining properties subject to state approval.[11] Similarly, Sweden in 1910 required that the principal officers of certain large corporations be Swedish citizens, while Czechoslovakia adopted restrictions on capital imports for fear of complications with foreign governments over their citizens' investments.

In less economically developed parts of the world, there were usually fewer indigenous corporations for *ueberfremdung* to be a concern. Nevertheless, foreign investment at times met stiff local resistance (occasionally prompting national governments to rescind permits and concessions), not necessarily because they were *foreign* investment, but because in the course of industrialization, capital—which happened to be mainly foreign—came into conflict with labor, or threatened traditional ways of life and existing socioeconomic structures; the fact of foreign ownership, however, often provided a convenient rallying cry for opponents.[12]

In sum, during this golden era of financial globalization, capital flows from the leading economies of the day helped finance the needs of industry and the state in the less developed parts of the world—the emerging markets of the era—though they likely contributed to periodic boom-bust cycles and financial panics as well. Capital flows were largely long term in nature.[13] There were few restrictions on either

---

Krupp AG (the largest company in Europe in the early twentieth century) to the *German Bank Inquiry of 1908–1909*: "I believe that the existing state of things suffices to enable the government to hold up undesirable loans or prevent them being placed at an inopportune moment" (Feis 1965, 168).

11. Even earlier, in 1824, Pennsylvania banned the transfer of bank stock to non-US citizens, and in 1825 prohibited foreigners (except Dutch citizens) from holding the stock of the Bank of North America unless the investor declared his intention of becoming a naturalized American (Staley 1935).

12. See Staley 1935, chapter 14.

13. Short-term flows in that period reflected seasonal balance of payments needs or "stabilizing speculation." As noted by Eichengreen (1992), the classical gold standard

capital inflows or outflows—though officialdom in each of the major capital exporters exercised varying degrees of influence over lending to foreign sovereigns, mostly for political reasons.

## 2.2.2   The Interwar Period

During World War I, private capital largely ceased to flow across national boundaries (especially from Europe, which had been the main source of global capital), and the gold standard effectively stopped operating. The cessation of hostilities revealed deep differences in attitudes toward restoring cross-border capital flows. At one extreme was the Soviet Union, which under an authoritarian and state socialist model had imposed tight controls on capital movements by 1919. At the other extreme were the private and central bankers of the leading economies of the day (including, preeminently, the United States, which had gone from being the world's largest debtor to the largest creditor), who sought to reestablish the previous liberal—and for the great banking houses, highly profitable—international monetary order. The Genoa Economic and Monetary Conference, meeting in 1922 to discuss Europe's postwar economic and financial reconstruction, thus resolved that "all artificial control of exchange . . . is futile and mischievous and should be abolished at the earliest possible date."[14]

Wartime dislocation, currency misalignments, and deficit financing of reparations and reconstruction costs delayed this process, especially in Europe.[15] But starting with the Dawes Plan in 1924 and the associated Dawes Loan (publicly endorsed but privately funded), Germany managed to stabilize its economy and put its new currency, the reichsmark,

---

was a highly credible target zone—with upper and lower bands determined by the gold import and export points. Such a regime will be characterized by stabilizing speculative flows because the exchange rate cannot help but appreciate as it approaches the lower band, thus attracting capital flows and thereby helping to strengthen the currency. Likewise, the exchange rate cannot help but depreciate when it reaches the upper band, thus discouraging further inflows.

14. Resolution 14 of the Financial Commission of the Genoa Economic and Monetary Conference; see Mills (1922, 366). In order to conserve scarce monetary gold, the conference also recommended that most central banks be on a gold *exchange* standard (backing their currencies with gold and foreign exchange), while only the major reserve currencies would be on a gold-coin or gold-bullion standard (i.e., payable in gold upon demand).

15. The London Conference, held in 1921, put Germany's responsibility for the war at 132 billion gold marks (the equivalent of US$32 billion, or more than 1.5 times Britain's prewar stock of net foreign assets). The actual schedule of reparations was 50 billion gold marks, or US$12 billion. During 1920–1924, world output grew at 16 percent, whereas European output grew at only 2 percent (League of Nations 1932).

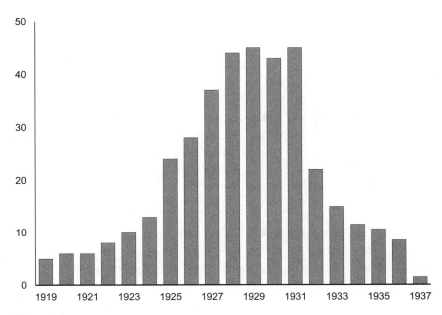

**Figure 2.2**
Rise and fall of the interwar gold standard (total number of major countries on gold/
gold exchange standard).
*Source*: Based on Eichengreen (1992).
*Note*: Out of 54 major economies.

on the gold standard. Britain returned to gold in 1925 at her prewar
parity. France also de facto returned to gold in 1926 (de jure in 1928),
albeit at a much depreciated exchange rate. By the late 1920s, most of the
world's major economies were back on the gold standard (figure 2.2).[16]

Buoyed by the success of the Dawes Loan, and underpinned by the
reestablished gold standard, American banks entered a period of massive private international lending, averaging about a billion dollars a
year over 1924–1929, half of which was destined for Europe, partly
intermediated by British banks (figure 2.3). Town halls in Germany were
said to be inundated by representatives of international banks offering
aggressively priced credits, spurring a huge economic and financial
boom.[17]

---

16. The United States maintained the gold standard almost throughout World War I,
suspending convertibility only twice in July 1914 as the war began, and then in 1917 as
the United States entered the war (Crabbe 1989).
17. See Brown (1987) and Eichengreen (1992) for a detailed account of that period. Over
1925–1929, European output grew at 31 percent (compared to 20 percent of world

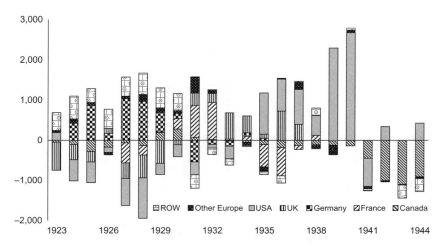

**Figure 2.3**
Net capital flows to selected countries, 1923–1944 (in millions of USD).
*Source*: League of Nations 1931, 1932, 1939, 1948.
*Notes*: Net capital flows include errors and omissions. Countries are included depending on data availability, as follows: Canada (1923–1944); France (1927–1938); Germany (1924–1935); UK (1923–1938); USA (1923–1944); Other Europe: Czecho-Slovakia (1925–1937), Denmark (1923–1939), Estonia (1924–1938), Greece (1929–1938), Hungary (1923–1937), Latvia (1923–1937), Netherlands (1929–1939), Norway (1923–1944), and Sweden (1923–1944); rest of the world (ROW): Argentina (1923–1944), Australia (1923–1937), Dutch Indies (1925–1939), India (1924–1938), Japan (1924–1936), New Zealand (1927–1937), South Africa (1923–1937), and Turkey (1926–1933).

But this resurrection of the liberal international order did not last long. The lending boom of the Dawes and other credits to Europe had not solved the underlying adjustment and transfer problem—whereby creditor nations were unwilling to increase imports to allow debtor countries to service their debts and reparations obligations. When a boom in the New York stock market (which ultimately ended spectacularly in the October 1929 crash) drew both domestic and foreign capital to the United States, Europe suffered an equally massive sudden stop (figure 2.3). By September 1930, Germany was experiencing funding difficulties and the reichsbank suffered a run, losing RM1 billion (US$250 million) in the last quarter of the year, with 10 percent of foreign exchange (FX) reserves lost in a single day.[18] A six-month loan (with up to three renewals) of US$125 million temporarily stabilized

---

output growth), while the demand for US machine tools rose by 87 percent (League of Nations 1932).
18. League of Nations 1932, 72–74.

the situation, but in May 1931 the Creditanstalt, a major Austrian bank, disclosed heavy losses. This triggered a global financial crisis as the unsustainability of the debts of Austria, Germany, and the countries of Eastern Europe became evident. With Germany unable to meet her short-term obligations to banks, the government declared a standstill on foreign payments and imposed exchange restrictions in July 1931.[19] This triggered a run on pound sterling, as British banks were known to be heavily exposed to Germany and Eastern Europe—forcing Britain off the gold standard in September 1931, with most of her dominions and numerous other countries following suit.[20]

What ensued was a decade of almost dizzying capital flight, hot-money flows, competitive devaluations, exchange restrictions and capital controls (nearly all on outflows), together with trade protectionism and imploding global trade.[21] The immediate impact of the pound sterling's devaluation was a drain of capital from the United States as investors, including central banks, lost confidence in the gold exchange standard and started hoarding gold instead of reserve currencies. In April 1933, the United States devalued the dollar. In turn, the dollar devaluation put speculative pressure on the Dutch florin and the Swiss franc (both of which continued to be pegged to gold at their prewar parities), and on the French franc (the largest economy still on gold) and the currencies of the other gold bloc countries, notably Belgium, Italy, and Portugal. In sequence, countries abandoned the gold standard and devalued their currencies, imposed exchange restrictions (of varying severity, depending on the availability of foreign exchange for capital and current account transactions), or did a combination of the two (figure 2.4).

Following the dollar devaluation, capital flows to the United States resumed as the country's economic recovery gained momentum and European political developments darkened. By 1935, flows to the United States—comprising mostly short-term funds—reached US$1.5

---

19. Brown (1987, 16) observes that Germany's chancellor and central bank president came to Paris in July 1931 to request short-term credits, and when denied them on acceptable terms, returned home to impose exchange restrictions. Thirty-seven years later, following the May 1968 riots, the French finance minister went to Bonn to request stand-by credits, and on being denied them, imposed exchange restrictions in France (see section 2.2.4).

20. The Bank of England's gold reserves fell from £163.2 million on July 1, 1931, to £133.6 million on September 23, 1931 (and further to £120.0 million by November 4, 1931). See Fanno (1939, 65) for a detailed discussion of "normal" and "abnormal" capital movements during the interwar period.

21. See, for example, League of Nations (1938, 1944), and Brown (1987, 18).

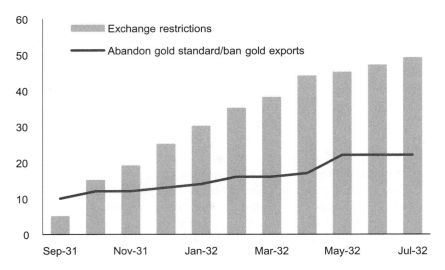

**Figure 2.4**
Exchange restrictions and abandoning of gold standard, September 1931–July 1932
(total number of major advanced and emerging market countries).
*Source*: League of Nations World Economic Survey, 1931–1932.
*Note*: Germany imposed exchange restrictions in July 1931.

billion, increasing to more than US$2 billion in 1939 (figure 2.5). These large inflows, especially during 1935–1937, concerned the US administration for several reasons. Foreign funds were believed to be contributing to an unhealthy speculative boom in the stock market. Inflows were also swelling the US banking system's excess reserves, which raised fears of an inflationary spiral and credit boom outside of the normal channels of control of the Federal Reserve. Equally worrying, there was a risk that foreign countries' loss of gold reserves through capital flight might prompt them to impose trade restrictions on US exports, undermining the nascent recovery. Finally, there was the possibility that foreigners might become large sellers in the event of war or other grave developments in Europe. Marriner Eccles, the chairman of the Federal Reserve, noted in 1937, "Since such inflows complicate the problem of achieving and maintaining a prosperous stability, constitute a source of embarrassment to many countries from which the capital is flowing, and . . . have nothing to do with foreign trade or the international division of labor, there appears to be a clear case for adopting measures designed to deter the growth of foreign capital holdings in our markets."[22]

---

22. *Fortune*, April 1937 (https://fraser.stlouisfed.org/docs/historical/eccles/068_05_0005
.pdf; last accessed on June 2, 2017).

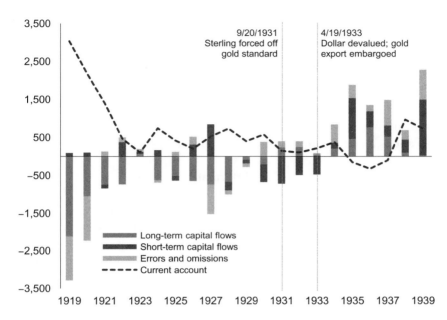

**Figure 2.5**
United States' balance of payments, 1919–1939 (in millions of USD).
*Source*: League of Nations 1938.
*Note*: Negative capital flows indicate outflows on a net basis.

Yet the United States did *not* impose controls on capital inflows.[23] Beyond certain practical difficulties in taxing foreigners, there was no significant precedent for inflow controls (the exception being Switzerland, which in 1937 abolished interest payments on nonresident deposits, levied a 1 percent commission, and required advance notice for withdrawals of such deposits).[24] Drawing on the experience of countries trying to control capital flight, there was also the belief that the restrictions would not be effective unless they were broad-based, covering both capital and current account transactions. Perhaps more importantly, there was a general distrust of any such restrictions, which in the minds of both the public and of policy makers were associated with the capital *outflow* restrictions imposed by undemocratic, dictatorial regimes (such as Austria, Germany, and the Soviet Union) in the

23. In an early example of responding to capital inflows, the Federal Reserve did, however, double reserve requirements of member banks in 1936–1937 to counteract the inflationary pressures of the large gold inflows.
24. Argentina and Sweden also reduced interest payments on nonresident deposits (Bloomfield 1950, 194).

interwar period. As Bloomfield (1950) notes: "Exchange control over capital movements and current account transactions alike was generally regarded in these circles as inherently objectionable and a perversion of the pattern of international payments worthy only of totalitarian countries or justifiable only under conditions of extreme necessity." Henry Morgenthau, the secretary of the Treasury, summed up the prevailing attitude when he wrote in 1937, "I am opposed to exchange control, except as a last resort. Frankly, I disapprove of exchange control."[25]

### 2.2.3 Bretton Woods and Its Aftermath

Beyond its intrinsic interest, and the cautionary tale of a boom-bust cycle in international lending, the interwar period is important because of the way it shaped thinking at the Bretton Woods Conference in July 1944, where delegates of 44 nations gathered to design a new international monetary system that would bring order to postwar economic relations and avoid the chaos of the interwar period. Tellingly, the main protagonists at the conference—John Maynard Keynes and Harry Dexter White—were Treasury men, not (private or central) bankers. The lesson that these men took from the interwar experience was that a regime of unfettered capital flows is fundamentally inconsistent with the macroeconomic management increasingly expected of governments (namely, to strive for full employment) or with a liberal international trade regime.[26] Given the choice, they preferred free trade to free capital flows, especially when it came to short-term hot-money flows and flight capital. Hence the emphasis in the IMF's Articles of Agreement—drawn up at the Bretton Woods Conference—on current rather than capital account convertibility, and the explicit recognition that countries may need to impose capital controls.

Keynes and White thus envisaged capital controls as a *structural* element of the international financial landscape, rather than as just temporary or transitional measures.[27] They also realized that capital controls

---

25. *New York Times*, February 16, 1937, 31; cited in Bloomfield (1950, 183).

26. Boughton (2002) argues that White and Keynes developed their views about capital controls independently of each other. For White, in his early thinking, controls were second best ("the best of the bad choices"), whereas for Keynes they were second nature.

27. In light of Morgenthau's avowed dislike of restrictions (see the quotation in section 2.2.2), it is perhaps ironic that he was the Secretary of the Treasury—notionally, the chief US negotiator—when the IMF Articles of Agreement were being framed at Bretton Woods. Steil (2013) suggests that Morgenthau had little understanding of technical issues related to international finance and delegated most of the negotiation to White. Moreover, Morgenthau was probably more receptive to the New York bankers' concerns and

would not be effective unless applied "at both ends" of the transaction, and their original plans therefore mandated IMF member countries to cooperate in enforcing each other's measures (partly in lieu of more draconian exchange restrictions that they thought would be necessary to make unilateral controls effective; Helleiner 2015).[28] Last-minute intervention by powerful New York bankers, however, succeeded in watering down these proposals, and in the final version of the IMF articles agreed at Bretton Woods, capital controls as a permanent feature of the international financial landscape were not included. Instead, Article VI.3 merely noted that "members may exercise such controls as are necessary to regulate international capital movements."[29] The requirement that member countries cooperate in enforcing each other's capital control measures was also dropped; according to Article VIII.2 (b), countries "may, by mutual accord, cooperate in measures for the purpose of making the exchange control regulations . . . more effective." Moreover, the IMF could not require a member country to impose controls on outflows when IMF resources were financing capital flight. It could only request that the country restrict outflows (and make the country ineligible for further use of IMF resources if it failed to do so).[30]

Despite this early push back by US banking interests, the Bretton Woods era was characterized by widespread use of restrictive measures

---

instrumental in agreeing to water down the proposals for capital controls in the original drafts of the articles prepared by Keynes and White.

28. The idea that cooperative controls might be much more effective was not unique to Keynes and White. Ragnar Nurkse wrote in his 1944 report *International Currency Experience: Lessons of the Inter-War Period*, "In considering the question whether it is possible to have a system of exchange control affecting capital movements alone—and particularly, of course, capital movements of the speculative or 'disequilibrating' kind—we should remember that the interwar period affords no experience of a generalized exchange control as exists today [1944]. Control was applied unilaterally by such individual countries as happened to be subject to a threat of capital flight. If control were exercised by capital-receiving as well as by capital-losing countries, the answer might be different" (League of Nations 1944, 164); see chapter 10.

29. The potential inconsistency between the freedom of IMF members to exercise controls under Article VI.3, and the prohibition under Article VIII.3 against discriminatory currency arrangements, was discussed by the IMF executive board on April 6, 1956. The board concluded that "Article VI.3 recognized the sovereign right of members to regulate international capital movements in any way that would not restrict current payments, including permitting discriminatory currency arrangements insofar as they were for the purpose of controlling capital movements" (Horsefield 1969, 404).

30. Because the articles do not explicitly address the use of inflow controls, there is the curious implication that, as part of its program conditionality, the IMF can require a country to impose controls on capital *inflows* under the general provisions of Article V Section 3(a)—see *Capital Movements: Legal Aspects of Fund Jurisdiction Under the Articles* (IMF SM/97/32, Supplement 3, February 21, 1997).

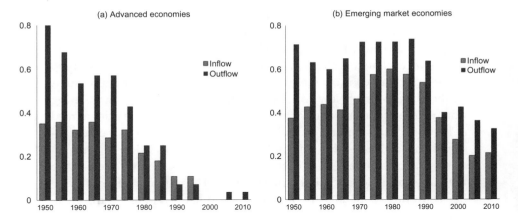

**Figure 2.6**
Capital inflow and outflow controls, 1950–2010.
*Source*: Authors' estimates based on various issues of the IMF's *AREAER*.
*Notes*: Advanced countries include the G7 countries (Canada, France, Germany, Italy, Japan, United Kingdom, and United States). EMs include the major emerging markets that were IMF members in 1950 (Argentina, Brazil, Chile, Colombia, Ecuador, Egypt, India, Indonesia, Korea, Malaysia, Mexico, Pakistan, Peru, the Philippines, South Africa, Thailand, Tunisia, Turkey, Uruguay, and Venezuela). Indices are averages for the respective country groups (where for each country, the restrictions are coded as 0 (none), 0.25 (mild), 0.75 (significant), 1 (extreme) based on authors' subjective judgment).

(figure 2.6). As in the interwar period, these measures were mainly controls on outflows rather than on inflows; unlike that period, they were typically not exchange restrictions but capital controls, since the IMF articles prohibit exchange restrictions on current account transactions (except transitionally or with the IMF's approval). The measures were also unilateral since the United States, which was the major recipient of capital flight, declined to cooperate in enforcing other countries' outflow restrictions.[31]

Britain provides a prominent example of the use of capital controls during that period. Following a disastrous "dash to convertibility" in 1947, which ended within six weeks with a run on the pound sterling, Britain imposed strict controls on capital outflows that were maintained until 1979 (current account convertibility, under IMF Article VIII, was achieved in 1961). Elsewhere in Europe (and Japan), current

---

31. Helleiner (1994) argues that this refusal to cooperate (which would have required furnishing foreign governments with information on their nationals' holdings of assets in the US) reflected the further reassertion of US banking interests, facilitated by changing attitudes within the US Treasury as Secretary Morgenthau was succeeded by Fred Vinson and, shortly later, by John Snyder, who was a former investment banker.

account convertibility was achieved by the late 1950s or early 1960s, but with the exception of Germany, full capital account liberalization had to await the 1980s. Indeed, during the initial postwar decades, advanced economies (with the exception of Canada, Germany, Switzerland, and the United States) were generally *more* restrictive in regard to capital flows than many developing and emerging market economies (figure 2.6).[32]

Nevertheless, the trend during the 1950s and 1960s in advanced economies was toward capital account liberalization—enshrined by the Organisation for Economic Co-operation and Development (OECD) in 1961 with its Code of Liberalization of Capital Movements. It is noteworthy, however, that at first the code explicitly excluded short-term capital flows from liberalization obligations. The trend was also occasionally interrupted as individual countries suffered balance of payments (BOP) difficulties. As early as 1963, for example, concerned by capital outflows that were causing persistent balance of payments deficits and undermining confidence in the dollar, the United States imposed the Interest Equalization Tax (IET) on foreign issuances in its markets. By 1970, as the US current account turned to deficit, this measure was broadened to incorporate both voluntary and mandatory foreign credit restraints, including an outright embargo on net direct investment outflows to continental Europe. At the other end, countries such as Australia, Germany, Japan, and Switzerland—recipients of increasingly large flows because of speculation that the dollar would be devalued—imposed restrictions on short-term inflows (table 2.2). Australia, for example, put an embargo on short-term borrowing and imposed deposit requirements on other borrowing. Japan tightened controls on portfolio inflows and imposed marginal reserve requirements on nonresident deposits. Germany imposed a cash deposit requirement (*Bardepot*) on foreign loans, suspended interest payments on nonresident deposits, and imposed marginal reserve requirements on the growth of banks' external liabilities.

---

32. Germany achieved currency convertibility in 1958, but occasionally imposed inflow controls in the late 1950s and the 1960s to deal with speculative capital movements (table 2.2). In 1957, for example, the German authorities imposed higher reserve requirements on nonresident bank deposits to prevent credit being extended against these deposits, which largely represented short-term speculative capital flows in anticipation of pound sterling devaluation and an appreciation of the deutsche mark (Goode and Thorn 1959). Then, in June 1960, an authorization requirement was imposed on the purchase of domestic money paper by nonresidents, and a ban was imposed on interest payments on nonresident bank deposits.

**Table 2.2**
Selected cases of inflow controls tightening in advanced countries.

| Country | Years | Measures | Context |
|---|---|---|---|
| Australia | 1972–1974 | Embargo on short-term borrowing | Restrict inflationary pressures and a stock market boom |
| | | Variable deposit requirement (VDR) on foreign borrowing[a] | |
| | 1977 | VDR on foreign borrowing[a] | |
| Austria | 1971–1975 | Reserve requirement (RR) on increase in nonresident deposits | Reduce inflationary pressures |
| Finland | 1985–1990 | Prohibition on sale of local currency bonds to nonresidents | Restrict domestic credit expansion |
| France | 1963–1967 | Prohibition on interest payment on nonresident deposits | Curb speculative inflows, and reduce upward pressure on the exchange rate |
| | | Prohibition on loans by nonresidents to residents | |
| | 1971–1973 | Minimum RR on external bank liabilities | |
| | | Prohibition on interest payment on nonresident deposits | |
| Germany | 1957 | Higher RR on nonresident deposits | Curb speculative inflows, reduce inflationary pressures and domestic credit extension |
| | 1960–1961 | Prohibition on sale of domestic money-market paper to nonresidents | |
| | | Prohibition on sale to nonresidents of domestic fixed-income securities with the obligation to reacquire the securities at a definitely fixed price | |
| | | Ban on interest payments on nonresident deposits | |
| | 1965 | Withholding tax on interest income on assets held by nonresidents | |
| | 1968–1973 | Minimum RR for any increase in external liabilities of domestic banks | |
| | | Cash deposit requirement in non–interest bearing account (*Bardepot*) of 40 percent on foreign loans | |

| | Year | Measure | Objective |
|---|---|---|---|
| | 1977–1978 | Suspension of interest payment on nonresident bank deposits | |
| | | Authorization requirement imposed on nonresidents' purchase of domestic fixed-interest securities (later extended to equities, mutual fund shares and borrowing above DM 50,000) | |
| | | Higher RR on nonresident deposits | |
| | | Authorization requirement for sale of securities with a maturity of less than four years to nonresidents | |
| Ireland | 1977 | RR on capital inflows to commercial banks | Restrict domestic credit growth |
| Japan | 1971–1972 | Restriction on nonresidents purchase of domestic bonds and equities | Reduce upward pressure on the exchange rate |
| | | Higher marginal RR on nonresident deposits | |
| | 1977–1978 | RR on foreign currency liabilities of foreign exchange banks, residents' external foreign currency deposits, and nonresident accounts | |
| Netherlands | 1971–1973 | Prohibition on interest payment on nonresident demand deposits | Curb short-term speculative capital movement, and reduce pressures on the exchange rate |
| | | Introduction of closed bond circuit system (O-guilder) for transactions in guilder-denominated securities, where purchase of such securities by nonresidents could be made only with funds from sales by nonresidents | |
| New Zealand | 1973–1985 | Approval requirements for foreign loans by companies | |
| Spain | 1989 | Imposition of nonremunerated RR on financial credits taken up abroad | Maintain monetary stability and reduce appreciation pressures |
| Switzerland | 1937–1939 | Charge on nonresident holders of short-term balances (equivalent of charging a negative rate of interest) | Stem short-term speculative inflows, reduce inflationary, and currency appreciation pressures |

(continued)

**Table 2.2** (continued)

| Country | Years | Measures | Context |
|---|---|---|---|
| | 1950–1951 | Charge on nonresident holders of short-term balances | |
| | 1955–1958 | Charge on nonresident holders of short-term balances | |
| | 1960 | Limits on the rights of nonresidents to hold sight deposits with domestic banks or to purchase domestic securities, and requirement that all foreign deposits be held for at least three months | |
| | 1971–1979 | Charge on nonresident holders of short-term balances, and payment of no interest on any foreign deposit | |
| | | RR on the growth and level of external liabilities | |
| | | Charge on nonresident accounts | |
| | | Authorization required for foreign borrowing by nonbank sectors | |
| United Kingdom | 1971 | Financial institutions prohibited from accepting deposits or loans from nonresidents of the sterling area[b] | Reduce inflationary pressures |
| | | Nonresidents of the sterling area prohibited from buying sterling securities having fixed maturity of less than five years | |
| | | Prohibition of interest payment on the increase in the balance of nonresidents' sterling accounts | |

*Sources:* IMF's *Annual Report on Exchange Arrangements and Exchange Restrictions* (various issues), Goode and Thorn 1959, Dorrance and Brehmer 1961, Australian Treasury 1999, and Bakker and Chapple 2002.

a. A proportion of borrowed funds had to be deposited in local currency with the central bank in an interest-free, nonassignable deposit account, until loan repayments were made. This was not applicable to the financing of normal foreign trade transactions; to borrowings of less than $100,000 in any 12-month period; or to existing portfolio position.

b. The sterling area comprised a group of countries that pegged their currencies to the pound sterling or used it as legal tender.

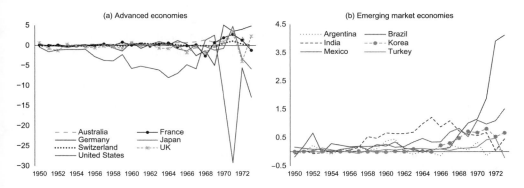

**Figure 2.7**
Net capital flows to selected countries, 1950–1973 (in billions of USD).
*Source*: IMF's *Balance of Payments Yearbook* (various issues).
*Note*: Statistics exclude reserves and related items, but include net errors and omissions.

Despite these increasingly desperate measures, the dollar was devalued in August 1971, and the major currencies were realigned when the Smithsonian Agreement was concluded in December. The effective devaluation of the dollar of around 10 percent, however, was insufficient to restore equilibrium in the US balance of payments, which came under renewed stress in 1972 and early 1973 (figure 2.7). Surprisingly, at that stage the United States not only declined to strengthen its outflow controls, but it actively opposed international cooperation in the administration of inflow and outflow controls, the approach being advocated by both the Japanese and the Europeans. Helleiner (1994) attributes this shift in attitude to the realization by US officials that unfettered private capital flows would be able to achieve in short order what they had failed to do after years of international negotiation: force currency appreciation in Japan and the European surplus countries, thus facilitating US external adjustment.[33]

By 1974, the United States had abandoned its outflow capital controls. Confident that the size and liquidity of US financial markets would always attract investors, American officials henceforth embraced—explicitly and unreservedly—a liberal international regime for private capital flows. The 1973 *Economic Report of the President* thus noted that "controls on capital transactions for balance-of-payments purposes should not be

---

33. Paul Volcker recounts the difficulties in persuading US trading partners to accept revaluations of their currencies at Smithsonian (Volcker and Gyohten 1992, 80–90). See Solomon (1982) for a discussion of earlier US efforts to engineer a revaluation of trading partners' currencies.

encouraged and certainly not required in lieu of other measures of adjustment, nor should they become the means of maintaining an undervalued or overvalued exchange rate."[34] The new doctrine also sought to eliminate the Bretton Woods bias of free trade over free capital flows: the 1973 *Economic Report* went on to argue that the new rules governing the international monetary system should recognize the parallelism between trade in financial assets and trade in goods and services. Accordingly, when the text of the amended IMF Articles of Agreement was being negotiated in 1978, the US delegation managed to insert the phrase "the essential purpose of the international monetary system is to provide a framework that facilitates the exchange of goods, services, *and capital* among countries."[35]

Interestingly, while advanced countries were changing course, the trend in developing and emerging market economies (EMEs) reversed toward greater restrictiveness in the late 1960s and 1970s. The military coup in Brazil in 1965 marked the turning point in Latin America, which had been significantly financially open before then. The new military regime developed an authoritarian, inward-looking model of industrialization, which implied stringent controls on merchandise trade and capital flows (Quinn 1997). The model was emulated broadly by other countries in the region as their own political climate changed. In South Asia, the level of financial openness had matched that of Great Britain—the colonial power—until independence in 1947. But as countries there experimented with inward-looking policy frameworks in the late 1950s and 1960s, they became financially more closed. In East Asia, countries had been, on average, relatively less financially open than their Latin American peers during the early Bretton Woods period, but several of them further tightened their capital account restrictions in the 1960s and 1970s as they pursued development through active government intervention (as in South Korea), or ran into balance of payments difficulties (as in Thailand).[36]

The restrictions in emerging markets were, again, mostly outflow controls, which were instrumental in meeting budgetary needs through financial repression. Even some of the measures that could be classified as inflow controls because they were likely to discourage inward

---

34. *Economic Report of the President* (1973, 128), cited in Helleiner (1994, 106).
35. Cited in Helleiner (1994), who adds the emphasis.
36. East Asia was characterized by different approaches to capital account openness in that period. For example, Hong Kong, Indonesia, and Singapore became less restrictive in the 1970s, while China remained largely closed.

investment—such as minimum investment periods or limits on the pace or amounts of repatriation—were intended to prevent sudden capital flow reversals and balance of payments deficits. In fact, until the 1970s, most inflow restrictions in EMEs took one of two forms: limitations on the amortization and repatriation of nonresidents' investments (to prevent sudden net flow reversals), or designation of specific sectors of the economy in which foreigners were not allowed to invest (in some cases, the set of sectors was sufficiently broad that the measure would likely have limited overall private external borrowing).[37]

### 2.2.4   Advent of Floating and the Washington Consensus

As advanced economies embraced greater capital account liberalization in the 1950s and 1960s, the new liberalism had started to gain a sounder footing intellectually as well (section 2.3 below reviews the evolution of the formal literature). In his 1953 *Essays in Positive Economics*, for example, Milton Friedman had argued—at that time, heretically—the benefits of floating exchange rates. With their advent in the early 1970s, the "impossible trinity" of monetary autonomy, free capital mobility, and fixed exchange rates was solved by dropping the latter in favor of exchange rate flexibility—thus allowing capital mobility and greater monetary autonomy.

The resulting exchange rate volatility after the collapse of the Bretton Woods system was, however, at odds with the desire for greater integration among European countries, which had embarked upon their common currency project with greater urgency in late 1960s. But various crises during its implementation delayed—and, at times, temporarily reversed—full capital account liberalization.[38] France is a case in point. Starting in the early 1960s, France began to liberalize its capital account, and—against the backdrop of a strengthening balance of payments and the desire to make the franc a global currency that could challenge the hegemony of the US dollar—it had removed most capital account restrictions by the end of 1966. But the Paris riots in May 1968 forced the authorities to reimpose outflow controls, invoking for the

---

37. Beginning in the 1970s, measures that were more explicitly prudential in nature began to appear. Brazil, for example, introduced safeguards against excessive use of foreign credits by commercial and investment banks by limiting the foreign obligations that each bank could assume. Venezuela introduced special regulations for foreign banks operating domestically, and Mexico limited banks' foreign currency liabilities from a single nonresident investor.

38. The first concrete articulation of the single currency project was the Werner Report in 1970.

first time the safeguards clause (which enabled member states to take protective measures when short-term capital movements of exceptional size seriously disrupted the conduct of monetary policy) under the European Economic Community (EEC) capital regime. These restrictions were maintained even as capital inflow measures—a 100 percent marginal reserve requirement on incremental nonresident franc deposits—had to be applied in 1971 to stem inflows speculating against the US dollar's devaluation.[39]

The situation reversed with the 1973 oil price shock, which resulted in safe haven flows to the United States, necessitating a further intensification of French outflow controls. These outflow measures, which were relatively effective (the differential between the on shore and off shore franc interest rate reached 5 percent per year), allowed France to pursue more expansionary policies than Germany during the latter half of the 1970s—though the franc was devalued twice (in January 1974 when it left the European "snake," and in March 1976 when it again left the snake less than a year after it had rejoined the mechanism).[40] Between 1976 and the establishment of the European Monetary System (EMS) in 1979, the franc depreciated by a further 30 percent against the deutsche mark despite successive efforts at tightening capital outflow restrictions.

Likewise, through the 1970s Japan sought to influence the value of its currency through the use of capital controls—notwithstanding the formal move to floating in February 1973. As mentioned above, when the yen experienced upward pressure because of speculative outflows from the United States in 1971, the authorities tightened controls on portfolio inflows (and relaxed outflow restrictions). But when the yen came under downward pressure following the first oil price shock in October 1973, restrictions on nonresident portfolio bond and equity purchases were eased, while residents were restricted in their purchases of short-term foreign currency securities. In 1977, as the yen strengthened, the pattern was reversed, with inflow restrictions applied more vigorously and controls on residents' outflows relaxed. Yet again, in 1979, when the yen came under downward pressure after the second oil price shock, inflow

---

39. The outflow controls were maintained because, despite the appreciation pressure against the dollar, the French franc tended to weaken against the deutsche mark (i.e., appreciation pressures on the mark were greater). See Bakker and Chapple (2002), who detail advanced economy experiences with the use of capital controls.

40. The "snake" refers to the decision by EEC countries in 1972 to maintain stable exchange rates after the collapse of the Bretton Woods system by preventing exchange rate fluctuations greater than 2.25 percent. The system was in place until March 1979, when it was replaced by the European Monetary System.

controls were lifted—though, in this instance, outflow controls were not reimposed. Attempts at fine-tuning the exchange rate by altering inflow and outflow restrictions then ended, paving the way for full capital liberalization during the 1980s.

A major turning point for continental Europe came in 1983 under French president François Mitterrand's *tournant de la rigueur* (that is, a turning away from inflationary policies and toward a *franc fort* firmly pegged to the deutsche mark), coupled with the realization that controls on capital outflows—which had been intensified during the economic crisis—disproportionately penalized middle-class investors, who were less able than the rich to evade them. Most French outflow controls were thus lifted during 1984–1986, with full capital account liberalization achieved by 1990.[41] This shift in attitude from a country that had long favored capital controls had major repercussions for both European and other advanced economies (Abdelal 2006). Jacques Delors, who had been Mitterrand's economics and finance minister went on to become the president of the European Commission, where he championed free movement of capital within the single market. His efforts culminated in 1988 with the European Council directive to "abolish restrictions on movements of capital taking place between persons resident in Member States" and to "endeavor to attain the same degree of liberalization . . . in respect of movements of capital to or from third countries."[42] Around the same time, Henri Chavranski, who had been a senior official in the French treasury in the Mitterrand administration, became the chairman of the OECD's committee on capital movements and invisible transactions, and from that vantage point helped to expand the Code of Liberalization to include all cross-border capital movements, including short-term flows that had been excluded from the original formulation of the code. (As recounted below, a third official from Mitterrand's administration, Michel Camdessus,

---

41. Abdelal (2006) suggests that one reason the French minister of economics and finance, Jacques Delors, championed free capital mobility was to provide Germany a *quid pro quo* for full monetary union.

42. EC council directive for the implementation of Article 67 of the Treaty (88/361/EEC). Article 67 of the Treaty of Rome had required member states to progressively abolish all restrictions on the movement of capital between themselves *to the extent necessary to ensure the proper functioning of the common market* (emphasis added). The new directive put transfers pertaining to capital movements on the same footing as those for current transactions, though Article 3 of the directive provides for temporary safeguards, not to be exercised for more than six months, in the face of "short-term capital movements of exceptional magnitude that impose severe strains on foreign exchange markets and lead to serious disturbances in the conduct of monetary and exchange rate policies."

became the managing director of the IMF, where he championed an amendment to the IMF articles that would give it the mandate to promote capital account liberalization—not just in Europe or among advanced economies, but in emerging markets and developing countries as well.)

Meanwhile, in the Anglo-Saxon countries, the impetus toward greater financial openness received a further boost in the early 1980s with the Reagan-Thatcher free-market doctrine. The United States abjured even FX intervention, and the UK finally liberalized its capital account. Moreover, such liberalism was increasingly incorporated in policy advice to emerging market and developing countries. While capital account liberalization was not a priority of the original Washington Consensus (see Williamson 1990), the idea of subjecting government policies to the discipline of the market was very much in the spirit of the reforms prescribed by the international community to emerging market and developing countries. As Summers (1998) argued, "market discipline is the best means the world has found to ensure capital is well used."

But as some emerging markets liberalized domestic financial markets and outflow controls toward the end of 1970s and early 1980s, they also tended to sweep away the prudential inflow measures that were already in place. Chile is a case in point. Until 1981, foreign borrowing by commercial banks required central bank approval, and all foreign borrowing with less than 5½-year maturity was subject to steep reserve deposit requirements, ranging from 10 percent to 25 percent. These restrictions were, however, removed or significantly reduced once Chile embarked on its financial liberalization program in the early 1980s. The result, as Diaz-Alejandro (1985) eloquently described, was "goodbye financial repression, hello financial crash"—a massive inflow surge (the current account deficit reached 14 percent of GDP), real exchange rate appreciation, and a credit boom (banking system credit to the private sector expanded 40 percent between end-December 1981 and June 1982) followed by a crash during which, by mid-1983, nonperforming loans reached 113 percent of bank capital. Much of the banking system had to be nationalized, and GDP contracted by 15 percent relative to 1981. Similar experiments in domestic-cum-external liberalization in Argentina and Uruguay ended equally disastrously.[43]

This experience helped shape policy responses when inflows to EMEs resumed in the early 1990s (once the Latin American debt crisis had been largely resolved), and led to a marked shift toward longer-

---

43. Reported statistics are from Díaz-Alejandro (1985).

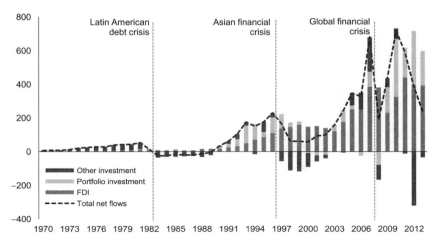

**Figure 2.8**
Net capital flows to EMEs by type of flow, 1970–2013 (in billions of USD).
*Sources*: IMF's International Financial Statistics and World Economic Outlooks databases.
*Notes*: Net capital flows exclude official liabilities of the general government (typically official loans) and foreign exchange reserves. Data are from World Economic Outlook database for 1970–1979, and from the International Financial Statistics database for 1980–2013.

term, nondebt flows (figure 2.8). In 1989, for example, as the Chilean economy overheated, the central bank tightened monetary policy; this, combined with a fall in world interest rates and improved market sentiment, resulted in a surge of capital inflows that further fueled the economic and financial boom. To reduce the volume of inflows and tilt their composition away from short-term debt flows, in June 1991 the central bank introduced a 20 percent unremunerated reserve requirement (URR) on foreign borrowing (for maturities of less than a year, this requirement applied for the duration of the inflow, but it lasted for one year on inflows of longer maturities), minimum stay requirements, regulatory requirements on corporate foreign borrowing, and extensive reporting requirements for banks' capital transactions (table 2.3).[44]

---

44. Initially, the URR covered foreign loans (except trade credits), but to prevent circumvention, coverage was later extended to foreign currency deposits, secondary American Deposit Receipts, and foreign direct investment deemed to be of a speculative nature (Ariyoshi et al. 2000). The URR was raised to 30 percent until capital inflows abated in the context of the 1997–1998 Asian crisis, at which point the URR was eliminated. A voluminous literature seeks to assess the effectiveness of the Chilean measures, and generally finds that the measures were effective in altering the composition of inflows (toward less risky forms of liabilities), but the evidence of the effect on aggregate flows or the exchange rate is mixed (see discussion in section 2.3.5).

**Table 2.3**
Selected cases of inflow controls tightening in EMEs.

| Country | Years | Measures | Context |
|---------|-------|----------|---------|
| Brazil | 1993–1997 | Set minimum term for external borrowing and external borrowing eligible for exemption on the income tax on interest | To avoid real exchange rate appreciation, overheating, and the fiscal costs associated with sterilization |
| | | Reduced (raised) limit on authorized banks' short (long) position in the forex market | |
| | | Imposed foreign transactions tax on proceeds from foreign borrowing | |
| | | Restricted portfolio investment by foreign investors in fixed-income instruments to a single class of fixed-income funds | |
| | | Increased the period for exchange contracting on exports to delay the flow of export revenues | |
| | 2008 | Tightened foreign exchange transaction tax[a] | |
| Chile | 1991–1998 | Introduced URR on foreign borrowing, later extended to cover nondebt flows, American Depository Receipts, and potentially speculative FDI | To avoid overheating, maintain competitiveness, and change the composition of inflows to favor equity over debt, and long-term financing over short-term financing |
| Colombia | 1993–1998 | Introduced URR on external borrowing (limited to loans with maturities up to 18 months), and later extended to cover certain trade credits | To control exchange rate appreciation and manage heavy capital inflow |
| | 2007–2008 | Introduced URR of 40 percent on foreign borrowing and portfolio inflows | |
| | | Imposed limits on the currency derivative positions of banks (500 percent of capital) | |
| Croatia | 2004–2008 | Introduced marginal reserve requirements (MRRs) on bank foreign financing. The MRRs were (1) 40 percent and unremunerated on the net increase in foreign liabilities, (2) 15 percent on the increase in nonresidents' funds, and (3) 55 percent on nonresidents' transactions | To slow down domestic credit growth and mitigate financial dollarization |

| | | | |
|---|---|---|---|
| Malaysia | 1994 | Banned sale to nonresidents of private and government debt securities with less than 12 months' maturity, and money-market instruments | To reestablish monetary control amid rising inflationary pressures and to limit financial sector risks |
| | | Banned commercial banks from performing non–trade related swaps or forward transactions with nonresidents | |
| | | Imposed ceilings on banks' net liability position (excluding trade related and FDI flows | |
| | | Imposed a non–interest bearing deposit requirement for commercial banks against ringgit funds of foreign banks[b] | |
| Thailand | 1995–1996 | Imposed URR on bank's nonresident baht accounts | Manage the volatility of large capital inflows and reduce currency-appreciation pressures |
| | | Introduced open-position limits for short and long positions with smaller limits on short foreign currency positions to discourage foreign borrowing | |
| | | Imposed reporting requirements for banks on risk control measures in forex and derivatives trading | |
| | 2006–2008 | Imposed a URR of 30 percent on foreign currencies sold or exchanged against baht with authorized financial institutions (except for FDI and amounts not exceeding US$20,000). Equity investments in companies listed on the stock exchange were exempt from the URR | |

*Sources:* IMF's *Annual Report on Exchange Arrangements and Exchange Restrictions* (various issues), Ariyoshi et al. 2000, and Magud and Reinhart 2007.

a. Stated aim of the increase in tax was to raise fiscal revenues.

b. Subsequently, banks' eligible liability base was redefined to include all inflows of funds from abroad, making them subject to reserve and liquid-asset requirements.

Chile was not the only country to experiment with inflow controls in the early 1990s—others included Brazil, Colombia, Malaysia, and Thailand. Starting in mid-1993, for example, the Brazilian authorities began to introduce various measures to deter short-term, fixed-income flows (having previously liberalized some inflow measures during 1987–1992); and extended the coverage of the measures to close various loopholes including through the use of sophisticated derivatives transactions. Additional restrictions to reduce the aggregate volume of inflows and alter their composition (such as taxes inversely related to maturities) were adopted in the context of the 1994 Real stabilization program, and further tightened in 1996–1997, before being relaxed as the Asian crisis unfolded in the late 1990s.

In the early 1990s, Thailand actively promoted capital inflows with a liberal inflow regime but kept intact its outflow restrictions. Flows were predominantly short-term borrowing by banks, especially through the Bangkok International Banking Facility (BIBF), which had been established in 1993 with various tax incentives to encourage residents to borrow from abroad. Then, in the face of growing and volatile flows, the authorities sought to stem inflows by imposing a reserve requirement (RR) whose effective cost to banks was greater for nonresident baht accounts (together with an asymmetric open FX position limit that penalized short foreign currency positions), and through moral suasion of BIBF banks to lengthen the maturity of their external borrowing. While the controls managed to reduce net inflows and improve their maturity structure (Ariyoshi et al. 2000), they did not manage to channel investment to foreign exchange–earning sectors and activities, and in 1996 Thailand became the first of the East Asian countries to suffer a major financial crisis that had widespread repercussions within the region—and for EMEs more generally.

**The IMF amendment and the Asian crisis**   Notwithstanding these experiments with inflow controls, the general trend during much of the 1990s was very much toward greater financial openness, culminating in 1995–1997 with an initiative by Michel Camdessus, managing director of the IMF, to amend the IMF's articles, and give it jurisdiction over the capital account in addition to the current account.[45] Abdelal (2006) quotes Camdessus as stating:

---

45. Formally, as discussed in section 2.2.3, the IMF has jurisdiction over payments for current account transactions rather than jurisdiction over the transactions themselves (which, at Bretton Woods, was to be the purview of the World Trade Organization).

Exchange controls may help insulate a country's authorities, but only for a very short time. Even the best conceived and effective exchange control system will be circumvented within six months. Speculators and crooks are extremely sophisticated. And then, after a year, exchange controls are effective only against the poor. The French experience of the beginning of the '80s had been extremely convincing for me. I preached on every possible occasion that you cannot trust exchange controls in the long term.

The proposed amendment would have given the IMF formal jurisdiction over members' financial regulations—generally prohibiting the imposition of new restrictions without its approval—as well as an explicit mandate to promote capital account liberalization. In practical terms, it would have allowed conditionality on capital account restrictions in IMF-supported programs. At the IMF's 1994 annual meetings in Madrid, the Fund's Interim Committee stated that it "welcomes the growing trend toward currency convertibility and encourages member countries to remove impediments to the free flow of capital."[46]

But the amendment was never passed. Opposition came from two quarters. Perhaps surprisingly, the US financial community—voicing its views through the Institute of International Finance (IIF)—opposed the initiative because it potentially gave the IMF too much power, including scope to legitimize capital controls of which the IMF did approve.[47] At the other end of the spectrum was opposition from developing and emerging market policy makers, alarmed by the unfolding East Asian financial crisis, and concerned that—even with transitional arrangements—the IMF would use this mandate to force premature liberalization on reluctant countries. Critics pointed to South Korea which, perversely, had liberalized short-term portfolio flows ahead of longer-term (and generally more stable) direct investment flows; though in fact the impetus for Korea's liberalization had been its desire to join the OECD, not prodding by the IMF.[48] Democrats in the US House of Representatives provided the final nail in the amendment's coffin when they threatened to withhold the US quota increase unless the

However, the proposed amendment to the IMF articles to cover capital movements would have given jurisdiction for both the associated payments and the underlying capital transactions.

46. IMF Press Release No. 94/69 (October 2, 1994).

47. Moreover, as Charles Dallara, the IIF managing director noted, "Although capital account openness is in the broad interest of financial institutions, bankers are much more interested in particular countries, rather than the system as a whole. And the economies that matter most are already mostly open." Quoted by Abdelal (2006).

48. IMF 2005b, 14.

US Treasury withdrew its (already lukewarm) support for the amendment, which it promptly did. That left only the European countries championing the amendment, and by 1999 the initiative was effectively dead.[49]

That the amendment failed to pass did not absolve the IMF from having to give advice on capital account management. Conceptually, what evolved on liberalization was the "integrated approach" of capital account measures and financial sector reforms.[50] Under this approach, capital account liberalization (together with various financial sector reforms) was recommended to proceed in three stages. In the first stage, inflows of foreign direct investment (FDI) should be allowed and restrictions on nonresidents' purchases of equity shares should be relaxed. Some short-term foreign exchange borrowing and lending by banks may also be permitted to facilitate the development of the interbank foreign exchange market, but with safeguards against excessive foreign currency exposure in the aggregate or on individual, unhedged balance sheets. In the second stage, as domestic financial market regulation and supervision improves, all longer-term and non-debt creating capital inflows (as well as FDI outflows) can be liberalized, while maintaining some controls on foreign borrowing, especially on short-term foreign currency debt by corporations. In the third stage, which was the eventual goal for all countries, the capital account would be fully liberalized for both inflows and outflows.

For countries that had already—largely or fully—liberalized, the IMF needed to provide advice on how best to respond to capital inflow surges. A subsequent Independent Evaluation Office (IEO) review of IMF country reports during the 1990s found that the staff had given advice on how to manage capital flows in nineteen episodes covering sixteen countries (out of a sample of twenty-seven EMEs) that experienced large inflows. Of those nineteen episodes, EMEs were counseled to tighten fiscal policy in twelve cases, allow greater exchange rate flexibility in fourteen cases, tighten monetary policy and/or sterilize intervention in seventeen cases, liberalize outflows in six cases, tighten prudential measures in four cases, and impose or tighten inflow controls in just two cases.[51]

It would be fair to say, therefore, that in terms of IMF policy advice, capital controls were very much a last resort. In a speech delivered in

49. For the European attitude toward the proposed amendment, see Communication from the Commission to the Council on *Amendment to the IMF Articles of Agreement on Capital Movements* (SEC 97, 1466, Brussels, 23.07.97).
50. Ishii and Habermeier (2002) discuss the integrated approach in detail.
51. IMF 2005b, 36.

Thailand in July 2007 (during the pre–global financial crisis inflow surge to EMEs), the IMF's managing director, Rodrigo de Rato, enumerated six policy actions—allowing the currency to appreciate, monetary and fiscal tightening, sterilized intervention, liberalization of outflows, and financial sector development—that countries should undertake before considering capital controls on inflows. Such controls, de Rato argued, "might succeed temporarily in reducing inflows and easing exchange market pressure. However, they are unlikely to do so for very long, and they also have important disadvantages. Controls tend to set central banks and private financial institutions against each other . . . and can also create distortions in the behavior of firms and individuals, and when imposed on short-term flows they can cause particular problems for companies that cannot get long-term finance—usually small businesses and start-up firms."[52]

The international community agreed with these views, yet some countries did impose controls on incoming capital as the flows surged into EMEs during the mid-2000s.[53] Colombia, for instance, imposed a URR on foreign borrowing and portfolio inflows in 2007 (while also limiting the currency derivative positions of banks), and Brazil tightened its foreign exchange tax on inflows in the run-up to the crisis in January 2008 (table 2.3). In some cases, however, attempts to impose such controls backfired. In Thailand, for example, concerned by the sharp rise of the Thai baht, the central bank imposed a 30 percent URR (with a 10 percent penalty if the funds were withdrawn in less than one year) on all foreign inflows in December 2006. Market reaction to this announcement was strongly negative: Thailand's stock market plunged 15 percent in less than one day, with indices in Malaysia, Singapore, India, and Indonesia declining by 2–3 percent in contagion selling. As the *New York Times* reported at the time, the episode "evoked memories of the currency crisis nearly a decade earlier," even though "the difference was that rather than trying to stop a plunge in the baht, Thailand was acting to stop sharp increases in its currency, which hit a nine-year high against the dollar Monday after rising 16 percent this

52. Remarks ("Capital Flows in an Interconnected World") delivered at the SEACEN Governors Conference, Bangkok, Thailand, July 28, 2007 (https://www.imf.org/external /np/speeches/2007/072807.htm).
53. Abdelal (2007, 196–199) suggests that following the Asian financial crisis, the IMF became more cautious about promoting capital account liberalization. This is distinct, however, from instances where countries that have already (largely or fully) liberalized their capital accounts reimpose controls or strengthen existing measures.

year."[54] Financial markets were thus sending the clear signal that they did not approve of the capital controls, whether on outflows or on inflows, to the point of not even bothering to distinguish between them.

It is therefore fair to say that by the eve of the global financial crisis in 2007, capital controls had become discredited and disreputable.

### 2.2.5 The Global Financial Crisis and Its Aftermath

The global financial crisis was a rude reminder that not all borrowing and lending decisions are rational, that markets can become overexuberant, and that unfettered flows can result in excessive volatility. With the collapse of Lehman Brothers in September 2008, capital flows suddenly reversed from EMEs, dropping by a staggering US$240 billion in net terms in one quarter (figure 2.9). Emerging Europe—which had been the most financially open in the run-up to the crisis—was hit the hardest, with net flows falling by about US$150 billion during the last two quarters of 2008.

By mid-2009, however, capital flows to EMEs rebounded sharply, driven by accommodative monetary policies in advanced economies and stronger growth prospects of EMEs. The IMF's managing director, Dominique Strauss-Kahn, directed the organization's research department to analyze how emerging markets should respond. The result was two influential staff papers (Ostry et al. 2010; Ostry, Ghosh, Habermeier et al. 2011) that explicitly acknowledged inflow controls as a legitimate part of the policy tool kit. The papers also established that macroprudential measures—commonly assumed to be more effective and efficient than capital controls—often had the same economic effects, leaving little reason to favor them over capital controls.[55]

Inside and outside the IMF, these papers helped spark debate about the appropriate role of capital controls and the optimal degree of capital account liberalization.[56] Meanwhile, emerging market countries began experimenting with a variety of responses to their increasingly volatile

---

54. *New York Times*, December 19, 2006.
55. In describing Ostry et al. (2010) as a fundamental "ideological swerve," *The Economist* (February 20, 2010) probably exaggerated, but the view articulated in that Staff Position Note was certainly contrary to popular *perception* of the IMF's attitude to capital controls.
56. Despite the explicit rubric that a Staff Position Note represents the views of the authors and not the official line, the papers were so controversial that the entire series had to be renamed "Staff Discussion Note" to emphasize that they did not represent the institutional position. On the internal institutional dynamics, see Chwieroth (2010), who focuses mostly on the pre–global financial crisis period, and Gallagher (2014).

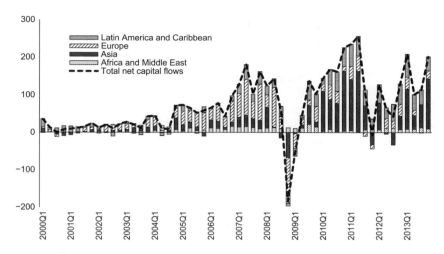

**Figure 2.9**
Net capital flows to EMEs, 2000Q1–2013Q4 (in billions of USD).
*Source*: IMF's International Financial Statistics database.
*Note*: Net capital flows exclude official liabilities of the general government (typically official loans) and foreign exchange reserves.

flows of capital, including prudential measures and capital controls (table 2.4). For the IMF's executive board, the issue of when (if ever) to impose capital controls (or currency-based prudential measures that could act the same way) became highly contentious. The views of the membership split almost perfectly between the advanced and emerging market/developing economies (Gallagher 2014). The executive directors representing EMEs, whose countries were the main recipients of capital inflows in 2009–2010, clung tenaciously to the Articles of Agreement, arguing that members' right to impose capital controls had been guaranteed in Article VI.3 ever since Bretton Woods.[57] They were also concerned that the board's deliberations might be used as the basis for issuing principles for the guidance of members" (PGMs) that could dictate the appropriate design of capital account policies in specified circumstances, as had been envisaged in a 2010 IMF board paper.[58]

---

57. The 1978 amendment of Article IV had already somewhat circumscribed that right, inasmuch as the amendment prohibits members "manipulating exchange rates or the international monetary system in order to prevent effective balance of payments adjustment or to gain an unfair competitive advantage over other members," and requires that they "collaborate with the Fund and other members to assure orderly exchange arrangements and promote a stable system of exchange rates."
58. IMF (2010b, 25) proposed "issuing principles on the appropriate design of capital account policies that would identify actions that members should take or refrain from

A compromise was hammered out after a remarkable internal effort at consensus building, complete with reassurances that the principles were not for the guidance of member countries but only to guide staff's policy advice. The principles were spelled out in a sequence of IMF board papers (IMF 2010a, b; 2011b, c, d; 2012b), culminating in the IMF's *Institutional View on the Liberalization and Management of Capital Flows* (IMF 2012a).[59] Crucially, the *Institutional View* recognizes that while capital flows can have substantial benefits, they also carry risks, and that "there is no presumption that full liberalization is an appropriate goal for all countries at all times." As regards capital inflow controls (and related prudential measures), the paper acknowledges that "in certain circumstances, capital flow management measures can be useful. They should not however substitute for warranted macroeconomic adjustment."[60] Moreover, for financial stability purposes, the *Institutional View* envisages that capital controls could be maintained over the longer term (provided that "no less discriminatory measure is available that is effective"), though it also notes that these should not substitute for efforts to improve supervision of the financial sector.[61]

---

taking in specified circumstances in order to assure orderly exchange arrangements and/ or promote a stable system of exchange rates. Such principles could extend beyond capital account policies to cover other policies, particularly macro-prudential ones that affect capital flows and have potential implications for the member's own domestic and external stability (and thereby systemic stability). The principles adopted for these purposes would thus provide guidance to members on the scope of their obligations under Article IV, Section 1." While disregard of such formal PGMs would not have automatically implied that the country was in breach of its obligations under the articles, it could have triggered the need for special consultations between the IMF and the member country.

59. Thus, IMF (2011d) clarified that "The framework proposed by staff would provide a basis for policy advice to members facing capital inflows . . . However, it is not proposed or contemplated that this policy framework would provide guidance on the scope of members' obligations under Article IV, as was foreshadowed last December in the context of *The Fund's Role Regarding Cross-Border Capital Flows* [IMF 2010b]."

60. In order to encompass both capital controls (i.e., residency-based measures) and macroprudential measures that affect capital flows, the IMF introduced the nomenclature "capital flow management (CFM)" measures. Capital controls are always CFMs, but whether a prudential measure constitutes a CFM depends on whether it was imposed in order to influence the volume of cross-border flows—i.e., it depends on the design intent of the measure, which is hard to prove. Since the label CFM does not have legal status within the IMF, this ambiguity is largely unimportant for the IMF's purposes—but the designation of a measure as a CFM by IMF staff can potentially cause difficulties for members who have other international obligations prohibiting the use of capital controls (e.g., the OECD Code of Liberalisation or the EU Treaty).

61. As shown in chapter 7, a capital control (that is, a residency-based measure) will generally be welfare superior to a liability-side currency-based prudential measure because it allows differentiation according to the residency of the investor.

**Table 2.4**
Post-crisis selected cases of measures to limit capital inflows in EMEs.

| Country | Year | Summary of measures |
|---------|------|---------------------|
| Brazil | 2009–2012 | A tax of 2 percent was levied on foreign portfolio equity and fixed-income inflows in October 2009. The tax rate was gradually increased to 6 percent and extended to cover other sources of foreign flows, such as the issuance of depository receipts (DRs) into local equities, borrowing abroad with a maturity of less than one year (later tightened to a maturity of less than two, three, and five years), and currency derivatives. A URR of 60 percent on banks' gross FX positions beyond US$3 billion (later tightened to US$1 billion) was also levied. |
| Costa Rica | 2014 | Activation (for a period of up to six months) of an increase in the income tax rate (from 8 to 33 percent) on interest earned on investments in fixed-income assets issued by private-sector entities to nonresidents; establishment of a URR for new investments in these financial instruments. |
| Indonesia | 2010–2011 | Imposition of a one-month minimum holding period on central bank bonds for all investors; a limit on the daily balance of banks' short-term external debt to 30 percent of capital; an increase in the reserve requirement on deposit accounts in foreign exchange from 1 to 5 percent. |
| Korea, S. | 2010–2011 | Setting the maximum limits on banks' foreign exchange derivative contracts at 50 percent (domestic banks) and 250 percent (foreign bank branches) of bank capital in the previous month; restoration of a 14 percent withholding tax on interest income on nonresident purchases of treasury and monetary stabilization bonds (a similar tax was already in place for domestic investors). |
| Peru | 2010–2011 | Extension of a 60 percent reserve requirement for new foreign holders of debt with maturity up to three years; extension of the application of income tax rate of 30 percent to all nonresident gains on financial derivatives transactions with residents. |
| Russia | 2011 | Increase in the reserve requirement for (1) liabilities to nonresident legal entities in rubles and foreign currency, from 2.5 to 3.5 percent; (2) liabilities to individuals in rubles and foreign currency, from 2.5 to 3.0 percent; and (3) other liabilities in rubles and in foreign currency, from 2.5 to 3.0 percent. |
| Thailand | 2010 | Restoration of a 15 percent withholding tax on nonresidents' interest earnings and capital gains on new purchases of government bonds. |
| Uruguay | 2012 | Introduction of a reserve requirement of 40 percent (later raised to 50 percent) on new foreign purchases of central bank notes and central government securities. |

*Source*: IMF country reports.

*Note*: Some measures do not discriminate between residents and nonresidents, but by their design (indirectly) target capital inflows.

While this document delineates the general conditions and circumstances under which IMF staff could recommend the use of certain tools and policies (including capital controls), by its very nature it does not provide an in-depth analysis of how these tools may interact with each other to better manage capital flows. That is the subject of this book.

## 2.3   The Academic Literature

Paralleling developments on the policy front have been advances in economic theory, and in the empirical analysis of capital flows and their management. Although the formal literature is vast, it can be grouped into two main strands. The first seeks to establish the benefits of capital flows (mostly from the perspective of the capital-importing country) for growth and economic development, as well as for risk sharing and consumption smoothing. Taking as given the ultimate goal of free capital mobility, a subbranch of this strand examines the optimal sequencing of liberalization—including between the current account and the capital account, between the capital account and the domestic financial markets, and among the various types of flows within the capital account.

The opposing strand, while acknowledging the benefits of foreign capital flows, emphasizes the macroeconomic challenges (including loss of monetary autonomy) and financial stability risks wrought by unfettered flows. A subbranch of this strand examines whether temporary or selective use of controls by countries that have largely or fully open capital accounts can help mitigate the adverse consequences of capital flows. Largely orthogonal, but crucial to the empirical analysis of either strand, are studies that try to measure—de jure or de facto—cross-border capital mobility (box 2.1).

### 2.3.1   Growth Benefits of Capital Flows

A large body of literature—often implicitly based on the Solow (1957) neoclassical growth model—seeks to establish how open capital accounts and the free flow of capital can foster economic growth. In the neoclassical model, an open capital account allows capital to flow from countries where it is abundant (and its marginal product is low) to countries where it is scarce (and its marginal product is correspondingly higher), resulting in an efficient allocation of resources and higher output (gross domestic product) in the capital-importing country and higher income (gross national product) for the capital-exporting

**Box 2.1**
Measures of capital controls.

Any empirical assessment of the effects of capital controls requires some way of measuring these policies. Unlike many other policy variables, such as interest rates or fiscal deficits, capital controls are difficult to quantify. Studies generally rely on the information contained in the IMF's *Annual Report on Exchange Arrangements and Exchange Restrictions (AREAER)* to construct de jure indices of capital controls, sometimes supplemented with news reports or information available from central bank websites.

The earlier literature (e.g., Epstein and Schor 1992; Alesina, Grilli, and Milesi-Ferretti 1993; Grilli and Milesi-Ferretti 1995) uses a (binary) summary indicator of "restrictions on residents' payments on capital transactions" to capture the existence of capital controls. This indicator, however, does not differentiate between inflow and outflow controls, between controls on different types of flows, or between partially and completely closed capital accounts. Several subsequent studies (e.g., Johnston and Tamirisa 1998; Brune and Guisinger 2007) take into account restrictions on different types of flows, and distinguish between inflow and outflow measures—taking the sum (or average) of the binary scores for restrictions on different categories to come up with an overall indicator of openness. But perhaps the most commonly used capital account openness measures are those by Chinn and Ito (2006) and Quinn and Toyoda (2008). Chinn and Ito use the *AREAER* to construct an "extensive" financial globalization indicator that is obtained from the principal component analysis of (binary indicators of) the existence of current account restrictions (including the presence of multiple exchange rates), and the five-year rolling average of a binary indicator of restrictions on the capital account. While the measure does not distinguish between inflow and outflow restrictions, it covers a wide range of countries over a long time period (it is updated periodically), which contributes to its broad appeal. By contrast, Quinn and Toyoda's capital account openness indicator is based on the coding of the information contained in the *AREAER* on restrictions on capital flows, while making a subjective assessment of the intensity of restrictions. Like the Chinn-Ito measure, it has a wide cross-country and time coverage.

In recent years, several other disaggregated de jure measures based on the *AREAER* have been developed (though their cross-country and time series coverage tends to be more limited than the Chinn-Ito and Quinn-Toyoda measures). Schindler (2009), for example, documents the existence of restrictions at the level of individual transactions (such as issue or purchase locally by nonresidents, sale or purchase abroad by residents) for different types of asset classes. Aggregating the codes over different subsets of transaction types, he obtains indices by types and direction of flows (as well as by the residency of the investor). His data set has been extended by Fernández et al. (2015) to cover additional asset

Box 2.1 (continued)

classes, countries, and years. Ostry et al. (2012) construct indicators of capital controls specific to the financial sector (such as restrictions on the financial sector from lending to nonresidents, or on maintenance of accounts abroad), as well as of foreign currency–related restrictions that may act like capital controls (such as restrictions on lending locally in foreign currency). Ahmed et al. (2015) and Forbes, Fratzscher, and Straub (2015) construct indicators of *changes* in capital controls at quarterly and weekly frequencies, respectively. The former covers the period 2002–2012, while the latter covers 2009–2011 only. These changes-based indices can better capture the tightening or loosening of controls—but still do not capture the intensity of the measure or even the degree to which it has been tightened (any tightening is coded as +1, any loosening as –1).

While de jure measures are a useful indicator of the extent of legal restrictions on capital account transactions in place in a country, they generally do not accurately reflect the intensity of restrictions (especially for cross-country comparative purposes) or whether or not those restrictions are binding. Therefore, some researchers use de facto measures or outcome variables, which capture actual flows or stocks of foreign assets and liabilities (e.g., Lane and Milesi-Ferretti 2001). A caveat to using de facto measures, however, is that they may capture the effect of factors other than legal restrictions, and of course they are of little use when the researcher is interested in the effect of capital controls on the outcome itself.

country.[62] While there are good theoretical reasons to believe the "global allocative efficiency" argument that flows to capital-scarce countries will, at least temporarily, raise the rate of output growth, the empirical evidence supporting this is surprisingly weak.[63]

In an early study, for example, Alesina, Grilli, and Milesi-Ferretti (1993) use a binary indicator of "restrictions on the payments for capital

62. In a famous paper, Lucas (1990) notes that in reality, capital flows from advanced to developing countries are far below the levels predicted by neoclassical theory. Several subsequent studies investigate this observation—often referred to as the Lucas Paradox—and argue that it can be explained by (1) differences in fundamentals that affect the production structure of the economy, such as differences in technology, quality of human capital, government policies, and institutions (e.g., Tornell and Velasco 1992; Alfaro, Kalemli-Ozcan, and Volosovych 2008); and (2) international capital market imperfections, notably sovereign risk and asymmetric information (Gertler and Rogoff 1990; Gordon and Bovenberg 1996).

63. The typical approach taken in empirical studies to assess the effect of capital mobility on economic growth is to regress annual or five-year output growth rates on an indicator of (the degree of) capital account openness, while controlling for a host of other typical growth determinants (à la Barro 1991).

transactions" in twenty OECD countries over 1950–1989 to examine the effect of capital account liberalization on economic growth, but they strongly reject the hypothesis that capital controls reduce growth. Using a similar method, but a larger sample of sixty-one advanced and developing countries, Grilli and Milesi-Ferretti (1995) also find that controls are not associated with lower output growth. By contrast, in a sample of sixty-four countries, and using a relatively detailed indicator of financial openness, Quinn (1997) purports to find that the *change* in capital account openness over 1958–1989 is robustly and positively associated with economic growth. Rodrik (1998), however, extends the sample to about 100 countries over 1975–1989, but concludes that "there is no evidence in the data that countries without capital controls have grown faster, invested more, or experienced lower inflation."[64]

In a survey of literature, Prasad et al. (2003) review fourteen studies examining the effect of capital account liberalization on output growth, and document that only three studies report unequivocally positive effects; the other eleven find no effects or mixed effects. Quinn and Toyoda (2008) use panel data spanning five decades and find that capital account liberalization has a significantly positive association with economic growth in both advanced and emerging market countries. Bonfiglioli (2008) finds that financial integration significantly increases productivity growth, but that it does not affect capital accumulation across countries. Using simulation analysis, however, Gourinchas and Jeanne (2006) argue that the welfare benefits from international real-location of capital are positive, but very modest for typical EMEs.

One reason for the widely differing findings may be that the effects of capital flows depend on recipient-country characteristics. Thus, using Quinn's (1997) measure of capital account restrictions, Edwards (2001) finds a positive interactive effect between income and capital account openness, whereas openness itself has a negative impact on growth—implying that it is only above a certain income threshold that openness is associated with faster GDP growth. Arteta, Eichengreen, and Wyplosz (2001) criticize Edwards' study on methodological grounds; nevertheless, the idea that countries need to achieve a certain level of economic, financial, and institutional development to benefit

---

64. Henry (2007) notes that since the neoclassical growth model would imply that gross domestic product (but not gross national product) should decline in the source country and increase in the recipient country, it is possible that studies whose samples include advanced and developing countries find no impact on output growth because of the offsetting effects on source and recipient countries.

from capital account liberalization recurs in the literature (e.g., Prasad et al. 2003; Dell'Ariccia et al. 2008). Klein and Olivei (2008), however, show that many emerging market and developing countries do not meet such thresholds, and that these results are mainly driven by developed countries. In fact, Prasad, Rajan, and Subramanian (2007) and Aizenman, Pinto, and Radziwill (2007) find that those emerging market and developing countries that rely more on foreign financing tend to experience *lower* long-run economic growth than their financially closed peers. Moreover, as Kose, Prasad, and Taylor (2010) note, it is very difficult to pinpoint the thresholds with any precision, and hence to give policy advice on when liberalization may be appropriate.

In addition to recipient-country characteristics, it is also intuitive that the benefits for output growth may depend upon the *nature* of the capital flows. Very short-term hot-money flows, for example, are unlikely to contribute directly to productive investment (though it is possible that they facilitate longer-term investment by providing liquidity), while FDI flows could conceivably bring larger direct growth benefits through transfer of technology and skills. Borensztein, De Gregorio, and Lee (1998) find that FDI indeed contributes significantly to higher economic growth, though the effect is conditional on the country's stock of human capital. Bekaert, Harvey, and Lundblad (2001) find that equity market liberalization—that is, allowing nonresidents to buy domestic equities—is associated with one percentage point per year higher output growth (over the five years following liberalization). Likewise, Henry (2007) reports lower cost of capital, higher investment, and faster output growth after equity market liberalization in EMEs. A meta-analysis by Jeanne, Subramanian, and Williamson (2012) concludes that there is little robust evidence of a positive relationship between financial globalization and growth, except possibly for equity market liberalization.

Beyond a direct, measurable impact on output growth, capital account openness may bring ancillary benefits such as financial development and policy and institutional discipline. Thus, Levine (2001) finds that the liberalization of foreign portfolio flows tends to enhance stock market liquidity and the efficiency of the domestic banking system, effects that spur economic growth. Edison et al. (2002) find that, although financial integration is not strongly correlated with higher output growth, it is associated with higher educational attainment, better institutional quality, and greater financial sector development. (For at least some of these variables, part of the correlation may reflect reverse causality. For example, more foreign capital is likely to flow to countries with a better educated labor force.) Likewise, Kaminsky and Schmukler (2008) and Kose et al. (2009) find more robust evidence that capital account openness produces indirect benefits—such as financial sector and institutional development—than that it directly promotes real GDP growth.

Rodrik and Subramanian (2009) conjecture why the empirical evidence is not fully supportive of the "global allocative efficiency" argument for capital account liberalization—whereby capital should flow from advanced to developing countries. Their explanation is that the traditional assumption underlying the neoclassical model that developing countries are saving-constrained (so that liberalization, by easing that constraint, should boost investment and growth) is incorrect. Rather, they argue, developing countries are investment-opportunity constrained, and inflows undercut growth by overvaluing the domestic currency, which inhibits investment in the crucial tradables sector.

By contrast, Henry (2007) criticizes the bulk of existing studies on the grounds that the neoclassical model, which the papers supposedly take as their basis, does not imply the phenomenon that the papers examine—namely, whether countries that are more financially open grow faster on average than those that are more financially closed. Rather, he maintains, the neoclassical model implies that an initial opening of the capital account will lead to a onetime decrease in the cost of capital and, in a frictionless world, to an instantaneous jump in the country's capital stock. It will therefore result in an instantaneously higher growth rate of output to a permanently higher level. Event studies that look at the growth impact in the immediate post-liberalization years, he reasons, thus provide a better test of the global allocative efficiency argument.

While event studies (e.g., Bekaert, Harvey, and Lundblad 2001; Henry 2007) do indeed tend to find that liberalization is followed by a short-term boost to the stock market or output growth, the issue in our view is *not* of a onetime increase in the growth rate. Few doubt that allowing capital inflows may boost investment and growth in the short run—in fact, one of the risks of capital account liberalization is excessive credit growth, which brings unsustainable consumption and investment booms (see chapter 4). The real question is how the economy behaves over the medium to long term; thus what needs to be established is that despite the greater macroeconomic and financial volatility typically associated with capital inflows and subsequent reversals, countries with open capital accounts *on average* grow faster than countries that are less financially open (such that, over a medium- to long-term horizon, the level of income will be higher in the former than in the latter). The empirical evidence discussed above suggests that this has been a hard case to make unequivocally.

### 2.3.2   Consumption Smoothing and Risk Sharing

In addition to the impact on growth, cross-border capital mobility is hypothesized to bring welfare gains from consumption smoothing and risk sharing. In the early 1980s, when policy circles had begun giving more credence to the idea that trade in capital assets should be on the same footing as trade in goods and services, intertemporal models of the current account (e.g., Sachs 1981) surfaced in the literature. In these models, the current account is not viewed as the excess of exports over imports and net factor payments, but rather as the excess of saving over investment—both of which are modeled as the optimal choice of the representative agent. A simple two-period diagram, in direct analogy to the trade literature, can then be used to establish that free capital mobility is optimal for a small open economy because it allows *intertemporal* trade.[65] In these models, capital flows allow the representative agent to smooth consumption against shocks to domestic output, and investment can be undertaken until the point at which the marginal product of capital equals the world interest rate. Developing countries, therefore, can invest and thereby converge to advanced economies' income levels faster than they would by relying on domestic saving alone (Bazdarich 1978; Lipton and Sachs 1983).

Related, but distinct, are the opportunities for risk sharing afforded by capital flows—whereby the home agent invests abroad and the foreign agent holds part of the domestic capital stock. Early work by Grubel (1968) applies Markowitz mean-variance portfolio optimization in an international framework to establish theoretically the benefits of cross-border risk diversification through gross capital flows. Stockman and Hernández D. (1988) examine the effects of restrictions (exchange controls and capital controls) on international financial markets in a general-equilibrium, rational expectations setting, and find that such restrictions

---

65. Although Bhagwati (1998)—a staunch defender of free trade in goods and services—explicitly rejects the analogy between "trade in widgets" and trade in assets on the grounds that the latter are susceptible to panics and manias (see discussion in section 2.3.4), and argues that any gains from free capital mobility must also consider the cost of the crises that often accompany free capital mobility.

reduce trade in goods and lower welfare. (The result is unsurprising since, in their setup, there are no distortions or externalities that call for government intervention; hence, any restrictions on the competitive equilibrium must be welfare deteriorating.) Obstfeld (1995) embeds the risk diversification of cross-border investment in a two-country model to establish the long-run growth benefits of asset trade, although Devereux and Smith (1994) obtain the opposite result—whereby risk diversification reduces precautionary saving and therefore investment and growth.

As with the growth literature, empirical studies on the consumption-smoothing or risk-diversification benefits of capital account openness are mixed. Ghosh (1995) finds that capital flows have generally been too volatile in industrialized countries to be consistent with optimal intertemporal consumption smoothing, while Ghosh and Ostry (1995) find that the current account in developing countries indeed acts as a buffer to smooth consumption in the face of shocks to output. Athana-soulis and van Wincoop (2000) evaluate the gains from global risk sharing and find large benefits to a typical country. By contrast, Kose, Prasad, and Terrones (2009) find that financial integration has at best led to a modest degree of risk sharing, with gains primarily accruing to advanced economies. They argue that one reason why EMEs have not benefited as much is that capital flows to these countries have been dominated by portfolio debt, which is not conducive to risk sharing. Other studies confirm a significant effect of financial integration on international risk sharing for advanced countries, but not so much for less economically developed countries (Artis and Hoffman 2006, 2007).

### 2.3.3 Sequencing of Liberalization

With liberalization accepted as a worthy long-run goal, a subbranch of the literature turned to the optimal sequencing of current and capital account liberalization—an issue of particular relevance in the 1970s and 1980s, when many EMEs had both trade and capital account restrictions. Several studies indicate two key reasons why trade should be liberalized before capital flows. First, the sectoral allocation of foreign savings may be inefficient in the presence of trade distortions; second, large capital inflows may appreciate the real exchange rate, damaging the tradable sector just as that sector needs to adjust to the loss of trade protection (McKinnon 1973; Rodrik 1987).[66] Calvo (1988) shows that

---

66. On the hysteresis effects of real appreciations on export performance, see Baldwin and Krugman (1989).

trade reform under an open capital account may be subject to self-fulfilling collapses, especially if the government's commitment to the reform program lacks credibility. Falvey and Kim (1992) recommend that current and capital account liberalization should proceed in phases, with macroeconomic stabilization, changes to the tariff structure, export incentives, and a government revenue scheme preceding capital account liberalization. McKinnon and Pill (1997) argue that successful capital account liberalization also requires establishing a sound banking system, especially effective prudential regulation. They show that in the presence of moral hazard in the financial sector, unrestrained capital inflows and domestic credit expansion can entail significant economic risks.

Building on these insights, a consensus seems to have emerged that current account liberalization should precede capital account liberalization, with the latter proceeding only gradually and according to an integrated approach that takes into account domestic financial and macroeconomic conditions and policies. The integrated approach thus envisions proceeding through successive, and often overlapping, phases of lifting controls on inflows and outflows (e.g., FDI inflows first, followed by long-term inflows and FDI outflows, and eventually short-term inflows and other outflows) that also entail supporting reforms to the legal, accounting, financial, and corporate frameworks (Johnston, Darbar, and Echeverria 1997; IMF 2012b).

### 2.3.4 Macroeconomic Challenges and Financial-Stability Risks

Despite the myriad potential benefits of capital mobility, there may also be significant costs. Foremost is the loss of policy autonomy, which is often cast in terms of the monetary policy "trilemma." Fleming (1962) and Mundell (1963) famously showed that countries with fixed exchange rates can enjoy monetary policy autonomy only by limiting capital mobility. (Some recent commentators go further, arguing that even countries with flexible exchange rates may be subject to the vagaries of capital flows and have limited scope for an independent monetary policy if their capital account is open; Rey 2013.) In the face of capital inflows, for instance, raising interest rates to cool an overheating economy may result in further inflows that will need to be monetized unless the intervention is sterilized. But the point is more general: unless the government is indifferent about the exchange rate, the scope for full policy autonomy will be limited when capital may enter or leave the country freely, which is partly why Keynes wanted controls to be a permanent feature of the international monetary architecture.[67]

In addition, as evident from the discussion in section 2.2, capital account openness also exposes the economy to the vicissitudes and vagaries of cross-border flows, and boom-bust cycles. Thus, Frank Taussig's insight from the late 1920s (the opening quote of this book) was amply confirmed during the interwar period, and painfully re-discovered by EMEs that liberalized rapidly in the 1980s and 1990s. Since then, several studies have formally documented how large capital inflows in the aftermath of financial liberalization are soon followed by sudden stops and financial crisis in EMEs, often with deep economic, social, and political costs (Diaz-Alejandro 1985; Kaminsky and Reinhart 1999; Demirguc-Kunt and Detragiache 1998; Kaminsky and Schmukler 2008).[68]

The volatility of cross-border capital flows has led some to propose that full financial integration may not be desirable when existing distortions and externalities imply that the assumptions of a first-best competitive equilibrium are violated. Cooper (1998), Rodrik (1998), and Stiglitz (2000), for instance, argue that in a world of imperfect information, free capital mobility may amplify existing distortions, encourage moral hazard and excessive risk taking, and expose countries to contagion/herding effects.[69] This literature has in recent years gained greater intellectual respectability as formal models have been developed in which the presence of domestic externalities results in excessive, and excessively risky external borrowing (Jeanne and Korinek 2010; Korinek 2011; Bianchi 2011). In these and other externality-based models (e.g., Ghosh and Kim 2008; Farhi and Werning 2013), the competitive equilibrium is inefficient, thus justifying the use of direct capital controls (or, in some cases, macroprudential measures) as a Pigouvian

---

67. This is contrary to the Fleming-Mundell model, where a fiscal expansion raises interest rates and strengthens the currency. More typically, fiscal expansion in developing and emerging market economies will lead to capital outflows and currency depreciation, thereby limiting the scope for countercyclical fiscal policy. The reason is that demand for government debt is lacking, often because the government lacks policy credibility.

68. By contrast, some studies, for example, Edwards (2005) and Glick, Guo, and Hutchison (2006) show that capital account openness is not associated with external or currency crises. Ranciere, Tornell, and Westermann (2006) theoretically decompose the effects of financial liberalization on economic growth and on the incidence of crises, and show that the direct effect on growth outweighs the indirect effect via a higher propensity to crisis.

69. On herding, Keynes (1936) compares cross-border capital flows to a beauty contest in which judges assess the contestants, not based on their own views, but how they believe other judges will vote.

tax against excessive inflows to attain the constrained optimum.[70] The tax is an *ex ante* measure, akin to Tobin's (1978, 1996) currency transactions tax, to prevent excessive inflows—which mitigates the impact of subsequent outflows, and may be a more effective strategy than trying to stop outflows when the reversal occurs.[71]

### 2.3.5  Managing Capital Inflows

While both theory and experience suggest that some restraint on cross-border capital flows may be desirable, few argue in favor of keeping the capital account fully closed. As a result, there is a burgeoning literature on the effectiveness of (usually temporary or cyclically varying) capital controls to mitigate the risks associated with unfettered flows in economies with largely open capital accounts (see chapter 9 for a detailed discussion). Unfortunately, many of these studies are not clear about the policy objective against which the measures are being assessed. In principle, there may be two broad objectives: reducing the volume of inflows and their associated consequences (currency appreciation, credit booms, overheating of the economy), or shifting the composition of the inflows so that the country ends up with a less risky external-liability structure (less FX exposure on unhedged balance sheets, less short-term debt, etc.).

Empirical studies also confront other difficulties in evaluating the effectiveness of capital controls, such as creating the counterfactual and contending with the fundamental identification problem whereby countries tend to impose controls precisely when they face large flows (which yields a spurious positive correlation, and biases estimates of the coefficient of interest toward zero). Notwithstanding these difficulties, the literature of the 1970s and 1980s, mostly in the context of advanced countries, generally finds that capital controls are able to insulate the economy—at least as measured by the wedge between domestic and international interest rates (Dooley 1996). For EMEs, perhaps the best-known (and most studied) instance of inflow con-

---

70. Gallagher (2014) provides a useful survey of the "prudential capital controls" literature. In addition to the externalities-based literature, some studies justify the use of capital inflow controls for dynamic terms-of-trade manipulation purposes (see, e.g., Costinot, Lorenzoni, and Werning 2011).

71. Empirical evidence on the effectiveness of outflow controls during market turbulence episodes suggests that they have little effect (Edison and Reinhart 2001). Comparing preventive outflow controls (intended to prevent a currency crisis) and curative controls (those imposed after the collapse), Edwards (1999) argues that the former have been largely ineffective, while evidence on the latter is mixed.

trols is Chile's adoption of an URR—commonly referred to as *encaje*—in the 1990s. Using high-frequency data, Edwards and Rigobon (2009) find that the tightening of Chile's inflow controls was associated with a depreciation of the exchange rate and with reduced sensitivity of the currency to external factors. But De Gregorio, Edwards, and Valdés (2000) claim that the *encaje* had no substantial impact on either the real exchange rate or the interest rate differential. They do, however, report more persistent and significant effects on the composition of capital inflows in favor of longer-maturity instruments.[72]

For other emerging markets, the findings are equally mixed. Examining Colombia's imposition of a Chilean-style URR during the 1990s, for example, Cardenas and Barrera (1997) find that there was little impact on the total volume of inflows, though the inflows' composition shifted toward longer-term—and, therefore, presumably safer—liabilities. Concha, Galindo, and Vasquez (2011), however, find no evidence that Colombia's controls over 1998–2008 were effective in reducing inflows and currency-appreciation pressures, or in changing the composition of inflows. By contrast, using monthly data for Brazil over 1983–1995, and estimating a vector autoregressive model to take into account endogeneity between variables, Cardoso and Goldfajn (1998) show that inflow controls do have a (lagged) impact on net flows.

In view of this very mixed evidence, Magud and Reinhart (2007) undertake a comprehensive review of (pre–global financial crisis) studies on the effectiveness of measures to control capital inflows. Their reading of the literature is that inflow controls tend to make monetary policy more independent and alter the composition of capital flows, with less clear effect on the volume of net flows or on real exchange rate dynamics. Subsequent to that review, Ostry et al. (2010, 2011, 2012) exploit the "natural experiment" afforded by the 2008 crisis to examine the results for EMEs that had capital controls (or currency-based prudential measures that may act like them) in place in the run-up to the crisis and those that did not. Their results show that both capital controls and currency-based prudential measures are associated with greater economic resilience (smaller output declines) during the crisis.

---

72. Controls that produce a safer external-liability structure or that temper volatile capital flows may reduce the economy's vulnerability to crisis. But they also have costs. In particular, they may disadvantage small- and medium-scale enterprises in obtaining credit (Forbes 2007; Alfaro, Chari, and Kanczuk 2014), though it is not clear that capital controls would be any worse than prudential measures in this respect (see chapter 11 for a discussion).

Moreover, they find that such measures significantly reduce financial-stability risks (such as FX lending by the domestic banking system, and portfolio debt in total external liabilities).

While the studies of Ostry et al. do not distinguish between long-standing and temporary capital controls, they renewed interest in examining the effectiveness of capital controls and prudential measures on capital flows and related macroeconomic concerns (such as currency appreciation), as well as on financial-stability risks. A large literature has since evolved that mostly focuses on the tightening of controls and prudential measures in the aftermath of the global financial crisis, especially in Brazil and South Korea. These studies tend to find that such measures are associated with a significant decrease in inflows, lower currency appreciation pressures, and greater monetary policy autonomy in Brazil (e.g., Forbes et al. 2012; Chamon and Garcia 2016), and with lower volatility of flows and lower financial-stability risks in Korea (Ree, Yoon, and Park 2012; Kim 2013; Bruno and Shin 2014). More generally, recent studies focusing on EMEs find a strong effect of capital controls and macroprudential policies in discouraging capital inflows (Ahmed and Zlate 2014), and in reducing financial fragilities (Forbes, Fratzscher, and Straub 2015).

## 2.4   Conclusion

Boom-bust cycles in cross-border capital flows are nothing new. They happened during the late–nineteenth century golden era of financial globalization, they were present in the interwar period, and they reemerged in the decades following World War II as capital account restrictions were dismantled and private capital flows resumed. But views about managing capital flows have swung markedly over this period—from the laissez-faire attitude of the nineteenth century, to the structural controls envisaged at Bretton Woods, to the free market principles and Washington Consensus of the 1980s and 1990s, and the recent reevaluation in light of the global financial crisis of 2008–2009.

It is clear, however, that many advanced economies used restrictions on capital inflows for prudential purposes—even as they pursued financial liberalization more broadly—until the 1980s, when capital account restrictions began to be swept away as part of broader liberalization efforts. Likewise, many emerging markets that had inflow controls for prudential reasons dismantled them when liberalizing domestic financial markets and controls over outflows. That the use of capital controls as a means of managing inflows is often viewed with suspicion may be partly a "guilt by association" with outflow controls and exchange restrictions. Historically these have been more prevalent and more intensive, and their purpose has been to prop up authoritarian regimes or poor macroeconomic policies, often affecting both current and capital transactions (Ghosh and Qureshi 2016).

For emerging market economies, the lesson from history and from the academic literature is that capital flows can bring myriad benefits—but that fully unfettered flows may not be optimal, and measures to manage them form a legitimate part of the policy tool kit. When and how such measures should be used, and how they fit with other policies—especially monetary, exchange rate, macroprudential—is the focus of the rest of this book.

# II  Surges and Consequences

# 3 Surges

## 3.1 Introduction

Capital flows to emerging markets have always been episodic, booms followed by busts. But, as discussed in chapter 1, both the amplitude and the frequency of swings appear to have increased markedly in recent years. Such volatility can pose policy challenges at both ends of the episode—when inflows surge as well as when they recede—but how the surge is managed is likely to have a significant bearing on how its end affects the economy. Since a first step to managing surges is understanding when and why they occur, our goal in this chapter is to identify their drivers, while in chapter 4 we look at their consequences and endings.

The literature on the topic has a long tradition of trying to identify push and pull factors of cross-border capital flows—yet in equilibrium, flows must reflect the confluence of supply and demand.[1] Hence there must be both push (supply-side) and pull (demand-side) factors at play, making it hard to attribute the observed flows to one side or the other. More meaningful, therefore, is to consider the determinants of *changes* in capital flows, which might be associated with changes in supply factors (and declining costs of funds), or changes in demand factors (and rising costs of funds), or both (with roughly constant costs). From a policy perspective, moreover, it is generally the large increases in inflows—surges—that are of particular importance because of their greater macroeconomic and financial-stability impact.

Since surges tend to be a distinct phenomenon from more normal flows (see appendix A.3.1), in studying them it is useful to distinguish

---

1. See, for example, Calvo, Leiderman, and Reinhart (1993); Chuhan, Claessens, and Mamingi (1993); Fernandez-Arias (1996); Taylor and Sarno (1997); Fratzscher (2011). Some recent studies focus on the characteristics of large inflows (Reinhart and Reinhart 2008; Cardarelli, Elekdag, and Kose 2009; Forbes and Warnock 2012; Ghosh et al. 2014).

between the factors associated with their occurrence and those that determine their magnitude. This gives some insight into which countries are likely to receive larger inflows when capital flows surge toward emerging market economies (EMEs). A further useful distinction is between asset- and liability-flow surges. While it is customary to think of inflow surges being the result of foreigners pouring money into the country (that is, increasing its external liabilities), from a balance of payments (BOP) perspective they could equally result from residents repatriating funds (or simply not investing as much abroad as usual), thus reducing the country's stock of external assets. The two types of surges may have different determinants—for instance, domestic investors may be more responsive to changes in local conditions because of informational advantages, while foreign investors may be more sensitive to global factors; they may thus require different policy responses. For example, while inflow controls could, at least in principle, be used against liability-flow surges, they could not easily be deployed against asset-flow surges, which would need some other policy measures.[2]

Our empirical analysis indeed finds differences in the roles of global and domestic factors in influencing the occurrence and the magnitude of surges. Global factors appear to matter more for the occurrence of surges—acting as gatekeepers in determining whether capital flows toward EMEs at all—while magnitude depends mostly on a given country's domestic characteristics. Our analysis also points to some differences between the characteristics of liability-flow surges (which reflect the portfolio decisions of foreign investors) and asset-flow surges (which reflect the investment decisions of residents). Surges driven by foreign investors appear to be more sensitive to global conditions (such as US interest rates and global market uncertainty), relative to those driven by domestic residents.

The remainder of this chapter is organized as follows. Section 3.2 describes how we define surges and presents some basic facts about their occurrence and magnitude. Section 3.3 examines the determinants of the occurrence of a surge, while section 3.4 looks at the factors that influence the magnitude of the flow conditional on surge occurrence. Section 3.5 distinguishes between surges driven by asset and liability flows. Section 3.6 concludes.

---

2. This is because, by definition, capital controls on inflows target nonresidents, limiting their acquisition of domestic assets. For the government to prevent residents from repatriating their foreign investments, it would either have to prevent the foreign investment in the first place—i.e., maintain restrictions on residents' outflows—or impose some form of tax on foreign exchange transactions related to capital movements.

## 3.2   Some Stylized Facts

Surges are exceptionally large capital flows into a country. This definition seems straightforward, but it leaves open many questions about how to define them. Much of the existing literature defines surges as instances in which flows exceed some threshold. Thus, Reinhart and Reinhart (2008) select a cutoff of the sample's twentieth percentile for net capital flows (in percent of gross domestic product, or GDP), while Cardarelli, Elekdag, and Kose (2009) use the criterion that the net flow exceed the country's trend by one standard deviation (or that it falls in the top quartile of the regional distribution). Forbes and Warnock (2012), by contrast, focus on gross flows and define a surge as an annual increase in inflows that is at least one standard deviation above the (five-year rolling) average, and at least two standard deviations above the average in at least one quarter.

Here we focus on net rather than on gross capital flows (i.e., the sum of liability and asset flows) because, as documented in chapter 1, surges to EMEs have largely been a net flow phenomenon. Moreover, although some financial-stability risks depend on the country's stock of gross external liabilities, most macroeconomic consequences of capital flows (such as exchange rate appreciation or macroeconomic overheating) are largely related to net capital flows (box 1.1).

Following the threshold approach, we define an observation to be a surge if it lies in the top thirtieth percentile of the country's own distribution of net capital flows (expressed in percent of GDP) *and* it falls in the top thirtieth percentile of the entire sample's distribution of net capital flows (again, in percent of GDP):

$$
S_{jt} = \begin{cases} 1 & \text{if } K_{jt} \in \{\text{top 30th percentile } (K_{jl})_{l=1}^{T}\} \\ & \qquad \cap \{\text{top 30th percentile } (K_{il})_{i=1,l=1}^{N,T}\} \\ 0 & \text{otherwise} \end{cases} \tag{3.1}
$$

where $S_{jt}$ is an indicator of whether there is a surge in country $j$ at time $t$, $K_{jt}$ denotes net capital flows in percent of GDP (positive values indicating inflows on a net basis) to country $j$ at time $t$, and $N$ and $T$ indicate the total number of countries and years in the sample, respectively. Our measure of net capital flows is computed from the IMF's *Balance of Payment Statistics* as total net financial flows excluding "other investment liabilities of the general government" (which are typically official loans rather than private inflows) and exceptional financing items (change in reserve assets and use of IMF credit); see data appendix for a detailed description of variables and data sources. We scale net flows by GDP to control for economic size—large inflows in absolute terms may not be of concern if the economy has a large absorptive capacity.

While the particular choice of algorithm to identify surges inevitably involves trade-offs, our threshold approach has the advantage of ensuring uniform treatment across countries while still allowing significant cross-country variation in the absolute threshold of a surge.[3] Moreover, we adopt a country-specific *and* sample-wide criterion in (3.1) to ensure that surges are large by the country's own experience but also by cross-country standards. This excludes from the surge sample instances where the country has capital outflows or very small net inflows through most of the sample and then experiences a minor inflow blip.[4] (In the robustness analysis presented in the chapter appendix, we also test the sensitivity of our results to using a purely country-specific criterion and find that the results hold.)

Applying the definition given in (3.1) to our sample of fifty-three emerging market economies yields 335 surge observations over 1980–2013 (presented in table 3.1).[5] On average, surges last two years, with a net capital inflow during the episode of around 10 percent of GDP. As a proportion of GDP, the largest surges are in the Middle East and in Africa (with an average net flow of around 14 percent of GDP, perhaps because of large resource-extraction investment projects), followed by emerging Europe. Surges have become more frequent in recent years, with the share of surge observations rising from 10 percent of the sample in the 1980s to more than 20 percent in the 1990s, and to almost 30 percent in the last decade (figure 3.1).

---

3. In our approach, the country-specific cutoff for identifying surges remains constant over the sample period, ensuring that exceptionally large capital inflows (in percent of GDP) are always coded as surges. This is in contrast to methods that use deviations from rolling averages (e.g., Forbes and Warnock 2012), which may take better account of drifts in capital flow volatility, but may not code large inflow observations as a surge if such flows have persisted for a few years. Conversely, rolling methods may identify a capital inflow as a surge even though it is small in absolute terms (and hence of little macroeconomic consequence) if flows have been low for a while but then there is a small jump in the series.

4. For example, Venezuela experienced capital outflows and only small inflows (on a net basis) through most of our sample period. The top thirtieth percentile of its net capital flows distribution thus includes some negative observations, and values less than 1 percent of GDP—which does not accord well with our criterion of exceptionally large inflows.

5. A comparison of our surge observations with those of Reinhart and Reinhart (2008) and Cardarelli, Elekdag, and Kose (2009)—who also look at large net flows (to GDP)—suggests broad overlap, particularly for well-known surge years, with an overall correlation of about 0.3–0.4.

**Table 3.1**
Identified surges in EMEs, 1980–2013.

| Country | Duration[a] | Avg. net capital flow (% of GDP)[a] | Country | Duration[a] | Avg. net capital flow (% of GDP)[b] | Country | Duration[a] | Avg. net capital flow (% of GDP)[b] |
|---|---|---|---|---|---|---|---|---|
| Albania | 1988–1989 | 9.9 | El Salvador | 2006 | 6.7 | Panama | 2010–2013 | 11.3 |
| Albania | 1997 | 5.1 | El Salvador | 2008 | 7.2 | Peru | 1994–1997 | 7.9 |
| Albania | 2006–2013 | 8.0 | El Salvador | 2012 | 7.4 | Peru | 2002 | 4.9 |
| Argentina | 1993 | 12.6 | Estonia | 1996–1997 | 13.4 | Peru | 2007–2008 | 10.5 |
| Argentina | 1997–1998 | 5.8 | Estonia | 2002–2004 | 12.2 | Peru | 2010–2013 | 8.4 |
| Armenia | 1996–2000 | 12.9 | Estonia | 2006–2007 | 16.5 | Philippines | 1980 | 6.1 |
| Armenia | 2009 | 11.5 | Georgia | 2004–2008 | 17.0 | Philippines | 1991 | 5.1 |
| Armenia | 2013 | 17.3 | Georgia | 2011 | 13.7 | Philippines | 1994–1997 | 9.1 |
| Belarus | 1997 | 4.8 | Guatemala | 1991–1993 | 7.8 | Philippines | 2010 | 5.8 |
| Belarus | 2002 | 5.1 | Guatemala | 1998 | 5.1 | Poland | 1995–1996 | 7.4 |
| Belarus | 2007 | 8.4 | Guatemala | 2000–2003 | 6.7 | Poland | 1998–2000 | 6.8 |
| Belarus | 2009–2011 | 9.4 | Hungary | 1993–1995 | 15.0 | Poland | 2005 | 7.1 |
| Belarus | 2013 | 9.5 | Hungary | 1998–2000 | 11.3 | Poland | 2007–2011 | 7.6 |
| Bosnia & Herzegovina | 2001 | 16.1 | Hungary | 2004–2006 | 11.5 | Romania | 1980 | 4.8 |
| Bosnia & Herzegovina | 2003–2005 | 13.6 | Hungary | 2008 | 8.7 | Romania | 1997–1998 | 5.1 |

(continued)

**Table 3.1** (continued)

| Country | Duration[a] | Avg. net capital flow (% of GDP)[a] | Country | Duration[a] | Avg. net capital flow (% of GDP)[b] | Country | Duration[a] | Avg. net capital flow (% of GDP)[b] |
|---|---|---|---|---|---|---|---|---|
| Bosnia & Herzegovina | 2007 | 13.6 | India | 2007 | 7.5 | Romania | 2001–2008 | 11.4 |
| Brazil | 1980–1981 | 6.7 | Indonesia | 1995–1996 | 5.1 | Russia | 2007 | 7.6 |
| Brazil | 1994 | 8.0 | Jamaica | 1984 | 9.3 | Serbia | 2007–2009 | 17.4 |
| Brazil | 2007 | 6.5 | Jamaica | 1996 | 7.2 | Slovak Rep. | 1996 | 11.3 |
| Bulgaria | 1992–1993 | 12.6 | Jamaica | 2001–2002 | 9.8 | Slovak Rep. | 1998 | 10.0 |
| Bulgaria | 2000–2008 | 19.7 | Jamaica | 2004–2009 | 11.3 | Slovak Rep. | 2002 | 22.7 |
| Chile | 1980–1981 | 12.8 | Jamaica | 2011 | 11.0 | Slovak Rep. | 2004–2005 | 13.2 |
| Chile | 1990 | 8.1 | Jordan | 1988 | 5.7 | Slovak Rep. | 2007 | 9.4 |
| Chile | 1992–1997 | 7.3 | Jordan | 1991–1992 | 31.4 | South Africa | 1997 | 5.4 |
| Chile | 2008 | 4.9 | Jordan | 1994 | 6.8 | South Africa | 2006–2007 | 6.9 |
| Chile | 2011 | 7.1 | Jordan | 2005–2011 | 16.2 | South Africa | 2009 | 6.6 |
| China | 1994 | 4.9 | Kazakhstan | 1996–1997 | 9.8 | South Africa | 2012 | 5.7 |
| China | 2004 | 5.6 | Kazakhstan | 2001 | 11.6 | Sri Lanka | 1980 | 5.0 |

| Country | Year | Value | Country | Year | Value | Country | Year | Value |
|---|---|---|---|---|---|---|---|---|
| China | 2010 | 4.8 | Kazakhstan | 2003–2004 | 9.9 | Sri Lanka | 1982 | 6.5 |
| Colombia | 1996–1997 | 5.9 | Kazakhstan | 2006 | 20.0 | Sri Lanka | 1989 | 5.0 |
| Colombia | 2007 | 4.9 | Korea, Rep. | 1980 | 7.6 | Sri Lanka | 1993–1994 | 6.5 |
| Colombia | 2013 | 4.9 | Latvia | 1995 | 11.7 | Sri Lanka | 2009–2013 | 6.3 |
| Costa Rica | 1980 | 6.5 | Latvia | 1999 | 10.3 | Thailand | 1981 | 6.2 |
| Costa Rica | 1999 | 4.8 | Latvia | 2001 | 10.9 | Thailand | 1988–1996 | 10.0 |
| Costa Rica | 2002 | 5.4 | Latvia | 2004–2007 | 21.4 | Thailand | 2010 | 7.8 |
| Costa Rica | 2006–2008 | 8.8 | Lebanon | 2003 | 29.0 | Tunisia | 1981–1982 | 6.2 |
| Costa Rica | 2011–2013 | 7.0 | Lebanon | 2007–2009 | 40.8 | Tunisia | 1984 | 5.4 |
| Croatia | 1996–1997 | 12.7 | Lithuania | 1997–1998 | 10.6 | Tunisia | 1993 | 6.5 |
| Croatia | 1999 | 13.9 | Lithuania | 2003 | 8.8 | Tunisia | 2006 | 9.5 |
| Croatia | 2001 | 11.8 | Lithuania | 2005–2007 | 13.7 | Tunisia | 2008–2009 | 6.6 |
| Croatia | 2003 | 12.5 | Macedonia, FYR | 2001 | 11.2 | Tunisia | 2012 | 6.0 |
| Croatia | 2006–2007 | 12.1 | Macedonia, FYR | 2004–2008 | 9.8 | Turkey | 2004–2007 | 7.5 |
| Czech Rep. | 1995–1996 | 9.1 | Malaysia | 1981–1983 | 9.1 | Turkey | 2010–2013 | 8.5 |
| Czech Rep. | 2000–2002 | 9.2 | Malaysia | 1985 | 10.6 | Ukraine | 2005 | 9.4 |
| Czech Rep. | 2004 | 5.8 | Malaysia | 1991–1993 | 14.5 | Ukraine | 2007–2008 | 8.9 |
| Dominican Rep. | 2000–2001 | 6.3 | Malaysia | 1995–1996 | 9.4 | Ukraine | 2013 | 8.9 |
| Dominican Rep. | 2008 | 7.2 | Mexico | 1981 | 8.2 | Uruguay | 1980 | 5.2 |
| Dominican Rep. | 2010–2011 | 7.9 | Mexico | 1991–1993 | 7.4 | Uruguay | 1982 | 10.4 |
| Dominican Rep. | 2013 | 6.6 | Mexico | 1997 | 5.0 | Uruguay | 2005–2008 | 9.6 |
| Ecuador | 1990–1992 | 8.4 | Morocco | 1994 | 5.5 | Uruguay | 2011–2013 | 8.3 |

(continued)

**Table 3.1** (continued)

| Country | Duration[a] | Avg. net capital flow (% of GDP)[a] | Country | Duration[a] | Avg. net capital flow (% of GDP)[b] | Country | Duration[a] | Avg. net capital flow (% of GDP)[b] |
|---|---|---|---|---|---|---|---|---|
| Ecuador | 1994 | 4.9 | Morocco | 2012–2013 | 6.1 | Venezuela | 1990 | 29.2 |
| Ecuador | 1998 | 5.3 | Pakistan | 2007–2008 | 5.4 | Venezuela | 1993 | 4.8 |
| Egypt, Arab Rep. | 2005 | 8.4 | Panama | 1997–1999 | 11.6 | Vietnam | 1996–1997 | 9.8 |
| Egypt, Arab Rep. | 2013 | 5.1 | Panama | 2001 | 11.0 | Vietnam | 2003 | 8.3 |
| El Salvador | 1998 | 7.3 | Panama | 2005 | 13.5 | Vietnam | 2007–2009 | 14.1 |
| El Salvador | 2003 | 6.7 | Panama | 2007–2008 | 10.8 | | | |

*Source:* Authors' calculations.

*Note:* Algeria is the only country in the sample with no surge identified based on the threshold approach.

a. Refers to the number of years the surge episode lasts.

b. Mean of net capital flow to GDP (in percent) received over the surge episode.

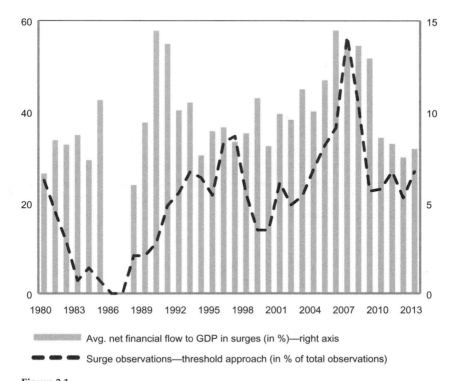

**Figure 3.1**
Surges of net capital flows to EMEs, 1980–2013.
*Source*: Authors' calculations based on the International Financial Statistics database.

An initial snapshot of the occurrence and magnitude of surges suggests three noteworthy points. First, surges tend to be synchronized internationally, generally corresponding to well-established periods of high global capital mobility: the early 1980s (just before the Latin American debt crisis), the mid-1990s (before the East Asian financial crisis and Russian default), and the mid-2000s in the run-up to the global financial crisis. This suggests that common factors are at play. Second, even in times of such global surges, not all EMEs are affected. In fact, the proportion of countries experiencing an inflow surge in any given year never exceeds one-half of the sample, with some experiencing them repeatedly. As such, conditions in the recipient countries must also be relevant. Third, there is considerable time-series and cross-sectional variation in the magnitude of flows during surges. For example, Asian countries experienced the largest surges (as a proportion of GDP) during the 1990s, whereas emerging Europe experienced the largest surges in the mid-2000s (figure 3.2).

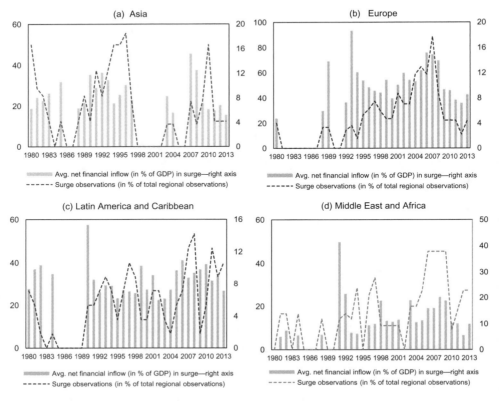

**Figure 3.2**
Surges by region, 1980–2013.
*Source*: Authors' calculations based on the International Financial Statistics database.

These statistics suggest that both global and domestic factors may
be at play, perhaps with global factors driving the overall volume of
flows to EMEs, and domestic factors influencing their allocation. What
are these factors? A simple tabulation of the values of various plausible
factors across surge and nonsurge observations is suggestive (table 3.2).
During surges, the US real interest rate and global market uncertainty
(S&P 500 index returns volatility) are significantly lower than at other
times, while recipient countries tend to have larger external financing
needs, faster output growth, more open capital accounts, less flexible
exchange rate regimes, and stronger institutions. These statistics are,
however, unconditional averages; in what follows, we conduct a more
formal examination of the factors associated with surge occurrence and
magnitude.

**Table 3.2**
Summary statistics of selected variables.

| | Obs. | Mean | Min | Max | Std dev. |
|---|---|---|---|---|---|
| Surge | | | | | |
| Net capital flows to GDP (in %) | 263 | 10.40*** | 4.75 | 53.86 | 6.68 |
| Real US interest rate (in %) | 263 | 0.73*** | −2.92 | 7.72 | 2.20 |
| S&P 500 returns volatility (in %) | 263 | 8.24*** | 2.94 | 22.59 | 4.46 |
| Commodity price index (% deviation) | 263 | 1.54*** | −19.00 | 22.66 | 1.54 |
| Real domestic interest rate (in %) | 263 | 3.02 | −21.80 | 96.63 | 8.21 |
| REER deviation from trend (in %) | 263 | 0.93** | −21.56 | 30.93 | 7.20 |
| Optimal current account (in % of GDP) | 263 | −2.44*** | −18.10 | 9.23 | 3.82 |
| Real GDP growth rate (in %) | 263 | 4.98*** | −12.40 | 12.55 | 3.33 |
| Real GDP per capita (Log) | 263 | 8.24*** | 6.15 | 9.52 | 0.69 |
| De facto exchange rate regime | 263 | 0.90* | 0.00 | 1.00 | 0.29 |
| Capital account openness index | 263 | 0.59*** | −1.86 | 2.44 | 1.49 |
| Institutional quality index | 263 | 0.67*** | 0.34 | 0.89 | 0.09 |
| Nonsurge | | | | | |
| Net capital flows to GDP (in %) | 872 | 1.02 | −35.14 | 22.75 | 4.27 |
| Real US interest rate (in %) | 872 | 1.20 | −2.92 | 7.72 | 2.52 |
| S&P 500 returns volatility (in %) | 872 | 9.24 | 2.94 | 22.59 | 4.20 |
| Commodity price index (% deviation) | 872 | −1.94 | −19.00 | 22.66 | 11.06 |
| Real domestic interest rate (in %) | 872 | 3.47 | −46.60 | 100.00 | 12.00 |
| REER deviation from trend (in %) | 872 | −0.49 | −56.55 | 50.13 | 9.79 |

(continued)

**Table 3.2** (continued)

| | Obs. | Mean | Min | Max | Std dev. |
|---|---|---|---|---|---|
| | Nonsurge | | | | |
| Optimal current account (in % of GDP) | 872 | 0.69 | −10.98 | 13.71 | 3.34 |
| Real GDP growth rate (in %) | 872 | 3.50 | −15.04 | 15.46 | 3.93 |
| Real GDP per capita (Log) | 872 | 8.00 | 5.71 | 10.00 | 0.87 |
| De facto exchange rate regime | 872 | 0.86 | 0.00 | 1.00 | 0.35 |
| Capital account openness index | 872 | 0.03 | −1.86 | 2.44 | 1.43 |
| Institutional quality index | 872 | 0.62 | 0.29 | 0.86 | 0.11 |

*Source:* Authors' calculations.

*Notes:* Observations restricted to the estimated sample as in table 3.3. Real domestic interest rate and real GDP growth rate have been rescaled using the formula $x/(1+x)$ if $x \geq 0$, and $x/(1-x)$ if $x < 0$ to transform the outliers. ***, **, * indicate significant difference between the surge and nonsurge observations at the 1, 5, and 10 percent levels, respectively.

### 3.3   Occurrence of Surges

To examine the factors associated with the occurrence of surges, we estimate a probit model of the following form:

$$\Pr(S_{jt} = 1) = F(x_t'\beta_1 + z_{jt}'\gamma_1) \tag{3.2}$$

where $S_{jt}$ is an indicator variable of whether a net inflow surge occurs in country $j$ in period $t$; and $x$ and $z$ are various global push and (lagged) domestic pull factors, respectively.

Existing literature has typically identified global factors as those driving the supply of capital. These factors are largely exogenous to emerging markets, but they underpin the provision of global liquidity and induce investors to increase exposure to EMEs. Neoclassical theory predicts that capital should flow from capital-abundant, low interest–rate advanced economies to capital-scarce, high-interest rate EMEs. Among global push factors, therefore, we include the US real interest rate (three-month US Treasury bill rate deflated by US inflation), with capital flows to EMEs expected to increase with lower US interest rates, and vice versa. In addition, to capture global "risk-on, risk-off" episodes, we include the volatility of the S&P 500 index returns as a proxy for global market risk aversion. Furthermore, we also consider world commodity prices (measured as the log difference between the actual and trend commodity price index) as a global push factor, to capture the effect of large movements in international commodity prices on capital flows to EMEs. Greater volatility of the S&P 500 index returns is likely to be associated with lower flows to emerging markets, since advanced economies are traditionally considered to be safe havens in times of heightened uncertainty. Higher commodity prices, by contrast, are likely to be positively correlated with inflows, inasmuch as they indicate a boom in demand for EME exports, and perhaps the recycling of income earned by commodity exporters.

Among pull factors, we include recipient-country characteristics that likely influence perceived risks and returns to investors, and that determine whether the country will be an attractive destination for investment flows. If capital flows indeed respond to expected return differentials, as predicted by neoclassical theory, then they should be an increasing function of the real interest rate in the emerging market, and a decreasing function of any expected real depreciation (which we proxy by the log difference between the real effective exchange rate, or REER, and its long-term trend).[6]

---

6. Neoclassical theory predicts the capital flows will respond positively to the interest rate differential, which is given by: $i_t - (i_t^* - (e_{t+1}^e - e_t))$, where $i_t$ is the domestic interest

Another important pull factor is the country's need for external financing. Early studies of private capital flows to developing countries often included the country's current account deficit as a measure of its financing need (Kouri and Porter 1974). But with the increasing importance of private (as opposed to official) flows, this approach becomes almost tautological: abstracting from changes in reserves, the current account deficit must be financed by private capital flows, and the observed net flows must correspond to the current account deficit. To get around this problem, and to see whether capital flows to EMEs respond to the macroeconomic fundamentals, we turn to a consumption-smoothing model of the current account (Ghosh 1995). In such a model, the current account responds only to temporary shocks, never to permanent ones. Since surges are defined as episodes of temporarily large capital inflows, they presumably correspond to temporary shocks to the domestic economy. Therefore, the financing need to which they are responding should be well captured by the consumption-smoothing current account deficit, which we include in our empirical model.[7]

Even if the country has an external financing need, however, it may not be met if the capital account is closed. To capture this possibility, we include a measure of (de jure) financial openness—taken from Chinn and Ito (2008)—which is based on the IMF's *Annual Report on Exchange Arrangements and Exchange Restrictions (AREAER)*. Fast-growing economies are more likely to experience large capital flows, not only because of their potentially large financing needs, but also because investors (especially for equity flows) may be attracted to the prospective productivity gains and corresponding returns. Likewise, they may feel more confident investing in countries with better institutional quality (Alfaro, Kalemli-Ozcan, and Volosovych 2008). Thus,

---

rate, $i_t^*$ is the foreign interest rate, and $e_t$ is the log of the exchange rate (an increase is an appreciation). Subtracting each country's inflation rate and defining the real exchange rate as $q_t = p_t + e_t - p_t^*$ (an increase in $q$ is a real appreciation) yields: $r_t - r_t^* + \Delta q_{t+1}^e$ ; finally, we proxy for the expected real appreciation by the extent of undervaluation (i.e., the deviation of the current real exchange rate from long-term trend, $\tilde{q}$ ) $\Delta q_{t+1}^e = \tilde{q} - q_t$ , so capital flows to EMEs should respond positively to domestic real interest rates, negatively to advanced-economy real interest rates, and positively to the degree of undervaluation (or negatively to the degree of overvaluation): $r_t - r_t^* - (q_t - \tilde{q}_t)$.

7. The consumption-smoothing current account balance can be shown to equal the present discounted value of expected changes in "national cash flow"—the difference between GDP, investment, and government consumption: $CA_t^* = -\sum_{j=1}^{\infty}(1+r)^{-j}E_t\{\Delta(Q_{t+j} - I_{t+j} - G_{t+j})\}$. The country's financing need is then defined as $-CA_t^*$. See Ghosh (1995) for details.

we include the real GDP growth rate as well as a measure of institutional quality among the pull factors. We also include the de facto exchange rate regime (taken from the IMF's *AREAER*, with one indicating a pegged regime and zero indicating a nonpegged regime) to capture the possibility that the implicit guarantee of a fixed exchange rate may encourage greater cross-border borrowing.

To address potential endogeneity concerns regarding the domestic pull factors in (3.2), we substitute current values of these variables by their (one-period) lagged values. Since many of the domestic pull factors change only slowly, and because we are interested in the effect of global factors that are common across recipient countries, we do not include country- or time-fixed effects but rather control for region-specific effects as well as (log) real per capita income. To take account of possible correlation in the error term, we cluster standard errors at the country level.

The coefficient estimates reported in table 3.3 indicate that global push factors are an economically important and statistically significant determinant of capital flow surges to EMEs. Against an unconditional surge probability of 22 percent, a 100 basis points (bps) rise in the US real interest rate is estimated to lower the likelihood of a surge by 3 percentage points (evaluated at mean values of other regressors). Likewise, global market uncertainty is associated with significantly lower likelihood of capital flowing to EMEs (a one-standard deviation increase in the volatility of the S&P 500 index returns reduces the probability of a surge by 3 percentage points) presumably because these countries have not traditionally been viewed as safe havens. Conversely, commodity price booms, which likely signal higher global demand for emerging market countries' exports, are positively correlated with surges (a one-standard deviation increase in commodity prices around the mean raises the surge likelihood by about 8 percentage points). While the individual coefficients are highly statistically significant, together these global factors have limited explanatory power: the pseudo-$R^2$ (which compares the log likelihood of the full model with that of a model with only a constant) is 6 percent, and the probit sensitivity (proportion of surges correctly called) is about 6.5 percent.

Turning to domestic pull factors, the external financing need implied by the consumption-smoothing current account is highly statistically significant, as is real GDP growth. A 1 percentage point increase in the country's real GDP growth rate, or an increase of 1 percent of GDP in the country's external financing need, raises the predicted likelihood

**Table 3.3**

Occurrence of surges in EMEs, 1980–2013.

| | (1) | (2) | (3) | (4) | (5) | (6) | (7) | (8) | (9) |
|---|---|---|---|---|---|---|---|---|---|
| Real US interest rate | -0.067** (0.027) | -0.067** (0.027) | -0.103*** (0.024) | -0.061** (0.027) | -0.050** (0.025) | -0.071*** (0.027) | -0.058** (0.027) | -0.067** (0.029) | -0.089*** (0.025) |
| S&P 500 volatility | -0.028*** (0.010) | -0.028*** (0.010) | -0.040*** (0.011) | -0.012 (0.010) | -0.027*** (0.010) | -0.029*** (0.010) | -0.024** (0.010) | -0.028*** (0.010) | -0.020* (0.012) |
| Commodity price index | 0.019*** (0.005) | 0.019*** (0.005) | 0.019*** (0.005) | 0.017*** (0.005) | 0.018*** (0.005) | 0.019*** (0.005) | 0.019*** (0.005) | 0.019*** (0.005) | 0.016*** (0.005) |
| Real domestic interest rate | | -0.001 (0.005) | | | | | | | 0.004 (0.006) |
| REER deviation from trend | | -0.000 (0.004) | | | | | | | -0.013** (0.005) |
| Optimal current account/GDP | | | -0.108*** (0.017) | | | | | | -0.109*** (0.016) |
| Real GDP growth | | | | 0.078*** (0.016) | | | | | 0.068*** (0.016) |
| Capital account openness | | | | | 0.106** (0.046) | | | | 0.063 (0.048) |
| Exchange rate regime | | | | | | 0.394** (0.163) | | | 0.380** (0.169) |
| Institutional quality index | | | | | | | 1.669** (0.657) | | 2.446*** (0.871) |
| Real GDP per capita (log) | | | | | | | | 0.003 (0.127) | -0.228 (0.153) |

| | | | | | | | | |
|---|---|---|---|---|---|---|---|---|
| Region-specific effects | Yes | Yes | Yes | Yes | Yes | Yes | Yes | Yes | Yes |
| Observations | 1,135 | 1,135 | 1,135 | 1,135 | 1,135 | 1,135 | 1,135 | 1,135 | 1,135 |
| Countries | 49 | 49 | 49 | 49 | 49 | 49 | 49 | 49 | 49 |
| Pseudo-$R^2$ | 0.062 | 0.075 | 0.062 | 0.122 | 0.092 | 0.072 | 0.069 | 0.073 | 0.173 |
| Wald-chi2 (p-value) | 0.00 | 0.00 | 0.00 | 0.00 | 0.00 | 0.00 | 0.00 | 0.00 | 0.00 |
| Percent correctly predicted | 77.18 | 77.53 | 76.92 | 78.59 | 77.80 | 76.21 | 76.74 | 76.30 | 79.21 |
| Sensitivity | 6.46 | 11.79 | 6.08 | 16.35 | 12.55 | 7.61 | 6.46 | 5.70 | 22.81 |
| Specificity | 98.51 | 97.36 | 98.28 | 97.36 | 97.48 | 96.90 | 97.94 | 97.59 | 96.22 |

*Notes:* Dependent variable is a binary variable equal to 1 if a surge occurs and 0 otherwise. All specifications are estimated using a probit model. Statistics reported in parentheses are clustered standard errors (at the country level). Constant and region-specific effects are included in all specifications. ***, **, * indicate significance at 1, 5, and 10 percent levels, respectively. Sensitivity (specificity) is the fraction of surge (nonsurge) observations that are correctly specified. All variables except for global factors (real US interest rate, S&P 500 returns volatility, and commodity price index) are lagged one period.

of a surge by some 2–3 percentage points. Higher real interest rates in the recipient country and the implied real exchange rate overvaluation (measured by the REER deviation from trend) are statistically insignificant (col. [2]), but the latter turns statistically significant when other domestic factors are included (col. [9]). Countries with more open capital accounts or better institutions are significantly more likely to experience an inflow surge (moving from the sample's twenty-fifth percentile to the seventy-fifth percentile on these indexes raises the predicted probability of a surge by some 6–7 percentage points), as are those that have less flexible exchange rate regimes. Including these factors together triples the pseudo-$R^2$ to 17 percent and raises the probit sensitivity—the proportion of surge observations correctly called—to 23 percent. Overall, the probit calls 80 percent of the observations correctly.

## 3.4   Magnitude of Flows during Surges

The probit model estimated above gives the likelihood of an inflow surge, but the magnitude of the surge varies considerably across countries, with a range of 50 percent of GDP between the smallest and the largest observations (table 3.2). Is it possible to say anything about the size of a surge, conditional on its occurrence? To this end, we estimate a regression over the sample of surge observations, of the following form:

$$K_{jt|S_{jt}=1} = x_t'\beta_2 + z_{jt}'\gamma_2 + \eta_{jt} \tag{3.3}$$

where $K_{jt|S_{jt}=1}$ is the net capital flow (in percent of GDP) to country $j$ in time $t$, conditional on the occurrence of a surge, $S$; $x$ and $z$ are the global push and (lagged) domestic pull factors, respectively; and $\eta$ is the random error term. We estimate (3.3) using ordinary least squares (OLS); as before, we include region-specific effects and cluster the standard errors at the country level.

The coefficient estimates, reported in table 3.4, suggest a more limited role for global factors in determining the magnitude of surges (as opposed to their occurrence). A 100 bps decline in the US real interest rate is associated with about 0.4 percent of GDP larger capital flows, and a one–standard deviation decrease in S&P 500 index returns' volatility increases the magnitude of the surge by 0.2 percent of GDP—though both effects are statistically insignificant, as is the estimated coefficient of commodity price booms in most specifications. These results, together with the findings of the probit model above, suggest that global factors act largely as "gatekeepers." That is, capital surges

**Table 3.4**
Magnitude of surge in EMEs, 1980–2013.

| | (1) | (2) | (3) | (4) | (5) | (6) | (7) | (8) | (9) |
|---|---|---|---|---|---|---|---|---|---|
| Real US interest rate | -0.045 | -0.039 | -0.073 | -0.038 | 0.123 | -0.096 | -0.051 | 0.033 | 0.114 |
| | (0.160) | (0.160) | (0.168) | (0.153) | (0.161) | (0.174) | (0.158) | (0.167) | (0.207) |
| S&P 500 volatility | -0.094 | -0.092 | -0.106 | -0.083 | -0.061 | -0.082 | -0.090 | -0.095 | -0.068 |
| | (0.079) | (0.093) | (0.084) | (0.082) | (0.084) | (0.075) | (0.079) | (0.080) | (0.090) |
| Commodity price index | 0.055 | 0.053 | 0.050 | 0.052 | 0.042 | 0.072* | 0.056 | 0.050 | 0.052* |
| | (0.037) | (0.037) | (0.035) | (0.039) | (0.033) | (0.039) | (0.037) | (0.036) | (0.031) |
| Real domestic interest rate | | -0.013 | | | | | | | 0.013 |
| | | (0.088) | | | | | | | (0.064) |
| REER deviation from trend | | -0.186** | | | | | | | -0.195** |
| | | (0.080) | | | | | | | (0.073) |
| Optimal current account/GDP | | | -0.152 | | | | | | -0.134 |
| | | | (0.134) | | | | | | (0.114) |
| Real GDP growth | | | | 0.081 | | | | | -0.018 |
| | | | | (0.240) | | | | | (0.206) |
| Capital account openness | | | | | 1.252*** | | | | 1.019*** |
| | | | | | (0.360) | | | | (0.329) |
| Exchange rate regime | | | | | | 4.784*** | | | 4.407*** |
| | | | | | | (0.999) | | | (1.037) |
| Institutional quality index | | | | | | | 3.192 | | -5.591 |
| | | | | | | | (5.863) | | (10.272) |

(continued)

**Table 3.4** (continued)

|  | (1) | (2) | (3) | (4) | (5) | (6) | (7) | (8) | (9) |
|---|---|---|---|---|---|---|---|---|---|
| Real GDP per capita (log) |  |  |  |  |  |  |  | 2.249 | 2.233 |
|  |  |  |  |  |  |  |  | (1.562) | (2.225) |
| Region-specific effects | Yes | Yes | Yes | Yes | Yes | Yes | Yes | Yes | Yes |
| Observations | 263 | 263 | 263 | 263 | 263 | 263 | 263 | 263 | 263 |
| Countries | 47 | 47 | 47 | 47 | 47 | 47 | 47 | 47 | 47 |
| $R^2$ | 0.095 | 0.132 | 0.103 | 0.097 | 0.165 | 0.137 | 0.097 | 0.097 | 0.259 |
| F-stat (p-value) | 0.00 | 0.00 | 0.00 | 0.00 | 0.00 | 0.00 | 0.00 | 0.00 | 0.00 |

*Notes:* Dependent variable is net capital flow to GDP conditional on surge occurrence. All specifications are estimated using OLS. Statistics reported in parentheses are clustered standard errors (at the country level). Constant and region-specific effects are included in all specifications. ***,**,* indicate significance at 1, 5, and 10 percent levels, respectively. All variables except for global factors (real US interest rate, S&P 500 returns volatility, and commodity price index) are lagged one period.

toward EMEs only when these global conditions permit, but once this hurdle is passed, the volume of capital that flows is largely independent of them.

Since countries that experience a surge already have the macroeconomic and structural characteristics identified above, several of the domestic pull factors are statistically insignificant in the magnitude regression. Nevertheless, the implied real exchange rate overvaluation, capital account openness, and nominal exchange rate regime are all highly significant. Countries whose currencies are overvalued by 10 percent experience surges that are, on average, smaller by 2 percent of GDP. Conversely, a country with a fixed exchange rate will experience a surge that is 4 percent of GDP larger than that of a country with a float, holding all else constant. Finally, countries with more open capital accounts tend to experience larger surges: moving from the twenty-fifth to the seventy-fifth percentile of the sample's capital account openness index is associated with surge inflows that are larger by 4 percent of GDP.

Overall, these findings are consistent with the results of previous studies and help to explain the stylized facts noted earlier. The finding that the likelihood of surge occurrence is influenced strongly by global factors—notably, US interest rates, as argued by Calvo, Leiderman, and Reinhart (1993) and Reinhart and Reinhart (2008), along with global risk and commodity price booms—explains the synchronicity of surges across regions, and highlights that sudden changes in these factors could trigger large swings in capital flows. Certain macroeconomic characteristics (in particular, growth and external financing need) and structural characteristics (notably, financial openness and institutional quality) are also important covariates with surge occurrence, which explains why not all countries experience a surge even when, in aggregate, capital is flowing toward EMEs. Further, among the countries that experience a surge, the magnitude of the flow appears to be strongly associated with their external financing need, exchange rate regime, and financial openness—with countries that have less flexible regimes, or those that are more financially open, experiencing larger surges. These results are generally robust, including to alternative methods of dating and classifying surges, model specification, and possible endogeneity of the domestic pull factors (see chapter appendix, A.3.1).

## 3.5   Asset- versus Liability-Flow Surges

The analysis thus far treats all surges as the same. But, as mentioned earlier, a net inflow surge may be the result of changes in the behavior of liability flows (foreigners investing in the home country) or changes in the behavior of asset flows (residents repatriating funds, or simply not investing as much abroad as usual) or possibly both. To see whether the two types of surges differ, we first classify each of our 335 surge observations according to whether the *change* in the asset or liability flow component of net flows is greater:[8]

$$AS_{jt} = \begin{cases} 1 & \text{if } \{S_{jt}=1\} \cap \{\Delta assetflow_{jt} > \Delta liabilityflow_{jt}\} \\ 0 & otherwise \end{cases} \tag{3.4}$$

$$LS_{jt} = \begin{cases} 1 & \text{if } \{S_{jt}=1\} \cap \{\Delta liabilityflow_{jt} > \Delta assetflow_{jt}\} \\ 0 & otherwise \end{cases} \tag{3.5}$$

where $AS_{jt}$ and $LS_{jt}$ indicate asset- and liability-flow dominated surges, respectively, in country $j$ at time $t$; $assetflow_{jt}$ is the (negative of) the change in the (stock of) foreign assets of country $j$'s residents at time $t$, expressed in percent of GDP; $liabilityflow_{jt}$ is the change in the (stock of) foreign liabilities of country $j$ at time $t$, expressed in percent of GDP; and $\Delta$ denotes the first difference operator. (In what follows, we refer to surges driven by increases in asset flows as asset-flow surges, and those driven by increases in liability flows as liability-flow surges.)

Classifying surges thus shows that, despite greater financial integration, it remains the case that most net inflow surges to emerging mar-

---

8. A simple way of classifying the (net inflow) surge observations would be according to whether it is the asset- or the liability-flow component of net flows that is larger. Such an approach, however, runs into two key problems. First, because liability flows to EMEs are nearly always larger than asset flows, almost all surges would be classified as liability-flow surges. Second, and more importantly, this approach does not always correctly capture *why* the observation is a surge. For example, suppose net capital flows are 4 percent of GDP in year $t$-1 (and suppose that is too low to qualify as a surge observation based on our definition [3.1]), consisting of 3 percent of GDP of liability flows and 1 percent of GDP of asset flows. In period $t$, net flows rise to 5 percent of GDP (which, suppose, is high enough to qualify as a surge), but liability flows remain unchanged (at 3 percent of GDP), while asset flows increase to 2 percent of GDP. If the relative level of asset versus liability flows is used for classification, then this surge would be classified as a liability-flow surge (since the 3 percent of GDP of liability flows still exceed the 2 percent of GDP of asset flows). But clearly it should be considered as an asset-flow surge because it is only the exceptional behavior of asset flows that results in the observation at time $t$ qualifying as a net inflow surge, whereas liability flows remain unchanged from the previous (nonsurge) year. Ghosh et al. (2014) discuss in more detail why it does not make sense to classify surges according to whether the *level* of asset or liability flows is greater.

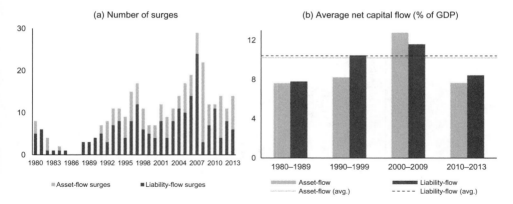

**Figure 3.3**
Types of surges, 1980–2013.
*Source*: Authors' estimates based on International Financial Statistics database.

kets (more than two-thirds) reflect increases in the country's liabilities rather than decreases in its external assets. Asset-flow surges dominate liability-flow surges in only two out of the thirty years of our sample—1982 and 2008, both of which were crisis years when residents repatriated the proceeds of foreign disinvestments (figure 3.3[a]).[9] On average, liability-flow surges are also somewhat larger than asset-flow surges, though the difference is not statistically significant (figure 3.3[b]).

Next we examine the drivers of asset- and liability-flow surges by estimating probit models similar to (3.2), but replacing the general surge variable with the specific types of surges. Table 3.5 (cols. [1]–[2]) reports the estimation results for the occurrence of asset-flow surges (as defined in [3.4], and where liability-flow surges are excluded from the sample), while cols. (3)–(4) report the corresponding results for liability-flow surges (as defined in [3.5], with asset-flow surges excluded from the sample).

The results show that US interest rates matter significantly for both asset- and liability-flow surges, though the impact is greater for the latter—a 100 bps increase in the US real rate (evaluated at mean values) lowers the predicted probability of a liability-flow surge by about 2 percentage points but that of an asset-flow surge by 1 percentage point. Global market uncertainty is also significantly associated with both types of surges, such that in times of increased global market uncertainty, foreign as well as domestic investors exit EMEs (and

9. This observation is in line with the well-established drawdown on residents' foreign assets during crises (Milesi-Ferretti and Tille 2011).

**Table 3.5**
Occurrence and magnitude: By surge type, 1980–2013.

| | Occurrence | | | | Magnitude | | | |
|---|---|---|---|---|---|---|---|---|
| | Asset-flow | | Liability-flow | | Asset-flow | | Liability-flow | |
| | (1) | (2) | (3) | (4) | (5) | (6) | (7) | (8) |
| Real US interest rate | −0.056* | −0.068* | −0.062** | −0.092*** | −0.169 | 0.034 | 0.043 | 0.175 |
| | (0.032) | (0.038) | (0.028) | (0.025) | (0.249) | (0.269) | (0.181) | (0.244) |
| S&P 500 volatility | −0.039*** | −0.033** | −0.023* | −0.020 | −0.151 | −0.090 | −0.087 | −0.093 |
| | (0.011) | (0.014) | (0.012) | (0.015) | (0.146) | (0.154) | (0.081) | (0.096) |
| Commodity price index | 0.025*** | 0.020*** | 0.011** | 0.010* | 0.099 | 0.066 | 0.028 | 0.024 |
| | (0.006) | (0.006) | (0.005) | (0.005) | (0.065) | (0.047) | (0.047) | (0.051) |
| Real domestic interest rate | | 0.003 | | 0.004 | | −0.017 | | 0.032 |
| | | (0.006) | | (0.006) | | (0.121) | | (0.064) |
| REER deviation from trend | | −0.009* | | −0.014*** | | −0.166** | | −0.235** |
| | | (0.005) | | (0.006) | | (0.080) | | (0.093) |
| Optimal current account/GDP | | −0.112*** | | −0.102*** | | −0.173 | | −0.146 |
| | | (0.022) | | (0.017) | | (0.174) | | (0.125) |
| Real GDP growth | | 0.078*** | | 0.054*** | | 0.216 | | −0.101 |
| | | (0.019) | | (0.016) | | (0.197) | | (0.262) |
| Capital account openness | | 0.115** | | 0.017 | | 1.678** | | 0.782** |
| | | (0.055) | | (0.048) | | (0.647) | | (0.347) |
| Exchange rate regime | | 0.296* | | 0.394** | | 5.388*** | | 3.158*** |
| | | (0.174) | | (0.193) | | (1.353) | | (1.084) |

| | (1) | (2) | (3) | (4) | (5) | (6) | (7) | (8) |
|---|---|---|---|---|---|---|---|---|
| Institutional quality index | | 2.672** | | 2.166*** | | -3.713 | | -7.008 |
| | | (1.077) | | (0.803) | | (10.687) | | (11.321) |
| Real GDP per capita (log) | | -0.295* | | -0.177 | | 1.322 | | 2.968 |
| | | (0.166) | | (0.144) | | (2.481) | | (2.332) |
| Observations | 977 | 977 | 1,031 | 1,031 | 104 | 104 | 158 | 158 |
| Pseudo-R² | 0.082 | 0.209 | 0.048 | 0.141 | 0.135 | 0.336 | 0.077 | 0.246 |
| Countries | 49 | 49 | 49 | 49 | 36 | 36 | 47 | 47 |
| Percent correctly predicted | 89.25 | 89.97 | 84.58 | 84.97 | | | | |
| Sensitivity | 0.00 | 10.48 | 0.00 | 9.43 | | | | |
| Specificity | 100.00 | 99.54 | 100.00 | 98.74 | | | | |

*Notes:* Dependent variable is a binary variable equal to one if an asset-flow surge occurs in cols. (1)–(2) and a liability-flow surge occurs in cols. (3)–(4); and zero otherwise. Dependent variable is defined as net financial flows to GDP if an asset-flow surge occurs in cols. (5)–(6) and a liability-flow surge occurs in cols. (7)–(8). Regressions are estimated using probit model in cols. (1)–(4) and with OLS in cols. (5)–(8), with clustered standard errors (at the country level) reported in parentheses. All variables except for real US interest rate, S&P 500 index returns volatility, and commodity price index are lagged one period. Constant and region-specific effects are included in all specifications. Pseudo-R² reported in cols. (1)–(4). ***,**,* indicate significance at 1, 5, and 10 percent levels, respectively.

presumably prefer to invest in safe-haven countries), but the impact is slightly larger for liability-flow surges. (A one–standard deviation increase in the volatility of the S&P 500 index around the mean reduces the probability of a liability-flow surge by about 2 percentage points, and that of an asset-flow surge by 1.5 percentage points). Conversely, booming commodity prices have a greater impact on the likelihood of asset-flow surges than on liability-flow surges.

Among the domestic pull factors, the external financing need, implied real exchange rate overvaluation, real GDP growth, exchange rate regime, and institutional quality show significant statistical association with both types of surges. Liability-flow surges are somewhat more sensitive to the recipient country's external financing need: an increase of 1 percent of GDP in the country's financing need raises the estimated likelihood of a liability-flow surge by about 1 percentage point more than it raises the likelihood of an asset-flow surge. Liability-flow surges also appear to be more sensitive to real exchange rate overvaluation, and the exchange rate regime (such that countries with less flexible exchange rate regimes, or those whose currencies are less overvalued, are more likely to experience a liability-flow surge). Capital account openness is strongly associated with asset-flow surges—moving from the twenty-fifth to the seventy-fifth percentile of the capital account openness index raises the estimated probability of an asset-flow surge by about 3 percentage points. This is intuitive because countries normally liberalize inflows before outflows, and it is only once outflows have been liberalized and residents have invested abroad that there can be repatriation that results in an asset-flow surge.

In terms of the magnitude of flows during surges, as before, several domestic macroeconomic and structural characteristics are statistically insignificant because, by definition, countries are sufficiently similar to have experienced a surge (table 3.5; cols. [5]–[8]). The results show that the estimated coefficients for global factors are statistically insignificant in the magnitude specifications of both asset- and liability-flow surges. Domestic factors, by contrast, do matter. The regressions imply that flows during a surge will be smaller if the real exchange rate is overvalued, the nominal exchange rate is more flexible, and the capital account is less open.

These results suggest that while asset- and liability-flow surges have many common factors, they also have some important differences. Liability-flow surges in particular seem to be more sensitive to US monetary policy than asset-flow surges. They are also more responsive to the external financing needs of the country, currency overvaluation, and the exchange rate regime.

## 3.6 Conclusion

In this chapter we set the stage for our subsequent discussion by characterizing the drivers of exceptionally large net capital flows—surges—to emerging market economies. The picture that emerges from our analysis is one in which global push factors, notably US interest rates and global market uncertainty, determine whether surges occur at all—which explains why surges tend to be synchronized across countries. Even during such episodes, however, a country that has no need for capital or that is an unattractive destination for investors is unlikely to experience an inflow surge. Hence pull factors (such as external financing needs, growth performance, the exchange rate regime, financial openness, and institutional quality) help determine which countries experience an inflow surge. Conditional on a surge occurring, moreover, it is mainly the domestic pull factors that determine its magnitude.

The analysis also indicates that most surges to emerging markets are driven by foreign investors rather than by retrenchment of domestic residents liquidating their investments abroad. Moreover, while both domestic and foreign investors respond to global and local factors, foreign investors tend to be more sensitive to global conditions, making them more flighty when conditions turn.

The upshot is that the occurrence of surges, being at least partly determined by global factors, is not under the control of emerging markets, and most of those factors that make individual destinations attractive to foreign capital such as good growth prospects, and strong institutions are hardly characteristics that the country would want to forgo purely for the sake of avoiding inflow surges. This puts a premium on identifying any negative repercussions of inflow surges and finding policy tools for managing them.

## Chapter 3 Appendix

This appendix establishes that surges are distinct from more normal capital flows, responding differently to various push and pull factors. It further reports various robustness tests on the main regressions in the text.

## A.3.1   Are Surges Different from Normal Flows?

To establish that large capital inflows to emerging markets are not just scaled-up normal flows but rather behave qualitatively differently, we estimate quantile regressions to compare the responsiveness of capital flows to different factors across the distribution:

$$K_{jt} = x'_t\beta_3^q + z'_{jt}\gamma_3^q + \varepsilon_{jt}; \quad q = 25, 30, 50, 70, 75, 90; \tag{A.3.1}$$

where $K_{jt}$ denotes net capital flows (positive values indicating inflows on a net basis), expressed in percent of GDP, to country $j$ at time $t$; $x$ and $z$ are global push and domestic pull factors, respectively; $q$ indicates the different quantiles of net capital flows (to GDP) based on the estimated sample; and $\varepsilon$ is the random error term.

We estimate (A.3.1) using the same sample (of fifty-three EMEs over 1980–2013) as in the main analysis. For comparative purposes, we first present the results for the ordinary least squares (OLS) regression estimated for the full (sample) distribution of net capital flows to GDP (table A.3.1, col. [1]). Most estimated coefficients are of the expected sign and are statistically significant. Among global push factors, higher US interest rates and greater volatility of the S&P 500 index returns are associated with lower capital flows into EMEs, while commodity price booms are associated with larger inflows. Among the domestic pull factors, greater financing needs (as captured by the consumption-smoothing current account), real GDP growth rate, less flexible exchange rate regimes, and greater financial openness are all associated with larger inflows. By contrast, real exchange rate overvaluation is associated with smaller inflows.

Going beyond the OLS results, quantile regressions suggest that the association between net capital flows and several of the push and pull factors depends on the magnitude of the flow (cols. [2]–[7]). For example, the coefficients on the US real interest rate, global risk aversion, and commodity prices are all larger for net flows that are at the upper end of the distribution (cols. [5]–[7]). Among pull factors, the coefficients on the real exchange rate overvaluation, exchange rate regime, capital account openness, and institutional quality also tend to be larger.

That the differences between several estimated coefficients across the inflow distribution are statistically significant is confirmed by the interquantile regressions (cols. [8]–[10]). Testing for the difference between the fiftieth and the ninetieth percentiles, for example, shows that four (out of a total of eleven) coefficients are statistically significantly different. (Comparing the results of twenty-fifth and ninetieth percentiles shows that six out of eleven estimated coefficients are statistically signifi-

**Table A.3.1**

Quantile regression estimates for net capital flows to GDP, 1980–2013.

| Estimation | OLS | Quantile regressions (percentiles) | | | | | | Interquartile regressions | | |
|---|---|---|---|---|---|---|---|---|---|---|
| | | 25th | 30th | 50th | 70th | 75th | 90th | 25th vs. 50th | 50th vs. 75th | 50th vs. 90th |
| | (1) | (2) | (3) | (4) | (5) | (6) | (7) | (8) | (9) | (10) |
| Real US interest rate | −0.329*** (0.092) | −0.312*** (0.077) | −0.310*** (0.074) | −0.278*** (0.042) | −0.331*** (0.074) | −0.328*** (0.080) | −0.403*** (0.123) | 0.035 (0.074) | −0.051 (0.068) | −0.126 (0.115) |
| S&P 500 volatility | −0.118*** (0.038) | −0.118** (0.055) | −0.076** (0.038) | −0.062** (0.030) | −0.078** (0.036) | −0.098*** (0.036) | −0.158** (0.076) | 0.056 (0.052) | −0.035 (0.032) | −0.095 (0.068) |
| Commodity price index | 0.066*** (0.015) | 0.052*** (0.017) | 0.048*** (0.011) | 0.041*** (0.011) | 0.055*** (0.015) | 0.054*** (0.018) | 0.077*** (0.030) | −0.011 (0.014) | 0.013 (0.014) | 0.036 (0.028) |
| Real domestic interest rate | 0.033 (0.023) | 0.025* (0.014) | 0.021* (0.011) | 0.016 (0.011) | −0.001 (0.015) | −0.002 (0.016) | −0.014 (0.019) | −0.009 (0.011) | −0.018 (0.013) | −0.030* (0.018) |
| REER deviation from trend | −0.056** (0.024) | 0.009 (0.022) | 0.016 (0.018) | 0.000 (0.015) | −0.028 (0.024) | −0.030 (0.020) | −0.065** (0.029) | −0.009 (0.018) | −0.031* (0.016) | −0.066** (0.026) |
| Optimal current account/GDP | −0.443*** (0.090) | −0.297*** (0.061) | −0.289*** (0.050) | −0.342*** (0.048) | −0.359*** (0.053) | −0.403*** (0.058) | −0.434*** (0.088) | −0.045 (0.051) | −0.061 (0.055) | −0.093 (0.088) |
| Real GDP growth | 0.278*** (0.079) | 0.283*** (0.067) | 0.299*** (0.062) | 0.259*** (0.038) | 0.252*** (0.052) | 0.217*** (0.058) | 0.151** (0.076) | −0.024 (0.050) | −0.042 (0.047) | −0.108 (0.073) |
| Exchange rate regime | 1.561** (0.648) | −0.204 (0.436) | 0.163 (0.344) | 0.840** (0.384) | 1.462*** (0.515) | 1.806*** (0.479) | 3.245*** (0.658) | 1.044** (0.434) | 0.966** (0.447) | 2.405*** (0.615) |
| Capital account openness | 0.629*** (0.225) | 0.270** (0.141) | 0.323** (0.127) | 0.425*** (0.091) | 0.472*** (0.136) | 0.699*** (0.148) | 0.746*** (0.213) | 0.155 (0.104) | 0.274** (0.132) | 0.321 (0.207) |

(continued)

**Table A.3.1** (continued)

| | | Quantile regressions (percentiles) | | | | | | Interquantile regressions | | |
|---|---|---|---|---|---|---|---|---|---|---|
| | OLS | 25th | 30th | 50th | 70th | 75th | 90th | 25th vs. 50th | 50th vs. 75th | 50th vs. 90th |
| Estimation | (1) | (2) | (3) | (4) | (5) | (6) | (7) | (8) | (9) | (10) |
| Institutional quality index | 5.925 | 6.311*** | 7.823*** | 7.505*** | 8.445*** | 7.973*** | 7.407** | 1.194 | 0.468 | −0.098 |
| | (5.247) | (2.374) | (1.993) | (1.448) | (1.823) | (2.018) | (3.352) | (1.697) | (1.689) | (3.255) |
| Real GDP per capita (log) | −0.527 | −1.358*** | −1.120*** | −0.791*** | −0.569 | −0.248 | 0.177 | 0.567** | 0.544 | 0.968* |
| | (0.917) | (0.344) | (0.256) | (0.188) | (0.441) | (0.399) | (0.617) | (0.267) | (0.344) | (0.565) |
| Region-specific effects | Yes | Yes | Yes | Yes | Yes | Yes | Yes | Yes | Yes | Yes |
| Observations | 1,135 | 1,135 | 1,135 | 1,135 | 1,135 | 1,135 | 1,135 | 1,135 | 1,135 | 1,135 |

*Notes*: Dependent variable is net capital flow to GDP. All variables except for real US interest rate, S&P 500 volatility, and commodity price index are lagged one period. Constant and regional specific effects are included in all specifications. The interquantile regressions (reported in cols. [8]–[10]) estimates regressions of the difference in quantiles (e.g., col. [8] indicates the difference between the estimates obtained for the 25th and 50th percentiles, and whether that difference is statistically significant). Clustered and bootstrapped standard errors (with 100 replications) reported in parentheses for OLS and quantile regressions, respectively. ***,**,* indicate significance at 1, 5, and 10 percent levels, respectively.

cantly different.) These findings suggest that there are indeed differences in the responsiveness of net capital flows to the various push and pull factors at different points along the net capital flow distribution. Large flows behave qualitatively and quantitatively differently from normal flows; as such, they merit separate treatment.

### A.3.2 Sensitivity Analysis

To check the robustness of our estimates reported in tables 3.3 and 3.4, we conduct a range of sensitivity tests regarding the dating and coverage of surge observations, the method of identifying surges, model specification, and the potential endogeneity of the regressors.

**Alternative surge definitions** To check whether our results are sensitive to the definition of surges, we employ three different approaches. First, since pinning down the exact timing (start and end) of surge episodes may not always be straightforward for countries receiving large net capital flows over several years, we construct a one-year window around our identified surge observations, and include the non-surge years immediately before and after the surge years (provided the net capital flow in those years is positive). We then reestimate all specifications with the push and pull factors using the extended surge variable. Tables A.3.2 and A.3.3 (col. [1]) present the estimation results for this exercise, which largely support the findings reported earlier. For surge likelihood, the estimated coefficients of US real interest rate, global market uncertainty and commodity price booms are statistically significant—while domestic factors such as the external financing need, real GDP growth rate, exchange rate regime, and institutional quality are also strongly significant. For surge magnitude, the implied exchange rate overvaluation, a less flexible exchange rate regime, and capital account openness are statistically significant in most cases, whereas the global factors remain largely statistically insignificant.

Second, we adopt a more novel, "clustering" approach, which avoids imposing ad hoc thresholds to identify surges. Specifically, we apply the *k-means* clustering technique on each country's (standardized) net flow to GDP observations, and group them into three clusters (surges, normal flows, and outflows), such that the within-cluster sum of squared differences from the mean is minimized (while the between-cluster difference in means is maximized). As a result, each observation belongs to the cluster with the nearest mean, and clusters comprise observations that

**Table A.3.2**
Likelihood of surge: Sensitivity analysis.

| | Surge definitions | | | Alternate regressors | | Additional regressors | | | | | Sample | |
|---|---|---|---|---|---|---|---|---|---|---|---|---|
| | Extended | Cluster | Country-specific | Real US 10yr yield | VXO | Trade openness | Reserves to GDP | Pvt. sector credit/GDP | Country-fixed effects | Regional contagion | 1990–2013 | 1980–2007 |
| | (1) | (2) | (3) | (4) | (5) | (6) | (7) | (8) | (9) | (10) | (11) | (12) |
| Real US interest rate | -0.088*** | -0.122*** | -0.126*** | -0.097*** | -0.072** | -0.086*** | -0.088*** | -0.091*** | -0.111*** | -0.079*** | -0.062* | -0.103*** |
| | (0.025) | (0.026) | (0.029) | (0.029) | (0.033) | (0.025) | (0.025) | (0.025) | (0.037) | (0.026) | (0.038) | (0.037) |
| S&P 500 index/VXO | -0.019* | -0.021* | -0.016 | -0.012 | -0.308** | -0.020 | -0.020* | -0.020* | -0.026* | -0.015 | -0.012 | -0.046*** |
| | (0.011) | (0.011) | (0.010) | (0.012) | (0.131) | (0.012) | (0.012) | (0.012) | (0.014) | (0.012) | (0.013) | (0.014) |
| Commodity price index | 0.016*** | 0.020*** | 0.018*** | 0.015*** | 0.016*** | 0.017*** | 0.016*** | 0.017*** | 0.018*** | 0.012** | 0.014** | 0.022*** |
| | (0.005) | (0.004) | (0.005) | (0.005) | (0.005) | (0.005) | (0.005) | (0.005) | (0.006) | (0.005) | (0.005) | (0.007) |
| Real domestic interest rate | 0.008 | 0.003 | 0.004 | 0.004 | 0.003 | 0.004 | 0.004 | 0.004 | 0.004 | 0.003 | -0.001 | 0.003 |
| | (0.008) | (0.005) | (0.006) | (0.006) | (0.007) | (0.006) | (0.006) | (0.006) | (0.010) | (0.006) | (0.008) | (0.006) |
| REER deviation from trend | -0.009 | -0.009* | -0.010** | -0.013** | -0.011** | -0.011** | -0.013** | -0.013*** | -0.017*** | -0.013*** | -0.017*** | -0.014** |
| | (0.006) | (0.005) | (0.005) | (0.005) | (0.005) | (0.005) | (0.005) | (0.005) | (0.006) | (0.005) | (0.006) | (0.006) |
| Optimal current account/GDP | -0.128*** | -0.106*** | -0.100*** | -0.111*** | -0.111*** | -0.108*** | -0.109*** | -0.109*** | -0.121*** | -0.111*** | -0.118*** | -0.134*** |
| | (0.021) | (0.019) | (0.017) | (0.017) | (0.018) | (0.016) | (0.016) | (0.016) | (0.017) | (0.016) | (0.017) | (0.023) |
| Real GDP growth | 0.069*** | 0.069*** | 0.047*** | 0.068*** | 0.069*** | 0.067*** | 0.068*** | 0.069*** | 0.075*** | 0.060*** | 0.065*** | 0.061*** |
| | (0.016) | (0.013) | (0.011) | (0.016) | (0.016) | (0.015) | (0.016) | (0.016) | (0.021) | (0.015) | (0.016) | (0.023) |
| Capital account openness | 0.076 | -0.004 | -0.015 | 0.063 | 0.056 | 0.041 | 0.062 | 0.057 | 0.034 | 0.051 | 0.034 | 0.074 |
| | (0.059) | (0.040) | (0.037) | (0.048) | (0.048) | (0.049) | (0.048) | (0.049) | (0.079) | (0.050) | (0.047) | (0.050) |

| | (1) | (2) | (3) | (4) | (5) | (6) | (7) | (8) | (9) | (10) | (11) | (12) |
|---|---|---|---|---|---|---|---|---|---|---|---|---|
| Exchange rate regime | 0.481** | 0.384** | 0.356** | 0.394** | 0.365** | 0.314* | 0.375** | 0.397** | 0.651*** | 0.416** | 0.411** | 0.532*** |
| | (0.208) | (0.187) | (0.152) | (0.165) | (0.169) | (0.177) | (0.171) | (0.172) | (0.247) | (0.165) | (0.175) | (0.203) |
| Institutional quality index | 2.830*** | 1.830** | 1.983*** | 2.286*** | 2.455*** | 0.314* | 0.375** | 0.397** | 0.651*** | 2.420*** | 0.411** | 0.532*** |
| | (1.017) | (0.736) | (0.579) | (0.873) | (0.907) | (0.177) | (0.171) | (0.172) | (0.247) | (0.906) | (0.175) | (0.203) |
| Real GDP per capita (log) | -0.229 | -0.112 | -0.195*** | -0.204 | -0.241 | -0.265* | -0.231 | -0.207 | -0.359 | -0.226 | -0.201 | -0.183 |
| | (0.187) | (0.095) | (0.072) | (0.150) | (0.151) | (0.142) | (0.156) | (0.168) | (0.362) | (0.159) | (0.148) | (0.161) |
| Regional dummies | Yes | Yes | Yes | Yes | Yes | Yes | Yes | Yes | Yes | Yes | Yes | Yes |
| Observations | 1,135 | 1,135 | 1,135 | 1,135 | 1,033 | 1,135 | 1,135 | 1,128 | 1,135 | 1,135 | 945 | 849 |
| Pseudo-R² | 0.192 | 0.146 | 0.118 | 0.172 | 0.166 | 0.177 | 0.173 | 0.174 | 0.241 | 0.180 | 0.159 | 0.231 |
| Countries | 49 | 49 | 49 | 49 | 49 | 49 | 49 | 49 | 49 | 49 | 49 | 49 |

*Notes:* Dependent variable is a binary variable (=1 if a surge occurs; 0 otherwise). All specifications are estimated using the probit model. Clustered standard errors (at the country level) are reported in parentheses. All variables except for real US interest rate, S&P 500 returns volatility and commodity price index are lagged one period. Constant and region-specific effects are included in all specifications. ***, **, * indicate statistical significance at 1, 5, and 10 percent levels, respectively. Extended = Surges identified using a one-year window (i.e., including the year before and after the surge if the net capital flow is positive), Cluster = Surges identified using the cluster approach, Country-specific = Surges identified using only country-specific top 30th percentile criteria, Real US 10yr yield = includes the real US 10-year government bond yield instead of the real US 3-month T-bill rate, VXO = Includes the (log) VXO available from 1986 onward, Trade openness = includes trade to GDP ratio in the specification, Reserves to GDP = includes the stock of foreign reserves to GDP ratio in the specification, Pvt. sector credit/GDP = includes domestic private sector credit to GDP ratio in the specification, Regional contagion = includes a proxy for occurrence of surges in regional neighbors. Country fixed effects = includes country fixed effects in the specification.

**Table A.3.3**
Magnitude of surge: Sensitivity analysis.

| | Surge definitions | | | Alternate regressors | | Additional regressors | | | | | Sample | |
|---|---|---|---|---|---|---|---|---|---|---|---|---|
| | Extended | Cluster | Country-specific | Real US 10yr yield | VXO | Trade openness | Reserves to GDP | Pvt. sector credit/GDP | Country-fixed effects | Regional contagion | 1990–2013 | 1980–2007 |
| | (1) | (2) | (3) | (4) | (5) | (6) | (7) | (8) | (9) | (10) | (11) | (12) |
| Real US interest rate | −0.048 (0.127) | 0.107 (0.159) | 0.033 (0.138) | 0.089 (0.233) | 0.418 (0.259) | 0.199 (0.194) | 0.455* (0.240) | 0.236 (0.203) | 0.378 (0.272) | 0.093 (0.210) | 0.499 (0.399) | −0.423* (0.232) |
| S&P 500 index/ VXO | −0.072 (0.051) | −0.067 (0.075) | −0.078* (0.046) | −0.080 (0.076) | 0.777 (1.902) | −0.051 (0.086) | −0.118 (0.081) | −0.070 (0.089) | −0.079 (0.090) | −0.087 (0.095) | 0.016 (0.124) | −0.273* (0.145) |
| Commodity price index | 0.047** (0.023) | 0.040* (0.024) | 0.041 (0.027) | 0.056* (0.031) | 0.032 (0.037) | 0.064* (0.033) | 0.002 (0.033) | 0.027 (0.028) | 0.061* (0.033) | 0.053* (0.031) | 0.028 (0.037) | 0.080 (0.063) |
| Real domestic interest rate | 0.006 (0.034) | −0.017 (0.068) | 0.023 (0.037) | 0.013 (0.064) | −0.003 (0.070) | 0.036 (0.065) | 0.017 (0.048) | 0.020 (0.063) | 0.095 (0.063) | 0.009 (0.065) | −0.007 (0.070) | −0.006 (0.051) |
| REER deviation from trend | −0.136*** (0.050) | −0.185** (0.069) | −0.127** (0.053) | −0.196** (0.073) | −0.200*** (0.072) | −0.122* (0.061) | −0.149** (0.068) | −0.188** (0.070) | −0.201** (0.098) | −0.202*** (0.073) | −0.196*** (0.065) | −0.137* (0.079) |
| Optimal current account/GDP | −0.183** (0.088) | −0.218* (0.112) | −0.241** (0.103) | −0.133 (0.116) | −0.170 (0.112) | −0.063 (0.116) | −0.108 (0.117) | −0.071 (0.106) | −0.216 (0.153) | −0.131 (0.113) | −0.163 (0.112) | −0.275 (0.234) |
| Real GDP growth | 0.070 (0.124) | −0.035 (0.217) | 0.080 (0.154) | −0.018 (0.207) | 0.004 (0.202) | −0.022 (0.204) | −0.015 (0.203) | −0.087 (0.208) | −0.086 (0.272) | −0.014 (0.206) | −0.002 (0.210) | −0.292 (0.253) |
| Capital account openness | 0.857*** (0.241) | 1.038*** (0.371) | 1.124*** (0.334) | 1.012*** (0.325) | 1.068*** (0.338) | 0.628* (0.316) | 0.659** (0.294) | 1.099*** (0.345) | 0.369 (0.796) | 0.993*** (0.326) | 1.060*** (0.347) | 0.641** (0.270) |

| | | | | | | | | | | | |
|---|---|---|---|---|---|---|---|---|---|---|---|
| Exchange rate regime | 3.348*** | 3.828*** | 3.576*** | 4.421*** | 4.253*** | 2.644*** | 3.149*** | 4.058*** | 1.081 | 4.279*** | 4.221*** | 5.818*** |
| | (0.689) | (1.126) | (0.848) | (1.039) | (1.034) | (0.853) | (0.682) | (0.992) | (1.269) | (1.037) | (1.009) | (0.830) |
| Institutional quality index | -1.624 | 0.273 | 1.838 | -5.234 | -7.240 | -11.888 | -12.543 | -8.400 | -8.846 | -5.098 | -8.893 | -3.371 |
| | (7.356) | (9.290) | (8.480) | (10.077) | (12.029) | (10.291) | (10.112) | (10.301) | (7.783) | (10.222) | (12.525) | (7.110) |
| Real GDP per capita (log) | 1.288 | 1.627 | 1.449 | 2.187 | 2.518 | 1.681 | 2.023 | 1.143 | 5.958** | 2.218 | 2.570 | 1.523 |
| | (1.615) | (1.878) | (1.698) | (2.200) | (2.454) | (1.774) | (1.676) | (2.208) | (2.221) | (2.213) | (2.391) | (1.617) |
| Regional dummies | Yes | Yes | Yes | Yes | Yes | Yes | Yes | Yes | Yes | Yes | Yes | Yes |
| Observations | 443 | 306 | 396 | 263 | 253 | 263 | 263 | 263 | 263 | 263 | 249 | 184 |
| $R^2$ | 0.199 | 0.278 | 0.265 | 0.255 | 0.266 | 0.341 | 0.385 | 0.281 | 0.632 | 0.122 | 0.270 | 0.317 |
| Countries | 48 | 49 | 49 | 47 | 47 | 47 | 47 | 47 | 47 | 47 | 47 | 46 |

*Notes:* Dependent variable is net financial flows to GDP conditional on surge occurrence. All specifications are estimated using OLS. Clustered standard errors (at the country level) are reported in parentheses. All variables except for real US interest rate, S&P 500 returns volatility and commodity price index are lagged one period. Constant and region-specific effects are included in all specifications. ***, **, * indicate statistical significance at 1, 5, and 10 percent levels, respectively. Extended=Surges identified using a one-year window (i.e., including the year before and after the surge if the net capital flow is positive), Cluster=Surges identified using the cluster approach, Country-specific=Surges identified using country-specific top 30th percentile criteria, Real US 10yr yield=includes the real US 10-year government bond yield instead of the real US 3-month T-bill rate, VXO=Includes the (log) VXO available from 1986 onward, Trade openness=includes trade to GDP ratio in the specification, Reserves to GDP=includes the stock of foreign reserves to GDP ratio in the specification, Pvt. sector credit/GDP=includes domestic private sector credit to GDP ratio in the specification, Country fixed effects=includes country fixed effects in the specification, Regional contagion=includes a proxy for spillovers from net capital flows to the regional neighbors.

are statistically similar.[10] Analysis of these surge observations yields a broadly similar picture to that obtained above (tables A.3.2 and A.3.3, col. [2]). The impact of both global and domestic factors is generally comparable to earlier estimates in terms of statistical significance and magnitude.

Third, we define surges based only on the country-specific criteria such that net capital flows falling in the top thirtieth percentile of the country's own distribution of net capital flows (expressed in percent of GDP) are identified as surges. The coefficient estimates obtained using this definition of surges (reported in col. [3] of tables A.3.2 and A.3.3) remain very similar to those reported above. The only notable difference is that, in the surge occurrence regression, the coefficient on the volatility of S&P 500 index returns variable turns marginally insignificant (p-value = 0.12).

**Alternative specifications**    While the estimations reported in tables 3.3 and 3.4 include a range of push and pull factors, other proxies and additional variables could also be added. To check the sensitivity of our results to alternative variable definitions of global factors, we use the ten-year US government bond yield (instead of the three-month US Treasury bill rate); and replace our S&P 500 index returns volatility measure with the VXO index—the precursor of VIX—for the pre-1990 years (higher values indicating greater volatility in international markets, and lower risk appetite). The revised estimation results reported in tables A.3.2 and A.3.3 (cols. [4]–[5]) show that using these alternate proxies does not have much impact on the results—both lower US interest rates and greater risk appetite (as measured by the VXO index) are associated with greater likelihood of a surge occurrence, but not with the magnitude, while the results of all other variables remain the same as before.

Columns (6)–(8) (in tables A.3.2 and A.3.3) include additional pull variables in our general specification to capture the effect of other potentially important domestic characteristics (for example, a country's trade openness and financial development may increase its attractiveness as an investment destination, and boost the likelihood and magnitude of surges), while column (9) includes country-fixed effects. The results for the additional variables (not reported here) show that trade openness is indeed associated with significantly higher surge likelihood, but the estimated coefficients for the stock of reserves and the

---

10. The total number of surge observations increases to 567, 373, and 486 under the first (extended surges), second (cluster), and third (country-specific) approaches, respectively.

proxy for financial sector development (private sector credit to GDP) are statistically insignificant in the surge-likelihood regression. These factors, however, do significantly increase the magnitude of the surge. The inclusion of these variables has little effect on the estimated magnitude and significance of the other pull factors in the regressions.

Recent literature finds strong contagion effects on capital flows, particularly in the context of economic and financial crises/sudden stops (Kaminsky, Lyons, and Schmukler 2001). But equally, there are several channels through which "positive" contagion could result in flows to one country leading to larger flows to regional neighbors. This could be through financial linkages (financial flows being on-lent from one EME to another), trade among EMEs, similar macroeconomic characteristics, or through investor-herding behavior more generally (Forbes and Warnock 2012). To capture such contagion, we also include a regional contagion variable in the occurrence and magnitude regressions.[11] The estimates show that regional contagion is strongly positively associated with surge occurrence—though including it lowers the estimated magnitude of the estimated coefficients of global factors (and slightly weakens their statistical significance), probably because global factors and surges to other countries in the region tend to be highly correlated (col. [10]). In the magnitude regression, however, the estimated coefficient of regional contagion is negative, but statistically insignificant. This finding, along with the positive estimated coefficient for the contagion variable in the surge occurrence regressions, suggests that there is positive contagion whereby investors discover a region. But then since many investors allocate funds regionally, the larger the flows going to one country, the smaller the amount left for other countries in the region.

Although, as shown in figure 3.1, a surge in international capital flows to the EMEs occurred in the early 1980s (as a continuation of the surge in late 1970s), surges in later years—particularly post–Latin American debt crisis—have been larger (in both absolute and relative to GDP terms), and have also involved more countries.[12] To examine

---

11. The regional contagion variable is defined as the proportion of other countries in the region experiencing a surge in the occurrence regression, and, correspondingly, as the average net flow (in percent of GDP) received by other countries in the region experiencing a surge in the magnitude regression.

12. Several studies (e.g., Chuhan, Claessens, and Mamingi 1993; and Taylor and Sarno 1997) note that the composition of flows in the surge of the 1990s and later years has also been different, with a pronounced increased in portfolio flows.

whether the role of global and local factors in later years has been any different, we reestimate our regressions for the 1990–2013 sample. Moreover, to ensure that our results are not driven by the dynamics of capital flows during and after the global financial crisis (with a prolonged period of accommodative monetary policy and quantitative easing in advanced countries), we also estimate the specification by restricting the sample to the pre–global financial crisis period. The results summarized in columns (9) and (10) (of tables A.3.2 and A.3.3), respectively, show a largely unchanged impact of global and local factors in these alternative samples.

**Endogeneity**    In the analysis presented above, we follow earlier studies in using one-year lagged values for domestic pull variables to mitigate potential endogeneity concerns. While using one-period lags as instruments is common, both because they are readily available and because persistence in most macro time series means that one-period lags tend to be highly correlated with the regressor, the validity of doing so rests on the assumption of a serially uncorrelated error term. If, however, the error term exhibits serial correlation (e.g., AR[1]), then one-period lags will not be valid instruments.

An obvious solution would be to use two-period lags. Results reported in table A.3.4 (cols. [1] and [3]) show that doing so has a minimal impact on the results. Regarding the pull factors, one finds that surge likelihood is strongly associated with the implied real exchange rate overvaluation, external financing need, real GDP growth rate, exchange rate regime, and institutional quality. Pull factors that affect magnitude of capital flows during a surge are real exchange rate overvaluation, capital account openness, and exchange rate regime.

In addition to using the two-period lag, we follow another, more novel approach: drawing on a unique database of IMF country-team projections, we construct instruments for macroeconomic variables such as real GDP growth and real exchange rate overvaluation—the explanatory variables for which endogeneity concerns are likely to be the most pertinent—using *projections* made in year *t*-1 or earlier for year *t* (specifically, we take the average of the projections made one, two, and three-periods ahead). Empirically, these projections are less likely to be correlated with the error term in the occurrence/magnitude regressions.[13] While endogeneity is of less concern using these instruments,

13. The IMF does not project REER overvaluation, only the nominal exchange rate (against the US dollar) and the consumer price index. Using the two series, we construct

**Table A.3.4**
Surge likelihood and magnitude: IV-2SLS estimations.

| | Surge likelihood | | Surge magnitude | |
|---|---|---|---|---|
| | Probit-two lags | Probit-IV | OLS-two lags | OLS-IV |
| | (1) | (2) | (3) | (4) |
| Real US interest rate | −0.115*** | −0.085* | 0.150 | 0.573 |
| | (0.026) | (0.047) | (0.261) | (0.499) |
| S&P 500 volatility | −0.040*** | −0.023 | −0.061 | −0.004 |
| | (0.012) | (0.016) | (0.092) | (0.135) |
| Commodity price index | 0.021*** | 0.008 | 0.038 | 0.020 |
| | (0.005) | (0.006) | (0.037) | (0.029) |
| Real domestic interest rate | 0.001 | −0.005 | −0.103 | −0.020 |
| | (0.006) | (0.008) | (0.085) | (0.080) |
| REER deviation from trend | −0.013** | 0.024 | −0.170** | −0.264 |
| | (0.006) | (0.025) | (0.069) | (0.252) |
| Optimal current account/GDP | −0.075*** | −0.132*** | −0.057 | −0.175 |
| | (0.013) | (0.021) | (0.086) | (0.129) |
| Real GDP growth | 0.054*** | 0.144*** | −0.044 | 0.187 |
| | (0.012) | (0.046) | (0.176) | (0.452) |
| Capital account openness | 0.043 | 0.029 | 0.943*** | 1.073*** |
| | (0.051) | (0.038) | (0.307) | (0.314) |
| Exchange rate regime | 0.303 | 0.382** | 3.584*** | 3.809*** |
| | (0.190) | (0.173) | (1.326) | (0.943) |
| Institutional quality index | 2.127** | 2.438*** | −9.808 | −6.978 |
| | (0.919) | (0.802) | (10.713) | (14.689) |
| Real GDP per capita (log) | −0.244 | −0.149 | 2.824 | 2.288 |
| | (0.148) | (0.115) | (2.463) | (2.779) |
| Region-specific effects | Yes | Yes | Yes | Yes |
| Observations | 1,090 | 861 | 252 | 231 |
| $R^2$ | 0.144 | . | 0.245 | 0.242 |

*Notes*: Dependent variable is a binary variable equal to 1 if a surge occurs and 0 otherwise in cols. (1)–(2), and net financial flows to GDP in a surge in cols. (3)–(4). Constant and region-specific effects are included in all specifications. ***,**,* indicate significance at 1, 5, and 10 percent levels, respectively. All variables except for real US interest rate, S&P 500 returns volatility, and commodity price index are lagged two periods in cols. (1) and (3). Two stage least squares-instrumental variable approach is applied in cols. (2) and (4), where the average of one-, two-, and three-period projected real GDP growth rates, and real exchange rate overvaluation, are used as instruments for real GDP growth rate and REER overvaluation, respectively (all other variables are lagged one period).

there is of course no guarantee that endogeneity problems have been fully addressed, and the reported results need to be treated with appropriate caution.

Unfortunately, these projections are only available from 1990 onward, so our sample size for these instrumental variable (IV) regressions is smaller (table A.3.4, cols. [2] and [4]). The results obtained from the Probit-IV model (col. [2]) show that the estimated effect of real GDP growth rate on surge likelihood remains significantly positive, but that of implied real exchange rate overvaluation turns statistically insignificant. For the IV regressions of surge magnitude, reported in col. (4), we do not find a strong association between implied real GDP growth or real exchange rate overvaluation and net flows, but the estimated coefficients (and significance) of other variables in the regression remain largely unaffected. Comparing the OLS and IV results, the only important difference is that the real exchange rate variable loses its statistical significance in the magnitude regression. Overall, therefore, our results appear to be robust to the potential endogeneity of the regressors.

the (projected) real exchange rate and compute the real exchange rate overvaluation with Hodrick-Prescott filter. Projections are not available for interest rates or other structural variables.

# 4    Consequences and Crashes

## 4.1    Introduction

Large and volatile capital flows can pose severe challenges for economic management. On the macroeconomic front, inflows can overheat
the economy and undermine inflation targets, fuel credit booms and
asset price bubbles, and damage the tradables sector through excessive
appreciation of the currency. Inflows may also exacerbate maturity mismatches and currency exposures on bank, corporate, or household balance sheets—leaving them vulnerable to the eventual reversal of capital
that, as documented in chapter 3, may be triggered by global factors
extraneous to the recipient economy.

While booms often end in bust, how the economy fares at the end of
an inflow surge depends, in part, on how well the inflow phase is managed. If macroeconomic discipline is lost and balance-sheet mismatches
are allowed to widen, there is a risk of a "crash landing"—financial crisis
and economic disruption.[1] Conversely, if the inflow surge is well managed, allowing the economy to take advantage of foreign finance while
avoiding macroeconomic and balance-sheet imbalances, then inflows
should in principle benefit the country.

The purpose of this chapter is to document the macroeconomic and
financial-stability consequences of capital inflows in emerging market
economies (EMEs), and how these translate into greater risk of crisis, both
generally and particularly after surge episodes. We begin in section 4.2
by establishing the relationship between capital inflows and various proxies of macroeconomic imbalances (overheating, currency overvaluation,
credit booms), and of balance-sheet vulnerabilities (domestic banking

---

1. Recent research points to deep and protracted recessions following financial crises
(Cerra and Saxena 2008; Reinhart and Rogoff 2009).

system leverage, captured by the loan-to-deposit ratio, and domestic banks' foreign currency–denominated lending). In section 4.3, we examine whether capital inflows are associated with a greater incidence of financial crises, and the channels through which this is likely to happen. To the extent that various macroeconomic and financial vulnerabilities are associated with financial crises, the implication is that safe management of capital inflows requires avoiding the buildup of such vulnerabilities—a point we establish more formally in section 4.4 by narrowing our focus on episodes of large capital inflows (or "surges" as defined in chapter 3), and distinguishing between those that end in a soft landing and those that end in a hard landing or a crash. Section 4.5 concludes.

## 4.2  Macroeconomic and Financial Vulnerabilities

A growing body of literature argues that—notwithstanding various benefits—capital inflows tend to be associated with macroeconomic and financial vulnerabilities in EMEs. Several studies, for instance, find that capital flows result in significant overvaluation of the currency—via inflation under fixed exchange rates, and via nominal appreciation under more flexible exchange rate regimes (Reinhart and Reinhart 2008; Combes, Kinda, and Plane 2012). Such appreciation raises competitiveness concerns and, even if temporary, can do lasting damage to the export sector through hysteresis effects (see box 4.1 for a discussion).

In addition to currency overvaluation, a common concern of emerging market policy makers is that large inflows fuel credit growth, thereby overheating the economy and resulting in widening output gaps and current account deficits, as well as in price inflation of both goods and assets. As discussed in chapter 5, the idea that inflows are expansionary is at odds with standard open-economy macro models (such as the Mundell-Fleming model) in which the currency appreciation causes deterioration in the current account and withdraws demand stimulus. While limited empirical analysis is available on whether inflows are in fact contractionary or expansionary, anecdotal evidence strongly supports the latter—presumably through some form of credit growth, either by borrowing directly from abroad or because flows are intermediated through the domestic banking system.[2]

---

2. On capital inflows and credit expansion in EMEs, see Mendoza and Terrones (2012); Dell'Ariccia et al. (2012); Furceri, Guichard, and Rusticelli (2012a); Calderon and Kubota (2012); and Elekdag and Wu (2013).

**Box 4.1**
Fear of appreciation.

Emerging market economies have become major global economic play-
ers over the last decade. While their share in world exports stood at
around 15 percent in the 1980s and 1990s, it doubled to 30 percent by
2007, and increased further to 35 percent in 2014. At the same time, the
average real GDP growth rate of EMEs has also more than doubled—
rising from about 3 percent per year in the 1980s and 1990s to 7 percent
per year before the global financial crisis. Given the well-established
strong association between exports and real GDP growth (e.g., Balassa
1978; Feder 1983; Frankel and Romer 1999)—also evident from box figure 4.1—it is not surprising that EMEs have become increasingly concerned that excessive exchange rate appreciation could dampen exports
and damage growth. This has made exchange rates perhaps the most
watched—and sensitive—asset price in EMEs.

Concern about exchange rate appreciation is, however, by no means
unique to EMEs. An important example is the Plaza Accord of 1985,
when the major advanced economies agreed to intervene in the foreign
exchange markets to depreciate the US dollar against the Japanese yen
and the German mark. More recently, concerns about export competitiveness in the face of a persistent strengthening of the currency prompted
Switzerland to peg the franc against the euro in 2011; meanwhile, the
persistent real appreciation of the US dollar since late 2014 (against

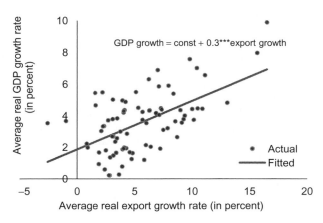

**Box Figure 4.1**
Export performance and growth, 2000–2013 (in percent).
*Source*: Authors' estimates

Box 4.1 (continued)

intensified quantitative easing by the euro area and Japan) has raised competitiveness concerns in the United States.[1]

But is there any merit to such concerns? The existing evidence is mixed—studies using aggregate or macro data generally find small or statistically insignificant effects of exchange rate movements on export quantities (Thursby and Thursby 1987; Hooper, Johnson, and Marquez 1998), while those using disaggregate or micro (e.g., firm-level) data typically find significantly large effects of exchange rate appreciation on exports (e.g., Campa 2004; Dekle, Jeong, Ryoo 2005; Das, Roberts, and Tybout 2007). Our own findings, using firm-level data from a sample of twenty-one advanced and twenty-one emerging market economies over 1985–2013, suggest an economically and statistically significant effect of currency appreciation on real export growth. Specifically, we estimate the following equation:

$$\Delta x_{ijt} = \alpha + \beta \Delta reer_{jt} + \sum_k \gamma_k z_{jkt} + \sum_l \delta_l w_{ilt} + \mu_i + \lambda_t + \varepsilon_{ijt} \qquad (1)$$

where $\Delta x$ is the real export growth (in percent) of firm $i$ in country $j$ at time $t$; $\Delta reer$ is the percentage change in the real effective exchange rate (REER) in country $j$ at time $t$ (an increase is an appreciation); $z$ represents a range of macroeconomic explanatory variables (such as real GDP growth, trade openness, real GDP per capita, and trading partner growth); $w$ is time-varying firm variables (such as firm size, investment, and industry effects); $\mu$ and $\lambda$ are time-invariant firm- and year-specific effects, respectively; and $\varepsilon$ is a random error term. The estimated $\beta$ for the full sample is −0.30 ($p$-value=0.00), implying that faster REER appreciation by 1 percentage point reduces firm-level real export growth rate by about one-third of 1 percentage point.

The effect is larger for EMEs compared to advanced economies: the estimated $\beta$ is −0.5 (p-value=0.00) for EMEs, and is −0.3 (p-value = 0.00) for advanced economies, while EME exporters are also hurt more by currency appreciation in the presence of already overvalued exchange rates. Thus, holding all other variables at their mean values, a 10 percent REER appreciation when the exchange rate is already 10 percent overvalued reduces export growth by 4 percentage points more than if the currency were not overvalued (box figure 4.2). Overall, financial development helps to mitigate the impact of currency appreciation—

1. The US dollar appreciated by about 12 percent (in real effective terms) between the first half of 2014 and 2015, while both the euro and yen depreciated by 10 percent. A survey of US exporters conducted in June 2015 suggests that the rise of the US dollar has hurt exporters and reduced their spending (Duke University/CFO Magazine Global Business Outlook Survey, June 2015. Available online at: http://www.cfosurvey.org/2015q2/Q2-2015-US-Key Numbers.pdf; last accessed on June 2, 2017).

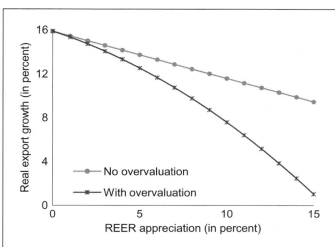

**Box Figure 4.2**
Predicted export growth in EMEs (in percent).
*Source*: Authors' estimates

presumably by providing hedging opportunities and easier access to finance to mitigate the adverse effects of appreciation—which may be why currency appreciation is usually of greater concern in EMEs than in advanced economies.

Not only do exchange rate movements affect export volumes, but our results for EMEs also support the hysteresis hypothesis, whereby even temporary movements in the exchange rate can have persistent effects (e.g., Baldwin 1988; Baldwin and Krugman 1989; Dixit 1989a, 1989b). Thus, estimating an augmented version of equation (1)—which includes two dummy variables, $D_1$ and $D_2$, indicating REER depreciation following a cumulative currency appreciation over the previous (for instance, three) years, and REER appreciation following a cumulative currency depreciation over the previous (three) years, respectively; and their interaction with $\Delta reer$—as follows:

$$\Delta x = \alpha + \beta \Delta reer + \varphi_1 D_1 + \varphi_2 D_1^* \Delta reer + \theta_1 D_2 + \theta_2 D_2^* \Delta reer + \sum_k \gamma_k z_k + \varepsilon \qquad (2)$$

we find that the estimated $\beta/\varphi_2$ is $-0.8$ ($p$-value $= 0.00$), $\varphi_2$ is $0.7$ ($p$-value $= 0.00$) and $\theta_2$ is $0.9$ ($p$-value $= 0.00$) for the EME sample. These estimates imply that the benefit for exports of an REER depreciation that occurs after persistent appreciation—relative to one that follows a previous depreciation—is almost negligible in EMEs. (Similarly, an REER appreciation followed by persistent depreciation in previous years has no strong economic impact on export growth.) Thus, a subsequent depreciation of the currency

Box 4.1 (continued)

following a period of appreciation does not help restore export growth—in other words, even temporary appreciations that are subsequently reversed can do lasting damage to the export sector. Moreover, we find that the magnitude of the appreciation also matters. The larger the cumulative appreciation in previous years, the smaller is the estimated effect of a subsequent depreciation in the EME sample. For advanced economy exports, by contrast, we find no evidence of hysteresis in the effects of exchange rates.

The easy availability of external financing may also induce banks to loosen lending standards, reduce loan quality, and fuel rapid asset price inflation that ultimately proves unsustainable. Moreover, capital flows could exacerbate maturity and currency mismatches on bank balance sheets (including through increased lending in foreign currency to unhedged borrowers), causing financial distress to the banking system when flows recede and the currency depreciates. In fact, Bruno and Shin (2014) find that capital flows tend to be associated with leverage buildup in the banking sector, which plays a key role in the international transmission of domestic financial conditions. Capital inflows may thus be associated with both macroeconomic overheating and rising financial-stability risks.

A first snapshot of the data for our sample of EMEs over 1980–2013 suggests that such concerns are well-founded (figure 4.1). Although net capital flows (lagged one period to mitigate potential endogeneity concerns) are associated with faster output growth, they are also associated with greater overvaluation of the real effective exchange rate and with larger positive output gaps, together with more rapid credit expansion, increased foreign currency lending, and greater increase in leverage of the domestic banking system.[3]

---

3. Data on capital flows are lagged one year to mitigate potential endogeneity concerns. (For instance, alongside the effect of inflows on currency appreciation, if exchange rate overvaluation discourages inflows, then the regression coefficient on inflows could be downward biased.) Results are robust to the exclusion of extreme observations—defined as those in the bottom and top 0.25th percentiles—from the sample. The findings for FX lending are also robust to the exclusion of countries with a 100 percent share of FX lending in total lending (mainly dollarized economies) from the sample.

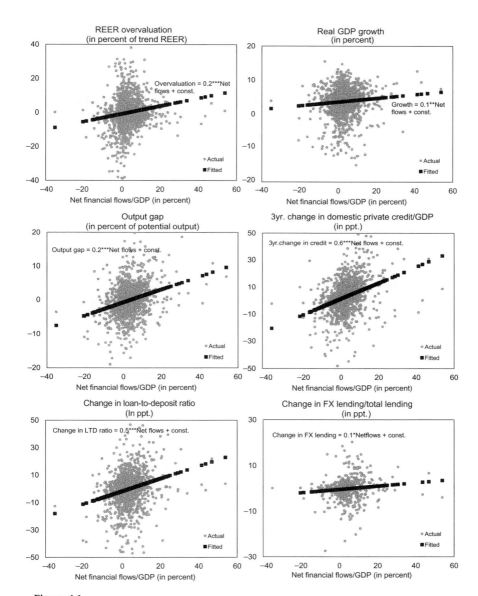

**Figure 4.1**
Macroeconomic and financial vulnerabilities and capital inflows, 1980–2013.
*Note*: Figure based on estimation results reported in cols. (1), (3), (5), (7), (9), and (11) in table 4.1. Net financial flows (to GDP) are lagged one period.

Table 4.1 undertakes a more formal analysis that controls (as appropriate) for other likely covariates of the various dependent variables—including the exchange rate regime, output growth, terms of trade, trade openness, trading partner country growth, initial conditions, as well as country- and year-fixed effects. The resulting estimates imply that a net capital inflow equal to 10 percent of GDP (the average inflow during a surge episode) is associated with about 2 percentage points greater currency overvaluation, a 2 percentage point widening of the output gap, a 1 percentage point increase in domestic credit growth (i.e., the annual change in the domestic credit-to-GDP ratio), a 4 percentage point increase in bank leverage growth (i.e., the annual change in banks' loan-to-deposit ratio), and about a 1 percentage point increase in the growth of foreign exchange (FX) lending (i.e., the annual change in the share of FX-denominated loans in total bank loans).[4]

While the estimated coefficients on capital flows are statistically significant in all specifications reported in table 4.1, they may be subject to endogeneity bias (despite the use of lagged regressors) if the error term is autocorrelated. To address this concern, we adopt the instrumental variable two-stage least squares (IV-2SLS) strategy and use capital flows to other countries in the region (in percent of regional GDP), as well as a de jure measure of capital account openness, as instruments for the net capital flow variable in the regression. These two variables are likely to be strongly correlated with flows to the recipient country but not with the dependent variables directly.[5] The resulting coefficients, reported in the appendix (table A.4.1), remain statistically significant but are generally larger.[6] Thus, according to the IV-2SLS estimates, a capital inflow equal to 10 percent of GDP is on average associated with

---

4. Looking at the relationship between capital inflows and inflation, we find a negative correlation for the full sample period, mainly because of the trend of rising capital inflows and declining inflation rates in the 1990s. Restricting the sample to the post-2005 period (when inflation rates in EMEs had been substantially reduced) yields the expected positive (and statistically significant) relation between inflation and capital flows.

5. That our instruments are valid is supported by the first-stage estimation results (reported in table A.4.2 in the chapter appendix), which show a highly statistically significant positive association between the instruments and net financial flows (to GDP) in all specifications, as well as a statistically insignificant test statistic for the Hansen's J-test for overidentifying restrictions (reported in the last row of table A.4.1). Overall, the instruments (together with control variables) fit the data reasonably well and explain about 40 percent of the variation in net capital flows to GDP.

6. In the case of currency overvaluation, this is intuitive since potential endogeneity (greater overvaluation is likely to decrease capital inflows as investors anticipate lower returns) would tend to bias toward zero the estimated coefficient on inflows. More puzzling is the increase in the estimated coefficient of capital flows on some of the other variables.

**Table 4.1**
Macroeconomic and financial vulnerabilities in EMEs and capital inflows, 1980–2013.

| | REER over-valuation | | Real GDP growth | | Output gap | | 3yr. change in credit/GDP | | 1yr. change in LTD ratio | | 1yr. change in FX loans/total loans | |
|---|---|---|---|---|---|---|---|---|---|---|---|---|
| | OLS | FE/TE | OLS | FE/TE | OLS | FE/TE | OLS | FE/TE | OLS | FE/TE | OLS | FE/TE |
| | (1) | (2) | (3) | (4) | (5) | (6) | (7) | (8) | (9) | (10) | (11) | (12) |
| Net financial flows/GDP | 0.229*** (0.084) | 0.211** (0.084) | 0.055*** | 0.065*** (0.018) | 0.193*** (0.032) | 0.196*** (0.036) | 0.600*** (0.134) | 0.402*** (0.113) | 0.460*** (0.101) | 0.410*** (0.099) | 0.072* (0.036) | 0.060* (0.031) |
| Exchange rate regime | | 2.961* (1.618) | | 0.389 (0.434) | | 0.953 (0.616) | | -0.417 (1.516) | | 3.385* (1.887) | | -0.079 (0.542) |
| Real GDP growth | | -0.035 (0.092) | | | | | | 0.016 (0.148) | | 0.449*** (0.140) | | -0.039 (0.073) |
| Terms of trade change | | 0.017 (0.022) | | 0.021** (0.010) | | 0.028** (0.011) | | -0.014 (0.027) | | 0.078 (0.062) | | 0.000 (0.029) |
| Trade openness | | -0.066** (0.029) | | 0.018* (0.010) | | -0.006 (0.011) | | -0.011 (0.043) | | -0.044 (0.031) | | -0.017 (0.023) |
| Real GDP per capita (log) | | 2.968* (1.554) | | -3.983*** (0.980) (0.163) | | 6.505*** (2.189) | | 20.115*** (3.941) | | 6.934** (2.733) | | 5.637** (2.521) |
| Initial condition[a] | | | | | | | | -0.443*** (0.055) | | -0.149*** (0.015) | | -0.124*** (0.023) |

(continued)

**Table 4.1** (continued)

| | REER over-valuation | | Real GDP growth | | Output gap | | 3yr. change in credit/ GDP | | 1yr. change in LTD ratio | | 1yr. change in FX loans/ total loans | |
|---|---|---|---|---|---|---|---|---|---|---|---|---|
| | OLS | FE/TE | OLS | FE/TE | OLS | FE/TE | OLS | FE/TE | OLS | FE/TE | OLS | FE/TE |
| | (1) | (2) | (3) | (4) | (5) | (6) | (7) | (8) | (9) | (10) | (11) | (12) |
| Country-fixed effects | No | Yes | No | Yes | No | Yes | No | Yes | No | Yes | No | Yes |
| Year effects | No | Yes | No | Yes | No | Yes | No | Yes | No | Yes | No | Yes |
| Observations | 1,349 | 1,349 | 1,403 | 1,403 | 1,403 | 1,403 | 1,295 | 1,295 | 1,276 | 1,276 | 489 | 489 |
| $R^2$ | 0.023 | 0.209 | 0.007 | 0.403 | 0.077 | 0.319 | 0.094 | 0.431 | 0.035 | 0.233 | 0.016 | 0.226 |
| Countries | 53 | 53 | 53 | 53 | 53 | 53 | 53 | 53 | 53 | 53 | 44 | 44 |

*Notes:* Dependent variable is REER overvaluation (defined as deviation of REER from trend REER, in percent of trend REER) in cols. (1)–(2); real GDP growth rate in cols. (3)–(4); output gap (defined as deviation of actual real GDP from trend real GDP, in percent of trend GDP) in cols. (5)–(6); 3-year cumulative change in domestic credit (in percent of GDP) in cols. (7)–(8); annual change in loan to deposit ratio (in ppt.) in cols. (9)–(10); and annual change in foreign currency loans to total loans (in ppt.) in cols. (11)–(12). All regressors (except for initial condition and trading partner growth) are lagged one period. OLS is estimation by ordinary least squares method (without including country- and year-fixed effects). FE/TE is estimation by ordinary least squares method including country- and year-fixed effects. Constant is included in all specifications. Clustered standard errors are reported in parentheses. ***, **, and * indicate statistical significance at 1, 5, and 10 percent levels, respectively.

a. Initial condition is three-period lagged domestic credit (in percent of GDP) in cols. (7)–(8), three-period lagged loan to deposit ratio (in percent) in cols. (9)–(10), and three-period lagged foreign currency loans (in percent of total loans) in cols. (9)–(10).

2.5 percentage points of faster output growth, but also with 14 percentage points of greater currency overvaluation, an 8 percentage point widening of the output gap, a 3 percentage point increase in credit growth, a 4 percentage point increase in banking system's leverage growth, and an 8 percentage point increase in FX lending growth. Thus, if anything, taking account of the possible endogeneity bias reinforces the association between capital inflows, on the one hand, and macroeconomic and balance-sheet vulnerabilities, on the other.

### 4.2.1   Disaggregating by Type of Capital Inflow

But are all types of capital flows equally problematic? Breaking down net capital flows into asset and liability flows, the macroeconomic and financial-stability consequences are broadly similar—although formal tests of coefficient equality imply that the effects of liability flows on real GDP growth, the output gap, and domestic credit expansion are (statistically) significantly larger (table 4.2). Thus, a 10 percent of GDP increase in liability flows would raise the real GDP growth rate by about 0.7 percentage points, while a corresponding increase in asset flows would raise the growth rate by 0.5 percentage points. Likewise, an increase of 10 percent of GDP in liability flows would increase domestic credit growth by 4 percentage points over three years, while the same increase in asset flows would raise lending by 3.5 percentage points.

While these differences are hardly dramatic, they suggest that the impact on the recipient country's economy may depend on the type of capital inflow. In this vein, Combes, Kinda, and Plane (2012) find that portfolio inflows lead to greater real appreciation of the currency than do foreign direct investment (FDI) flows, while Calderon and Kubota (2012) find that the likelihood of credit booms (and, in particular, those that end in crisis) is significantly higher if the surge is driven by private "other investment" (mainly cross-border bank flows). The same applies, though to a lesser extent, if the surge mainly reflects portfolio investment. Similarly, Furceri, Guichard, and Rusticelli (2012a) find that debt inflows have the largest impact on domestic credit growth, as opposed to portfolio equity or FDI flows.

Consistent with these studies, the estimates reported in table 4.2 suggest that the consequences of capital inflows indeed depend on their type. Thus, FDI has the largest impact on real GDP growth and the output gap, but is not statistically significantly associated with currency overvaluation, domestic credit growth, bank leverage growth, or a higher

**Table 4.2**
Macroeconomic and financial vulnerabilities by type of capital inflows, 1980–2013.

| | REER over-valuation | | Real GDP growth | | Output gap | | 3yr. change in credit/GDP | | 1yr. change in LTD ratio | | 1yr. change in FX lending | |
|---|---|---|---|---|---|---|---|---|---|---|---|---|
| | (1) | (2) | (3) | (4) | (5) | (6) | (7) | (8) | (9) | (10) | (11) | (12) |
| Asset flows/GDP | 0.229** (0.087) | | 0.047** (0.018) | | 0.161*** (0.036) | | 0.357*** (0.122) | | 0.443*** (0.094) | | 0.052 (0.046) | |
| Liability flows/GDP | 0.208** (0.084) | | 0.065*** (0.018) | | 0.197*** (0.035) | | 0.408*** (0.111) | | 0.405*** (0.100) | | 0.062* (0.031) | |
| Net FDI flows/GDP | | -0.007 (0.130) | | 0.207*** (0.056) | | 0.246*** (0.063) | | 0.247 (0.242) | | 0.062 (0.169) | | 0.035 (0.073) |
| Net portfolio flows/GDP | | 0.287* (0.143) | | 0.064* (0.036) | | 0.092* (0.054) | | 0.185 (0.158) | | 0.333** (0.151) | | 0.116* (0.064) |
| Net other inv. flows/GDP | | 0.254*** (0.087) | | 0.024 (0.024) | | 0.204*** (0.048) | | 0.506*** (0.139) | | 0.535*** (0.136) | | 0.055 (0.044) |
| Exchange rate regime | 2.949* (1.619) | 3.142* (1.624) | 0.385 (0.432) | 0.271 (0.428) | 0.951 (0.617) | 0.903 (0.622) | -0.402 (1.520) | -0.246 (1.486) | 3.375* (1.890) | 3.708* (1.873) | -0.071 (0.544) | -0.088 (0.547) |
| Real GDP growth | -0.024 (0.094) | -0.026 (0.092) | 0.020* (0.010) | 0.021* (0.010) | 0.027** (0.012) | 0.025** (0.012) | -0.016 (0.154) | 0.007 (0.148) | 0.471*** (0.145) | 0.452*** (0.140) | -0.041 (0.074) | -0.034 (0.073) |
| Terms of trade change | 0.018 (0.022) | 0.020 (0.022) | 0.020* (0.010) | 0.021* (0.010) | 0.027** (0.012) | 0.025** (0.012) | -0.012 (0.027) | -0.014 (0.028) | 0.076 (0.062) | 0.078 (0.062) | 0.001 (0.029) | 0.002 (0.029) |

| | | | | | | | | | | | |
|---|---|---|---|---|---|---|---|---|---|---|---|
| Trade openness | -0.066** | -0.065** | 0.018* | 0.017 | -0.006 | -0.006 | -0.010 | -0.012 | -0.044 | -0.043 | -0.017 | -0.014 |
| | (0.029) | (0.029) | (0.010) | (0.010) | (0.011) | (0.011) | (0.043) | (0.043) | (0.031) | (0.030) | (0.024) | (0.023) |
| Real GDP per capita (log) | 3.012* | 2.935* | -4.026*** | -3.939*** | 6.414*** | 6.501*** | 20.113*** | 19.840*** | 7.038** | 6.717** | 5.562** | 5.647** |
| | (1.569) | (1.510) | (0.995) | (0.961) | (2.160) | (2.195) | (3.923) | (3.889) | (2.751) | (2.791) | (2.456) | (2.545) |
| Trading partner growth | | | 0.945*** | 0.936*** | | | | | | | | |
| | | | (0.162) | (0.162) | | | | | | | | |
| Initial condition | | | | | | | -0.445*** | -0.436*** | -0.149*** | -0.148*** | -0.124*** | -0.125*** |
| | | | | | | | (0.055) | (0.056) | (0.015) | (0.015) | (0.022) | (0.023) |
| Country-fixed effects | Yes | Yes | Yes | Yes | Yes | Yes | Yes | Yes | Yes | Yes | Yes | Yes |
| Year effects | Yes | Yes | Yes | Yes | Yes | Yes | Yes | Yes | Yes | Yes | Yes | Yes |
| Observations | 1,349 | 1,349 | 1,403 | 1,403 | 1,403 | 1,403 | 1,295 | 1,295 | 1,276 | 1,276 | 489 | 489 |
| $R^2$ | 0.210 | 0.212 | 0.406 | 0.410 | 0.329 | 0.324 | 0.433 | 0.436 | 0.234 | 0.237 | 0.226 | 0.226 |
| Countries | 53 | 53 | 53 | 53 | 53 | 53 | 53 | 53 | 53 | 53 | 53 | 44 |
| *Test of coefficient equality (p-value):* | | | | | | | | | | | | |
| Asset vs. liability flows | 0.085 | 0.000 | 0.000 | | 0.034 | | 0.104 | | 0.799 | | | |

*Notes:* See table 4.1 for variable descriptions. Constant is included in all specifications. Clustered standard errors (at the country level) are reported in parentheses. ***, **, and * indicate statistical significance at 1, 5, and 10 percent levels, respectively.

share of FX-denominated lending.[7] (This is intuitive inasmuch as FDI is more likely than the other types of flows to be used directly to finance imports—e.g., of capital goods—rather than to be deposited in the domestic banking system where it could finance domestic lending.) By contrast, other investment flows (which typically take the form of bank deposits) are strongly associated with currency overvaluation, output expansion, domestic credit booms, and bank leverage growth.[8] Similarly, portfolio flows are associated—albeit only at the 10 percent significance level—with currency overvaluation, positive output gaps, and economic growth, as well as with FX-denominated lending and increased bank leverage (at the 5 percent significance level). Splitting portfolio flows further into debt and equity shows that currency overvaluation and financial-stability risks stem mainly from the former, while output expansion tends to be associated with the latter (table A.4.3).

In sum, capital inflows can amplify macroeconomic imbalances and financial sector vulnerabilities, with certain types of flows—especially debt flows—being particularly pernicious, while FDI seems to contribute to output growth with few untoward consequences.

### 4.3   Crisis Likelihood

To what extent do the imbalances and vulnerabilities associated with capital inflows translate into crisis? Existing studies find that they often do—notably, credit growth and real exchange rate overvaluation turn out to be strong predictors of banking and currency crises in EMEs (Demirgüç-Kunt and Detragiache 1998; Gourinchas and Obstfeld 2012; Ghosh, Ostry, and Qureshi 2015).[9] Caballero (2016) finds that large capital inflows are associated with systemic banking crises even in

---

7. Some caution is required in interpreting the results for disaggregated flows, as the net concept refers to nonresidents' purchases of that type of domestic liability plus the repatriated proceeds of residents' sale of that type of foreign asset—regardless of how those proceeds are used (i.e., whether or not they are invested in the same type of asset domestically). Further disaggregating individual net flows into asset and liability flows, we find that where the estimated coefficients are statistically significant in table 4.2, the effect is generally driven by both asset and liability flows.

8. The estimated coefficient of net other investment flows (lagged) is statistically insignificant in the real-GDP growth estimations, but becomes significant and larger in magnitude if contemporaneous flows are used, or in IV-2SLS regressions using as instruments net flows to the region (in percent of regional GDP) and the de jure capital account openness index.

9. Analyzing data for fourteen advanced countries from 1870–2008, Schularick and Taylor (2012) find that faster credit growth and higher leverage in the financial system are strongly associated with financial crises in advanced economies as well.

the absence of lending booms, but that the likelihood of a crisis magnifies threefold in the presence of a credit boom. Similarly, Calderon and Kubota (2012) find that surges in gross inflows are a good predictor of credit booms that end up in a financial crisis, and this remains true even after controlling for currency appreciation and the buildup of leverage.

To establish the link between capital inflows and financial (i.e., banking or currency) crises, we estimate the following model:

$$\Pr(Crisis_{jt} = 1) = F(\beta k_{jt} + z'_{jt}\gamma) \qquad (4.1)$$

where $Crisis_{jt}$ is an indicator variable of whether a banking or currency crisis occurs in country $j$ in period $t$; $k$ indicates net capital flows (in percent of GDP) prior to the onset of the crisis; and $z$ includes other relevant explanatory variables such as (lagged) real GDP growth, fiscal balance, stock of foreign exchange reserves (in percent of GDP), inflation, exchange rate regime, real GDP per capita, as well as country-specific and year effects.[10] The banking and currency crisis variables are taken from the database of Laeven and Valencia (2013), who define systemic banking crises as those in which significant signs of financial distress appear in the banking system, requiring significant policy interventions in response to significant losses. Currency crises are defined following Frankel and Rose (1996) and comprise nominal exchange rate depreciations against the US dollar of at least 30 percent that are also at least 10 percentage points greater than the previous year's depreciation. We estimate (4.1) using the probit model, and cluster the standard errors at the country level.

The results imply (against an unconditional crisis probability of about 4 percent, and evaluating the effects around the mean values of all explanatory variables) that if net capital flows increase by 5 percent of GDP, then the probability of banking and currency crises goes up by about 1 percentage point, though the effect is statistically insignificant for currency crises (table 4.3, cols. [1] and [3]). Much of this increase in crisis likelihood, however, stems from just two variables: currency overvaluation and the change in the ratio of domestic credit to GDP.

---

10. We use one-period lagged net financial flow (in percent of GDP) in the banking crisis estimations, and two-period lagged net financial flow (in percent of GDP) in the currency crisis estimations. This is because typically a currency crisis happens after the onset of outflows. Thus, the one-year lag probably reflects the fact that countries with larger outflows (or lower net inflows) experience a currency crisis, as opposed to capturing that larger inflows *eventually* lead to crisis.

**Table 4.3**
Crisis probability and capital inflows in EMEs.

| | Banking | | | Currency | | |
|---|---|---|---|---|---|---|
| | (1) | (2) | (3) | (4) | (5) | (6) |
| Net financial flows/GDP | 0.031*** | 0.014 | 0.024 | 0.021 | 0.003 | 0.045* |
| | (0.012) | (0.014) | (0.023) | (0.014) | (0.012) | (0.026) |
| REER overvaluation | | 0.026*** | 0.024** | | 0.045*** | 0.058*** |
| | | (0.009) | (0.011) | | (0.011) | (0.011) |
| Domestic credit boom | | 0.025*** | 0.032*** | | 0.009 | 0.006 |
| | | (0.005) | (0.009) | | (0.009) | (0.008) |
| Exchange rate regime | 0.756* | 0.642 | 0.242 | 0.367 | 0.270 | −0.455 |
| | (0.397) | (0.437) | (0.667) | (0.283) | (0.308) | (0.551) |
| Real GDP growth | −0.013 | −0.004 | −0.028 | −0.006 | 0.016 | 0.066** |
| | (0.016) | (0.018) | (0.032) | (0.019) | (0.021) | (0.028) |
| Reserves/GDP | −0.027*** | −0.027** | −0.030 | −0.050*** | −0.042** | −0.099* |
| | (0.009) | (0.011) | (0.026) | (0.017) | (0.019) | (0.051) |
| Trade openness | −0.002 | −0.002 | −0.008 | −0.002 | −0.001 | −0.001 |
| | (0.002) | (0.002) | (0.010) | (0.003) | (0.003) | (0.014) |
| Real GDP per capita (log) | 0.100 | 0.092 | 1.774** | 0.228** | 0.219** | 5.530*** |
| | (0.072) | (0.066) | (0.734) | (0.111) | (0.099) | (1.515) |
| Fiscal balance/GDP | 0.005 | −0.011 | −0.022 | −0.032* | −0.037** | −0.126*** |
| | (0.016) | (0.018) | (0.039) | (0.016) | (0.018) | (0.035) |
| Inflation | 0.003 | 0.006** | −0.008 | 0.004 | 0.012*** | 0.003 |
| | (0.004) | (0.003) | (0.007) | (0.003) | (0.004) | (0.007) |
| Country-fixed effects | No | No | Yes | No | No | Yes |
| Year effects | No | No | Yes | No | No | Yes |
| Observations | 1,177 | 1,177 | 1,177 | 1,158 | 1,158 | 1,158 |
| Countries | 53 | 53 | 53 | 53 | 53 | 53 |
| Pseudo-$R^2$ | 0.060 | 0.139 | 0.412 | 0.110 | 0.218 | 0.543 |
| Wald-chi2 (p-value)[a] | 0.00 | 0.00 | 0.00 | 0.00 | 0.00 | 0.00 |

*Notes:* Dependent variable is a binary variable equal to one if there is a banking or currency crisis in cols. (1)–(3) and (4)–(6), respectively. All specifications are estimated using the probit model. All regressors are lagged one period, except for net financial flows to GDP in cols. (4)–(6), which is lagged two periods. Constant is included in all specifications. Clustered standard errors (at the country level) are reported in parentheses. ***, **, and * indicate statistical significance at 1, 5, and 10 percent levels, respectively.
a. Test of joint significance of regressors.

When these variables are included in the probit, the estimated coefficient on net capital flows becomes statistically insignificant for banking crises (col. [2]). A 10 percentage point increase in real exchange rate overvaluation, for instance, raises the likelihood of a banking or a currency crisis by about 2 percentage points, while a 10 percentage point expansion of domestic credit over a three-year period raises the likelihood of a banking crisis by about 1 percentage point (domestic credit expansion is not a statistically significant explanatory variable for currency crises).

Moreover, these results hold when we include year-fixed effects to capture common shocks across countries. With this addition, the estimated coefficient of capital flows on currency crises becomes statistically significant at the 10 percent level (cols. [3] and [6]). Thus, beyond the effects of exchange rate overvaluation and credit expansion, there appears to be some residual risk of capital flows (such as currency mismatches on private sector balance sheets) that magnifies the risk of currency crises. Among the other variables in the probit, a larger stock of foreign exchange reserves, a higher fiscal balance, and lower inflation are associated with a lower likelihood of a currency crisis.

### 4.3.1 Disaggregating by Type of Capital Inflow

Disaggregating net flows once again into asset flows and liability flows, we find that both have a similar effect on crisis likelihood. An increase of 5 percent of GDP in capital inflows, for instance, by either domestic residents (asset flows) or by foreigners (liability flows) raises the probability of a banking crisis by about 1 percentage point (table 4.4, col. [1]). (This also holds for currency crises, although in that case the estimated coefficient on both asset and liability flows is statistically insignificant without country-fixed and year effects; col. [7].) The estimated coefficient for both types of flows turns statistically insignificant when measures of currency overvaluation and credit expansion are included in the probit for banking crises, implying that both work mainly through these channels (cols. [2]–[3]). In the case of currency crises, however, once country-fixed and year effects are included in the model, the estimated coefficients on asset and liability flows turn statistically significant despite the inclusion of currency overvaluation and credit expansion (col. [9]).

Analogous to the exercise above, further disaggregating flows suggests that the type of capital inflow matters for the likelihood of a subsequent

**Table 4.4**
Crisis probability by type of capital inflows, 1980–2013.

| | Banking | | | | | | Currency | | | | | |
|---|---|---|---|---|---|---|---|---|---|---|---|---|
| | (1) | (2) | (3) | (4) | (5) | (6) | (7) | (8) | (9) | (10) | (11) | (12) |
| Asset flows/ GDP | 0.033*** (0.013) | 0.018 (0.014) | 0.026 (0.023) | | | | 0.020 (0.015) | 0.002 (0.012) | 0.114* (0.064) | | | |
| Liability flows/GDP | 0.031*** (0.012) | 0.015 (0.013) | 0.025 (0.023) | | | | 0.021 (0.014) | 0.003 (0.012) | 0.045* (0.026) | | | |
| Net FDI flows/GDP | | | | -0.042 (0.036) | -0.071* (0.037) | -0.150** (0.076) | | | | 0.010 (0.028) | -0.018 (0.033) | -0.083 (0.067) |
| Net portfolio flows/GDP | | | | 0.039** (0.019) | 0.019 (0.022) | -0.011 (0.026) | | | | 0.041* (0.023) | 0.022 (0.018) | 0.020 (0.029) |
| Net other inv. flows/GDP | | | | 0.049*** (0.015) | 0.038** (0.016) | 0.051** (0.025) | | | | 0.021 (0.016) | 0.007 (0.016) | 0.104** (0.047) |
| REER overvaluation | | 0.027*** (0.009) | 0.024** (0.011) | | 0.029*** (0.009) | 0.024** (0.012) | | 0.045*** (0.011) | 0.060*** (0.012) | | 0.046*** (0.011) | 0.063*** (0.013) |
| Domestic credit boom | | 0.026*** (0.005) | 0.032*** (0.009) | | 0.025*** (0.006) | 0.033*** (0.009) | | 0.009 (0.009) | 0.007 (0.008) | | 0.009 (0.009) | 0.008 (0.008) |
| Exchange rate regime | 0.754* (0.397) | 0.637 (0.438) | 0.240 (0.666) | 0.762* (0.393) | 0.657 (0.445) | 0.222 (0.698) | 0.367 (0.283) | 0.270 (0.308) | -0.537 (0.558) | 0.374 (0.282) | 0.282 (0.309) | -0.513 (0.574) |
| Real GDP growth | -0.012 (0.016) | -0.001 (0.018) | -0.025 (0.034) | -0.010 (0.017) | -0.002 (0.018) | -0.017 (0.034) | -0.007 (0.019) | 0.016 (0.021) | 0.071** (0.029) | -0.007 (0.019) | 0.016 (0.021) | 0.082*** (0.027) |
| Reserves/ GDP | -0.027*** (0.009) | -0.027** (0.011) | -0.030 (0.026) | -0.022*** (0.008) | -0.021** (0.010) | -0.023 (0.027) | -0.050*** (0.017) | -0.043** (0.019) | -0.095* (0.050) | -0.049*** (0.017) | -0.040** (0.020) | -0.091* (0.049) |

| | (1) | (2) | (3) | (4) | (5) | (6) | (7) | (8) | (9) | (10) | (11) | (12) |
|---|---|---|---|---|---|---|---|---|---|---|---|---|
| Trade openness | -0.002 | -0.002 | -0.008 | -0.002 | -0.001 | -0.013 | -0.002 | -0.001 | -0.002 | -0.002 | -0.000 | -0.002 |
| | (0.002) | (0.002) | (0.010) | (0.002) | (0.002) | (0.010) | (0.003) | (0.003) | (0.014) | (0.003) | (0.002) | (0.014) |
| Real GDP per capita (log) | 0.102 | 0.095 | 1.772** | 0.095 | 0.072 | 1.664** | 0.227** | 0.219** | 5.651*** | 0.223** | 0.214** | 5.752*** |
| | (0.071) | (0.066) | (0.731) | (0.074) | (0.067) | (0.739) | (0.111) | (0.099) | (1.506) | (0.112) | (0.099) | (1.560) |
| Fiscal balance/GDP | 0.004 | -0.011 | -0.023 | 0.008 | -0.006 | -0.026 | -0.032* | -0.037** | -0.130*** | -0.030* | -0.035* | -0.134*** |
| | (0.016) | (0.018) | (0.039) | (0.015) | (0.018) | (0.041) | (0.016) | (0.018) | (0.033) | (0.017) | (0.018) | (0.036) |
| Inflation | 0.003 | 0.007** | -0.007 | 0.003 | 0.007** | -0.008 | 0.004 | 0.012*** | 0.003 | 0.004 | 0.012*** | 0.002 |
| | (0.004) | (0.003) | (0.007) | (0.003) | (0.003) | (0.007) | (0.003) | (0.004) | (0.007) | (0.003) | (0.004) | (0.007) |
| Country-fixed effects | No | No | Yes | No | No | Yes | No | No | Yes | No | No | Yes |
| Year effects | No | No | Yes | No | No | Yes | No | No | Yes | No | No | Yes |
| Observations | 1,177 | 1,177 | 1,177 | 1,177 | 1,177 | 1,177 | 1,158 | 1,158 | 1,158 | 1,158 | 1,158 | 1,158 |
| Countries | 53 | 53 | 53 | 53 | 53 | 53 | 53 | 53 | 53 | 53 | 53 | 53 |
| Pseudo-$R^2$ | 0.061 | 0.140 | 0.412 | 0.079 | 0.160 | 0.434 | 0.110 | 0.218 | 0.546 | 0.113 | 0.220 | 0.551 |
| Wald-chi2 (p-value)[a] | 0.00 | 0.00 | 0.00 | 0.00 | 0.00 | 0.00 | 0.00 | 0.00 | 0.00 | 0.00 | 0.00 | 0.00 |

*Notes:* Dependent variable is a binary variable equal to one if there is a banking or currency crisis in cols. (1)–(6) and (7)–(12), respectively. All specifications are estimated using the probit model. All regressors are lagged one period, except for the net financial flow to GDP variables in cols. (7)–(12), which are lagged two periods. Constant is included in all specifications. Clustered standard errors (at the country level) are reported in parentheses. ***, **, and * indicate statistical significance at 1, 5, and 10 percent levels, respectively.

a. Test of joint significance of regressors.

financial crisis. Net portfolio flows significantly increase the probability of banking and currency crises, though the association becomes statistically insignificant when currency overvaluation and credit expansion are included in the model (table 4.4; cols. [4]–[6] and [10]–[12]). Other investment flows (mainly banking flows) also significantly raise the crisis probabilities; importantly, the estimated coefficient stays statistically significant despite controlling for currency overvaluation and domestic credit expansion, suggesting that such flows pose some residual risks. Interestingly, the estimates for FDI flows imply that, if anything, they lower the probability of crisis, though the estimated coefficient is negative and statistically significant only for banking crises (cols. [5]–[6]).

A further breakdown of net portfolio flows into equity and debt suggests that—consistent with the results reported in table A.4.3—it is mainly debt flows that raise the crisis likelihood (table A.4.4). These findings resonate with those of existing studies (e.g., Furceri, Guichard, and Rusticelli 2012b), which tend to find that large capital inflows, especially debt-driven inflows, substantially increase the probability of banking and currency crises, whereas portfolio equity or FDI have a negligible effect on crisis likelihood.

### 4.4  Surges, Soft Landings, and Crashes

The implications of the findings above are clear: capital inflows can lead to macroeconomic imbalances and balance-sheet vulnerabilities, raising the likelihood of financial crisis. If that is true in general, then it should be especially true of large inflow, or surge, episodes. In this section, we sharpen the analysis by focusing on surges (as identified in chapter 3), distinguishing between those that end in crisis (a crash) and those that end with little or no disruption (a soft landing).

A first observation, consistent with the discussion above, is that macroeconomic and balance-sheet vulnerabilities are indeed higher during surges than in nonsurge years. Figure 4.2, for example, shows that real exchange rate overvaluation, the output gap, and real GDP growth rate are about 2 percentage points higher, while the growth of bank leverage and of banking system credit are some 3–5 percentage points greater in surge years than in nonsurge years.[11] Grouping con-

---

11. The 2 percentage point average overvaluation during surges seems somewhat low, but this average reflects several episodes in which the real exchange rate appreciates during the first half of the year, and then depreciates sharply as capital flows reverse.

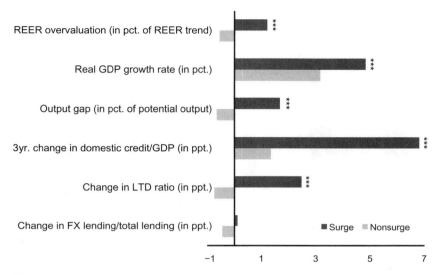

**Figure 4.2**
Macroeconomic and financial vulnerabilities in surges vs. nonsurges.
*Notes*: Figure based on surges identified in chapter 3 (table 3.1). *** indicates difference between the means of the two groups (surges, nonsurges) is statistically significant at the 1 percent level.

secutive surge years, we obtain 167 surge *episodes* (listed in table 3.1); excluding the fourteen episodes that are ongoing at the end of the sample, leaves 153 episodes, of which thirty experienced a banking crisis within two years of the end of the surge, nineteen experienced a currency crisis, and twelve experienced a twin banking-currency crisis.[12] The implied probabilities—20 percent, 12 percent, 8 percent—are all substantially (and statistically significantly) higher than the corresponding frequencies in the full sample, which range from about 1 to 4 percent (figure 4.3). The likelihood that a country experiences some form of financial crisis in the aftermath of a surge episode is thus *three to five times* greater than in nonsurge years.

---

12. See chapter appendix for the list of identified surge episodes ending with a currency or banking crisis. Using our definition to identify crash endings, we find two cases—Hungary (2006–2008) and the Slovak Republic (1996–1998)—in which a banking crisis is associated with two surge episodes that are separated by one year. Classifying just one episode (either the first or the second) as a crash landing does not affect the empirical results.

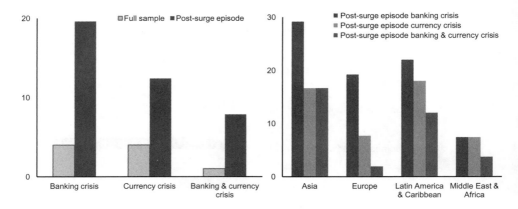

**Figure 4.3**
Banking and currency crisis probability (in percent).
*Notes*: Post-surge crisis probability is defined as a (banking/currency) crisis occurring within two years after a surge episode ends. Surge episodes are those identified in chapter 3 (table 3.1), and banking and currency crises are those identified by Laeven and Valencia (2013).

Yet, clearly not all surge episodes end in crisis. In 2007, for instance, Russia and Ukraine recorded inflows of about 10 percent of GDP; with the onset of the global financial crisis the following year, both experienced banking crises. But during the same period, several other emerging markets—including Brazil, India, South Africa, and Turkey—experienced similarly large capital inflows but did not suffer a subsequent banking crisis (overall, of the thirty EMEs that had an inflow surge in the run up to the GFC, five experienced a financial crisis in 2008–2009).

To establish what determines whether a surge ends gracefully or in crisis, we estimate the following probit model over the sample of 153 surge episodes:

$$\Pr(Crisis_{jt|S_{jt-1}=1} = 1) = F(\Delta x'_{jt}\, \delta + \Delta z'_{jt}\, \eta + z'_{jt}\, \xi) \tag{4.2}$$

where $Crisis_{jt|S_{jt-1}=1}$ is an indicator variable of whether country $j$ experiences a (banking or currency) crisis in period $t$ or $t+1$, conditional on its inflow surge ending in period $t-1$; $\Delta x$ is the change in global conditions (US real interest rate, global risk aversion, commodity prices) that trigger the end of the episode for country $j$ in period $t$; $\Delta z$ is the change in domestic conditions (current account balance, real GDP growth, financial-stability conditions, etc.) over the surge episode; and $z$ includes domestic factors whose level (at the end of the surge episode) may make the country more vulnerable to crisis (current account balance and fiscal balance, degree of currency overvaluation, stock of foreign exchange reserves, external debt, etc.). In addition, we include regional dummies in (4.2) to capture any contagion from crises in neighboring countries, as well as per capita real GDP to control for differences in institutional development across countries.

A tricky issue in specifying the empirical model concerns the timing of the variables (and the period over which their change should be measured). The change in global conditions, for example, could either be defined as the change between the average value during the surge and the value in the year(s) following the surge, or as the change between the value in the last year of the surge episode and the year(s) that follow. To be consistent with our definition of a crash ending—a crisis occurring within two years of the end of the surge—we define changes in global conditions as the average over the two post-surge years relative to the average during the surge episode. Changes in domestic conditions could in principle be defined the same way, but using the post-surge value gives rise to a potentially serious endogeneity problem: domestic variables such as the interest rate, output growth, or the current account balance can (and generally do) move in response to the occurrence of a crisis. For this reason, we define changes in domestic variables as the average conditions prevailing over the surge episode relative to those in the year before the episode began.[13] This allows us to assess the impact of policies pursued over the surge episode on the outcome. Finally, for the variables in levels that may affect investor sentiment or otherwise affect the likelihood of a crisis, we use the value in the last year of the surge episode.[14]

We begin by considering the impact of changes in global conditions on the likelihood of a crash landing, controlling only for region-specific effects, and the country's initial (pre-surge) per capita real GDP. The results presented in table 4.5 (col. [1]) show that changes in global conditions, specifically the US real interest rate, commodity prices, and investor risk aversion, are strongly associated with a crisis occurring after the surge episode. Against an unconditional probability of 24 percent, the predicted probability of a crisis (keeping other variables at their mean value) increases by 9 percentage points if US real interest

---

13. Changes in domestic variables could also be defined as the difference between the last year of the surge episode and the year before the surge episode began; using this alternate definition mostly yields similar results.
14. For both changes and levels of domestic factors, we exclude outliers that are in the top and bottom 0.25th percentile of the distribution.

**Table 4.5**
Post-surge episode crisis probability.

| | (1) | (2) | (3) | (4) | (5) | (6) | (7) |
|---|---|---|---|---|---|---|---|
| US real interest rate[a] | 0.279*** (0.091) | 0.265*** (0.091) | 0.280*** (0.096) | 0.298*** (0.092) | 0.311*** (0.100) | 0.253*** (0.092) | 0.326*** (0.121) |
| Commodity prices[a] | −0.039*** (0.009) | −0.038*** (0.009) | −0.042*** (0.010) | −0.038*** (0.009) | −0.041*** (0.010) | −0.041*** (0.010) | −0.041*** (0.011) |
| S&P 500 returns' volatility[a] | 0.046* (0.024) | 0.048* (0.025) | 0.026 (0.025) | 0.052** (0.025) | 0.044* (0.025) | 0.035 (0.026) | 0.045 (0.031) |
| Real GDP per capita (log)[b] | 0.029 (0.199) | 0.025 (0.203) | −0.088 (0.217) | 0.044 (0.213) | −0.051 (0.199) | 0.048 (0.220) | −0.087 (0.215) |
| Change in current acc. bal./GDP[c] | | 0.037 (0.046) | | | | | |
| Change in credit/GDP[c] | | | 0.032** (0.013) | | | | |
| Change in real GDP growth rate[c] | | | | −0.058* (0.032) | | | |
| Change in bank foreign liab./GDP[c] | | | | | 0.043* (0.022) | | |
| Change in exchange rate regime[c] | | | | | | −0.778* (0.425) | |
| Change in institutional quality[c] | | | | | | | −8.490** (4.212) |
| Current account balance/GDP[d] | | | | | | | |
| FX reserves/GDP[d] | | | | | | | |
| Overvaluation[d] | | | | | | | |
| External debt/GDP[d] | | | | | | | |
| FDI-dominated surge[e] | | | | | | | |
| Other inv. liab.-dominated surge[e] | | | | | | | |
| Region-specific effects | Yes | Yes | Yes | Yes | Yes | Yes | Yes |
| Observations | 142 | 141 | 141 | 141 | 141 | 142 | 120 |
| Countries | 51 | 51 | 51 | 51 | 50 | 51 | 48 |
| Pseudo-$R^2$ | 0.182 | 0.176 | 0.207 | 0.188 | 0.213 | 0.207 | 0.207 |
| Wald-chi2 (p-value) | 0.00 | 0.00 | 0.00 | 0.00 | 0.00 | 0.00 | 0.01 |
| Percent correctly predicted | 80.99 | 81.56 | 80.85 | 82.98 | 82.98 | 82.39 | 85.83 |
| Sensitivity | 33.33 | 34.38 | 31.25 | 31.25 | 39.39 | 39.39 | 42.31 |

*Notes:* Dependent variable is a binary variable equal to 1 if a banking or currency crisis happened within two years after a surge episode ended. All specifications include a constant and are estimated using the probit model. Clustered standard errors (at the country level) are reported in parentheses. *, **, and *** indicate statistical significance at 10, 5, and 1 percent levels, respectively.
a. Difference between the two-year average after the end of the surge episode, and the average over the surge episode.
b. Level in the year before the surge episode started.

| (8) | (9) | (10) | (11) | (12) | (13) | (14) | (15) | (16) |
|---|---|---|---|---|---|---|---|---|
| 0.271*** | 0.298*** | 0.296*** | 0.372*** | 0.237** | 0.268*** | 0.251** | 0.250** | 0.607** |
| (0.094) | (0.099) | (0.094) | (0.087) | (0.093) | (0.092) | (0.114) | (0.118) | (0.242) |
| −0.038*** | −0.034*** | −0.032*** | −0.044*** | −0.037*** | −0.036*** | −0.030*** | −0.033*** | −0.050*** |
| (0.010) | (0.010) | (0.010) | (0.009) | (0.010) | (0.009) | (0.011) | (0.012) | (0.014) |
| 0.047* | 0.060** | 0.042 | 0.062** | 0.049* | 0.051** | 0.039 | 0.038 | 0.070 |
| (0.024) | (0.025) | (0.027) | (0.025) | (0.026) | (0.025) | (0.031) | (0.031) | (0.060) |
| 0.020 | 0.280 | −0.046 | 0.033 | −0.107 | −0.004 | 0.105 | 0.129 | −0.147 |
| (0.195) | (0.240) | (0.222) | (0.201) | (0.197) | (0.205) | (0.274) | (0.266) | (0.293) |
|  |  |  |  |  |  | 0.034* | −0.007 | 0.042* |
|  |  |  |  |  |  | (0.018) | (0.019) | (0.025) |
|  |  |  |  |  |  | −0.065 | −0.081* | −0.071 |
|  |  |  |  |  |  | (0.044) | (0.046) | (0.052) |
|  |  |  |  |  |  | 0.112*** |  |  |
|  |  |  |  |  |  | (0.036) |  |  |
|  |  |  |  |  |  | −1.285** | −1.377*** | −0.985** |
|  |  |  |  |  |  | (0.571) | (0.530) | (0.494) |
|  |  |  |  |  |  |  |  | −19.830** |
|  |  |  |  |  |  |  |  | (7.994) |
| 0.013 |  |  |  |  |  | 0.047 | 0.071* | 0.029 |
| (0.032) |  |  |  |  |  | (0.035) | (0.040) | (0.053) |
|  | −0.050** |  |  |  |  | −0.041** | −0.043** | −0.019 |
|  | (0.020) |  |  |  |  | (0.020) | (0.021) | (0.019) |
|  |  | 0.063*** |  |  |  | 0.063*** | 0.068*** | 0.087*** |
|  |  | (0.017) |  |  |  | (0.022) | (0.022) | (0.023) |
|  |  |  | 0.004 |  |  |  |  | 0.018** |
|  |  |  | (0.004) |  |  |  |  | (0.007) |
|  |  |  |  | −0.650** |  |  |  |  |
|  |  |  |  | (0.253) |  |  |  |  |
|  |  |  |  |  | 0.488** |  |  |  |
|  |  |  |  |  | (0.223) |  |  |  |
| Yes | Yes | Yes | Yes | Yes | Yes | Yes | Yes | Yes |
| 142 | 142 | 142 | 141 | 142 | 142 | 140 | 139 | 117 |
| 51 | 51 | 51 | 51 | 51 | 51 | 51 | 50 | 48 |
| 0.183 | 0.226 | 0.270 | 0.216 | 0.215 | 0.203 | 0.372 | 0.408 | 0.480 |
| 0.00 | 0.00 | 0.00 | 0.00 | 0.01 | 0.01 | 0.00 | 0.00 | 0.00 |
| 81.69 | 82.39 | 85.21 | 79.43 | 80.28 | 79.58 | 86.43 | 86.33 | 88.89 |
| 36.36 | 39.39 | 54.55 | 31.25 | 36.36 | 33.33 | 58.06 | 54.84 | 69.57 |

c. Difference between the average over the surge episode and the year before the surge started.

d. Level in the last year of the surge episode.

e. FDI-dominated surge is defined as one where the average net FDI flow received during the surge episode is larger than the average net portfolio or other investment liability flow. Similarly, other investment liability–dominated surge is one where the average net other investment liability flow during the surge episode is larger than the other types of net flows.

rates rise by 100 basis points relative to no change in interest rates at all.[15] Similarly, doubling (relative to the average increase) the increase in global risk aversion when the surge ends, raises the probability of crisis by 2 percentage points. Conversely, the probability of a crash landing is about 12 percentage points lower if commodity prices are 10 percent higher (relative to no change) at the end of the surge episode. Taken together, changes in global conditions explain surge endings rather well—the global factors are jointly highly statistically significant (Wald test $p$-value=0.00) with a pseudo-$R^2$ of 18 percent, and 33 percent of crash endings called correctly.

Next, we add changes in domestic factors. Cols. (2)–(5) in table 4.5 indicate that the post-surge crisis probability is not significantly affected by changes in the current account balance (presumably because most countries in the sample experience little improvement in the current account balance over the surge episode), but is significantly higher for episodes with greater credit expansion and accumulation of bank foreign liabilities, as well as for those with slower real GDP growth. Thus, for example, the probability of a crash landing is 5 percentage points higher after a surge episode in which expansion in domestic credit (in percent of GDP) is higher by 10 percentage points (rather than about 5 percentage points, which is the average credit expansion observed during a surge). By contrast, episodes where the (de facto) exchange rate regime—captured by a discrete variable, with 1, 2, and 3 indicating fixed, intermediate, and floating regimes, respectively—becomes more flexible, or where the institutional quality improves, are less likely to experience a subsequent crisis (cols. [6]–[7]).

Turning to domestic variables whose end-surge level may affect the crisis likelihood, we find that real exchange rate overvaluation strongly raises the probability of a crash landing, whereas a larger stock of foreign exchange reserves reduces it (cols. [8]–[11]). Neither the current account balance nor the level of external debt comes out to be a statistically significant determinant, though the latter turns significant when other domestic factors are included (col. [16]). In addition, surges that are dominated by FDI are less likely to experience a crisis, while those dominated by other investment liabilities are more likely to end in crisis (cols. [12]–[13]).[16] Including both global and domestic factors, the esti-

---

15. In about one-fifth of the surge endings, US interest rates (in real terms) rise by at least 100 basis points.

16. FDI-dominated surges are defined as those where the average net FDI flow received during the surge episode is larger than both (average) net portfolio and other investment liability flows. Similarly, other investment liability dominated surges are where the aver-

mated coefficients remain largely the same in magnitude and statistical significance while the pseudo-$R^2$ jumps to 37 percent, and the percentage of crash endings correctly predicted rises to 58 percent (col. [14]).

Finally, it is noteworthy that when both the change in bank foreign liabilities and the change in domestic credit are included in the probit, the latter's coefficient falls to almost zero and turns wholly statistically insignificant (col. [15]). This suggests that much of the effect of credit expansion is the result of accumulation of foreign liabilities by domestic banks (deposits or debt), which makes bank flows one of the riskiest types of flows. (Or, to put it the other way around, credit booms that correspond to an expansion of the banking system's domestic liabilities seem less dangerous than those associated with an expansion of foreign liabilities.) This result thus helps explain why net other investment liability flow–dominated episodes are risky—because they largely comprise cross-border bank flows such as intra and interbank loans, which contribute to vulnerabilities in the financial system.[17]

## 4.5   Conclusion

Capital inflows can lead to macroeconomic imbalances—positive output gaps and overheating of the economy, currency appreciation, and excessive credit growth—as well as to balance-sheet vulnerabilities. While global variables, beyond the control of EMEs, are a major factor of when and how surges end, they are not fully determinative of the eventual outcome. Put differently, there are measures—short of imposing full financial autarky—that EMEs can take to reduce the likelihood that the surge ends in a crash. In particular, domestic credit expansion and currency overvaluation are the principal macroeconomic imbalances that raise the risk of a subsequent financial crisis—the obvious

age net other investment liability flow during the surge episode is larger than the other types of net flows.

17.  In addition to the variables presented in table 4.5, we also consider (changes in, and the level of) several other variables, such as domestic real interest rates, government overall and primary fiscal balance (in percent of GDP), short-term debt (in percent of GDP), and capital account openness (measured by the Chinn-Ito openness index), but these turn out to be statistically insignificant. The results presented here hold when we control for surge duration as well as the cumulative (or average) net flow received in the surge episode. They are also generally robust to defining the regressors over alternate periods; estimating separate models for banking and currency crisis; using alternate variables to proxy global conditions (such as oil prices instead of commodity prices, the Chicago Board Options Exchange Volatility Index instead of the S&P 500 index returns volatility measure); as well as to including country-fixed effects.

implication being that policy should try to limit these during an inflow surge.

Even so, there may be residual risks that are likely related to balance-sheet vulnerabilities. In this regard, other investment (i.e., bank) flows and portfolio debt appear to be the most risky types of inflows, while FDI seems to be the safest. Another main implication of the analysis, therefore, is that policy should try to shift the composition of inflows away from the relatively risky flows toward safer types of liabilities. In the remainder of this book, we discuss how policy makers may limit both macroeconomic imbalances and balance-sheet vulnerabilities.

# Chapter 4 Appendix

**Table A.4.1**

Macroeconomic and financial vulnerabilities and capital inflows: IV-2SLS estimates.

| | REER overvaluation | | Real GDP growth | | Output gap | | 3yr. change in credit/GDP | | 1yr. change in LTD ratio | | 1yr. change in FX lending | |
|---|---|---|---|---|---|---|---|---|---|---|---|---|
| | IV[a] (1) | IV[b] (2) | IV[a] (3) | IV[b] (4) | IV[a] (5) | IV[b] (6) | IV[a] (7) | IV[b] (8) | IV[a] (9) | IV[b] (10) | IV[a] (11) | IV[b] (12) |
| Net financial flows/GDP | 1.445* (0.836) | 1.361** (0.540) | 0.381*** (0.126) | 0.239** (0.098) | 0.999*** (0.251) | 0.795*** (0.206) | 0.614 (0.662) | 1.258* (0.676) | 1.244** (0.547) | 1.311** (0.506) | 0.182 (0.194) | 0.263 (0.165) |
| Exchange rate regime | 0.753 (2.321) | 0.916 (1.964) | −0.137 (0.537) | −0.028 (0.369) | −0.671 (1.158) | −0.297 (1.020) | −0.851 (1.634) | −1.760 (1.621) | 2.037 (2.184) | 1.944 (2.234) | −0.410 (1.054) | −0.594 (1.031) |
| Real GDP growth | −0.440* (0.243) | −0.414** (0.179) | | | 0.016 (0.017) | 0.021 (0.014) | −0.034 (0.296) | −0.280 (0.310) | 0.129 (0.277) | 0.075 (0.266) | −0.084 (0.134) | −0.118 (0.118) |
| Terms of trade change | 0.012 (0.030) | 0.012 (0.028) | 0.017 (0.012) | 0.014 (0.011) | | | −0.017 (0.033) | 0.000 (0.030) | 0.091 (0.064) | 0.090 (0.063) | 0.003 (0.031) | 0.004 (0.031) |
| Trade openness | −0.058 (0.044) | −0.062 (0.043) | 0.015 (0.013) | 0.026** (0.010) | −0.008 (0.018) | −0.005 (0.019) | −0.016 (0.045) | −0.017 (0.052) | −0.036 (0.044) | −0.035 (0.045) | −0.028 (0.031) | −0.036 (0.031) |
| Real GDP per capita (log) | 4.897* (2.823) | 5.501** (2.500) | −3.528*** (0.988) | −3.983*** (0.985) | 8.014*** (2.641) | 7.373*** (2.518) | 20.420*** (4.325) | 19.566*** (4.606) | 8.771** (3.368) | 9.057** (3.464) | 5.758** (2.796) | 5.491** (2.782) |
| Trading partner growth | | | 0.608*** (0.183) | 0.633*** (0.171) | | | | | | | | |
| Initial condition[c] | | | | | | | −0.422*** (0.074) | −0.382*** (0.071) | −0.141*** (0.016) | −0.142*** (0.016) | −0.115*** (0.030) | −0.107*** (0.028) |

(continued)

Table A.4.1 (continued)

| | REER overvaluation | | Real GDP growth | | Output gap | | 3yr. change in credit/GDP | | 1yr. change in LTD ratio | | 1yr. change in FX lending | |
|---|---|---|---|---|---|---|---|---|---|---|---|---|
| | $IV^a$ (1) | $IV^b$ (2) | $IV^a$ (3) | $IV^b$ (4) | $IV^a$ (5) | $IV^b$ (6) | $IV^a$ (7) | $IV^b$ (8) | $IV^a$ (9) | $IV^b$ (10) | $IV^a$ (11) | $IV^b$ (12) |
| Country-fixed effects | Yes | Yes | Yes | Yes | Yes | Yes | Yes | Yes | Yes | Yes | Yes | Yes |
| Year effects | Yes | Yes | Yes | Yes | Yes | Yes | Yes | Yes | Yes | Yes | Yes | Yes |
| Observations | 1,346 | 1,332 | 1,400 | 1,375 | 1,400 | 1,375 | 1,292 | 1,283 | 1,273 | 1,264 | 488 | 483 |
| $R^2$ | −0.158 | −0.109 | 0.244 | 0.325 | −0.537 | −0.160 | 0.335 | 0.183 | 0.086 | 0.072 | 0.103 | 0.062 |
| Countries | 53 | 52 | 53 | 52 | 53 | 52 | 53 | 52 | 53 | 52 | 44 | 43 |
| Weak identification test[b] | 15.77 | 8.824 | 14.63 | 9.332 | 18.26 | 11.01 | 14.29 | 8.097 | 16.08 | 8.529 | 18.70 | 10.77 |
| Hansen J stat. (p-value)[d] | . | 0.844 | . | 0.0228 | . | 0.0962 | . | 0.278 | . | 0.882 | . | 0.375 |

Notes: See table 4.1 for variable descriptions. All estimates are obtained from the instrumental variable two-stage least squares (IV-2SLS) regressions where the instrumented variable is net financial flows to GDP (in percent). All regressors (except for trading partner growth and initial condition) are lagged one period. Net financial flows to GDP is the predicted value obtained from first-stage regression with instrument(s) and all other regressors (as well as country-fixed and year effects) included. Constant is included in all specifications. Clustered standard errors (at the country level) are reported in parentheses. ***, **, and * indicate statistical significance at 1, 5, and 10 percent levels, respectively.

a. Net financial flows to other countries in the region (in percent of regional GDP) is used as an instrument in the first stage.

b. Net financial flows to other countries in the region (in percent of regional GDP), and the Chinn-Ito (de jure) capital account openness index are used as instruments in the first stage.

c. Initial condition is three-period lagged domestic credit (in percent of GDP) in cols. (7)–(8), and three-period lagged loan to deposit ratio (in percent) in cols. (9)–(10).

d. Overidentification test of instruments (with the null hypothesis that the full set of orthogonality conditions are valid).

**Table A.4.2**
IV-2SLS regressions: First-stage estimates.

| | REER overvaluation | | Real GDP growth | | Output gap | | 3yr. change in credit/GDP | | 1yr. change in LTD ratio | | 1yr. change in FX lending | |
|---|---|---|---|---|---|---|---|---|---|---|---|---|
| | (1) | (2) | (3) | (4) | (5) | (6) | (7) | (8) | (9) | (10) | (11) | (12) |
| Net financial flows to region | 0.424*** (0.109) | 0.401*** (0.112) | 0.478*** (0.127) | 0.414*** (0.119) | 0.595*** (0.142) | 0.520*** (0.132) | 0.391*** (0.106) | 0.366*** (0.105) | 0.457*** (0.116) | 0.420*** (0.113) | 0.782*** (0.229) | 0.802*** (0.229) |
| Capital acc. openness index | | 0.784** (0.320) | | 0.830** (0.320) | | 0.879*** (0.316) | | 0.718** (0.319) | | 0.779** (0.323) | | 0.996** (0.460) |
| Exchange rate regime | 1.667** (0.783) | 1.842** (0.748) | 1.641** (0.743) | 1.942** (0.757) | 1.880** (0.760) | 2.147*** (0.773) | 1.397* (0.809) | 1.553* (0.789) | 1.432* (0.823) | 1.602* (0.793) | 2.529** (1.154) | 2.588** (1.138) |
| Real GDP growth | 0.308*** (0.073) | 0.311*** (0.077) | | | | | 0.306*** (0.074) | 0.300*** (0.075) | 0.353*** (0.084) | 0.346*** (0.082) | 0.359** (0.145) | 0.363** (0.142) |
| Terms of trade change | -0.006 (0.011) | -0.006 (0.011) | 0.006 (0.011) | -0.006 (0.011) | 0.006 (0.011) | -0.007 (0.011) | -0.031** (0.014) | -0.028** (0.013) | -0.034** (0.013) | -0.030** (0.013) | -0.028 (0.030) | -0.033 (0.029) |
| Trade openness | -0.007 (0.022) | -0.004 (0.021) | 0.004 (0.018) | -0.002 (0.019) | 0.000 (0.018) | -0.005 (0.019) | 0.005 (0.022) | 0.009 (0.024) | -0.008 (0.022) | -0.004 (0.022) | 0.104** (0.049) | 0.106** (0.048) |
| Real GDP per capita (log) | -0.922 (1.413) | -0.327 (1.352) | -0.839 (1.351) | -0.154 (1.263) | -1.041 (1.422) | -0.393 (1.320) | 1.603 (1.596) | 2.064 (1.645) | -0.755 (1.794) | -0.013 (1.640) | 3.446 (4.016) | 2.608 (3.866) |

(continued)

**Table A.4.2** (continued)

| | REER overvaluation | | Real GDP growth | | Output gap | | 3yr. change in credit/GDP | | 1yr. change in LTD ratio | | 1yr. change in FX lending | |
|---|---|---|---|---|---|---|---|---|---|---|---|---|
| | (1) | (2) | (3) | (4) | (5) | (6) | (7) | (8) | (9) | (10) | (11) | (12) |
| Trading partner growth | | | 0.776*** (0.186) | 0.748*** (0.201) | | | | | | | | |
| Initial condition | | | | | | | −0.062** (0.024) | −0.060** (0.025) | −0.006 (0.009) | −0.008 (0.008) | −0.078* (0.042) | −0.084** (0.041) |
| Country-fixed effects | Yes | Yes | Yes | Yes | Yes | Yes | Yes | Yes | Yes | Yes | Yes | Yes |
| Year effects | Yes | Yes | Yes | Yes | Yes | Yes | Yes | Yes | Yes | Yes | Yes | Yes |
| Observations | 1,346 | 1,332 | 1,400 | 1,375 | 1,400 | 1,375 | 1,292 | 1,283 | 1,273 | 1,264 | 488 | 483 |
| $R^2$ | 0.412 | 0.422 | 0.383 | 0.403 | 0.370 | 0.391 | 0.434 | 0.442 | 0.421 | 0.430 | 0.613 | 0.620 |
| F-stat (p-value)[a] | 0.00 | 0.00 | 0.00 | 1.00 | 0.00 | 0.00 | 0.00 | 0.00 | 0.00 | 0.00 | 0.00 | 0.00 |

*Notes:* First-stage estimates obtained from the instrumental variable two-stage least squares (IV-2SLS) regression. See table 4.1 for variable descriptions. All regressors (except for net financial flows to the region, in percent of regional GDP; capital account openness index, trading partner growth, and initial condition) are lagged one period. Constant included in all specifications. Clustered standard errors are reported in parentheses. ***, **, and * indicate statistical significance at 1, 5, and 10 percent levels, respectively.

a. Test of joint significance of regressors.

**Table A.4.3**
Macroeconomic and financial vulnerabilities by type of portfolio flow.

| | REER over-valuation | Real GDP growth | Output gap | 3yr. change in credit/ GDP | 1yr. change in FX lending |
|---|---|---|---|---|---|
| | (1) | (2) | (3) | (4) | (5) |
| Net FDI flows/GDP | −0.002 (0.129) | 0.208*** (0.056) | 0.246*** (0.063) | 0.231 (0.243) | 0.037 (0.072) |
| Net portfolio equity flows/GDP | 0.173 (0.255) | 0.169** (0.064) | 0.087 (0.129) | 0.095 (0.324) | 0.014 (0.088) |
| Net portfolio debt flows/GDP | 0.305* (0.180) | 0.047 (0.044) | 0.091 (0.059) | 0.198 (0.167) | 0.145 (0.087) |
| Net other inv. flows/GDP | 0.256*** (0.090) | 0.023 (0.025) | 0.204*** (0.049) | 0.506*** (0.139) | 0.055 (0.046) |
| Exchange rate regime | 3.136* (1.584) | 0.233 (0.423) | 0.901 (0.615) | −0.119 (1.491) | −0.083 (0.539) |
| Real GDP growth | −0.022 (0.095) | | | 0.001 (0.149) | −0.029 (0.075) |
| Terms of trade change | 0.020 (0.022) | 0.020* (0.011) | 0.025** (0.012) | −0.013 (0.027) | 0.001 (0.029) |
| Trade openness | −0.066** (0.030) | 0.017 (0.010) | −0.006 (0.011) | −0.010 (0.044) | −0.014 (0.025) |
| Real GDP per capita (log) | 2.893* (1.469) | −3.925*** (0.958) | 6.497*** (2.203) | 19.795*** (3.893) | 5.637** (2.506) |
| Trading partner growth | | 0.937*** (0.162) | | | |
| Initial condition | | | | −0.435*** (0.058) | −0.125*** (0.023) |
| Country-fixed effects | Yes | Yes | Yes | Yes | Yes |
| Year effects | Yes | Yes | Yes | Yes | Yes |
| Observations[a] | 1,345 | 1,399 | 1,399 | 1,291 | 486 |
| $R^2$ | 0.213 | 0.411 | 0.324 | 0.430 | 0.227 |
| Countries | 53 | 53 | 53 | 53 | 44 |

*Notes:* See table 4.1 for variable descriptions. Constant is included in all specifications. Clustered standard errors are reported in parentheses. ***, **, and * indicate statistical significance at 1, 5, and 10 percent levels, respectively.
a. Number of observations is slightly fewer than in table 4.2, as breakdown of portfolio flows into equity and debt flows is unavailable in these cases.

**Table A.4.4**
Crisis probability by type of portfolio flow.

| | Banking | | | Currency | | |
|---|---|---|---|---|---|---|
| | (1) | (2) | (3) | (4) | (5) | (6) |
| Net FDI flows/GDP | −0.042 | −0.071* | −0.145* | 0.012 | −0.017 | −0.099 |
| | (0.036) | (0.037) | (0.078) | (0.028) | (0.034) | (0.082) |
| Net portfolio equity flows/GDP | 0.013 | −0.023 | −0.045 | 0.114 | 0.079 | 0.288 |
| | (0.099) | (0.075) | (0.096) | (0.085) | (0.057) | (0.270) |
| Net portfolio debt flows/GDP | 0.042** | 0.025 | −0.005 | 0.035* | 0.016 | 0.006 |
| | (0.017) | (0.021) | (0.026) | (0.020) | (0.017) | (0.019) |
| Net other inv. flows/GDP | 0.050*** | 0.038** | 0.052** | 0.018 | 0.004 | 0.106** |
| | (0.015) | (0.016) | (0.025) | (0.015) | (0.016) | (0.049) |
| REER overvaluation | | 0.029*** | 0.024** | | 0.046*** | 0.064*** |
| | | (0.009) | (0.012) | | (0.011) | (0.013) |
| Domestic credit boom | | 0.025*** | 0.033*** | | 0.009 | 0.006 |
| | | (0.006) | (0.009) | | (0.009) | (0.008) |
| Exchange rate regime | 0.760* | 0.663 | 0.256 | 0.395 | 0.292 | −0.453 |
| | (0.391) | (0.450) | (0.719) | (0.279) | (0.308) | (0.570) |
| Real GDP growth | −0.010 | −0.001 | −0.018 | −0.008 | 0.015 | 0.080*** |
| | (0.017) | (0.018) | (0.034) | (0.019) | (0.021) | (0.027) |
| Reserves/GDP | −0.022*** | −0.021** | −0.023 | −0.049*** | −0.040** | −0.089* |
| | (0.008) | (0.010) | (0.028) | (0.018) | (0.021) | (0.049) |
| Trade openness | −0.002 | −0.001 | −0.013 | −0.002 | 0.000 | −0.003 |
| | (0.002) | (0.002) | (0.010) | (0.003) | (0.003) | (0.014) |
| Real GDP per capita (log) | 0.092 | 0.065 | 1.677** | 0.225** | 0.216** | 5.922*** |
| | (0.075) | (0.070) | (0.734) | (0.110) | (0.098) | (1.590) |
| Fiscal balance/GDP | 0.008 | −0.006 | −0.025 | −0.031* | −0.036** | −0.143*** |
| | (0.016) | (0.018) | (0.041) | (0.017) | (0.018) | (0.038) |
| Inflation | 0.003 | 0.007** | −0.008 | 0.004 | 0.012*** | 0.001 |
| | (0.004) | (0.003) | (0.007) | (0.003) | (0.004) | (0.007) |
| Country-fixed effects | No | No | Yes | No | No | Yes |
| Year effects | No | No | Yes | No | No | Yes |
| Observations[a] | 1,173 | 1,173 | 1,173 | 1,149 | 1,149 | 1,149 |
| Countries | 53 | 53 | 53 | 53 | 53 | 53 |
| Pseudo-$R^2$ | 0.079 | 0.161 | 0.434 | 0.113 | 0.220 | 0.553 |
| Wald-chi2 (p-value)[b] | 0.00 | 0.00 | 0.00 | 0.00 | 0.00 | 0.00 |

*Notes:* Dependent variable is a binary variable equal to one if there is a banking or currency crisis in cols. (1)–(3) and (4)–(6), respectively. All specifications are estimated using the probit model. All regressors are lagged one period, except for net financial flow to GDP variables in cols. (4)–(6), which are lagged two periods. Constant is included in all specifications. Clustered standard errors (at the country level) are reported in parentheses. ***, **, and * indicate statistical significance at 1, 5, and 10 percent levels, respectively.
a. Number of observations is slightly fewer than in table 4.4 as breakdown of net portfolio flows into equity and debt flows is unavailable in these cases.
b. Test of joint significance of regressors.

**Table A.4.5**
Post-surge banking and currency crisis.

| Country | Last year of surge episode | Year of banking crisis | Year of currency crisis |
|---|---|---|---|
| Albania | 1997 | | 1997 |
| Argentina | 1993 | 1995 | |
| Belarus | 1997 | | 1997 |
| Belarus | 2007 | | 2009 |
| Brazil | 1981 | | 1982 |
| Brazil | 1994 | 1994 | |
| Chile | 1981 | 1981 | 1982 |
| Colombia | 1997 | 1998 | |
| Costa Rica | 1980 | | 1981 |
| Croatia | 1997 | 1998 | |
| Czech Rep. | 1996 | 1996 | |
| Dominican Rep. | 2001 | 2003 | 2003 |
| Ecuador | 1998 | 1998 | 1999 |
| Hungary | 2006 | 2008 | |
| Hungary | 2008 | 2008 | |
| Jamaica | 1996 | 1996 | |
| Jordan | 1988 | 1989 | 1989 |
| Jordan | 1996 | | |
| Kazakhstan | 1997 | | 1999 |
| Kazakhstan | 2006 | 2008 | |
| Indonesia | 1996 | 1997 | 1998 |
| Latvia | 1995 | 1998 | |
| Latvia | 2007 | 2008 | |
| Malaysia | 1996 | 1997 | 1998 |
| Mexico | 1981 | 1981 | 1982 |
| Mexico | 1993 | 1994 | 1995 |
| Philippines | 1997 | 1997 | 1998 |
| Russia | 2007 | 2008 | |
| Slovak Rep. | 1996 | 1998 | |
| Slovak Rep. | 1998 | 1998 | |
| Sri Lanka | 1989 | 1989 | |
| Thailand | 1981 | 1983 | |
| Thailand | 1996 | 1997 | 1998 |
| Ukraine | 2008 | 2008 | 2009 |
| Uruguay | 1980 | 1981 | |
| Uruguay | 1982 | | 1983 |
| Venezuela | 1993 | 1994 | 1994 |
| Vietnam | 1997 | 1997 | |

*Source:* Authors' estimates.

# III    Policy Framework

# 5    Managing Macroeconomic Imbalances: A Simple Model

## 5.1    Introduction

The literature survey in chapter 2 and the empirical evidence presented in chapter 4 suggest that capital flows to emerging markets can result in macroeconomic imbalances (overheating, currency overvaluation, excessive credit growth) and balance-sheet vulnerabilities (currency, maturity, and debt-equity mismatches). This chapter and the next discuss how policy makers might address macroeconomic imbalances, while chapter 7 turns to balance-sheet vulnerabilities.

The analysis of chapter 4 shows that the macroeconomic impact of different types of capital flows is not identical. Some types of flow, such as foreign direct investment (FDI), bring a high ratio of benefits to costs, perhaps expanding physical and human capital and correspondingly potential output. But other types—highly speculative, short-term capital—may be more trouble than they are worth. For policy makers, the goal would presumably be to try to alter the composition of inflows in a way that favors good flows over bad flows; policies designed to lengthen the maturity of inflows (e.g., a toll tax or an unremunerated reserve requirement) have often been used with this compositional goal in mind. But for a given composition of flows, policy makers may still want to mitigate any adverse effects of the flows—either by addressing specific consequences or by managing the volume of flows.

The discussion in this chapter takes as given the composition of inflows and does not consider policies to alter it. Our focus here is on cyclical tools—be they macroeconomic policies (monetary policy, FX intervention, macroprudential measures) or capital controls to tame the risks associated with capital inflows. The use of more structural capital controls and prudential measures to shift the composition of inflows toward less risky types of liabilities (or discourage certain transactions, such as FX-denominated lending to unhedged borrowers), are taken up later in the book (chapters 7 and 11). In other words, here we assume that structural measures designed to achieve a desirable composition of flows are in place to the degree possible, and consider how emerging market policy makers should manage the cyclical risks associated with volatile capital flows.

We begin in this chapter by developing a simple theoretical framework linking capital flows and various policy measures to macroeconomic outcomes. The model is based on an open-economy investment-saving liquidity preference-money supply (IS-LM) framework (the Mundell-Fleming model) with three important tweaks. In the standard model, a capital inflow appreciates the exchange rate and deteriorates the current account balance, thus reducing aggregate demand. But most of the emerging market evidence, including that presented in chapter 4, points to capital inflows being *expansionary*, presumably through some form of credit growth that boosts private consumption and investment—allowing for such a credit channel on output is therefore our first tweak.[1] If such a channel indeed exists, then this also implies that sterilized intervention—which absorbs the capital inflow—and macroprudential measures (that reduce the rate at which domestic banks can create credit) will also affect aggregate demand.

The second tweak concerns the process governing capital flows. In the Mundell-Fleming model, capital is "perfectly mobile," implying a potentially infinite flow that drives expected rate-of-return differentials to zero instantaneously. While this may be a reasonable assumption for advanced economies, it is probably more realistic to think of capital responding to the rate-of-return differential (net of any capital controls) at a finite pace in EMEs, as investors adjust portfolio allocations. An

---

1. As shown in chapter 4, the degree to which inflows are expansionary may depend on the form of the inflow, with equity or bank flows being more likely to stimulate the economy than portfolio debt flows (especially government bonds). Blanchard et al. (2015) argue that the differential effect occurs because the purchase of government bonds by foreign investors bids up their price and reduces their rate of return. If the central bank sets the short-term interest rate through its policy rate, and does not allow the interest rate to decline (i.e., does not engage in expansionary monetary policy), then the only effect of the inflow will be to appreciate the currency—which is likely to be contractionary. Conversely, if investors are purchasing equity (or other assets that are not close substitute for bonds), they drive down the price, making it easier for borrowers to obtain financing, which is likely to be expansionary (perhaps sufficiently so to counteract the effect of the currency appreciation).

important consequence of this assumption is that sterilized intervention is feasible in the model.

The third tweak, more technical in nature, is that the central bank is assumed to set the interest rate directly—as most modern central banks do—rather than controlling the money supply or domestic credit (as in the original Mundell-Fleming model).

With this framework, we are able to analyze the impact of various policy measures—monetary, exchange rate, nondiscriminatory macro-prudential, and capital controls (or currency-based prudential measures that, as noted in chapter 1, can act like capital controls by having a substantial impact on capital flows). Although fiscal tightening—particularly when capital inflows are driven by the public sector's borrowing—should constitute a natural policy response, political considerations and implementation lags may limit the scope for fiscal consolidation. (As discussed in chapter 8, in practice few countries tighten fiscal policy in the face of capital inflows.) Fiscal policy in the form of aggregate spending or taxation is therefore not analyzed here (though, to the extent that capital controls or prudential measures involve some form of taxation, they constitute "fiscal measures" in the strict sense of the term).

The rest of this chapter is organized as follows. Section 5.2 lays out the model. Section 5.3 discusses the initial pre–capital inflow surge equilibrium. Section 5.4 considers the impact of an inflow surge. Section 5.5 describes the effects of individual policy instruments. Section 5.6 discusses how policy makers should respond when some instruments are unavailable, and the possible role of cyclical capital controls. Section 5.7 concludes.

## 5.2   The Model

The economy is assumed to be small, taking as given the world interest rate. Aggregate demand comprises domestic absorption, $a^d$, plus net exports, $ca$. Domestic absorption depends on output, $y$, and via the impact on consumption and investment, on domestic credit, $x$. Net exports depend negatively on the real exchange rate, $e$ (an increase is an appreciation), and on the level of output:

$$y = a^d(y, x) + ca(e, y); \quad 0 < a_y^d < 1, a_x^d \geq 0, ca_e < 0, ca_y < 0 \tag{5.1}$$

Credit to the private sector, $x$, depends upon capital inflows, $\Delta k$ (minus the proportion that is absorbed by sterilized intervention, $\Delta R$), the policy interest rate, $r$, and nondiscriminatory macroprudential measures (such as maximum loan-to-value ratios [LTVs] or countercyclical capital requirements on banks), $\mu$:[2]

$$x = x(\Delta k - \Delta R, r, \mu) \; x_k > 0, \; x_r < 0, \; x_\mu < 0 \qquad (5.2)$$

where, in what follows, we set $k_{-1} = 0$ and $R_{-1} = 0$.

Since capital flows depend on the expected relative return on domestic assets, they are assumed to be an increasing function of the domestic interest rate, and a decreasing function of the current level of the exchange rate and of an exogenous (to the country) shift variable, $r^*$, which represents the world interest rate (or, more generally, changes in investors' preferences, global interest rates and growth rates, global market risk aversion). Capital flows also depend upon the capital account openness of the country, $\gamma$, which is taken to be a structural parameter of the economy (fixed for the duration of the analysis), and upon cyclical capital controls (or currency-based prudential measures that may deter inflows), $\tau$, that can be varied as a policy instrument:

$$\Delta k = k - k_{-1} = k = \gamma(r - e - \tau - r^*), \; \gamma > 0 \qquad (5.3)$$

Hence, credit growth can be written as:

$$x = x(\gamma(r - e - \tau - r^*) - R, r, \mu) \; x_k > 0, \; x_r < 0, \; x_\mu < 0 \qquad (5.4)$$

where the effect of a higher policy rate is potentially ambiguous, attracting capital inflows, but stemming credit growth for a given inflow. The latter is assumed to dominate (thus, we assume that $|x_r| > x_k\gamma$).

As output increases, credit is required to help finance productive economic activity. Demand for credit is therefore assumed to be an increasing function of real output:

$$\Phi(y) = x, \; \Phi_y > 0 \qquad (5.5)$$

with financial-stability risks rising to the extent that credit growth exceeds this stable demand.

The balance of payments (BOP) identity equates the sum of the current and capital accounts to the change in reserves:

$$ca(y, e) + \gamma(r - e - \tau - r^*) = R - R_{-1} \qquad (5.6)$$

---

2. Nondiscriminatory macroprudential measures are applied to the domestic regulated financial system (principally banks) and do not discriminate on the basis of the currency or residency of the parties to the capital transaction.

Sterilized FX intervention is captured by a change in $R$ for a given policy rate; as above, $R_{-1}=0$ in this static version of the model.

The Phillips curve gives inflation as a function of expected inflation as well as firms' real marginal cost. This reflects the fact that, in the open economy, marginal cost depends not only on output, but also on the real exchange rate: an appreciation leads to a decrease in the product wage given the consumption wage (or a decrease in the cost of imported intermediate inputs), decreasing marginal cost, and hence raising aggregate supply.[3] For given aggregate demand, therefore, inflation is decreasing in the real exchange rate.[4]

$$\pi - \pi^e(+1) = f(y, e); \quad f_y > 0, f_e < 0 \tag{5.7}$$

The model thus captures in a rough way the effects of the policy rate, FX intervention, macroprudential measures, and capital controls. The relevant distortions (Dutch disease, financial-stability risks) are implicit in the central bank's objective function, which is to meet its inflation target (i.e., ensure nonaccelerating inflation) and achieve a zero output gap, stabilize the exchange rate around its equilibrium value, and avoid excessive credit growth that could undermine financial stability.

## 5.3   Initial Equilibrium

To solve for output and the exchange rate in the short run, we rewrite the investment-saving (IS) curve to get a relation between output and the exchange rate, for given policies:

$$\begin{aligned} y &= a^d(y, x\,(\gamma(r - e - \tau - r^*) - R, r, \mu)) + ca(e, y) \\ &= y\,(e, r, \tau, R, r^*, \mu); \; y_e < 0, \; y_r < 0, \; y_{r^*} < 0, \; y_\tau < 0, \; y_\mu < 0, \; y_R < 0 \end{aligned} \tag{5.8}$$

Since the marginal propensity to consume is less than unity, the left-hand side of (5.8) is increasing in income, while the right-hand side is

---

3. A real appreciation lowers the price of imported goods in workers' consumption basket, hence their nominal wages can decline (or not rise as fast) while still protecting their living standards. The lower nominal wage translates into a lower real product wage faced by the employer, resulting in higher employment and aggregate supply.

4. Capital flows could also raise aggregate supply by increasing physical investment, but this effect would operate with a lag, and is thus not relevant to the analysis here. Potentially more relevant is the possibility that inflows reduce the cost of working capital and thereby raise aggregate supply; for simplicity, here this is subsumed in the exchange rate effect on aggregate supply.

decreasing in the exchange rate (an appreciation lowers demand), so the IS curve slopes downward. An increase in the interest rate slows credit expansion and depresses demand and output, but also induces larger capital inflows, which contribute to faster credit expansion. It seems reasonable to assume that the first effect dominates, so the net effect of a higher policy interest rate is contractionary. A rise in the world interest rate (or global risk aversion) or the imposition of capital controls reduces inflows and domestic credit, while a more open capital account increases the sensitivity of output to these variables $y_{r^*\gamma} < 0$, $y_{\tau\gamma} < 0$. Finally, tightening macroprudential regulations restrains credit expansion, dampening aggregate demand.

We solve the BOP relation to get a second relation between the exchange rate and output, again for given policies:

$$e = e(y, r, r^*, \tau, R); \quad e_y < 0, e_r > 0, e_{r^*} < 0, e_R < 0, e_\tau < 0 \tag{5.9}$$

An increase in income worsens net exports, requiring a depreciation to attract capital and narrow the current account deficit. An increase in the policy rate induces larger capital inflows and an appreciation of the currency; an increase in the foreign interest rate does the opposite. Central bank intervention (accumulation of reserves) depreciates the currency, as does the imposition of controls on capital inflows. Greater capital account openness raises the sensitivity of the exchange rate to the imposition of capital controls.[5]

For given settings of the policy instruments, the two schedules determine output and the exchange rate in the short run (figure 5.1). In $(e,y)$ space, both schedules will be downward sloping, and a stability condition ensures that the IS curve be steeper than the BOP curve.[6] Given this level of output and the exchange rate, there will be implications for inflation, credit growth, and the exchange rate. The Phillips curve (5.7), denoted $\Pi$, defines the combinations of $(e,y)$ that are consistent with stable inflationary expectations: a higher level of output without a corresponding appreciation of the currency overheats the economy, potentially sparking an inflationary spiral. Therefore, to the right of the $\Pi$ schedule, inflation is rising, and inflationary expectations are at risk of

---

5. The partial effect of imposing capital controls on the exchange rate is: $e_\tau = \partial e/\partial \tau = \gamma/(ca_e - \gamma) < 0$. Differentiating with respect to $\gamma$ yields: $\partial e_\tau/\partial \gamma = ca_e/(ca_e - \gamma)^2 < 0$.

6. Along the IS curve, $de/dy = (1 - a_y^d - ca_y)/(ca_e - \gamma x_k a_x^d) < 0$; along the BOP curve, $de/dy = ca_y/(\gamma - ca_e) < 0$. Hence: $de/dy|_{IS} < de/dy|_{BOP} \Leftrightarrow (1 - a_y^d - ca_y)/(ca_e - \gamma a_x^d x_k) < ca_y/(\gamma - ca_e)$ or: $(1 - a_y^d) > \gamma ca_y (a_x^d x_k - 1)/(ca_e - \gamma)$, which is a stability condition that we will assume.

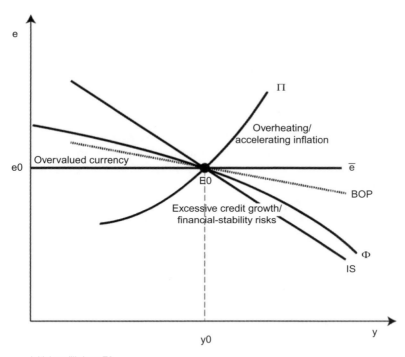

Initial equilibrium: E0
Above ē: currency overvalued
Right of Π: overheating, accelerating inflation
Below Φ: excessive credit growth, financial-stability risks

**Figure 5.1**
Initial equilibrium.
*Source*: Authors' illustration.

becoming unanchored. Likewise, for a given level of output, an exchange
rate appreciation stems capital inflows and curbs credit growth, so that
below the financial-stability schedule, Φ, the economy is at greater risk
of financial crisis. Finally, even if there is no specific exchange rate target,
there may be a point (denoted by ē) beyond which the currency becomes
sufficiently overvalued that any further appreciation, even if temporary,
could inflict lasting damage to the traded goods sector. When the exchange
rate is above ē, therefore, the currency is overvalued.

## 5.4    Capital Inflow Shock

Against this backdrop, a decrease in the world interest rate or in global risk aversion will result in a rightward shift of the IS curve (for a given exchange rate, capital inflows stimulate aggregate demand) and an upward shift of the BOP curve (for a given level of output, inflows appreciate the currency). If capital flows have little impact on aggregate demand (either because demand is not credit-sensitive, or because inflows do not translate into greater lending to domestic entities), then the IS curve will shift by less than the BOP curve and output will decline. More plausibly, capital inflows will be expansionary even taking into account the negative effect on aggregate demand of the currency appreciation, shifting the equilibrium from $E_0$ to $E_1$ in figure 5.2. The condition for inflows to be expansionary is readily obtained by totally differentiating the IS curve (5.8) and setting policy responses to zero:

$$dy(1 - a_y^d - ca_y) = (ca_e - a_x^d x_k \gamma)de - a_x^d x_k \gamma dr^* \tag{5.10}$$

Totally differentiating the BOP curve (5.6):

$$de = (\gamma dr^* - ca_y dy)/(ca_e - \gamma) \tag{5.11}$$

and substituting (5.11) into (5.10):

$$dy[1 - a_y^d - \gamma ca_y (a_x^d x_k - 1)/(ca_e - \gamma)] = (1 - a_x^d x_k)ca_e \gamma dr^*/(ca_e - \gamma) \tag{5.12}$$

Therefore, $dy/dr^* < 0$—lower world interest rates will lead to expansionary capital inflows—as long as $a_x^d x_k > 1$ (i.e., the effects of capital inflows on credit expansion, and of credit expansion on aggregate demand, are sufficiently large), and the stability condition $(1 - a_y^d) > \gamma ca_y (a_x^d x_k - 1)/(ca_e - \gamma)$ is satisfied.

The condition $a_x^d x_k > 1$ has an intuitive explanation: from the BOP identity, in the absence of intervention, an increase in capital inflows must be matched by a corresponding current account deficit. If capital flows rise by 1 percent of GDP, for instance, then in equilibrium the current account deficit must widen by 1 percent of GDP as well. From the IS curve, this deterioration of the current account balance withdraws 1 percent of GDP of demand stimulus. For capital flows to have an expansionary effect on aggregate demand, therefore, the direct impact on domestic demand must be greater. In the formal model, this direct impact is assumed to come from some channel for domestic credit expansion. More generally, it may reflect banking system credit,

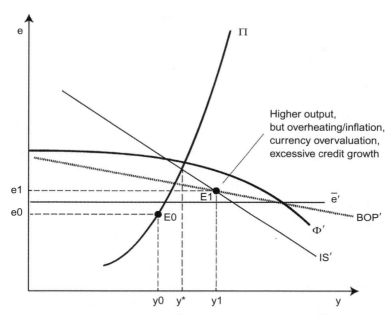

Expansionary inflows shifts IS curve to IS', BOP to BOP', and Φ curve to Φ'
At new equilibrium: E1:
Output is higher at y1; exchanged rate appreciates to e1
Since E1 is to the right of Π: overheating, accelerating inflation
Since E1 is below Φ: excessive credit growth, financial-stability risks
If increase in output were limited to y*, then aggregate supply
would match aggregate demand, and no inflationary pressures

**Figure 5.2**
Expansionary capital inflow.
*Source*: Authors' illustration.

direct borrowing from abroad, or wealth effects associated with the real exchange rate appreciation—all of which will boost private consumption and investment, contributing to greater domestic demand. The empirical evidence presented in chapter 4 points to capital inflows being expansionary—so, in what follows, we concentrate on this case. We also assume, plausibly, that the capital inflow appreciates the exchange rate, which imposes a slightly more stringent restriction than the stability condition assumed above.[7]

---

7. The expression for the change in the exchange rate is: $de = -\gamma dr^* \{(1 - a_y^d) + ca_y(a_x^d x_k - 1)\}$ $\{(1 - a_y^d)(\gamma - ca_e) + \gamma ca_y(a_x^d x_k - 1)\}^{-1}$ ; hence $de/dr^* < 0$ (capital inflows appreciate the exchange rate), provided the term in the first set of curly brackets is positive (the term in the second set of brackets is positive by the stability condition). If $a_x^d x_k < 1$ (i.e., inflows are

Since the world interest rate does not enter the Phillips curve, the $\Pi$ schedule remains constant. The financial-stability schedule shifts upward by the decline in the world interest rate; in other words, if the economy could not handle (any) further credit expansion without the risk of asset price bubbles, the exchange rate would need to appreciate to choke off the capital inflow (by making domestic assets more expensive).[8] More generally, to the extent that the exchange rate is below the $\Phi$ schedule, there is greater risk of financial crisis. Most of the rise of capital inflows during the surge will, by definition, be cyclical (since surges are instances of exceptionally large inflows), but there may be a structural ("permanent") component as well. To the extent that there is such a structural component, the equilibrium real exchange rate appreciates to a level such as $\bar{e}'$.

The inflow of capital is itself partly welcome, raising both aggregate demand and aggregate supply. If the increase in output were limited to $y^*$, the higher aggregate supply would match the rise in aggregate demand, and there would be no inflationary pressures (though even at $y^*$, the currency would be overvalued and there would be excessive credit growth). In general, as depicted, the inflow may cause three macroeconomic imbalances: first, the new equilibrium, $E_1$, may not lie on the $\Pi$ schedule, so the economy is overheating, and inflationary expectations are at risk of becoming unanchored. Second, to the extent that the currency strengthens beyond the increase in the equilibrium real exchange rate ($\bar{e}$), it is overvalued. Third, the credit expansion associated with the inflow of foreign capital raises financial-stability risks, with the new equilibrium lying below the $\Phi'$ schedule.

## 5.5    Effects of Policies

We begin by cataloging the effects of various policy instruments individually on the key macroeconomic targets: output, inflation, the exchange rate, and financial stability.

---

contractionary), then this condition is necessarily satisfied. If $a_x^d x_k > 1$ then, for expansionary inflows to appreciate the exchange rate requires that $ca_y > (a_y^d - 1)/(a_x^d x_k - 1)$ since $ca_y < 0$. This means that the absolute value of the income elasticity of the current account not be too large. The intuition is that if inflows are sufficiently expansionary, and the income elasticity of the current account is large, then the deterioration of the current account may exceed the capital inflow, necessitating a depreciation of the currency. For reasonable parameters, this is implausible, and we do not consider this perverse case further.

8. In the static model, where the exchange rate is expected to return to its baseline value next period, the upward shift of the $\Phi$ schedule is equal to the decline in foreign interest rates: from (5.4), $dx = 0 \Rightarrow de = -dr^*$.

### 5.5.1 Raising the Policy Interest Rate

Faced by expansionary capital flows that create inflationary pressures $(E_1)$, the central bank will want to raise the policy interest rate in order to meet its inflation target. Differentiating the IS and BOP curves with respect to the policy interest rate gives:

$$dy(1 - a_y^d - ca_y) = a_x^d(x_k\gamma + x_r)dr + (ca_e - \gamma a_x^d x_k)de \qquad (5.13)$$

$$de = (ca_y dy + \gamma dr)/(\gamma - ca_e) \qquad (5.14)$$

Substituting (5.14) into (5.13) yields:

$$dy[1 - a_y^d - ca_y\gamma(a_x^d x_k - 1)/(ca_e - \gamma)] = a_x^d[\gamma x_k ca_e/(ca_e - \gamma) + x_r]dr \qquad (5.15)$$

The term multiplying $dy$ will be positive under the stability condition above, while the term multiplying $dr$ will be negative provided the direct contractionary effect of higher interest rates on domestic credit expansion outweighs the induced effect through capital inflows; assuming this to be the case, $dy/dr < 0$ so from (5.14), $de/dr > 0$—a higher policy interest rate appreciates the exchange rate (recall, we assumed that $|x_r| > x_k\gamma$).

Graphically, as shown in figure 5.3, an increase in the policy rate shifts the IS curve rightward $(E_2)$, raises the BOP schedule (as the higher policy rate induces further capital inflows), and lowers the $\Phi$ schedule (notwithstanding the induced inflows, tighter monetary policy is assumed to curb credit growth). Thus, although the central bank is able to meet its inflation target ($E_2$ lies on the $\Pi$ schedule), it must tolerate an even more appreciated real exchange rate than that implied by the original capital inflow ($e_2 > e_1$). Moreover, while the monetary tightening does curb credit growth, the latter may still be excessive, with some residual financial stability risks.

### 5.5.2 Sterilized FX Intervention

FX intervention (sterilized, so the policy interest rate remains unchanged) stems the currency appreciation. To the extent that such intervention absorbs the capital inflow, it diminishes—and could even eliminate—the effect on credit growth. Again, differentiating the IS and BOP curves, now with respect to FX intervention:

$$dy(1 - a_y^d - ca_y) = (ca_e - \gamma a_x^d x_k)de - a_x^d x_k dR \qquad (5.16)$$

$$de = (dR - ca_y dy)/(ca_e - \gamma) \qquad (5.17)$$

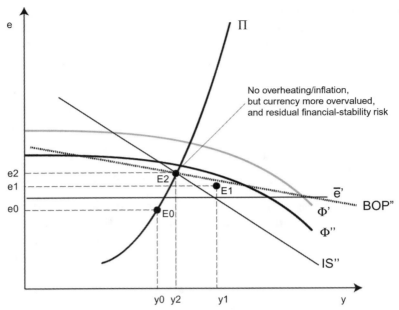

Expansionary inflow shifted the equilibrium from E0 to E1
Higher policy interest rate shifts the IS' curve down to IS", Φ' down to Φ"; BOP up to BOP"
At new equilibrium, E2:
Output is lower at y2 than post-inflow level, y1, but highter than y0
Inflationary pressure of capital inflow is eliminated
Exchange rate at e2 is more appreciated than it was at post-inflow level, e1
Financial-stability risk has been reduced (Φ" is closer to E2 than Φ' is to E1)

**Figure 5.3**
Monetary tightening.
*Source*: Authors' illustration.

and substituting (5.17) into (5.16) yields:

$$dy[1 - a_y^d - \gamma ca_y(a_x^d x_k - 1)/(ca_e - \gamma)] = ca_e(a_x^d x_k - 1)/(\gamma - ca_e)dR \qquad (5.18)$$

Hence $dy/dR < 0$, although FX intervention depreciates the currency, boosting exports and aggregate demand, it also absorbs the capital inflow, curbing domestic credit growth. Since the credit expansion effect of capital inflows is assumed to dominate (which is why the initial capital inflow was expansionary), it follows that sterilized intervention will be contractionary. Finally, substituting (5.18) into (5.17) gives:

$$de = -dR[1 - a_y^d + ca_y(a_x^d x_k - 1)]/[(1 - a_y^d)(\gamma - ca_e) - \gamma ca_y(1 - a_x^d x_k)] \qquad (5.19)$$

Thus, under the conditions assumed above, purchases of foreign exchange (FX) will depreciate the currency $de/dR < 0$.

The effects of sterilized intervention (FX purchases) are illustrated in figure 5.4. Intervention shifts the BOP schedule down and the IS schedule to the left (the exchange rate depreciation raises aggregate demand, but the credit contraction has a larger impact). Moreover, by curbing credit growth, the financial-stability schedule shifts down from $\Phi'$ to $\Phi''$. FX intervention is thus a powerful policy tool, potentially eliminating the currency overvaluation while also reducing financial-stability risks and inflationary pressures (though, as illustrated, at the new equilibrium exchange rate there may remain some financial-stability risks and inflationary pressures—that is, $E_2$ lies below $\Phi''$ and to the right of the $\Pi$ schedule).

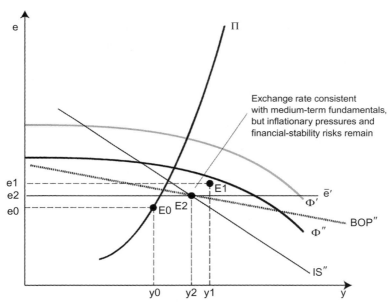

Expansionary inflow shifted the equilibrium from E0 to E1
FX intervention shifts the IS' curve down to IS", BOP' down to BOP"
effect on $\Phi$ curve is ambiguous, but likely shifts $\Phi'$ curve down to $\Phi''$
At new equilibrium, E2:
Output is lower at y2 than post-inflow level, y1, but higher than y0
Inflationary pressures are reduced relative to post-inflow level
Exchange rate at e2 is less appreciated than it was at post-inflow level, e1
Financial-stability risk has likely been reduced ($\Phi''$ closer to E2 than $\Phi'$ is to E1)

**Figure 5.4**
Foreign exchange (FX) intervention.
*Source*: Authors' illustration.

### 5.5.3   Macroprudential Regulation

Tightening macroprudential regulations would curb credit growth and, in turn, dampen aggregate demand. Proceeding as above yields:

$$dy(1 - a_y^d - ca_y) = (ca_e - \gamma a_x^d x_k)de + a_x^d x_\mu d\mu \tag{5.20}$$

$$de = ca_y dy/(\gamma - ca_e) \tag{5.21}$$

$$dy[1 - a_y^d - \gamma ca_y(a_x^d x_k - 1)/(ca_e - \gamma)] = a_x^d x_\mu d\mu \tag{5.22}$$

Hence, $dy/d\mu < 0$ and $de/d\mu > 0$. That is, tightening macroprudential policies curbs credit growth and aggregate demand, while appreciating the real exchange rate (ceteris paribus, lower aggregate demand improves the current account so the exchange rate must appreciate for the current account deficit to match the capital inflow). Graphically, the financial-stability schedule shifts downward from $\Phi'$ to $\Phi''$, and the IS curve shifts leftward to IS'' (figure 5.5). However, tightening macroprudential regulation sufficiently to reduce financial-stability risks may contract aggregate demand to the point of creating deflationary pressures, as in $E_2$. Dampen-

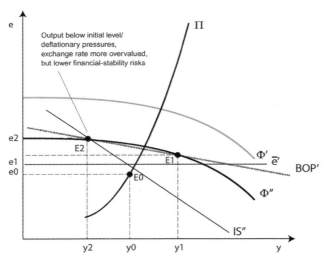

Expansionary inflow shifted the equilibrium from E0 to E1
Macroprudential tightening shifts the IS' curve down to IS'' and $\Phi'$ curve down to $\Phi''$
At new equilibrium, E2:
Output is lower at y2 than post-inflow level, y1, and lower than y0
Economy experiences deflationary pressures
Exchange rate at e2 is more appreciated than it was at post-inflow level, e1
Financial-stability risk due to inflow has been eliminated (E2 lies on $\Phi''$)

**Figure 5.5**
Macroprudential regulation.
*Source*: Authors' illustration.

ing aggregate demand, moreover, means that the current account can support a more appreciated real exchange rate while still satisfying the BOP identity. Accordingly, aggregate demand consistent with financial stability may be below full employment, and the real exchange rate will become even more appreciated when macroprudential measures are applied $(e_2 > e_1 > e_0)$.

### 5.5.4 Capital Controls

Finally, imposing capital controls (e.g., an interest rate equalization tax) reverses the effect of the initial capital inflow. Differentiating (5.8) and (5.6) with respect to capital controls:

$$dy(1 - a_y^d - ca_y) = (ca_e - \gamma a_x^d x_k)de - \gamma a_x^d x_k d\tau \tag{5.23}$$

$$de = (\gamma d\tau - ca_y dy)/(ca_e - \gamma) \tag{5.24}$$

which implies:

$$dy[1 - a_y^d - \gamma ca_y(a_x^d x_k - 1)/(ca_e - \gamma)] = \gamma ca_e(a_x^d x_k - 1)/(\gamma - ca_e)d\tau \tag{5.25}$$

Hence, $dy/d\tau < 0$. That is, since capital inflows finance domestic credit expansion and boost aggregate demand, choking them off by imposing capital controls will be contractionary. Substituting (5.25) into (5.24) yields:

$$de = -(1 - a_y^d - ca_y(1 - a_x^d x_k))\gamma d\tau/[(\gamma - ca_e)(1 - a_y^d) - \gamma ca_y(1 - a_x^d x_k)] \tag{5.26}$$

The denominator of (5.26) is positive under the stability condition, while the numerator will be negative provided $1 - a_y^d > ca_y(1 - a_x^d x_k)$, as was assumed earlier. The direct impact of controls on capital inflows is to depreciate the exchange rate, but because controls are contractionary, they reduce imports and improve the current account balance, thus supporting a more appreciated exchange rate. We assume the former effect dominates, so $de/d\tau < 0$, which seems intuitive and conforms to empirical evidence.[9]

In the limiting case that controls are able to choke off the capital inflow entirely, the economy returns to the pre-shock equilibrium, $E_0$ (figure 5.6). While this addresses all of the concerns (overheating, overvaluation, financial stability), it also means that the economy forgoes the higher output—aggregate supply and aggregate demand—that the inflow could have afforded.[10]

---

9. In chapter 9, we present evidence that the tightening of capital controls significantly reduces the rate of currency appreciation.

10. Since (leaving aside the impact on various macroeconomic imbalances) capital inflows here are beneficial (they raise aggregate supply and demand), in principle the optimal capital control could be negative. As depicted, the Π curve is upward sloping,

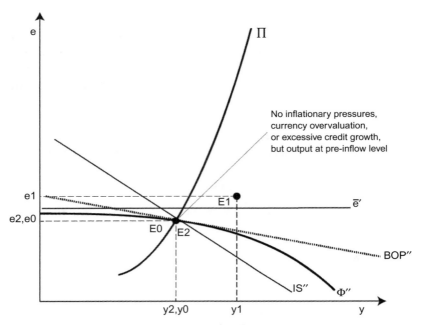

Expansionary inflow shifted the equilibrium from E0 to E1
Capital controls return the economy to E2 = E0, thus eliminating
inflationary pressures, currency overvaluation and excessive credit growth,
but at the cost of foregoing any increase in output

**Figure 5.6**
Capital controls.
*Source*: Authors' illustration.

## 5.6   Unavailability of Conventional Policy Instruments and the Use of Cyclical Capital Controls

Thus far we have considered the effects of one policy instrument at a time, in which case there is a natural mapping: the policy interest rate for inflation and economic overheating, FX intervention for limiting the currency appreciation, and macroprudential measures to curb excessive credit growth. If one or more of the imbalances is not present—there are few signs of inflationary pressures, the currency appre-

and at some point would be vertical, so sufficiently large inflows eventually become unproductive. Nonetheless, it is possible that a negative tax—a subsidy—on inflows would be beneficial, a possibility that we do not consider here. In practice, governments do sometimes "subsidize" certain types of highly beneficial capital inflow—for instance, by providing tax breaks or other incentives to FDI-financed corporations.

ciation does not appear to be denting exports, or credit growth appears moderate—then the corresponding instrument need not be used. Alternatively, it might be used in the opposite direction to normal. For instance, if the inflow is leading to currency overvaluation but not to overheating of the economy or to excessive credit growth, then the policy interest rate could be lowered (rather than raised), thus complementing the effects of FX intervention. As a general principle, moreover, when there is uncertainty about the effects of policy instruments, it is preferable to use multiple instruments less intensively than to rely exclusively on any single instrument (Brainard 1967). Thus, if credit growth appears excessive, then in addition to macroprudential measures, the central bank might undertake some sterilized intervention to absorb part of the capital inflow.

But what about the opposite case: where there is an imbalance, but the corresponding policy instrument is unavailable (or too costly to use)? Below (and further in chapter 11) we argue that the other available macroeconomic instruments should not be diverted from their primary objectives if doing so would jeopardize meeting those objectives. For instance, if the currency is appreciating rapidly but sterilized intervention is considered too costly, then the central bank might be tempted to lower the policy rate (or at least not raise it as much as it otherwise would)—at the cost of missing its inflation target. In our view, it would be preferable for the policy interest rate to be subordinated to meeting the inflation target, and if there remain macroeconomic imbalances (e.g., the exchange rate is, or becomes more, overvalued), then capital controls can be brought into play.

How far can the central bank get in addressing all three imbalances with a limited set of macroeconomic instruments? We consider two cases. Since the use of macroprudential measures is relatively new (although at least for some instruments—such as reserve requirements—less so than others), the authorities may simply lack sufficient instruments or experience to calibrate them correctly to allow productive finance while pricking incipient asset price bubbles. Hence, in the first case, we assume that only the policy interest rate and FX intervention are available to the policy maker. In the second example, we assume that high capital mobility and asset substitutability renders sterilized FX intervention ineffective, so the only two instruments are the policy interest rate and macroprudential regulation. (The third logical possibility, that the only available instruments are FX intervention and macroprudential measures, is not considered here as it is unlikely that the central bank would not be able to use the policy interest rate—except, possibly, in a monetary union or dollarized economy. We also do not consider the use of capital controls, which—as shown in section 5.5.4—can, in principle, substitute for all instruments by simply cutting off the capital inflow.)

### 5.6.1 Policy Interest Rate cum FX Intervention

We begin with the case where the central bank may have only the policy interest rate and FX intervention to deal with the consequences of inflows. The mechanics in the face of an inflow shock are as follows (figure 5.7).

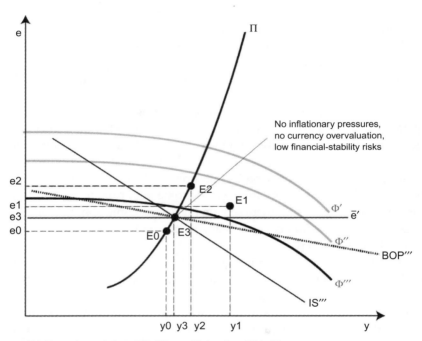

E1: Expansionary inflow shifted the equilibrium from E0 to E1
E2: Higher policy interest rate reduces output (y2), inflationary pressures, and financial-stability risks (E2 is closer to Φ″ than E1 is to Φ′), but also appreciates the currency to e2
E3: FX intervention depreciates the currency to e3 (so that it is no longer overvalued) but also reduces output (and keeps financial-stability risks roughly the same as E2).

**Figure 5.7**
Monetary tightening with FX intervention.
*Source*: Authors' illustration.

Starting at the post-inflow equilibrium, $E_1$, the higher policy interest rate reduces aggregate demand and helps reduce credit growth, bringing the economy to a point such as $E_2$, where the inflation target is met and financial-stability risks are diminished, but where the currency is more appreciated because the higher interest rate induces further inflows. This appreciation can then be countered through FX intervention. The resulting depreciation reduces aggregate supply, while the intervention also curbs credit growth, and therefore aggregate demand and financial-stability risks. While, as depicted, there may remain some residual financial-stability risks at the new equilibrium, $E_3$, the central bank is able to achieve much of its objective of curbing inflationary pressures, currency overvaluation, and excessive credit growth with these two instruments.

### 5.6.2   Policy Interest Rate cum Macroprudential Regulation

If the policy interest rate and macroprudential regulation are available (but FX intervention is not), then the policy interest rate can be assigned to the external balance objective (reducing capital inflows) and macroprudential policy to the internal balance objective (cooling aggregate demand and maintaining financial stability). While it would be unusual to use macroprudential policies to manage aggregate demand in advanced economies, central banks in emerging markets do alter reserve requirements—a form of macroprudential tool—countercyclically (Federico, Vegh, and Vuletin 2014; see also chapter 8). In fact, if macroprudential regulation is viewed here as a substitute for fiscal policy (that, as noted above, may be politically too difficult to adjust rapidly), then this would be in the spirit of Meade's (1951) assignment of monetary policy to the external balance and fiscal policy to internal balance. As Meade notes, "while monetary and fiscal methods of inflating domestic expenditure will have broadly similar results . . . the monetary method of reducing interest rates may cause a significantly larger increase in the transfer of capital funds abroad and . . . [thus] a larger unfavorable movement in its total balance of payments."[11]

Under this assignment, however, in sharp contrast to the analysis above, the policy interest rate would be *lowered* in the face of capital inflows (despite overheating of the economy), while macroprudential

---

11. The problem here is one of capital inflows (rather than capital outflows, which was Meade's concern), but the principle remains the same: lowering the interest rate may have greater effect on reducing capital inflows than tightening macroprudential measures.

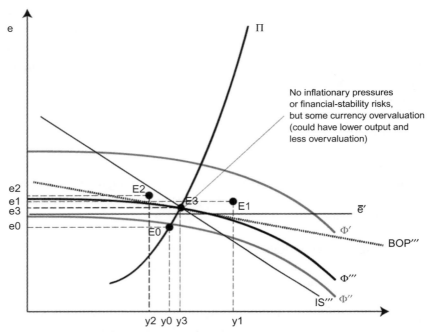

E1: Expansionary inflow shifted the equilibrium from E0 to E1
E2: Macroprudential measures reduce output (y2),
reduce inflation (to the point of deflationary pressures), and
financial-stability risks (E2 is above Φ″ whereas E1 is below Φ′), but also
appreciates the further to e2
E3: Lower policy interest rate raises output (y3), restores the inflation
target, depreciates the currency, but reduces the margin of financial
stability; as depicted, some overvaluation of the currency
(or could have lower output)

**Figure 5.8**
Macroprudential regulation and monetary loosening.
*Source*: Authors' illustration.

regulation would be tightened—offsetting both the impact of the initial
capital inflow and the additional stimulus from the lower policy rate
(figure 5.8). Tightening of macroprudential regulation shifts the IS
curve to the left so that it intersects the unchanged BOP curve at a point
like $E_2$, where output is lower (there is an output gap), the exchange
rate is more appreciated, and financial-stability risks are reduced (the
Φ curve shifts down). Monetary easing then raises output, depreciates
the currency, but also increases credit growth, $E_2$. With careful calibra-
tion, the central bank could achieve its inflation and financial-stability
objectives. As regards output and the exchange rate, however, the cen-

tral bank faces a trade-off: to the extent it strives for a higher level of output (still consistent with nonaccelerating inflation—i.e., satisfies the Phillips Curve, Π), it will have to tolerate a stronger currency.

### 5.6.3 The Role of Capital Controls

In the natural mapping proposed above, there is little need for capital controls. Three instruments allow policy makers to address three macroeconomic imbalances perfectly; even two instruments may afford them significant scope for mitigating the untoward consequences of capital inflows. (In terms of the assignment of instruments, each of the three macro policies can be assigned to one of the macroeconomic imbalances; capital controls could then be reserved for altering the *composition* of inflows—as discussed in chapter 7—without necessarily altering their volume.) A diametrically opposite approach would be to impose or tighten controls in order to prevent or reduce volume of the inflow surge in the first place, thus obviating the need for any macroeconomic policy response. While this would simplify macroeconomic management, it would also mean forgoing any of the benefits of the higher capital inflows.

Between these two extremes is the tack suggested here: macroeconomic instruments should be used to mitigate macroeconomic imbalances, with capital controls used as a backstop when those instruments are unavailable, ineffective, insufficient, or excessively costly.[12] Yet there is a considerable element of judgment required in deciding whether, or at what stage, to deploy capital controls. The advantage of capital controls is that they help tackle all three macroeconomic imbalances simultaneously; that is also their disadvantage, inasmuch as the optimal size of capital inflow from the inflation-growth trade-off perspective need not (and, in general, will not) coincide with that from the perspective of overvaluation-growth trade-off, or that of the excessive credit expansion-growth trade-off. In other words, capital controls may be too blunt an instrument for addressing individual macroeconomic imbalances.[13] A further drawback of capital controls is that they could be inflexible, requiring relatively long lags for implementation, especially in countries that lack the necessary administrative infrastructure to implement controls (macroprudential measures suffer from a similar drawback). By

---

12. Capital controls could be applied broadly, or selectively against particular types of inflows that are causing macroeconomic imbalances (use of capital controls to alter the composition of capital flows is discussed further in chapters 7 and 11).

13. Admittedly, each of the other instruments may also affect the volume of capital inflows (e.g., raising the policy interest or FX intervention are likely to encourage further inflows); capital controls, however, do so by design.

contrast, a decision on monetary policy or FX intervention can be made from one day to the next.

The upshot is that when there are large capital inflows that will either overwhelm the ability of macroeconomic policies to address the resulting imbalances, or that will require the intensive use of all these instruments when their costs are convex, then cyclical capital controls should be brought into play. Conversely, when the surge seems more limited, or the types of capital inflows (e.g., FDI) are less likely to result in macroeconomic imbalances, then controls should not be used and the authorities should rely on macroeconomic instruments instead.

## 5.7  Conclusion

In the face of macroeconomic imbalances, policy makers need to decide whether to try to reduce the volume of flows or to tackle any collateral damage that they may cause. If the inflows are such that they bring little genuine benefit to the recipient country, then the obvious solution is to try to stop them entering the economy in the first place. But inasmuch as the capital inflow is considered to be beneficial, then dealing with any negative repercussion would naturally be the preferred option. To this end, the central bank—or national authorities more generally—have potentially three instruments at their disposal: the policy interest rate, FX intervention, and macroprudential measures. These instruments map naturally to maintaining price stability, curbing the appreciation of the currency, and safeguarding financial stability.

Even with this mapping, however, "the left hand must know what the right hand does"—because each instrument has implications for the other targets (and consequently for how the other instruments should be deployed), there needs to be coordination across the various decision makers (whether they are spread across agencies or are located within a single agency, typically the central bank).[14] For example, raising the policy interest rate to achieve the inflation target may induce further inflows that appreciate the currency, in turn calling for more FX interven-

---

14. For instance, in October 2012, Central Bank of Uruguay (CBU) imposed a 40 percent reserve requirement that applied to all institutions with a position in securities issued by the CBU denominated in local currency or inflation index units for nonresidents, but the Ministry of Finance did not apply the same tax on (essentially equivalent) government bonds. It was not until August 2013 that a reserve requirement of 50 percent on government securities was introduced, at which time the reserve requirement on CBU securities was also raised from 40 percent to 50 percent (information based on the IMF's *Annual Report on Exchange Arrangements and Exchange Restrictions, 2013*).

tion; conversely, a higher policy rate may give scope for relaxing macroprudential measures. (In technical terms, the matrix of instruments to targets is not diagonal—each instrument has some impact beyond its primary target.) Moreover, in a world of instrument uncertainty—that is, the effects of policies on targets are not known precisely—it is generally preferable to use multiple instruments to a lesser degree than to rely solely on any one instrument.

This mapping leaves little room for capital controls to affect aggregate flows, except as a backstop to the other policies (assuming the flows are themselves welcome). The basic principle here is that macro tools—the policy interest rate, FX intervention, nondiscriminatory macroprudential—should be directed at macroeconomic or aggregate problems that capital inflows might bring. When these macroeconomic tools are available and effective, it seems natural to rely on them to address individual macroeconomic imbalances. When some instruments are unavailable, and others need to be geared to their primary objectives, or when the intensive use of the three instruments is excessively costly, then capital controls should be brought into play.

The prescription here presumes that policy makers would want to make use of all available macroeconomic instruments. Yet, this is not uncontroversial. For inflation-targeting (IT) central banks, in particular, it is often argued that they should abjure foreign exchange intervention, allowing the currency to float freely, and subordinate the policy interest rate to the inflation target exclusively. In the following chapter, we examine whether FX intervention (and, more generally, the wider use of policy instruments such as macroprudential measures or capital controls) is consistent with inflation targeting, especially when the central bank has limited credibility.

# 6 Should Inflation Targeters Intervene in the Foreign Exchange Market?

## 6.1 Introduction

In chapter 5, we proposed a schema for managing some of the less desirable consequences of capital inflows without necessarily closing off the economy entirely. The underlying premise is that the central bank has (implicit or explicit) objectives of price stability, external competitiveness, and financial stability—and that it should be willing to use all of the various instruments in its policy tool kit. But a contrary view is that modern central banks, especially those with an inflation-targeting (IT) framework, should focus exclusively on (goods' price) inflation—responding to asset prices (most notably the exchange rate) only to the extent that they affect expected inflation. Having multiple objectives, the argument goes, can undermine the credibility of the central bank's inflation target because there may be times when the various objectives are in conflict. In the face of capital inflows, for instance, the central bank may hesitate to raise its policy interest rate to combat economic overheating for fear of exacerbating competitiveness concerns. Once the private sector harbors doubt that the central bank will always gear its policies to meet the inflation target, much of the benefit of an IT framework for anchoring expectations may be lost.

This alternative view rests on the presumption that modern central banks typically have *one* instrument, the policy interest rate, and hence can have only one objective. As Freedman and Ötker-Robe (2010) argue:

A number of emerging economies have chosen to have targets for both inflation and the exchange rate, especially in the initial period after the adoption of IT. This has a number of disadvantages. It can leave the public and the financial markets unclear as to which will dominate when the two are in conflict. And the central bank will be unable to communicate nearly as clearly the way in which policy will be conducted as it could in a full-fledged IT environment with a single target. As a result, the central bank will lose many of the benefits that arise from anchoring the public's inflation expectations to the inflation target . . . In sum, attempting to operate a system with more than one target tends to have many disadvantages and relatively few advantages.

Mishkin (2000), a strong advocate of inflation targeting, makes a similar point about the inconsistency between the central bank having both an inflation and exchange rate target, noting that "inflation targeting necessarily requires nominal exchange rate flexibility."[1] Despite the credibility benefits that an IT framework can bestow, Mishkin concludes that such a regime may not be viable in emerging market economies (EMEs) "unless there are stringent prudential regulations on, and strict supervision of, financial institutions that ensure the system is capable of withstanding exchange rate shocks." Since, historically, EMEs have been—and most remain—sensitive to large and abrupt exchange rate movements, the upshot of this line of reasoning is that they must choose between the credibility benefits of an IT regime and the flexibility to respond to capital flow shocks as proposed in chapter 5.

In this chapter, we confront the question of whether foreign exchange (FX) intervention (and, more generally, activist policies including the use of macroprudential measures and capital controls) is really incompatible with IT. This issue is of growing relevance to EMEs as increasing numbers adopt IT frameworks (table 6.1). Certainly, early adopters of IT in advanced economies (New Zealand, Sweden, and United Kingdom) took the view that a high degree of exchange rate flexibility was integral to successful inflation targeting, and indeed allowing the currency to float freely is considered by many to be a litmus test of a country's commitment to a credible IT regime (Masson, Savastano, and Sharma 1997). Even where exchange rate pass-through to domestic prices may be high, there are concerns that systematic interventions in the foreign exchange rate market could undermine the credibility of the IT framework (Mishkin and Savastano 2001).

Nevertheless, here we argue that provided the central bank genuinely has a second instrument (e.g., FX intervention), there is no reason why inflation targeting should be incompatible with an exchange rate objective (likewise, if it has macroprudential tools, then it can target financial stability independently of price stability).[2] Indeed, our sense is that the

---

1. See also Nordstrom et al. (2009).
2. IMF (2015) argues that—beyond the tightening required to meet the inflation target—the policy interest rate should not be raised to curb credit growth to address financial-stability risks.

**Table 6.1**
EMEs with inflation-targeting frameworks.

| Country | Year of adoption | Country | Year of adoption |
|---|---|---|---|
| Albania | 2008 | Korea, S. | 2001 |
| Armenia | 2013 | Mexico | 2001 |
| Brazil | 1999 | Peru | 2002 |
| Chile | 1999 | Philippines | 2002 |
| Colombia | 2000 | Poland | 2000 |
| Czech Republic | 1998 | Romania | 2008 |
| Dominican Republic | 2011 | Serbia | 2000 |
| Georgia | 2013 | Slovak Republic | 2005 |
| Guatemala | 2012 | South Africa | 2000 |
| Hungary | 2002 | Thailand | 2000 |
| Indonesia | 2013 | Turkey | 2002 |

*Source:* IMF's *Annual Report on Exchange Arrangements and Exchange Restrictions* (various issues).

use of additional instruments to meet the central bank's broader objectives may actually enhance the credibility of its inflation target. This is because policy is not made in a vacuum. When the exchange rate moves strongly out of line with fundamentals, the central bank inevitably comes under pressure to do something about it. Obstinately refusing to acknowledge the problem and the need for policy adjustments likely undermines credibility because private agents realize that the stance is untenable. By acknowledging that the exchange rate has moved too far or too abruptly, and by undertaking FX intervention to counter it, an inflation-targeting central bank's claim that it will respect its inflation target arguably becomes more—not less—credible.

To examine this matter more formally, we embed the macroeconomic model of chapter 5 in the literature's workhorse model for analyzing monetary policy credibility issues—the Barro and Gordon (1983) framework. In the Barro-Gordon setting, the central bank has the incentive to create surprise inflation in order to cut real wages and thereby boost aggregate supply, output, and employment. Since this incentive is perfectly anticipated by wage setters, however, in equilibrium the central bank does not succeed in boosting output, but its inability to commit not to try to do so imparts an inflationary bias to the economy. In these circumstances, an IT framework can provide the necessary commitment device to avoid this inflationary bias, while constraining the central bank's ability to respond to certain shocks. The latter turns out not to matter in closed-economy New Keynesian models that exhibit "divine coincidence" between the output gap and the inflation target because the central bank would not want to respond to such shocks anyway. But in an open economy, where the central bank has the additional objective of stabilizing the exchange rate around some equilibrium value, the constraints on responding to aggregate demand or capital inflow shocks under IT do bind and they impose a corresponding welfare cost. There is then a trade-off between the credibility and discipline of IT and the greater scope for responding to shocks under discretionary policy regimes. When the central bank's credibility is low, and the economy's inflationary bias is correspondingly large, the IT framework is preferable; when the central bank has considerable credibility but shocks are large, then discretionary policies dominate.

Within this framework, we show that the central bank having an exchange rate objective indeed diminishes the attractiveness of IT relative to discretionary monetary policy because the "divine coincidence" across the central bank's various objectives breaks down. But the addition of a second instrument—FX intervention—is by no means inconsistent with IT. On the contrary, it strengthens the case for IT by increasing the range of parameters over which it will be preferable to discretionary policies. Moreover, the welfare gain from switching from IT to discretionary monetary policy will be smaller when the central bank has both the policy interest rate and sterilized intervention at its disposal than when it has only the policy interest rate. We conclude that, inasmuch as exchange rate misalignment or volatility has real consequences in EMEs, even central banks that have formal IT frameworks can usefully intervene in the FX markets (and deploy other policy instruments) as proposed in chapter 5.

The remainder of this chapter is organized as follows. Section 6.2 lays out the basic analytical framework. Section 6.3 establishes the conditions under which discretionary monetary policy will be preferable to inflation targeting when the central bank has an exchange rate objective but only one instrument, the policy interest rate. Section 6.4 shows that the addition of FX intervention to the policy tool kit raises welfare under both discretionary monetary policy and under inflation targeting, though the gain is larger under the latter. Section 6.5 compares the various policy regimes and shows that intervention strengthens the case for inflation targeting in the sense that it widens the range of parameters over which IT will be welfare superior to discretionary policy (and reduces the stabilization gain associated with switching from IT to discretionary policies). Section 6.6 simulates a dynamic version of the model to gain some further insights about optimal policy in the face of volatile capital flows. Section 6.7 discusses more generally the costs and benefits of EME central banks intervening in the FX market. Section 6.8 extends the model simulation to include domestic macroprudential policies and capital controls. Section 6.9 concludes.

## 6.2 The Setup

The basic macroeconomic model is an extension of that developed in chapter 5. Aggregate demand, $y$, consists of domestic absorption, $a^d$, and the current account, $ca$:

$$y = a^d + ca \tag{6.1}$$

Aggregate supply is assumed to be constant and is normalized to zero (the mechanism of chapter 5, whereby the exchange rate appreciation increases aggregate supply, is suppressed here for convenience. Hence, regardless of the effects of the capital inflow on aggregate supply, $y$ can be interpreted as the excess of aggregate demand over aggregate supply, i.e., the output gap). Via domestic credit growth, absorption depends on the real interest rate and capital flows net of central bank reserve accumulation, as well as on a random shock, $u$:

$$a^d = a^d_x x_r r + a^d_x x_k (\Delta k - \Delta R) + u \tag{6.2}$$

where $r$ is the real interest rate, $\Delta k$ is capital flows, $\Delta R$ is the change in central bank reserves, and $a^d_x, x_r, x_k$ are parameters satisfying $a^d_x \geq 0$, $x_r \leq 0$, $x_k \geq 0$. The current account is a decreasing function of the real exchange rate: $ca = ca_e e$, where $ca_e < 0$, where an increase in $e$ is an appreciation.

The expectations-augmented Phillips curve relates actual inflation, $\pi$, to the private sector's expectation of inflation, $\pi^e$, and the output gap:

$$\pi = \pi^e + y \tag{6.3}$$

Capital flows respond to the expected return differential, albeit at a finite pace:

$$\Delta k = \gamma(r - r^* + (e^e_{t+1} - e_t)) \tag{6.4}$$

where $r^*$ is the world real interest rate, $e_t$ is the real exchange rate, and $e^e_{t+1}$ is the expected value of the exchange rate. The balance of payments (BOP) identity implies:

$$\Delta R = \Delta k + ca = \Delta k + ca_e e \tag{6.5}$$

We consider two types of exogenous shocks: a change in aggregate demand, $u$, and a change in the world interest rate, $r^*$, where (6.4) implies that, other things being equal, a decline in the world interest rate ($\Delta r^* < 0$) will induce a capital inflow $\Delta k > 0$. The shocks are assumed to have mean zero, $E(r^*) = E(u) = 0$, and to be mutually and serially uncorrelated: $E(r^{*2}) = \sigma_{r^*}^2$; $E(u^2) = \sigma_u^2$; $E(ur^*) = 0$. The assumption that shocks are serially uncorrelated means that the real exchange rate is expected to return to its steady state value (here normalized to zero) so that capital flow equation, suppressing time subscripts, becomes:

$$\Delta k = \gamma(r - r^* - e) \tag{6.6}$$

In the static model, $k_{-1} = R_{-1} = 0$, and to simplify the algebra, we set $\gamma = 1$, $a_x^d = 1$, $x_r = -1$, $ca_e = -1$; the simulation analysis below relaxes these assumptions and shows that they are unimportant for our main results. The real exchange rate is then given by:

$$e = (r - R - r^*)/2 \tag{6.7}$$

Writing $(1 + 2\lambda) \equiv a_x^d x_k$, and substituting (6.2) and the BOP identity into (6.1) yields:

$$y = -r - (1 + 2\lambda)ca + ca + u = -r - 2\lambda ca + u \tag{6.8}$$

Finally, using (6.5)–(6.6) gives the semireduced form for output:

$$y = -(1 - \lambda)r - \lambda(R + r^*) + u \tag{6.9}$$

The parameter $\lambda$ thus governs whether inflows ($\Delta r^* < 0$) are, on net, expansionary ($\lambda > 0$), contractionary ($\lambda < 0$), or neutral ($\lambda = 0$). The discussion in chapter 4 suggests that $\lambda \geq 0$ is the pertinent case for EMEs, but all we require here as a stability condition is $\lambda < 1$.

As is standard in such models, the central bank is assumed to penalize deviations of inflation from its target level (here, normalized to zero) and deviations of output from its target level, $\bar{y} \geq 0$, where the target may exceed the aggregate supply attainable at workers' desired real wage (aggregate supply is also normalized to zero). When $\bar{y} > 0$, the central bank has a time consistency (or a credibility) problem: its inability to commit to pursuing low-inflation policies will impart an inflationary bias to the economy even though, in equilibrium, this inflation will be fully anticipated by wage setters and thus not result in any higher output or employment. Of course, it is unlikely that a central bank would knowingly pursue a futile inflationary policy. But in reality the nonaccelerating inflation level of output will not be known with certainty, and the central bank is often under political pressure not to raise interest rates when the economy is booming.[3] It is this slippery slope that is captured here, either by the central bank genuinely aiming for some $\bar{y} > 0$, or by the central bank not having the credibility to convince the private sector that it will not pursue inflationary policies (in other words, $\bar{y} = 0$ but $\bar{y}^e > 0$).

Departing from the advanced-economy literature, the central bank is assumed—in addition to its inflation/output objectives—to penalize the volatility of the real exchange rate around its medium-term fundamentals value (zero). This assumption can be justified on competitiveness concerns whereby even temporary appreciations may do lasting damage to the tradables sector (as discussed in chapter 4), while sharp depreciations can lead to widespread bankruptcies if the private sector has unhedged balance-sheet exposures. The central bank, however, also seeks to minimize its foreign exchange intervention—due to the costs of sterilization on the accumulation side, and due to the risk of exhausting the stock of reserves on the decumulation side. (Although the objectives are specified symmetrically, our concern here is with capital inflows, which will tend to appreciate the exchange rate and lead to reserve accumulation when the central bank intervenes.)

The objective function of the central bank may therefore be written:

$$L = Min \frac{E}{2}\left\{(y - \bar{y})^2 + a(\pi)^2 + 4b(e)^2 + cR^2\right\} \tag{6.10}$$

where $a$, $4b$, and $c$ are the central bank's welfare weights (relative to a 1 percent of GDP output gap) on the deviation of inflation, the exchange rate, and accumulation of reserves from their targets, respectively.[4]

The timing of the model is such that the private sector (e.g., wage setters) must decide on their expectation of inflation before the demand and capital inflow shocks are realized. The central bank, however, is able to choose its optimal policies in light of the realized shocks. We consider a $2 \times 2$ matrix of possible regimes. The first dimension concerns the choice between discretionary monetary policy (whereby the central

---

3. Alternatively, the government may pressure the central bank not to raise interest rates because of adverse implications for public debt dynamics.

4. The model formulation and objective function (6.10) is ad hoc in the tradition of the Barro-Gordon model, but Alla, Espinoza, and Ghosh (2015) develop a fully microfounded model in which (the second-order approximation of) the representative agent's utility function can be written as (6.10).

bank makes no commitments and simply optimizes policy according to its objective function) and inflation targeting, whereby the central bank is committed to deliver the inflation target—assumed to be zero here—based on available information (i.e., the realization of the stochastic shocks, $u$ and $r^*$). The second dimension pertains to the central bank's instruments—whether it uses only the policy interest rate, $r$, or it employs sterilized intervention, $R$, as well.

### 6.3 Discretion versus Inflation Targeting: The Policy Interest Rate

We begin by comparing inflation targeting to discretionary monetary policy when the central bank uses only the policy interest rate.

### 6.3.1 Discretionary Monetary Policy

Under discretionary policies, the central bank chooses the interest rate to minimize the loss function (6.10); since it does not intervene in the foreign exchange market, $R=0$. The first-order condition for the optimal monetary policy implies:

$$r = \frac{[b-(1+a)\lambda(1-\lambda)]r^* + (1+a)(1-\lambda)u}{[(1+a)(1-\lambda)^2 + b]} \tag{6.11}$$

In response to a positive aggregate demand shock, $u>0$, monetary policy should be tightened, though the degree to which the interest rate should be raised depends on the extent to which capital inflows are expansionary. If expansionary, $\lambda>0$ then the increase should be correspondingly *smaller* as higher interest rates attract foreign capital, which exacerbates the economy's overheating problem. The response to an inflow shock itself, $\Delta r^* < 0$, depends critically on whether inflows are expansionary or contractionary. In the benchmark case where inflows are neither expansionary nor contractionary, $\lambda=0$, the policy rate would nevertheless be *lowered* because inflows appreciate the currency—which, if the central bank cares about the exchange rate, $b>0$, is costly. If inflows are sufficiently expansionary, however, then the policy rate needs to be increased in order to dampen economic activity and inflationary pressures. Corresponding to this policy setting, output, inflation, and the exchange rate are given by:

$$y = \frac{b(u-r^*)}{(1+a)(1-\lambda)^2 + b}; \quad \pi = (\bar{y}/a) + \frac{b(u-r^*)}{(1+a)(1-\lambda)^2 + b};$$
$$e = \frac{(1/2)(1+a)(1-\lambda)(u-r^*)}{(1+a)(1-\lambda)^2 + b} \tag{6.12}$$

Somewhat surprisingly, therefore, regardless of whether inflows themselves are expansionary or contractionary, the central bank's optimal policy implies that—even disregarding the inflationary bias, $\bar{y}$—an inflow shock will result in a positive output gap and inflation, together with a currency appreciation. The logic of this result is that, if inflows are expansionary, then the central bank's scope for raising the policy rate will be limited because doing so further appreciates the exchange rate, which is costly if $b > 0$. Hence, the central bank must tolerate some inflation and a positive output gap. Conversely, if inflows are contractionary, then the central bank lowers the policy rate to close the negative output gap and limit the currency appreciation—and will do so to the point that there is a small positive output gap whose marginal welfare cost equals the corresponding cost of the currency appreciation. Of course, if the central bank does not care about the exchange rate ($b=0$), then the policy interest rate is sufficient to ensure that neither aggregate demand nor capital inflow shocks have any effect on inflation. Thus the existence of the exchange rate objective worsens the economy's inflation performance.

The associated welfare loss when the central bank pursues discretionary policy (and has only the interest rate as an instrument) is:

$$L_r^D = \frac{1}{2}\left\{ \frac{(\sigma_u^2 + \sigma_{r*}^2)(1+a)b}{(1+a)(1-\lambda)^2 + b} + \bar{y}^2(1+1/a) \right\} \tag{6.13}$$

The first term of (6.13) arises because, with only one instrument, the central bank cannot fully insulate the economy from the effects of shocks as its output/inflation objectives do not coincide with its exchange rate objective (the term becomes zero if the central bank does not care about stabilizing the exchange rate, $b=0$). The second term derives from the central bank's (futile) attempt at boosting output, where its inability to *commit* to low inflation results in the additional cost $(1/2)(\bar{y}^2/a)$. [5]

### 6.3.2  Inflation Targeting
Under inflation targeting, the central bank commits to a monetary policy that is expected, on the basis of its available information, to deliver the inflation target (here, equal to zero). The central bank's commitment is assumed to pin down the private sector's inflationary expectations

---

5. If the central bank does not actually have the incentive to boost output, but lacks the credibility to convince the private sector that it will not try to do so, then the second term in (6.13) becomes $[(\bar{y}^e)^2/a)] > 0$, where $\bar{y}^e$ is the private sector's belief about the central bank's preferences.

($\pi^e = 0$). From (6.9), this implies that the policy interest rate must be raised in the face of demand shocks and, depending on whether capital inflows are expansionary or contractionary, in response to capital inflows:

$$r = (u - \lambda r^*)/(1 - \lambda) \tag{6.14}$$

Output, inflation, and the exchange rate are then given by:

$$y = 0; \; \pi = 0; \; e = (1/2)[(u - r^*)/(1 - \lambda)] \tag{6.15}$$

with associated welfare loss:

$$L_r^{IT} = \frac{1}{2} \left\{ \bar{y}^2 + b \frac{(\sigma_u^2 + \sigma_{r^*}^2)}{(1 - \lambda)^2} \right\} \tag{6.16}$$

Again, when $b = 0$, there is no welfare loss associated with the aggregate demand or capital inflow shocks (and if the central bank does not have the incentive to try to boost output, then the first term becomes zero as well).

### 6.3.3 Discretion versus Inflation Targeting with One Instrument

The essential trade-off between inflation targeting and discretionary monetary policy is that the IT framework pins down the private sector's inflationary expectations whereas discretion gives the central bank greater scope to respond to shocks that affect its other objectives. The latter has no value in standard New Keynesian models where there is "divine coincidence" between the central bank's two objectives (output gap and inflation), but it is valuable when the central bank has other objectives that do not coincide with its inflation goal, as is the case here with the exchange rate.

The welfare gain of switching from IT to discretionary monetary policy is:

$$G_r^{IT \to D} = L_r^{IT} - L_r^D = \frac{1}{2} \left\{ \frac{b^2(\sigma_u^2 + \sigma_{r^*}^2)}{(1 - \lambda)^2((1 + a)(1 - \lambda)^2 + b)} - \frac{\bar{y}^2}{a} \right\} \tag{6.17}$$

where the first term is the gain from being able to respond to shocks to the exchange rate (which is zero if the central bank does not care about exchange rate volatility, $b=0$), and the second term is the loss due to the inflationary bias of the discretionary regime.[6]

---

6. This term becomes $(\bar{y}^e/a) > 0$ if the central bank does not actually have the incentive to boost output but lacks credibility under the discretionary policy regime.

## 6.4 Discretion versus Inflation Targeting: The Policy Rate and FX Intervention

The drawback of IT, as identified above, is that it does not allow the central bank to respond to shocks that affect its other objectives, such as the level or volatility of the exchange rate. But what if the central bank has a second instrument? In this section, we introduce the possibility of sterilized intervention and ask whether it is compatible with inflation targeting and what the gains are relative to using just the policy interest rate. As before, we begin by characterizing the discretionary policy regime to provide a benchmark.

### 6.4.1 Discretionary Monetary Policy and Sterilized Intervention

The central bank's objective remains the same, but it now chooses both the policy interest rate and sterilized intervention:

$$L = Min_{r,R} \frac{E}{2}\{(y - \bar{y})^2 + a(\pi)^2 + 4b(e)^2 + cR^2\} \tag{6.18}$$

Substituting (6.3), (6.7), and (6.9) into (6.18), and taking the first-order conditions with respect to $r$ and $R$, yields the optimal policies:

$$r = \frac{(b - (1+a)\lambda(1-\lambda))cr^*}{(1+a)[b + c(1-\lambda)^2] + bc} + \frac{(1+a)(b + c(1-\lambda))u}{(1+a)[b + c(1-\lambda)^2] + bc} \tag{6.19}$$

$$R = \frac{-b(1+a)r^*}{(1+a)[b + c(1-\lambda)^2] + bc} + \frac{b(1+a)u}{(1+a)[b + c(1-\lambda)^2] + bc} \tag{6.20}$$

If intervention is not costly, $c=0$, then there is no need for the policy interest rate to respond to capital inflows, regardless of whether they are expansionary or contractionary. With intervention being costless, it is used to fully offset the inflow, freeing the central bank from having to take into account the impact of capital flows on output or inflation. More realistically, however, there will be some cost or limit to how much sterilized intervention the central bank wants to undertake, in which case the policy interest rate needs to be brought into play. If flows are neither expansionary nor contractionary, $\lambda=0$, but the central bank cares about exchange rate volatility ($b>0$), then the policy rate should be lowered to curb inflows and stem the currency appreciation. If, however, inflows are expansionary, then the policy interest rate will need to be raised to reduce inflationary pressures. Since inflows appreciate the exchange rate, the central bank will always want to do at least some sterilized intervention to offset the impact of the inflow if it cares about the exchange rate. It is also noteworthy that optimal FX intervention responds not only to capital inflows, but also to aggregate demand shocks. In other words, there is not a simple assignment of the policy rate to the inflation target and intervention to the exchange rate goal.

The corresponding outcomes for output, inflation, and the exchange rate are:

$$y = \frac{bc(u-r^*)}{(1+a)[b+c(1-\lambda)^2]+bc} ; \quad \pi = \frac{\bar{y}}{a} + \frac{bc(u-r^*)}{(1+a)[b+c(1-\lambda)^2]+bc} ;$$
$$e = \frac{(c/2)(1+a)(1-\lambda)(u-r^*)}{(1+a)[b+c(1-\lambda)^2]+bc} \tag{6.21}$$

Again, regardless of whether inflows are themselves expansionary ($\lambda > 0$) or contractionary ($\lambda < 0$) optimal monetary policy will result in capital inflows being associated with a positive output gap and inflation (except when the central bank does not care about the exchange rate [$b=0$] or in the limit that intervention becomes costless [$c=0$] so that the capital inflow can be fully absorbed by the central bank's reserve accumulation). Comparing (6.21) and (6.12) shows that, when the central bank has both policy instruments, then not only will the currency appreciation be smaller, but inflation will be lower as well.[7] Substituting (6.21) into (6.18) yields:

$$L_{r,R}^D = \frac{1}{2} \left\{ \frac{(\sigma_u^2 + \sigma_{r^*}^2)(1+a)bc}{(1+a)[b+c(1-\lambda)^2]+bc} + \bar{y}^2(1+(1/a)) \right\} \tag{6.22}$$

From the loss function, if the central bank did not care about the exchange rate ($b=0$) or intervention were costless ($c=0$), there would be no welfare loss from the exogenous shocks, and the only cost would arise from the (unattainable) output objective and the inflationary bias that results from the central bank's inability to commit to low inflation under discretionary policies.

---

7. The inflation response to a capital inflow shock when the central bank has one instrument is $\dfrac{b}{(1+a)(1-\lambda)^2+b}$ whereas the corresponding term when the central bank has both instruments is $\dfrac{bc}{(1+a)[b+c(1-\lambda)^2]+bc}$. Then it is readily seen that the inflationary response will be greater when the central bank has only the policy interest rate:

$$\frac{b}{(1+a)(1-\lambda)^2+b} > \frac{bc}{(1+a)[b+c(1-\lambda)^2]+bc} \Leftrightarrow (1+a)[b+c(1-\lambda)^2]+bc > c[(1+a)(1-\lambda)^2+b]$$
$$\Leftrightarrow (1+a)b > 0.$$

### 6.4.2 Inflation Targeting and Sterilized Intervention

Under IT, the central bank's commitment to the inflation target implies that its interest rate and intervention policies must satisfy:

$$r = \frac{-\lambda R - \lambda r^* + u}{1 - \lambda} \tag{6.23}$$

Notice that the settings of the two policy instruments are interdependent. While it is common for the central bank to determine both monetary and exchange rate policies, if the responsibilities are split between different agencies, then those agencies would at least need to be aware of, and take into account, each other's actions.

Substituting (6.23) and the rest of the model into (6.18), taking the first-order condition with respect to R, and solving the resulting equations, yields as optimal policies:

$$r = \frac{-\lambda c(1-\lambda)r^* + (b + c(1-\lambda))u}{b + c(1-\lambda)^2}; \quad R = \frac{-b(r^* - u)}{b + c(1-\lambda)^2} \tag{6.24}$$

Again, if sterilized intervention is costless, then it can be used to offset capital inflows fully, obviating the need for the policy interest rate to respond. More generally, the policy rate will be raised or lowered according to whether inflows are expansionary or contractionary. Although the central bank achieves its inflation target, it must tolerate an appreciation of the currency in the face of inflow or aggregate demand shocks:

$$e = \frac{(c/2)(1-\lambda)(u - r^*)}{[b + c(1-\lambda)^2]} \tag{6.25}$$

with associated welfare cost:

$$L_{r,R}^{IT} = \frac{1}{2}\left\{ \bar{y}^2 + \frac{bc(\sigma_u^2 + \sigma_{r^*}^2)}{b + c(1-\lambda)^2} \right\} \tag{6.26}$$

### 6.4.3 Discretion versus Inflation Targeting with Two Instruments

The welfare gain associated with switching from inflation targeting to discretionary monetary policy (together with sterilized intervention under either regime) is given by:

$$G_{r,R}^{IT \to D} = \frac{1}{2}\left\{ \frac{b^2 c^2 (\sigma_u^2 + \sigma_{r^*}^2)}{(b + c(1-\lambda)^2)((1+a)[b + c(1-\lambda)^2] + bc)} - \frac{\bar{y}^2}{a} \right\} \tag{6.27}$$

The first term, which is nonnegative, represents the central bank's welfare gain from being able to offset shocks to the exchange rate under discretionary monetary policy. This term will be zero if intervention is costless (in which case shocks to the exchange rate can be fully offset even under IT) or if the central bank does not care about exchange rate volatility. The second term is the usual welfare loss associated with the inflationary bias of the discretionary policy regime.

## 6.5   Comparison of Regimes

With these preliminaries, it is straightforward to compare the properties of the various policy regimes. The two dimensions of regime choice are inflation targeting versus discretionary monetary policy, and the use of only one instrument (the policy interest rate) versus the use of both the policy interest rate and sterilized FX intervention.

Regardless of whether the central bank uses one or both instruments, the choice between IT and discretion boils down to whether the time consistency or credibility problem outweighs the welfare loss that results from the central bank being less able to respond to shocks that affect the exchange rate. If there is no time-consistency or credibility problem ($\bar{y} = 0$), then from (6.17) and (6.27) discretion dominates regardless of whether the central bank uses one or both instruments. This is not the case in standard New Keynesian models, where the central bank is assumed to care only about the output gap and inflation, so "divine coincidence" implies that it can meet all its objectives under an IT framework. If the central bank does not care about the exchange rate, or if it can fully offset shocks to the exchange rate through sterilized intervention, then again discretion offers no benefit relative to IT.

What about the choice between using only the policy interest rate or a combination of the policy rate and sterilized intervention? From the mathematics of optimization, it may seem obvious that the central bank must be better off if it has two instruments instead of one (since it could always choose not to use the second instrument), but that is not necessarily the case in a model with forward-looking agents (here, the wage setters). While it is true that if the set of constraints (i.e., the behavior of the private sector) facing the central bank were to remain invariant across regimes, then the central bank must be better off with two instruments rather than one—the essence of the Lucas critique is that, under rational expectations, the private sector's behavior may change, possibly to the detriment to the central bank achieving its objectives. For instance, in a very similar setup with forward looking wage setters, Rogoff (1985) shows that international policy coordination—which essentially entails expanding the set of instruments available to policy makers—can be counterproductive. Here, however, neither the existence of the exchange rate target, nor the possibility of sterilized intervention, affects the output-inflation trade-off or the central bank's incentive to generate surprise inflation under discretionary policies.

Proponents of strict IT often argue that the central bank should allow the exchange rate to float freely, as intervention in the currency markets could undermine the credibility of its inflation target. It turns out, however, that both under discretion and under IT, adding the second instrument improves welfare. Subtracting (6.22) from (6.13), the gain from adding sterilized intervention to the central bank's policy tool kit under discretionary policies is given by:

$$G_{r \to r, R}^{D} = L_r^{D} - L_{r, R}^{D}$$
$$= \frac{1}{2} \left\{ \frac{(\sigma_u^2 + \sigma_{r^*}^2)(1+a)^2 b^2}{[(1+a)(1-\lambda)^2 + b][(1+a)(b+c(1-\lambda)^2)+bc]} \right\} > 0 \qquad (6.28)$$

Similarly, the gain under IT is:

$$G_{r \to r, R}^{IT} = L_r^{IT} - L_{r, R}^{IT} = \frac{1}{2} \left\{ \frac{b^2(\sigma_u^2 + \sigma_{r^*}^2)}{(1-\lambda)^2 [b+c(1-\lambda)^2]} \right\} > 0 \qquad (6.29)$$

Thus, not only is sterilized intervention fully consistent with inflation targeting, it is welfare improving if there are costs of exchange rate volatility. Indeed, the welfare gain from adding sterilized intervention as an additional instrument is *greater* for an inflation-targeting central bank than for a central bank that pursues discretionary monetary policy:

$$G_{r \to r, R}^{IT} - G_{r \to r, R}^{D}$$
$$= \frac{1}{2} \left\{ \frac{b^3(\sigma_u^2 + \sigma_{r^*}^2)\{c(1+a)(1-\lambda)^2 + (1+a)[b+c(1-\lambda)^2]+bc\}}{(1-\lambda)^2(b+c(1-\lambda)^2)([(1+a)(1-\lambda)^2 + b][(1+a)(b+c(1-\lambda)^2)+bc])} \right\}$$
$$> 0 \qquad (6.30)$$

The intuition for this result is that, under discretion, the policy interest rate is already chosen optimally to minimize the loss function (6.10), so the addition of a second, optimally chosen, instrument yields relatively little welfare gain.[8] By contrast, under IT, the policy interest rate is geared solely to the ad hoc objective of delivering the inflation target, so the addition of a second instrument whose setting is chosen optimally to minimize the central bank's loss function provides a larger welfare gain.

Moreover, FX intervention supports inflation targeting in the sense that its addition to the tool kit increases the range of parameters over

---

8. Strict concavity of the objective function (as in quadratic utility used here) will suffice for this result.

which IT will be preferable to discretion, and reduces the stabilization gain from switching to discretionary policies. To understand why, figure 6.1 shows the welfare loss under the various regimes, which are all an increasing function of the central bank's time-consistency/credibility problem, $\bar{y}$. The lines marked D1 and IT1 indicate the welfare loss when the central bank has only the policy interest rate as an instrument. From (6.17), when $\bar{y}$ exceeds the critical value $\bar{y}_1$, the time consistency problem is sufficiently severe that IT will be welfare superior to discretionary monetary policy. The addition of FX intervention to the policy maker's tool kit reduces the welfare loss under both IT and discretion (lowering them to IT2 and D2 respectively), but as noted above in (6.30), the welfare gain will be larger for an inflation-targeting central bank. There is thus a greater downward shift of the IT curve compared to the discretion curve, with a corresponding leftward shift of their intersection to $\bar{y}_2$. Whereas with one instrument, the time consistency problem had to be greater than $\bar{y}_1$ for IT to be preferable to discretionary policies, with two instruments, it need only be greater than $\bar{y}_2 (< \bar{y}_1)$ for IT to dominate discretion.

A slightly different way of seeing the same result is to note that the welfare gain (in terms of being able to better offset shocks to the exchange rate) of switching from IT to discretionary policies is greater when an inflation-targeting central bank has only the policy interest rate than when it also has sterilized intervention in its arsenal:

$$G_r^{IT \to D} - G_{r,R}^{IT \to D}$$
$$= \frac{1}{2} \left\{ \frac{b^3\{(1+a)(b+2c(1-\lambda)^2)+bc\}(\sigma_u^2 + \sigma_{r*}^2)}{(1-\lambda)^2[(1+a)(1-\lambda)^2+b][b+c(1-\lambda)^2][(1+a)(b+c(1-\lambda)^2)+bc]} \right\}$$
$$> 0 \tag{6.31}$$

Finally, even ignoring the time consistency problems associated with discretionary monetary policy, an IT central bank will likely benefit more from adding sterilized intervention to its tool kit than from switching to discretionary policies; from (6.29) and (6.17)[9]:

$$G_{r \to r, R}^{IT} - G_r^{IT \to D} = \frac{1}{2} \left\{ \frac{b^2(\sigma_u^2 + \sigma_{r*}^2)(1+a-c)}{[b+c(1-\lambda)^2][(1+a)(1-\lambda)^2+b]} + \frac{\bar{y}^2}{a} \right\} \tag{6.32}$$

---

9. Although the first term of (6.32) is potentially ambiguous, for any reasonable central bank objective function, it will be positive as $c$ represents the welfare cost of sterilizing an additional 1 percent increase in the stock of reserve holdings (which average around 20 percent of GDP for EMEs) relative to the welfare cost of a 1 percent of GDP output gap (which is normalized to unity), hence $c \ll 1$; in the simulations below, we use $c = 0.01$.

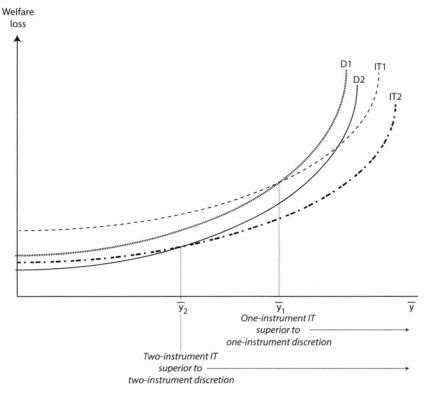

D1 Discretionary policy with one instrument
IT1 Inflation targeting with one instrument
D2 Discretionary policy with two instruments
IT2 Inflation targeting with two instruments

**Figure 6.1**
Welfare comparisons across regimes.
*Source*: Authors' illustration.

## 6.6 Some Simulations

In this section, we relax the parameter assumptions that we made earlier for algebraic simplicity and simulate a dynamic version of the model. The equations describing the model now become:

$$y = a^d + ca \tag{6.33}$$

$$a^d = a_x^d x_r r + a_x^d x_\mu \, \mu + a_x^d x_k (\Delta k - \Delta R) + u \tag{6.34}$$

$$ca = ca_y \, y + ca_e e \tag{6.35}$$

where $\mu$ *is* macroprudential policy (for the moment, set to zero), and the current account balance is a decreasing function of income $ca_y < 0$. Substituting (6.34)–(6.35) into (6.33) yields:

$$y_t = \Phi_r\, r_t + \Phi_\mu \mu_t + \Phi_k\, (\Delta k_t - \Delta R_t) + \Phi_e e_t + \Phi_u u_t \qquad (6.36)$$

where $\Phi_r \equiv a_x^d x_r/(1-ca_y)$; $\Phi_\mu \equiv a_x^d x_\mu/(1-ca_y)$; $\Phi_k \equiv a_x^d x_k/(1-ca_y)$; $\Phi_e \equiv ca_e/(1-ca_y)$; $\Phi_u \equiv 1/(1-ca_y)$

Capital account dynamics are given by:

$$\Delta k_t = \gamma_r (r_t - r_t^* + (e_{t+1}^e - e_t) - \tau_t) - \gamma_k k_{t-1} \qquad (6.37)$$

where $\tau$ is the capital control (also set to zero). The expectations-augmented Phillips curve is:

$$\pi_t = \beta \pi_{t+1}^e + \kappa y_t \qquad (6.38)$$

and the model is closed with the BOP identity:

$$ca + \Delta k = \Delta R \qquad (6.39)$$

The capital inflow shock and the aggregate demand shock are assumed to follow autoregressive processes:

$$r_t^* = \rho_{r^*} r_t^* + \varepsilon_t^{r^*}; \quad u_t = \rho_u u_t + \varepsilon_t^u \qquad (6.40)$$

The central bank's objective function is:

$$L = Min \frac{E}{2} \left\{ (y - \bar{y})^2 + a(\pi)^2 + b(e)^2 + c(R)^2 + d_\mu(\mu)^2 + d_\tau(\tau)^2 \right\} \qquad (6.41)$$

To abstract from time-consistency issues, we set $\bar{y} = 0$; the other parameters are chosen to mimic a typical EME (see Ghosh, Ostry, and Chamon 2015), and are given in table 6.2.

### 6.6.1  Monetary Policy and FX Intervention

We begin by considering policies and outcomes under the discretionary and IT regimes when the central bank has only the interest rate as its policy instrument. In the face of a capital inflow shock that is expansionary ($\Phi_k = 1.2$), the policy interest rate is raised under both discretion and under IT, but more so under the latter, as the central bank is committed to delivering its inflation target (figure 6.2, dashed lines). The higher interest rate under IT translates into a (slightly) larger cumulative capital inflow and greater real exchange rate appreciation compared to the discretionary regime. The greater exchange rate appreciation under IT then implies lower welfare.

**Table 6.2**
Parameter values for dynamic simulation.

| | |
|---|---|
| Capital flow equation: | $\gamma_r = 2; \gamma_k = 0.5; \rho_{r^*} = 0.9$ |
| Current account equation: | $ca_y = -0.3; ca_e = -0.15$ |
| Phillips Curve: | $\beta = 0.99; \rho_u = 0.75; k = 1$ |
| Aggregate demand: | $\Phi_r = -0.8; \Phi_\mu = -0.8; \Phi_e = -0.1; \Phi_u = 0.8; \Phi_k = 1.2$ or 0.4. |
| Objective function: | $a = 1; b = 0.1; c = 0.01; d_r = 0.1; d_\mu = 0.1$ |

*Source:* Authors' estimates.

What happens when FX intervention is added to the policy tool kit? Policy interest rates are again raised, but by less than the increase when the central bank does not intervene in the FX market (in figure 6.2, the solid lines are below the corresponding dashed lines). Of the two regimes, IT still has a higher interest rate than discretion. The main welfare benefit of adding intervention to the tool kit is that the currency appreciation is smaller. The smaller exchange rate appreciation implies that the cumulative capital inflows is greater, but much of it is absorbed by reserves accumulation (the higher interest rate under IT means both a larger capital inflow and more FX intervention). By construction, IT delivers zero inflation and a zero output gap. Under discretionary monetary policy, inflation and the output gap are *lower* when the central bank also intervenes in the FX market; this is because sterilized intervention absorbs some of the domestic credit growth, reducing aggregate demand pressures. An interesting insight from the simulation is that the stock of reserves returns to its baseline (here normalized to zero) as the inflow shock peters out. In other words, even though there are never capital outflows in the simulation, the central bank undertakes two-way intervention: first buying reserves and then selling them.

In broad terms, the same pattern holds in the case of contractionary inflows (figure 6.3). Of course, the policy interest rate is now lowered rather than raised—more so under discretion than under IT, and more so (for both regimes) when the central bank has only the policy interest rate as its instrument. The (relatively) higher policy rate when the central bank has both instruments implies a larger cumulative capital inflow, but much of it is absorbed by FX intervention, resulting in a smaller real exchange rate appreciation. As discussed above, even though the parameter values are such that the inflow itself would be contractionary $(a_x^d x_k < 1)$, the decline in the policy interest rate under discretion is sufficient to ensure that there is a net expansionary impact on the economy (under IT, the central bank delivers $\pi = y = 0$, regardless of

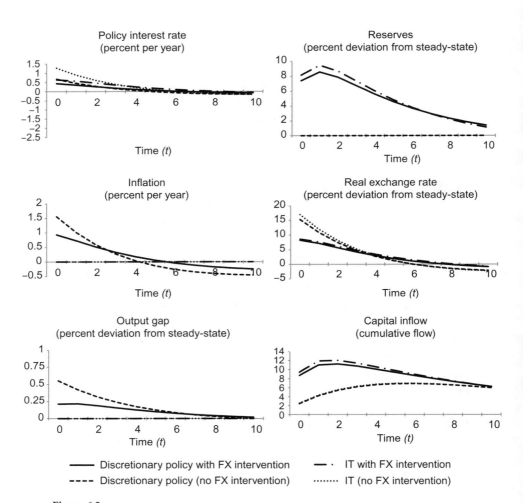

**Figure 6.2**
Responding to expansionary inflows.
*Source*: Authors' calculations.

whether the inflows are expansionary or contractionary). Again, inflation is lower and the output gap smaller when the central bank has both instruments, though now the explanation is that the policy interest rate is reduced by less under the two-instrument regime.

Since the simulations abstract from central bank credibility/time consistency issues, welfare under discretionary policies will necessarily be higher than under IT, and welfare when the central bank uses both instruments is higher than when the central bank uses only the policy

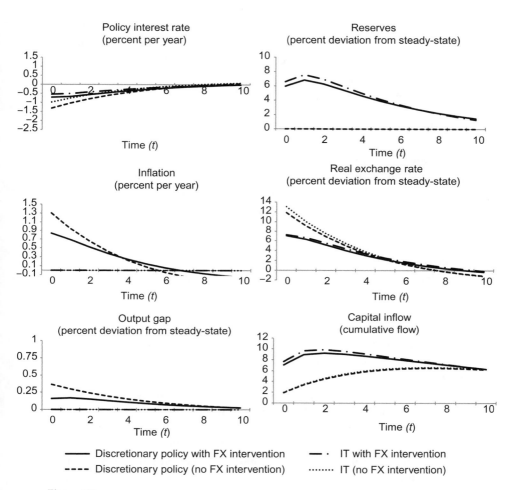

**Figure 6.3**
Responding to contractionary inflows.
*Source*: Authors' calculations.

interest rate. Measured in arbitrary but consistent units, welfare loss under each regime is: one-instrument IT, $L_r^{IT} = 6.00$; one-instrument discretion, $L_r^{D} = 5.68$; two-instrument IT, $L_{r,R}^{IT} = 2.77$; two-instrument discretion, $L_{r,R}^{D} = 2.70$. Therefore, consistent with the simple theoretical model above, (1) discretion dominates inflation targeting when there are no time-consistency issues; (2) the welfare gain associated with adding intervention to the available instruments is greater for IT than it is for discretion: $G_{r \to r,R}^{IT} = 3.23 > G_{r \to r,R}^{D} = 2.98$; (3) the gain associated with shifting from IT to discretion is greater when the IT central bank has only the policy interest rate than when it has both instruments: $G_r^{IT \to D} = 0.33 > G_{r,R}^{IT \to D} = 0.07$; and (4) the gain associated with adding the second instrument to IT is greater than the gain associated with shifting to discretion: $G_{r \to R}^{IT} = 3.23 > G_r^{IT \to D} = 0.03$.

## 6.7   FX Intervention: Welfare Gains

Both the theoretical model and the simulation analysis suggest that more activist policies—supplementing IT (or discretionary monetary policies) with FX intervention—is likely to be beneficial when the central bank has a target or comfort zone for the exchange rate. But what would the welfare gain depend upon? And what might be the drawbacks of such a strategy?

Beyond the importance of exchange rate stability in the central bank's objective function, the welfare gain from FX intervention depends on the nature and characteristics of the capital inflows. Two parameters are key: the interest rate sensitivity of capital flows ($\gamma_r$) and the persistence of capital inflows ($\rho_r$). As capital flows become more sensitive to the return differential, sterilized intervention becomes more difficult (a given quantity of intervention has a smaller impact on the exchange rate); in the limiting case of perfect capital mobility ($\gamma \to \infty$), sterilized intervention becomes impossible. Not surprisingly, therefore, greater sensitivity of capital flows to the return differential means that the central bank must tolerate a larger real appreciation and—proportional to the capital flow—undertake less intervention, as illustrated in figure 6.4 (right panel). The absolute amount of reserve accumulation is nonmonotonic in the return sensitivity of capital flows, $\gamma_r$. When this sensitivity is small, the initial change in reserves is also small (since the return differential has little impact on inflows). As $\gamma_r$ increases, FX intervention initially increases, but eventually starts to decline (since intervention becomes ineffective as $\gamma_r \to \infty$). Conversely, the greater the responsiveness of capital flows to the return differential, the more the policy rate is lowered. In other words, as the economy moves toward the limiting case of perfect capital mobility and asset substitutability, the central bank must increasingly rely on interest rate changes rather than on FX intervention to influence the exchange rate.

The other key parameter is the persistence of the shock. The less persistent the inflow shock, the smaller should be the policy response. The key insight of this experiment, however, is that—as a proportion of the initial capital inflow—the initial intervention (i.e., accumulation

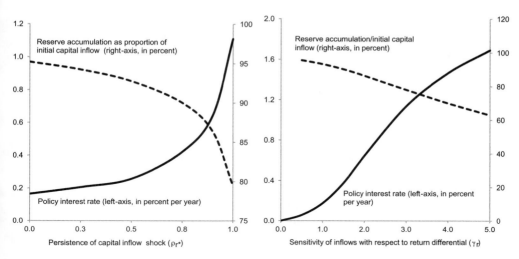

**Figure 6.4**
Relative use of FX intervention and policy interest rate.
*Source*: Authors' calculations.

of reserves) is *greater* when inflows are expected to be *less* persistent. In fact, the degree of intervention (as a proportion of the initial inflow) is monotonically decreasing in the expected persistence of the inflows, as illustrated in figure 6.4 (left panel). Moreover, when the shock is more persistent, the policy interest rate will be raised by more, thus playing a larger role relative to FX intervention. This accords with the usual intuition that the central bank should allow the economy to adjust to permanent shocks (including capital inflows) but intervene to absorb temporary shocks that move the economy away from its medium-term equilibrium. While the logic is clear, in practice the central bank may have significant difficulty in judging whether the shock is likely to be temporary or persistent, especially given its likely dependence on a host of factors, including global risk aversion and the monetary policies of advanced economies.

Although having the second instrument can clearly be welfare enhancing, it is also important to recognize that there may be drawbacks (beyond the sterilization costs, which are already implicitly incorporated in the analysis) to the central bank intervening in the FX market. One concern is the potential endogeneity of investor behavior. The simulations take the sensitivity of capital flows to the rate of return as given and constant across regimes; in practice, greater certainty on the part of investors that they will obtain a higher rate of return would likely increase the sensitivity of capital flows to the return differential. It is noteworthy in this regard that, in most of the simulations, the response to a capital inflow shock is to allow a jump in real exchange rate appreciation (albeit smaller than in the absence of intervention), followed by a gradual depreciation. In other words, the optimal intervention typically does not offer investors an anticipated appreciation. This is precisely because doing so would induce greater capital inflows, which is what the central bank wants to avoid. Nevertheless, as stressed by the Lucas critique, a shift in policy regime can endogenously alter the private sector's behavior—in this case, making investors more responsive to the return differential, thus rendering sterilized intervention less effective (and even counterproductive in a limiting case where flows respond very strongly to the combination of a significant interest rate differential with a stable exchange rate).

Purist advocates of inflation targeting also worry that the market could interpret the adoption of a second target (the exchange rate) as a softening of the central bank's commitment to low inflation. Using a formal model in which the private sector has rational expectations, we showed that, under discretionary policies, the central bank having an exchange rate target does lead to higher inflation, but that the addition of FX intervention results in lower inflation compared to the one-instrument case. Moreover, under an IT framework, the central bank is able to deliver the targeted inflation rate regardless of its exchange rate objective. But this conclusion is predicated on sterilized intervention being effective (see chapter 9), and on the central bank being able to reliably identify the equilibrium real exchange rate for the economy. If that is not the case, or is only the case to a limited degree, then having an exchange rate target could undermine the credibility of the inflation target. An effective communication strategy that stresses the precedence of the inflation target is thus critical.

A related but somewhat distinct concern is that the central bank will come under political pressure not to raise the policy interest rate, despite inflationary pressures, in the face of capital inflows that are strengthening the currency. In such a situation, would the availability of sterilized intervention as an additional policy instrument enhance or undermine the inflation target? In the standard Mundell-Fleming model, where capital inflows are contractionary, FX intervention would tend to exacerbate the inflationary pressures by limiting the currency appreciation (which would otherwise lower the price of imports). But when inflows are expansionary, the credit channel of aggregate demand is more important than the current account channel of currency appreciation. Sterilized intervention becomes contractionary, reducing aggregate demand and inflation. Hence, provided that inflows are expansionary, sterilized intervention works in the same direction as raising the policy interest rate—and when the latter cannot be used due to political constraints, intervention can help the central bank adhere to its inflation target. If flows are contractionary, then the opposite is true—however, the issue becomes moot since the central bank would not need to raise its policy interest rate in the face of contractionary inflows, so the political constraint on tightening monetary policy would not apply.

## 6.8   Expanding the Policy Tool Kit

What happens if the policy tool kit is augmented to include nondiscriminatory macroprudential measures and capital controls ($\mu$ and $\tau$, respectively)? In figure 6.5, we simulate the optimal response to an expansionary capital inflow under inflation targeting: the dotted and short-dashed lines reproduce the one- and two-instrument inflation-targeting response from figure 6.2; the long-dashed and solid lines show how policies and outcomes differ with the addition of macroprudential measures and capital controls.

When the central bank has only its policy rate (dotted line), the primacy of the inflation target requires that the interest rate be raised sharply in response to an expansionary capital inflow. While the higher interest rate attracts more capital, the inflow is choked off by the real exchange rate appreciation. The central bank thus delivers its zero inflation/output gap target, but at the cost of substantial overvaluation of the currency. Adding FX intervention (dashed line), the policy interest rate can be increased by less than when the central bank has only one instrument because sterilized intervention absorbs part of the inflow (the total inflow is larger when the central bank intervenes to limit the currency appreciation, but credit growth—which depends on the inflow net of intervention—is smaller). When the central bank has macroprudential policies available (dashed and dotted line), the response of the policy interest rate flips sign: as discussed in chapter 5, the policy interest rate can be *lowered* (thus reducing the inflow of capital), with macroprudential policies (and FX intervention) being employed to curb credit growth and prevent overheating of the economy. The lower policy interest rate (and hence smaller capital inflow) when macroprudential policies are applied also means that the central bank can undertake less FX intervention while still achieving a smaller

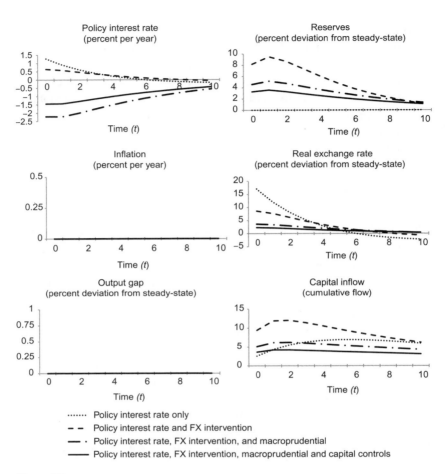

**Figure 6.5**
Responding to expansionary flows: Inflation targeting with additional instruments.
*Source*: Authors' calculations.

appreciation of the currency. Finally, if capital controls are used as well (solid line), the cumulative capital inflow is smaller, allowing the central bank to reduce interest rates by less and undertake less FX intervention while still achieving the inflation/output gap target and a smaller real appreciation.

In broad terms, the picture is much the same under discretionary monetary policy (figure 6.6), except that the inflation/output gap target is not met perfectly (as it is under IT). When the central bank has only the policy interest rate and FX intervention in its tool kit, the policy interest rate is raised—though by less than it would under inflation targeting (inflation is correspondingly higher under discretionary monetary policy). The lower interest rate than under inflation targeting implies a smaller capital inflow and a smaller real appreciation, with correspondingly less need for FX intervention. Nevertheless, credit growth and aggregate demand, and hence inflation, are lower when the central bank intervenes in the FX market than when it uses only its policy interest rate.

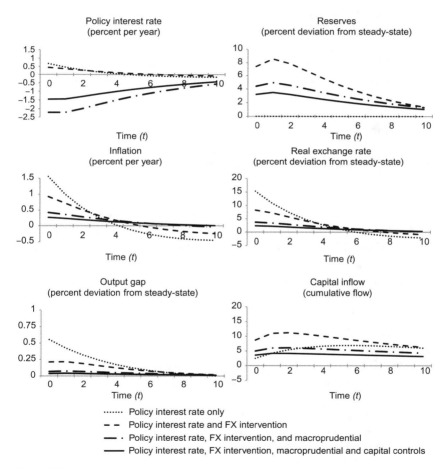

**Figure 6.6**
Responding to expansionary flows: Discretionary monetary policy with additional instruments.
*Source*: Authors' calculations.

Again, when macroprudential measures are applied (dashed and dotted line), the use of the policy interest rate can flip its sign, being lowered instead of raised, and thus reducing the incentive for inflows. This allows for less FX intervention while still achieving a smaller real appreciation and better inflation performance (by curbing credit growth). This is reinforced by the application of capital controls (solid line), which further reduce inflows without the need to lower interest rates by as much, while achieving a smaller real exchange rate appreciation and lower inflation.

Finally, comparing discretionary policies to inflation targeting, it is noteworthy that FX intervention, macroprudential measures, and capital controls are all (optimally) used *more intensively under IT*. Thus, while the addition of these instruments raises welfare under either regime, they are particularly useful for central banks with inflation-targeting frameworks.

### 6.9   Conclusion

This chapter examined how policy might respond to macroeconomic imbalances—inflation, currency appreciation, and credit growth—that result from capital inflows. While a purist view of inflation targeting would argue for the central bank to use only its policy interest rate, and to target only the inflation rate, a broader perspective is that policy makers should try to address all of the various macroeconomic imbalances associated with large inflows—not just consumer price inflation— and should make use of all of the relevant policy instruments. Focusing on the use of sterilized intervention to manage the exchange rate, we showed that having a second instrument and a second objective is not at all inconsistent with the central bank attaining its inflation target. If anything, it makes inflation-targeting more attractive and enhances welfare if exchange rate movements are costly.

Sterilized intervention, by partly absorbing the impact of capital inflows on credit growth, can also serve as a macroprudential tool. More generally, the use of multiple instruments (FX intervention, macroprudential policies, capital controls) will tend to enhance, rather than reduce, the central bank's credibility. This is because policy is not made in a vacuum. When the exchange rate moves strongly in either direction, the central bank inevitably comes under pressure to do something about it. Obstinately refusing to acknowledge that there is a problem, and that the central bank will eventually need to make policy adjustments, likely undermines the central bank's credibility because the public realizes that the stance is politically untenable. By acknowledging that the exchange rate is moving out of its comfort zone (or doing so too abruptly), and by openly undertaking foreign exchange intervention, an inflation-targeting central bank's claim that it will respect its inflation target arguably becomes more—not less—credible.

# 7     Balance-sheet Vulnerabilities

## 7.1   Introduction

The framework adopted in chapter 5 is useful for thinking about how policies might respond to the macroeconomic imbalances that are typically associated with capital inflows—inflation, currency overvaluation, and credit booms. But as flows cumulate into stocks, they can also widen mismatches on domestic balance sheets, increasing their vulnerability to a sudden stop or reversal of capital inflows. For instance, since emerging markets usually borrow in foreign currency, large inflows may leave borrowers dangerously exposed to a subsequent depreciation of the exchange rate. For this reason, virtually every emerging market has imposed limits on banks' open foreign exchange (FX) positions, but if the ultimate borrowers (households and corporations) are unhedged, then this merely transforms banks' FX risk into credit risk.[1] Likewise, wholesale funding or other short-term debt may leave domestic balance sheets exposed to maturity mismatches. Indeed, debt financing will tend to raise leverage (i.e., widen the debt-equity mismatch), exposing the borrower to solvency risk if there is a revaluation of liabilities relative to assets or earning capacity. Whereas macroeconomic imbalances are largely related to the volume of *net* capital flows, balance-sheet vulnerabilities depend more on the magnitude and composition of the country's *gross* liability position. This chapter provides a welfare-theoretic framework for considering optimal policies to address such balance-sheet vulnerabilities, while practical considerations in the application of these policies are taken up in chapter 11.

---

1. Another possible vulnerability to banks' balance sheets arises from relaxed lending standards during credit booms; financial-stability risks arising from rapid credit expansion were considered in chapters 5 and 6, and are not discussed here.

In principle, balance-sheet mismatches are just part of ordinary commercial risk and do not call for any government intervention. In practice, however, there are at least two reasons why the government may want to intervene. First, there is plenty of anecdotal evidence that markets often underestimate or underprice salient risks. The most obvious example is households who, in fixed exchange rate countries, prefer foreign currency–denominated mortgages on grounds that they are cheaper—not recognizing that the reason that domestic interest rates are higher is that there is a risk of currency devaluation.[2] Second, even if individuals assess risks correctly, they may fail to take account of the externalities associated with their borrowing decisions, resulting in excessively large, and excessively risky, liabilities for the economy as a whole. This is where recent theories of prudential capital controls (Jeanne and Korinek 2010; Korinek 2011; Bianchi 2011) come in. In these models, the amount that can be borrowed is limited by a collateral constraint, where the collateral consists of traded and nontraded goods so its value depends on the real exchange rate (the relative price of nontraded goods). Since atomistic borrowers take the collateral constraint as given, they fail to recognize that in a sudden stop, when debt cannot be rolled over, repayment of their own borrowing depreciates the real exchange, thus tightening the collateral constraint for all borrowers. Therefore, *ex ante*, the decentralized economy ends up with too much external debt. The optimal intervention is to tax borrowing to prevent this excessive debt buildup, with the tax calibrated to the riskiness of the liabilities incurred.

This chapter begins by reviewing in section 7.2 the reasons why certain external liability structures may be more risky than others. Section 7.3 lays out a formal welfare-theoretic framework for analyzing government intervention in borrowing-lending decisions. Section 7.4 discusses to what extent various real-world measures—such as capital controls or prudential policies—are able to replicate the theoretically optimal measure. Section 7.5 concludes with a summary of the chapter's main findings.

---

2. From the borrower's perspective, it may still be rational if—as in the case of Argentina's "pessofication" in 2002—the government *ex post* forces the banks to convert the debt into local currency at the pre-devaluation exchange rate or otherwise bails out the borrower.

## 7.2 Riskiness of External Liabilities

There is ample empirical evidence, including that presented in chapter 4, that external liabilities make emerging market economies (EMEs) more vulnerable to crisis. The degree of vulnerability, however, depends on the structure of those liabilities, with some instruments having worse risk-sharing characteristics than others. The key issue is how large a transfer of resources the debtor needs to make—and how painful that transfer is to effect—in the face of shocks to (tradable) output or to capital inflows (sudden stops).[3] There are then three characteristics of the liability that are relevant to an instrument's riskiness: the conjunction of currency denomination and residency of the creditor, its maturity, and whether it takes the form of debt or equity.

### 7.2.1 Creditor Residency and Currency Denomination

To see why the currency denomination of a liability matters, it is useful to consider a "real" model (i.e., one without money) of a small open economy that produces traded and nontraded goods, and that is inhabited by a single representative borrower who produces and consumes both goods (appendix A.7.1 formalizes the model). Since there are no nominal quantities in this setup, "foreign currency" and "local currency" debt correspond to the claim being denominated in the traded and the nontraded good, respectively. The claim can then be classified in a $2 \times 2$ matrix according to whether it is owed to external (i.e., nonresident) or to domestic (i.e., resident) creditors, and whether it is denominated in foreign or in local currency (table 7.1). Thus, the four quadrants of the matrix are (1) foreign currency/nonresident creditor, (2) foreign currency/resident creditor, (3) local currency/nonresident creditor, and (4) local currency/resident creditor.

Starting with the first quadrant (foreign currency/nonresident creditor), the point to note is that, by definition, a nonresident creditor can only consume traded goods. Therefore, to effect a repayment, the debtor must either borrow more (roll over the debt or borrow from another creditor) or generate a current account surplus through a combination of lower consumption and higher production of traded

---

3. Sudden stops are episodes in which there is an abrupt loss of confidence in the currency (or in the country), capital inflows come to a halt, and foreign creditors (sometimes joined by domestic investors) rush for the exit. As a result, far from being able to roll over its maturing debts, the economy is forced to generate a current account surplus to repay them.

**Table 7.1**
Currency denomination of liability and creditor residency.

|  |  | Creditor residency | |
|---|---|---|---|
|  |  | *Nonresident creditor* | *Resident creditor* |
| **Currency denomination of liability** | *Foreign currency* | (1) Foreign currency liability and nonresident creditor | (2) Foreign currency liability and resident creditor |
|  | *Local currency* | (3) Local currency liability and nonresident creditor | (4) Local currency liability and resident creditor |

*Source:* Authors' illustration.

goods. During a sudden stop, the only option (barring default) is to run a current account surplus as the country is unable to borrow more or to roll over its debt. The larger the requisite current account surplus, the greater the real exchange rate depreciation required to induce the shift of consumption and production. Since the country is constrained in its external borrowing, the marginal utility of traded goods will be high—which is what makes it painful to repay the external creditor in traded goods at that time.[4] Put differently, generating the current account surplus requires the price of nontraded goods to decline—but part of the debtor's income derives from nontraded goods. It is thus the combination of a nonresident creditor and the foreign currency ("traded good") denomination of the claim that makes it so pernicious.

By contrast, in the second quadrant, where the foreign currency–denominated debt is owed to a resident creditor (who consumes both traded and nontraded goods), effecting the debt repayment may require little or no change in the real exchange rate.[5] In essence, a resident

---

4. Even if the economy is able to shift resources from the nontraded to the traded sector, there will be diminishing returns, especially in the short run when not all factors are mobile, so this shift is costly in terms of aggregate output. In practice, the only way an economy is able to generate a large current account surplus in the short run is through import compression, which further depresses output.

5. In the limiting case that the domestic borrower and creditor have identical, homothetic preferences, the real exchange rate would be constant. Of course, it is *possible* that the resident creditor consumes only the traded good, but that would be an extreme assumption, whereas it is necessarily true that nonresident creditors can only consume traded goods. Conversely, if the resident creditor is as likely as a nonresident creditor to rush for the exit and transfer his capital abroad (in effect, consumes only the traded good), then it makes no difference whether the creditor is a resident or a nonresident.

creditor can be partly repaid in nontraded goods, even though his claim is formally denominated in traded goods.

If the debt were owed to a nonresident creditor but denominated in local currency (quadrant III), its repayment would still necessitate a real exchange rate depreciation (which would be especially sharp during a sudden-stop episode). But the value of the creditor's claim—and thus the current account surplus needed to repay it—would decrease correspondingly as the currency weakened. Denominating external debt in local currency therefore reduces the real value of the transfer that the debtor must make to the creditor precisely when his marginal utility of consumption is high—namely, during a sudden stop. This would also seem to imply that local currency debt owed to nonresidents (quadrant III) is *less* risky than local currency debt owed to residents (quadrant IV) because, conditional on a sudden stop, the real value of the former declines during a sudden stop whereas the latter does not. While true given the sudden stop, this does not take into account the empirical observation that sudden stops are much more frequent in cross-border capital flows than in domestic borrowing-lending relationships. Thus, debt owed to nonresident creditors is generally more risky than that owed to residents, and debt owed in foreign currency is more risky than that owed in local currency—it follows that foreign currency–denominated debt owed to nonresidents is the *most* risky form of liability.

### 7.2.2  Maturity

Turning to the maturity of external liabilities (regardless of currency denomination), those with longer maturity (e.g., medium- and long-term debt) are preferable to short-term instruments. With short-term liabilities, the economy is subject to the risk that it is unable to roll over its debt and is therefore forced to suddenly generate a large current account surplus to repay the maturing debt. With longer-term instruments, although nonresident creditors may still rush for the exit—thus forcing the economy to run a current account surplus to repay them—they must first sell their claims to domestic residents, in the process suffering a capital loss as the attempt to sell the assets depresses their price. As with local currency liabilities, therefore, longer-dated instruments imply a larger decline in the value of the creditor's claim during periods of crisis, and a correspondingly smaller transfer of real resources from the debtor. (That the value of creditors' claims declines during the rush for the exit might, to some degree, also dissuade them from trying to exit the country.)

### 7.2.3 Debt versus Equity

The third dimension relevant to the riskiness of an external liability is its form: debt or equity. This determines the degree to which the creditor shares the risk of the individual investment, but not necessarily the aggregate external risk of the economy (i.e., the risk that the real exchange rate will need to depreciate and that a current account surplus will have to be generated). To the extent that returns are correlated across projects within a country, however, equity instruments imply that creditors are also sharing in the aggregate risk since the value of their claims—and therefore the current account surplus required to pay them—diminishes in times of crisis.

Finally, it is often asserted that foreign direct investment (FDI) is safer than portfolio investment—though it is not clear why, in principle, that should be the case independently of the form (i.e., debt versus equity) of the claim. However, FDI may be less risky for the borrowing country (and indeed we find this to be the case in chapter 4) because the creditor is less likely to rush for the exit during a crisis—either because the nature of the investment (e.g., green field or physical plant and equipment) makes it difficult to liquidate quickly without suffering a significant loss, or because the company is trying to build brand loyalty in the country, and therefore places a premium on remaining in the market.[6]

In sum, nonresident creditors are likely to be more skittish than resident creditors (partly because, lacking political representation, they may be more susceptible to implicit or explicit expropriation). They will rush for the exit precisely when the economy is suffering a sudden stop or other negative shock. Unless the country happens to have sufficient foreign reserves, repaying these creditors requires the economy to generate a current account surplus (with the corresponding real depreciation) whose magnitude depends on the risk-sharing characteristics of the liability. Repayment of short-term debt instruments in a foreign currency is the worst because the value of the creditor's claim is preserved even as the real exchange rate depreciates. But in itself, this would not justify government intervention because instruments

---

6. The one exception is FDI in the financial sector, where empirical evidence suggests that it may be more risky than portfolio flows (Reinhardt and Dell'Erba 2013). A possible explanation is that if the foreign investment takes the form of bank capital, it can have an amplified effect on domestic lending, potentially fueling a credit boom. Such risks, however, are more in the nature of flow imbalances (discussed in chapter 5) than balance-sheet vulnerabilities.

that preserve the value of the creditor's claim will also be the cheapest in which to borrow. Wedges (in the form of residency-based capital controls or currency-based prudential measures) between the market interest rate and the rate paid by domestic borrowers are only appropriate if the decentralized economy misprices or underestimates the risks. In the next section, we draw on recent models of prudential capital controls to flesh out a framework in which a Pigouvian tax on borrowing is optimal because atomistic individuals do not fully internalize the risks associated with their borrowing. (Throughout this chapter, we refer to a "tax," though the actual measure could be any equivalent administrative or quantitative restriction; indeed, for financial regulation, quantitative measures are commonly employed.)

## 7.3 A Welfare-Theoretic Framework

In standard welfare economics, where agents are assumed to be fully rational, the only justification for government intervention in the free market is the existence of externalities. In the real world, of course, there may be many borrowing and lending decisions that even *ex ante* are dubious, and *ex post* end in tears. Recent models of (prudential) capital controls nevertheless rest on the assumption that individual agents, though acting rationally, are led to borrow more than is socially optimal because they fail to take into account the externalities associated with their decisions. In this section, we draw on the work of Jeanne and Korinek (2010), Korinek (2011), and Bianchi (2011) to lay out such a theory of capital controls. (The same framework will form the basis of our discussion of multilateral considerations in chapter 10.)

### 7.3.1 Capital Controls

We consider a three-period $(-1, 0, +1)$ model of a representative agent who inhabits a small open economy. There is a traded good $(T)$ and a nontraded good $(N)$; to simplify, and without loss of generality, the latter is produced and consumed only in period 0 (the key action will take place in period 0). The representative agent maximizes his lifetime utility:

$$V_{-1} = Max \; u(c_{-1}^T) + \beta[u(c_0^T) + w(c_0^N)] + \beta^2 u(c_1^T) \tag{7.1}$$

subject to a sequence of flow budget constraints:

$$c_{-1}^T = y_{-1}^T + b_{-1} \tag{7.2}$$

$$c_0^T + pc_0^N = y_0^T + py_0^N + b_0 - (1+r)b_{-1} \tag{7.3}$$

$$c_1^T = y_1^T - (1+r)b_0 \tag{7.4}$$

where $V_{-1}$ is the value function (i.e., maximized value of utility) as of period $-1$, $c$ is consumption, $y$ is the endowment, $b$ is end-period debt, $(1+r)$ is the world interest rate, $p$ is the real exchange rate (price of nontraded goods relative to traded goods), $\beta$ is the agent's subjective discount rate, and $u(c^T)$ and $w(c^N)$ are components of his utility function, satisfying $u'(c^T) > 0$, $u''(c^T) < 0$ and $w'(c^N) > 0$, $w''(c^N) < 0$. Borrowing takes the form of one-period bonds, denominated in the traded good, and since there is a single representative agent, there is no distinction between net and gross liabilities.[7]

Market clearing in the nontraded good requires that consumption equal production:

$$c_0^N = y_0^N \tag{7.5}$$

In addition, there is a collateral constraint on borrowing such that the stock of outstanding liabilities at the end of period 0 must be less than some proportion, $\theta$, of income:

$$b_0 \leq \Theta = \theta(y_0^T + py_0^N) \tag{7.6}$$

Following Mendoza (2002) and Jeanne and Korinek (2010), the logic of this constraint is that borrowers can threaten to default at the end of period 0. In the event of default, creditors can at most seize some fraction $\theta$ of the borrower's income, convert it into traded goods at the prevailing exchange rate, and repatriate the funds.[8] An alternative, largely equivalent, interpretation is that borrowers need to post collateral, at least some of which—such as real estate—is nontradable.

The model is solved via dynamic programming, starting with period 1, and working backward. In period 1, the agent inherits an amount of debt $b_0$ as a result of his borrowing during period 0, so the value function is simply:

$$V_1(b_0) = u(y_1^T - (1+r)b_0)$$

---

7. Inasmuch as balance sheets cannot be consolidated across different agents in the economy (i.e., it does not help an indebted individual that his neighbor owns foreign assets), $b$ should be interpreted as gross liabilities.

8. In this literature, the results turn out to be quite sensitive to the exact specification of the collateral constraint (for instance, that it depends on the value of the collateral being a function of the current, rather than the future, real exchange). The model should therefore be considered as merely illustrative.

Stepping back in time, the period 0 value function is given by:

$$V_0(b_{-1}) = Max \ u(c_0^T) + w(c_0^N) + \beta V_1(b_0)$$

**Unconstrained equilibrium**  If the collateral constraint (7.6) does not bind, then the standard Euler equation obtains:

$$u_c(c_0^T) = \beta(1+r)u_c(c_1^T) \tag{7.7}$$

while intratemporal optimization implies:

$$pu_c(c_0^T) = w_c(c_0^N)$$

The impact of higher inherited debt may be found by totally differentiating (7.7), and using the budget constraint (7.3) and the market clearing condition for nontraded goods (7.5):

$$\frac{db_0}{(1+r)db_{-1}} = \frac{u_{cc}(c_0^T)}{u_{cc}(c_0^T) + \beta(1+r)^2 u_{cc}(c_1^T)} > 0 \tag{7.8}$$

$$0 > \frac{dc_0^T}{(1+r)db_{-1}} = \frac{-\beta(1+r)^2 u_{cc}(c_1^T)}{u_{cc}(c_0^T) + \beta(1+r)^2 u_{cc}(c_1^T)} > -1 \tag{7.9}$$

$$\frac{dp}{db_{-1}} = \frac{-pu_{cc}(c_0^T)}{u_c(c_0^T)} \frac{dc_0^T}{db_{-1}} < 0 \tag{7.10}$$

These comparative statics imply that if the borrower inherits more debt from period −1, he will want to roll over some of that debt by borrowing more in period 0 (cutting consumption, but by less than one-for-one with the larger stock of inherited debt). In turn, to induce the agent to reduce consumption of the traded good, its relative price must increase; that is, the real exchange rate (the price of nontraded goods) must depreciate. Finally, the marginal effect of higher inherited debt on the period 0 value function is:

$$\frac{dV_0}{db_{-1}} = u_c(c_0^T)\frac{dc_0^T}{db_{-1}} - \beta(1+r)u_c(c_1^T)\frac{db_0}{db_{-1}} \quad \text{or} \quad \frac{dV_0}{(1+r)db_{-1}} = -u_c(c_0^T) \tag{7.11}$$

That is, the cost of inheriting an additional dollar of debt is simply the marginal utility of the traded good.

**Constrained equilibrium**  If the collateral constraint (7.6) *does* bind, then $b_0 = \Theta = \theta(y_0^T + py_0^N)$, and the consumer's only first-order condition is:

$$pu_c(c_0^T) = w_c(c_0^N)$$

The individual agent takes the real exchange rate, and thus the collateral constraint as given; for the atomistic agent, therefore, the collateral constraint is a fixed number ($\Theta = \bar{\Theta}$), invariant to the agent's actions. The budget constraint (7.3) then implies:

$$\left.\frac{dc_0^T}{(1+r)db_{-1}}\right|_{\Theta=\bar{\Theta}} = -1; \quad \left.\frac{db_0}{(1+r)db_{-1}}\right|_{\Theta=\bar{\Theta}} = 0 \tag{7.12}$$

Thus, at the margin, consumption of the traded good must take the full brunt of the higher inherited debt, as no further borrowing is possible when the collateral constraint is binding. The marginal impact of inheriting more debt in period 0, *as evaluated by the atomistic agent*, is:

$$\left.\frac{dV_0}{(1+r)db_{-1}}\right|_{\Theta=\bar{\Theta}} = -u_c(c_0^T) \tag{7.13}$$

In equilibrium, however, the real exchange rate must depreciate:

$$dp = \frac{-pu_{cc}(c_0^T)}{u_c(c_0^T)} dc_0^T < 0 \tag{7.14}$$

In turn, the real depreciation tightens the collateral constraint, so the *equilibrium* effect of inheriting more debt on period 0 consumption, and on period 0 borrowing is:

$$\frac{dc_0^T}{(1+r)db_{-1}} = -\left(1 + \theta y_0^N \frac{pu_{cc}(c_0^T)}{u_c(c_0^T)}\right)^{-1} < -1 = \left.\frac{dc_0^T}{(1+r)db_{-1}}\right|_{\Theta=\bar{\Theta}} \tag{7.15}$$

$$\frac{db_0}{(1+r)db_{-1}} = \theta y_0^N dp < 0 \tag{7.16}$$

Contrasting (7.15)–(7.16) to (7.8)–(7.9), when the collateral constraint binds, the contractionary impact of inheriting more debt is amplified: consumption falls by more than one-for-one, the real exchange rate depreciation is greater, and the resulting tightening of the collateral constraint means that borrowing in period 0 must *decrease* rather than increase as it would in the unconstrained equilibrium. Notice, moreover, that this effect arises because part of the borrower's income and collateral consists of nontraded goods ($y_0^N > 0$). If the borrower was fully hedged (both his debt and his income were denominated in traded goods, or both were denominated in nontraded goods), then this tightening of the collateral constraint—and the inefficiency of the decentralized economy (as described below)—would not arise.

The effect on the value function is:

$$dV_0 = u_c(c_0^T)dc_0^T - \beta(1+r)u_c(c_1^T)db_0 = u_c(c_0^T)dc_0^T + \lambda db_0 \qquad (7.17)$$

where $\lambda \equiv u_c(c_0^T) - \beta(1+r)u_c(c_1^T) > 0,$ because when the collateral constraint binds, period 0 consumption is lower than it would be optimally and the marginal utility of consumption is correspondingly higher, $u_c(c_0^T) > \beta(1+r)u_c(c_1^T)$. Substituting (7.15) and (7.16) into (7.17) yields:[9]

$$\frac{dV_0}{(1+r)db_{-1}} = -u_c(c_0^T) + \lambda \frac{db_0}{(1+r)db_{-1}} \qquad (7.18)$$

If the collateral constraint does not bind, then $\lambda = 0$, and the marginal impact of higher inherited debt is simply the marginal utility of traded-good consumption. If the constraint does bind, however, then the marginal impact of inheriting more debt on welfare is greater (more negative) since from (7.16), $db_0/[(1+r)\,db_{-1}] < 0$.

**Optimal intervention in the decentralized economy**   As demonstrated above, the disutility of inheriting more debt is greater if the collateral constraint binds in the current period. In itself, that does not justify government intervention. The critical insight, however, comes from comparing (7.18) to (7.13). When the constraint does not bind, then the welfare impact of higher debt as evaluated by atomistic agents (7.13) coincides with its equilibrium effect (7.18). But when the constraint does bind, since $\lambda = 0$ and $db_0 < 0$, the *equilibrium (negative) effect of higher inherited debt is greater than that calculated by atomistic agents.*

In essence, the decentralized economy underestimates the value of liquidity because atomistic agents do not take full account of the impact of higher debt on the collateral constraint via the real exchange rate. This has important implications for domestic balance sheets. First, the decentralized economy will have too much debt. This can be seen by considering the first-order condition for the borrowing decision in period −1:

$$u_c(c_{-1}^T) = -\beta(dV_0/db_{-1})|_{\Theta = \bar{\Theta}}$$

If the collateral constraint binds in period 0 (or if there is some likelihood that it will bind, so $dV_0/db_{-1}$ is the probability weighted average

---

9.   $dV_0 = u_c(c_0^T)dc_0^T - \beta(1+r)u_c(c_1^T)db_0 = u_c(c_0^T)dc_0^T - u_c(c_0^T)db_0 + u_c(c_0^T)db_0 - \beta(1+r)u_c(c_1^T)db_0,$ or $dV_0 = u_c(c_0^T)[dc_0^T - db_0] + \lambda db_0,$ then from the budget constraint (7.3), and market clearing in nontraded goods, $dc_0^T - db_0 = -(1+r)db_{-1};$ hence $dV_0/(1+r)db_{-1} = -u_c(c_0^T) + \lambda db_0/(1+r)db_{-1}.$

of the binding and nonbinding cases), then $-\beta(dV_0/db_{-1})$ as calculated by the social planner is greater than the value calculated by the decentralized economy. It follows that consumption in period $-1$, and therefore borrowing in period $-1$, will be *lower* under the social planner's solution. This excessive borrowing by the decentralized economy is the basis for imposing capital controls (a tax on external borrowing) in period $-1$.

The intuition is that when the constraint binds, it is endogenous to the real exchange rate: a more depreciated exchange rate ($dp < 0$) tightens the collateral constraint. But individual borrowers take the real exchange rate as given when making their borrowing decisions. Therefore, they do not recognize that bequeathing more debt to period 0 will have an amplified effect on the collateral constraint—tightening it not only one-for-one by the higher inherited debt, but also by reducing the collateral value of nontraded output as the lower net supply of the traded good depreciates the real exchange rate. As noted above, none of these effects would obtain if the borrower's income consisted entirely of traded goods (i.e., if $y^N = 0$); the more unhedged the borrower, the greater the inefficiency of the decentralized equilibrium—and the higher the tax required to align private and social valuations.

To derive the optimal policy, consider the period $-1$ budget constraint (7.2), amended to include a tax on borrowing (with the revenue rebated lump sum to the representative agent):

$$c_{-1}^T = y_{-1}^T + (1 - \tau)b_{-1}$$

So the agent's first-order condition becomes: $(1 - \tau)u_c(c_{-1}^T) = -\beta(dV_0/db_{-1})|_{\Theta=\bar{\Theta}}$, whereas the social planner would set $u_c(c_{-1}^T) = -\beta(dV_0/db_{-1})$. Thus a tax equal to:

$$\tau = 1 - \frac{(dV_0/db_{-1})|_{\Theta=\bar{\Theta}}}{(dV_0/db_{-1})}$$

would implement the social planner's optimum. Since $(dV_0/db_{-1})|_{\Theta=\bar{\Theta}}/(dV_0/db_{-1}) \leq 1$, the optimal tax will be nonnegative, $\tau \geq 0$. It bears emphasizing that the tax is imposed *ex ante* in order to reduce borrowing to the level that would be undertaken by a social planner who takes into account the effect of such borrowing on the likelihood that the collateral constraint will bind in the future. Once the collateral constraint does bind, the social planner's borrowing and that of the decentralized economy essentially coincide (both are limited by the collateral constraint) and the tax can be set to zero.[10] The optimal tax on external borrowing is therefore cyclical—rising during surges, and falling when inflows subside and the financing constraint binds—although simulations by Bianchi (2011) suggest that much of the welfare gains can be captured by a constant tax.

As Korinek (2011) notes, not only will the decentralized economy have too much external debt, the structure of its liabilities will be sub-optimally risky as well. Suppose, for instance, that there are two types of liabilities: liability $B$ that pays $(1+r_b)$ in the bad state of the world, and nothing in the good state—where the bad state, which occurs with probability $\rho$, means that output is low, $y^T = y_b^T$ (or the marginal utility of consumption is high). Liability $G$ pays $(1+r_g)$ in the good state and nothing in the bad state, where the good state, which occurs with probability $(1-\rho)$, means that output is high (or the marginal utility of consumption is low), $y^T = y_g^T > y_b^T$. In general, different types of liabilities can be modeled as combinations of these two fundamental liabilities, $B$ and $G$. Thus FX-denominated debt, which—barring default—makes the same payout in the good and bad states of the world, can be viewed as an equally weighted average of $B$ and $G$ liabilities; local currency debt, or equity, pays less in the bad state of the world and would be more in the nature of a $G$ liability. In the bad state, where output is low, the collateral constraint (7.6) is assumed to bind; in the good state, it does not. In addition, creditors are assumed to be risk averse and willing to pay a premium against the bad state of the world in the sense that they are willing to accept a lower expected return for the $B$ liability (because it pays out in the bad state of the world): $\rho(1+r_b)<(1-\rho)(1+r_g)$.[11]

Now in period −1, the borrower must decide not only how much to borrow, but also the financing mix between $B$- and $G$-type liabilities:

$$V_{-1} = Max\ u(y_{-1}^T + b_{-1}^B + b_{-1}^G) + \beta(\rho V_0(y_B, (1+r_b)b_{-1}^B)$$
$$+ (1-\rho)V_0(y_G, (1+r_g)b_{-1}^G))$$

---

10. If the collateral constraint may be more binding in the future, then the social planner would want to maintain some positive tax to reduce borrowing below the constrained amount, but this tax would nevertheless be lower than it would be in normal times or during a surge.

11. As a result, it would be cheaper (*ex ante*) to borrow in the form of $B$-liabilities, though from the borrower's perspective they have worse risk-sharing characteristics (e.g., the popularity of FX-denominated mortgages in Eastern Europe before the global financial crisis in 2008–2009 because borrowing in euros or Swiss Francs was cheaper than borrowing in local currency).

The first-order conditions characterizing the decentralized economy's issuance of each type of debt are:

$$u_c(c_{-1}^T) = -(1 - \rho)(1 + r_g)\beta(dV_0/db_{-1}^G)_{\Theta=\bar{\Theta}}$$

$$u_c(c_{-1}^T) = -\rho(1 + r_b)\beta(dV_0/db_{-1}^B)_{\Theta=\bar{\Theta}}$$

In the good state, the collateral constraint does not bind, so the decentralized economy and the social planner evaluate the effect of higher debt equally. But in the bad state, it does bind, so the decentralized economy underestimates the (negative) impact of the debt on marginal utility $|(dV_0/db_{-1}^B)_{\Theta=\bar{\Theta}}| < |(dV_0/db_{-1}^B)|$. Since $u_{cc}(c_{-1}^T) < 0$, and $c_{-1}^T$ is increasing in $b_{-1}$, it follows that, relative to the decentralized economy, the social planner would choose to borrow less in the form of liabilities that have to pay out in the bad state of the world, such as FX-denominated debt, and relatively more in those types of liabilities that pay in the good state of the world, such as local currency debt or equity. (Since the collateral constraint might bind for the $B$-liability, the social planner would also choose to borrow less in absolute terms.) Therefore, the tax necessary to make atomistic borrowers correctly internalize the effect of their borrowing will be increasing in the riskiness of the liability. By means of illustration, Korinek (2011) calculates the *ex ante* optimal taxes that should have prevailed in Indonesia prior to the 1997 crisis on various types of liabilities. Based on his calculations, the highest tax rate, at 1.5 percent, should have been applied to US dollar–denominated debt, one of the riskiest forms of liabilities; the optimal tax on local currency (rupiah) debt would be considerably lower, at 0.4 percent. Even equity should be subject to some tax, as international investors generally sell stocks during a crisis (despite realizing a loss) and seek to repatriate the proceeds, putting downward pressure on the exchange rate. The optimal tax rate on equity (0.3 percent), however, is lower than that on local currency debt, reflecting its better risk-sharing properties. To the extent that FDI is less subject to such panic liquidation and repatriation, the optimal tax would be yet lower.

## 7.4 Capital Controls versus Prudential Measures

The model presented above provides a formal, welfare-theoretic justification for capital controls—that is, wedges between resident borrowers and the nonresident creditors. But since (as is typical of such models) it assumes that all liabilities consist of one-period debt that is both denominated in foreign currency and owed to a nonresident creditor, it conflates the various dimensions of the liability's riskiness. Thus, the model cannot tell us whether the optimal intervention is a capital control (a wedge between borrowers and lenders that depends on the residency of the parties to the transaction), a currency-based prudential measure (a wedge that depends on the currency denomination of the transaction), or a nondiscriminatory macroprudential measure (a wedge that depends on neither). Of course, there may be instances where it makes no practical difference which measure is applied. For instance, if only nonresidents lend in foreign currency, and nonresidents lend only in foreign currency, then it is immaterial whether the country imposes a capital control or a currency-based prudential measure.[12] But in general, the optimal tax rate will depend on *each* of the dimensions discussed in section 7.2—the form (debt or equity) and maturity of the liability, the degree to which the liability is hedged (i.e., the currency denomination of the liability relative to that of the borrower's assets or income), and whether the liability is owed to resident or to nonresident creditors.

While the optimal wedge should be calibrated to each of these dimensions, many commonly used measures differentiate according to only a subset of them—so in principle multiple measures may need to be applied to achieve the theoretically optimal policy intervention. In reality, this may not be practical: the administrative, compliance, and distortionary costs will outweigh the benefits—and for a variety of reasons, some measures may not be available or implementable. In chapter 11, we discuss how policy makers might proceed pragmatically with the available instrument set. Here we simply catalog the extent to which various measures can differentiate between the risk characteristics of the transaction—which depends, also, on whether there is a direct relationship between the creditor and the end-borrower (e.g., firms or households borrowing directly from foreign banks (or their branches), and corporate issuances on foreign capital markets), or whether the flows are being intermediated through the domestic banking system (see figure 7.1 and table 7.2).

---

12. By analogy, in trade theory, there are circumstances in which optimal intervention is a consumption tax, but it may make no practical difference whether the government imposes a consumption tax or a tariff when the country does not produce the imported good and there is no import-competing sector.

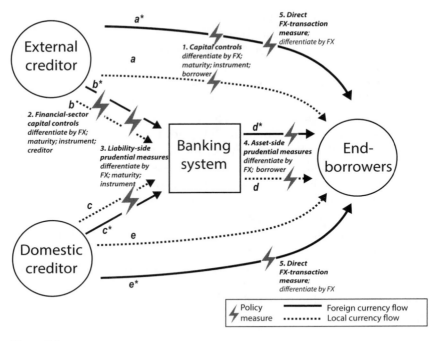

**Figure 7.1**
Capital flows and policy measures.
*Source*: Authors' illustration.

### 7.4.1 Capital Controls

Controls on capital inflows apply to cross-border flows between non-resident creditors and resident borrowers. When flows take the form of direct borrowing from abroad by the household or corporate sectors (denoted $a$ and $a^*$ for flows denominated in local and foreign currency, respectively, in figure 7.1), a capital control can be applied to tax such flows. This would automatically differentiate between loans from resident creditors (to which the capital control does not apply) and those from nonresident creditors—which, as the discussion in section 7.2 suggests, would be appropriate inasmuch as the latter are more risky. Moreover, the tax rate could be varied according to the currency denomination of the liability, its form (portfolio debt, portfolio equity, foreign direct investment), and maturity—and the extent to which the borrower is hedged (for instance, households could be prohibited from borrowing in foreign currency, whereas firms—especially those with export revenues—could be allowed greater latitude).

**Table 7.2**
Potential differentiation of policy measures by risk characteristics of liability flows.

| Measure | When applied to | Example | Allows differentiation by | | | |
|---|---|---|---|---|---|---|
| | | | Instrument or maturity | Currency | Creditor | End-borrower |
| *Capital control* | | | | | | |
| Economy-wide | Direct lending from abroad | Tax or URR | Yes | Yes | Yes | Yes |
| Financial sector–specific | External lending intermediated through domestic banking system | Prohibition or limit on external borrowing | Yes | Yes | Yes | No |
| *Prudential measure* | | | | | | |
| Liability-side | External lending intermediated through domestic banking system | RR | Yes | Yes | No | No |
| | Domestic lending intermediated through domestic banking system | RR | Yes | Yes | No | No |
| Asset-side | External lending intermediated through domestic banking system | Capital charges | Yes | Yes | No | Yes |
| | Domestic lending intermediated through domestic banking system | Capital charges | Yes | Yes | No | Yes |
| *Direct foreign currency—transactions measure* | Domestic or external FX-denominated lending | Prohibition on FX contracts for capital transactions | No | Yes | No | No |

*Source:* Authors' illustration.
*Notes:* URR = unremunerated reserve requirement; RR = reserve requirement.

Capital controls on direct borrowing from abroad are thus highly customizable to the riskiness of the liability; at least in principle, therefore, they may be calibrated to the theoretically optimal intervention. At the same time, it is worth noting that if there are other risky flows— for instance, foreign currency–denominated lending by residents (flows $c^*$ and $e^*$ in figure 7.1), who might also rush for the exit during a sudden stop or crisis—then capital inflow controls will not suffice: prudential or other measures will be required as well.[13]

When flows are intermediated through the domestic banking system (flows $b$ and $b^*$), capital controls can still be applied, though in this case they could be financial-sector specific measures that apply to banks' own borrowing from abroad (of course, these could be a subset of economy-wide measures that apply to both the financial and the nonfinancial sectors). These measures can be calibrated to the currency denomination and form or maturity of the liability (e.g., to penalize banks' excessive reliance on wholesale funding), but they do not differentiate according to the end-borrower's characteristics (e.g., whether the funds are being on-lent to firms that have foreign exchange receipts or to poorly hedged households). For the latter, the capital control would need to be combined with a prudential measure that applies to the asset side of banks' balance sheets (see discussion below). Furthermore, as above, if there are risky flows from resident creditors that are intermediated through the domestic banking system (e.g., foreign currency deposits), $c^*$, then (liability-side) prudential measures will be required as well.

### 7.4.2 Prudential Measures

Prudential measures, by definition, apply only to flows (whether from resident or nonresident creditors) that are intermediated by the banking system, possibly differentiating by the currency denomination of the flow (flows $b$ and $b^*$, $c$ and $c^*$). They may operate on the liability side, or on the asset side of banks' balance sheets:

• *Liability-side prudential measures*, such as higher reserve requirements on foreign currency deposits or on noncore liabilities, can differentiate by currency denomination and the form of the liability. The advantage

---

13. To reiterate, here we are discussing only *ex ante* measures intended to mitigate the impact on the economy of a sudden stop (or capital flow reversal). In the event of a crisis, other measures—e.g., controls on capital outflows—might need to be considered, but that is beyond the scope of this book.

of these measures is that they cover risky lending by both resident and nonresident creditors. Their disadvantage is that they do not allow differentiation between resident and nonresident creditors, as would be optimal if nonresident creditors are more likely to rush for the exit, and repaying them entails a larger real depreciation. (If a prudential measure does differentiate between resident and nonresident creditors, then it constitutes a capital control.) Moreover, as with financial-sector specific capital controls, liability-side prudential measures do not allow differentiation across end-borrowers (e.g., to distinguish between unhedged households and hedged corporations).

• *Asset-side prudential measures*, such as capital charges, apply to flows between the banking system and end-borrowers (flows $d$ and $d^*$). Such measures allow the implicit tax rate to be calibrated to the risk posed to the ultimate borrower's balance sheet—for instance, higher capital charges might be applied on foreign currency–denominated loans to unhedged borrowers. What these measures do not allow is differentiation according to the riskiness of the original sources of the funds—for instance, short-term foreign currency deposits of nonresidents compared with local currency savings of residents. To protect the bank's own balance sheet, open FX limits need to be imposed in addition to any asset-side prudential measures—but there are other risks such as maturity mismatches (short-term liabilities, long-term assets) to which banks might still be exposed.

### 7.4.3 Direct Foreign-Currency Transactions Measures

Although most lending is intermediated by the domestic banking system, there may be instances where foreign currency flows from both resident and nonresident creditors bypass the banking system (flows $a^*$ and $e^*$). While capital controls can be applied to prevent unhedged borrowers from assuming excessive FX risk on loans from nonresident creditors (as discussed above), the only way to do so on loans from resident creditors would be a general ban on foreign currency–denominated capital transactions. In some countries, for instance, it is unlawful to write contracts denominated in foreign currency (i.e., such contracts are unenforceable in the law courts). The disadvantage of such measures is that they cannot differentiate according to either the characteristics of the borrower or the residency of the creditor, and thus constitute a relatively blunt tool.

## 7.5   Conclusion

As capital inflows accumulate into stocks of liabilities, they can result in balance-sheet vulnerabilities: heavy indebtedness or maturity or currency mismatches relative to the balance sheet or repayment capacity of the borrower. Existing mismatches may be exacerbated by large inflows, but these balance-sheet vulnerabilities are distinct from the macroeconomic imbalances analyzed in chapters 5 and 6, which are largely a flow phenomenon (i.e., occurring over an interval of time) rather than a stock phenomenon.

Formal models imply that atomistic agents in a decentralized economy will borrow too much, and will choose an excessively risky liability structure because they fail to internalize the impact of their borrowing decisions on the economy-wide real exchange rate and collateral constraint. There is thus a role for policy; specifically, some form of Pigouvian tax (or equivalent quantitative measure) that acts as a wedge between creditors and borrowers, calibrated to the likelihood that the collateral constraint will become binding, and to the magnitude of adjustment that the economy will need to undertake in the event of a sudden stop in which investors rush for the exit.

The theoretically optimal tax would vary according to the stock of liabilities (in relation to the borrower's capacity to repay, such as income or assets); the composition of the liability, whether the liability is owed to resident or to nonresident creditors; and the extent to which the end-borrower is hedged against the relevant currency risk. Against highly risky forms of liabilities, there may be structural (i.e., permanent) measures—capital controls or prudential policies (e.g., a ban on foreign currency–denominated lending to unhedged borrowers). But typically the measure should include a cyclical component. This is because the optimal tax depends on the cyclical position of capital flows, as the likelihood that the country suffers a *future* sudden stop is at maximum at the peak of the cycle. (Likewise, the tax could be removed or reduced if and when the sudden stop occurs.) More generally, the willingness of the authorities to tolerate risky liabilities might be a function of how urgently the country needs foreign funds. If there is a dearth of external financing, policy makers might be willing to accept more risky forms of liabilities; if a surfeit, there would be less reason to do so, and the tax could be raised correspondingly. Real-world measures achieve the appropriate differentiation to varying degrees, and the ultimate choice of measure must take into account not only the most pertinent risk but also practical, legal, and institutional considerations; these are taken up in chapter 11.

## Chapter 7 Appendix: Risk-Sharing Characteristics of External Liabilities

In this appendix, we show formally why external liabilities—that is, those owed to nonresidents—denominated in foreign currency ("traded goods") have worse risk-sharing characteristics than the same liabilities owed to residents. In particular, the marginal disutility of effecting the requisite transfer to nonresident creditors will be greater because of the "transfer problem" (i.e., the borrower would have to generate a current account surplus by squeezing consumption of the traded good, whose marginal utility will be higher during a sudden stop).

### A.7.1   Nonresident Creditor

The representative agent lives for three periods $-1$, $0$, $+1$. Period $-1$ is not modeled explicitly, but the representative agent is assumed to have contracted some debt during that period, which must be repaid in period 0. Depending on whether there is a sudden stop, he may or may not be able to borrow again in period 0 (essentially rolling over the inherited debt). There are two goods in the economy (traded and nontraded); for simplicity, and without loss of generality, the agent is assumed to consume only the traded good ($T$) in period $+1$.

The agent's maximization problem is therefore:

$$V = Max\ u(c_0^T) + w(c_0^N) + \beta u(c_1^T) \tag{7.19}$$

Subject to the flow budget constraints:

$$c_1^T = y_1^T - (1 + r)b_0 \tag{7.20}$$

$$c_0^T + pc_0^N = y_0^T + py_0^N + b_0 - (1 + r)b_{-1} \tag{7.21}$$

where $c^T$, $c^N$ are consumption of the traded and nontraded goods, respectively; $b_{-1}$ and $b_0$ are the stocks of debt at the end of periods $-1$ and $0$, respectively; $\rho$ is the real exchange rate (the relative price of nontraded goods); and $y_0^T, y_0^N, y_1^T$ are fixed endowments of the goods.

In addition to the flow budget constraints, the agent may face a sudden-stop constraint in period 0—an exogenous limit on end-period

0 debt that applies even if the agent respects the intertemporal budget constraint (7.20)–(7.21). The sudden-stop constraint is simply:

$$b_0 \le \bar{b}_0 \tag{7.22}$$

Market clearing in the nontraded good implies:

$$c_0^N = y_0^N$$

**Unconstrained equilibrium**   When the sudden-stop constraint does not bind, the standard first-order conditions apply:

$$u_c(c_0^T) = \beta(1+r)u_c(c_1^T) \tag{7.23}$$

$$pu_c(c_0^T) = w_c(c_0^N) \tag{7.24}$$

The effect of inheriting more debt in period 0 from period $-1$ can be calculated as:

$$dV = u_c(c_0^T)dc_0^T + w_c(c_0^N)dc_0^N + \beta u_c(c_1^T)dc_1^T \tag{7.25}$$

Using (7.20)–(7.21) to substitute for $dc_0^T$ and $dc_1^T$:

$$dV = u_c(c_0^T)[db_0 - (1+r)db_{-1}] - \beta(1+r)u_c(c_1^T)db_0 \tag{7.26}$$

Finally, using the first-order condition (7.23) yields:

$$dV = -u_c(c_0^T)(1+r)db_{-1} \tag{7.27}$$

**Constrained equilibrium**   Proceeding as above for the case where the sudden-stop constraint *does* bind:

$$d\bar{V} = u_c(\bar{c}_0^T)[db_0 - (1+r)db_{-1}] - \beta(1+r)u_c(\bar{c}_1^T)db_0 \tag{7.28}$$

where bars indicate constrained-equilibrium values. Rearranging (7.28):

$$d\bar{V} = -(1+r)u_c(\bar{c}_0^T)db_{-1} + [u_c(\bar{c}_0^T) - \beta(1+r)u_c(\bar{c}_1^T)]db_0 \tag{7.29}$$

When constraint binds, $[u_c(\bar{c}_0^T) - \beta(1+r)u_c(\bar{c}_1^T)] > 0$ but $db_0 = 0$, therefore:

$$d\bar{V} = -u_c(\bar{c}_0^T)(1+r)db_{-1} \tag{7.30}$$

Comparing (7.27) and (7.30), since $\bar{c}_0^T < c_0^T$ when the borrowing constraint binds (because period 0 consumption of the traded good must take the full brunt of the higher inherited debt, since $db_0 = 0$, hence

$dc_0^T = -(1+r)db_{-1})$, the marginal utility is higher $u_c(\overline{c}_0^T) > u_c(c_0^T)$, and therefore repaying the inherited debt is more costly in utility terms during a sudden stop.

## A.7.2   Resident Creditor

Suppose that the agent owes the debt to a resident creditor rather than to a nonresident creditor, and that the resident creditor has homothetic preferences identical to those of the debtor. In that case, even if the debt is denominated in the traded good, once the debtor makes the payment to the creditor, the creditor spends it on the same basket of traded and nontraded goods. Let the domestic agents (both debtors and creditors) spend a fraction $\mu$ of their income on the traded good, and $(1-\mu)$ on the nontraded good. The debt repayment can then be modeled as an equivalent decrease in the borrower's endowments of the two goods, where the real exchange rate is constant because preferences of the domestic borrower and creditor are assumed to be identical and homothetic:

$$dy_0^{*T} = -\mu(1+r)db_{-1}; \quad d(py_0^{*N}) = (1-\mu)(1+r)db_{-1} \tag{7.31}$$

**Unconstrained equilibrium**   When the sudden-stop constraint does not bind, the equilibrium is identical to the unconstrained equilibrium with a nonresident creditor. Denoting the equilibrium when the creditor is a domestic resident by an asterisk, the effect on utility of the same higher inherited debt, $db_{-1}$, is given by:

$$dV^* = u_c(c_0^{*T})dc_0^{*T} + w_c(c_0^{*N})dc_0^{*N} + \beta u_c(c_1^{*T})dc_1^{*T} \tag{7.32}$$

Using $dc_0^{*N} = dy_0^{*N}$; $dc_0^{*T} = dy_0^{*T} + db_0^*$ :

$$dV^* = u_c(c_0^{*T})db_0^* - \mu(1+r)u_c(c_0^{*T})db_{-1} \\ -(1-\mu)(1+r)w_c(c_0^{*N})db_{-1}/p^* + \beta u_c(c_1^{*T})dc_1^{*T} \tag{7.33}$$

From the intratemporal first-order condition: $p^* u_c(c_0^{*T}) = w_c(c_0^{*N})$

$$dV^* = u_c(c_0^{*T})db_0^* - u_c(c_0^{*T})(1+r)db_{-1} + \beta u_c(c_1^{*T})dc_1^{*T} \tag{7.34}$$

and since $dc_1^{*T} = -(1+r)db_0^*$:

$$dV^* = u_c(c_0^{*T})db_0^* - u_c(c_0^{*T})(1+r)db_{-1} - \beta(1+r)u_c(c_1^{*T})db_0^* \tag{7.35}$$

Finally, the Euler condition implies $u_c(c_0^{*T}) = \beta(1+r)u_c(c_1^{*T})$

$$dV^* = -u_c(c_0^{*T})(1+r)db_{-1} \tag{7.36}$$

In the unconstrained equilibrium, the borrower's consumption of traded goods in period 0 is the same regardless of whether the creditor is nonresident or resident: $c_0^{*T} = c_0^T$, hence $dV^* = dV$; the marginal disutility of inheriting more debt is therefore the same regardless of the identity of the creditor.

**Constrained equilibrium**    Next consider the case where the sudden-stop constraint (now on borrowing from the resident) does bind. From (7.35):

$$d\bar{V}^* = u_c(\bar{c}_0^{*T})db_0^* - u_c(\bar{c}_0^{*T})(1+r)db_{-1} - \beta(1+r)u_c(\bar{c}_1^{*T})db_0^* \qquad (7.37)$$

But when the sudden-stop constraint binds, $db_0^* = 0$, so:

$$d\bar{V}^* = -u_c(\bar{c}_0^{*T})(1+r)db_{-1} \qquad (7.38)$$

Comparing (7.38) to (7.30), $\bar{c}_0^{*T} > \bar{c}_0^T$ because from (7.31), $|dy_0^T| < -(1+r)db_{-1}$. Recall that $dc_0^{*T} = dy_0^{*T} + db_0^*$, but when the constraint binds, $db_0^* = 0$, so $d\bar{c}_0^{*T} = dy_0^{*T}$ and since $dy_0^{*T} = -\mu(1+r)db_{-1}$, $d\bar{c}_0^{*T} = -\mu(1+r)db_{-1} > -(1+r)db_{-1} = d\bar{c}_0^T$. In response to higher inherited debt, the decline in period 0 consumption of the tradable good is smaller when the debt is owed to a resident creditor than when it is owed to a nonresident creditor (who can only consume traded goods). Since the *decline* in period 0 consumption is smaller when debt is owed to a domestic creditor, the level of consumption will be higher, $\bar{c}_0^{*T} > \bar{c}_0^T$, and the marginal utility of consumption correspondingly lower $u_c(\bar{c}_0^{*T}) < u_c(\bar{c}_0^T)$. It follows from (7.30) and (7.38) that $d\bar{V}^* > d\bar{V}$: when the sudden-stop constraint binds, the marginal *disutility* of inheriting more traded-good liabilities to nonresident creditors is greater than the marginal disutility of owing the same liabilities to resident creditors.

The intuition is simple. Since nonresident creditors can only consume traded goods, repaying the debt entails a depreciation of the real exchange rate when the sudden-stop constraint binds. But part of the borrower's income is in the form of nontraded goods. The example here is extreme in that the resident creditor is assumed to have identical preferences to the domestic borrower, so repaying to the resident creditor entails no depreciation of the real exchange rate. However, the result is general inasmuch as, even if the resident creditor consumes only a small proportion of nontraded goods, the nonresident creditor necessarily consumes none. Therefore, only in the limiting case in which the resident creditor consumes none of the nontraded good would the FX-denominated liabilities owed to resident creditors be as risky as the FX-denominated liabilities owed to nonresidents.

# 8    What Do Countries Do?

## 8.1   Introduction

In the preceding chapters, we laid out the theoretical foundation of how various macroeconomic policies, macroprudential measures, and capital controls can help mitigate the imbalances and vulnerabilities associated with capital flows. It is worth noting, however, that our prescription is quite at odds with the standard policy advice given to emerging market economies (EMEs) for coping with capital inflows. Traditionally, emerging markets were counseled not to impede inflows nor to intervene in the foreign exchange (FX) market, but rather to allow the currency to appreciate freely, and to tighten fiscal policy to counter overheating pressures if necessary. (Even monetary tightening was considered inadvisable lest it attract further inflows.[1]) But what do emerging markets do in practice? Have they been following the traditional advice, or do they come closer to behaving as the policy framework in chapters 5–7 suggests they should? That is the question we take up in this chapter.

Anecdotal evidence suggests that policy makers rely on a variety of instruments—at times deployed in combination—to deal with capital inflows. In the post–global financial crisis surge, for instance, EMEs adopted a host of policy tools to tackle the possible macroeconomic and financial-stability risks (table 8.1). Thus, Brazil intervened in the currency markets to stem appreciation pressures, raised the policy rate

---

1. IMF (2005b) reports that during the 1990s, the IMF staff gave advice on managing capital inflows to sixteen EMEs (out of a sample of twenty-seven EMEs), covering nineteen episodes of large inflows. In twelve of the cases, EMEs were explicitly advised to tighten fiscal policy; in fourteen cases, to allow greater exchange rate flexibility; in four cases, to tighten monetary policy; in nine cases, to sterilize intervention; in six, to liberalize capital outflows; in four cases, to tighten prudential measures; and in two cases, to tighten inflow controls.

**Table 8.1**
Policy responses in post–global financial crisis inflow surge, 2009Q2–2011Q2.

| | Magnitude of net inflows (in pct. of GDP)[a] | Reserve accumulation (in pct. of GDP)[b] | Policy rate[c] | Capital controls[d] | Macroprudential policies[e] |
|---|---|---|---|---|---|
| Brazil | 7.8 | 4.7 | Raised | Yes | Yes |
| India | 5.4 | 1.5 | Raised | Yes | Yes |
| Indonesia | 4.7 | 5.6 | Lowered | Yes | Yes |
| Korea, South | 2.3 | 4.5 | Raised | Yes | Yes |
| Peru | 11.1 | 6.7 | Raised | Yes | Yes |
| Poland | 11.4 | 5.0 | Raised | No | Yes |
| South Africa | 6.3 | 2.2 | Lowered | No[f] | No |
| Thailand | 5.9 | 10.6 | Raised | Yes | Yes |
| Turkey | 9.5 | 2.0 | Lowered | Yes | Yes |

*Sources:* IMF's IFS and WEO databases, Ahmed et al. 2015, and Akinci and Olmstead-Rumsey 2015.
a. Average quarterly net financial flows (in percent of GDP) over 2009Q2–2011Q2.
b. Average quarterly reserve flows (in percent of GDP) over 2009Q2–2011Q2.
c. Change in central bank policy rate between 2009Q2 and 2011Q2.
d. Tightening of capital controls (including measures that may act like them, e.g., foreign currency–based measures) over 2009Q2–2011Q2.
e. Tightening of macroprudential measures over 2009Q2–2011Q2.
f. South Africa liberalized controls on outflows in response to the surge in capital inflows.

in response to economic overheating, tightened macroprudential measures to address financial-stability risks, and introduced capital controls on debt and equity flows. During the same period, however, Indonesia responded by intervening in the FX markets, and by tightening both capital controls and macroprudential measures, but also by *lowering* the policy interest rate—while Poland relied on FX intervention and tightened monetary and macroprudential policies, but did not introduce capital controls.

As discussed earlier, this "portfolio" approach of using multiple instruments in the face of capital inflows makes sense when policy makers have several targets, there are (possibly convex) costs associated with the use of each instrument, and there is uncertainty about the effects of the instrument on the intended target. Nevertheless, the differences in specific instruments employed suggest that economic and structural considerations, as well as historical and institutional factors, may be at play in determining policy responses in practice.

Recognizing that the tools employed will depend on country circumstances, this chapter seeks to document systematic patterns in how emerging markets respond to capital inflows. One finding bears mentioning at the outset: we find no evidence that emerging market policy makers tighten aggregate fiscal policy in the face of capital inflows (see chapter appendix; table A.8.1 and figure A.8.1). By contrast, there is plenty of evidence that they use other policies—especially FX intervention—to manage the risks from capital inflows. While it is well known that fiscal levers take time to pull, budgets have their own cycles, and the whole budgetary process is often politically fraught, it is nonetheless striking that practice should differ so dramatically from the standard policy advice.

The rest of this chapter is organized as follows. Section 8.2 explores how monetary and exchange rate policies respond to capital inflows. Section 8.3 drills down to see whether this response differs according to the type of inflow. Section 8.4 turns to the less orthodox part of the tool kit—capital controls and macroprudential measures—to see how often these instruments are used in the face of inflows. Section 8.5 discusses whether, consistent with our prescription, policies are deployed in conjunction—especially in the face of inflow surges. Section 8.6 concludes.

## 8.2 Macroeconomic Policy Response

To track policy responses to capital inflows, we use quarterly data for the EMEs in our sample over the period 2005Q1–2013Q4.[2] A first look at the data suggests that both central bank policy rates and FX intervention—defined here as the change in foreign reserve assets (excluding valuation effects) scaled by GDP—react to capital flows in EMEs (figure 8.1). Changes in reserves tightly follow the ebbs and flows of capital, with a strong positive correlation between reserve accumulation and capital inflows. For the policy interest rate, the pattern is less clear, with the raw correlation suggesting mild countercyclicality whereby the policy rate increases during periods of inflows and decreases during reversals.

---

2. The sample period is selected to maximize cross-country coverage, as most EMEs have only recently begun to report the balance of payment (BOP) and national account statistics on a quarterly basis.

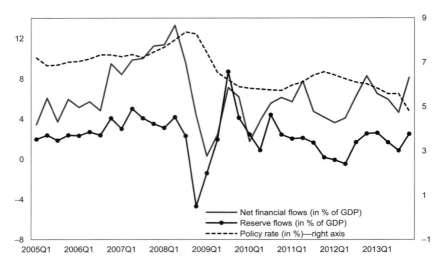

**Figure 8.1**
Capital flows, reserve accumulation, and policy rate in EMEs, 2005Q1–2013Q4.
*Source*: Authors' calculations based on the IMF's International Financial Statistics database.
*Notes*: Net financial flows exclude other investment liabilities of the general government. Statistics represent the average for the countries included in the sample.

### 8.2.1 Monetary Policy

More formal regression analysis, controlling for various exogenous factors such as US interest rates, global market volatility (proxied by the VIX index), and commodity prices, as well as for country-specific and quarter effects, suggests that EMEs typically raise policy rates in the face of capital inflows, with the effect statistically significant at the 5 percent level (table 8.2). Since inflows are usually expansionary and inflationary, this implies that the policy interest rate is used counter-cyclically, as an inflation-targeting framework would imply.[3] Yet looking at (selected) individual country policy response functions, it is apparent that many of the estimated coefficients are either negative or statistically insignificant (though all of the statistically significant coefficients are positive). This diversity is not surprising: where the inflows

---

3. Focusing on a subsample of eighteen EMEs with explicit inflation-targeting frameworks, the estimated coefficient on net capital flows (in percent of GDP) is positive but statistically insignificant (the policy interest rate does, however, respond to inflation and the output gap). Moreover, segmenting the full sample into periods of capital inflows versus outflows shows that the policy rate response is stronger to inflows than to outflows.

**Table 8.2**

Net capital flows and policy interest rate in EMEs, 2005Q1–2013Q4.

| | Net capital flows/GDP | Policy rate (lagged) | US interest rate | Global market volatility | Commodity prices | GFC | Obs. | $R^2$ |
|---|---|---|---|---|---|---|---|---|
| Full sample | 0.006** | 0.915*** | 0.055*** | 0.153 | 0.310*** | −0.456*** | 1,318 | 0.978 |
| | (0.002) | (0.018) | (0.010) | (0.099) | (0.092) | (0.141) | | |
| *Asia* | | | | | | | | |
| India | 0.002 | 0.759*** | 0.027 | −0.465 | 1.183*** | −0.419 | 36 | 0.916 |
| | (0.022) | (0.078) | (0.025) | (0.307) | (0.336) | (0.376) | | |
| Indonesia | −0.038 | 0.823*** | 0.012 | −0.910* | −0.093 | 0.311 | 36 | 0.884 |
| | (0.025) | (0.088) | (0.052) | (0.518) | (0.586) | (0.539) | | |
| Korea, South | 0.056*** | 0.976*** | 0.015 | −0.443** | 0.697*** | −0.236 | 36 | 0.950 |
| | (0.013) | (0.047) | (0.019) | (0.178) | (0.217) | (0.241) | | |
| Malaysia | −0.004 | 0.780*** | 0.025 | −0.236 | 0.478 | −0.363 | 20 | 0.908 |
| | (0.007) | (0.160) | (0.027) | (0.267) | (0.365) | (0.343) | | |
| Philippines | 0.024** | 0.885*** | 0.120*** | 0.407* | 0.709** | −0.389* | 36 | 0.896 |
| | (0.009) | (0.065) | (0.017) | (0.212) | (0.295) | (0.198) | | |
| Thailand | 0.007 | 0.839*** | 0.024 | −0.462* | 0.164 | −0.229 | 36 | 0.897 |
| | (0.007) | (0.065) | (0.029) | (0.247) | (0.279) | (0.313) | | |
| *Europe* | | | | | | | | |
| Czech Rep. | −0.001 | 1.067*** | 0.003 | −0.212 | 0.275 | −0.411 | 36 | 0.964 |
| | (0.005) | (0.039) | (0.021) | (0.177) | (0.188) | (0.275) | | |
| Hungary | 0.009 | 0.843*** | 0.075 | 0.759 | 0.182 | −0.030 | 36 | 0.849 |
| | (0.015) | (0.126) | (0.060) | (0.463) | (0.507) | (0.635) | | |
| Poland | 0.039*** | 0.887*** | 0.042*** | 0.086 | 0.493* | −0.443* | 36 | 0.900 |
| | (0.009) | (0.063) | (0.015) | (0.193) | (0.250) | (0.238) | | |
| Romania | 0.040** | 0.589*** | 0.060 | 0.777 | −0.317 | 0.354 | 36 | 0.883 |
| | (0.016) | (0.143) | (0.053) | (0.456) | (0.778) | (0.422) | | |

(continued)

**Table 8.2** (continued)

| | Net capital flows/GDP | Policy rate (lagged) | US interest rate | Global market volatility | Commodity prices | GFC | Obs. | $R^2$ |
|---|---|---|---|---|---|---|---|---|
| Russia | 0.005 (0.007) | 0.833*** (0.096) | -0.045* (0.025) | -0.104 (0.207) | -0.006 (0.273) | 1.257*** (0.291) | 36 | 0.937 |
| Turkey | -0.069 (0.051) | 0.965*** (0.047) | 0.260*** (0.079) | 0.314 (0.767) | 1.741* (0.938) | -2.552** (0.929) | 36 | 0.967 |
| *Latin America* | | | | | | | | |
| Brazil | -0.011 (0.050) | 0.962*** (0.068) | 0.036 (0.070) | -0.091 (0.577) | 0.872 (0.940) | -0.436 (0.949) | 36 | 0.925 |
| Chile | -0.001 (0.021) | 0.817*** (0.114) | 0.150** (0.071) | -0.193 (0.621) | 1.410 (1.006) | -1.371** (0.646) | 36 | 0.846 |
| Colombia | -0.009 (0.046) | 1.062*** (0.040) | 0.101** (0.037) | 0.083 (0.346) | 0.719 (0.492) | -1.695*** (0.427) | 36 | 0.963 |
| Mexico | 0.012 (0.012) | 1.188*** (0.074) | 0.102*** (0.023) | 0.448 (0.289) | 0.624 (0.439) | -1.642*** (0.350) | 23 | 0.977 |
| Peru | 0.002 (0.017) | 0.917*** (0.110) | 0.105* (0.056) | 0.269 (0.434) | 0.628 (0.514) | -0.997 (0.981) | 36 | 0.816 |
| *Middle East and Africa* | | | | | | | | |
| Jordan | -0.002 (0.004) | 0.896*** (0.050) | 0.030 (0.019) | -0.382* (0.196) | -0.266 (0.210) | -0.139 (0.220) | 36 | 0.950 |
| Morocco | -0.002 (0.003) | 0.872*** (0.160) | 0.010* (0.005) | -0.001 (0.045) | 0.045 (0.096) | -0.001 (0.061) | 36 | 0.804 |
| South Africa | -0.005 (0.014) | 1.164*** (0.033) | 0.072*** (0.020) | -0.216 (0.190) | 0.759*** (0.188) | -1.552*** (0.200) | 36 | 0.987 |

*Notes:* Dependent variable is central bank policy rate (in percent). Net capital flows are in percent of GDP. Global market volatility is log of VIX index. Commodity prices are in logs. US interest rate is inflation-adjusted 3-month T-bill rate. GFC is a binary variable (=1) for the global financial crisis (2008Q4–2009Q1). Total number of countries in the full sample is 41. All regressions include a constant and quarter effects. Full sample specification also includes country-fixed effects. Clustered (robust) standard errors reported in parentheses for panel (individual country) specifications. ***, **, and * indicate statistical significance at the 1, 5 and 10 percent levels, respectively.

are not especially expansionary, or if inflation nevertheless remains within target, the policy rate need not be increased (and may be lowered to reduce the incentive for capital to flow into the country). Indeed, as discussed in chapters 5 and 6, even in the face of inflationary pressures the optimal response may allow for monetary easing to reduce the incentive for further inflows when the policy interest rate is being used in conjunction with other policies that depress aggregate demand.

Whatever impact capital flows have on the policy interest rate, it comes through the behavior of inflation, the output gap, or the real exchange rate. Table 8.3 augments the specification with these three variables and shows that policy rates are raised in response to higher inflation or a larger output gap (i.e., GDP above potential), and lowered in response to real exchange rate appreciation (the latter effect being weaker but nevertheless statistically significant at the 10 percent level in the full sample). Adding these variables renders the coefficient on capital flows utterly insignificant in the panel specification, as well as in the vast majority of individual country regressions. Thus, with capital inflows generally being expansionary, the central bank tightens monetary policy to offset overheating of the economy; given inflation and the output gap, however, the central bank lowers its policy interest rate in the face of real exchange rate appreciation—as the framework developed in chapter 5 suggests that it should.

Among the other factors, the central bank policy rate responds positively to commodity prices and to US interest rates, but also exhibits a high degree of persistence (reflected by the estimated coefficient of the lagged policy rate term).[4] The coefficient on the dummy variable for the global financial crisis (GFC) shows that, controlling for other factors, policy rates were on average lowered significantly during the crisis.

A potential concern with these estimates is that capital flows may be responding to the domestic interest rate, in which case the estimated coefficients would be subject to endogeneity bias (with the bias going in *favor* of finding a spurious positive coefficient on the net capital flows variable). Instrumenting net capital flows with flows to other emerging markets in the region and applying the instrumental variable two-stage least squares (IV-2SLS) method, however, makes little difference to the

---

4. The fixed-effects estimation of models with lagged dependent variable can produce biased estimates (the Nickell bias). The bias (equal to $1/T$) is serious for short panels, but disappears as $T \to \infty$ (for our sample, $T=36$; so the fixed-effects estimator is likely to perform at least as well as many alternatives; Judson and Owen 1999). The results remain similar if the GMM estimation method for dynamic panels is applied.

**Table 8.3**

Net capital flows and policy interest rate in EMEs: Additional covariates.

| | Net capital flows/GDP | Policy rate (lagged) | US interest rate | Global market vol. | Commodity prices | GFC | Output gap | Change in REER | Inflation | Obs. | R² |
|---|---|---|---|---|---|---|---|---|---|---|---|
| Full sample | 0.002 (0.004) | 0.845*** (0.039) | 0.040*** (0.010) | 0.058 (0.079) | 0.012 (0.086) | -0.461*** (0.129) | 0.037* (0.020) | -0.007* (0.004) | 0.090*** (0.030) | 1,318 | 0.981 |
| *Asia* | | | | | | | | | | | |
| India | 0.004 (0.020) | 0.641*** (0.088) | 0.028 (0.019) | -0.433 (0.296) | 1.493** (0.639) | -0.001 (0.312) | 0.105 (0.062) | -0.005 (0.006) | -0.070 (0.063) | 36 | 0.961 |
| Indonesia | -0.046** (0.021) | 0.458*** (0.075) | -0.010 (0.037) | -0.268 (0.324) | -0.512 (0.450) | -0.412 (0.358) | 0.173 (0.185) | 0.009** (0.004) | 0.272*** (0.023) | 36 | 0.969 |
| Korea, South | 0.028*** (0.008) | 0.918*** (0.071) | 0.004 (0.014) | -0.305 (0.224) | 0.072 (0.208) | 0.044 (0.136) | 0.194*** (0.052) | 0.009** (0.004) | 0.038 (0.055) | 36 | 0.974 |
| Malaysia | -0.004 (0.006) | 0.686*** (0.162) | 0.017 (0.024) | -0.154 (0.307) | -0.229 (0.467) | 0.006 (0.509) | 0.113 (0.064) | 0.002 (0.012) | -0.027 (0.059) | 20 | 0.946 |
| Philippines | 0.018*** (0.007) | 0.670*** (0.102) | 0.086*** (0.025) | 0.248 (0.188) | 0.290 (0.281) | -0.549** (0.243) | 0.011 (0.057) | 0.002 (0.009) | 0.157* (0.083) | 36 | 0.919 |
| Thailand | 0.007 (0.010) | 0.799*** (0.048) | -0.017 (0.027) | -0.516* (0.256) | -0.090 (0.214) | 0.067 (0.365) | -0.020 (0.025) | -0.003 (0.008) | 0.151*** (0.036) | 36 | 0.947 |
| *Europe* | | | | | | | | | | | |
| Czech Rep. | -0.003 (0.005) | 0.879*** (0.096) | 0.012 (0.019) | -0.033 (0.149) | -0.098 (0.308) | -0.252 (0.234) | 0.077** (0.034) | 0.011* (0.006) | -0.036 (0.049) | 36 | 0.972 |
| Hungary | -0.013 (0.011) | 0.694*** (0.109) | 0.011 (0.067) | 0.967** (0.443) | -0.646 (0.487) | 0.436 (0.674) | 0.221*** (0.038) | 0.002 (0.007) | 0.101 (0.072) | 36 | 0.927 |
| Poland | 0.003 (0.008) | 0.749*** (0.053) | 0.024** (0.011) | 0.157 (0.206) | 0.324 (0.209) | -0.460*** (0.137) | 0.225*** (0.046) | 0.005 (0.004) | 0.131** (0.058) | 36 | 0.965 |

| | (1) | (2) | (3) | (4) | (5) | (6) | (7) | (8) | (9) | N | R² |
|---|---|---|---|---|---|---|---|---|---|---|---|
| Romania | 0.016 (0.016) | 0.499*** (0.171) | 0.059 (0.056) | 1.070 (0.762) | -1.073 (0.789) | -0.077 (0.592) | 0.101* (0.056) | 0.008 (0.016) | 0.121* (0.065) | 36 | 0.903 |
| Russia | 0.003 (0.009) | 0.874*** (0.127) | -0.052* (0.028) | -0.221 (0.318) | -0.124 (0.397) | 1.279*** (0.350) | 0.020 (0.028) | -0.001 (0.003) | 0.001 (0.044) | 36 | 0.938 |
| Turkey | -0.052 (0.054) | 0.905*** (0.075) | 0.254** (0.092) | 0.598 (0.784) | 0.219 (1.305) | -1.643 (1.024) | 0.127 (0.086) | -0.016** (0.008) | 0.032 (0.112) | 36 | 0.975 |
| *Latin America* | | | | | | | | | | | |
| Brazil | -0.039 (0.043) | 0.760*** (0.059) | 0.012 (0.041) | -0.651 (0.394) | -2.173** (0.787) | 0.139 (0.486) | 0.455*** (0.065) | -0.002 (0.006) | 0.413*** (0.094) | 36 | 0.977 |
| Chile | 0.009 (0.014) | 0.416*** (0.103) | 0.074** (0.034) | -0.409 (0.497) | 1.058* (0.529) | -0.579 (0.479) | 0.241** (0.109) | -0.020* (0.011) | 0.260*** (0.082) | 36 | 0.945 |
| Colombia | 0.000 (0.024) | 0.610*** (0.085) | 0.078*** (0.024) | 0.122 (0.265) | 0.283 (0.278) | -1.633*** (0.348) | 0.194** (0.075) | -0.002 (0.004) | 0.549*** (0.130) | 36 | 0.985 |
| Mexico | 0.016 (0.015) | 1.068*** (0.103) | 0.093*** (0.026) | 0.447 (0.332) | 0.151 (1.104) | -1.457*** (0.312) | 0.064 (0.059) | -0.001 (0.004) | 0.099 (0.178) | 23 | 0.981 |
| Peru | -0.005 (0.014) | 0.683*** (0.110) | 0.054 (0.036) | -0.205 (0.487) | -0.082 (0.499) | -0.605 (0.794) | 0.273*** (0.073) | -0.003 (0.015) | 0.127 (0.106) | 36 | 0.912 |
| *Middle East and Africa* | | | | | | | | | | | |
| Jordan | -0.002 (0.004) | 0.879*** (0.051) | 0.010 (0.023) | -0.415* (0.235) | -0.477 (0.304) | -0.149 (0.222) | 0.004 (0.050) | 0.004 (0.010) | 0.029 (0.022) | 36 | 0.956 |
| Morocco | -0.002 (0.003) | 0.790*** (0.197) | 0.006 (0.005) | 0.018 (0.054) | 0.002 (0.118) | -0.002 (0.058) | 0.007 (0.008) | -0.006 (0.004) | 0.020 (0.020) | 36 | 0.826 |
| South Africa | 0.004 (0.013) | 1.018*** (0.066) | 0.064*** (0.017) | 0.020 (0.201) | 0.112 (0.324) | -1.258*** (0.205) | 0.170** (0.068) | 0.000 (0.002) | 0.009 (0.012) | 36 | 0.991 |

*Notes:* See table 8.2 for variable descriptions. All regressions include a constant and quarter effects. Full sample specification also includes country-fixed effects. Clustered (robust) standard errors reported in parentheses for panel (individual country) specifications. ***, **, and * indicate statistical significance at the 1, 5, and 10 percent levels, respectively.

results. In the full sample, the estimated coefficient for net capital flows remains positive and statistically significant, and implies that a 10 percent of GDP increase in net capital flows would elicit about a 0.2 percentage point increase in the policy rate (see chapter appendix; table A.8.2, col. [1]). As with the OLS estimates reported in table 8.3, the effect becomes much smaller and loses statistical significance when the output gap, inflation, and change in real exchange rate are included in the model (col. [2]).

### 8.2.2 Foreign Exchange Intervention

Turning to FX intervention, the regressions confirm that reserve accumulation—which is nearly always sterilized—is strongly associated with capital inflows (table 8.4).[5] The estimates imply that, on average, EME central banks purchase around 40 percent of the inflow, with significant variation across countries. South Africa is well known for allowing the exchange rate to respond freely to capital flows; among the major Latin American countries in the sample, Chile, Colombia, and Mexico undertake the least intervention, while Brazil and Peru undertake the most. Asian central banks generally intervene heavily, as do most central banks in our emerging Europe sample. These findings resonate with those reported in existing studies documenting central bank surveys, which show that most EME central banks intervene frequently in currency markets to stabilize the exchange rate (Mihaljek 2005; Mohanty and Berger 2013).

Controlling for the effect of capital inflows, higher commodity prices are, on average, associated with sales of reserves—presumably as central banks in commodity-importing countries try to offset the effects of the terms of trade shock. In addition, EME central banks sold reserves during the global financial crisis in the face of fleeing capital and depreciation pressures (indeed, if the data are segmented into net inflow and outflow observations, a larger coefficient is obtained for outflow episodes relative to inflows, and the difference is statistically significant).

Instrumenting capital flows to address potential endogeneity concerns (that capital flows may be responding to the FX intervention, as the theoretical model of chapter 5 implies they would) makes little

---

5. The extent to which this reserve accumulation is sterilized may be gauged by regressing the change in broad money, measured in percent of GDP, on capital inflows or on the change in reserves (also measured in percent of GDP). The resulting coefficients (not reported here) are very small—thus, much of the impact of the reserve accumulation on monetary aggregates is sterilized.

**Table 8.4**
Net capital flows and FX intervention in EMEs, 2005Q1–2013Q4.

| | Net capital flows/GDP | US interest rate | Global market volatility | Commodity prices | GFC | Obs. | $R^2$ |
|---|---|---|---|---|---|---|---|
| Full sample | 0.402*** (0.041) | -0.125 (0.091) | -0.408 (0.878) | -2.232** (0.864) | -1.759* (0.990) | 1,707 | 0.349 |
| *Asia* | | | | | | | |
| India | 0.835*** (0.202) | 0.115 (0.116) | -0.012 (1.626) | -6.674*** (1.824) | 0.858 (1.989) | 36 | 0.612 |
| Indonesia | 0.732*** (0.178) | 0.101 (0.191) | 3.637 (2.414) | -6.005** (2.295) | -3.121 (2.548) | 36 | 0.424 |
| Korea, South | 0.688*** (0.121) | -0.446** (0.175) | -2.646 (1.948) | 0.915 (2.164) | 0.957 (2.508) | 36 | 0.714 |
| Malaysia | 0.901*** (0.109) | -0.349 (0.427) | 0.624 (4.646) | 16.040*** (4.776) | 1.781 (4.599) | 20 | 0.964 |
| Philippines | 0.582*** (0.157) | -0.425** (0.188) | 2.388 (1.818) | 0.959 (2.184) | -2.152 (2.312) | 36 | 0.704 |
| Thailand | 0.618*** (0.113) | -0.112 (0.282) | 8.313** (3.617) | -6.760** (3.258) | -3.447 (3.952) | 36 | 0.714 |
| *Europe* | | | | | | | |
| Czech Rep. | 0.645*** (0.208) | -0.268 (0.214) | -1.548 (2.493) | 1.170 (2.925) | 1.035 (2.543) | 36 | 0.598 |
| Hungary | 0.663*** (0.177) | -0.512 (0.522) | 10.853* (5.830) | -4.379 (5.617) | 4.018 (7.495) | 36 | 0.571 |
| Poland | 0.519*** (0.095) | -0.385* (0.225) | -1.618 (2.377) | -1.464 (1.878) | -2.465 (2.836) | 36 | 0.725 |

(continued)

**Table 8.4** (continued)

| | Net capital flows/GDP | US interest rate | Global market volatility | Commodity prices | GFC | Obs. | $R^2$ |
|---|---|---|---|---|---|---|---|
| Romania | 0.309*** | −0.628* | −4.867 | −3.782 | 1.750 | 36 | 0.508 |
| | (0.098) | (0.318) | (3.117) | (3.103) | (4.604) | | |
| Russia | 1.024*** | 0.540** | 3.195 | 4.031 | −4.539 | 36 | 0.944 |
| | (0.074) | (0.219) | (2.335) | (2.508) | (2.704) | | |
| Turkey | 0.528*** | −0.066 | −0.992 | −5.668*** | 2.352 | 36 | 0.650 |
| | (0.101) | (0.132) | (1.867) | (2.008) | (1.879) | | |
| *Latin America* | | | | | | | |
| Brazil | 0.882*** | 0.198* | 0.818 | −6.348*** | −1.239 | 36 | 0.800 |
| | (0.091) | (0.098) | (1.083) | (1.509) | (1.131) | | |
| Chile | 0.435*** | 0.270 | 3.476 | −1.381 | −3.924 | 36 | 0.561 |
| | (0.112) | (0.276) | (2.878) | (3.131) | (2.970) | | |
| Colombia | 0.453*** | 0.061 | −0.675 | −0.318 | −0.188 | 36 | 0.766 |
| | (0.098) | (0.064) | (0.689) | (1.080) | (0.778) | | |
| Mexico | 0.140 | 0.124 | 2.005* | 1.569 | −4.472*** | 36 | 0.546 |
| | (0.091) | (0.118) | (1.155) | (1.078) | (1.300) | | |
| Peru | 0.823*** | 0.022 | 0.819 | −6.000* | −4.456 | 36 | 0.798 |
| | (0.104) | (0.317) | (3.106) | (3.454) | (3.998) | | |
| *Middle East and Africa* | | | | | | | |
| Jordan | 0.840*** | −0.570 | −5.015 | −18.725** | 8.980 | 36 | 0.573 |
| | (0.241) | (0.592) | (11.690) | (8.920) | (12.762) | | |
| Morocco | 0.699*** | 0.217 | −3.006 | −13.498*** | −4.332 | 36 | 0.514 |
| | (0.243) | (0.300) | (3.057) | (3.989) | (3.249) | | |
| South Africa | 0.151* | −0.003 | 0.087 | −1.698 | −0.288 | 36 | 0.277 |
| | (0.077) | (0.127) | (0.975) | (1.441) | (1.190) | | |

*Notes:* Dependent variable is change in reserves (excluding valuation changes) in percent of GDP. See table 8.2 for descriptions of other variables. Full sample comprises 51 countries for which data is available. All regressions include a constant and quarter effects. Full sample specification also includes country-fixed effects. Clustered (robust) standard errors reported in parentheses for panel (individual country) specifications. ***, **, and * indicate statistical significance at the 1, 5, and 10 percent levels, respectively.

difference to our findings (table A.8.2). Although the instrumental variable estimate is slightly lower, at around 30 percent, the coefficient remains highly statistically significant (col. [3]).

## 8.3 Macroeconomic Policy Response by Type of Flow

Given that the consequences of capital flows tend to differ across the types of flows (as documented in chapter 4), the policy response may also depend on the type of inflow. Breaking down the net capital flow variable into asset flows and liability flows, for example, shows that the policy rate reacts more strongly to liability flows than to asset flows (table 8.5, col. [1]). This may be because, on a net basis, large flows in EMEs tend to be driven by foreign investors, while retrenchment by domestic residents (asset flows) in many cases happens when the economy is experiencing a negative shock (and the policy rate needs to be lowered).[6] Disaggregating flows by asset type, the policy rate reacts more strongly to foreign direct investment (FDI) and to other investment flows than it does to portfolio flows (col. [2]). A 10 percent of GDP increase in net FDI flows, for example, results in the policy rate being raised by some 0.3 percentage points, while a similar increase in net portfolio flows has—on average—no significant impact on the policy rate. Inasmuch as FDI and other investment flows tend to be the most expansionary (as documented in chapter 4), this finding makes intuitive sense: policy makers try to cool down an overheating economy by tightening monetary policy. This conclusion is reaffirmed when the output gap, real exchange rate appreciation, and inflation are added to the specification, as their inclusion renders the estimated coefficient on the flow variables statistically utterly insignificant (cols. [3]–[4]).

Turning to FX intervention, the policy response seems to be symmetric to asset and liability flows—with the central bank, on average, purchasing some 40 percent of the inflow (table 8.5, col. [5]). Considering the findings in chapter 4 that both asset and liability flows are about equally likely to appreciate the exchange rate, this result is not surprising. Central banks tend to intervene to stem currency appreciation pressures in the face of all types of flows—but they intervene most

---

6. In the estimation sample, for example, the correlation between total net flows (in percent of GDP) and asset flows (in percent of GDP) is only 0.2, while that between net flows and liability flows is 0.7. The mean net capital flow is also significantly larger (about 6 percent of GDP) when liability flows are positive relative to when asset flows are positive (about −0.7 percent of GDP).

**Table 8.5**
Policy rate, FX intervention, and composition of flows, 2005Q1–2013Q4.

| | Policy rate | | | | FX intervention | |
|---|---|---|---|---|---|---|
| | (1) | (2) | (3) | (4) | (5) | (6) |
| Asset flows/GDP | 0.002 | | 0.001 | | 0.428*** | |
| | (0.003) | | (0.004) | | (0.040) | |
| Liability flows/GDP | 0.007*** | | 0.003 | | 0.395*** | |
| | (0.002) | | (0.004) | | (0.041) | |
| Net FDI flows/GDP | | 0.026** | | 0.012 | | 0.309*** |
| | | (0.011) | | (0.008) | | (0.068) |
| Net portfolio flows/GDP | | 0.000 | | 0.002 | | 0.536*** |
| | | (0.003) | | (0.004) | | (0.047) |
| Net other inv. flows/GDP | | 0.004* | | 0.001 | | 0.394*** |
| | | (0.002) | | (0.004) | | (0.046) |
| Policy rate (lagged) | 0.915*** | 0.910*** | 0.845*** | 0.844*** | | |
| | (0.018) | (0.017) | (0.039) | (0.039) | | |
| US interest rate | 0.054*** | 0.053*** | 0.039*** | 0.039*** | −0.115 | −0.097 |
| | (0.010) | (0.010) | (0.010) | (0.010) | (0.089) | (0.084) |
| Global market volatility | 0.157 | 0.134 | 0.060 | 0.054 | −0.438 | −0.241 |
| | (0.098) | (0.091) | (0.079) | (0.077) | (0.882) | (0.811) |
| Commodity prices | 0.300*** | 0.301*** | 0.013 | 0.011 | −2.145** | −2.463*** |
| | (0.092) | (0.090) | (0.086) | (0.084) | (0.867) | (0.895) |
| GFC | −0.441*** | −0.446*** | −0.457*** | −0.455*** | −1.857* | −1.721* |
| | (0.139) | (0.139) | (0.129) | (0.128) | (1.000) | (0.959) |
| Output gap | | | 0.036* | 0.036* | | |
| | | | (0.020) | (0.020) | | |
| Change in REER | | | −0.007* | −0.006* | | |
| | | | (0.004) | (0.004) | | |
| Inflation | | | 0.089*** | 0.087*** | | |
| | | | (0.030) | (0.029) | | |
| Country-fixed effects | Yes | Yes | Yes | Yes | Yes | Yes |
| Quarter effects | Yes | Yes | Yes | Yes | Yes | Yes |
| Observations | 1,318 | 1,318 | 1,318 | 1,318 | 1,707 | 1,707 |
| $R^2$ | 0.978 | 0.978 | 0.981 | 0.981 | 0.350 | 0.363 |

*Notes:* Dependent variable is central bank policy rate (in percent) in cols. (1)–(4), and change in reserves (excluding valuation changes) in percent of GDP in cols. (5)–(6). All regressions include a constant. Clustered standard errors by country reported in parentheses. ***, **, and * indicate statistical significance at the 1, 5, and 10 percent levels, respectively.

heavily for portfolio flows, followed by other investment flows (col. [6]). Again, this finding is intuitive since—as documented earlier—these flows are also the most prone to causing currency overvaluation. Moreover, as the model of chapter 5 implied, and as we establish empirically in chapter 9, sterilized intervention also helps absorb the capital inflow, in particular its impact on domestic credit growth. Since chapter 4 showed that other investment flows (which are predominantly cross-border bank flows) are the most important contributor to credit growth, sterilized intervention may have a macroprudential motive as well.

## 8.4   Macroprudential Measures and Capital Controls

The results presented above suggest that policy makers indeed use macroeconomic policies to respond to capital flows. But what about the less orthodox part of the policy tool kit—that is, nondiscriminatory macroprudential measures and capital controls on inflows?

While often lumped together, a key conceptual difference between nondiscriminatory macroprudential measures and capital controls (as mentioned in earlier chapters) is that the former are intended to mitigate the consequences of capital inflows—such as credit booms, inflation/ overheating, and general financial instability—whereas the latter are intended to target the capital inflow itself (its volume or composition).[7] At a practical level, an important problem in trying to identify responses that involve macroprudential policies or capital controls is that these tend to be discrete administrative measures that do not lend themselves to easy quantification. Indeed, as discussed in chapter 2 (box 2.1), the available indices for capital controls are rather crude—indicating only the presence of restrictions and not their intensity. Thus, they cannot pick up the cyclical variations (tightening and easing) in the use of capital controls. The same is generally true of indices of macroprudential measures, which mostly reflect the presence of a measure and not its intensity (e.g., Lim et al. 2011; Ostry et al. 2012; Cerutti, Claessens, and Laeven 2015).

As is evident from table 8.1, however, EMEs have been resorting to macroprudential measures and capital controls in the face of large inflows. To capture these instances, we rely on data from a variety of sources. For macroprudential measures, we use quarterly information on

---

7. Currency-based prudential measures are in between nondiscriminatory macroprudential measures and capital controls. Primarily intended to reduce the foreign currency risks associated with capital flows, they are also likely to affect the volume of capital flows; they are thus included with capital controls for analytical purposes.

*changes* in seven different types of measures—countercyclical capital requirements, dynamic loan-loss provisioning, caps on loan-to-value (LTV) and debt-to-income (DTI) ratios, limits on credit growth and consumer loans, and other housing sector–related measures—compiled by Akinci and Olmstead-Rumsey (2015) for twenty-seven EMEs in our sample.[8] Using this information, we construct binary measures to indicate the tightening of individual policies (with +1 coded as tightening, and zero otherwise), as well as an overall binary measure to capture the tightening of *any* of the macroprudential policies.

While the binary macroprudential measures capture the tightening of policies, they still suffer from the caveat of not capturing the intensity of the measure, or even the degree to which the measures have been tightened (since any tightening, regardless of magnitude, is coded as +1). We thus supplement our change-based indicators with a more continuous measure of (quarterly) legal reserve requirements (RRs) on local currency liabilities, developed by Federico, Vegh, and Vuletin (2014) for 35 EMEs in our sample.[9] Since RRs are directly quantifiable, using them has the distinct advantage of capturing the intensity of the macroprudential policy, as well as the extent of any changes to it. Moreover, RRs are a more widely deployed tool, having been used by central banks for decades; their cross-country coverage is therefore broader than that of other types of macroprudential measures.[10]

For capital controls, we rely on change-based measures developed by Ahmed et al. (2015), who record changes in capital inflow controls (as well as in currency-based prudential measures that may act like capital controls) at quarterly frequency for seventeen EMEs in our sample. Using this information, we create binary measures for tightening of capital controls on cross-border portfolio equity and debt flows, as well as on bank flows (with a tightening coded as +1, and zero otherwise), and an overall binary measure to indicate if *any* type of capital control was tightened.

---

8. Other housing-related measures include higher regulatory risk weights for mortgage loans, quantitative limits on mortgage lending, property gains taxes, and stricter requirements for mortgage borrower creditworthiness.

9. We consider local currency RRs (and not those on foreign currency deposits) to capture prudential measures that are purely domestic in nature, and not likely to directly affect capital flows. This also helps to mitigate endogeneity concerns in estimations related to the impact of prudential measures on capital flows.

10. While the earlier conception of RRs was that of a monetary policy tool, in recent years they have been used more from a macroprudential perspective as well (Tovar, Garcia-Escribano, and Martin 2012; Cordella et al. 2014).

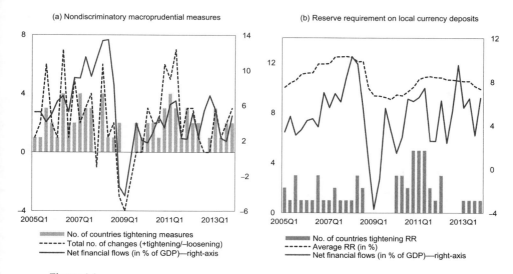

**Figure 8.2**
Capital flows and macroprudential measures in EMEs, 2005Q1–2013Q4.
*Sources*: Authors' calculations based on the IMF's IFS database; Federico et al. 2014; and Akinci, and Olmstead-Rumsey 2015.
*Note*: Net financial flows (in percent of GDP) are the average for countries for which information on respective macroprudential policies is available.

To what extent do EMEs respond to inflows by imposing or tightening nondiscriminatory macroprudential measures? A simple snapshot of changes in macroprudential policies suggests that both the number of countries tightening policies, as well as the total number of policy tightenings (net of easings) across countries, is positively correlated with net capital flows (figure 8.2[a]). Thus, countries tighten macroprudential policies as inflows surge, and relax policies when flows abate or reverse. Importantly, this correlation has become more pronounced since the global financial crisis, indicating a greater usage of macroprudential measures by EMEs in recent years to mitigate the adverse consequences of inflows.[11] A similar picture emerges when reserve requirements are considered: the total number of countries raising RRs, and the average RR across countries track closely the movement in net capital flows (figure 8.2[b]). In the post–global financial crisis surge, for example, several large EMEs—including Brazil, China, India, and

---

11. See chapter appendix (tables A.8.3 and A.8.4) for the list of countries that have tightened macroprudential policies during the sample period.

**Table 8.6**
Net capital flows and macroprudential policy response in EMEs, 2005Q1–2013Q4.

| | Overall | CCR | LLP | Consumer loan limit | Credit growth limit | DTI | LTV | Other housing-related | RR |
|---|---|---|---|---|---|---|---|---|---|
| | (1) | (2) | (3) | (4) | (5) | (6) | (7) | (8) | (9) |
| Net capital flows/GDP | 0.017* | 0.010 | 0.012 | 0.047 | 0.019 | 0.077** | 0.030** | -0.038* | 0.014** |
| | (0.009) | (0.011) | (0.010) | (0.029) | (0.016) | (0.030) | (0.012) | (0.022) | (0.005) |
| US interest rate | 0.042 | 0.058** | 0.064 | 0.050 | -0.088 | -0.062 | -0.054 | -0.225* | 0.013 |
| | (0.030) | (0.030) | (0.046) | (0.111) | (0.085) | (0.062) | (0.046) | (0.127) | (0.030) |
| Global market volatility | 0.289 | 1.253*** | -0.272 | 0.464 | -1.038 | -0.158 | -0.957** | 1.178*** | -0.459 |
| | (0.278) | (0.371) | (0.420) | (0.536) | (1.320) | (0.775) | (0.406) | (0.454) | (0.365) |
| Commodity prices | -0.142 | -0.005 | -0.228 | -0.292 | -1.053* | -0.948*** | 0.230 | -0.327 | -0.102 |
| | (0.433) | (0.646) | (0.453) | (0.646) | (0.600) | (0.260) | (0.729) | (0.939) | (0.199) |
| GFC | -0.905*** | -1.298*** | -0.244 | -5.697*** | -4.453*** | -5.057*** | 0.253 | -5.552*** | -0.247 |
| | (0.308) | (0.321) | (0.402) | (0.879) | (0.885) | (0.630) | (0.500) | (0.908) | (0.208) |
| Real GDP growth | -0.009 | 0.067 | -0.021 | -0.104*** | 0.157 | -0.241** | -0.028 | -0.054 | 0.046 |
| | (0.049) | (0.082) | (0.071) | (0.020) | (0.116) | (0.101) | (0.057) | (0.042) | (0.040) |
| Initial RR | | | | | | | | | 0.915*** |
| | | | | | | | | | (0.013) |
| Country-fixed effects | Yes | Yes | Yes | Yes | Yes | Yes | Yes | Yes | Yes |
| Quarter effects | Yes | Yes | Yes | Yes | Yes | Yes | Yes | Yes | Yes |
| Observations | 924 | 924 | 924 | 924 | 924 | 924 | 924 | 924 | 968 |
| $R^2$ | 0.165 | 0.271 | 0.206 | 0.414 | 0.487 | 0.484 | 0.332 | 0.473 | 0.960 |
| Countries | 27 | 27 | 27 | 27 | 27 | 27 | 27 | 27 | 32 |

*Notes:* In cols. (1)–(8), the dependent variable is a binary variable equal to one if macroprudential policy is tightened, and zero otherwise. In col. (9), the dependent variable is average reserve requirement on local currency liabilities. Overall indicates tightening of any macroprudential policy; CCR = countercyclical capital requirements; LLP = dynamic loan-loss provisioning rules; DTI = debt-to-income ratio; LTV = loan-to-value ratio; RR = average reserve requirement on local currency liabilities. Cols. (1)–(8) are estimated using a probit model. Pseudo-$R^2$ is reported in cols. (1)–(8). Initial RR is one-period lagged RR. All regressions include a constant. Clustered standard errors reported in parentheses. ***, **, and * indicate statistical significance at the 1, 5, and 10 percent levels, respectively.

Turkey—increased RRs multiple times to preserve macroeconomic and financial stability.

More formal analysis—controlling for global factors such as US interest rates, global market volatility, and commodity prices, as well as for real GDP growth, the global financial crisis, and country-specific and quarter effects—confirms the positive association between capital flows and tightening of macroprudential policies (table 8.6). Thus, credit-related policies such as limits on DTI and LTV ratios—as well as liquidity-related measures such as reserve requirements—react strongly to capital inflows. Specifically, against an unconditional probability of policy tightening of about 8 percent, an increase by 10 percent of GDP in net capital flows raises the likelihood that macroprudential policy will be tightened by about 0.3 percentage points (though statistically significant, the coefficient is small because it is only in the more recent years of the sample that such measures have been widely used). For reserve requirements, the estimates suggest that (controlling for the initial level of reserve requirement) an increase by 10 percent of GDP in net flows typically elicits a 0.1 percentage point increase in reserve requirements (RRs) in EMEs.

Among individual countries, tightening of macroprudential policies is generally positively correlated with capital flows, though the association is statistically significant only for Croatia (results for selected countries are presented in chapter appendix; table A.8.5). Given the relatively short time span over which such measures have been employed, it is unsurprising that the time-series data are insufficient to identify the effect of capital flows on their use. Similarly, RRs respond positively to capital inflows in most countries in our sample, but the estimated coefficient is statistically significant only for Brazil, Turkey, and Uruguay.

In terms of the types of flows to which policy makers respond, the results reported in table 8.7 show that they react similarly to asset flows and to liability flows. The macroprudential response is stronger, however, for portfolio and other investment flows as compared to FDI. Since portfolio and other investment flows are also the most prone to causing domestic credit booms and financial-stability risks, it is natural that policy makers tighten macroprudential policies more aggressively in response to them.

Turning to capital controls, their use across countries has been relatively limited, but the tightening (and easing) that is observed corre-

**Table 8.7**

Macroprudential policies and composition of flows, 2005Q1–2013Q4.

| | Overall | | DTI | | LTV | | RR | |
|---|---|---|---|---|---|---|---|---|
| | (1) | (2) | (3) | (4) | (5) | (6) | (7) | (8) |
| Asset flows/GDP | 0.015 (0.010) | | 0.080** (0.035) | | 0.026** (0.013) | | 0.026* (0.013) | |
| Liability flows/GDP | 0.017* (0.009) | | 0.077** (0.031) | | 0.030** (0.012) | | 0.012** (0.005) | |
| Net FDI flows/GDP | | 0.001 (0.017) | | 0.069 (0.055) | | | | -0.007 (0.026) |
| Net portfolio flows/GDP | | 0.038*** (0.014) | | 0.077** (0.035) | | | | 0.015 (0.011) |
| Net other inv. flows/GDP | | 0.020* (0.010) | | 0.087*** (0.031) | | | | 0.018*** (0.005) |
| US interest rate | 0.042 (0.030) | 0.046 (0.029) | -0.059 (0.064) | -0.073 (0.067) | -0.056 (0.047) | -0.054 (0.047) | 0.018 (0.029) | 0.013 (0.030) |
| Global market volatility | 0.292 (0.275) | 0.323 (0.269) | -0.172 (0.778) | -0.243 (0.747) | -0.953** (0.402) | -1.017** (0.403) | -0.461 (0.365) | -0.464 (0.357) |

| | (1) | (2) | (3) | (4) | (5) | (6) | (7) | (8) |
|---|---|---|---|---|---|---|---|---|
| Commodity prices | -0.145 | -0.205 | -0.948*** | -0.909*** | 0.229 | 0.144 | -0.067 | -0.071 |
| | (0.431) | (0.436) | (0.260) | (0.250) | (0.729) | (0.772) | (0.188) | (0.196) |
| GFC | -0.905*** | -0.891*** | -5.077*** | -5.576*** | 0.263 | 0.153 | -0.282 | -0.242 |
| | (0.308) | (0.296) | (0.665) | (1.065) | (0.503) | (0.504) | (0.219) | (0.207) |
| Real GDP growth | -0.010 | -0.008 | -0.247** | -0.275*** | -0.027 | -0.034 | 0.051 | 0.046 |
| | (0.049) | (0.050) | (0.107) | (0.102) | (0.056) | (0.067) | (0.044) | (0.043) |
| Initial RR | | | | | | | 0.918*** | 0.918*** |
| | | | | | | | (0.015) | (0.016) |
| Country-fixed effects | Yes | Yes | Yes | Yes | Yes | Yes | Yes | Yes |
| Quarter effects | Yes | Yes | Yes | Yes | Yes | Yes | Yes | Yes |
| Observations | 924 | 924 | 924 | 924 | 924 | 924 | 968 | 968 |
| $R^2$ | 0.165 | 0.170 | 0.485 | 0.490 | 0.332 | 0.351 | 0.960 | 0.960 |

*Notes*: In cols. (1)–(6), the dependent variable is a binary variable equal to one if macroprudential policy is tightened, and zero otherwise. In cols. (7)–(8), the dependent variable is average RR on local currency liabilities. See table 8.6 for variable descriptions. Cols. (1)–(6) are estimated using a probit model and pseudo-$R^2$ is reported. All regressions include a constant. Clustered standard errors are reported in parentheses. ***, **, and * indicate statistical significance at the 1, 5, and 10 percent levels, respectively.

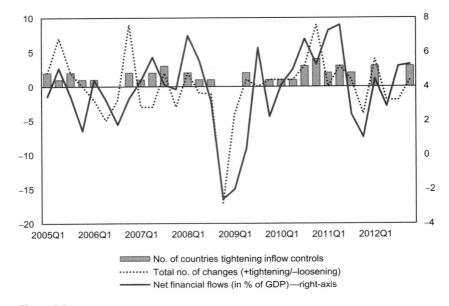

**Figure 8.3**
Capital flows and inflow controls in EMEs, 2005Q1–2012Q4.
*Sources*: Authors' calculations based on the IMF's International Financial Statistics database and Ahmed et al. 2015.
*Note*: Net financial flows (in percent of GDP) are the average for countries for which data on changes in capital controls are available.

sponds to capital inflows—albeit, apparently, with some lag (figure 8.3).[12] Within our sample of major emerging markets, Brazil has been the most active country in terms of calibrating its controls to inflow surges, adjusting them both before the global financial crisis and during the post–global financial crisis surge. In October 2009, for example, Brazil imposed a 2 percent financial transactions tax (Imposto Sobre Operações Financeiras—IOF) on portfolio flows, later raising the rate to 4 percent and shortly afterward to 6 percent on portfolio debt flows (figure 8.4). The Brazilian authorities also adopted a number of other controls, including a 6 percent tax on short-term external borrowing (initially on loans of up to one-year maturity, later extended to up to five years), limits on banks' gross FX positions to discourage them

---

12. The lag is more pronounced for tightening of measures in the face of large inflows presumably because of administrative and institutional delays, but perhaps also because national authorities have often been reluctant to impose them due to the reputational risk (as discussed in chapter 2).

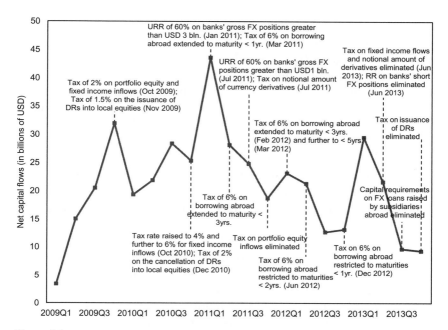

**Figure 8.4**
Brazil: Net capital flows and capital controls, 2009Q1–2013Q4.
*Sources*: IMF's International Financial Statistics database, and Chamon and Garcia 2015.
*Notes*: Nonexhaustive list of capital controls; DRs = depository receipts; URR = unremunerated reserve requirements; RR = reserve requirements.

from channeling offshore carry trades, and a tax on the notional amount of derivative transactions to discourage onshore carry trades. Other recent cases of inflow controls include Indonesia's measures to limit banks' external borrowing, and the removal of withholding exemptions on nonresident investors by Korea and Thailand.[13] (In EMEs where the capital account has not yet been fully liberalized—for example, India and South Africa—the general trend in the face of inflows has been to liberalize outflows, instead of further tightening residency-based inflow restrictions.)

Probit estimates—controlling for global conditions, relevant domestic factors such as institutional quality and the general level of capital

---

13. See chapter appendix (table A.8.6) for the list of inflow control–tightening episodes in the sample. Measures were also taken by some countries to make central bank paper less attractive to foreigners, without explicitly discriminating against them. Thus, Bank Indonesia imposed a minimum holding period for central bank bills and lengthened the tenor of those instruments to make them less attractive for carry trade.

account openness, as well as for country-specific and quarter effects—confirm that some countries indeed respond to capital flows by tightening inflow controls (table 8.8).[14] The coefficient on capital flows is statistically significant but quantitatively small: against an unconditional probability of 8 percent in the full sample, the predicted probability of tightening inflow controls increases by about 0.2 percentage points if (lagged) flows are 10 percentage points higher than the mean value (of 3.7 percent of GDP). (Lagged net capital flows are included in the estimations based on the observation in figure 8.3 that controls respond to flows with a lag. This also helps to mitigate endogeneity concerns that capital flows are affected by changes in capital controls. Using contemporaneous flows instead, however, barely changes the estimated coefficient.)

While many countries appear not to use inflow controls (perhaps for the historical, institutional, or political economy reasons mentioned in chapter 2), among countries that did impose or tighten inflow controls, that policy action is statistically significantly related to net capital inflows in Brazil, Indonesia, and the Philippines.[15] These findings contradict those of recent studies (e.g., Eichengreen and Rose 2014; Fernandez, Rebucci, and Uribe 2015) who claim that capital controls are acyclical and do not respond to macroeconomic activity. One reason why these studies obtain different results is that they rely on slow-moving capital account openness indices based on the presence of restrictions, instead of the more relevant change-based measures employed here. As such, while they capture broad trends in liberalization, they miss the finer cyclical variations in the use of capital account restrictions.

As discussed in chapters 5–7, it makes sense to use capital controls against flows that bring fewer perceived benefits but cause greater

---

14. We control for institutional quality as some studies (e.g., Grilli and Milesi-Ferretti 1995) find that countries that have lower institutional quality are more likely to implement capital controls. In addition, we include a measure of overall capital account openness to capture the fact that more liberalized economies are more likely to implement temporary controls than mostly closed countries (although it could also be argued that relatively closed economies may find it more convenient and politically palatable to impose additional controls.) Results remain essentially the same if other control variables such as monetary freedom and real GDP growth are also included in the estimations.

15. In the individual country estimations, we do not include quarter effects and the indices for capital account openness and institutional quality (which are slow-moving, largely time-invariant variables), since their inclusion leads to "perfect prediction" of the model in most cases.

**Table 8.8**

Net capital flows and inflow controls in EMEs, 2005Q1–2012Q4.

| | Net capital flows/GDP | US interest rate | Global market volatility | Commodity prices | GFC | Capital acc. openness | Institutional quality | Obs. | Pseudo-$R^2$ |
|---|---|---|---|---|---|---|---|---|---|
| Full sample | 0.039** (0.019) | -0.091*** (0.025) | -0.995** (0.465) | 0.465 (0.383) | 0.804 (0.601) | 0.155 (0.217) | -7.625* (4.222) | 533 | 0.256 |
| *Individual countries* | | | | | | | | | |
| Brazil | 0.333** (0.138) | 0.024 (0.166) | -0.212 (1.306) | 1.006 (1.814) | -4.926** (2.393) | | | 32 | 0.397 |
| Colombia | 0.114 (0.142) | 0.020 (0.154) | -1.673** (0.841) | 2.190 (1.697) | -3.931** (1.731) | | | 32 | 0.208 |
| India | 0.023 (0.067) | 0.062 (0.095) | 0.583 (1.868) | -2.038 (1.403) | -5.015* (2.629) | | | 32 | 0.103 |
| Indonesia | 0.180* (0.096) | -0.400** (0.195) | -1.854 (1.452) | -1.897 (2.046) | -3.988*** (1.308) | | | 32 | 0.301 |
| Korea, South | 0.007 (0.079) | 0.004 (0.114) | 1.179 (1.256) | 0.473 (1.487) | -5.869*** (1.865) | | | 32 | 0.140 |
| Philippines | 0.087* (0.052) | 0.383* (0.209) | -7.274 (5.387) | 11.445 (7.202) | -7.216*** (2.158) | | | 32 | 0.457 |
| Thailand | 0.096 (0.069) | -0.380 (0.245) | -8.049 (7.449) | 2.114 (3.250) | 3.001 (6.526) | | | 32 | 0.299 |
| Turkey | 0.031 (0.066) | -0.271* (0.152) | -0.143 (1.249) | 0.985 (1.748) | 1.374 (1.587) | | | 32 | 0.196 |
| Romania | -0.356 (0.435) | 0.868 (1.481) | -15.905 (17.012) | -28.301 (42.789) | 10.520 (19.268) | | | 32 | 0.692 |

*Notes:* Dependent variable is a binary variable equal to one for tightening of capital inflow controls. Net capital flows (in percent of GDP) is lagged one period. Full sample comprises seventeen countries. All regressions include a constant and are estimated as a probit model. Full sample specification includes country-fixed and quarter effects. Clustered (robust) standard errors reported in parentheses for full sample (individual country) specifications. ***, **, and * indicate statistical significance at the 1, 5, and 10 percent levels, respectively.

**Table 8.9**
Inflow controls composition of flows, 2005Q1–2012Q4.

| | Overall | | Equity | Bond | Financial sector |
|---|---|---|---|---|---|
| | (1) | (2) | (3) | (4) | (5) |
| Asset flows/GDP | 0.033 | | | | |
| | (0.024) | | | | |
| Liability flows/GDP | 0.041* | | | | |
| | (0.021) | | | | |
| Net FDI flows/GDP | | 0.050 | 0.651*** | 0.121* | 0.039 |
| | | (0.061) | (0.138) | (0.062) | (0.058) |
| Net portfolio flows/GDP | | 0.061* | 0.342*** | 0.048 | 0.064** |
| | | (0.036) | (0.043) | (0.043) | (0.028) |
| Net other inv. flows/GDP | | 0.027 | 0.365* | 0.075* | 0.005 |
| | | (0.024) | (0.187) | (0.043) | (0.026) |
| Global market volatility | −0.992** | −0.989** | 0.052 | −0.670 | −0.750* |
| | (0.466) | (0.457) | (1.254) | (0.620) | (0.403) |
| Commodity prices | 0.441 | 0.409 | −5.221*** | 0.718 | 0.394 |
| | (0.365) | (0.410) | (1.317) | (0.585) | (0.560) |
| US interest rate | −0.093*** | −0.088*** | −0.473*** | −0.133*** | −0.038 |
| | (0.025) | (0.024) | (0.129) | (0.045) | (0.043) |
| GFC | 0.823 | 0.791 | −0.137 | 0.556 | 0.414 |
| | (0.579) | (0.621) | (1.496) | (0.815) | (0.509) |
| Capital account openness | 0.165 | 0.150 | 1.859*** | 0.713** | −0.156 |
| | (0.223) | (0.213) | (0.376) | (0.298) | (0.224) |
| Institutional quality | −7.693* | −8.002* | 5.096 | −1.769 | −11.115** |
| | (4.141) | (4.181) | (14.327) | (6.490) | (5.229) |
| Country-fixed effects | Yes | Yes | Yes | Yes | Yes |
| Quarter effects | Yes | Yes | Yes | Yes | Yes |
| Observations | 533 | 533 | 533 | 533 | 533 |
| $R^2$ | 0.256 | 0.259 | 0.682 | 0.349 | 0.263 |
| Countries | 17 | 17 | 17 | 17 | 17 |

*Notes*: Dependent variable is a binary variable equal to one for tightening of inflow controls. Capital flows are lagged one period. All regressions include a constant and are estimated as a probit model. Clustered standard errors reported in parentheses. ***, **, and * indicate significance at the 1, 5, and 10 percent levels, respectively.

macroeconomic imbalances or exacerbate balance-sheet mismatches. There is some evidence that EME policy makers are more likely to adopt controls in the face of certain types of flows. Disaggregating by the type of flow, it is apparent that countries tighten inflow controls in response to large liability flows (which is intuitive as flows driven by domestic residents will not be affected by residency-based restrictions that target nonresidents), especially portfolio flows (table 8.9, cols. [1]–[2]). Moreover, there appears to be some—albeit imperfect—mapping between the tightening of specific types of controls (equity, bond, and financial-sector related), and the nature of the inflow (cols. [3]–[5]). Equity controls thus respond strongly to net FDI and portfolio flows, financial sector-related restrictions respond more to portfolio flows, while bond controls react to other investment flows as well as to FDI flows. (The findings by type of inflow control should be interpreted with caution since—as reported in table A.8.6—for equity and bond controls, there are few instances of tightening in the sample.)

## 8.5 Policy Combinations

Evidently, EME policy makers do respond to capital inflows—more frequently with macroeconomic policies (monetary and exchange rate) than with macroprudential measures or capital controls, but there are examples of each of these instruments being used. A key insight of chapters 5–7, however, is that multiple objectives (to meet the inflation target, keep the currency competitive, and maintain financial stability) call for multiple instruments. To examine whether this happens on a systematic basis, here we narrow our focus to policy responses to large inflows—specifically, the surge observations identified in chapter 3.

With our strict definition of a surge (that the net inflow in percent of GDP lie in both the country's own, and in the full sample's, top thirtieth percentile), there are a total of 151 annual surge observations occurring in forty-three countries during 2005–2013 (listed in table A.3.1). Of these observations, we have data available on *all* four policy measures—the policy rate, FX intervention, tightening of macroprudential measures, and capital controls—for only twenty-six surge observations, occurring in Brazil, Chile, Colombia, India, the Philippines, Poland, Romania, Thailand, and Turkey. (Correspondingly, out of a total of 326 non-surge observations over 2005–2013, we have data available on all policy measures for seventy-three observations.)

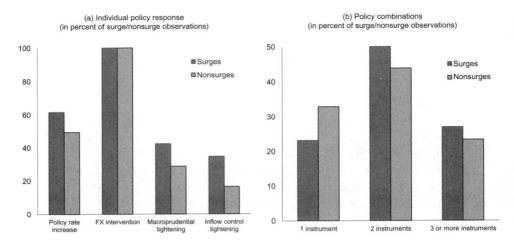

**Figure 8.5**
Policy responses in inflow surges in EMEs.
*Source*: Authors' estimates.
*Notes*: Policy response is classified for surges identified in chapter 3 (table A.3.1) over 2005–2013 for which data on all policy instruments is available. Panel (a) shows the percentage of surges in which the respective policy instruments were deployed. Panel (b) shows the percentages of surges by the number of policy instruments deployed.

During the twenty-six surges, FX intervention is always used—even by inflation targeters—so there are no instances in our data of policies not responding at all during periods of large capital inflows (figure 8.5[a]).[16] Monetary tightening is the second-most commonly used tool, occurring in some 60 percent of surges, whereas in the remaining 40 percent of cases monetary policy is either loosened or stays unchanged. (Consistent with the results presented in tables 8.2 and 8.3, the output gap is the key distinguishing feature between instances when the policy rate is raised and when it is lowered; in the latter case, the gap is more than 1 percentage point smaller.) Macroprudential policies are the next-most popular tool, tightened in about 42 percent of surges; these are followed by inflow controls, which are tightened in 35 percent of cases. It is noteworthy that when inflow controls are imposed or tightened, at least one other instrument is also deployed. This suggests that cyclical capital controls are mainly used to buttress the effects of other instruments, as implied by the theoretical analysis in chapter 5.

16. A policy instrument is deemed to have been used if it was deployed in at least one quarter in the identified surge year.

With the exception of FX intervention, which is used equally often in the face of large or more normal flows, the use of policy tools is greater in surges than in non-surge periods. This pattern also holds when we look at policy combinations (figure 8.5[b]). Thus, the share of observations in which only one policy instrument is used (FX intervention) is smaller for surges (23 percent) than it is for non-surge observations (33 percent). By contrast, two instruments (FX intervention, and usually, but not always, the policy interest rate) are used in 50 percent of surges, compared to 44 percent of non-surge cases, while three or more instruments are deployed in 27 percent of surges but in only 23 percent of non-surge observations.

The difference in the number of policy tools to deal with large inflows relative to more normal flows is even starker if we consider a more relaxed definition of surges, used in the robustness analysis of chapter 3, that defines surges in country-specific terms only (such that the net inflow in percent of GDP is in the country's top thirtieth percentile, but not necessarily in the full sample's top thirtieth percentile). This definition almost doubles the number of surge observations, but the results clearly indicate that when inflows surge, EME policy makers are more than twice as likely to respond with multiple instruments (three or more) than during normal times (chapter appendix; figure A.8.2).[17]

## 8.6 Conclusion

Confronted by an inflow surge, national authorities respond through a combination of policy instruments—both macroeconomic tools and less orthodox measures. While the thrust of the policy responses across countries is largely the same, there are differences in the specific instruments deployed that likely depend on economic, historical, and institutional characteristics. Central banks seem to use the policy interest rate to address inflation and overheating concerns associated with capital inflows, and (to a lesser degree) to reduce currency appreciation. Most emerging market central banks intervene quite heavily in the face

---

17. As discussed in Ghosh, Ostry, and Qureshi (2017), the use of these instruments also corresponds to the natural mapping laid out in chapter 5: the policy interest rate is used in the face of overheating pressures, FX intervention is used when the real exchange rate is appreciating, and macroprudential measures are tightened when there is rapid credit growth. Inflow controls are typically deployed when there are multiple imbalances and vulnerabilities.

of inflows, nearly always sterilizing that intervention. Finally, EMEs also seem to be using capital controls and macroprudential measures in the face of large inflows, but capital controls appear less frequently, often acting as a backstop to other measures. While these results accord with the theoretical framework laid out in chapters 5–7, they are still surprising, given that they are so contrary to the more traditional policy advice offered to EMEs facing large capital inflows. But how effective are these policy instruments in practice? That is the issue we take up next.

## Chapter 8 Appendix

**Table A.8.1**
Fiscal policy response and net capital flows in EMEs, 1985–2013.

|                              | FE (1)    | IV (2)    | FE (3)    | IV (4)    |
| ---------------------------- | --------- | --------- | --------- | --------- |
| Govt. expenditure/GDP (lagged) | 0.731*** | 0.708*** | 0.731*** | 0.708*** |
|                              | (0.056)   | (0.042)   | (0.053)   | (0.040)   |
| Net capital flows/GDP        | 0.000     | 0.001     | 0.002     | 0.010     |
|                              | (0.017)   | (0.019)   | (0.076)   | (0.181)   |
| Output gap                   |           | 0.024     |           | 0.020     |
|                              |           | (0.052)   |           | (0.107)   |
| Change in REER               |           | −0.045*   |           | −0.046    |
|                              |           | (0.023)   |           | (0.033)   |
| Inflation                    |           | −0.060*** |           | −0.060*** |
|                              |           | (0.021)   |           | (0.020)   |
| Country-fixed effects        | Yes       | Yes       | Yes       | Yes       |
| Year effects                 | Yes       | Yes       | Yes       | Yes       |
| Observations                 | 914       | 914       | 914       | 914       |
| $R^2$                        | 0.932     | 0.934     | 0.677     | 0.683     |
| Countries                    | 53        | 53        | 53        | 53        |

*Notes*: Dependent variable is government expenditure to GDP. Net capital flows (excluding other investment liabilities of the general government) are measured in percent of GDP. Output gap is measured in percent of potential GDP. FE is estimation by ordinary least squares method including country-fixed effects. IV refers to instrumental variable-two stage least squares (IV-2SLS) estimations. In IV estimations, net capital flows to the region (in percent of regional GDP) is used as the instrument. Constant is included in all specifications. All data is at annual frequency. Clustered standard errors by country are reported in parentheses. ***, **, and * indicate statistical significance at the 1, 5, and 10 percent levels, respectively.

**Table A.8.2**
Net capital flows and policy response in EMEs: IV–2SLS.

| | Policy rate | | FX intervention |
|---|---|---|---|
| | (1) | (2) | (3) |
| Net capital flows | 0.024** | 0.009 | 0.311*** |
| | (0.010) | (0.016) | (0.081) |
| Policy rate (lagged) | 0.906*** | 0.843*** | |
| | (0.023) | (0.036) | |
| US interest rate | 0.053*** | 0.041*** | −0.110 |
| | (0.009) | (0.012) | (0.082) |
| Global market volatility | 0.200** | 0.075 | −0.518 |
| | (0.088) | (0.086) | (0.870) |
| Commodity prices | 0.240** | 0.010 | −1.954** |
| | (0.120) | (0.082) | (0.847) |
| GFC | −0.412*** | −0.456*** | −1.882* |
| | (0.140) | (0.124) | (1.018) |
| Output gap | | 0.028 | 0.288 |
| | | (0.027) | (0.662) |
| Change in real ER | | −0.007** | 0.383 |
| | | (0.003) | |
| Inflation | | 0.089*** | |
| | | (0.031) | |
| Country-fixed effects | Yes | Yes | Yes |
| Quarter effects | Yes | Yes | Yes |
| Observations | 1,318 | 1,318 | 1,707 |
| R² | 0.841 | 0.868 | 0.289 |
| Countries | 41 | 41 | 51 |

*Notes*: Dependent variable is central bank policy rate (in percent) in cols. (1)–(2), and change in reserves (excluding valuation changes) in percent of GDP in col. (3). All specifications are estimated using IV-2SLS approach with net financial flows to the region (in percent of regional GDP) used as an instrument for net capital flows (in percent of GDP). See table 8.2 for descriptions of other variables. Clustered standard errors reported in parentheses. ***, **, and * indicate statistical significance at the 1, 5, and 10 percent levels, respectively.

**Table A.8.3**

Episodes of tightening of macroprudential policies in EMEs: 2005Q1–2013Q4.

| Countercyclical requirement | | Credit growth limits | | Consumer loan limits | | Loan-loss provisioning | | Debt-to-income cap | | Loan-to-value cap | | Other housing measures | |
|---|---|---|---|---|---|---|---|---|---|---|---|---|---|
| Brazil | 2007Q3 | Bulgaria | 2005Q2 | Brazil | 2010Q4 | Bulgaria | 2005Q4 | Croatia | 2006Q4 | Bulgaria | 2005Q2 | Brazil | 2007Q3 |
| Brazil | 2010Q4 | Bulgaria | 2006Q1 | Hungary | 2010Q1 | China | 2010Q3 | Hungary | 2010Q1 | Bulgaria | 2006Q2 | China | 2010Q2 |
| Brazil | 2011Q4 | Croatia | 2007Q1 | Indonesia | 2012Q2 | Colombia | 2007Q2 | Korea | 2005Q3 | China | 2010Q2 | China | 2010Q3 |
| Bulgaria | 2006Q2 | Romania | 2005Q3 | Thailand | 2005Q1 | Colombia | 2008Q2 | Korea | 2006Q2 | China | 2010Q3 | China | 2011Q1 |
| China | 2010Q3 | Turkey | 2010Q2 | Thailand | 2007Q2 | Croatia | 2006Q2 | Korea | 2006Q4 | China | 2011Q1 | China | 2013Q1 |
| Colombia | 2008Q4 | Turkey | 2011Q2 | Turkey | 2010Q2 | India | 2005Q4 | Korea | 2007Q1 | China | 2013Q1 | Hungary | 2010Q3 |
| Croatia | 2006Q2 | | | Turkey | 2011Q2 | India | 2006Q2 | Korea | 2007Q3 | China | 2013Q4 | India | 2011Q4 |
| Croatia | 2008Q1 | | | Turkey | 2013Q4 | India | 2007Q1 | Korea | 2009Q3 | Croatia | 2006Q4 | Mexico | 2011Q1 |
| India | 2005Q3 | | | | | India | 2010Q4 | Korea | 2011Q2 | Hungary | 2010Q1 | Serbia | 2011Q2 |
| India | 2006Q2 | | | | | Korea | 2006Q4 | Latvia | 2007Q3 | India | 2010Q4 | | |
| Peru | 2011Q3 | | | | | Mexico | 2009Q3 | Latvia | 2008Q1 | India | 2013Q2 | | |
| Poland | 2012Q2 | | | | | Mexico | 2011Q1 | Poland | 2010Q4 | Indonesia | 2012Q2 | | |
| Romania | 2008Q1 | | | | | Peru | 2006Q3 | Poland | 2011Q4 | Indonesia | 2013Q3 | | |
| Russia | 2010Q1 | | | | | Peru | 2008Q4 | Romania | 2005Q3 | Korea, S. | 2005Q3 | | |
| Russia | 2011Q4 | | | | | Romania | 2005Q3 | | | Korea, S. | 2006Q4 | | |
| Russia | 2012Q1 | | | | | Romania | 2008Q1 | | | Korea, S. | 2009Q3 | | |
| Russia | 2013Q3 | | | | | Romania | 2012Q1 | | | Korea, S. | 2009Q4 | | |
| Turkey | 2007Q2 | | | | | Russia | 2013Q1 | | | Latvia | 2007Q3 | | |
| Turkey | 2008Q1 | | | | | Serbia | 2008Q3 | | | Poland | 2011Q1 | | |
| Turkey | 2011Q2 | | | | | Turkey | 2011Q2 | | | Poland | 2013Q1 | | |
| | | | | | | Turkey | 2013Q4 | | | Romania | 2011Q1 | | |
| | | | | | | Ukraine | 2007Q1 | | | Serbia | 2008Q3 | | |
| | | | | | | Uruguay | 2006Q3 | | | Serbia | 2011Q2 | | |
| | | | | | | | | | | Serbia | 2012Q4 | | |

*Source:* Akinci and Olmstead-Rumsey 2015.

**Table A.8.4**
Episodes of increase in reserve requirements in EMEs: 2005Q1–2013Q4.

| Country | Quarter | Country | Quarter | Country | Quarter |
| --- | --- | --- | --- | --- | --- |
| Argentina | 2006Q2 | Guatemala | 2012Q1 | Peru | 2008Q3 |
| Argentina | 2006Q3 | Hungary | 2010Q4 | Peru | 2010Q3 |
| Belarus | 2011Q1 | India | 2006Q4 | Peru | 2010Q4 |
| Belarus | 2012Q1 | India | 2007Q1 | Philippines | 2005Q3 |
| Brazil | 2010Q1 | India | 2007Q2 | Philippines | 2011Q2 |
| Brazil | 2010Q2 | India | 2007Q3 | Philippines | 2011Q3 |
| Brazil | 2011Q1 | India | 2007Q4 | Poland | 2011Q1 |
| Brazil | 2011Q3 | India | 2008Q2 | Romania | 2006Q3 |
| China | 2010Q1 | India | 2008Q3 | Sri Lanka | 2011Q2 |
| China | 2010Q2 | India | 2010Q1 | Turkey | 2010Q3 |
| China | 2010Q4 | India | 2010Q2 | Turkey | 2010Q4 |
| China | 2011Q1 | Indonesia | 2010Q4 | Turkey | 2011Q1 |
| China | 2011Q2 | Indonesia | 2013Q3 | Turkey | 2011Q2 |
| Colombia | 2007Q2 | Indonesia | 2013Q4 | Turkey | 2013Q1 |
| Costa Rica | 2005Q3 | Latvia | 2005Q3 | Uruguay | 2008Q2 |
| Croatia | 2005Q1 | Latvia | 2006Q1 | Uruguay | 2011Q2 |
| Croatia | 2005Q2 | Macedonia | 2005Q1 | Uruguay | 2013Q2 |
| Croatia | 2005Q4 | Pakistan | 2006Q3 | Venezuela | 2006Q3 |
| Croatia | 2011Q4 | Peru | 2008Q1 | | |
| Croatia | 2012Q1 | Peru | 2008Q2 | | |

*Source:* Based on Frederico, Vegh, and Vuletin (2014).

**Table A.8.5**
Capital flows and macroprudential policy response by country, 2005Q1–2013Q4.

| | Net capital flows/GDP | US interest rate | Global market vol. | Commodity prices | GFC | Real GDP growth | Initial RR | Obs. | $R^2$ |
|---|---|---|---|---|---|---|---|---|---|
| *(a) Overall change in macroprudential policy* | | | | | | | | | |
| Brazil | −0.155 (0.136) | −0.414 (0.380) | 3.436** (1.379) | −1.580 (1.259) | −10.653*** (3.494) | −0.542 (0.428) | | 36 | 0.313 |
| Colombia | −0.236 (0.181) | 0.032 (0.124) | −0.165 (1.115) | 2.498 (2.440) | 0.058 (1.404) | −1.224*** (0.469) | | 36 | 0.310 |
| Croatia | 0.270* (0.149) | 0.560 (0.443) | −5.184 (3.673) | 4.988** (2.510) | −2.154 (6.066) | 0.302 (0.420) | | 36 | 0.726 |
| Hungary | −0.012 (0.075) | 0.040 (0.185) | 2.543*** (0.938) | −2.447 (2.298) | −8.377*** (1.903) | −0.260 (0.253) | | 36 | 0.199 |
| India | −0.124 (0.094) | −0.056 (0.150) | −0.206 (1.205) | −1.981 (1.321) | −7.417*** (2.241) | −0.641 (0.422) | | 36 | 0.204 |
| Indonesia | 0.046 (0.068) | 0.384** (0.192) | −0.003 (1.419) | 8.014** (3.380) | −9.500*** (2.833) | −1.965 (2.281) | | 36 | 0.285 |
| Korea, South | 0.134 (0.101) | 0.015 (0.110) | 0.324 (1.272) | −1.887 (1.924) | −6.281*** (1.968) | −0.452 (0.552) | | 36 | 0.207 |
| Poland | −0.018 (0.060) | −0.404 (0.347) | 1.555 (1.463) | 3.034* (1.727) | −5.171** (2.442) | −1.606** (0.651) | | 36 | 0.399 |
| Romania | 0.020 (0.028) | −0.272 (0.187) | −0.770 (0.981) | 0.475 (1.621) | −3.413*** (0.608) | 0.201 (0.292) | | 36 | 0.190 |
| Turkey | 0.027 (0.078) | 0.134 (0.121) | 0.504 (1.459) | 2.011 (1.583) | −6.190*** (1.768) | 0.107 (0.144) | | 36 | 0.110 |

*(b) Reserve requirements*

| | | | | | | | | |
|---|---|---|---|---|---|---|---|---|
| Brazil | 0.059* | −0.816* | 0.858* | −0.012 | −0.140 | 0.740*** | −0.063 | 36 | 0.898 |
| | (0.034) | (0.399) | (0.500) | (0.031) | (0.507) | (0.149) | (0.102) | | |
| Colombia | 0.193 | 1.475 | −4.898 | 0.378 | −3.494 | 0.784*** | −0.082 | 36 | 0.624 |
| | (0.185) | (1.843) | (3.569) | (0.263) | (2.547) | (0.197) | (0.851) | | |
| Croatia | 0.014 | −0.158 | 0.044 | 0.075 | 0.029 | 0.787*** | 0.045 | 36 | 0.844 |
| | (0.015) | (0.406) | (0.524) | (0.076) | (0.642) | (0.148) | (0.071) | | |
| Hungary | 0.032 | −8.953 | −2.850 | 0.050 | −1.894 | 0.858*** | 0.903 | 36 | 0.911 |
| | (0.063) | (5.940) | (5.590) | (0.543) | (5.159) | (0.093) | (0.756) | | |
| India | 0.017 | −0.722 | 0.532 | −0.013 | −0.284 | 1.118*** | 0.229*** | 36 | 0.851 |
| | (0.033) | (0.460) | (0.482) | (0.046) | (0.415) | (0.137) | (0.079) | | |
| Peru | 0.086 | 1.139 | 1.854 | −0.065 | −1.727 | 0.862*** | −0.277 | 36 | 0.929 |
| | (0.069) | (1.271) | (2.867) | (0.169) | (1.407) | (0.074) | (0.284) | | |
| Poland | −0.000 | −0.181 | 0.174 | −0.009 | 0.249 | 0.732*** | 0.034 | 36 | 0.715 |
| | (0.005) | (0.119) | (0.114) | (0.008) | (0.160) | (0.170) | (0.033) | | |
| Romania | 0.014 | −0.158 | 0.044 | 0.075 | 0.029 | 0.787*** | 0.045 | 36 | 0.844 |
| | (0.015) | (0.406) | (0.524) | (0.076) | (0.642) | (0.148) | (0.071) | | |
| Turkey | 0.057* | −0.640 | 0.993 | −0.098 | 1.264 | 0.767*** | 0.016 | 36 | 0.870 |
| | (0.029) | (0.584) | (0.707) | (0.060) | (0.743) | (0.137) | (0.060) | | |
| Uruguay | 0.032* | −0.688* | 0.342 | −0.074* | 1.623** | 0.834*** | 0.058 | 32 | 0.814 |
| | (0.018) | (0.357) | (0.583) | (0.041) | (0.680) | (0.151) | (0.098) | | |

*Notes:* In top panel (a), the dependent variable is a binary variable equal to one if any macroprudential policy was tightened, and zero otherwise. In bottom panel (b), the dependent variable is average reserve requirement (RR) on local currency liabilities. All estimations in the top panel are conducted using a probit model, and pseudo-$R^2$ is reported. Initial RR is one-period lagged RR. All regressions include a constant. Robust standard errors are reported in parentheses. ***, **, and * indicate statistical significance at the 1, 5, and 10 percent levels, respectively.

**Table A.8.6**
Episodes of capital inflow control tightening in EMEs: 2005Q1–2012Q4.

| Equity | | Bond | | Financial sector | | | |
|---|---|---|---|---|---|---|---|
| Country | Quarter | Country | Quarter | Country | Quarter | Country | Quarter |
| Argentina | 2005Q2 | Argentina | 2005Q2 | Argentina | 2008Q3 | Korea, South | 2007Q3 |
| Argentina | 2005Q4 | Argentina | 2005Q4 | Argentina | 2012Q1 | Korea, South | 2008Q1 |
| Argentina | 2009Q2 | Argentina | 2009Q2 | Brazil | 2007Q2 | Korea, South | 2010Q1 |
| Brazil | 2009Q4 | Argentina | 2012Q1 | Brazil | 2007Q3 | Korea, South | 2010Q3 |
| Brazil | 2010Q4 | Brazil | 2008Q1 | Brazil | 2008Q1 | Korea, South | 2010Q4 |
| Colombia | 2007Q2 | Brazil | 2009Q4 | Brazil | 2011Q1 | Korea, South | 2011Q3 |
| Colombia | 2008Q2 | Brazil | 2010Q4 | Brazil | 2011Q2 | Mexico | 2012Q4 |
| | | Colombia | 2007Q2 | Brazil | 2011Q3 | Philippines | 2012Q4 |
| | | Colombia | 2008Q2 | Brazil | 2012Q1 | Thailand | 2006Q4 |
| | | Indonesia | 2010Q3 | Colombia | 2007Q2 | Turkey | 2009Q2 |
| | | Indonesia | 2011Q2 | India | 2007Q1 | Turkey | 2010Q2 |
| | | Korea, South | 2010Q4 | India | 2007Q3 | Turkey | 2010Q3 |
| | | Korea, South | 2011Q3 | Indonesia | 2005Q1 | Turkey | 2010Q4 |
| | | Korea, South | 2012Q1 | Indonesia | 2005Q3 | Turkey | 2011Q2 |
| | | Thailand | 2006Q4 | Indonesia | 2010Q3 | Turkey | 2012Q4 |
| | | Thailand | 2010Q4 | Indonesia | 2011Q1 | Romania | 2005Q1 |
| | | | | Indonesia | 2011Q2 | Romania | 2005Q3 |
| | | | | Korea, South | 2006Q4 | Romania | 2006Q1 |

*Source:* Based on Ahmed et al. (2015).

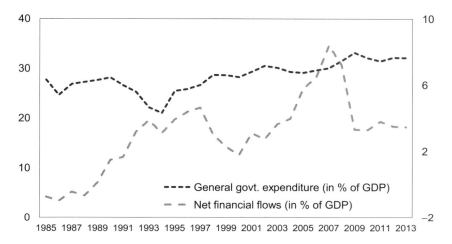

**Figure A.8.1**
Fiscal policy and net capital flows to EMEs, 1985–2013.
*Sources*: Authors' calculations based on the IMF's International Financial Statistics and
World Economic Outlook databases.
*Notes*: General government expenditure (in percent of GDP) taken as a proxy for fiscal
policy. Chart shows the average net financial flows and general government expenditure
for the countries included in the sample.

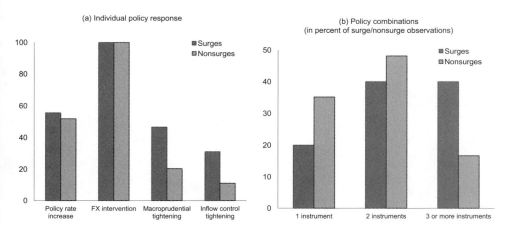

**Figure A.8.2**
Policy responses in inflow surges in EMEs.
*Notes*: Policy response is classified for surges identified using the country-specific criteria
(that the net inflow in percent of GDP lie in country's top thirtieth percentile of the
distribution) over 2005–2013 for which data on all policy instruments is available. Panel
(a) shows the percentage of surges in which the respective policy instruments were deployed.
Panel (b) shows the percentages of surges by the number of policy instruments deployed.

# IV    Policy Considerations

# 9 Effectiveness of Policy Instruments

## 9.1 Introduction

In previous chapters, we argued that emerging markets facing capital inflows should, and indeed do, deploy a variety of policy instruments. But do these instruments actually work? With the exception of the policy interest rate, there is considerable doubt and debate about the effectiveness of various instruments, most notably about capital controls. It is true that, given the incentive to circumvent capital controls, markets will try to find ways around them—often displaying remarkable ingenuity—but the same is true of any other tax or regulation. Therefore, it is far from obvious why capital controls should be singled out as being especially susceptible to evasion or circumvention. As discussed in chapter 2, part of the perception may stem from historical experience with the use of *outflow* controls—yet individuals trying to protect their savings from expropriation, devaluation, or other loss are a far cry from institutional investors making a cost-benefit analysis of where to place their funds.

Sterilized intervention is the other instrument whose effectiveness is often questioned. Yet the very fact that central banks of most emerging market economies (EMEs) intervene regularly (as shown in chapter 8) suggests that at least they believe it to be effective in their own markets. By contrast, there appears to be inordinate faith, relative to available evidence, in the ability of macroprudential measures to maintain financial stability. Since much of our policy prescription depends on the ability of the various instruments to act, in this chapter we review existing studies and present our own empirical research on the effectiveness of foreign exchange (FX) intervention, capital controls, and macroprudential measures.[1]

---

1. There is little debate about the effectiveness of monetary policy in achieving its objectives of price and output stability in EMEs (see Leiderman, Maino, and Parrado 2006;

A key difficulty in evaluating the effectiveness of policy instruments is determining the authorities' intended objective. Thus, capital controls might be imposed to curb the aggregate volume of inflows (for instance, to stem currency appreciation, as in chapter 5) or to alter the composition of flows toward less risky liabilities (as in chapter 7). Likewise, FX intervention might be undertaken to alter the level of the exchange rate, or to reduce its volatility, or simply to slow the pace of appreciation or depreciation. This conceptual problem is compounded by several practical difficulties in assessing effectiveness. First, as documented in chapter 8, measures are often imposed in tandem—as part of an overall package of policy responses to deal with a surge in capital inflows—so it is inherently difficult to isolate the effect of any individual measure, let alone attribute observed outcomes to it. Second, the econometrician faces a fundamental identification problem: policies tend to be adopted in *response* to capital inflows (as we saw in chapter 8), which will tend to give rise to a spurious positive correlation between their imposition and the magnitude or consequence of the inflows, thus biasing the estimates toward *not* finding any effect of the policies. (Conversely, in some cases policy may respond when the tide has already turned, and the outcome could be erroneously attributed to the measure. In such instances, it is imperative to control for the factors that contributed to the reversal in the first place.) Third, as noted earlier, there are measurement problems—many capital controls and prudential measures are discrete in nature and do not lend themselves easily to quantification.

Notwithstanding these difficulties, a voluminous literature seeks to analyze the efficacy of various policy tools in EMEs. This chapter reviews that literature, but also lays out stylized facts based on our data. Section 9.2 examines the impact of sterilized FX intervention on the exchange rate and then considers its implications for domestic credit growth. Section 9.3 assesses the effectiveness of macroprudential measures in dampening domestic credit cycles. Section 9.4 explores whether capital account regulations (both residency-based capital controls and currency-based prudential measures) can help address macroeconomic imbalances—currency-appreciation pressures and domestic credit growth—as well as limit balance-sheet vulnerabilities. Section 9.5 concludes.

---

Saizar and Chalk 2008; Acosta-Ormaechea and Coble 2011); hence we do not consider the issue of its effectiveness here.

## 9.2   Sterilized FX Intervention

The argument, which we made in chapter 6, that EME central banks—
even those with inflation-targeting frameworks—might usefully intervene in the FX markets (and can do so without jeopardizing their inflation
target) is predicated on sterilized intervention actually having an effect
on the exchange rate. The literature has identified two main ways
through which this might happen: the portfolio balance channel and
the signaling channel. The former relies on intervention altering the
relative supplies of domestic and foreign currency-denominated assets
in the market. If the assets are perfect substitutes (so uncovered interest
rate parity holds), then changes in their relative supplies will not affect
the exchange rate. Under imperfect substitutability, however, rates of
return must adjust to induce investors to shift their portfolios toward
the asset whose relative supply has increased; given interest rates, this
requires an adjustment of the exchange rate. There are reasons to be
skeptical about the quantitative importance of this channel in the case
of advanced economies, where bond markets are so huge that even massive intervention barely makes a dent on the relative supply of assets. In
the case of EMEs, however, interventions can amount to a significant
share in local bond markets, and this channel can be correspondingly
stronger.[2]

The signaling channel affects the exchange rate through a change in
market expectations about future fundamentals (including the stance
of monetary policy). If the central bank has better information about
fundamentals—which is certainly the case regarding its own future
monetary stance—then intervention can influence today's exchange
rate by signaling changes in future fundamentals. Unlike the portfolio
balance channel, it is not clear a priori whether this channel should be
stronger in EMEs or in advanced economies. Arguably, moreover, if
sterilized intervention operates exclusively by signaling future monetary policy, then it does not represent an independent policy tool.[3]

---

2. Indeed, studies analyzing sterilized FX intervention in the context of advanced economies find limited evidence of effectiveness (e.g., Dominguez 1990, 1998; Dominguez and
Frankel 1993; Ghosh 1992; Kaminsky and Lewis 1996).

3. Ghosh (2002) develops a model in which secret intervention by the central bank allows
it to optimally signal its private information about a future shock (rather than about
future monetary policy). In that model, however, such signaling only works in a rational-
expectations setting if there exists some (however small) portfolio balance effect as well,
so that intervention is not working solely through signaling.

Existing studies are hardly unanimous, but overall they present a relatively favorable picture about the effectiveness of sterilized FX intervention in emerging markets (table 9.1). Within the literature, the findings of individual country case studies are generally more mixed than those based on cross-country/panel data. Domaç and Mendoza (2004), for instance, use daily intervention data from Mexico and Turkey and find that foreign exchange sales have a statistically significant effect on both the level and the volatility of exchange rate. But using similar data, Guimarães and Karacadag (2004) conclude that FX intervention affects the level of the exchange rate in Mexico (but not in Turkey), while reducing its volatility in Turkey (but not in Mexico). Similarly, Kamil (2008) finds that interventions have been somewhat effective in Colombia if done during episodes of monetary easing—but not when the economy is overheating and monetary policy is being tightened—while Rincón and Toro (2010) find FX intervention to have been effective in Colombia when capital inflow controls have been in place.

Panel data seem to yield less equivocal results. Adler and Tovar (2011) estimate the effect of intervention in a group of fifteen (mostly Latin American) EMEs, and find that intervention can slow the pace of currency appreciation—especially when the currency is already overvalued—but that it is less effective in countries with more open capital accounts. Likewise, in a sample of eighteen EMEs, Daude, Levy-Yeyati and Nagengast (2014) find that FX intervention is, on average, effective—and becomes more so the larger the deviation of the exchange rate from its equilibrium. Using a sample that consists mainly of EMEs, Blanchard, Adler, and de Carvalho Filho (2015) find that intervention can significantly reduce currency appreciation in the face of capital inflows.

### 9.2.1 Some Empirics
In order to examine this issue ourselves, we turn to the data set used in chapter 8 and estimate the following model:

$$\Delta er_{it} = \beta_0 + \beta_{FX}FX_{it} + \sum_{m=1}^{n} \beta_m Z_{mit} + \mu_i + \varepsilon_{it} \tag{9.1}$$

where $\Delta er$ is the quarterly change in the real effective exchange rate; $FX$ is the proxy for intervention (quarterly change in reserves excluding valuation changes, scaled by GDP); $Z$ includes other relevant explana-

**Table 9.1**
Selected studies on effectiveness of FX intervention.

| Country | Study | Did FX intervention affect exchange rate | |
| --- | --- | --- | --- |
| | | Level | Volatility |
| Brazil | Stone, Walker, and Yasui (2009) | Yes | Yes |
| | Chamon, Garcia, and Souza (2015) | Yes (mixed) | No |
| Chile | Tapia and Tokman (2004) | Yes | |
| Colombia | Mandeng (2003) | | Yes (moderate) |
| | Kamil (2008) | Yes (mixed) | Yes |
| | Rincón and Toro (2010) | Yes (mixed) | Yes (mixed) |
| Czech | Gersl and Holub (2006) | Yes (ST) | Yes (ST) |
| Republic | Disyatat and Galati (2005) | Yes | No |
| | Dominguez, Fatum, and Vacek (2013) | Yes (mixed) | |
| Hungary | Barabás (2003) | Yes | |
| India | Pattanaik and Sahoo (2003) | Yes (weak) | Yes |
| Korea, S. | Rhee and Song (1999) | Yes | |
| Mexico and Turkey | Domaç and Mendoza (2004) | Yes | Yes |
| | Guimarães and Karacadag (2004) | Yes (mixed) | Yes (mixed) |
| Philippines | Abenoja (2003) | Yes (mixed) | Yes |
| | Guinigundo (2013) | | Yes |
| Peru | Lahura and Vega (2013) | Yes | |
| | Tashu (2014) | Yes | Yes |
| Poland | Adam, Koziński, and Zieliński (2013) | Yes | Yes |
| Thailand | Sangmanee (2001) | No | |
| Cross-country evidence | | | |
| | Adler and Tova (2011) | Yes | |
| | Broto (2013) | Yes (mixed) | Yes (mixed) |
| | Daude, Levy-Yeyati, and Nagengast (2014) | Yes | |
| | Adler, Lisack, and Mano (2015) | Yes | |
| | Blanchard et al. (2015) | Yes | |

*Notes*: A blank entry reflects that the particular relationship was not analyzed. ST indicates cases where only short-term effects were detected. Mixed indicates that findings on effectiveness reported in the study were not conclusive.

tory variables such as net capital flows (scaled by GDP), global market volatility, a dummy for the global financial crisis, and the lagged dependent variable (to capture persistence in exchange rate movements); $\mu$ is country-specific effects; and $\varepsilon$ is the random error term. In addition, we include quarter-specific effects in (9.1) to control for any seasonal factors influencing the exchange rate.

The results are disappointing: the coefficient on intervention, though negative, is both economically and statistically insignificant (table 9.2, col. [1]). But restricting the sample to episodes of foreign exchange purchases (i.e., reserve accumulation), the coefficient increases substantially in magnitude and turns highly statistically significant. Against an average rate of *appreciation* of 6 percent per quarter in the (restricted) sample, reserve accumulation in the order of 10 percent of GDP would be associated with a quarterly rate of *depreciation* of 0.4 percent. More telling, the coefficient on reserve accumulation is of equal magnitude, but of opposite sign, to that on capital inflows (where the latter itself is also highly significant). Thus, the impact of any given capital inflow on the exchange rate can be *fully offset* if the central bank is willing to undertake a corresponding amount of FX intervention.[4]

These results hold when the regression includes the central bank policy rate—which allows us to interpret the results as pertaining to sterilized intervention (in practice, almost all of the intervention is sterilized, so the inclusion of the policy rate makes little difference)—as well as the US interest rate (col. [3]). They are also robust to taking into account changes in commodity prices (to capture any terms of trade effects), the overall trade openness of the economy, and to the inclusion of lagged FX intervention, which we find to be statistically insignificant (col. [4]). That FX intervention may have stronger effects against currency appreciation pressures than depreciation dynamics is plausible since a lower bound on the stock of reserves may constrain the central bank's ability to defend the exchange rate. If anticipated by markets, this could imply that FX sales would have a more limited impact.[5]

---

4. Looking at individual countries, however, the picture is less clear-cut (results are not reported here). FX intervention appears to be significantly effective in countries with pegged exchange rates in emerging Europe (e.g., Belarus, Bulgaria, Estonia, Latvia, Lithuania, Macedonia, and Slovakia), as well as in some countries with more flexible exchange rate regimes (e.g., Brazil, Jordan, Paraguay, the Philippines, and Turkey), but less so in others. 5. Among existing studies using panel data, Daude, Levy-Yeyati, and Nagengast (2014) find some evidence of FX intervention being more effective in limiting currency appreciation, but Adler, Lisack, and Mano (2015) do not find evidence in support of asymmetric effects in their sample (which comprises both advanced and emerging market countries).

**Table 9.2**
FX intervention, exchange rate, and domestic credit in EMEs, 2005Q1–2013Q4.

| | Change in REER | | | | Domestic credit growth | | | |
|---|---|---|---|---|---|---|---|---|
| | Full sample (1) | FX purchase (2) | FX purchase (3) | FX purchase (4) | Full sample (5) | FX purchase (6) | FX purchase (7) | FX purchase (8) |
| FX intervention | -0.001 (0.018) | -0.039* (0.020) | -0.037* (0.021) | -0.040* (0.022) | -0.036* (0.019) | -0.076** (0.034) | -0.072** (0.032) | -0.070** (0.031) |
| Net capital flows/GDP | 0.037*** (0.010) | 0.032*** (0.011) | 0.028** (0.011) | 0.030** (0.011) | 0.058*** (0.017) | 0.076*** (0.022) | 0.081*** (0.022) | 0.087*** (0.023) |
| Global market volatility | -0.895** (0.416) | -0.500 (0.358) | -0.188 (0.517) | 0.025 (0.521) | -1.799*** (0.377) | -1.835*** (0.423) | -0.612 (0.483) | -0.176 (0.463) |
| GFC | 0.132 (0.339) | 0.354 (0.594) | -0.185 (0.736) | -0.259 (0.744) | 0.241 (0.329) | -0.131 (0.402) | -1.773*** (0.562) | -2.385*** (0.496) |
| Change in REER (lagged) | 0.155*** (0.026) | 0.164*** (0.028) | 0.159*** (0.027) | 0.160*** (0.027) | | | | |
| Credit growth (lagged) | | | | | 0.347*** (0.057) | 0.365*** (0.069) | 0.340*** (0.067) | 0.310*** (0.061) |
| Policy rate | | | 0.105 (0.076) | | | | -0.244 (0.158) | -0.250* (0.141) |
| US interest rate | | | 0.059 (0.057) | | | | 0.277*** (0.052) | 0.280*** (0.053) |

(continued)

**Table 9.2** (continued)

| | Change in REER | | | | Domestic credit growth | | | |
|---|---|---|---|---|---|---|---|---|
| | Full sample (1) | FX purchase (2) | FX purchase (3) | FX purchase (4) | Full sample (5) | FX purchase (6) | FX purchase (7) | FX purchase (8) |
| Commodity prices | | | | −0.642 (0.485) | | | | −2.429*** (0.759) |
| Trade openness | | | | 0.017* (0.008) | | | | −0.011 (0.013) |
| FX reserves/GDP (lagged) | | | | 0.009 (0.013) | | | | 0.032 (0.020) |
| Country-fixed effects | Yes | Yes | Yes | Yes | Yes | Yes | Yes | Yes |
| Quarter effects | Yes | Yes | Yes | Yes | Yes | Yes | Yes | Yes |
| Observations | 1,504 | 1,034 | 1,034 | 1,032 | 1,504 | 1,034 | 1,034 | 1,032 |
| $R^2$ | 0.071 | 0.128 | 0.135 | 0.143 | 0.312 | 0.378 | 0.402 | 0.423 |
| Countries | 46 | 45 | 45 | 45 | 46 | 45 | 45 | 45 |

*Notes:* Dependent variable is quarterly change in REER (in percent) in cols. (1)–(3); and quarterly real domestic credit growth (in percent) in cols. (4)–(6). Full sample includes all observations. FX purchase restricts sample to include reserves accumulation observations only. All regressions include a constant. Clustered standard errors (by country) are reported in parentheses. ***, **, and * indicate significance at the 1, 5, and 10 percent levels, respectively.

Beyond its primary purpose—influencing the exchange rate—sterilized intervention also has implications for banking system credit creation. Table 9.2 (col. [4]) shows that while capital inflows have a positive and highly significant impact on credit expansion (as documented also in chapter 4), reserve accumulation has a *negative* and highly statistically significant impact on credit expansion. In other words, capital inflows expand banking system credit to the economy, but by undertaking sterilized intervention the central bank can absorb that inflow (parking it in FX reserves) and its impact on the real economy. This justifies our choice in chapter 5 of modeling credit expansion as a function of $\Delta k - \Delta R$ (as well as our reasoning that sterilized intervention may help limit excessive credit growth).

### 9.3 Macroprudential Measures

In the wake of the global financial crisis, the use of macroprudential policies to tame the risks associated with domestic credit growth have risen to the forefront of the policy discourse.[6] As documented in chapter 8, emerging market policy makers are now proactively deploying macroprudential tools in various forms, which has led to a burgeoning literature exploring their effectiveness.

Broadly speaking, existing studies on the topic can be grouped into two categories—those that examine the effectiveness of macroprudential measures by lumping them into aggregate indices, and those that analyze the effectiveness of individual measures.[7] The first group of studies finds that macroprudential measures are in general effective in limiting credit booms (e.g., Ostry et al. 2012; Dell'Ariccia et al. 2012), while the second group nuances this conclusion by establishing that the effectiveness of instruments varies within, and across, countries (table 9.3). Thus, for example, Igan and Kang (2011) find that caps on loan-to-value (LTV)

---

6. Policy discussions paid little attention to credit booms in the run-up to the global financial crisis as the increasing popularity of the inflation-targeting framework implied that monetary policy focused mostly on interest rates (rather than on monetary aggregates), while regulatory policy focused more on individual institutions, and was more microprudential in nature (Dell'Ariccia et al. 2012). Moreover, there was also the view that since "bad" credit booms were difficult to distinguish from "good" credit booms in real time, policy should deal with the bust instead of trying to prevent the boom (Greenspan 2002).

7. A parallel strand of literature theoretically evaluates the effectiveness of macroprudential policies in different settings (see, for example, Acharya 2009; Hanson, Kashyap, and Stein 2011; Goodhart 2008; Goodhart et al. 2012; Hahm et al. 2012; De Nicolò, Favara, and Ratnovski 2012; Shin 2013). Galati and Moessner (2012) provide a detailed literature review of the objectives of macroprudential policy, its interaction with monetary policy, and the operational issues involved in its implementation.

**Table 9.3**
Selected studies on effectiveness of macroprudential measures.

| Country | Study | Macroprudential measure | Did macroprudential measures reduce | |
|---|---|---|---|---|
| | | | Domestic credit growth | Asset price inflation |
| Brazil | Glocker and Towbin 2012 | RR | Yes | |
| | Afanasieff et al. 2015 | Risk weight on high LTV auto loans | Yes[a] | |
| Croatia | Kraft and Galac 2011 | Limits on bank credit growth | Yes (mixed) | |
| Korea, S. | Igan and Kang 2011 | LTV and DTI ratios | | Yes |
| | Lee 2013 | DC liquidity ratio; LTV and DTI ratios | Yes | Yes (mixed) |
| Peru | Terrier et al. 2011 | RR | Yes | |
| | Pérez-Forero and Vega 2014 | RR | Yes | |
| Uruguay | Camors and Peydró 2014 | RR and liquidity requirement | Yes | |
| *Cross-country evidence* | | | | |
| | Lim et al. 2011 | LTV; DTI; credit growth limit; RR; DP rules | Yes | |
| | Ostry et al. 2012 | Index (LTV; credit concentration limits; RR) | Yes | |
| | Dell'Ariccia et al. 2012 | Index (differential treatment of deposits; RR; liquidity requirements; interest rate and credit controls; open FX position limits) | Yes | |
| | Vandenbussche, Vogel, and Detragiache 2012 | Marginal RR; minimum CARs | | Yes |
| | Tovar, Garcia-Escribano and Martín 2012 | RR | Yes (ST) | |

| Study | Measures | | |
|---|---|---|---|
| Claessens, Ghosh, and Mihet 2013 | LTV; DTI; credit growth limit; RR; dynamic provisioning rules | | |
| Kuttner and Shim 2013 | LTV; DTI; exposure limits to housing sector; housing-related taxes | Yes (mixed) | Yes (mixed) |
| Akinci and Olmstead-Rumsey 2015 | LTV; DTI; capital requirements; DP rules | Yes | Yes |
| Cerutti, Claessens, and Laeven 2015 | LTV; DTI; leverage ratio; DP; RR; taxes on banks; CAR; limits on DC and FX loans; limits on interbank exposure; concentration limits | Yes | No |
| Zhang and Zoli 2014 | Index of housing-related measures (LTV; DTI; higher risk weight and DP rules on mortgage loans; housing-related taxation); index of other measures (RR; consumer loan measures; credit limits; CAR; DP rules; liquidity tools) | Yes[b] | Yes |

*Notes:* A blank entry reflects that the study did not analyze the particular relationship. Cross-country studies (except for Ostry et al. [2012]) generally include both advanced countries and EMEs in the sample. DP = dynamic provisioning; LTV = loan-to-value ratio; DTI = debt-to-income ratio; DC = domestic currency; RR = reserve requirements; CAR = capital adequacy ratio; SIFI = systemically important financial institutions. (ST) indicates that the effect was short-lived. (Mixed) indicates that studies report mixed findings on the effectiveness of the particular measure.

a. Measure reduced the origination of new auto loans with long maturities and high LTV.

b. Specifically, index of housing-related measures significantly reduces real credit growth and house price growth.

and debt-to-income (DTI) ratios imposed in South Korea were significantly associated with a decline in house price appreciation and the volume of transactions, but Vandenbussche, Vogel, and Detragiache (2012) find that such measures did not have a strong impact on house prices in emerging Europe. Instead they show that minimum capital adequacy ratios, together with changes in marginal reserve requirements linked to credit growth, have a statistically and economically significant impact on house price inflation. That the same policies may have different effects is plausible since institutional capacity, the level of financial development and sophistication of the markets (which may affect the scope for circumvention), and the coverage and intensity of the measures naturally vary across countries.

More generally, studies using cross-country/panel data find that credit and liquidity-related macroprudential measures such as limits on credit growth, caps on LTV and DTI ratios, and reserve requirements are effective in dampening domestic credit cycles and in limiting financial-stability risks (e.g., Lim et al. 2011; Claessens, Ghosh, and Mihet 2013; Akinci and Olmstead-Rumsey 2015; Cerutti, Claessens, and Laeven 2015). There is also some evidence of asymmetry in their efficacy, with a tightening of the measures being more effective in reducing credit growth in upturns than their relaxation in stimulating credit growth during downturns.

### 9.3.1   Some Empirics

A snapshot of our own data supports these findings and shows that real domestic private sector credit growth indeed falls after macroprudential measures are tightened, but that the impact varies across instruments (figure 9.1). Thus, for example, based on the overall indicator of macroprudential measures, credit growth drops by about 0.8 percentage points in the quarter in which the measure is tightened ($t$) and remains fairly constant at this reduced rate in the next three quarters (figure 9.1, panel [a]). Looking at individual instruments, however, the (unconditional) drop in credit growth appears to be the most pronounced, not surprisingly, for credit-related instruments such as limits on credit growth and caps on LTV and DTI ratios, and the least for other housing-related measures. In some cases (for example, in panels [c] and [d]), credit growth appears to be higher in the quarter the measure is introduced, but this may simply be a result of endogeneity (whereby measures tend to be tightened precisely when domestic credit is growing rapidly), which induces the spurious positive correlation. The time series presented in figure 9.1 also suggests that there

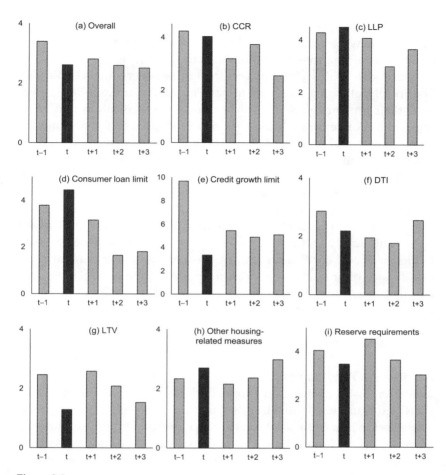

**Figure 9.1**
Macroprudential measures and domestic credit growth in EMEs, 2005Q1:2013Q4 (in percent).
*Source*: Authors' estimates.
*Note*: The figure presents real domestic private sector credit growth (on a quarterly basis) before the macroprudential measure is tightened (t–1), the quarter in which the measure is tightened (t), and the three quarters after the measure is tightened.

may be some lag before the full impact of policies is realized as new measures may be phased in gradually, or there may be a response lag on the part of financial institutions and their borrowers.

Regression analysis broadly confirms these observations (table 9.4). Specifically, allowing measures to have an impact up to four quarters after their implementation, and choosing the specification that minimizes the Akaike Information Criterion (AIC), we find that limits on credit growth and caps on LTV and DTI ratios are negatively correlated with real credit growth—though the coefficient is statistically significant only for the LTV ratio (col. [7]). Liquidity-related measures such as reserve requirements (RRs) also significantly reduce credit growth, albeit with a lag of three quarters (col. [9]). That we do not find a statistically significant coefficient on other macroprudential measures does not necessarily imply that they are ineffective; rather, endogeneity issues (which will bias coefficients toward zero) are daunting here, and the significance of at least some measures points to the potentially useful role that macroprudential policies can play in dampening credit cycles and economic overheating.

## 9.4   Capital Controls

As discussed in chapter 2, there is a vast literature analyzing the effectiveness of controls on capital inflows in EMEs, which can be classified into three main strands. The first, and predominant, group analyzes the impact of capital controls on the total volume of inflows, currency-appreciation pressures, and composition of flows. Much of the earlier literature—conducted in the context of EME surges during the 1990s and mid-2000s—is of this variety. Examining mostly Latin American inflow control episodes (notably in Brazil, Chile, and Colombia), this literature generally finds that capital controls successfully alter the composition of capital flows toward longer-term and less risky types of flows (such as foreign direct investment, or FDI), but only mixed evidence that they affect either the exchange rate or aggregate flows (table 9.5). Taken at face value, the finding of no impact on the total volume of flows, but a change in its composition, implies that there must be perfect substitutability across different asset classes. But this seems implausible: while some investors may be willing and able to jump across asset classes, it is very unlikely that they can all do so. The lack of convincing evidence on the effectiveness of controls in reducing the aggregate volume of inflows can therefore likely be

**Table 9.4**

Macroprudential measures and domestic credit in EMEs, 2005Q1–2013Q4.

| | Overall (1) | CCR (2) | LLP (3) | Consumer loan limit (4) | Credit growth limit (5) | DTI (6) | LTV (7) | Other housing-related (8) | RR (9) |
|---|---|---|---|---|---|---|---|---|---|
| Macroprudential measure | −0.492 (0.561) | 0.474 (0.701) | 0.949* (0.515) | 0.971 (0.597) | −2.696 (4.377) | −0.484 (0.709) | −1.786* (1.041) | 0.768 (1.191) | 0.048 (0.063) |
| Macroprudential measure (1-period lagged) | | | | | | | | | 0.081 (0.094) |
| Macroprudential measure (2-periods lagged) | | | | | | | | | −0.028 (0.072) |
| Macroprudential measure (3-periods lagged) | | | | | | | | | −0.084** (0.034) |
| Net capital flows/GDP | 0.075*** (0.014) | 0.074*** (0.014) | 0.074*** (0.014) | 0.074*** (0.014) | 0.074*** (0.014) | 0.074*** (0.014) | 0.076*** (0.014) | 0.074*** (0.014) | 0.040** (0.016) |
| Global market volatility | −1.622*** (0.450) | −1.648*** (0.454) | −1.601*** (0.457) | −1.631*** (0.453) | −1.639*** (0.460) | −1.627*** (0.451) | −1.666*** (0.451) | −1.641*** (0.456) | −1.822*** (0.387) |
| GFC | 0.412 (0.372) | 0.457 (0.380) | 0.419 (0.379) | 0.447 (0.376) | 0.427 (0.377) | 0.430 (0.373) | 0.456 (0.376) | 0.453 (0.378) | 0.358 (0.309) |

(continued)

**Table 9.4** (continued)

| | Overall (1) | CCR (2) | LLP (3) | Consumer loan limit (4) | Credit growth limit (5) | DTI (6) | LTV (7) | Other housing-related (8) | RR (9) |
|---|---|---|---|---|---|---|---|---|---|
| Credit growth (lagged) | 0.294*** (0.083) | 0.292*** (0.083) | 0.292*** (0.083) | 0.293*** (0.083) | 0.300*** (0.079) | 0.293*** (0.083) | 0.291*** (0.082) | 0.293*** (0.083) | 0.361*** (0.081) |
| Country-fixed effects | Yes | Yes | Yes | Yes | Yes | Yes | Yes | Yes | Yes |
| Quarter effects | Yes | Yes | Yes | Yes | Yes | Yes | Yes | Yes | Yes |
| Observations | 924 | 924 | 924 | 924 | 924 | 924 | 924 | 924 | 1,033 |
| $R^2$ | 0.294 | 0.294 | 0.295 | 0.294 | 0.296 | 0.294 | 0.298 | 0.294 | 0.335 |
| Countries | 27 | 27 | 27 | 27 | 27 | 27 | 27 | 27 | 32 |

*Notes:* Dependent variable is quarterly real domestic private credit growth (in percent). Overall indicates tightening of any macroprudential policy; CCR = countercyclical capital requirements; LLP = dynamic loan loss provisioning rules; LTV = loan-to-value ratio; RR = average reserve requirement on local currency liabilities. All regressions include a constant. In col. (9), observations pertaining to Croatia for the year 2008 are excluded from the estimation because of an extremely large reduction (outlier of 41 percentage points) in the RR ratio during the global financial crisis. Clustered standard errors reported in parentheses. ***, **, and * indicate statistical significance at the 1, 5, and 10 percent levels, respectively.

**Table 9.5**
Selected studies on capital inflow controls and macro outcomes.

| Country | Duration of controls | Study | Did controls on inflows | | |
| --- | --- | --- | --- | --- | --- |
| | | | Reduce the volume of flows | Reduce currency pressures | Change composition |
| Brazil | 1993–1997 | Cardoso and Goldfajn 1998 | Yes (ST) | | Yes (ST) |
| | | Reinhart and Smith 1998 | No | | Yes (ST) |
| | | Ariyoshi et al. 2000 | No | No | No |
| | | Edison and Reinhart 2001 | | No | |
| | | Carvalho and Garcia 2008 | Yes (ST) | | |
| | 2008 | Baba and Kokenyne 2011 | No | No | No |
| | 2009–2012 | Forbes et al. 2012 | | | |
| | | Chamon and Garcia 2016 | | Yes | Yes |
| Chile | 1991–1998 | Valdes-Prieto and Soto (1998) | No | No | Yes |
| | | Le Fort and Budnevich 1997 | No | Yes | |
| | | Larraín, Laban, and Chumacero 1997 | No | | Yes |
| | | Cardoso and Laurens 1998 | Yes (ST) | No | Yes |
| | | Reinhart and Smith 1998 | Yes | | Yes (ST) |
| | | Edwards 1999 | No | No | Yes |
| | | Gallego, Hernández, and Schmidt-Hebbel 1999 | Yes (ST) | No | Yes (ST) |
| | | Ariyoshi et al. 2000 | No | No | No |
| | | De Gregorio, Edwards, and Valdés 2000 | No | Yes (ST) | Yes |
| | | Edwards and Rigobon 2009 | | Yes | |

(continued)

**Table 9.5** (continued)

| Country | Duration of controls | Study | Did controls on inflows | | |
|---|---|---|---|---|---|
| | | | Reduce the volume of flows | Reduce currency pressures | Change composition |
| Colombia | 1993–1998 | Le Fort and Budnevich 1997 | Yes (ST) | Yes | Yes |
| | | Cardenas and Barrera 1997 | No | | Yes |
| | | Reinhart and Smith 1998 | No | | Yes |
| | | Ariyoshi et al. 2000 | No | No | No |
| | 2007–2008 | Concha, Galindo, and Vasquez 2011 | No | | Yes |
| | | Cardenas 2007 | No | | Yes (ST) |
| | | Clements and Kamil 2009 | No | No | Yes |
| | | Baba and Kokenyne 2011 | Yes (ST) | No | Yes (ST) |
| Croatia | 2004–2008 | Jankov 2009 | | | Yes |
| Malaysia | 1994 | Reinhart and Smith 1998 | Yes | | Yes |
| | | Ariyoshi et al. 2000 | Yes | Yes (ST) | Yes |
| | | Tamirisa 2004 | | No | |
| | | Goh 2005 | Yes | | Yes |
| Thailand | 1995–1996 | Ariyoshi et al. 2000 | Yes | Yes | Yes |
| | 2006–2008 | Baba and Kokenyne 2011 | Yes | No | |
| *Cross-country evidence* | | | | | |
| | | Montiel and Reinhart 1999 | No | | Yes (ST) |
| | | Binici, Hutchison, and Schindler 2010[a] | No | | No |
| | | Ghosh, Qureshi, and Sugawara 2014[a] | Yes | | |
| | | Forbes, Fratzscher, Straub 2015 | | Yes (mixed) | Yes |

*Notes*: A blank entry refers to the cases where the study in question did not analyze the particular relationship. (ST) refers to cases where only short-term effects were detected.
a. Use indices of the general presence of capital controls.

attributed to the policy endogeneity-identification problem discussed above.[8]

Recognizing that capital inflows may have (direct or indirect) implications for financial stability, the second group of studies—which mostly evolved in the aftermath of the global financial crisis—focuses explicitly on the link between inflow restrictions and various measures of financial stability. This literature generally uses a broader definition of capital controls and considers not only residency-based restrictions, but also currency-based prudential measures that may act like capital controls (table 9.6). The main finding of these studies is that such measures can significantly reduce banks' balance-sheet vulnerabilities in EMEs (Ostry et al. 2012; Forbes, Fratzscher, and Straub 2015).

A third group of studies leaps to the next logical step, namely the link between (the absence of) capital controls and the occurrence and severity of crises. Inasmuch as inflow controls limit macroeconomic imbalances and financial-stability risks, they should be associated with a lower incidence and depth of crises. Yet evidence on this is mixed. Some studies (e.g., Gupta, Mishra, and Sahay 2007) find that countries with more open capital accounts experience larger output declines in financial crises, while others (e.g., Glick, Guo, and Hutchinson 2006) find that such economies are less prone to crisis. Part of the reason for this discrepancy is that these studies use aggregate measures of capital controls that do not distinguish between inflow and outflow controls: some of the countries that experienced crises were poorly managed, with very restrictive controls on capital outflows (that helped prop up poor policies), rather than largely open economies that had imposed inflow controls for prudential reasons or because of widening macroeconomic imbalances. Using disaggregated measures of capital controls that do distinguish between inflow and outflow controls, Ostry et al. (2010, 2012) find that countries with greater restrictions on inflows in the run-up to the global financial crisis were more resilient during the crisis.

Related to this discussion is the distinction between studies that consider the impact of episodic, short-term controls ("gates") and those based on the analysis of long-standing measures ("walls"). Most of the

---

8. Cordella (2003) presents a theoretical framework in which short-term capital controls on inflows reduce the vulnerability of emerging markets to financial crises, thereby inducing foreign lenders to invest in long-term instruments in EMEs and increasing the total volume of capital inflows. The proposed mechanism, however, presumes that investors are willing to substitute riskier types of assets for other types of flows.

**Table 9.6**
Selected studies on capital account–related measures and financial-stability risks.

| Country | Study | Measure | Did measure reduce | |
|---|---|---|---|---|
| | | | Level/ volatility of targeted flows | Other financial-stability risks |
| Croatia | Jankov 2009 | Financial sector capital controls; currency-based prudential | Yes | Yes |
| Korea, S. | Bruno and Shin 2014 | Financial sector capital controls | Yes | |
| Peru | Pérez-Forero and Vega 2014 | Currency-based prudential | | Yes |
| *Cross-country evidence* | | | | |
| | Lim et al. 2011 | Currency-based prudential | | Yes |
| | Ostry et al. 2012 | Capital controls; Currency-based prudential | | Yes |
| | Claessens, Ghosh, and Mihet 2013 | Currency-based prudential | | Yes |
| | Vandenbussche, Vogel, and Detragiache 2012 | Currency-based prudential | | Yes |
| | Bruno, Shim, and Shin 2015 | Financial sector capital controls | Yes (mixed) | |
| | Ghosh, Qureshi, and Sugawara 2014 | Capital controls; currency-based prudential | Yes | |
| | Akinci and Olmstead-Rumsey 2015 | Financial sector capital controls | | Yes |
| | Forbes, Fratzscher, and Straub 2015 | Capital controls; currency-based prudential | Yes | Yes |
| | Zhang and Zoli 2014 | Capital controls; currency-based prudential | Yes | Yes |

*Note*: A blank entry reflects that the study did not analyze the particular relationship.

literature in the first strand falls in the former category, seeking to analyze the effect of temporary capital inflow controls in mitigating risks from surges in largely open economies.[9] The issue of effectiveness is especially pertinent here because it is often argued that episodic controls will have less traction in more open economies as evasion is easier, and because such countries may not have in place the requisite infrastructure of monitoring, reporting, and enforcement (Klein 2012). By contrast, studies in the second and third groups mostly consider long-standing capital account–related measures, and exploit their cross-country variation, as their interest lies in analyzing the link between the general restrictiveness of capital inflows and the buildup of financial vulnerabilities (in stock terms).

Against this backdrop, we use two approaches to examine the effectiveness of capital controls in our data set. First, we use the quarterly data on episodes of *tightening* of inflow controls (employed in chapter 8) to assess the impact of temporary capital controls on macroeconomic imbalances (such as currency appreciation and domestic credit cycle). Next, we use annual data on the *presence* of inflow controls over a longer horizon to examine their link with financial fragilities and ultimately with crisis resilience.

### 9.4.1 Macroeconomic Imbalances

A first look at our data suggests that inflow controls may well play a role in limiting macroeconomic imbalances (figure 9.2). Currency-appreciation pressures appear to drop sharply after the introduction of capital controls, with some lagged effects as well (panel [a]). Thus, the real exchange rate (REER) turns from a rate of *appreciation* of about 1.5 percent per quarter before controls are tightened to a rate of *depreciation* of similar magnitude by the third quarter following the tightening (i.e., a 3–percentage point swing in the quarterly rate of change of the real exchange rate). This pattern is apparent for all types of capital controls—portfolio equity, bond, and financial sector-related measures—suggesting that when the source of appreciation is a particular type of

---

9. Exceptions to this include Binici, Hutchison, and Schindler (2010), who use panel data to examine the link between the general presence of inflow controls and the volume/composition of flows. To the extent that such studies include country-fixed effects in their regressions, the results could be interpreted as capturing the effect of within-country changes in capital controls (i.e., the effects of imposing or tightening inflow measures).

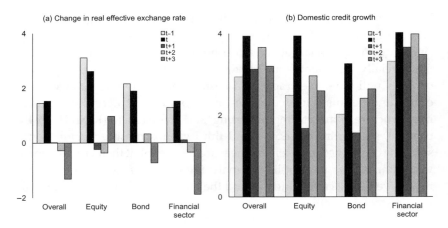

**Figure 9.2**
Capital controls, exchange rate, and credit growth in EMEs, 2005Q1:2013Q4 (in percent).
*Source*: Authors' estimates.
Note: The figure presents change in real effective exchange rate and real domestic private
sector credit growth (on a quarterly basis) before the tightening of capital inflow controls (t–1),
in the quarter of tightening (t), and three quarters after tightening.

capital inflow (such as portfolio or cross-border bank flows), then more
targeted measures could be effective as well.[10]

These observations hold in regressions controlling for other factors
(table 9.7). Thus, taking into account the potential lagged effects of a
policy tightening (where the lag length is again selected based on the
AIC), the REER depreciates by about 3 percent some three quarters
after capital controls have been tightened (col. [1]). Among the individual
types of controls, the impact of portfolio equity and bond controls appears
fully one quarter after the tightening, while that of financial sector–related
controls takes longer (2–3 quarters). This may be because the latter include
currency-based prudential measures that typically do not target inflows
directly; hence their (indirect) effects may become apparent with some
delay.

Evidence of an effect of capital controls on banking system credit
growth, by contrast, is at best mixed. While the unconditional plot suggests that there is some reduction in the pace of credit expansion fol-

---

10. But more targeted measures may have to be used more intensively as well. Also,
circumvention of narrowly targeted measures may be easier and could eventually lead
to a widening of the regulatory perimeter. These considerations are discussed further in
chapter 11.

**Table 9.7**

Capital controls, exchange rate, and domestic credit growth in EMEs, 2005Q1–2013Q4.

| | Change in REER | | | | Domestic credit growth | | | |
|---|---|---|---|---|---|---|---|---|
| | Overall (1) | Equity (2) | Bond (3) | Financial sector controls (4) | Overall (5) | Equity (6) | Bond (7) | Financial sector controls (8) |
| Inflow controls | 0.887 (0.564) | 0.576 (2.775) | 0.677 (1.481) | 0.973* (0.537) | 0.977** (0.335) | 0.653** (0.260) | 0.727 (0.505) | 0.908** (0.428) |
| Inflow controls (1-period lagged) | -0.591 (0.648) | -3.029*** (0.563) | -1.468*** (0.461) | 0.156 (0.909) | | -1.858*** (0.593) | -1.193 (0.781) | |
| Inflow controls (2-periods lagged) | -1.316** (0.508) | -1.704 (1.369) | | -1.148*** (0.389) | | -0.073 (0.865) | | |
| Inflow controls (3-periods lagged) | -2.011** (0.855) | -0.564 (0.465) | | -2.529** (1.051) | | 0.176 (0.917) | | |
| Net capital flows/GDP | 0.054 (0.032) | 0.056 (0.034) | 0.053 (0.033) | 0.054 (0.032) | 0.057 (0.040) | 0.061 (0.040) | 0.060 (0.040) | 0.058 (0.040) |
| Global market volatility | -3.154*** (0.614) | -3.430*** (0.582) | -3.390*** (0.623) | -3.194*** (0.607) | -1.134** (0.399) | -1.161** (0.398) | -1.126** (0.396) | -1.142** (0.399) |
| GFC | 0.680 (0.676) | 1.021 (0.658) | 0.976 (0.667) | 0.762 (0.694) | -0.115 (0.426) | -0.120 (0.407) | -0.160 (0.411) | -0.108 (0.422) |
| Change in REER (lagged) | 0.106*** (0.036) | 0.124*** (0.032) | 0.127*** (0.034) | 0.108*** (0.036) | | | | |
| Credit growth (lagged) | | | | | 0.237** (0.104) | 0.243** (0.105) | 0.244** (0.104) | 0.236** (0.104) |

(continued)

Table 9.7 (continued)

| | Change in REER | | | | Domestic credit growth | | | |
|---|---|---|---|---|---|---|---|---|
| | Overall | Equity | Bond | Financial sector controls | Overall | Equity | Bond | Financial sector controls |
| | (1) | (2) | (3) | (4) | (5) | (6) | (7) | (8) |
| Country-fixed effects | Yes | Yes | Yes | Yes | Yes | Yes | Yes | Yes |
| Quarter effects | Yes | Yes | Yes | Yes | Yes | Yes | Yes | Yes |
| Observations | 532 | 532 | 532 | 532 | 532 | 532 | 532 | 532 |
| $R^2$ | 0.196 | 0.179 | 0.174 | 0.195 | 0.248 | 0.247 | 0.248 | 0.247 |
| Countries | 27 | 27 | 27 | 27 | 27 | 27 | 27 | 27 |

*Notes:* Dependent variable is quarterly change in real effective exchange rate (in percent) in cols. (1)–(4), and quarterly domestic private sector credit growth (in percent) in cols. (5)–(8). Overall indicates tightening of any type of capital inflow control. Lag length is chosen based on the Akaike Information Criterion (AIC). All regressions include a constant. Clustered standard errors (by country) reported in parentheses. ***, **, and * indicate statistical significance at the 1, 5, and 10 percent levels, respectively.

lowing the tightening of capital controls (figure 9.2, panel [b]), regressions show that the impact is statistically significant only for equity controls (table 9.7, col. [5]). Credit growth thus declines by about 2 percentage points one quarter after the tightening of equity controls and does not rebound afterwards. The impact of bond controls is also negative—suggesting a decline in credit growth by about 1 percentage point—but the coefficient is marginally statistically insignificant. Surprisingly, the estimated coefficient on financial sector capital controls is positive and significant, suggesting an *increase* in credit growth after such controls are tightened. Considering that restrictions on the financial sector are more likely to be imposed when credit growth is of particular concern, the most likely explanation of this perverse result is that the endogeneity of the policy measures is confounding estimates of their effects. Beyond using lags, however, we are unable to address endogeneity issues here because of a lack of valid instruments at a quarterly frequency.

### 9.4.2 Financial Fragilities
To examine whether having capital controls in place can help prevent the buildup of balance-sheet vulnerabilities, we use annual data over 1995–2012 on de jure measures of capital controls on inflows, and currency-based macroprudential measures described in chapter 1. Specifically, for capital controls, we employ an overall measure of restrictiveness, as well as controls disaggregated by asset class (i.e., on bond, equity, direct investment, and financial credit inflows). For currency-based prudential measures, we consider restrictions on lending locally in FX, restrictions on the purchase of locally issued securities denominated in FX, and open FX position limits. (See data appendix for details on the construction of these variables.)

An initial snapshot is afforded by figure 9.3, which compares various financial-stability risks with below- and above-median capital controls and currency-based prudential measures for the EMEs in our sample. On average, the share of debt liabilities in total external liabilities, the financial sector's borrowing from abroad, and FX-denominated domestic lending are all significantly lower in the presence of capital account restrictions.

Regressions controlling for relevant factors such as real GDP per capita, the level of financial development, institutional quality, exchange rate regime, and time- and region-specific effects show that capital inflow controls indeed tilt the composition of external liabilities away

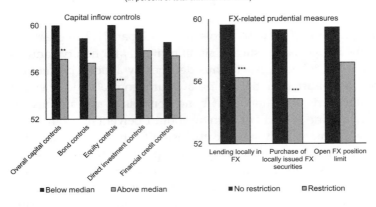

(a) Debt liabilities
(in percent of total external liabilities)

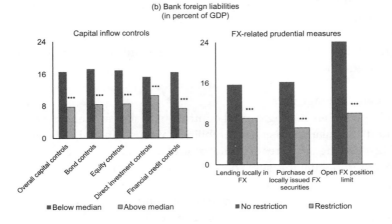

(b) Bank foreign liabilities
(in percent of GDP)

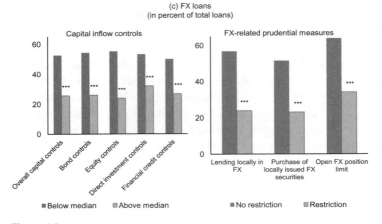

(c) FX loans
(in percent of total loans)

**Figure 9.3**
Financial fragilities and capital account–related measures, 1995–2012.
*Notes*: All policy measures are lagged one period. ***, **, and * indicate statistically significant different means between the two groups at the 1, 5, and 10 percent levels, respectively.

from debt liabilities (table 9.8; col. [1]).[11] The estimates imply that moving from the sample's twenty-fifth to seventy-fifth percentile on the overall capital controls index lowers the share of debt liabilities by about 6 percentage points (the sample average for debt share is about 58 percent, while the sample average for total liabilities is 87 percent of GDP). This result seems to be driven by bond, equity, and financial credit controls.[12]

Among the other explanatory variables, we find institutional quality to be an important factor in influencing the composition of external liabilities—countries with better institutions appear to rely less heavily on debt financing, presumably because foreign investors are less reluctant to lend to such countries on a risk-sharing basis (e.g., equity). This finding resonates with that of Wei (2001), who argues that weak institutions increase the relative importance of debt in total liabilities, but reduce that of FDI, as foreign banks are more likely to be bailed out than foreign direct investors in the event of a crisis. (FDI could also be lower in institutionally weak countries if foreign investors are concerned about corruption and red tape.)[13] Countries with more developed financial markets (proxied by the M2 to GDP ratio), and flexible exchange rate regimes also have a lower share of debt liabilities, though the estimated coefficients for these variables are mostly statistically insignificant.

Along with capital controls, the presence of currency-based prudential measures is also associated with a lower share of debt liabilities, though the estimated coefficient is only statistically significant for restrictions on the purchase of locally issued securities denominated in FX (table 9.8, col. [7]).

What happens if capital controls and currency-based prudential measures are considered together? To analyze which one dominates, we create two indices of currency-based prudential measures: *FX reg1* is an average of restrictions on lending locally in foreign exchange and the presence of open FX position limits, and *FX reg2* is an average of

---

11. Since capital controls and currency-based prudential measures are slow-moving variables, we do not include country-fixed effects, but control for region-specific effects. Moreover, we use lagged values of the policy variables to mitigate endogeneity concerns, and to take into account possible lagged effects.
12. The sample size varies across estimations depending on data availability of different variables.
13. By contrast, Razin, Sadka, and Yuen (1998, 2000) argue that institutionally vulnerable countries are likely to have a higher share of FDI in total external liabilities since FDI is relatively difficult to expropriate.

**Table 9.8**
Debt liabilities and capital account-related measures, 1995–2012.

| | Inflow controls | | | | | Currency-based prudential | | | Controls and currency-based | |
|---|---|---|---|---|---|---|---|---|---|---|
| | (1) | (2) | (3) | (4) | (5) | (6) | (7) | (8) | (9) | (10) |
| Overall | −9.505** (3.830) | | | | | | | | −8.541** (4.087) | −6.556 (4.196) |
| Bond | | −4.530* (2.642) | | | | | | | | |
| Equity | | | −9.489*** (3.217) | | | | | | | |
| Direct investment | | | | −3.494 (3.022) | | | | | | |
| Financial credit | | | | | −4.667** (2.312) | | | | | |
| Lending locally in FX | | | | | | −3.156 (2.822) | | | | |
| Purchase local FX sec. | | | | | | | −5.975** (2.927) | | | |
| Open FX position limit | | | | | | | | −3.767 (3.176) | | |
| FX reg1 | | | | | | | | | −2.112 (3.297) | |

FX reg2

| | (1) | (2) | (3) | (4) | (5) | (6) | (7) | (8) | (9) | (10) |
|---|---|---|---|---|---|---|---|---|---|---|
| Real GDP per capita | -3.363 (3.135) | -3.950 (3.331) | -3.948 (3.192) | -3.001 (3.475) | -3.598 (3.367) | -3.466 (3.283) | -4.874 (3.303) | -2.956 (3.389) | -3.806 (3.335) | -5.234 (4.117) |
| Institutional quality | -55.779*** (17.857) | -50.171** (19.863) | -52.097*** (18.836) | -53.867*** (19.080) | -48.033** (19.758) | -52.728** (20.024) | -43.875** (21.607) | -50.732** (19.399) | -57.306*** (18.786) | -49.623** (20.734) |
| M2/GDP | -0.017 (0.083) | -0.019 (0.085) | -0.004 (0.084) | -0.034 (0.083) | -0.028 (0.084) | -0.033 (0.081) | -0.026 (0.087) | -0.031 (0.085) | -0.016 (0.083) | -0.014 (0.085) |
| Exchange rate regime | -2.094 (2.117) | -2.459 (2.205) | -1.446 (2.118) | -2.775 (2.149) | -2.208 (2.082) | -2.064 (2.191) | -1.971 (2.061) | -2.347 (2.224) | -1.847 (2.156) | -1.545 (2.098) |
| Trade openness | -0.014 (0.057) | -0.002 (0.062) | -0.018 (0.058) | -0.000 (0.059) | -0.007 (0.059) | 0.008 (0.061) | -0.008 (0.060) | -0.010 (0.061) | -0.020 (0.058) | -0.022 (0.058) |
| Region effects | Yes | Yes | Yes | Yes | Yes | Yes | Yes | Yes | Yes | Yes |
| Year effects | Yes | Yes | Yes | Yes | Yes | Yes | Yes | Yes | Yes | Yes |
| Observations | 700 | 663 | 692 | 698 | 688 | 675 | 658 | 669 | 663 | 647 |
| $R^2$ | 0.485 | 0.445 | 0.477 | 0.466 | 0.458 | 0.453 | 0.452 | 0.438 | 0.462 | 0.448 |
| Countries | 45 | 45 | 45 | 45 | 45 | 45 | 45 | 45 | 45 | 45 |

*Notes:* Dependent variable is debt liabilities to total foreign liabilities (in percent). All variables are lagged one period. All regressions include a constant. Clustered standard errors (by country) are reported in parentheses. *, **, and *** indicate statistical significance at the 10, 5, and 1 percent levels, respectively.

all the three measures (restrictions on lending locally in FX, open FX position limits, and restrictions on purchase of locally issued FX securities). When included jointly in the regression, the results show that the statistical significance of the association between capital controls and a lower share of debt liabilities survives with *FX reg1* (col. [9]), while it turns marginally statistically insignificant with *FX reg2* (p-value = 0.12, col. [10]); the coefficient on FX indices however becomes insignificant in both cases. That capital controls turn out to be dominant makes intuitive sense inasmuch as currency-based prudential measures can, at most, affect flows that are intermediated through the banking system, whereas capital controls potentially apply to all flows. These findings are generally robust to inclusion of other independent variables in the regression and to the use of instrumental variables to help address potential endogeneity concerns (see chapter appendix for details). They are also in line with previous studies, as reported in table 9.6 above, which tend to find quantitatively important effects of capital controls on the *composition* of inflows.

Regarding the vulnerability of the domestic banking system, the results reported in table 9.9 suggest that foreign borrowing by domestic banks is also significantly lower when capital controls on inflows (especially, bond, equity, and financial credit controls), as well as currency-based prudential measures, are in place (cols. [1]–[8]). Specifically, moving from the twenty-fifth to the seventy-fifth percentile on the capital controls measures implies a reduction in banks' foreign liabilities by 8–9 percentage points of GDP, while the presence of currency-based prudential measures (such as restrictions on domestic FX lending or on the purchase of locally issued FX-denominated securities) imply a reduction by about 5 percentage points.[14] Among other independent variables, we find that banks in countries with more developed financial markets, as well as those with a less flexible exchange rate regime, are more likely to borrow from abroad.

When capital controls and the composite measures of prudential regulations are included together in the regressions, once again we find that capital controls dominate and that their estimated coefficients remain statistically significant, while those of currency-based prudential measures turn insignificant (cols. [9]–[10]). This suggests that by targeting the risk directly, capital controls have a stronger effect on

---

14. Since nearly all EMEs also impose open FX position limits on banks, restrictions on banks' FX lending will also curtail their foreign borrowing as that is mostly in FX.

**Table 9.9**
Banks' foreign liabilities and capital account–related measures, 1995–2012.

| | Inflow controls | | | | | Currency-based prudential | | | Controls and currency-based | |
|---|---|---|---|---|---|---|---|---|---|---|
| | (1) | (2) | (3) | (4) | (5) | (6) | (7) | (8) | (9) | (10) |
| Overall | −14.319** (6.302) | | | | | | | | −10.539** (4.109) | −9.623** (3.956) |
| Bond | | −8.323* (4.262) | | | | | | | | |
| Equity | | | −9.260** (3.956) | | | | | | | |
| Direct investment | | | | −6.296 (4.752) | | | | | | |
| Financial credit | | | | | −7.982** (2.991) | | | | | |
| Lending locally in FX | | | | | | −4.526* (2.678) | | | | |
| Purchase local FX sec. | | | | | | | −5.846** (2.893) | | | |
| Open FX position limit | | | | | | | | −9.743 (7.376) | | |
| FX reg1 | | | | | | | | | −6.217 (5.936) | |

(continued)

**Table 9.9** (continued)

| | Inflow controls | | | | | Currency-based prudential | | | Controls and currency-based | |
|---|---|---|---|---|---|---|---|---|---|---|
| | (1) | (2) | (3) | (4) | (5) | (6) | (7) | (8) | (9) | (10) |
| FX reg2 | | | | | | | | | | -6.522 (5.668) |
| Real GDP per capita | 4.214* (2.411) | 3.597 (2.527) | 3.764 (2.474) | 4.769* (2.474) | 4.665* (2.613) | 3.186 (2.307) | 2.477 (2.582) | 3.678 (2.416) | 3.803 (2.372) | 3.583 (2.599) |
| Institutional quality | -4.404 (14.730) | 1.360 (16.323) | -0.997 (16.471) | -1.284 (16.756) | -1.419 (15.745) | 14.183 (20.561) | 16.026 (23.491) | 14.553 (19.506) | 5.975 (17.136) | 6.432 (20.143) |
| M2/GDP | 0.216*** (0.078) | 0.208** (0.081) | 0.215*** (0.079) | 0.191** (0.072) | 0.194** (0.074) | 0.178** (0.070) | 0.182** (0.073) | 0.184** (0.071) | 0.203*** (0.068) | 0.202*** (0.070) |
| Exchange rate regime | -6.214** (3.065) | -6.627** (3.255) | -5.881* (3.127) | -7.389** (3.514) | -6.373* (3.320) | -5.969* (3.053) | -6.102** (2.989) | -5.566** (2.571) | -5.022** (2.475) | -5.139** (2.518) |
| Trade openness | -0.011 (0.060) | 0.008 (0.064) | -0.000 (0.062) | 0.011 (0.057) | 0.005 (0.057) | 0.016 (0.061) | 0.004 (0.065) | -0.016 (0.067) | -0.017 (0.059) | -0.016 (0.060) |
| Region effects | Yes | Yes | Yes | Yes | Yes | Yes | Yes | Yes | Yes | Yes |
| Year effects | Yes | Yes | Yes | Yes | Yes | Yes | Yes | Yes | Yes | Yes |
| Observations | 770 | 733 | 762 | 768 | 758 | 745 | 728 | 739 | 733 | 717 |
| $R^2$ | 0.368 | 0.345 | 0.343 | 0.336 | 0.352 | 0.355 | 0.365 | 0.378 | 0.405 | 0.403 |
| Countries | 44 | 44 | 44 | 44 | 44 | 44 | 44 | 44 | 44 | 44 |

*Notes*: Dependent variable is bank foreign liabilities to GDP (in percent). All variables are lagged one period. All regressions include a constant. Clustered standard errors (by country) are reported in parentheses. *, **, and *** indicate statistical significance at the 10, 5, and 1 percent levels, respectively.

banks' foreign borrowing than relatively indirect prudential measures on the asset side of the balance sheet.

Turning to asset-side vulnerabilities of bank balance sheets, we find that countries with greater restrictions on capital inflows have significantly lower foreign currency–denominated lending (table 9.10, cols. [1]–[8]). Interestingly, both capital controls and currency-based prudential measures retain their (strong) statistical significance when included jointly in the regression (cols. [9]–[10]): moving from the twenty-fifth to seventy-fifth percentile of these indices is associated with about 10–15 percentage point reduction in the share of foreign currency–denominated lending in total bank lending. While the magnitude of the effects appears to be large, they are plausible since, as discussed earlier, currency-based prudential measures can have a direct impact on FX lending by domestic banks (sufficiently restrictive measures can in principle drive such lending to zero).[15] Similarly, capital controls that impede external borrowing will also tend to reduce FX lending since EME banks' borrowing abroad is typically in foreign currency.

### 9.4.3 Crisis Resilience

To the extent that the balance-sheet vulnerabilities considered above—excessive debt liabilities, banks' foreign liabilities, and FX lending—can exacerbate financial fragilities, policy measures that reduce them should be associated with greater resilience of the economy in the event of a financial crisis. To test whether this hypothesis holds true, we exploit the "natural experiment" afforded by the global financial crisis, which—exogenous to the EMEs—triggered downturns of varying intensities across different countries, and examine whether those that had capital inflow controls and currency-based prudential measures in place *before* the crisis fared better during the crisis. We also test this idea using a panel data set of previous EME financial crises over 1995–2008.

To estimate the effect of policy measures on the output decline experienced during the global financial crisis, we compute the change in real GDP growth in 2009 relative to the country's average growth over 2004–2008. Capital controls and currency-based prudential measures are averaged over 2003–2007 to capture the presence of such measures

---

15. Of course, that could come at a cost in terms of the volume of credit, and may cause lending to migrate to unregulated corners of the financial sector. These issues are discussed in detail in chapter 11.

**Table 9.10**
FX lending and capital account-related measures, 1995–2012.

| | Inflow controls | | | | | Currency-based prudential | | | Controls and currency-based | |
|---|---|---|---|---|---|---|---|---|---|---|
| | (1) | (2) | (3) | (4) | (5) | (6) | (7) | (8) | (9) | (10) |
| Overall | −35.847*** (6.620) | | | | | | | | −24.361*** (6.518) | −18.217** (8.031) |
| Bond | | −22.899*** (6.665) | | | | | | | | |
| Equity | | | −28.754*** (7.024) | | | | | | | |
| Direct investment | | | | −22.125*** (7.405) | | | | | | |
| Financial credit | | | | | −18.184*** (4.244) | | | | | |
| Lending locally in FX | | | | | | −24.808*** (6.180) | | | | |
| Purchase local FX sec. | | | | | | | −21.199*** (7.194) | | | |
| Open FX position limit | | | | | | | | −20.744* (10.952) | | |
| FX reg1 | | | | | | | | | −28.868*** (9.939) | |
| FX reg2 | | | | | | | | | | −33.759*** (10.997) |

| | | | | | | | | | |
|---|---|---|---|---|---|---|---|---|---|
| Real GDP per capita | −1.693 | −1.966 | −3.501 | −2.865 | −0.486 | −1.644 | −4.452 | −3.121 | 0.470 | −0.603 |
| | (9.060) | (9.303) | (9.238) | (8.235) | (8.924) | (9.491) | (8.617) | (9.147) | (9.584) | (9.336) |
| Institutional quality | −49.970 | −38.564 | −41.273 | −39.403 | −35.479 | −23.867 | −21.448 | −31.937 | −57.554 | −50.948 |
| | (59.752) | (63.165) | (59.344) | (57.059) | (60.553) | (61.291) | (59.548) | (60.668) | (54.781) | (53.003) |
| M2/GDP | 0.081 | 0.063 | 0.102 | 0.052 | 0.023 | 0.034 | 0.033 | 0.034 | 0.075 | 0.070 |
| | (0.162) | (0.168) | (0.162) | (0.157) | (0.152) | (0.139) | (0.163) | (0.160) | (0.148) | (0.152) |
| Exchange rate regime | −11.385** | −12.619** | −9.692 | −14.731** | −13.241** | −9.941* | −11.762** | −11.027* | −7.089 | −7.213 |
| | (5.605) | (5.984) | (5.823) | (5.775) | (5.805) | (5.165) | (5.189) | (6.468) | (5.352) | (5.028) |
| Region effects | Yes | Yes | Yes | Yes | Yes | Yes | Yes | Yes | Yes | Yes |
| Year effects | Yes | Yes | Yes | Yes | Yes | Yes | Yes | Yes | Yes | Yes |
| Observations | 516 | 500 | 515 | 516 | 515 | 507 | 505 | 501 | 499 | 498 |
| $R^2$ | 0.414 | 0.370 | 0.391 | 0.401 | 0.364 | 0.407 | 0.388 | 0.348 | 0.488 | 0.496 |
| Countries | 37 | 37 | 37 | 37 | 37 | 37 | 37 | 37 | 37 | 37 |

*Notes:* Dependent variable is foreign currency lending in total lending (in percent). All variables are lagged one period. All regressions include a constant. Clustered standard errors (at country level) are reported in parentheses. *, **, and *** indicate statistical significance at the 10, 5, and 1 percent levels, respectively.

before the crisis. Controlling for real per capita GDP, change in terms of trade, and real GDP growth of trading partners, the results reported in table 9.11 indicate that both capital controls on inflows and currency-based prudential measures are associated with improved growth resilience—countries that had these measures in place in the years leading up to the global financial crisis fared significantly better during the crisis.[16] Moving from the twenty-fifth to the seventy-fifth percentile of the overall capital inflow controls index, for instance, reduces the growth decline in the aftermath of the crisis by about 2 percentage points (the average growth decline in the sample is 7 percentage points). Regressions for individual components of capital controls show that this result is largely driven by controls on bond and equity inflows (cols. [2]–[3]).

Evidence from past (pre–global financial crisis) episodes (in table 9.12) supports the association of capital controls with growth resilience. Specifically, among EMEs that experienced banking or currency crises (as identified by Laeven and Valencia [2013]), those that had more restrictive capital accounts in the years prior to their crisis experienced smaller growth declines when the crisis occurred. Thus, while the jury is still out on whether capital account restrictiveness is good for growth in non-crisis times, our results suggest that such measures—by reducing financial vulnerabilities—can help countries avoid some of the worst outcomes when a crisis occurs.

These results are generally robust to the inclusion of other potentially relevant factors (such as pre-crisis measures of financial soundness and stability, and stock of reserves to GDP) in the regression equations, as well as to the exclusion of Baltic countries from the sample; these countries had experienced some of the largest output declines during the global financial crisis. (See chapter appendix [table A.9.1] for details.)

## 9.5  Conclusion

This chapter assessed the effectiveness of different instruments in the policy tool kit—FX intervention, nondiscriminatory macroprudential policies, capital controls, and currency-based prudential measures. The

---

16. Similar to the growth decline variable, the change in terms of trade, and real GDP growth of trading partners are computed as the difference between 2009 and the average over 2004–2008.

**Table 9.11**

Crisis resilience and capital account–related measures: Global financial crisis.

| | Inflow controls | | | | | Currency-based prudential | | | Controls and currency-based | |
|---|---|---|---|---|---|---|---|---|---|---|
| | (1) | (2) | (3) | (4) | (5) | (6) | (7) | (8) | (9) | (10) |
| Overall | 3.996*<br>(2.303) | | | | | | | | 5.153**<br>(2.185) | 5.549**<br>(2.225) |
| Bond | | 3.349*<br>(1.764) | | | | | | | | |
| Equity | | | 4.314**<br>(1.816) | | | | | | | |
| Direct investment | | | | 2.132<br>(1.295) | | | | | | |
| Financial credit | | | | | 0.310<br>(1.434) | | | | | |
| Lending locally in FX | | | | | | −1.437<br>(1.342) | | | | |
| Purchase local FX sec. | | | | | | | 0.390<br>(1.378) | | | |
| Open FX position limit | | | | | | | | −0.502<br>(1.323) | | |
| FX reg1 | | | | | | | | | −3.684**<br>(1.800) | |
| FX reg2 | | | | | | | | | | −3.492*<br>(1.872) |

(continued)

**Table 9.11** (continued)

| | Inflow controls | | | | | Currency-based prudential | | | Controls and currency-based | |
|---|---|---|---|---|---|---|---|---|---|---|
| | (1) | (2) | (3) | (4) | (5) | (6) | (7) | (8) | (9) | (10) |
| Terms of trade change | 0.098** | 0.096** | 0.102** | 0.083* | 0.078* | 0.076* | 0.108*** | 0.074* | 0.101** | 0.135*** |
| | (0.043) | (0.041) | (0.041) | (0.043) | (0.043) | (0.043) | (0.034) | (0.041) | (0.044) | (0.034) |
| Trading-partner growth | 1.427*** | 1.452*** | 1.377*** | 1.551*** | 1.712*** | 1.935*** | 1.687*** | 1.778*** | 1.727*** | 1.601*** |
| | (0.465) | (0.481) | (0.454) | (0.500) | (0.502) | (0.491) | (0.479) | (0.537) | (0.514) | (0.488) |
| Real GDP per capita | -0.002 | 0.215 | -0.158 | -0.325 | -0.374 | -0.547 | -0.342 | -0.379 | -0.152 | -0.328 |
| | (1.050) | (1.079) | (1.017) | (1.026) | (1.033) | (0.930) | (1.090) | (1.026) | (0.943) | (0.951) |
| Observations | 47 | 47 | 47 | 47 | 47 | 47 | 46 | 47 | 47 | 46 |
| R² | 0.619 | 0.623 | 0.639 | 0.609 | 0.586 | 0.594 | 0.608 | 0.586 | 0.643 | 0.665 |

*Notes:* Dependent variable is the difference between real GDP growth rate in 2009 and the average growth rate over previous 5 years (in percentage points). All regressions include a constant and region-specific effects. Capital control and currency-based prudential measures are averaged over 2003–2007. Real GDP per capita (log) is lagged one period. Robust standard errors are reported in parentheses. *, **, and *** indicate statistical significance at the 10, 5, and 1 percent levels, respectively.

**Table 9.12**

Crisis resilience and capital account–related measures: Past crises.

| | Inflow controls | | | | | Currency-based prudential | | | Controls and currency-based | |
|---|---|---|---|---|---|---|---|---|---|---|
| | (1) | (2) | (3) | (4) | (5) | (6) | (7) | (8) | (9) | (10) |
| Overall | 5.675** (2.067) | | | | | | | | 5.550* (2.923) | 5.195** (2.316) |
| Bond | | 0.790 (2.722) | | | | | | | | |
| Equity | | | 1.864 (2.018) | | | | | | | |
| Direct investment | | | | 2.048 (2.013) | | | | | | |
| Financial credit | | | | | 5.847*** (1.430) | | | | | |
| Lending locally in FX | | | | | | 2.395 (1.600) | | | | |
| Purchase local FX sec. | | | | | | | 1.428 (2.394) | | | |
| Open FX position limit | | | | | | | | −3.726*** (1.207) | | |
| FX reg1 | | | | | | | | | −2.905 (4.253) | |
| FX reg2 | | | | | | | | | | −2.906 (4.130) |

(continued)

**Table 9.12** (continued)

| | Inflow controls | | | | | Currency-based prudential | | | Controls and currency-based | |
|---|---|---|---|---|---|---|---|---|---|---|
| | (1) | (2) | (3) | (4) | (5) | (6) | (7) | (8) | (9) | (10) |
| Terms of trade change | 0.187* (0.099) | 0.055 (0.139) | 0.134 (0.111) | 0.157 (0.114) | 0.164* (0.087) | 0.115 (0.105) | 0.069 (0.115) | 0.010 (0.122) | 0.112 (0.150) | 0.099 (0.126) |
| Trading partner growth | 2.570*** (0.524) | 2.027** (0.728) | 2.613*** (0.657) | 2.491*** (0.630) | 1.933*** (0.491) | 2.214*** (0.527) | 2.736*** (0.680) | 1.951** (0.726) | 2.529*** (0.635) | 2.318*** (0.656) |
| Real GDP per capita | -2.004** (0.860) | -1.548 (1.348) | -2.327* (1.309) | -2.887** (1.332) | -1.604 (1.045) | -2.002 (1.197) | -2.308 (1.920) | -1.411 (1.422) | -1.886 (1.209) | -2.015 (1.524) |
| Observations | 21 | 17 | 20 | 21 | 21 | 20 | 19 | 17 | 17 | 17 |
| $R^2$ | 0.588 | 0.360 | 0.477 | 0.465 | 0.714 | 0.494 | 0.493 | 0.386 | 0.426 | 0.424 |

*Notes*: Dependent variable is the difference between real GDP growth rate in crisis year and the average growth rate over previous five years (in percentage points). All regressions include a constant. Capital control and currency-based prudential measures, and real GDP per capita (log) are lagged one period. Crisis is defined as pre-2008 banking or currency crisis identified by Laeven and Valencia (2013), where only the first year of crisis is considered when banking and currency crisis occur in successive years. Robust standard errors are reported in parentheses. *, **, and *** indicate statistical significance at the 10, 5, and 1 percent levels, respectively.

review of literature, as well as empirical analysis based on our own data, point to the effectiveness of these measures in EMEs. While the lack of valid instruments precludes addressing the endogeneity problem for high-frequency policy measures—thus biasing estimated coefficients toward zero—we nevertheless find at least some evidence of the effectiveness of each of the policy instruments.

The empirical analysis here thus suggests that the "natural mapping" of instruments proposed in chapters 5–7 could be implemented. When it comes to macroeconomic imbalances, for instance, sterilized FX intervention can be used to mitigate currency-appreciation pressures, and both sterilized intervention and macroprudential measures to curb domestic credit growth. Remaining imbalances can be addressed by imposing or tightening capital controls.

As regards financial fragilities, capital controls can be used to tilt the composition of external liabilities away from riskier (i.e., debt) flows, and restrict excessive foreign borrowing by the financial sector, with currency-based macroprudential measures another, albeit less effective, alternative. Conversely, to limit foreign currency–denominated lending in the economy, currency-based macroprudential measures are strongly effective, with capital controls on inflows a possible alternative. Consistent with these results, our findings also show a significant association between the economy's resilience during crises and residency-based capital controls or currency-based prudential measures that help prevent the buildup of balance-sheet vulnerabilities. Overall, therefore, emerging market policy makers would appear to have a potent tool kit at their disposal for coping with capital inflows.

## Chapter 9 Appendix

This appendix establishes the robustness of the results obtained above regarding capital controls and financial fragilities by conducting a battery of sensitivity checks—including estimating alternative specifications of the benchmark models with additional control variables and different samples, and addressing potential endogeneity concerns through the use of instrumental variable two-stage least squares (IV-2SLS) estimation.

**Alternative specifications and samples**   While the regressions reported in tables 9.8–9.12 include several relevant explanatory variables, to ensure that the strong association between our policy measures and financial fragilities/crisis resilience is not driven by omitted variables, we also estimate alternative specifications with additional explanatory variables to capture relevant country characteristics such as the level of financial development (as proxied by stock market capitalization and deposit bank assets to GDP), soundness of the financial system (proxied by bank return on assets and equity), financial sector concentration, and the stock of foreign reserves to GDP. We find that the benchmark result generally survives the addition of these other explanatory variables. Specifically, capital controls remain associated with a lower proportion of debt liabilities, bank foreign liabilities, and FX lending, as well as with improved crisis resilience, while currency-based prudential measures have a strong dampening effect on FX lending (table A.9.1).

In addition to model specification, we check the sensitivity of our results to the sample composition. Some recent studies (e.g., Cline 2010) find no relationship between capital account openness and the output decline during the global financial crisis in EMEs, and question whether such a relationship exists (or whether it is driven by the experience of the Baltic countries in the EME sample). While we believe that including the Baltic countries in the sample is important, as they suffered some of the largest output declines during the crisis, and as such their experience is informative, we reestimate our specifications without the three Baltic countries (Estonia, Latvia, and Lithuania) in the sample.

As shown in table A.9.1 (panel [d], col. [8]), excluding the Baltic countries from the sample leaves the sign and magnitude of the overall capital controls measure unchanged, but marginally reduces the statistical significance (p-value=0.103). This is scarcely surprising, however. The Baltic countries suffered the largest output declines in the crisis and excluding them means throwing out highly informative crisis observations. Nevertheless, despite dropping the Baltic countries, there remains a statistically significant association between resilience during the global financial crisis and controls on bond and equity inflows.

Since the concern pertaining to the Baltic countries is that these are essentially small economies, and lest that be the cause of their larger output decline, we also conduct another exercise. Rather than simply excluding the Baltic countries from the sample, we retain them but control explicitly for the size of the economy. This is done in col. (9), where the precrisis U.S. dollar–value of GDP is added as a regressor. Doing so leaves the coefficient on overall capital controls largely unchanged: positive and statistically significant.

**Table A.9.1**

Financial fragilities and crisis resilience: Robustness analysis.

| | Baseline | Stock market capitalization | Deposit bank assets/GDP | Return on assets | Return on equity | Bank concentration | FX reserves to GDP | Excluding Baltics | Economic scale |
|---|---|---|---|---|---|---|---|---|---|
| | (1) | (2) | (3) | (4) | (5) | (6) | (7) | (8) | (9) |
| *(a) Debt liabilities* | | | | | | | | | |
| Overall capital controls | -9.505** | -8.130** | -9.552** | -8.095* | -8.360* | -8.972** | -10.180** | | |
| Bond controls | -4.530* | -4.337 | -4.560* | -4.096 | -4.233 | -4.371 | -4.911 | | |
| Equity controls | -9.489*** | -9.109** | -9.256*** | -9.704** | -9.737** | -10.950*** | -9.955*** | | |
| Direct investment controls | -3.494 | -2.680 | -2.910 | -2.181 | -2.042 | -2.991 | -4.051 | | |
| Financial credit controls | -4.667** | -2.002 | -3.963 | -4.517* | -4.418* | -4.264* | -4.867** | | |
| Lending locally in FX | -3.156 | 0.364 | -1.173 | -3.493 | -3.700 | -3.158 | -3.881 | | |
| Purchase of local FX sec. | -5.975** | -4.421 | -4.511 | -5.550* | -5.551* | -5.468* | -6.234** | | |
| Open FX position limit | -3.767 | -3.496 | -3.085 | -4.005 | -4.331 | -4.123 | -3.272 | | |
| *(b) Bank foreign liabilities* | | | | | | | | | |
| Overall capital controls | -14.319** | -12.208** | -14.338** | -8.583 | -8.865* | -12.686** | -10.085 | | |
| Bond controls | -8.323* | -6.196 | -8.602** | -3.982 | -4.030 | -7.017 | -5.161 | | |

(continued)

**Table A.9.1** (continued)

| | Baseline | Stock market capitalization | Deposit bank assets/GDP | Return on assets | Return on equity | Bank concentration | FX reserves to GDP | Excluding Baltics | Economic scale |
|---|---|---|---|---|---|---|---|---|---|
| | (1) | (2) | (3) | (4) | (5) | (6) | (7) | (8) | (9) |
| Equity controls | −9.260** | −6.638* | −10.291** | −4.759 | −4.873 | −8.118* | −5.651 | | |
| Direct investment controls | −6.296 | −5.288 | −5.230 | −4.321 | −4.327 | −5.417 | −6.047 | | |
| Financial credit controls | −7.982** | −7.555** | −8.162** | −7.175*** | −7.175** | −8.012*** | −7.257** | | |
| Lending locally in FX | −4.526* | −3.003 | −5.347 | −5.124 | −5.207* | −5.398* | −3.508 | | |
| Purchase of local FX sec. | −5.846** | −5.349* | −5.644* | −4.916 | −5.009 | −6.143 | −5.014 | | |
| Open FX position limit | −9.743 | −10.187 | −9.875 | −10.755 | −10.706 | −12.035 | −10.193 | | |
| *(c) FX lending* | | | | | | | | | |
| Overall capital controls | −35.847*** | −35.232*** | −36.924*** | −34.519*** | −35.710*** | −35.745*** | −36.795*** | | |
| Bond controls | −22.899*** | −24.443*** | −24.946*** | −21.984*** | −22.642*** | −22.827*** | −24.371*** | | |
| Equity controls | −28.754*** | −30.486*** | −27.746*** | −26.783*** | −27.279*** | −28.052*** | −28.420*** | | |
| Direct investment controls | −22.125*** | −17.002* | −20.688*** | −21.266*** | −21.580*** | −21.640*** | −22.471*** | | |
| Financial credit controls | −18.184*** | −14.058*** | −17.009*** | −18.628*** | −18.859*** | −19.259*** | −20.738*** | | |
| Lending locally in FX | −24.808*** | −21.400*** | −23.973*** | −25.502*** | −25.868*** | −25.727*** | −27.593*** | | |

| | (1) | (2) | (3) | (4) | (5) | (6) | (7) | (8) | (9) |
|---|---|---|---|---|---|---|---|---|---|
| Purchase of local FX sec. | −21.199*** | −18.242*** | −18.394*** | −19.935** | −20.762** | −20.579*** | | | −22.573*** |
| Open FX position limit | −20.744* | −16.842* | −17.949* | −19.650* | −19.690* | −18.972 | | | −19.632* |
| *(d) Crisis resilience* | | | | | | | | | |
| Overall capital controls | 3.996* | 2.599 | 2.453 | 3.930* | 3.954 | 5.756** | 4.122* | 3.980 | 4.269* |
| Bond controls | 3.349* | 2.243 | 2.022 | 3.375* | 3.327* | 4.524** | 3.473* | 3.261* | 3.382* |
| Equity controls | 4.314** | 3.012 | 3.018* | 4.263** | 4.294** | 6.093*** | 4.112** | 4.032** | 4.945** |
| Direct investment controls | 2.132 | 1.826 | 1.835 | 2.076* | 2.130 | 2.562* | 2.506* | 3.004** | 2.247* |
| Financial credit controls | 0.310 | 0.760 | 0.623 | 0.267 | 0.262 | 0.698 | 0.446 | 0.230 | 0.308 |
| Lending locally in FX | −1.437 | −1.064 | −0.647 | −1.643 | −1.427 | −1.976 | −1.202 | −1.238 | −1.448 |
| Purchase of local FX sec. | 0.390 | −0.267 | −0.171 | 0.183 | 0.390 | 0.688 | 0.432 | 0.599 | 0.384 |
| Open FX position limit | −0.502 | −0.163 | −0.246 | −0.980 | −0.547 | −0.308 | −0.131 | −0.688 | −0.557 |

*Notes*: Debt liabilities is the share of debt liabilities in total external liabilities (in percent). FX lending is the share of FX loans in total loans (in percent). Crisis resilience is the difference between real GDP growth rate in 2009 and the average over 2004–2008. Standard errors are clustered at the country level. *, **, and *** indicate statistical significance at the 10, 5, and 1 percent levels, respectively. Values in cells indicate the estimated coefficients for relevant policy measures indicated in row headers when the benchmark specification is augmented with additional control variable specified in cols. (2)–(7) and col. (9), and by dropping the Baltic countries in col. (8).

**Endogeneity**   As mentioned above, one concern when estimating the effect of capital controls on the aggregate stock or flow of external liabilities relates to reverse causality—that is, countries may strengthen capital account restrictions in response to a surge in capital inflows, which could give rise to a spurious positive association between controls and inflows. While such endogeneity concerns may be less pertinent when considering the impact of controls on the *composition*, rather than on the overall level or flow of liabilities, endogeneity bias—if it exists—would tend to reduce the estimated effects of capital controls and other prudential measures. Again, the relatively strong findings above are therefore despite—rather than because of—any potential endogeneity bias.

Nevertheless, we use lagged values of the capital controls index in all estimations to mitigate the endogeneity concerns. In addition, we apply an IV-2SLS approach, whereby we consider the presence of a democratic left-wing government in the recipient in that year as our instrument. Existing studies (e.g., Grilli and Milesi-Ferretti 1995) find this variable to be an important determinant of capital controls: countries with a left-wing government are more likely to implement capital controls. There is, however, no a priori reason to believe that this variable would be directly related to the stock or flow of external liabilities (especially since we include for per capita income as a proxy for institutional quality in all specifications).

We obtain information on the presence of a left-wing government from Beck et al. (2001), which is summarized as a binary variable (with one indicating a left-wing government, and zero otherwise). While the sample size drops by one-third because information on the presence of left-wing government is not available for all countries in the sample, the validity of our instrument is supported by the results from the first stage of the IV-2SLS regression (tables A.9.2–A.9.4, panel [a]). The estimated coefficient of left-wing government is positive and highly statistically significant in almost all specifications, indicating greater prevalence of capital controls in countries with a left-wing government. Among the other explanatory variables, we find institutional quality and trade openness to be mostly statistically significant, implying a lower prevalence of capital controls in countries with stronger institutions and greater trade openness (results not shown here). The $F$-test of the hypothesis that the estimates in the first-stage regression are jointly equal to zero is thus strongly rejected, and the R-squared across specifications is between 0.3–0.4, offering evidence on the appropriateness of our instrument and the overall fit of the first-stage regression.[17]

The results obtained from the second stage of the estimation—using the predicted values of the policy measures from the first-stage regression—support the strong negative association between capital controls or currency-based prudential measures and financial fragilities (tables A.9.2–A.9.4, panel [b]). Specifically, the composition of external liabilities is less risky with greater prevalence of policy measures: moving from the twenty-fifth to the seventy-fifth percentile on the (predicted) capital inflow controls index, for instance, implies a reduction in the share of debt liabilities by about 16 percentage points. Similarly, the banking sector's foreign liabilities and domestic lending in foreign currency are also lower by 15 and 21 percentage points, respectively, if capital inflow controls are increased from the twenty-fifth to the seventy-fifth percentile. The benchmark results are thus robust to addressing potential endogeneity concerns through the instrumental variable approach.

---

17. Including the lagged dependent variable in the first-stage regressions to account for persistence in the policy measures does not affect the result much. The estimated coefficient for left-wing government in some of the first-stage regressions turns marginally statistically insignificant as it is highly correlated with the lagged policy measure, yet both variables remain jointly significant, and the results of the second stage estimation remain largely the same.

**Table A.9.2**
Debt liabilities and capital account–related measures: IV-2SLS estimates.

*(a) First-stage regression*[a]

| Dependent variable | Overall controls | Bonds controls | Equity controls | Direct investment | Financial credit | Local FX lending | Purchase of local FX sec. | Open FX position limit |
|---|---|---|---|---|---|---|---|---|
| | (1) | (2) | (3) | (4) | (5) | (6) | (7) | (8) |
| Left-wing government | 0.163*** | 0.186** | 0.166** | 0.067 | 0.182** | 0.148 | 0.286*** | −0.031 |
| | (0.054) | (0.071) | (0.063) | (0.111) | (0.085) | (0.094) | (0.103) | (0.077) |
| Observations | 490 | 464 | 489 | 490 | 486 | 472 | 461 | 468 |
| $R^2$ | 0.363 | 0.323 | 0.425 | 0.089 | 0.272 | 0.343 | 0.391 | 0.194 |
| F-test (p-value) | 0.00 | 0.00 | 0.00 | 0.00 | 0.00 | 0.00 | 0.00 | 0.00 |

*(b) Second-stage regression*[b]

| | | | | | | | | |
|---|---|---|---|---|---|---|---|---|
| Overall controls | −61.427*** | | | | | | | |
| | (21.114) | | | | | | | |
| Bond controls | | −56.074** | | | | | | |
| | | (23.092) | | | | | | |
| Equity controls | | | −60.591*** | | | | | |
| | | | (22.440) | | | | | |

| | Direct investment controls | Financial credit controls | Lending locally in FX | Purchase of local FX securities | Open FX position limits |
|---|---|---|---|---|---|
| Direct investment controls | −148.296 (226.695) | | | | |
| Financial credit controls | | −55.841** (26.230) | | | |
| Lending locally in FX | | | −71.199* (42.688) | | |
| Purchase of local FX securities | | | | −37.883*** (13.628) | |
| Open FX position limits | | | | | 353.773 (854.318) |
| Region effects | Yes | Yes | Yes | Yes | Yes |
| Year effects | Yes | Yes | Yes | Yes | Yes |
| Observations | 490 | 486 | 472 | 461 | 468 |
| Countries | 39 | 39 | 39 | 39 | 39 |

a. Panel (a) reports the first-stage estimation results where the presence of a left-wing government is used as an instrument for capital controls and prudential measures. Other exogenous variables included are the same as in table 9.8. All regressors are lagged one period. Constant, region-specific, and year effects are included in all specifications. F-test (p-value) reports the joint significance of all regressors. Clustered standard errors (by country) are reported in parentheses. ***, **, and * indicate statistical significance at the 1, 5, and 10 percent levels, respectively.

b. Panel (b) reports the instrumental variable two-stage least squares (IV-2SLS) estimates with debt liabilities to total foreign liabilities (in percent) as the dependent variable. Capital controls and prudential measures are predicted values obtained from the corresponding first-stage regression in Panel A. Control variables as specified in table 9.8, as well as a constant are included in all specifications. Clustered standard errors (by country) are reported in parentheses. ***, **, and * indicate statistical significance at the 1, 5, and 10 percent levels, respectively.

**Table A.9.3**

Bank foreign liabilities and capital account-related measures: IV-2SLS estimates.

| Dependent variable | Overall controls | Bonds controls | Equity controls | Direct investment | Financial credit | Local FX lending | Purchase of local FX sec. | Open FX position limit |
|---|---|---|---|---|---|---|---|---|
| | (1) | (2) | (3) | (4) | (5) | (6) | (7) | (8) |
| *(a) First-stage regression*[a] | | | | | | | | |
| Left-wing government | 0.150** | 0.176** | 0.154** | 0.042 | 0.171* | 0.138 | 0.278*** | −0.020 |
| | (0.056) | (0.072) | (0.064) | (0.110) | (0.085) | (0.095) | (0.100) | (0.077) |
| Observations | 502 | 476 | 501 | 502 | 498 | 484 | 473 | 480 |
| $R^2$ | 0.309 | 0.278 | 0.385 | 0.088 | 0.241 | 0.326 | 0.370 | 0.191 |
| F-test (p-value) | 0.00 | 0.00 | 0.00 | 0.00 | 0.00 | 0.00 | 0.00 | 0.00 |
| *(b) Second-stage regression*[b] | | | | | | | | |
| Overall controls | −60.755** | | | | | | | |
| | (26.233) | | | | | | | |
| Bond controls | | −52.707** | | | | | | |
| | | (26.010) | | | | | | |
| Equity controls | | | −59.618** | | | | | |
| | | | (27.191) | | | | | |
| Direct investment controls | | | | −218.693 | | | | |
| | | | | (543.308) | | | | |

| | | | | | | | | |
|---|---|---|---|---|---|---|---|---|
| Financial credit controls | | | | | -52.687* | | | |
| | | | | | (27.703) | | | |
| Lending locally in FX | | | | | | -65.467 | | |
| | | | | | | (45.048) | | |
| Purchase of local FX securities | | | | | | | -31.795** | |
| | | | | | | | (14.872) | |
| Open FX position limits | | | | | | | | 472.130 |
| | | | | | | | | (1,764.594) |
| Region effects | Yes | Yes | Yes | Yes | Yes | Yes | Yes | Yes |
| Year effects | Yes | Yes | Yes | Yes | Yes | Yes | Yes | Yes |
| Observations | 502 | 476 | 501 | 502 | 498 | 484 | 473 | 480 |
| Countries | 38 | 38 | 38 | 38 | 38 | 38 | 38 | 38 |

a. Panel (a) reports the first-stage estimation results where the presence of a left-wing government is used as an instrument for capital controls and prudential measures. Other exogenous variables included are the same as in table 9.9. All regressors are lagged one period. Constant, region-specific, and year effects are included in all specifications. F-test (p-value) reports the joint significance of all regressors. Clustered standard errors (by country) are reported in parentheses. ***, **, and * indicate statistical significance at the 1, 5, and 10 percent levels, respectively.

b. Panel (b) reports the instrumental variable two-stage least squares (IV-2SLS) estimates with bank foreign liabilities to GDP (in percent) as the dependent variable. Capital controls and prudential measures are predicted values obtained from the corresponding first-stage regression in Panel A. Control variables as specified in table 9.9, as well as a constant are included in all specifications. Clustered standard errors (by country) are reported in parentheses. ***, **, and * indicate statistical significance at the 1, 5, and 10 percent levels, respectively.

**Table A.9.4**

FX lending and capital account-related measures: IV-2SLS estimates.

(a) *First-stage regression*[a]

| Dependent variable | Overall controls | Bonds controls | Equity controls | Direct investment | Financial credit | Local FX lending | Purchase of local FX sec. | Open FX position limit |
|---|---|---|---|---|---|---|---|---|
| | (1) | (2) | (3) | (4) | (5) | (6) | (7) | (8) |
| Left-wing government | 0.132* | 0.097 | 0.131* | 0.089 | 0.192* | 0.084 | 0.302*** | −0.047 |
| | (0.066) | (0.065) | (0.071) | (0.127) | (0.111) | (0.090) | (0.109) | (0.076) |
| Observations | 354 | 347 | 354 | 354 | 353 | 348 | 347 | 343 |
| $R^2$ | 0.331 | 0.323 | 0.387 | 0.114 | 0.255 | 0.346 | 0.417 | 0.279 |
| F-test (p-value) | 0.00 | 0.00 | 0.00 | 0.00 | 0.00 | 0.00 | 0.00 | 0.00 |

(b) *Second-stage regression*[b]

| | Overall controls | Bonds controls | Equity controls | | | | | |
|---|---|---|---|---|---|---|---|---|
| Overall controls | −101.689** | | | | | | | |
| | (40.662) | | | | | | | |
| Bond controls | | −143.772* | | | | | | |
| | | (76.162) | | | | | | |
| Equity controls | | | −99.571** | | | | | |
| | | | (41.793) | | | | | |

|                                      | (1)                  | (2)                | (3)                 | (4)                   | (5)                    |
| ------------------------------------ | -------------------- | ------------------ | ------------------- | --------------------- | ---------------------- |
| Direct investment<br>controls        | −163.671<br>(206.025) |                    |                     |                       |                        |
| Financial<br>credit controls         |                      | −69.419*<br>(39.158) |                     |                       |                        |
| Lending<br>locally in FX             |                      |                    | −175.092<br>(146.071) |                       |                        |
| Purchase of local<br>FX securities   |                      |                    |                     | −46.914***<br>(17.359) |                        |
| Open FX<br>position limits           |                      |                    |                     |                       | 429.537<br>(1,057.338) |
| Region effects                       | Yes                  | Yes                | Yes                 | Yes                   | Yes                    |
| Year effects                         | Yes                  | Yes                | Yes                 | Yes                   | Yes                    |
| Observations                         | 354                  | 353                | 348                 | 347                   | 343                    |
| Countries                            | 32                   | 32                 | 32                  | 32                    | 32                     |

a. Panel (a) reports the first-stage estimation results where the presence of a left-wing government is used as an instrument for capital controls and prudential measures. Other exogenous variables included are the same as in table 9.10. All regressors are lagged one period. Constant, region-specific, and year effects are included in all specifications. F-test (p-value) reports the joint significance of all regressors. Clustered standard errors (by country) are reported in parentheses. ***, **, and * indicate statistical significance at the 1, 5, and 10 percent levels, respectively.
b. Panel (b) reports the instrumental variable two-stage least squares (IV-2SLS) estimates with foreign currency lending in total lending (in percent) as the dependent variable. Capital controls and prudential measures are predicted values obtained from the corresponding first-stage regression in panel (a). Control variables as specified in table 9.10, as well as a constant are included in all specifications. Clustered standard errors (by country) are reported in parentheses. ***, **, and * indicate statistical significance at the 1, 5, and 10 percent levels, respectively.

# 10 Multilateral Considerations

## 10.1 Introduction

Thus far, we have largely taken the individual country's perspective when discussing how to manage capital flows. Yet, by definition, capital flows involve at least two parties. Indeed, there may be interactions not only between borrowers and creditors, but also among borrowers (and, for that matter, among creditors—though these are not the subject of this book). As such, there is an inherent multilateral dimension to the management of cross-border capital flows, which we take up in this chapter. The discussion here is cast in terms of capital controls, but it bears emphasizing that exactly the same analysis applies to *any* policy (interest rates, foreign exchange [FX] intervention, prudential measures) that affect the volume of capital inflows, whether by intent or incidentally. (A rather different multilateral aspect of the policy response—via the exchange rate on trading partners—is discussed in chapter 11.)

When a country imposes a capital control (or any other measure that reduces inflows), there are two possible effects. One is a decrease in global demand for capital, which shifts the intertemporal terms of trade in favor of borrowers. The other is a deflection of some of the capital toward other borrowers. All borrowers benefit from the lower interest rate, but those contending with their own capital inflow problem may not welcome the larger volume of flows. These borrowers might respond by imposing their own capital controls, deflecting some of the flows back to the original borrower, who could reply by raising its controls further. The successive rounds of tit-for-tat could degenerate into a full-blown capital controls war. A natural question is whether such an outcome is Pareto efficient—and, if not, whether capital-receiving countries may benefit from coordinating their policy responses.

Any such cooperation, however, would be quite different from that envisaged by Keynes and White at Bretton Woods, which concerned source and recipient countries "controlling capital at both ends" (see chapter 2). While it would be natural for the borrower to want to shift part of the burden of managing capital flows onto lenders, the creditor's incentive is less obvious. Nonetheless, cooperation may benefit source countries as well. For instance, it could reduce the likelihood of an eventual financial crisis in recipient countries, one that could inflict losses on source-country financial institutions (and hence on their taxpayers) or even threaten the stability of the international monetary system. Limiting outflows may also make accommodative monetary policy more effective in stimulating the source-country economy by preventing leakage of liquidity abroad. Further, as we establish below, the creditor may have an incentive to restrict outflows to manipulate the terms of trade (i.e., the world interest rate) in its favor, even if doing so incurs a distortionary or administrative cost. From a global perspective, if the distortionary costs associated with capital controls are convex (increasing at an increasing rate in the tax rate), as seems plausible—or, more generally, if the sum of distortionary costs of inflow and outflow measures is less than the cost of inflow measures alone to achieve a given reduction in inflows—then the efficient arrangement would be to control capital flows at both ends.

Theory aside, there is little empirical evidence concerning the multilateral aspects of capital controls. To begin with, only a few studies examine spillovers from borrowers imposing controls on inflows to other borrowers, and they present mixed findings. More compelling is the evidence on source-country policies, with many studies (including the analysis in chapter 3) reporting that a key determinant of capital flows to emerging market economies (EMEs) is the interest rates of advanced countries (especially the United States). But there is much less evidence that quantitative measures—capital controls and currency-based prudential policies—in source countries have an impact on capital flows. The problem confronting the empirical researcher is that, except in times of crisis (which typically have their own dynamics), there are few instances of countries imposing outflow controls—and even fewer cases of simultaneous source- and recipient-country measures.[1]

---

1. As recounted in chapter 2, the United States declined to cooperate in the enforcement of capital controls, both when it was the major recipient of flight capital during the interwar period and when it was the major source of capital outflows at the time of the collapse of Bretton Woods.

In this chapter, we establish theoretically the conditions under which recipient-recipient and source-recipient cooperation in managing capital flows would be desirable (section 10.2). Next we examine empirically whether such cooperation would be feasible (section 10.3). For that purpose, we exploit annual bilateral data on cross-border bank flows to see whether there are spillovers from capital controls in recipient countries, and also whether outflow and inflow measures imposed by source and recipient countries, respectively, are *simultaneously* effective in influencing the volume of cross-border flows. We conclude with a discussion of the policy implications of the analysis (section 10.4).

## 10.2 Analytical Framework

In this section, we lay out a simple analytical framework for discussing multilateral aspects of managing the capital account. Our starting point is the analysis of chapter 7, where we showed that the decentralized economy will over-borrow—justifying a tax on such borrowing. Here we consider how the intervention that is optimal from a unilateral perspective gets modified once global interdependencies are taken into account.

We summarize the welfare effect of the decentralized economy's excessive borrowing by a function $\xi(b_{-1})$, that increases with the amount of borrowing, $\xi(b_{-1}) = \xi b_{-1}$, $\xi \geq 0$, which may represent the adverse consequences of either balance-sheet vulnerabilities or macroeconomic imbalances or both. Since the purpose of this framework is to analyze the impact of capital controls that are *ex ante* intended to prevent excessive borrowing, all of the action takes place between periods −1 and 0, and without loss of generality, period +1 can be suppressed.

### 10.2.1 The Setup

The representative agent lives for two periods, maximizing lifetime utility:

$$V(R, I) = Max \; u(c_{-1}) + \beta u(c_0) \tag{10.1}$$

where $R = (1+r)$ is the gross interest rate faced by the domestic agent, $I$ is his lifetime income, and $c_{-1}$, $c_0$ are consumption in each period. The static budget constraints are:

$$c_{-1} = y_{-1} + b_{-1} \tag{10.2}$$

$$c_0 = y_0 - Rb_{-1} + T - \xi(b_{-1}) - \delta(\tau) \tag{10.3}$$

where $y_{-1}$ and $y_0$ are the endowments of income in each period, $b_{-1}$ is borrowing (as well as end-period debt), $T$ is the lump sum transfer from the government (in equilibrium, equal to the revenue raised by the tax on inflows, $T = \tau b_{-1}$, where $\tau$ is a proportional tax on borrowing), $\xi(b_{-1})$ is the externality associated with excessive borrowing, and $\delta(\tau)$ is the distortionary cost of capital controls, which is assumed to satisfy $\delta(\tau) \geq 0$, $\delta''(\tau) \geq 0$, $\delta(0) = \delta'(0) = 0$. The interest rate faced by the domestic agent is the world interest rate, $\hat{R}$, plus the inflow tax:

$$R = \hat{R} + \tau \tag{10.4}$$

The agent's income is:

$$I = Ry_{-1} + y_0 + T - \xi(b_{-1}) - \delta(\tau) \tag{10.5}$$

The atomistic agent ignores the externality associated with excessive borrowing, and treats $\bar{z} = T - \xi(b_{-1}) - \delta(\tau)$ as a fixed quantity. The agent therefore maximizes his utility subject to his intertemporal budget constraint:

$$Rc_{-1} + c_0 = I = Ry_{-1} + y_0 + \bar{z} \tag{10.6}$$

The first-order conditions characterizing the agent's optimum are given by:

$$u_c(c_{-1}) = R\lambda \tag{10.7}$$

$$\beta u_c(c_0) = \lambda \tag{10.8}$$

where $\lambda$ is the Lagrange multiplier associated with the intertemporal budget constraint.

Combining (10.7)–(10.8) yields the familiar Euler equation:

$$u_c(c_{-1}) = \beta R u_c(c_0) \tag{10.9}$$

Totally differentiating (10.9) and substituting (10.2)–(10.3) yields:

$$db_{-1} = \frac{\beta(u_c(c_0) - b_{-1}(\hat{R} + \tau)u_{cc}(c_0))}{(u_{cc}(c_{-1}) + \beta(\hat{R} + \tau)^2 u_{cc}(c_0))}(d\hat{R} + d\tau) \tag{10.10}$$

$$\equiv b_{\hat{R}}d\hat{R} + b_\tau d\tau; \quad b_{\hat{R}} = b_\tau < 0$$

Intuitively, an exogenous increase in the world interest rate or in the tax on capital inflows reduces borrowing.

With this set up, we first derive the optimal policy for an individual capital-recipient country acting on its own. Next we consider the interaction between recipient countries. Finally, we discuss how responsibility for the management of cross-border flows may be split optimally between the source and recipient countries.

### 10.2.2 Individual Government's Optimal Capital Controls

The government is assumed to be benevolent in the sense that it maximizes the representative agent's welfare while taking into account the externality that results in socially excessive borrowing. The government's problem is therefore:

$$Max_\tau \ V(R, I)$$

subject to the budget constraints (10.2) and (10.3), and the private sector's behavior, as summarized in (10.9). The first-order condition for the government's optimization problem, $dV/d\tau = 0$, may be written:

$$\frac{dV}{d\tau} = \frac{dV}{dR}\frac{dR}{d\tau} + \frac{dV}{dI}\frac{dI}{d\tau} = 0$$

Exploiting Roy's identity[2] and differentiating (10.5) with respect to $\tau$ yields:

$$\frac{dV}{d\tau} = \left(-c_{-1}\frac{dV}{dI}\right)\frac{dR}{d\tau} + \frac{dV}{dI}\left(y_{-1}\frac{dR}{d\tau} + b_{-1} + (\tau - \xi)\frac{db_{-1}}{d\tau} - \delta'(\tau)\right) = 0$$

Using $y_{-1} - c_{-1} = -b_{-1}$, this expression may be simplified:

$$\frac{dV}{d\tau} = \frac{dV}{dI}\left\{b_{-1}\left(1 - \frac{dR}{d\tau}\right) + (\tau - \xi)\frac{db_{-1}}{d\tau} - \delta'(\tau)\right\} = 0$$

The first term is simply the increase in the agent's utility from an extra dollar of income, and equals the Lagrange multiplier, which is positive $dV/dI = \lambda > 0$, while from (10.4), $1 - dR/d\tau = -d\hat{R}/d\tau$.

Hence the optimal capital control may be written as:

$$\tau = \left(\frac{b_{-1}(d\hat{R}/d\tau)}{(db/d\tau)}\right) + \xi - \left(\frac{\delta'(\tau)}{-(db/d\tau)}\right) \tag{10.11}$$

Each of the terms in brackets is positive. The first term corresponds to the "optimal tariff" or terms-of-trade manipulation in trade theory:

---

2. Note that $\partial V/\partial R = u_c\,(c_{-1})\partial c_{-1}/\partial R + \beta u_c\,(c_0)\partial c_0/\partial R$. Substituting (10.7)–(10.8) yields $\partial V/\partial R = \lambda[R(\partial c_{-1}/\partial R) + (\partial c_0/\partial R)]$. Differentiating the budget constraint (10.6), we obtain: $(R\partial c_{-1}/\partial R) + (\partial c_0/\partial R) = -c_{-1}$, which, upon substitution, yields Roy's identity: $\partial V/\partial R = -\lambda c_{-1} = -(\partial V/\partial I)c_{-1}$.

by imposing an inflow control, the government of a capital-recipient country reduces global demand for capital, and therefore the world interest rate—shifting the terms of trade in its favor. The second term is the borrowing externality. The third term encapsulates the cost-benefit trade-off: imposing controls incurs a distortionary cost but reduces borrowing by $db/d\tau$. The capital control chosen by the government will thus be higher: the greater the perceived impact on the terms of trade, the larger the borrowing externality and the greater the perceived effect of the inflow tax on reducing private sector borrowing. Conversely, the higher the distortionary cost of the capital control, the lower the optimal tax.

### 10.2.3   Coordination among Capital-Recipient Countries

The optimal capital control formula derived above pertains to an individual borrowing country. In this section, we embed the individual country in a wider world economy in which there are $n$ (identical) borrowers whose total mass sums to unity $\left(\sum_{i=1}^{n}(1/n)=1\right)$. The world interest rate is an increasing function of the global demand for capital $\hat{R}\left(\sum_{i=1}^{n}(b_i/n)\right)$, $\hat{R}'(b) > 0$.

**Noncooperative equilibrium**   If the borrowing countries do not coordinate their response to capital flows, then each individual borrower chooses its capital control according to (10.11), where in evaluating the expressions $(db/d\tau)$ and $(d\hat{R}/d\tau)$ each government makes the Nash conjecture that other borrowers will not respond to its policy: $\partial \tau_j / \partial \tau_i = 0 \; \forall j \neq i$.

Totally differentiating the world interest rate schedule:

$$d\hat{R} = \hat{R}_b\left(\sum_{i=1}^{n}(b_{\hat{R}}^i/n)d\hat{R} + \sum_{i=1}^{n}(b_{\tau}^i/n)d\tau^i\right)$$

or:

$$d\hat{R} = \frac{\hat{R}_b\left(\sum_{i=1}^{n}(b_{\tau}^i/n)d\tau^i\right)}{\left(1 - \hat{R}_b\sum_{i=1}^{n}(b_{\hat{R}}^i/n)\right)} \tag{10.12}$$

The perceived impact of a change in the home country's capital control on the world interest rate in the Nash equilibrium is thus:

$$(d\hat{R}/d\tau)^N = \frac{\hat{R}_b(b_{\tau}/n)}{\left(1 - b_{\hat{R}}\right)} \leq 0 \tag{10.13}$$

where $\hat{R}_b > 0$, and from (10.10), $b_\tau < 0$, $b_{\hat{R}} < 0$. In the limiting case of infinitely many atomistic borrowers, each borrower acts as though it has no impact on the world interest rate: $\lim_{n \to \infty}(d\hat{R}/d\tau)^N \to 0$.

The effect of raising the capital inflow tax on the country's borrowing is then evaluated as:[3]

$$(db_{-1}/d\tau)^N = b_{\hat{R}}\left(1 + \frac{\hat{R}_b(b_\tau/n)}{(1-b_{\hat{R}})}\right) < 0 \tag{10.14}$$

Since $b_\tau < 0$, the term in brackets is less than unity. Therefore, as capital-recipient countries become atomistic and ignore the impact of their controls on the world interest rate, their perceived effect on borrowing is correspondingly greater:

$$\lim_{n \to \infty}(db/d\tau)^N = b_{\hat{R}}$$

Substituting (10.13) and (10.14) into (10.11) yields the optimal inflow control under noncooperative behavior:

$$\tau^N = b\left(\frac{\dfrac{\hat{R}_b(b_\tau^i/n)}{(1-b_{\hat{R}})}}{b_{\hat{R}}\left(1 + \dfrac{\hat{R}_b(b_\tau/n)}{(1-b_{\hat{R}})}\right)}\right) + \xi - \left(\frac{\delta'(\tau)}{-b_{\hat{R}}\left(1 + \dfrac{\hat{R}_b(b_\tau/n)}{(1-b_{\hat{R}})}\right)}\right) \tag{10.15}$$

In the limiting case of atomistic borrowers, the term for terms of trade manipulation becomes zero, and the optimal capital control is simply:

$$\lim_{n \to \infty}\tau^N = \xi - \left(\frac{\delta'(\tau)}{-b_{\hat{R}}}\right)$$

**Coordination among borrowers**   If borrowers coordinate their policy responses, they recognize that they all face the same incentive and will act symmetrically; therefore, $\partial\tau_j/\partial\tau_i = 1 \; \forall j \neq i$. Substituting into (10.12):

$$(d\hat{R}/d\tau)^C = \frac{\hat{R}_b b_\tau}{(1-b_{\hat{R}})} \leq 0 \tag{10.16}$$

Comparing (10.13) and (10.16), when borrowers coordinate, their (actual and perceived) impact on the world interest rate is $n$ times greater than perceived in the Nash equilibrium.

---

3. We assume that $\hat{R}_b < -(1 - b_{\hat{R}})/b_{\hat{R}}$ as a stability condition to ensure that higher inflow taxes do not depress global interest rates to such an extent that the imposition of controls actually increases borrowing.

The corresponding impact on borrowing is:

$$(db_{-1}/d\tau)^C = b_{\hat{R}}\left(1 + \frac{\hat{R}_b b_\tau}{\left(1 - b_{\hat{R}}\right)}\right) < 0$$

So the optimal capital control under cooperation (which is invariant to the size of individual countries, as indexed by $n$) is:

$$\tau^C = b\left(\frac{\dfrac{\hat{R}_b b_\tau}{\left(1 - b_{\hat{R}}\right)}}{b_{\hat{R}}\left(1 + \dfrac{\hat{R}_b b_\tau}{\left(1 - b_{\hat{R}}\right)}\right)}\right) + \xi - \left(\frac{\delta'(\tau)}{-b_{\hat{R}}\left(1 + \dfrac{\hat{R}_b b_\tau}{\left(1 - b_{\hat{R}}\right)}\right)}\right) \qquad (10.17)$$

Comparing (10.15) and (10.17), the first term corresponds to the incentive to manipulate the terms of trade, which is larger when borrowing countries band together (and act as a monopsonist) than when they act individually. Indeed, in the Nash equilibrium this term goes to zero as countries become atomistic. In reality, even if capital-recipient countries coordinate their policy responses, it is unlikely that they would impose controls for the sole purpose of manipulating the terms of trade in their favor—in which case, this term becomes irrelevant under the coordinated equilibrium as well.

The second and third terms in (10.15) and (10.17) correspond to the use of capital controls to reduce the financial-stability risks associated with excessive external borrowing. For a given financial-stability risk associated with such borrowing, $\xi$, there is a trade-off between the economic distortions caused by imposing capital controls and the benefit in terms of reducing borrowing. The latter is (perceived) to be greater under the Nash equilibrium, where atomistic countries ignore their impact on the world interest rate (though, in equilibrium, their capital controls depress the world interest rate and thereby induce more borrowing). This is the crux of the deflection problem: in the Nash equilibrium, each government imposing capital controls overestimates the extent to which its tax will reduce inflows because it fails to take into account that (part of) the capital will be deflected back as other countries respond with their own controls. This effect leads to higher capital controls in the Nash equilibrium than in the coordinated equilibrium.

Moreover, contrary to common intuition, the inefficiency of the uncoordinated equilibrium does not diminish as countries become atomistic. On the contrary, the divergence between the Nash and cooperative tax rates increases as each country becomes a smaller player (Ghosh 1991). Finally, from (10.15) and (10.17), abstracting from any terms of trade manipulation, there are two instances in which the Nash and cooperative policies coincide, so there would be no gains from coordination. First, when there is no financial-stability risk ($\xi = 0$), and abstracting from terms-of-trade manipulation, the optimal capital control under Nash or cooperative behavior is zero, so there can be no gains from coordination. Second, when capital controls are not costly ($\delta = 0$), although each country in Nash equilibrium imposes controls without regard to the spillover to others, those countries can respond by raising their own controls without incurring any cost. Thus, in the Nash equilibrium capital controls are higher than they would be under cooperation, but this carries no welfare implication when controls are not costly. Both these cases are examples of the general result that when governments have as many instruments as targets, there are no gains from coordination (Ghosh and Masson 1994). Once governments wish to offset the financial-stability risk while also minimizing the distortionary cost of controls, they have fewer instruments than targets and therefore have an incentive to coordinate.[4]

### 10.2.4 Cooperation between Borrowers and Creditors
Beyond coordination among capital-receiving countries, there may also be circumstances under which cooperation between borrowers and creditors is globally efficient and perhaps mutually beneficial. To examine this, we now explicitly model the behavior of creditors.

As before, in the borrowing country, the representative agent maximizes:

$$V(R, I) = Max \; u(c_{-1}) + \beta u(c_0)$$

subject to:

$$c_{-1} = y_{-1} + b_{-1}$$

$$c_0 = y_0 - Rb_{-1} + \bar{z} = y_0 - Rb_{-1} + \tau b_{-1} - \xi(b_{-1}) - \delta(\tau)$$

---

4. Terms-of-trade manipulation always gives an incentive to coordinate (in effect, to act as a monopsonist) because implicitly there are two objectives that are in tension in any such manipulation: to reduce global demand for capital and thereby lower the world interest rate, but also to maintain the same level of borrowing (and thus benefit from the lower cost of borrowing).

where $R = \hat{R} + \tau$ , and where the agent's lifetime income is given by:

$$I = R y_{-1} + y_0 + \tau b_{-1} - \xi(b_{-1}) - \delta(\tau)$$

In the creditor country, the representative agent's problem is:

$$V^*(R^*, I^*) = Max\ u(c_{-1}^*) + \beta^* u(c_0^*)$$

subject to:

$$c_{-1}^* = y_{-1}^* - b_{-1}$$

$$c_0^* = y_0^* + R^* b_{-1} + \bar{z}^* = y_0^* + R^* b_{-1} + \tau^* b_{-1} - \delta^*(\tau^*)$$

where $R^* = \hat{R} - \tau^*$, and where the agent's lifetime income is given by:

$$I^* = R^* y_{-1}^* + y_0^* + \tau^* b_{-1} - \delta^*(\tau^*)$$

$\tau^*$ is a tax on capital outflows (thus reducing the rate of return to the creditor below the world interest rate), and it is assumed that lending does not incur financial-stability risks, though there may be distortionary costs associated with outflow measures.

We set $y_{-1} = y_0^* = 0$; $y_0 = y_{-1}^* > 0$; $\beta = \beta^* = 1$, which simplifies the algebra by ensuring that the home country is the debtor, and the foreign country is the creditor, but that the countries are otherwise fully symmetric. The global planner takes account of the welfare of both the borrower and the lender, with weights $\omega$ and $(1-\omega)$, respectively.

$$W = \{\omega V(R, I) + (1 - \omega)V^*(R^*, I^*)\} \tag{10.18}$$

A natural welfare weight to choose would be such that $\omega/(1 - \omega) = (dV^*/dI^*)/(dV/dI)$ so that an extra dollar is equally valuable to each party (given the assumed symmetry, this will imply $\omega \approx 1/2$).[5]

The planner's first-order conditions imply:

$$dW/d\tau = \omega(dV/dI)\big((y_{-1} - c_{-1})dR/d\tau + b_{-1} + (\tau - \xi)(db_{-1}/d\tau) - \delta'(\tau)\big)$$
$$+ (1 - \omega)(dV^*/dI^*)\Big(y_{-1}^* - c_{-1}^*\Big)(dR^*/d\tau) = 0 \tag{10.19}$$

$$dW/d\tau^* = \omega(dV/dI)\big((y_{-1} - c_{-1})dR/d\tau^*\big) + (1 - \omega)(dV^*/dI^*)$$
$$\times \Big(\big(y_{-1}^* - c_{-1}^*\big)(dR^*/d\tau^*) + b_{-1} + \tau^*(db_{-1}/d\tau^*) - \delta^{*'}(\tau^*)\Big) = 0 \tag{10.20}$$

---

5. The countries are not quite symmetric here since the debtor incurs a financial-stability cost associated with its borrowing, whereas the creditor does not. The source country is therefore inherently "wealthier."

Using $\omega(dV/dI)=(1-\omega)(dV^*/dI^*)$, $1-(dR/d\tau)=-d\hat{R}/d\tau$, and $1+(dR^*/d\tau)=d\hat{R}/d\tau$, these may be simplified to:

$$\frac{dW}{d\tau}=\frac{dV}{dI}\left(b_{-1}\left(\frac{dR^*}{d\tau}-\frac{d\hat{R}}{d\tau}\right)+(\tau-\xi)\left(\frac{db_{-1}}{d\tau}\right)-\delta'(\tau)\right)=0 \qquad (10.21)$$

$$\frac{dW}{d\tau^*}=\frac{dV}{dI}\left(b_{-1}\left(\frac{d\hat{R}}{d\tau^*}-\frac{dR}{d\tau^*}\right)+\tau^*\left(\frac{db_{-1}}{d\tau^*}\right)-\delta^{*\prime}(\tau^*)\right)=0 \qquad (10.22)$$

The global planner's first-order conditions (10.21)–(10.22) constitute a pair of simultaneous equations that define the optimal inflow and outflow taxes. Even without specific functional forms, some further insight can be gained by adding them and exploiting the symmetry of the model, which implies that $dR^*/d\tau=dR/d\tau^*$; $db_{-1}/d\tau=db_{-1}/d\tau^*$. Hence:

$$\tau+\tau^*=\xi-\frac{[\delta'(\tau)+\delta^{*\prime}(\tau^*)]}{-(db/d\tau)} \qquad (10.23)$$

Since the global planner cares equally about the borrower and the lender, there is no terms-of-trade manipulation in (10.23), and if there was no financial-stability cost of excessive borrowing, $\xi'=0$, then the optimal solution would involve neither inflow nor outflow controls, $\tau=\tau^*=0$. More generally, condition (10.23) tells the global planner that, given the financial-stability risks associated with excessive borrowing, the *sum* of inflow and outflow controls in the borrowing and lending countries, respectively, should be chosen so as to trade off their distortionary cost against the reduced capital flows—but it does not specify how the burden should be split between the borrower and the lender.

The planner's objective function (10.18) for $\omega \in (0, 1)$ traces out the Pareto locus between the borrower and lender so any deviation from the resulting equilibrium cannot make them both better off. Condition (10.23) implies global efficiency, but whether the borrower and lender individually gain relative to the counterfactual depends on the allocation between inflow and outflow taxes, and on the corresponding distortionary costs.

Suppose the global planner were to impose only inflow controls. This would reduce borrowing and thus the financial-stability risks for the debtor, as well as shift the terms of trade in the debtor's favor—but at the distortionary cost of inflow controls. Meanwhile, the creditor would lose because of the reduction in the world interest rate. Conversely, if the planner used only outflow controls the debtor would gain because financial-stability risks would be lowered without it having to incur the distortionary costs of imposing inflow taxes, but it would also lose because of the higher world interest rate. Meanwhile, the creditor would gain from the higher world interest rate, but at the expense of incurring the distortionary cost of imposing outflow controls. The global optimum will lie between these two extremes (i.e., will involve both inflow and outflow controls) because the distortionary costs are assumed to be convex—increasing at an increasing rate in the tax rate—so the total cost of achieving a given reduction in global flows is smaller if a combination of inflow and outflow controls is used than if the planner operates at only one end of the transaction.

Figure 10.1 shows the optimal inflow and outflow controls when the counterfactual is no inflow or outflow controls (and thus no terms-of-trade manipulation), and the planner gives equal weight to the welfare gain of the borrower and the creditor relative to the benchmark of neither inflow nor outflow controls. Even though it is only the borrower who faces the financial-stability risk associated with excessive capital flows, the optimal policy calls for almost equal inflow and outflow controls—indeed outflow controls are used more intensively than inflow controls as $\xi$ becomes sufficiently large and the borrower becomes correspondingly "poorer."

Despite its simplicity, the analytical framework developed here provides some useful insights. First, and most basically, it serves as a useful reminder that, by definition, capital flows involve more than one party, and responses to them will typically have multilateral implications. When a borrowing country imposes capital controls (or adopts any other policy measure to deter inflows) part of the flows will be deflected to other capital-recipient countries. If they follow suit in imposing barriers, part of the capital will be deflected back again, eliciting a further increase in capital controls. A capital controls war might ensue, with the net result that if capital-recipient countries do not coordinate their responses to generalized flows, they will end up with controls that are—from their own perspective—too high and too costly.[6]

---

6. It is important to recognize that multiple countries imposing/intensifying controls simultaneously (or in rapid sequence) is not necessarily indicative of a capital control war and may simply be the appropriate response of each country to the excessive inflows it is facing. It is only a capital control war when the escalation of controls is in response to deflected flows.

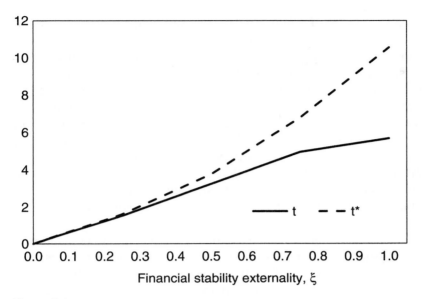

**Figure 10.1**
Optimal source- and recipient-country capital controls.
*Source*: Authors' estimates.
*Notes*: Optimal recipient-country inflow $(\tau)$, and source-country outflow $(\tau^*)$ controls as a function of the financial-stability risk in the recipient country, $\xi$. The example assumes logarithmic utility with no discounting and unit levels of output $(y_{-1} = 0, y_{-1}^* = 1; \quad y_0 = 1, y_0^* = 0)$.

If the distortionary cost of capital controls is convex, as seems plausible, then cooperation between borrowers and lenders is also possible, with the borrower gaining because it does not have to impose such draconian inflow controls, and the lender gaining because restricting outflows shifts the terms of trade in its favor (or protects its financial institutions' balance sheets from potentially risky assets).

## 10.3   Some Empirics

While the theoretical argument for greater cooperation among recipient—and between source and recipient—countries is clear, the case for any such coordination in practice rests upon cross-country spillovers being empirically relevant. A prerequisite for spillovers from the recipient country's capital inflow controls is for them to be effective—in the sense that at least the country imposing the measure should experience a smaller volume of inflows. If this does not hold, then controls obviously cannot have any spillover effects. The evidence presented in chapter 9 suggests that capital controls and currency-based prudential measures reduce macroeconomic imbalances and balance-sheet vulnerabilities; therefore most likely they affect the magnitude of at least some forms of capital flows. But it does not follow that there are economically important spillovers among capital-recipient countries. Some recent studies report mixed results for the existence of spillovers. For example, analyzing the effect of Brazil's imposition of inflow controls in 2009–2011, Forbes et al. (2012) find deflection toward some countries, but no overall impact on EMEs. By contrast, Lambert, Ramos-Tallada, and Rebillard (2011) find evidence of significant spillovers from Brazilian controls to other EMEs in the region.

As for the possibility of source- and recipient-country cooperation, a prerequisite is for spillovers to exist from source-country policies (e.g., monetary policies). But if such cooperation is achieved through the imposition of capital controls, then another requirement is for source-country restrictions on capital *outflows* to be effective. While a voluminous literature, including that presented in chapter 3, finds evidence of spillovers from monetary policies in source countries (especially the US), there are virtually no studies about the effectiveness of outflow controls—except in the context of measures imposed in the midst of crisis (e.g., Malaysia in 1998), where the dynamics are likely to be very different.[7]

In what follows, we first take up the case for coordination among recipient countries, for which we examine the effectiveness of capital controls in recipient countries in discouraging inflows, and then explore the existence of spillovers from such restrictions. We then turn to the case for cooperation between source countries and recipient countries by examining whether source-country outflow measures and recipient-country inflow measures *simultaneously* affect cross-border flows.

**Data and stylized facts**    For our analysis, we rely on annual data on bilateral cross-border bank flows from thirty-one major source countries

---

7. An exception to this is Binici, Hutchison, and Schindler (2010), who examine the effectiveness of outflow controls more generally and find that they are associated with significantly lower outflows in advanced economies.

to forty-seven emerging market recipient countries over 1995–2012, obtained from the Bank for International Settlements (BIS). Flows are estimated by the BIS as the exchange rate–adjusted changes in gross international financial claims on the bank and nonbank sectors of recipient countries by resident banks in the reporting country (i.e., as changes in the total outstanding stock of reporting-country banks' foreign assets, accounting for repayments and exchange rate effects).[8] To the extent that such flows tend to be highly procyclical—with the potential to create serious economic and financial instabilities (Milesi-Ferretti and Tille 2011; Brunnermeier et al. 2012; Bruno and Shin 2015)—they are particularly relevant for analyzing whether policy coordination could help in better regulating cross-border capital flows.[9]

By any estimate, cross-border bank flows to EMEs have ballooned over the past couple of decades. Total bank-asset flows from reporting advanced countries to EMEs increased from about US$59 billion in 1995 to US$414 billion in 2007, before dropping sharply during the global financial crisis in 2008–2009 (figure 10.2[a]). Recovery has been gradual and volatile, with flows totaling about US$150 billion in 2010, but falling again in 2011–2012. The post-crisis bounce back in flows has also not been uniform across regions: Latin America and Asia have been the major recipients, with total flows received in 2010 close to the pre-crisis peak, while recovery in emerging Europe has lagged. Flows from (reporting) EMEs to other EMEs also increased sharply before the global financial crisis and have picked up since the steep fall in 2009 (figure 10.2[b]). In terms of stocks, the increase in such liabilities is also striking—with claims on EMEs rising threefold, from less than US$1 trillion in 1995 to about US$3 trillion in 2012 (representing around 20 percent of EMEs' total external liabilities).

The importance of bank flows has increased not only in absolute terms but also in relation to other flows. By the eve of the crisis in

---

8. The data—originally compiled by reporting-country central banks and then provided to the BIS—cover over 90 percent of the international assets of the domestic banking institutions, and comprise cross-border bank loans, bank credit lines (used portions), and trade-related credit, as well as debt securities, equity holdings, and participations of banks.

9. Also, bilateral data on other types of flows (e.g., portfolio flows) is mostly available for advanced economies and not for EMEs. More recently, the IMF has initiated coordinated investment surveys that document the total stock of direct and portfolio investment assets/liabilities of reporting countries against major partner countries, but the cross-country and time coverage of this data is limited.

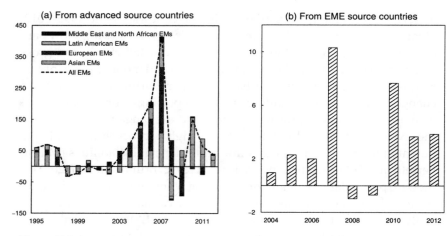

**Figure 10.2**
Total cross-border bank-asset flows to EMEs, 1995–2012 (in billions of USD).
*Source*: Bank for International Settlements Locational Statistics.
*Note*: Source countries include those for which data is available.

2007, they accounted for about 40 percent of gross inflows to EMEs (figure 10.3). The starkest increase was in emerging Europe, where the share of bank flows in total flows doubled from about 20 percent in 1995 to over 40 percent just before the crisis. Not only are banking claims a significant component of capital flows to EMEs, they are also among the most procyclical and volatile, with surges in bank inflows often followed by sharp declines (such as in Asia and Latin America in the late 1990s, and more generally across all countries in the global financial crisis). Indeed, of the surge episodes identified in chapter 3, around two-fifths are driven by corresponding surges in bank flows.

### 10.3.1   Coordination among Recipient Countries
**Recipient-country effects**   We begin by examining the impact of restrictions on flows to the country imposing them. From figure 10.4, EMEs with greater restrictions on capital inflows appear to receive smaller cross-border bank flows on a bilateral basis.[10] On average, flows are

---

10. Flows are presented in logarithmic terms. Following existing literature (e.g., Papaio-annou 2009; Herrmann and Mihaljek 2010), when taking the log, the negative asset flow observations are transformed by taking the log of the absolute value and then changing the sign. This transformation preserves the original sign on the flow observations, and retains symmetry in the data.

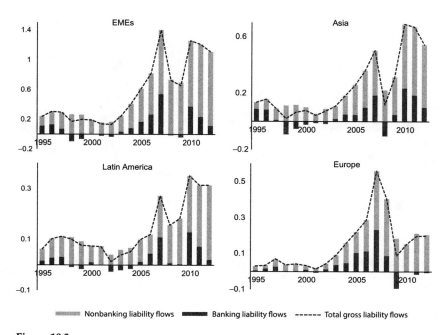

**Figure 10.3**
Total cross-border bank and nonbank liability flows to EMEs, 1995–2012 (in trillions of USD).
*Source*: Bank for International Settlements Locational Statistics and International Financial Statistics database.
*Notes*: Bank-liability flows for recipient regions are computed as the sum of gross bank-asset flows from all source countries to that region. Nonbank-liability flows are computed as the difference between total (gross) liability flows to the region (obtained from the IFS) and bank-liability flows.

about 25–45 percent lower if above-median capital inflows controls or currency-based prudential measures are in place in recipient countries (though, among the latter, the difference is statistically significant only for restrictions on lending locally in FX, and on the purchase of locally issued securities denominated in FX). These statistics are, however, unconditional averages. To analyze the association between bilateral bank flows and capital account regulations in EMEs more rigorously, we estimate the following gravity-type model:

$$F_{ijt} = X'_{it}\beta_i + X'_{jt}\beta_j + \gamma R_{jt} + \mu_{ij} + \lambda_t + \varepsilon_{ijt} \tag{10.24}$$

where $F_{ijt}$ is (the log of) bank flows from source country $i$ to recipient country $j$ in year $t$; $R_j$ is the capital inflow related policy measure in the recipient country; $X_i$ and $X_j$ are additional explanatory variables

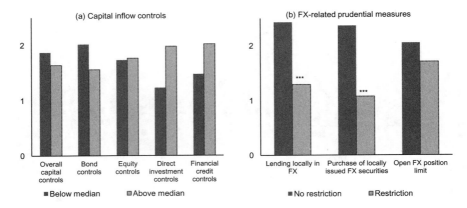

**Figure 10.4**
Cross-border bank flows and capital account–related measures, 1995–2012.
*Source*: Authors' estimates.
*Notes*: Bank flows are measured as log of exchange rate–adjusted changes in the total stock (amounts outstanding) of assets. All policy measures are lagged one period. *** indicates statistically significant different means between the two groups at the 1 percent level.

characterizing source and recipient countries, respectively; $\mu_{ij}$ are the source-recipient country specific effects to capture time-invariant factors that may affect bilateral flows (such as geographical distance, political and cultural ties, etc.); $\lambda_t$ are time effects to capture common shocks across country pairs; and $\varepsilon_{ijt}$ is a random error term.

Similar to the analysis in chapter 9 (section 9.4.2), the capital inflow regulations considered here include an overall measure of capital inflow controls, as well as controls disaggregated by asset class (i.e., on bond, equity, direct investment and financial credit inflows). For prudential measures, we consider restrictions on lending locally in FX; restrictions on the purchase of locally issued securities denominated in FX; and open FX position limits. The list of explanatory variables in (10.24) includes proxies for source-country push and recipient-country pull factors such as real GDP per capita, real GDP growth rate, real interest rate, and real GDP (to control for the economic size). In addition, as in chapter 3, the current account balance in percent of GDP (to capture the external financing need), and the exchange rate regime (equal to one if the country has a pegged regime, and zero otherwise) of the recipient country are also included in the model.[11]

---

11. See data appendix for details on variable definitions and data sources.

While the cross-border bank flows data that we use is bilateral in nature, the explanatory variables as well as the capital account regulations included in (10.24) are in aggregate terms, which tend to respond to the total, rather than the bilateral, volume of flows. Econometrically, this helps to mitigate the endogeneity problem, making it easier to identify the impact of policy measures on the volume of cross-border banking flows; we nevertheless lag all source and recipient country–specific variables by one period when estimating (10.24) to further mitigate potential reverse causality concerns (endogeneity is also addressed through the use of instrumental variables in the chapter appendix). In addition, we include the recipient-country capital account regulations in (10.24) individually to avoid multicollinearity problems.

The estimation results for (10.24) show that the presence of capital controls is significantly associated with a reduction in cross-border bank inflows: moving from the twenty-fifth to seventy-fifth percentile on the overall capital inflow control index lowers flows by about 80 percent (table 10.1, col. [1]). This result, however, appears to be driven mainly by controls on bond inflows—moving from the twenty-fifth to seventy-fifth percentile on the bond controls index reduces inflows by some 87 percent (col. [2]). The estimated coefficients on equity, direct investment and financial credit control indices are negative, but statistically insignificant (cols. [3]–[5]).

Going beyond capital controls, we find that all currency-based prudential measures are strongly associated with lower cross-border bank flows. Inflows are, for example, about 100 percent lower in the presence of restrictions on lending locally in FX. Inasmuch as domestic lending in foreign currency largely relies on foreign (especially, bank) financing—as in emerging Europe before the global financial crisis—this finding is intuitive, and reaffirms earlier assertions that such prudential measures could also indirectly limit inflows. Similarly, the estimated coefficients on restrictions on the purchase of locally issued securities denominated in FX, and on net open FX position limits in the recipient countries, are negative and statistically significant, implying a reduction in cross-border bank inflows of about 80–90 percent.

Among the other explanatory variables, cross-border flows are increasing in the recipient country's economic size, real GDP growth, and real interest rate. Greater external financing need and a pegged exchange rate in the recipient country also imply significantly larger inflows. These findings are robust to other econometric specifications. For instance, including proxies for recipient-country financial development, financial

**Table 10.1**
Cross-border bank flows and capital inflow regulations in EMEs, 1995–2012.

| | Capital controls | | | | Prudential measures | | | |
|---|---|---|---|---|---|---|---|---|
| | (1) | (2) | (3) | (4) | (5) | (6) | (7) | (8) |
| Log (real GDP)$_i$ | 13.976 (9.941) | 14.176 (9.914) | 14.010 (9.948) | 13.928 (9.955) | 13.900 (9.949) | 14.360 (9.870) | 14.201 (9.988) | 14.113 (9.967) |
| Log (real GDP)$_j$ | 22.386*** (5.205) | 21.361*** (5.108) | 20.343*** (5.104) | 20.196*** (5.094) | 20.784*** (5.148) | 19.864*** (5.040) | 22.721*** (5.206) | 21.287*** (5.165) |
| Log (real GDP per capita)$_i$ | −21.917* (12.162) | −22.176* (12.140) | −21.969* (12.186) | −21.886* (12.192) | −21.867* (12.184) | −22.535* (12.060) | −22.270* (12.211) | −22.126* (12.202) |
| Log (real GDP per capita)$_j$ | −7.898* (4.713) | −6.606 (4.591) | −5.694 (4.619) | −5.484 (4.603) | −6.176 (4.645) | −6.307 (4.519) | −8.562* (4.715) | −6.903 (4.688) |
| Real GDP growth$_i$ | 0.144 (0.121) | 0.144 (0.121) | 0.143 (0.121) | 0.143 (0.121) | 0.142 (0.121) | 0.145 (0.120) | 0.143 (0.121) | 0.143 (0.121) |
| Real GDP growth$_j$ | 0.376*** (0.059) | 0.369*** (0.059) | 0.364*** (0.059) | 0.361*** (0.059) | 0.367*** (0.059) | 0.396*** (0.059) | 0.356*** (0.059) | 0.363*** (0.059) |
| Real interest rate$_i$ | −0.117 (0.131) | −0.116 (0.131) | −0.115 (0.131) | −0.116 (0.131) | −0.116 (0.131) | −0.113 (0.130) | −0.117 (0.132) | −0.117 (0.131) |
| Real interest rate$_j$ | 0.114*** (0.044) | 0.122*** (0.044) | 0.124*** (0.044) | 0.121*** (0.044) | 0.115** (0.045) | 0.104** (0.044) | 0.112** (0.044) | 0.118*** (0.044) |
| Exchange rate regime$_j$ | 1.655*** (0.615) | 1.627*** (0.613) | 1.524** (0.618) | 1.544** (0.618) | 1.575** (0.618) | 1.394** (0.610) | 1.615*** (0.614) | 1.534** (0.619) |
| Current account bal./GDP$_j$ | −0.081* (0.047) | −0.088* (0.047) | −0.085* (0.047) | −0.086* (0.047) | −0.081* (0.047) | −0.064 (0.047) | −0.078* (0.047) | −0.087* (0.047) |
| Overall inflow controls$_j$ | −2.666** (1.176) | | | | | | | |

| | (1) | (2) | (3) | (4) | (5) | (6) | (7) |
|---|---|---|---|---|---|---|---|
| Bond inflow controls$_j$ | −2.075*** (0.800) | | | | | | |
| Equity inflow controls$_j$ | | −1.170 (1.020) | | | | | |
| Direct investment inflow controls$_j$ | | | −0.366 (0.827) | | | | |
| Financial credit inflow controls$_j$ | | | | −0.556 (0.577) | | | |
| Lending locally in FX$_j$ | | | | | −4.256*** (0.772) | | |
| Purchase of local FX securities$_j$ | | | | | | −1.986** (0.891) | |
| Open FX position limits$_j$ | | | | | | | −1.766* (0.972) |
| Country-pair effects | Yes | Yes | Yes | Yes | Yes | Yes | Yes |
| Year effects | Yes | Yes | Yes | Yes | Yes | Yes | Yes |
| Observations | 12,194 | 12,194 | 12,194 | 12,194 | 12,194 | 12,194 | 12,194 |
| Country pairs | 1,127 | 1,127 | 1,127 | 1,127 | 1,127 | 1,127 | 1,127 |
| $R^2$ | 0.047 | 0.047 | 0.046 | 0.046 | 0.047 | 0.046 | 0.046 |
| Source countries | 31 | 31 | 31 | 31 | 31 | 31 | 31 |
| Recipient countries | 47 | 47 | 47 | 47 | 47 | 47 | 47 |

*Notes*: Dependent variable is (log of) bank-asset flows from country i to country j. All variables are lagged one period. Constant is included in all specifications. Reported $R^2$ is the within $R^2$. Clustered standard errors (at the country-pair level) are reported in parentheses. ***, **, and * indicate statistical significance at the 1, 5, and 10 percent levels, respectively.

soundness, trade openness, and fiscal balance to GDP, we find that the estimated coefficients of capital account–related measures remain similar to those in table 10.1 (see chapter appendix). In addition, the results remain mostly the same if the sample is restricted to advanced economies as source countries only; or if offshore financial centers and post-global financial crisis years (when international bank deleveraging occurred) are excluded from the sample. The results also hold when potential endogeneity concerns are addressed through the instrumental variable two-stage least squares (IV-2SLS) approach—where the presence of a democratic left-wing government is used as an instrument for the presence of capital controls.

To gauge the economic significance of the estimates obtained above, we simulate some counterfactual scenarios in which EMEs are assumed to have imposed greater inflow restrictions than were actually in place on the eve of the global financial crisis in 2007. Our results suggest that if all recipient countries had in place capital controls (i.e., had a score of 1 on our overall inflow controls index), then the outstanding stock of foreign bank claims would have been around 3 percent of GDP lower in emerging Europe and in Latin America, and about 1 percent of GDP lower in Asia (figure 10.5).[12] Likewise, nonresident banks' financial claims on emerging Europe would have been about 2 percent of GDP lower (about 0.5 percent of GDP lower for Latin America and emerging Asia) if all recipient countries had adopted some form of currency-based prudential restriction (e.g., on lending locally in FX).

**Deflection to other capital-recipient countries**   While recipient-country restrictions reduce the volume of cross-border bank inflows, do they do so by deflecting flows to other capital-receiving countries? To examine this possibility, we augment (10.24) to include a measure of inflow restrictions in *other* recipient countries:

$$F_{ijt} = X'_{it}\beta_i + X'_{jt}\beta_j + \gamma R_{jt} + \theta R_{kt} + \mu_{ij} + \lambda_t + \varepsilon_{ijt} \tag{10.25}$$

where $R_{kt}, k \neq j$ is the average inflow restriction in "neighboring" countries (lagged one period). Neighbors are defined in two ways: geographically—the average of restrictions in countries in the same geographic region;

---

12. The smaller impact for Asia is because many of these countries actually had inflow measures in place; hence raising their index to 1 in the counterfactual exercise implies only a modest increase in restrictiveness and a correspondingly small impact on the stock of claims.

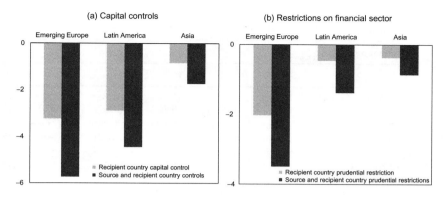

**Figure 10.5**
Potential impact of capital account restrictions on financial claims of nonresident banks (in percent of GDP).
*Source*: Authors' estimates.
*Note*: (a) and (b) panels show the change in predicted financial claims of nonresident banks (in percent of recipient region's GDP) if either all recipient countries or if all source and recipient countries had imposed capital controls, or financial sector-specific restrictions, respectively, in 2007.

and in terms of economic similarity (per capita income; real GDP growth; institutional quality). For the latter, we use $k$-means clustering to define two (similar) groups of countries for three sub-periods (1995–99; 2000–04; 2005–12), and calculate the distance-weighted average of inflow restrictions in countries within the same group. (The obtained country groupings are reported in the chapter appendix.)

The regression results for (10.25) suggest rather strong spillovers to a recipient country from inflow restrictions imposed by its neighbors—regardless of the method used to define neighborhood. Table 10.2 (cols. [1]–[7]), for instance, shows a positive coefficient on the regional inflow restrictions measure, which is highly statistically significant. The estimate implies that raising the average inflow control in regional neighbors from the sample median to the seventy-fifth percentile increase bank flows to the recipient country (controlling for its own restrictions) by about 80 percent. Similar results are found using the economic-similarity criterion of neighboring countries (table 10.4 cols. [8]–[14]). Moreover, the inclusion of inflow restrictions in neighboring countries makes little difference to the estimated coefficient on the country's own inflow restrictions in terms of economic and statistical significance. These results suggest that policy coordination among recipient countries could be worthwhile when dealing with unwelcome capital inflows.

**Table 10.2**
Spillovers of inflow restrictions to EMEs, 1995–2012.

| | Regional neighbors | | | | | | | |
|---|---|---|---|---|---|---|---|---|
| | (1) | (2) | (3) | (4) | (5) | (6) | (7) | (8) |
| Log (real GDP$_i$) | 13.906 (9.923) | 14.074 (9.904) | 13.914 (9.924) | 13.847 (9.927) | 13.842 (9.920) | 14.286 (9.847) | 14.131 (9.959) | 14.047 (9.937) |
| Log (real GDP$_j$) | 15.729*** (5.689) | 15.082*** (5.545) | 13.336** (5.508) | 12.841** (5.478) | 13.565** (5.576) | 13.236** (5.422) | 15.419*** (5.548) | 13.916** (5.519) |
| Log (real GDP per capita$_i$) | −21.903* (12.159) | −22.118* (12.143) | −21.933* (12.175) | −21.859* (12.178) | −21.867* (12.170) | −22.512* (12.051) | −22.262* (12.197) | −22.122* (12.186) |
| Log (real GDP per capita$_j$) | −1.513 (5.364) | −0.643 (5.180) | 0.988 (5.176) | 1.481 (5.121) | 0.727 (5.226) | −0.001 (5.044) | −1.649 (5.191) | 0.070 (5.182) |
| Real GDP growth$_i$ | 0.141 (0.121) | 0.142 (0.121) | 0.140 (0.121) | 0.140 (0.121) | 0.140 (0.121) | 0.142 (0.120) | 0.140 (0.121) | 0.140 (0.121) |
| Real GDP growth$_j$ | 0.377*** (0.059) | 0.371*** (0.059) | 0.367*** (0.059) | 0.365*** (0.059) | 0.369*** (0.059) | 0.399*** (0.059) | 0.360*** (0.059) | 0.367*** (0.059) |
| Real interest rate$_i$ | −0.115 (0.131) | −0.114 (0.131) | −0.114 (0.131) | −0.115 (0.131) | −0.114 (0.131) | −0.112 (0.130) | −0.116 (0.132) | −0.115 (0.131) |
| Real interest rate$_j$ | 0.134*** (0.046) | 0.140*** (0.045) | 0.144*** (0.045) | 0.142*** (0.045) | 0.138*** (0.046) | 0.123*** (0.045) | 0.133*** (0.045) | 0.140*** (0.045) |
| Exchange rate regime$_j$ | 1.460** (0.616) | 1.444** (0.613) | 1.337** (0.619) | 1.339** (0.619) | 1.369** (0.619) | 1.211** (0.612) | 1.411** (0.614) | 1.327** (0.619) |
| Current account bal./GDP$_j$ | −0.076 (0.047) | −0.082* (0.047) | −0.078* (0.047) | −0.078* (0.047) | −0.075 (0.047) | −0.057 (0.047) | −0.070 (0.047) | −0.080* (0.047) |
| Neighbors controls$_j$ | 7.333** (3.183) | 7.151** (3.179) | 8.167*** (3.134) | 8.709*** (3.136) | 8.240*** (3.153) | 7.815** (3.092) | 8.662*** (3.123) | 8.755*** (3.124) |
| Overall controls$_j$ | −2.153* (1.204) | | | | | | | |
| Bond controls$_j$ | | −1.722** (0.821) | | | | | | |
| Equity controls$_j$ | | | −0.747 (1.023) | | | | | |
| Direct investment controls$_j$ | | | | −0.577 (0.831) | | | | |
| Financial credit controls$_j$ | | | | | −0.363 (0.578) | | | |
| Lending locally in FX$_j$ | | | | | | −4.191*** (0.773) | | |

Economic neighbors

| (9) | (10) | (11) | (12) | (13) | (14) | (15) | (16) |
|---|---|---|---|---|---|---|---|
| 15.005 | 15.139 | 14.953 | 14.895 | 14.906 | 15.392 | 15.219 | 15.084 |
| (10.037) | (10.020) | (10.038) | (10.036) | (10.034) | (9.973) | (10.072) | (10.047) |
| 18.245*** | 17.406*** | 16.002*** | 15.757*** | 16.208*** | 16.610*** | 18.500*** | 16.571*** |
| (5.699) | (5.509) | (5.512) | (5.440) | (5.585) | (5.382) | (5.574) | (5.468) |
| −22.813* | −22.994* | −22.762* | −22.691* | −22.719* | −23.431* | −23.136* | −22.940* |
| (12.296) | (12.283) | (12.312) | (12.310) | (12.307) | (12.197) | (12.331) | (12.320) |
| −4.457 | −3.445 | −2.234 | −2.036 | −2.469 | −3.677 | −5.362 | −3.370 |
| (5.167) | (4.944) | (4.981) | (4.903) | (5.040) | (4.821) | (5.034) | (4.948) |
| 0.158 | 0.158 | 0.157 | 0.157 | 0.157 | 0.159 | 0.158 | 0.157 |
| (0.123) | (0.123) | (0.123) | (0.123) | (0.123) | (0.122) | (0.123) | (0.123) |
| 0.363*** | 0.358*** | 0.354*** | 0.352*** | 0.355*** | 0.386*** | 0.346*** | 0.355*** |
| (0.060) | (0.059) | (0.059) | (0.059) | (0.059) | (0.059) | (0.059) | (0.059) |
| −0.082 | −0.081 | −0.080 | −0.080 | −0.080 | −0.079 | −0.082 | −0.081 |
| (0.134) | (0.134) | (0.134) | (0.134) | (0.134) | (0.133) | (0.134) | (0.134) |
| 0.112** | 0.117*** | 0.119*** | 0.117*** | 0.115** | 0.099** | 0.106** | 0.114** |
| (0.045) | (0.044) | (0.044) | (0.045) | (0.046) | (0.044) | (0.045) | (0.045) |
| 1.600*** | 1.576** | 1.498** | 1.504** | 1.521** | 1.376** | 1.581** | 1.485** |
| (0.616) | (0.614) | (0.620) | (0.620) | (0.619) | (0.612) | (0.615) | (0.620) |
| −0.081* | −0.086* | −0.083* | −0.083* | −0.081* | −0.063 | −0.074 | −0.084* |
| (0.047) | (0.047) | (0.047) | (0.047) | (0.047) | (0.047) | (0.047) | (0.047) |
| 7.058* | 7.136** | 8.274** | 8.698** | 8.304** | 6.483* | 8.842** | 9.593*** |
| (3.651) | (3.592) | (3.623) | (3.487) | (3.604) | (3.477) | (3.475) | (3.510) |
| −1.954 | | | | | | | |
| (1.239) | | | | | | | |
| | −1.529* | | | | | | |
| | (0.839) | | | | | | |
| | | −0.479 | | | | | |
| | | (1.061) | | | | | |
| | | | −0.406 | | | | |
| | | | (0.826) | | | | |
| | | | | −0.256 | | | |
| | | | | (0.590) | | | |
| | | | | | −4.048*** | | |
| | | | | | (0.781) | | |

(continued)

**Table 10.2** (continued)

| | Regional neighbors | | | | | | | |
|---|---|---|---|---|---|---|---|---|
| | (1) | (2) | (3) | (4) | (5) | (6) | (7) | (8) |
| Purchase of local FX securities$_j$ | | | | | | | −2.024** (0.897) | |
| Open FX position limits$_j$ | | | | | | | | −1.857* (0.975) |
| Country-pair effects | Yes | Yes | Yes | Yes | Yes | Yes | Yes | Yes |
| Year effects | Yes | Yes | Yes | Yes | Yes | Yes | Yes | Yes |
| Observations | 12,194 | 12,194 | 12,194 | 12,194 | 12,194 | 12,194 | 12,194 | 12,194 |
| Country pairs | 1,127 | 1,127 | 1,127 | 1,127 | 1,127 | 1,127 | 1,127 | 1,127 |
| R² | 0.047 | 0.047 | 0.047 | 0.047 | 0.047 | 0.050 | 0.047 | 0.047 |

*Notes:* Dependent variable is (log of) bank-asset flows from country i to j. Source- and recipient-country control variables (lagged one period), as in table 10.1, and constant are included in all specifications. Inflow controls in regional neighbors are defined as the average of the overall capital inflow controls index in EMEs in the same region. Inflow controls in economic neighbors is the distance-weighted average of countries with similar economic (per capita real income, real GDP growth, and institutional) characteristics as the recipient country. Sample size is reduced slightly in cols. (9)–(16) as institutional quality index is unavailable for Georgia and Macedonia. See table A.10.3 for country groupings by economic characteristics. Clustered standard errors (at the country-pair level) are reported in parentheses. ***, **, and * indicate statistical significance at the 1, 5, and 10 percent levels, respectively.

### 10.3.2   Cooperation between Source and Recipient Countries

What about cooperation between source and recipient countries? To examine whether cross-border capital flows could indeed be regulated "at both ends" of the transaction, we include in (10.24) a measure for source-country restrictions on capital outflows:

$$F_{ijt} = X'_{it}\beta_i + X'_{jt}\beta_j + \gamma R_{jt} + \delta S_{it} + \mu_{ij} + \lambda_t + \varepsilon_{ijt} \qquad (10.26)$$

where $S_i$ is the source country's capital account regulation that is likely to affect its bank outflows, while the definition of all other variables remains the same as in (10.24). Similar to recipient-country measures, the source-country measures that we consider here include an overall measure of capital controls on outflows, as well as controls disaggregated by asset class (i.e., on bond, equity, direct investment and financial credit inflows). For prudential measures, we consider

| Economic neighbors | | | | | | | |
| (9) | (10) | (11) | (12) | (13) | (14) | (15) | (16) |
| --- | --- | --- | --- | --- | --- | --- | --- |
|  |  |  |  |  |  | −2.138** |  |
|  |  |  |  |  |  | (0.908) |  |
|  |  |  |  |  |  |  | −2.079** |
|  |  |  |  |  |  |  | (0.982) |
| Yes | Yes | Yes | Yes | Yes | Yes | Yes | Yes |
| Yes | Yes | Yes | Yes | Yes | Yes | Yes | Yes |
| 11,944 | 11,944 | 11,944 | 11,944 | 11,944 | 11,944 | 11,944 | 11,944 |
| 1,092 | 1,092 | 1,092 | 1,092 | 1,092 | 1,092 | 1,092 | 1,092 |
| 0.048 | 0.048 | 0.048 | 0.048 | 0.048 | 0.051 | 0.048 | 0.048 |

restrictions on lending to nonresidents; restrictions on the maintenance of accounts abroad; and limits on banks' open FX positions.[13]
As before, we lag $S_i$ to mitigate potential endogeneity concerns.

The estimation results, reported in table 10.3, show that outflow
restrictions in the source country, and inflow restrictions in the recipient country, are *simultaneously* effective in reducing cross-border flows.
Thus, the coefficients on both the overall inflow and outflow control
indices are negative and statistically significant in col. (1), as are those
on bond inflow and outflow controls in col. (2). Similarly, several other
combinations of capital account regulations in both source and recipient countries are effective in reducing the volume of cross-border capital flows (cols. [6]–[9]). It seems plausible, however, that the effects of
inflow and outflow measures are not *fully* additive since they will (to
some extent) hit the same potential capital flow. Indeed, by construction,

13. Open FX position limits in source countries have a potentially ambiguous effect on the
volume of flows: if source-country banks have few FX-denominated deposits or other liabilities, then such limits will tend to decrease cross-border flows as the bank would be limited
in the foreign currency (and hence foreign) assets it could acquire. Conversely, if FX deposits
in source-country banks are plentiful, then FX limits would force banks to acquire foreign-
currency assets, which may well take the form of cross-border claims. Moreover, open FX
limits may be less relevant in reserve currency countries such as the United States since
many US banks' cross-border claims are in their domestic currency (i.e., the US dollar).

**Table 10.3**
Cross-border bank flows and restrictions at both ends, 1995–2012.

| | (1) | (2) | (3) | (4) | (5) | (6) | (7) | (8) | (9) |
|---|---|---|---|---|---|---|---|---|---|
| Log (real GDP$_i$) | 12.615 | 12.991 | 11.723 | 13.157 | 12.704 | 18.343* | 12.970 | 12.842 | 12.750 |
| | (9.988) | (9.940) | (10.012) | (9.978) | (10.008) | (9.889) | (9.921) | (10.032) | (10.010) |
| Log (real GDP$_j$) | 22.237*** | 21.172*** | 20.125*** | 20.283*** | 20.647*** | 19.804*** | 19.698*** | 22.570*** | 21.136*** |
| | (5.206) | (5.115) | (5.114) | (5.063) | (5.150) | (4.991) | (5.042) | (5.211) | (5.168) |
| Log (real GDP per capita$_i$) | −19.994 | −20.227* | −18.888 | −20.506* | −20.376* | −26.240** | −20.572* | −20.349* | −20.200* |
| | (12.229) | (12.187) | (12.276) | (12.246) | (12.245) | (12.122) | (12.133) | (12.273) | (12.261) |
| Log (real GDP per capita$_j$) | −7.707 | −6.400 | −5.459 | −5.533 | −6.011 | −6.150 | −6.100 | −8.372* | −6.712 |
| | (4.706) | (4.593) | (4.622) | (4.572) | (4.639) | (4.473) | (4.513) | (4.713) | (4.684) |
| Real GDP growth$_i$ | 0.160 | 0.149 | 0.156 | 0.148 | 0.156 | 0.110 | 0.162 | 0.160 | 0.159 |
| | (0.121) | (0.121) | (0.121) | (0.121) | (0.122) | (0.120) | (0.121) | (0.122) | (0.122) |
| Real GDP growth$_j$ | 0.375*** | 0.368*** | 0.364*** | 0.360*** | 0.366*** | 0.394*** | 0.395*** | 0.355*** | 0.362*** |
| | (0.059) | (0.059) | (0.059) | (0.059) | (0.059) | (0.059) | (0.059) | (0.059) | (0.059) |
| Real interest rate$_i$ | −0.111 | −0.120 | −0.100 | −0.103 | −0.119 | −0.176 | −0.107 | −0.112 | −0.111 |
| | (0.131) | (0.132) | (0.132) | (0.131) | (0.131) | (0.130) | (0.130) | (0.131) | (0.131) |
| Real interest rate$_j$ | 0.114*** | 0.122*** | 0.124*** | 0.121*** | 0.115** | 0.103** | 0.103** | 0.112** | 0.118*** |
| | (0.044) | (0.044) | (0.044) | (0.044) | (0.045) | (0.043) | (0.044) | (0.044) | (0.044) |
| Exchange rate regime$_j$ | 1.653*** | 1.621*** | 1.516** | 1.560** | 1.569** | 1.414** | 1.390** | 1.612*** | 1.531** |
| | (0.615) | (0.612) | (0.617) | (0.617) | (0.617) | (0.608) | (0.610) | (0.613) | (0.618) |
| Current account bal./GDP$_j$ | −0.081* | −0.089* | −0.086* | −0.083* | −0.081* | −0.065 | −0.063 | −0.078* | −0.087* |
| | (0.047) | (0.047) | (0.047) | (0.047) | (0.047) | (0.046) | (0.047) | (0.047) | (0.047) |
| Overall outflow controls index$_i$ | −2.243* | | | | | | −2.291* | −2.241* | −2.248* |
| | (1.300) | | | | | | (1.296) | (1.305) | (1.310) |
| Overall inflow controls index$_j$ | −2.681** | | | | | | | | |
| | (1.179) | | | | | | | | |
| Bond outflow controls index$_i$ | | −2.003* | | | | | | | |
| | | (1.074) | | | | | | | |
| Bond inflow controls index$_j$ | | −2.092*** | | | | | | | |
| | | (0.803) | | | | | | | |

| | (1) | (2) | (3) | (4) | (5) | (6) | (7) |
|---|---|---|---|---|---|---|---|
| Equity outflow controls index$_i$ | −2.435** (1.113) | | | | | | |
| Equity inflow controls index$_j$ | −1.193 (1.024) | | | | | | |
| Direct investment outflow controls index$_i$ | | −3.048** (1.431) | | | | | |
| Direct investment inflow controls index$_i$ | | −0.351 (0.825) | | | | | |
| Financial credit outflow controls index$_i$ | | | −0.887 (0.678) | | | | |
| Financial credit inflow controls index$_j$ | | | −0.556 (0.578) | | | | |
| Lending to nonresidents$_i$ | | | | −6.846*** (1.598) | | | |
| Lending locally in FX$_i$ | | | | −4.223*** (0.769) | −4.266*** (0.774) | | |
| Purchase of local FX securities$_j$ | | | | | | −1.995** (0.889) | |
| Open FX position limits$_j$ | | | | | | | −1.783* (0.969) |
| Country-pair effects | Yes | Yes | Yes | Yes | Yes | Yes | Yes |
| Year effects | Yes | Yes | Yes | Yes | Yes | Yes | Yes |
| Observations | 12,194 | 12,194 | 12,194 | 12,194 | 12,194 | 12,194 | 12,194 |
| Country pairs | 1,127 | 1,127 | 1,127 | 1,127 | 1,127 | 1,127 | 1,127 |
| $R^2$ | 0.047 | 0.047 | 0.046 | 0.051 | 0.050 | 0.047 | 0.047 |
| Source countries | 31 | 31 | 31 | 31 | 31 | 31 | 31 |
| Recipient countries | 47 | 47 | 47 | 47 | 47 | 47 | 47 |

*Notes:* Dependent variable is (log of) bank-asset flows from country i to country j. All variables are lagged one period. Constant is included in all specifications. $R^2$ is the within $R^2$. Clustered standard errors (at the country-pair level) are reported in parentheses. ***, **, and * indicate statistical significance at the 1, 5, and 10 percent levels, respectively.

the log specification implies that the effects are not fully additive: in table 10.3 (col. [1]), for instance, moving from the twenty-fifth to the seventy-fifth percentile on the source-country overall outflow control index (holding the recipient-country inflow index constant) is associated with an 80 percent reduction in flows, while a similar increase for the recipient-country bond inflow controls index (holding the source-country outflow index constant) is associated with a reduction in flows by about 50 percent—but the impact of both measures combined is a 90 percent (and not 130 percent) reduction in the volume of flows.

To explore this issue further, table 10.4 re-estimates the impact of source and recipient-country measures by segmenting the data according to whether the other end is relatively more or less open (that is, the overall controls index is below or above the seventy-fifth percentile). The top panel of table 10.4 shows that outflow related measures generally have a quantitatively larger and statistically significant impact when the recipient country is more open to inflows (cols. [1]–[8]) than when it is already mostly closed (cols. [9]–[16]). Likewise, the bottom panel of table 10.4 shows that inflow restrictions have a quantitatively larger and statistically significant impact when the source country is more open to outflows, than when it is mostly closed. The effect of both inflow and outflow restrictions thus seems to lose its statistical significance once the other side is already relatively closed. This is intuitive in that the *incremental impact* of a restriction is likely to be small if the capital account at the other end is already closed.

Importantly, however, our findings do not imply that inflow and outflow restrictions are mutually redundant. Rather, the results remain statistically significant if we exclude the fully open recipient countries (i.e., those with no inflow restrictions) when estimating the effect of outflow measures, and exclude fully open source countries (i.e., those with no outflow restrictions) when estimating the effect of inflow measures (table 10.5). While the number of observations declines when we do so, the estimated impact and statistical significance of the different measures are barely affected. Effectiveness of inflow or outflow restrictions therefore does not depend on the other side of the transaction being *fully* open—only on the other side not being fully closed.[14]

---

14. We draw similar implications if instead of splitting the sample by openness, we include an interaction term between the measures and a dummy variable indicating if the other side is more open/closed (where the dummy variable is equal to one if the other side is more closed, and zero otherwise).

The upshot of these findings is that it should be possible to influence the volume of cross-border bank flows through outflow or inflow restrictions, or by some combination of the two. Imposing measures on both sides allows a further reduction in flows, or possibly the same reduction but achieved by using the measures less intensively. Thus, undertaking a counterfactual exercise similar to that conducted above, we find that the stock of financial claims of nonresident banks on emerging Asia, Latin America, and emerging Europe would have been some 2–6 percent of GDP lower than the actual levels if the relevant (economy-wide) capital controls had been in place in both source *and* recipient countries in 2007 (figure 10.5). Financial sector–specific restrictions at both ends—such as source country's restrictions on banks' lending to nonresidents, and recipient country's restrictions on banks' lending domestically in FX would also have translated into a significant reduction (about 3.5 percent of GDP for emerging Europe, 1.5 percent of GDP for Latin America, and 1 percent for Asia of GDP) in nonresident banks' claims. If the distortionary costs associated with restrictions are convex in the "tax" rate, then—as shown above—it may be globally more efficient to use a combination of low outflow and inflow restrictions than to put the full burden at either end. Conversely, when it is not possible to operate at one end—either because the administrative capacity is lacking or because international treaty obligations prohibit the use of such restrictions—then it would nevertheless still be possible to reduce flows by imposing the relevant restrictions at the other end.

## 10.4 Conclusion

This chapter considered some of the multilateral aspects of capital account management. Theory and empirics suggests that recipient countries would benefit from coordinating their policy responses to capital inflows. Specifically, because of spillovers of one country's measures on another, uncoordinated responses might result in barriers that—abstracting from terms of trade effects—are inefficiently high, reducing both global and recipient-country welfare.

Theory also suggests that, under plausible conditions, it would be globally efficient if source and recipient countries could act "at both ends" in managing cross-border capital flows. For the recipient country, there would be a clear benefit if part of the distortive cost of capital controls (or the economic cost of diverting other instruments from their primary tar-

**Table 10.4**
Cross-border bank flows and restrictions by openness, 1995–2012.

| | More open recipient countries | | | | | | | |
| --- | --- | --- | --- | --- | --- | --- | --- | --- |
| | (1) | (2) | (3) | (4) | (5) | (6) | (7) | (8) |
| *Source-country outflow restrictions* | | | | | | | | |
| Overall controls$_i$ | −2.723* (1.444) | | | | | | | |
| Bond controls$_i$ | | −2.207* (1.167) | | | | | | |
| Equity controls$_i$ | | | −2.752** (1.202) | | | | | |
| Direct investment$_i$ | | | | −4.603*** (1.644) | | | | |
| Financial credit$_i$ | | | | | −1.109 (0.751) | | | |
| Lending to nonresidents$_i$ | | | | | | −7.691*** (1.972) | | |
| Accounts abroad$_i$ | | | | | | | −2.571 (1.588) | |
| Open FX position limits$_i$ | | | | | | | | 1.286 (0.987) |
| Country-pair effects | Yes | Yes | Yes | Yes | Yes | Yes | Yes | Yes |
| Year effects | Yes | Yes | Yes | Yes | Yes | Yes | Yes | Yes |
| Observations | 9,273 | 9,273 | 9,273 | 9,273 | 9,273 | 9,273 | 9,273 | 9,273 |
| Country pairs | 979 | 979 | 979 | 979 | 979 | 979 | 979 | 979 |
| $R^2$ | 0.041 | 0.041 | 0.041 | 0.041 | 0.041 | 0.042 | 0.041 | 0.041 |

| | More open source countries | | | | | | | |
| --- | --- | --- | --- | --- | --- | --- | --- | --- |
| | (1) | (2) | (3) | (4) | (5) | (6) | (7) | (8) |
| *Recipient-country inflow restrictions* | | | | | | | | |
| Overall controls$_j$ | −2.978** (1.209) | | | | | | | |
| Bond controls$_j$ | | −2.318*** (0.810) | | | | | | |
| Equity controls$_j$ | | | −1.075 (1.076) | | | | | |
| Direct investment$_j$ | | | | −0.401 (0.869) | | | | |

Less open recipient countries

| (9) | (10) | (11) | (12) | (13) | (14) | (15) | (16) |
|---|---|---|---|---|---|---|---|
| 0.522<br>(3.253) | | | | | | | |
| | −0.982<br>(2.683) | | | | | | |
| | | −0.909<br>(2.838) | | | | | |
| | | | 2.663<br>(3.093) | | | | |
| | | | | 0.229<br>(1.650) | | | |
| | | | | | −4.324<br>(2.738) | | |
| | | | | | | 4.159<br>(3.744) | |
| | | | | | | | −0.956<br>(1.735) |
| Yes | Yes | Yes | Yes | Yes | Yes | Yes | Yes |
| Yes | Yes | Yes | Yes | Yes | Yes | Yes | Yes |
| 2,921 | 2,921 | 2,921 | 2,921 | 2,921 | 2,921 | 2,921 | 2,921 |
| 412 | 412 | 412 | 412 | 412 | 412 | 412 | 412 |
| 0.096 | 0.097 | 0.097 | 0.097 | 0.096 | 0.097 | 0.097 | 0.097 |

Less open source countries

| (9) | (10) | (11) | (12) | (13) | (14) | (15) | (16) |
|---|---|---|---|---|---|---|---|
| 5.240<br>(5.470) | | | | | | | |
| | 3.270<br>(4.229) | | | | | | |
| | | −0.429<br>(3.706) | | | | | |
| | | | 2.474<br>(3.668) | | | | |

(continued)

**Table 10.4** (continued)

| | More open source countries | | | | | | | |
| | (1) | (2) | (3) | (4) | (5) | (6) | (7) | (8) |
|---|---|---|---|---|---|---|---|---|
| Financial credit$_j$ | | | | | −0.636 (0.604) | | | |
| Lending locally in FX$_j$ | | | | | | −4.909*** (0.803) | | |
| Purchase of local FX securities$_j$ | | | | | | | −2.272** (0.887) | |
| Open FX position limits$_j$ | | | | | | | | −1.615 (1.028) |
| Country-pair effects | Yes | Yes | Yes | Yes | Yes | Yes | Yes | Yes |
| Year effects | Yes | Yes | Yes | Yes | Yes | Yes | Yes | Yes |
| Observations | 10,805 | 10,805 | 10,805 | 10,805 | 10,805 | 10,805 | 10,805 | 10,805 |
| Country pairs | 994 | 994 | 994 | 994 | 994 | 994 | 994 | 994 |
| $R^2$ | 0.053 | 0.054 | 0.053 | 0.053 | 0.053 | 0.057 | 0.054 | 0.053 |

*Notes*: Dependent variable is (log of) bank-asset flows from country i to country j. More (less) open recipient countries are those with the overall inflow controls index below (above) the seventy-fifth percentile. More (less) open source countries are those with the overall outflow controls index below (above) the seventy-fifth percentile. All specifications include control variables as in tables 10.1–10.3. All variables are lagged one period. Constant is included in all specifications. Reported $R^2$ is the within $R^2$. Clustered standard errors (at the country-pair level) are reported in parentheses. ***, **, and * indicate statistical significance at the 1, 5, and 10 percent levels, respectively.

gets) could be shifted to the source country. Even though source countries might incur some economic or administrative cost in managing outflows, they would benefit from the terms of trade improvement (i.e., the higher world interest rate). More generally (and perhaps more pertinently), creditor countries would benefit inasmuch as their banks—and ultimately their tax payers—are less likely to incur losses if financial-stability risks in recipient countries are reduced through better management of volatile capital flows. Such cooperation would also be very much in the spirit of Keynes' and White's proposal at the time of Bretton Woods.

Testing the feasibility of this proposal directly is difficult because, historically, there have been few instances of such cooperation. Nonetheless, exploiting bilateral data on cross-border bank flows, we are able to establish that recipient- and source-country capital controls and prudential

| Less open source countries | | | | | | | |
| --- | --- | --- | --- | --- | --- | --- | --- |
| (9) | (10) | (11) | (12) | (13) | (14) | (15) | (16) |
| | | | | 0.334 (2.070) | | | |
| | | | | | 1.024 (2.708) | | |
| | | | | | | 7.979* (4.328) | |
| | | | | | | | −3.656 (2.848) |
| Yes | Yes | Yes | Yes | Yes | Yes | Yes | Yes |
| Yes | Yes | Yes | Yes | Yes | Yes | Yes | Yes |
| 1,389 | 1,389 | 1,389 | 1,389 | 1,389 | 1,389 | 1,389 | 1,389 |
| 294 | 294 | 294 | 294 | 294 | 294 | 294 | 294 |
| 0.057 | 0.057 | 0.056 | 0.056 | 0.056 | 0.056 | 0.059 | 0.057 |

measures can simultaneously be effective in affecting the volume of these flows—which, as discussed in earlier chapters, are among the most volatile and risky. In turn this implies that if—for legal or administrative reasons—it is impossible to operate at one end of the flow, then it should be possible to manage the flow from the other end. Or, if the distortive and administrative costs of restrictive measures are increasing in their intensity and coverage, then more globally efficient outcomes can be achieved by splitting the burden between source and recipient countries.

But what would this mean in practice? First, as regards cooperation between source countries and recipient countries, there are times when specific bilateral flows are problematic, and where cooperation between source- and recipient-country regulators may be beneficial, especially in regard to bank flows (which is part of the reason why we focused on these flows in the empirical analysis above). In the run-up to the global financial crisis, for instance, Swedish banks contributed to rapid credit growth in the Baltic countries (Estonia, Lithuania, and Latvia). When the Estonian supervisors, however, asked the Swedish authorities to impose stricter capital requirements on the Swedish banks' affiliates, the Swedish Financial Supervisory Authority declined to do so, on

**Table 10.5**
Restrictions by openness (excluding fully open), 1995–2012.

| | More open recipient countries | | | | | | | |
| | (1) | (2) | (3) | (4) | (5) | (6) | (7) | (8) |
|---|---|---|---|---|---|---|---|---|
| Overall controls | −3.301**<br>(1.648) | | | | | | | |
| Bond controls | | −2.686**<br>(1.354) | | | | | | |
| Equity controls | | | −3.236**<br>(1.397) | | | | | |
| Direct investment | | | | −4.665***<br>(1.805) | | | | |
| Financial credit | | | | | −1.478*<br>(0.847) | | | |
| Lending to nonresidents | | | | | | −8.943***<br>(2.290) | | |
| Accounts abroad | | | | | | | −4.129**<br>(1.770) | |
| Lending locally in FX | | | | | | | | |
| Purchase of local FX securities | | | | | | | | |
| Open FX position limits | | | | | | | | 2.053*<br>(1.147) |
| Country-pair effects | Yes | Yes | Yes | Yes | Yes | Yes | Yes | Yes |
| Year effects | Yes | Yes | Yes | Yes | Yes | Yes | Yes | Yes |
| Observations | 7,572 | 7,572 | 7,572 | 7,572 | 7,572 | 7,572 | 7,572 | 7,572 |
| Country pairs | 876 | 876 | 876 | 876 | 876 | 876 | 876 | 876 |
| $R^2$ | 0.041 | 0.041 | 0.042 | 0.042 | 0.041 | 0.044 | 0.042 | 0.041 |

*Notes*: Dependent variable is (log of) bank-asset flows from country i to country j. More open recipient countries are those with the overall inflow controls index below the seventy-fifth percentile but excluding those with no restrictions on inflows. More open source countries are those with the overall outflow controls index below the seventy-fifth percentile but excluding those with no restrictions on outflows. Restrictions refer to those in source countries in cols. (1)–(8), and those in recipient countries in cols. (9)–(16). All specifications include control variables as in tables 10.1–10.3. All variables are lagged one period. Constant is included in all specifications. Reported $R^2$ is the within $R^2$. Clustered standard errors (at the country-pair level) are reported in parentheses. ***, **, and * indicate statistical significance at the 1, 5, and 10 percent levels, respectively.

| More open source countries | | | | | | | |
| --- | --- | --- | --- | --- | --- | --- | --- |
| (9) | (10) | (11) | (12) | (13) | (14) | (15) | (16) |
| −4.248** | | | | | | | |
| (1.887) | | | | | | | |
| | −3.113** | | | | | | |
| | (1.292) | | | | | | |
| | | −1.109 | | | | | |
| | | (1.615) | | | | | |
| | | | −0.638 | | | | |
| | | | (1.311) | | | | |
| | | | | −0.484 | | | |
| | | | | (0.823) | | | |
| | | | | | −5.440*** | | |
| | | | | | (1.059) | | |
| | | | | | | −3.671*** | |
| | | | | | | (1.352) | |
| | | | | | | | −2.470** |
| | | | | | | | (1.258) |
| Yes | Yes | Yes | Yes | Yes | Yes | Yes | Yes |
| Yes | Yes | Yes | Yes | Yes | Yes | Yes | Yes |
| 6,045 | 6,045 | 6,045 | 6,045 | 6,045 | 6,045 | 6,045 | 6,045 |
| 737 | 737 | 737 | 737 | 737 | 737 | 737 | 737 |
| 0.066 | 0.066 | 0.065 | 0.065 | 0.065 | 0.070 | 0.067 | 0.066 |

grounds that the groups' capital, on a consolidated basis, already exceeded the required minimum (Gronn and Fredholm 2013). Likewise, with credit expanding at annual rate of more than 30 percent, the problem in Latvia, as IMF (2005a) notes, was that the "exposure of foreign banks' subsidiaries or branches to Latvia represent[ed] only a very small share of their portfolios, while profits derived from this business constitute a far greater fraction of their consolidated profit. This could induce foreign banks to assume greater risk than is beneficial from the Latvian perspective." As in the case of Estonia, the Latvian authorities were barred from imposing capital controls by European Union (EU) regulations, but at the same time were handicapped in their inability to impose prudential measures on foreign (Swedish) banks.

In such circumstances, which may be quite frequent in EMEs with a large foreign banking presence, the home country regulators might usefully cooperate with host country regulators. More recently, Basel III mandates "reciprocity" in the application of counter-cyclical capital buffers. Under such reciprocity, home country regulators are required to impose the same capital buffers on their international banks' credit exposures in the host country (up to a level of 2.5 percent) as are being imposed by host country regulators on their own domestic banks. In essence, therefore, Basel III enjoins source-country regulators to cooperate in the prudential management of cross-border banking flows—at least in this limited regard (within the EU, the same principle is being applied more broadly; European Systemic Risk Board 2014)

As regards coordination among recipient countries on inflow controls, in the face of a generalized surge toward EMEs that is likely to elicit policy responses from multiple countries (because each is concerned about the macroeconomic or financial-stability risks), a useful role could be played by a multilateral organization like the IMF. IMF surveillance and policy advice can help ensure that countries imposing or intensifying controls calibrate them appropriately—that is, take account of the likely response of other countries to the deflected flows.[15] In practice, this would simply mean that recipient countries would be counseled to

15. In a world with both destabilizing and beneficial flows (say hot-money flows and foreign direct investment), and imperfect targeting of flows by capital account restrictions, measures imposed by one country may actually deflect "good flows" to other countries. Our assumption here is that deflection of good flows—the collateral damage from the measure—is smaller than deflection of bad flows.

adopt somewhat less intensive controls than would be the case if the inflow surge was not generalized (and large flows were only going to one or two countries), thus avoiding the risk of an escalating capital control "war."

## Chapter 10 Appendix

This appendix establishes the robustness of the results obtained above regarding capital controls and financial fragilities by conducting a battery of sensitivity checks—including estimating alternate specifications of the benchmark models with additional control variables and different samples, and addressing potential endogeneity concerns through the use of IV-2SLS estimation.

**Alternate specifications and samples**   While the gravity-type benchmark specification (10.24) that we use to examine the association between cross-border bank flows and capital controls or currency-based prudential measures already takes into account a range of global and domestic factors, here we include several other variables in the model that could potentially affect the volume of cross-border bank flows. Table A.10.1 shows that the benchmark results reported in table 10.1 generally remain robust to this exercise. For example, controlling for source and recipient-country institutional quality; financial development (proxied by private credit-to-GDP); financial soundness (proxied by bank return on equity), contagion effects through a common lender (i.e., exposure of source country to other countries experiencing a financial crisis; Herrmann and Mihaljek 2010), and trade openness, we find that the estimated coefficients of capital account–related measures remain mostly similar to those in table 10.1 in both magnitude and statistical significance (cols. [2]–[7]).

In addition, the results hold if we restrict the source countries to advanced economies only (col. [8]), or if we exclude offshore financial centers (both advanced and emerging markets) or post-global financial crisis years from the sample (cols. [8]–[10]). Defining the dependent variable in (log) real terms (deflated by US CPI) does not have much impact on the results either (col. [11]), nor does using data on total cross-border *stock* of bank assets instead of flows (col. [12]). In fact, in the latter case, we find that the (negative) estimated coefficient of financial credit controls turns statistically significant at the 1 percent level,

**Table A.10.1**
Cross-border bank flows: Robustness analysis.

| | Benchmark | Inst. quality[a] | Financial development[b] | Financial soundness[c] | Fiscal balance[d] | Common lender[e] |
|---|---|---|---|---|---|---|
| | (1) | (2) | (3) | (4) | (5) | (6) |
| Overall capital controls$_j$ | −2.666** | −2.063* | −3.015** | −1.890 | −2.962** | −2.662** |
| Bond controls$_j$ | −2.075*** | −1.705** | −2.526*** | −2.072** | −2.274*** | −2.074*** |
| Equity controls$_j$ | −1.170 | −1.026 | −1.029 | −0.588 | −1.465 | −1.166 |
| Direct investment controls$_j$ | −0.366 | −0.259 | 0.458 | 0.227 | −0.301 | −0.366 |
| Financial credit controls$_j$ | −0.556 | −0.175 | −0.398 | −0.255 | −0.591 | −0.555 |
| Lending locally in FX$_j$ | −4.256*** | −4.053*** | −2.917*** | −4.005*** | −4.075*** | −4.249*** |
| Purchase of local FX securities$_j$ | −1.986** | −1.897** | −2.678*** | −2.786*** | −1.780** | −1.991** |
| Open FX position limit$_j$ | −1.766* | −1.836* | −3.090*** | −2.344** | −1.999** | −1.755* |
| Country-pair/year effects | Yes | Yes | Yes | Yes | Yes | Yes |
| Observations | 12,194 | 11,867 | 10,382 | 10,977 | 12,164 | 12,194 |
| Country pairs | 1,127 | 1,092 | 1,106 | 1,124 | 1,125 | 1,127 |

*Notes*: Table presents robustness results for benchmark model. Dependent variable is (log of) bank-asset flows from country i to j unless otherwise stated. All specifications include control variables listed in table 9.8, and country-pair and year effects. Sample size varies across specifications based on data availability for the variables. Standard errors are clustered at country-pair level in all specifications. *, **, and *** indicate statistical significance at 10, 5, and 1 percent levels, respectively.

a. Institutional quality for source and recipient countries is added to the benchmark specification (reported in table 10.2).

b. Bank private credit to GDP for source and recipient countries is added to the benchmark specification.

c. Bank return on equity for source and recipient countries is added to the benchmark specification.

d. Fiscal balance to GDP ratio for source and recipient countries is added to the benchmark specification.

e. Common lender variable is added to the benchmark specification.

f. Trade openness variable for source and recipient countries is added to the benchmark specification.

g. Sample excludes EME source countries.

h. Sample excludes those source and recipient countries that are offshore financial centers.

i. Estimated sample is restricted up to pre–global financial crisis years (i.e., 1995–2007).

j. Dependent variable is (log) real flows from source country i to recipient country j.

k. Dependent variable is (log) total stock of bank assets (amount outstanding) of source country in recipient country.

l. Alternate capital controls indices with mild restrictions treated as zero are used.

| Trade openness[f] | Adv. source[g] | Excl. offshore[h] | Pre-GFC sample[i] | Real flows (log)[j] | Stock of assets[k] | Alt. policy measures[l] |
|---|---|---|---|---|---|---|
| (7) | (8) | (9) | (10) | (11) | (12) | (13) |
| −2.669** | −2.948** | −3.545*** | −4.127*** | −2.668** | −0.479*** | −2.662** |
| −2.074*** | −2.232*** | −2.421*** | −1.682* | −2.082*** | −0.146* | −2.074*** |
| −1.301 | −0.922 | −1.373 | −1.877 | −1.177 | −0.076 | −1.166 |
| −0.442 | −0.847 | −0.342 | −1.455 | −0.368 | −0.050 | −0.366 |
| −0.568 | −0.700 | −0.881 | −2.274*** | −0.555 | −0.198*** | −0.555 |
| −4.524*** | −4.497*** | −4.878*** | −4.295*** | −4.259*** | −0.184*** | |
| −2.024** | −2.295** | −2.836*** | −4.044*** | −1.999** | −0.283*** | |
| −1.793* | −1.757* | −2.242** | −1.582 | −1.767* | −0.267*** | |
| Yes | Yes | Yes | Yes | Yes | Yes | Yes |
| 12,194 | 10,741 | 9,542 | 7,555 | 12,194 | 11,834 | 12,194 |
| 1,127 | 881 | 867 | 992 | 1,127 | 1,114 | 1,127 |

implying a lower stock of cross-border bank liabilities in recipient countries when such controls are in place.

As noted above, our capital control measures are based on the existence of a restriction, with no differentiation by their intensity. While this is unavoidable considering the nature of available information, some restrictions are less likely to be material or binding, with a correspondingly lower impact on flows. As a robustness test, we also construct some alternative capital control measures, where relatively mild regulations such as registration requirements or restrictions on investments in only a few selected sectors for national security purposes are deemed to be "no restrictions"; the results remain similar to those reported above (col. [13]).

**Endogeneity**  An important concern when estimating the effect of capital controls and prudential measures on capital flows is that of reverse causality—i.e., countries may strengthen such measures in response to a surge in capital inflows. Since we focus on bilateral components of total capital flows (whereas the imposition of policy measures tends to be in response to the aggregate volume of flows), reverse causality is less likely to be a concern in our case than if the aggregate volume of flows were the dependent variable (only in the limiting case that bilateral flows happened to be perfectly correlated across country pairs would the endogeneity problem be the same). Moreover, to the extent that there is any such endogeneity, it is likely to *reduce* the estimated coefficients of capital controls and prudential measures. The strong findings above on both source and recipient-country restrictions are therefore despite, rather than because of, any potential endogeneity (which would tend to bias the results toward finding no effect).

Nevertheless, we use the first lag of capital controls and prudential measures in all of the estimations above to mitigate potential endogeneity concerns. Here we also apply the IV-2SLS approach similar to that used in chapter 9, where we take the presence of a democratic left-wing government in the recipient country as the instrument for capital controls. The validity of our instrument is supported by the results from the first stage of the IV-2SLS estimation: the estimated coefficient of left-wing government is negative and statistically significant (at the 1 percent level) in almost all specifications, indicating greater prevalence of capital controls and prudential measures in countries with a left-wing government (table A.10.2, panel [a]). The other control variables included in the first-stage regression for inflow restrictions are those relevant for the recipient countries—such as economic size, real GDP growth rate, real per capita income, real interest rate, exchange rate regime, and current account balance—and are also generally statistically significant (results not shown).[16] The F-test of the hypothesis that the estimates in the first-stage regression are jointly equal to zero is thus strongly rejected, and the R-squared across specifications is about 0.9, offering evidence on the appropriateness of our instrument and the overall fit of the first-stage regression.

The results obtained from the second stage of the estimation—using the predicted values of the policy measures from the first-stage regression—are mostly in line with the benchmark results reported in table 9.8. The overall restrictiveness on capital inflows remains statistically significant, as do bond inflow restrictions (table A.10.2, panel [b]). In addition, the estimated coefficient on financial credit inflow controls also turns statistically significant at the 10 percent level. Among currency-based prudential measures, the estimated coefficients of all restrictions remain negative and statistically significant (at the 1 percent level). Together these estimates imply a reduction in inflows by some 70–100 percent if restrictions are raised from the lower to the top quartile of the (predicted) measures.

Overall, these findings support the robustness of our results to potential endogeneity bias, and suggest that both residency-based capital controls and currency-based prudential measures in recipient countries can play an important role in moderating large cross-border bank flows.

---

16. We do not include country-fixed effects in the first-stage regression because our instrument is a slow moving variable, but include region-specific and year effects, as well as the first lag of capital controls and prudential measures to capture their persistence.

**Table A.10.2**
Cross-border bank flows: IV-2SLS estimates.

*(a) First-stage estimates*[a]

| Dependent variable | Overall controls | Bonds | Equity | Direct investment | Financial credit | Local FX lending | Purchase of local FX sec. | Open FX position limit |
|---|---|---|---|---|---|---|---|---|
| | (1) | (2) | (3) | (4) | (5) | (6) | (7) | (8) |
| Left-wing government | 0.005** | 0.015*** | 0.022*** | 0.010*** | 0.019*** | 0.010*** | −0.018*** | −0.001 |
| | (0.002) | (0.003) | (0.003) | (0.003) | (0.005) | (0.004) | (0.003) | (0.003) |
| Observations | 8,027 | 8,027 | 8,027 | 8,027 | 8,027 | 8,027 | 8,027 | 8,027 |
| $R^2$ | 0.922 | 0.880 | 0.905 | 0.896 | 0.864 | 0.884 | 0.937 | 0.841 |
| F-test (p-value) | 0.00 | 0.00 | 0.00 | 0.00 | 0.00 | 0.00 | 0.00 | 0.00 |

*(b) Second-stage estimates*[b]

| | (1) | (2) | (3) | (4) | | | | |
|---|---|---|---|---|---|---|---|---|
| Overall controls$_j$ | −4.411*** | | | | | | | |
| | (1.365) | | | | | | | |
| Bond controls$_j$ | | −3.298*** | | | | | | |
| | | (0.946) | | | | | | |
| Equity controls$_j$ | | | −1.336 | | | | | |
| | | | (1.237) | | | | | |
| Direct investment controls$_j$ | | | | −1.509 | | | | |
| | | | | (1.127) | | | | |

| | (1) | (2) | (3) | (4) | (5) | (6) | (7) | (8) |
|---|---|---|---|---|---|---|---|---|
| Financial credit controls$_j$ | | | | | −1.384* (0.755) | | | |
| Lending locally in FX$_j$ | | | | | | −5.337*** (1.077) | | |
| Purchase of local FX securities$_j$ | | | | | | | −4.398*** (1.403) | |
| Open FX position limits$_j$ | | | | | | | | −3.823*** (1.471) |
| Country pair / year effects | Yes | Yes | Yes | Yes | Yes | Yes | Yes | Yes |
| Year effects | Yes | Yes | Yes | Yes | Yes | Yes | Yes | Yes |
| Observations | 8,027 | 8,027 | 8,027 | 8,027 | 8,027 | 8,027 | 8,027 | 8,027 |
| $R^2$ | 0.043 | 0.044 | 0.042 | 0.042 | 0.042 | 0.046 | 0.044 | 0.043 |

a. Panel (a) reports the first-stage estimation results where the presence of a left-wing government in the recipient country is used as an instrument. Log of real GDP and real GDP per capita, real GDP growth, real interest rate, current account balance, exchange rate regime, lagged capital control/prudential measure, and regional dummies for the recipient countries are included. All regressors are lagged one period. Constant and year effects are included in all specifications. F-test (p-value) reports the joint significance of all regressors. Robust standard errors are reported in parentheses. *** indicates statistical significance at the 1 percent level.

b. Panel (b) reports the IV-2SLS estimates with (log of) bank-asset flows from country i to country j as the dependent variable. Capital controls and prudential measures are predicted values obtained from the corresponding first-stage regression in panel (a). Control variables as specified in table 10.2 (lagged real GDP [log], real per capita income [log], real GDP growth rate, and real interest rate of both source and recipient countries; current account balance and exchange rate regime of recipient country; country pair and year effects) and the constant are included in all specifications. Standard errors computed with jackknife are reported in parentheses. ***, **, and * indicate statistical significance at the 1, 5, and 10 percent levels, respectively.

**Table A.10.3**
Recipient-country groupings by economic characteristics.

| 1995–1999 | 2000–2004 | 2005–2012 |
|---|---|---|
| *Group I* | *Group I* | *Group I* |
| Argentina | Argentina | Argentina |
| Chile | Brazil | Bulgaria |
| Croatia | Bulgaria | Chile |
| Czech Republic | Chile | Croatia |
| Estonia | Costa Rica | Czech Republic |
| Hungary | Croatia | Estonia |
| Korea, S. | Czech Republic | Hungary |
| Lebanon | Estonia | Korea, S. |
| Lithuania | Hungary | Latvia |
| Malaysia | Korea, Rep. | Lebanon |
| Mexico | Latvia | Lithuania |
| Poland | Lebanon | Malaysia |
| Slovak Republic | Lithuania | Mexico |
| Turkey | Malaysia | Panama |
| Uruguay | Mexico | Poland |
| Venezuela, RB | Panama | Romania |
| | Poland | Russia |
| | Romania | Slovak Republic |
| | Russia | Turkey |
| | Slovak Republic | Uruguay |
| | South Africa | Venezuela, RB |
| | Turkey | |
| | Uruguay | |
| | Venezuela | |
| *Group II* | *Group II* | *Group II* |
| Algeria | Algeria | Algeria |
| Armenia | Armenia | Armenia |
| Brazil | China | Brazil |
| Bulgaria | Colombia | China |
| China | Dominican Republic | Colombia |
| Colombia | Ecuador | Costa Rica |
| Costa Rica | Egypt | Dominican Republic |
| Dominican Republic | El Salvador | Ecuador |
| Ecuador | Guatemala | Egypt |
| Egypt | India | El Salvador |
| El Salvador | Indonesia | Guatemala |
| Guatemala | Jamaica | India |
| India | Jordan | Indonesia |

**Table A.10.3** (continued)

| 1995–1999 | 2000–2004 | 2005–2012 |
|---|---|---|
| *Group II* | *Group II* | *Group II* |
| Indonesia | Morocco | Jamaica |
| Jamaica | Pakistan | Jordan |
| Jordan | Peru | Morocco |
| Latvia | Philippines | Pakistan |
| Morocco | Sri Lanka | Peru |
| Pakistan | Thailand | Philippines |
| Panama | Tunisia | South Africa |
| Peru | Ukraine | Sri Lanka |
| Philippines | | Thailand |
| Romania | | Tunisia |
| Russia | | Ukraine |
| South Africa | | |
| Sri Lanka | | |
| Thailand | | |
| Tunisia | | |
| Ukraine | | |

# 11 Toward the Policy Maker's Vade Mecum

## 11.1 Introduction

So how should emerging market policy makers respond to capital inflows? The theoretical frameworks developed in chapters 5, 6, and 7 laid the groundwork for discussing which tools to use when addressing macroeconomic imbalances and financial vulnerabilities. Going beyond theory, there are several practical considerations and complications that need to be taken into account in deploying these tools. That is the subject of this chapter, which seeks to translate the analytical insights from the earlier chapters into a pragmatic vade mecum for the EME policy maker contending with capital inflows.

To begin with, certain types of flows—very short-term, highly speculative, hot-money flows—may be such that their costs (in terms of the imbalances and vulnerabilities that they are likely to engender) exceed their benefits. Provided such flows can be identified and targeted sufficiently precisely, it may make sense to have structural (i.e., noncyclically varying) capital controls to discourage them, thus tilting the composition of capital inflows toward more desirable forms of liabilities.[1] Likewise, certain prudential measures might be structural—for instance, a ban on domestic banks providing FX-denominated property mortgages. To the extent that these structural measures are adopted, this would imply that the capital account is not fully liberalized in the steady state. In our view, that is not a problem: financial openness is a means to achieving certain economic objectives, not an end in itself,

---

1. An example of such a measure could be a financial transactions tax (à la Tobin 1978) or a "toll tax" (a fixed ad valorem tariff levied when foreign investors purchase or sell securities), which automatically imposes a higher tax rate on short-term instruments—though, in reality, the mechanism could not be so simple as certain short-term flows, such as trade credits, would need to be exempt.

and there is no *inherent* virtue to a fully open capital account. Indeed, most economies in the world—including advanced economies—are not *fully* liberalized in that they often restrict foreign investment in some important sectors (such as transportation, communications, and public utilities) for strategic purposes.[2] Controlling highly volatile and potentially disruptive flows that confer fewer benefits than costs would likewise be in the broader national interest.[3] That said, in practice the set of flows that can *ex ante* be identified as being more trouble than they are worth may be limited.

Beyond such structural measures, policy makers may want to respond to sudden and sharp increases in capital flows. At least conceptually, the nature of the response will depend on whether the inflows are exacerbating macroeconomic imbalances (chapters 5 and 6) or balance-sheet vulnerabilities (chapter 7)—though in reality the same measure may be used for both, tailored to whichever is the predominant concern.[4] In determining the particular configuration of the policy response, three basic considerations need to be borne in mind: the availability of policy tools in the context of the different objectives of economic policy; the cost-benefit trade-off of their deployment; and the multilateral implications of their use.

In EMEs with relatively less developed financial markets, for instance, macroprudential measures could be considered to be unavailable if the financial regulatory and supervisory framework is weak, hindering their effective implementation. In such cases, policy makers may have to rely more on other tools—monetary policy, FX intervention, capital controls—to limit financial vulnerabilities. In a similar vein, while technically available, the costs of sterilized intervention for countries that have abundant reserves may be deemed too high relative to the benefits, and other policy tools could be preferred instead. Finally,

---

2. Some other measures of a prudential nature adopted by advanced economies also constitute impediments to cross-border capital flows. For example, several European Union (EU) countries restrict investment by institutional investors in non-EU assets.

3. The IMF's *Institutional View* (IMF 2012a), discussed in chapter 2, recognizes that full liberalization is not an appropriate goal for all countries at all times.

4. In the case of capital controls (or currency-based prudential measures that act like them), for example, while there is an analytical distinction between imposing them as a backstop against macroeconomic imbalances, and their use to address balance-sheet vulnerabilities (tailored for a specific purpose), in practice it makes sense to target the riskiest forms of liabilities first—even when the main purpose is to stem the overall volume of inflows. This is because, as shown in chapter 4, the riskiest forms of liabilities from the balance-sheet perspective are also often the most prone to causing macroeconomic imbalances.

even if a measure is available and beneficial for the country on a net basis, its potential multilateral implications—most notably, through its impact on the exchange rate—should be taken into account.[5] Thus, if the currency is undervalued, then FX intervention or capital controls to resist the appreciation could constitute a beggar-thy-neighbor policy.[6]

The remainder of this chapter is organized as follows. Section 11.2 elaborates on the three overarching considerations for policy response: availability, cost-benefit trade-off, and multilateral implications. Section 11.3 lays out a logical sequence of policy actions to deal with macroeconomic imbalances. Section 11.4 undertakes the same exercise for addressing balance-sheet vulnerabilities. Section 11.5 concludes.

## 11.2 Responding to Capital Inflows: Overarching Considerations

Faced by an observed uptick of capital inflows, the basic question confronting the policy maker is whether to respond. This, in turn, will depend on the magnitude of the surge, its expected duration, and associated consequences.[7] A general dictum of macroeconomic policy is that the economy may be shielded from temporary shocks but should be allowed to adjust to permanent shocks. (Recall that in the model of chapter 5, the equilibrium real exchange rate appreciated in the face of the permanent component of the capital inflow, with FX intervention used to prevent overvaluation relative to the new equilibrium exchange rate.) Thus, if there is a step (permanent) increase in the volume of capital flows, the medium-term equilibrium real exchange rate will appreciate correspondingly, and the currency should be allowed to

---

5. This is not a self-evident proposition: if other (source or recipient) countries are ignoring the multilateral implications of their policies, then each individual country will be better off by acting unilaterally in its own interest. Such thinking, however, leads to globally inefficient outcomes, of which the interwar period (see chapter 2) was perhaps the starkest example.

6. There is some asymmetry between exchange rate policy (i.e., FX intervention) and monetary or fiscal policy: the former is subject to formal multilateral obligations under the IMF's Articles of Agreements and is subject to the charge of currency manipulation, while the latter are viewed as domestic policies and generally get a free pass multilaterally (even though they may affect the exchange rate and thus have multilateral implications).

7. As discussed in chapters 4 and 7, the consequences are likely to depend on the type of flow. Thus, foreign direct investment (FDI) is associated with economic overheating, portfolio—especially debt—and other investment flows are associated with currency appreciation, credit growth, and balance-sheet vulnerabilities.

strengthen to this new level (though not necessarily beyond it). But when the shock is expected to be temporary, allowing the exchange rate to appreciate will induce resources to move out of the tradable sector, which may have permanent costs if hysteresis effects mean that the loss of jobs, capital, and global market share persists even after the currency returns to a more depreciated level. In the face of inflow shocks that are expected to be relatively short-lived, therefore, the equilibrium real exchange rate would not adjust, requiring FX intervention to prevent temporary overvaluation. (Of course, if the duration of the surge is extremely short—say, a few days or weeks—then the damage to the tradable sector is likely to be limited, and there is correspondingly less need to stem the currency appreciation. In practice, as mentioned in chapter 3, the average duration of a surge is about two years, so an intermediate course—allowing some appreciation but also undertaking some sterilized intervention—is likely to be appropriate.)

In the real world, emerging markets confront two key challenges in determining their response. First, it is hard to detect in real time how long the surge will last. At least in the initial phases of the surge, therefore, unless macroeconomic imbalances are already evident (the economy is booming, the currency overvalued, credit expansion rampant), it may make sense to do nothing at all and adopt a wait-and-see attitude. Second, capital inflows may not be permanent but still highly persistent. In fact, as the post-independence experience of the Baltic states suggests, countries may receive large inflows for several years that can lull them into (falsely) believing that the increase in capital inflows represents a permanent shift.[8] For highly persistent flows, to the extent that the equilibrium real exchange rate also appreciates, countries may allow the exchange rate to adjust to reach the new level, but intervene to prevent overvaluation beyond that. The effect of the persistence of the shock on other targets is more ambiguous. To the extent that the currency is allowed to appreciate (given a permanent or highly persistent shock), this should help choke off part of the capital inflow (as domestic assets become more expensive). Conversely, the longer the shock persists, the larger the cumulative capital inflow and the possible impact on macroeconomic imbalances such as the output gap and domestic credit growth (unless the economy's ability to safely

---

8. Net capital flows to the Baltic states—Estonia, Latvia, and Lithuania—remained elevated throughout the 2000s until the eve of the global financial crisis, averaging almost 13 percent of GDP. The tide turned with the onset of the crisis, and an equally large capital flow reversal followed in 2009–2010.

absorb, and productively use, inflows rises sufficiently over time), and balance-sheet vulnerabilities.[9] As a rule of thumb, however, the larger the initial surge, and the longer it is expected to last, the greater the need for a policy response.

Assuming a surge merits a policy response, the authorities have, potentially, five main instruments—monetary policy, fiscal policy, FX intervention, macroprudential measures, and capital controls—from which to choose. Besides the particular risk being targeted, the decision to deploy any individual policy tool depends on three main factors: its availability, its cost-benefit trade-off, and its multilateral implications.

### 11.2.1 Availability

The availability of a policy tool rests on the institutional, political, and legal setup, as well as (to some degree) on past experience with its use. In some instances, the country may lack the necessary institutional and administrative capacity to implement certain policies (such as macro-prudential measures if the financial regulatory and supervisory framework is rudimentary, or capital controls if there are insufficient technical and human resources to monitor flows).[10] It could also be that the institutions exist, yet flows are channeled to the domestic economy in a manner that makes certain measures inoperative. For example, pruden-tial measures will have no traction if flows bypass the regulated financial system; similarly, capital controls cannot (technically) be applied if inflows are driven by the domestic residents repatriating funds.

Countries might also be constrained in their choice of policy tools because of international agreements or treaty obligations (membership in the European Union [EU] or the Organisation for Economic Co-operation and Development [OECD], or certain bilateral trade or investment treaties with the US; box 11.1), or because of domestic politi-cal constraints. The latter is particularly relevant for fiscal policy, where political economy considerations and implementation lags may limit the scope for discretionary fiscal measures. Where the central bank is

---

9. The economy's ability to absorb the capital inflow may also increase over time. For instance, aggregate supply may increase as working capital and investment raise the pro-ductive capacity of the economy, narrowing the output gap. This is less likely to be true of balance-sheet vulnerabilities, which tend to cumulate and widen the longer the inflow surge lasts.

10. Other things equal, countries should opt for measures that play to their relative admin-istrative strengths. In the case of capital controls, for example, if the foreign exchange administration capacity at the central bank is weak, then a tax on inflows implemented by the fiscal authorities may be more effective.

**Box 11.1**
International arrangements restricting the use of capital controls.

Several countries have assumed legal obligations to liberalize capital movements under different international arrangements, which may constrain their ability to use capital controls. Prudential regulations that do not discriminate between residents and nonresidents—and, as such, do not constitute capital controls—may still be available, though that depends on their legal interpretation. In general, these undertakings are much more restrictive than the IMF's *Institutional View*, which imposes no obligations on IMF members, and does not even constitute formal "principles for the guidance of members" under IMF surveillance.

**WTO/GATS**: Members only incur obligations to remove restrictions on capital flows if they have made commitments in the financial services sector. But even then, these constraints are limited in scope; the commitments are subject to periodic rounds of negotiation; are of a qualified nature; and are subject to prudential carve-outs. There is also a general balance-of-payments clause that allows the use of capital controls under specific circumstances.

**Bilateral Investment Treaties (BITs) and Free Trade Agreements (FTAs)**: There are over 2,500 BITs, as well as bilateral and regional trade agreements that provide legal protection for foreign investments. These agreements usually liberalize inward investments and provide for the free repatriation of that investment. They typically include most-favored-nation clauses. Most BITs and FTAs either provide temporary safeguards on capital inflows and outflows to prevent or mitigate financial crises, or defer that matter to the host country's legislation. However, BITs and FTAs to which the United States is a party usually do not permit restrictions on either capital inflows or outflows.[1]

**OECD**: The OECD's Code of Liberalisation of Capital Movements is the only legally binding instrument that focuses exclusively and comprehensively on cross-border capital movements. It covers all types of capital flows, but its framework enables members to remove restrictions on capital movements in a progressive manner. Members are permitted to lodge reservations with respect to specific transactions at the time of joining the OECD (and in the case of some transactions considered short-term in nature, these reservations can be reintroduced at any time). The code also provides a temporary derogation for capital flows (for reasons arising from "serious economic and financial disturbances" and for balance of payments reasons).

**EU**: Members of the EU are prohibited from imposing any restrictions on cross-border movements of capital among EU members and third countries. There are safeguards that allow for the temporary imposition of restrictions. But once an EU member joins the currency union, these safeguards may only be imposed by the EU Council and are limited to restrictions vis à vis nonmembers.

---

1. See Gallagher (2010, 2013) for a detailed discussion on the provisions related to capital controls in trade and investment treaties.

not fully independent, the government may attempt to exercise its influence over the use of monetary policy as well—for example, by limiting the scope for monetary tightening in the face of overheating concerns (in which case the central bank may have to rely on macroprudential measures as an alternate instrument). Even the use of capital controls might be hostage to the domestic political process if changes in tax rates require parliamentary approval.[11]

Another consideration is the character and quality of the country's governance. Measures may be subject to dilution or exemption through lobbying, or they may be administered in an arbitrary or corrupt manner. In addition, historical experience tends to play an important role in determining the availability of some tools. Policy makers may be reluctant to use measures that have proved highly unpopular or ineffective in the past. Conversely, they may be more inclined to rely on instruments that worked well previously, and for which the relevant institutional and administrative infrastructure remains intact. In this respect, inflow controls may be more effective in countries that deploy them frequently (e.g., Brazil), as opposed to those that use them as one-off measures, because they maintain the necessary monitoring and reporting infrastructure. (Conversely, however, the market has greater scope for finding ways to avoid or evade the controls in such cases.)

### 11.2.2   Cost

Policy adjustments in response to capital inflows may inevitably entail some costs. In determining which policy tool to adopt, therefore, its costs need to be evaluated against the benefits, as well as against the costs and benefits of other tools. For instance, sterilized FX intervention may be prohibitively costly when there is a large difference between the interest rate paid on domestic sterilization bonds and that earned on foreign reserves; monetary policy tightening to address inflationary concerns may have unintended financial costs (e.g., by raising the incidence of nonperforming loans); and macroprudential policies (particularly in the form of reserve requirements) could lead to undesirable financial disintermediation. Likewise, while it is usually desirable to tighten fiscal policy in response to capital inflows, high-frequency adjustments in taxes and spending (beyond the operation of automatic stabilizers) are likely to be distortionary, as well as economically and

---

11. In some cases, the legislature approves a maximum tax rate, leaving it to the ministry of finance to set the rate within the permissible range.

politically costly—making it a tool to be used from a medium-term perspective (including to ensure debt sustainability), but not necessarily to manage short-term surges in inflows.

Traditionally, capital controls are considered the costliest of all the instruments in the policy tool kit. It is often argued, for example, that they are administratively burdensome, distortionary, encourage regulatory arbitrage, hurt small businesses more than large firms, damage liquidity, and encourage rent-seeking. Yet, it is clear that these critiques apply just as much to other policy tools. For instance, setting up a macroprudential policy framework and applying it effectively also entails costs (just as collection of taxes for fiscal purposes may be administratively costly). Likewise, macroprudential and fiscal policies may also encourage offshore activity and regulatory arbitrage (e.g., the case of Croatia discussed in box 11.2). And while studies have shown that capital controls can make access to financing more difficult for domestically owned and smaller firms (Harrison, Love, McMillian 2004; Forbes 2007), prudential measures curbing credit growth could also disproportionately affect small and medium-size enterprises (SMEs) because these tend to rely more on bank financing and are not as able to borrow directly from abroad. (In fact, given that only large firms have access to the international capital markets, imposing controls on direct borrowing abroad arguably creates a more level playing field for SMEs than macroprudential regulations that curtail domestic bank lending—unless SMEs receive preferential treatment.)[12]

Which policy tool to use should thus be based on an informed and unbiased assessment of its costs (while its benefits can be judged by its effectiveness in addressing the targeted imbalance and vulnerability). This may need to be a dynamic assessment, with policy instruments applied with varying degrees of intensity. Moreover, inasmuch as the cost of using a tool is convex (rising at an increasing rate in the intensity of the measure), it may make sense to bring multiple tools into play to address a given risk.

### 11.2.3  Multilateral Considerations

While a policy response might make sense from an individual country's perspective, it may also have multilateral consequences. Some of these were explored in chapter 10, namely the impact of imposing

---

12. It is striking that the literature has tended to focus exclusively on the costs of capital controls while ignoring the costs associated with other policy measures.

**Box 11.2**
Bypassing macroprudential regulation: The case of Croatia.

Foreign-owned banks have dominated the Croatian banking system since 2000 and have played a key role in bringing foreign capital into Croatia (see Jankov 2009). The surge in capital inflows during the early 2000s, however, raised macroeconomic and financial-stability concerns, especially since an important part of the inflows corresponded to household consumer borrowing.

Given the constraints on monetary policy implied by the exchange rate regime, the Croatian National Bank (CNB) responded to capital inflows chiefly by adopting various prudential measures on the financial sector, some of which included an element of capital control. In 2003, the CNB introduced a speed limit to bank lending and a rule on minimum retained earnings if bank lending exceeded a certain threshold. Banks responded to the limit by selling part of their loan portfolio to affiliated leasing companies (to get around the bank lending limits) and by transferring credit risk to the books of their foreign parents (thanks to an accounting loophole).

The speed limit regulation was replaced in July 2004 by a capital control on domestic banks—the marginal reserve requirement (MRR)—which required them to make additional non–interest bearing deposits with the CNB if their foreign liabilities increased above their value recorded at the end of June 2004. The MRR rate was increased through time, and the CNB continually refined the regulation to close loopholes exploited by banks (e.g., by applying the MRR to affiliated leasing companies, off–balance sheet items related to the selling of credit risk, and to debt securities issued). By 2008, banks were required to place 72 percent of the increase in foreign liabilities with the CNB, or in liquid foreign assets, while the remaining 28 percent was available for lending to clients. Despite the extremely high reserve requirements, banks' domestic lending continued to increase.

Capital adequacy rules were also tightened. As of mid-2006, risk weights applied to bank loans in foreign exchange, and to loans in kuna indexed to foreign currency but granted to unhedged clients, were set above the minimum Basel II standards. Yet the combination of higher bank reserve requirements and capital adequacy requirements failed to curtail capital inflows or domestic lending.

To reduce the buildup of external vulnerabilities associated with the rapid growth of domestic lending, the CNB reintroduced a speed limit to bank lending in 2007 but this time designed the regulation so that it also covered the selling of credit portfolios and credit risk. As bank lending is an important source of household credit, this limit caused a significant decline in household credit growth. But enterprises continued to be able to get credit as borrowing from local banks was replaced by direct foreign borrowing.

**Box 11.2** (continued)

---

In 2008, the CNB introduced minimum capital requirements that were differentiated by credit growth rates. Banks with credit growth below 12 percent per year had to satisfy a minimum capital adequacy rate of 12 percent, while banks growing faster faced higher capital adequacy requirements. In addition, risk weights and minimum retained-earnings ratios were increased for fast-growing banks. Higher risk weights applied to bank loans in FX, as well as those in kuna indexed to FX and granted to unhedged clients.

The Croatian experience shows that it can be very difficult to curtail credit growth associated with a surge in capital flows without economy-wide capital controls. Croatia was not in a position to use exchange rate policy to stem capital inflows. Prudential measures had some traction in reducing the growth of bank credit, and they also reduced capital inflows for a short period. However, credit remained readily available as domestic bank credit was partly replaced by direct lending from abroad, thereby altering the structure of capital inflows to channels not covered by the prudential policies or capital controls that were specific to banks.

---

capital controls on other capital-recipient countries. (Though, in reality, any such effects are likely to be dwarfed by the impact of policies in capital-source countries that push capital toward EMEs in the first instance.)

A more direct multilateral impact on the country's trading partners is through the exchange rate. Clearly, to the degree that the currency is undervalued relative to some notion of multilaterally consistent medium-term equilibrium (see Lee et al. 2008; Phillips et al. 2013), the first-best policy is to allow it to strengthen in response to capital inflows (to the extent that global current account imbalances are a problem, this would also help to narrow those imbalances).[13] Indeed, Article IV of the IMF's Articles of Agreement prohibits exchange rate manipulation—

---

13. This prescription, however, is much less clear-cut than it seems. There may be valid domestic reasons to pursue an exchange rate that is undervalued from a multilateral perspective. One example would be if there is a domestic distortion or externality that causes the tradables sector to be smaller than its socially optimal level (Ghosh and Kim 2008; Rodrik 2008). Put differently, a genuine multilaterally consistent equilibrium exchange rate calculation would take into account the relative magnitudes of such domestic externalities across countries to arrive at a globally efficient configuration of equilibrium exchange rates. Of course, this would be all but impossible in practice, not least because it would be hard to verify countries' claims about the existence or magnitude of such domestic externalities.

and, inasmuch as the currency is undervalued, resisting the appreciation is a potentially beggar-thy-neighbor policy.

This suggests an "exchange rate test" that should be applied before deploying policies (FX intervention and capital controls) that would limit appreciation of the currency—namely, that the currency first be allowed to appreciate to its multilaterally consistent medium-term value. Of course, that is easier said than done, since determining the (multilaterally consistent) medium-term equilibrium exchange rate is no easy task. Exercises such as the IMF's external balance assessment (EBA) can give some reasonable estimates of the equilibrium exchange rate, but even the most sophisticated techniques leave substantial margins for error.[14]

In principle, the same exchange rate test should apply to other policy instruments intended to address macroeconomic imbalances. In practice, raising the policy interest rate or tightening nondiscriminatory macroprudential measures will tend to appreciate the exchange rate (see chapter 5). So, if anything, these policies will move an undervalued exchange rate in the direction mandated by multilateral considerations and there is no reason to wait for the currency to appreciate before deploying them.

What about capital controls imposed (or tightened) for balance-sheet vulnerabilities? Our view is that the impact on the exchange rate is likely to be small to the extent that the controls are of a targeted nature and mainly intended to address balance-sheet vulnerabilities by shifting the composition of inflows toward less risky liabilities (rather than by reducing the volume of aggregate inflows). The undervaluation of the currency should thus *not* preclude the use of such measures.[15] This is a matter of judgment, of course, and depends inter alia on how broadly the measure is applied. (If the measure is narrowly applied and targets only specific types of highly risky flows, then passing the exchange rate test is not relevant. If applied so broadly that the measure

---

14. The EBA uses panel regressions to model the determinants of the real exchange rate using both policy variables (e.g., fiscal policy, capital controls, foreign exchange market intervention, credit growth, and public health expenditure) and nonpolicy fundamentals (e.g., income level, demographics, commodity terms of trade). To ensure multilateral consistency, the explanatory variables in the regression are expressed as the difference between the country's own values and the weighted average of the values of its main trading partners (see Phillips et al. 2013). The equilibrium real exchange rate is then constructed as the predicted value of the regression using actual values for the nonpolicy fundamentals and desirable settings for policies.

15. As discussed in chapter 4, however, certain types of flows are more strongly associated with currency overvaluation, so shifting the composition of inflows, even for a given volume, will likely have at least some impact on the exchange rate.

significantly reduces the volume of inflows, then there is a stronger case for taking multilateral considerations into account.)

## 11.3   Macroeconomic Imbalances

With these broad principles in mind, how should policy makers address macroeconomic imbalances associated with capital inflows?

### 11.3.1   Currency Overvaluation

A useful starting point in any policy response is the exchange rate test mentioned above—an assessment of whether, prior to the inflow surge, the currency was significantly undervalued. If so, then the appreciation resulting from the inflow should not be resisted through FX intervention or capital controls until the exchange rate has reached its medium-term fundamentals value (i.e., the equilibrium real exchange rate that is expected to prevail once the temporary surge recedes). Beyond the multilateral considerations discussed above, the exchange rate appreciation will make domestic assets look expensive, which should help stem the inflow. (However, the opposite is at least theoretically possible. In collateral models of the type examined in chapter 7, for example, the appreciation raises the value of domestic collateral, increasing the scope for foreign borrowing if that was a binding constraint.)

If the currency is considered undervalued, then it should be allowed to appreciate, but that does not preclude raising the policy interest rate to cool an overheating economy or applying macroprudential measures to curb excessive credit growth in the meantime. If the currency is not undervalued (or if it has been allowed to appreciate such that it is no longer undervalued), a judgment needs to be made about how much (further) to let the currency strengthen, given the impact on the traded-goods sector. Exporters of manufactures, who tend to face downward sloping demand curves because of product differentiation, are more sensitive to exchange rate movements than commodity exporters, for whom prices are set in dollar terms in international markets. While emerging markets differ in the composition of their exports, the general finding is that even temporary appreciations (especially when the currency is already overvalued) can have hysteresis effects and do lasting damage to the exportable sector. This damage does not reverse when the currency depreciates again (see chapter 4, box 4.1).

How much to resist the appreciation through intervention will then depend on the country's initial reserve holdings compared with standard country insurance metrics, its need to accumulate additional reserves against the new liabilities it is incurring (which in turn depends on the nature of the flows), and the fiscal costs of sterilizing its intervention.[16] (Although intervention need not be sterilized, inflationary pressures associated with expansionary inflows mean that there is typically very limited scope for unsterilized intervention, and empirically EMEs nearly always sterilize their intervention.) At the same time, it is important that the central bank not chase its own tail, whereby intervention (by preventing currency appreciation) perpetuates even larger flows. This is especially important if markets come to believe that, because of the fiscal costs or otherwise, the intervention will eventually be abandoned, at which point speculators would reap a discrete capital gain.[17]

### 11.3.2 Overheating and Credit Expansion

Inasmuch as the inflow is overheating the economy, thus jeopardizing the central bank's inflation target, or threatening financial stability by fueling credit growth and asset price inflation, monetary and (domestic) macroprudential policies need to be brought into play. Whether, or to what extent, monetary policy should be used as a macroprudential tool, or conversely, macroprudential measures can be used to manage aggregate demand, has become a hotly debated question since the global financial crisis. The issue is partly semantic: reserve requirements, for instance, have traditionally been considered part of monetary policy, but more recently, they have tended to be classified as part of the macroprudential tool kit. The underlying question is whether it is all right to mix and match, to use business-cycle tools to tame the financial cycle, and vice versa.

The issue is largely moot when the business cycle and financial cycle coincide (in which case, the policy rate would probably suffice), but it becomes more pertinent when they do not (e.g., when there are few signs of goods price inflation but credit and asset prices are rising rapidly).

---

16. On country insurance metrics, see Becker et al. (2007); IMF (2011a, 2013a). There is considerable debate on how to measure the welfare costs of sterilization (which would be zero if lump-sum taxes are available), but most measures are based on the difference between the rate of return that the central bank earns on its foreign assets and either an estimate of the opportunity cost of those funds, or the return it must pay on the domestic sterilization bonds. Other forms of sterilization include raising reserve requirements (that could also be considered as a macroprudential tool; Federico, Vegh, and Vuletin 2014), which does not entail a quasi-fiscal cost (if banking system reserves at the central bank are not remunerated), but may lead to undesirable disintermediation.

17. A notable example is the Swiss National Bank's abandonment of its currency ceiling in January 2015, a move that resulted in an immediate 30 percent appreciation of the Swiss franc against other currencies.

Several commentators (e.g., Greenspan 2002; Mishkin 2008; Svensson 2015) have argued that it hardly ever makes sense to gear the policy interest rate to the financial cycle and that macroprudential measures should be used instead. Fischer (2015) agrees in principle, but points out that such tools may not always be available or effective (e.g., because of regulatory arbitrage). The converse proposition—that macroprudential tools can be used to moderate the business cycle—receives less attention, except in regard to the use of reserve requirements (Federico, Vegh, and Vuletin 2014). Likewise, the idea that sterilized FX intervention can serve as a macroprudential tool (a point that we have emphasized in earlier chapters) has received almost no play in literature. Possibly this is because it applies only in regard to a capital inflow–fueled credit boom and is predicated on inflows being expansionary (which, we have argued, is the empirically relevant case for EMEs, but perhaps not for advanced economies).

### 11.3.3  Interaction of Instruments
The discussion thus far illustrates that the interaction between the policy interest rate, domestic macroprudential tools, and FX intervention to help tame both the business and financial cycles in the face of capital inflows is likely to be complex and country-specific. (Discretionary countercyclical fiscal measures may also play a useful role, provided the political process does not make fiscal policy too inflexible.) The "natural mapping" proposed in chapter 5—whereby the policy interest rate is geared toward achieving the inflation target, macroprudential tools are deployed to curb excessive credit growth or asset price inflation, and sterilized intervention is used to prevent the currency from departing significantly from its medium-term equilibrium value—is certainly a useful starting point, but it may need to be modified and adapted according to the particular challenges posed by the inflow surge and the efficacy of the available instruments (figure 11.1).

What these instruments should *not* be used for is to curb capital inflows directly or, as argued earlier, to achieve other goals if doing so jeopardizes that instrument's primary goal. For instance, it may be tempting to lower the policy interest rate to reduce the incentive for capital to flow into the country (thus, for example, relieving the burden on FX intervention to curb currency appreciation), but that should not be at the cost of missing the inflation target.[18] Likewise, if macropru-

---

18. The tension between the exchange rate and inflation objectives is mitigated to some extent by bond inflows being less expansionary but more likely to respond to higher

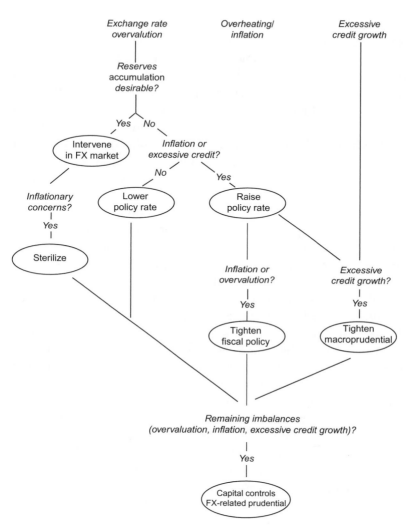

**Figure 11.1**
Responding to macroeconomic imbalances.
*Source*: Authors' illustration.

dential measures are not effective, the central bank may feel forced to
pursue a monetary policy that, from the perspective of meeting the
inflation or output gap target, is excessively tight. In our view, the

interest rates, whereas equity flows are more likely to be expansionary but less likely to
be attracted by higher interest rates (see, e.g., Blanchard et al. 2016).

basic principle is that when at least one macroeconomic imbalance (overheating, currency overvaluation, excessive credit growth) cannot be addressed with the available macroeconomic instruments (policy interest rate, FX intervention, macroprudential measures), then it is generally preferable to deploy capital controls to curb the capital inflow than to deflect another instrument from its primary goal (if doing so means that goal will not be fully met). Put differently, where legal or other impediments do not preclude their use, capital controls represent an additional tool that should be brought into play when standard macroeconomic policies are unavailable, ineffective, insufficient, or excessively costly.[19]

### 11.3.4  Design of Capital Controls for Macroeconomic Imbalances

How should capital controls be designed when they are used against macroeconomic imbalances? As a first principle, such measures should be temporary. Put more precisely, they should be state-contingent: in place while the surge is leading to macroeconomic imbalances, removed as the surge recedes (even if flows do not reverse into actual outflows) and the imbalances narrow or disappear. If imposed purely for macroeconomic imbalances, then these measures would also have to be broad-based, since most types of flows will contribute to such imbalances. But to the extent that some types of flows contribute more to macro imbalances than others, as shown in chapter 4, it makes sense to at least start with the most problematic types of inflow (such as debt flows that may also be problematic from the balance-sheet perspective).

Capital controls may be price-based (e.g., a tax) or quantitative (e.g., ceilings/limits, authorization requirements, or outright prohibitions on certain flows). Economists' usual instinct based on the trade literature is that, while it is always possible to find equivalent price and quantitative controls, the former are preferable because they raise revenue and are less opaque and/or subject to arbitrary enforcement.[20] Price-based

---

19. Capital controls will have an additional benefit of making monetary and exchange rate (i.e., sterilized intervention) policy more effective.

20. Tariffs automatically generate revenues for the government, whereas quantitative restrictions generate rents that accrue to whoever holds the quota (though the government can try to recapture those rents by auctioning the quota instead of allocating it; see Schuknecht 1999). By analogy, taxes on inflows generate revenues, whereas quantitative restrictions or outright prohibitions do not. But this is a double-edged sword—government's reliance on such revenues may be an impediment to the removal of the taxes when they are no longer necessary.

**Box 11.3**
Taxes vs. URRs.

The textbook examples of price-based capital controls are taxes on inflows and unremunerated reserve requirements (URRs). URRs have a similar effect to taxes by requiring that part of the inflow be deposited in an unremunerated account for a period of time. Both types of controls place a larger burden on short-term flows (e.g., paying an entry tax has a larger impact on the net return on a one-year flow than on a ten-year investment). While URRs have an administrative (i.e., quantitative) element, it is straightforward to compute a tax-equivalent rate for the URR, which will be a function of the level of the URR as a proportion of the investment, and the opportunity cost of those funds:[1]

$$\tau = \frac{r(i^* + s)T/(1-r)}{D}$$

where $\tau$ represents the implied tax rate, $r$ is the URR rate, $i^*$ is the nominal interest rate for the currency in which the URR is constituted, $s$ is the premium applied to the investor when borrowing funds to cover the URR (i.e., country risk premium plus specific credit risks for the investor), $T$ is the duration of the URR, and $D$ is the duration of the foreign investment.

There are pros and cons associated with both taxes and URRs. URRs can create liquidity costs, since part of the funds is not available immediately to the investor, and the URR deposit is not useful as collateral to a counterparty other than the central bank. While this acts as a deterrent to capital flows, it also involves a deadweight loss (in the sense that it would be more efficient to discourage flows through a higher tax rate, which does not create illiquidity).[2] On the other hand, URRs that are deposited in foreign exchange immediately reduce the exchange rate pressure by the amount of the deposit, while the tax, which is generally paid in local currency, requires conversion of FX into local currency, with the resulting exchange rate pressure. Given the similarity between URRs and inflow taxes, the choice between the two is usually driven by administrative considerations. Typically, the central bank has authority to impose a URR but does not have authority to levy taxes. This explains why most countries adopt URRs in the face of temporary inflow surges. Unlike a tax, a URR can usually be removed (or set to zero) more easily because the budget is not directly reliant on its revenues; however, it may be more burdensome to administer than a tax.

**Selected examples of URRs and taxes:**
• Chile set up a URR in 1991 at a 20 percent rate (with varying lengths depending on the maturity of the credit). The rate was subsequently

---

1. Ariyoshi et al. 2000.
2. In a low interest rate environment, a substantial deposit may be required for the URR to be effective, exacerbating liquidity concerns.

**Box 11.3** (continued)

increased to 30 percent and the deposit period was set at one year, regardless of the credit's maturity. The coverage of the URR was also expanded. The rate was reduced to zero in 1998.

• Colombia applied a 40 percent, six-month URR in 2007. Withdrawals before the six-month period were subject to substantial penalties. In June 2007 equities issued abroad were exempted; in December the URR on initial public offerings was eliminated and early-withdrawal penalties were reduced. Persistent appreciation pressures led to an increase in the URR to 50 percent in May 2008. To prevent circumvention, a two-year minimum-stay requirement was implemented on inward FDI.

• Thailand implemented a 30 percent-one year URR in late 2006. Early withdrawals were subject to approval by the Bank of Thailand and were penalized by withholding one-third of the deposit. Debt flows that were fully hedged were later exempted from the URR. Ultimately, the URR was eliminated in March 2008.

• Russia introduced a number of different URRs in 2004: a 3 percent, 365-day URR on foreign borrowing; a 20 percent, 365-day URR on transactions with government bonds; and a 3 percent, 365-day URR for transactions with other securities.

• Brazil implemented a tax (Imposto Sobre Operações Financeiras—IOF) on certain capital inflows in March 2008, at a 1.5 percent rate. The tax was eliminated at the onset of the global crisis, but reintroduced in October 2009, with a 2 percent tax on foreign equity and fixed-income inflows and a 1.5 percent tax applied when foreign investors convert American Depository Receipts (ADRs) into receipts for shares issued locally. Subsequently, the tax rate was increased in two steps to 6 percent for fixed-income inflows and extended to derivatives. The tax rate was reduced to zero in 2013. (In the case of Brazil, the tax exists, and the Ministry of Finance has the authority to adjust the tax rate.)

measures may be easier to adjust cyclically, as well as simpler to administer.[21] Indeed, one option is to keep the administrative apparatus and institutional arrangements permanently in place, so as to be able to implement a tax or unremunerated reserve requirement (URR) when appropriate, reducing the rate (possibly to zero) when it is not required.

---

21. In practice, countries often introduce price and quantitative measures simultaneously. For example, Colombia (2004), Russia (2004), and Thailand (2008) adopted quantitative restrictions along with a URR. But partially liberalized countries with an extensive system of quantitative controls in place may find it easier to strengthen the existing controls in response to an inflow surge.

Among price-based measures, a further choice is between a tax and a URR. Whereas there are pros and cons to each (see box 11.3), URRs that are deposited in foreign exchange may immediately reduce the exchange rate pressure by the amount of the deposit, while the tax, which is generally paid in local currency, requires conversion of FX into local currency, with the resulting exchange rate pressure. Another potential advantage of the URR is that it is typically set by the central bank, whereas in most countries, changes in tax rates require parliamentary approval (in some cases, the legislature approves a maximum tax rate, leaving it to the ministry of finance to set the rate within the permissible range). In general, therefore, URRs can be changed more quickly in response to changes in inflows. At the same time, they may require a more complex administrative apparatus because the deposited amount has to be returned to the investor after the expiry of the reserve period.

## 11.4 Balance-sheet Vulnerabilities

Beyond macroeconomic imbalances, policy makers need to be aware of existing balance-sheet mismatches in the economy, and the extent to which they are being exacerbated by capital inflows. While, as discussed above, allowing the currency to strengthen makes domestic assets more expensive, and hence should reduce capital inflows, it also raises the foreign currency value of domestic collateral. This allows unhedged borrowers to take on more FX-denominated debt—in turn, making them more vulnerable to a sudden capital flow reversal and currency depreciation. As balance-sheet mismatches widen to the point that they raise concern, currency-based prudential measures or capital controls may be required to shift the composition of the inflows toward safer forms of liabilities.

In applying policy measures, a primary consideration is whether the flows are being intermediated by, or correspond to the borrowing of, the domestic regulated financial system (which comprise mostly banks, but can include other financial institutions). If so, prudential measures or financial-sector specific capital controls are at least a viable policy option; if not, then the only effective instrument would be an economy-wide capital control. As noted in chapter 7, the appropriate choice of instrument depends on the nature of the risk. In principle, the policy intervention should differentiate according to each dimension of the transaction (resident/nonresident creditor, currency denomination relative to borrower's income or assets, debt or equity instrument). In practice, however, this may lead to an excessively complex set of regulations. Policy makers therefore need to be pragmatic, focusing on the most salient risks and deploying such tools as are available and effective.

### 11.4.1  Flows Intermediated by the Regulated Financial System

When flows are intermediated through the regulated financial system (domestic banks), they may be associated with widening risks on both the liability and the asset sides of the balance sheet (figure 11.2[a]). Bank liabilities could be excessively risky because of maturity and currency mismatches, while bank assets could become excessively risky because of the credit risk associated with them.

1. Excessively risky bank *liabilities*

   • *Maturity mismatch*: banks may be relying excessively on short-term external funding (wholesale or foreign deposits) to finance longer-term assets, leading to maturity mismatches. To address this risk, it is possible to use a capital control that, for example, limits short-term external borrowing or imposes higher reserve requirements on short-term liabilities to nonresidents. If capital controls cannot be applied because of international legal obligations, prudential measures (such as a tax on banks' noncore liabilities; Shin 2010) might be able to achieve the same end. A notable example is South Korea's imposition of currency-based prudential measures in 2010, which could be considered as a substitute for capital controls to reduce external borrowing by domestic banks, given the country's obligations under the OECD Code of Liberalization (see box 11.4).

   • *FX exposure*: banks may have excessive foreign currency exposure. If the main concern is the currency denomination of bank liabilities (whether owed to residents or to nonresidents), then a targeted prudential measure, such as currency-dependent liquidity requirements, or open FX position limits (in relation to bank capital), would be preferable. As a practical matter, however, most FX-denominated funding will be from nonresidents. Therefore, if the prudential measure cannot be applied or would be ineffective, a capital control that penalizes foreign liabilities denominated in FX would be another option.

2. Excessively risky bank *assets*

   • *FX-denominated lending and unhedged borrowers*: when the ultimate borrower (a firm or household) contracts FX debt but has income

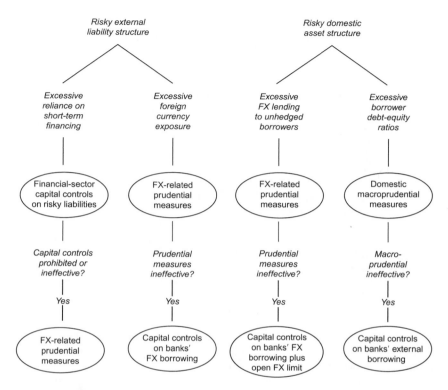

**Figure 11.2(a)**
Responding to flows intermediated through the domestic banking system.
*Source*: Authors' illustration.

only in local currency, it is exposed to currency fluctuations, which creates a credit risk for the banks.[22] Appropriate steps may include more stringent currency-based regulations on banks (such as higher capital requirements on FX loans) or limits and even outright prohibition on loans to borrowers who cannot demonstrate a natural hedge.[23] If such prudential measures cannot be applied effectively, and if banks' foreign currency–denominated funds are mostly external,

---

22. Ranciere, Tornell, and Vamvakidis (2010) show that FX lending to unhedged borrowers is associated with more severe financial crises, but that it also spurs economic growth by easing financing constraints. The regulation on FX loans should thus strike a balance between the competing objectives of resilience and credit availability.
23. Residents may try to circumvent such a measure by borrowing directly from abroad. While this would address the credit risk of local banks, the currency risk of the ultimate borrowers would remain.

**Box 11.4**
South Korea—Substituting capital controls with macroprudential measures.

Following the surge of capital flows to EMEs in the aftermath of the global financial crisis, South Korean authorities grew concerned about the extent of short-term external borrowing by the country's banks. The obvious measure would have been a financial sector–specific capital control restricting such borrowing, but this was barred by South Korea's obligations under the OECD Code of Liberalisation. Further examination showed that banks' external borrowing corresponded to hedging operations on behalf of exporters—suggesting that a currency-based prudential measure could effectively substitute for a capital control.

South Korean exporters have traditionally sought to hedge future export receipts. This has especially been the case with shipbuilders, who face lengthy but predictable lags on dollar receipts related to the long gestation period for shipbuilding. Exporters will want to hedge by selling their dollars forward and buying Korean won, but when there are broad expectations of won appreciation, they may be tempted to overhedge (speculate) to take advantage of any appreciation beyond the interest differential. The exporter's counterparty will typically be an onshore bank, which would take the opposite position—buying dollars forward and selling the Korean won forward (see box figure 11.1).

To do this, onshore banks (mostly branches of foreign banks) borrow dollars from offshore banks, including their parent banks (a capital inflow in the balance of payments, *a*, in the figure), exchange the dollars in the spot market for won to cover their long dollar positions (*b*), and invest the proceeds in domestic assets for forward delivery to the exporter (*c*). At time of delivery, banks liquidate their local currency investment and use the proceeds to deliver the local currency promised to the exporter (*d*). In exchange, the exporter delivers the US dollars, which the bank uses to repay its US dollar loan (*e*). The onshore banks are thus fully hedged against FX risk, but they have large short-term dollar loans. (Regardless of their transactions with shipbuilders, South Korean banks could engage in "carry trade," borrowing in FX and investing in local currency assets in the expectation of a currency appreciation. But this would expose them to FX risk and bring them up against their open FX position limits.)

In June 2010, the Korean authorities announced a package of prudential measures to "prevent excessive foreign exchange leverage." These strengthened some measures that had been implemented the previous year. (A November 2009 measure had already required banks to gradually raise their long-term FX borrowing from 80 to 90 percent—later raised to 100 percent—of their long-term FX lending, which had succeeded in reducing banks' short-term borrowing.) The authorities imposed these measures because they did not want a repeat of what had happened in the run-up to the global financial crisis, when FX derivatives trading

**Box 11.4** (continued)

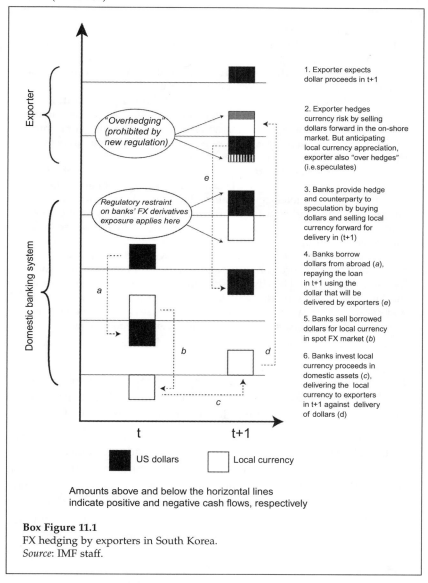

**Box Figure 11.1**
FX hedging by exporters in South Korea.
*Source*: IMF staff.

**Box 11.4** (continued)

between banks and firms had led to an excessive increase in short-term external borrowing, in turn exposing the banks to a sudden stop when dollar funding contracted globally during the global financial crisis. (The dollar shortage was addressed, in part, through the dollar swap line extended by the US Federal Reserve to the Bank of Korea.)

The 2010 measures included ceilings on FX derivative positions of banks (expressed in relation to bank capital), tighter restrictions on the provision of FX-denominated loans, and stricter liquidity ratios for domestic banks. Banks were also prohibited from overhedging underlying transactions of forward contracts with exporters.

The measures succeeded in preventing banks' external debt from returning to precrisis levels, but because of their targeted nature did not substantially reduce total capital inflows (IMF 2011a). They did, however, succeed in significantly lowering the *sensitivity* of capital flows into South Korea to global conditions (Bruno and Shin 2014). The narrow scope of the measures (in light of South Korea's open capital account) allowed corporates to hedge their positions offshore, with offshore banks still be able to offset their short Korean won positions resulting from the nondeliverable forwards (NDFs) by investing in the onshore government bond market. The authorities also reinstated nondiscriminatory withholding and capital gains taxes on nonresident purchases of government and central bank securities, to which residents were already subject.

then another option would be to impose a capital control on banks' FX-denominated foreign borrowing, together with a limit on their open FX positions, which would implicitly cap their FX lending.

• *Debt-equity mismatch of the borrower*: a generalized credit boom, even if all debt is contracted in local currency, may lead to excessive leverage (debt-equity ratio) of the borrower. Prudential rules that reduce the risk of a lending boom can be an appropriate response; examples include increasing reserve requirements on banks' liabilities, raising risk weights in capital adequacy calculations for certain types of lending, and tightening loan classification rules. Likewise, if lending fuels an asset price boom (giving a false sense of security because measured debt-equity ratios are unsustainably low), the response could include strengthening prudential measures, such as countercyclical capital requirements, lower maximum loan-to-value ratios (especially for real estate loans), and higher margin requirements (for equity-related lending).[24]

---

24. While cast here as a balance-sheet vulnerability due to a debt-equity mismatch, in essence this risk is the same as excessive credit growth in the economy, which we earlier

The bottom line is that when flows are intermediated through the regulated banking system, some combination of financial sector–specific capital controls and prudential measures may be required.[25] To the extent that the risk arises mainly from the external nature of the liability, a capital control would be appropriate. But if the currency denomination is of concern, then a currency-based prudential measure would be preferable (although in practice it may make little difference, as most of the problematic liabilities are likely to be both denominated in foreign currency and owed to nonresidents). If the concern is excessive credit growth (general, or in specific asset categories) then nondiscriminatory prudential measures might be applied.

What other factors might tip the balance among these types of measures? First, concerns about the efficiency of financial sector supervision may favor more rudimentary measures, such as capital controls. Second, as discussed below, prudential measures on regulated financial institutions (such as banks) may cause flows to be intermediated through the unregulated financial sector (e.g., finance companies). This may argue for capital controls, or a customized mix of capital controls on the unregulated financial sector and of prudential measures on the regulated financial entities, geared to country circumstances (including the sophistication of domestic financial markets and the scope for regulatory arbitrage) that could both reduce distortions and limit circumvention.

### 11.4.2 Flows Bypassing the Regulated Financial System

What if capital flows bypass the domestic banking system? This may be because of direct lending from abroad, such as corporate issuance or cross-border lending by foreign banks, or because domestic banks channel the funds through unregulated financial entities (sometimes precisely to avoid prudential regulations, as in the case of Croatia discussed in box 11.2).[26] The short answer is that, unless the regulatory perimeter can be expanded to include the unregulated financial sector (or the end borrowers themselves), capital controls are the only option, since by definition prudential measures apply only to regulated financial institutions (figure 11.2[b]). Three risks are noteworthy:

---

looked at as a macroeconomic imbalance. Not surprisingly, therefore, the solution is the same: a nondiscriminatory macroprudential measure.

25. It bears emphasizing that not all increases in credit relative to the previous trend are problematic. The goal of policy is to prevent unhealthy booms and busts, not to stop a normal process of financial deepening that is essential to economic development and convergence.

26. Recent research by Reinhardt and Sowerbutts (2015) suggests that tightening of capital regulation of domestic banks may lead to increased lending by foreign banks.

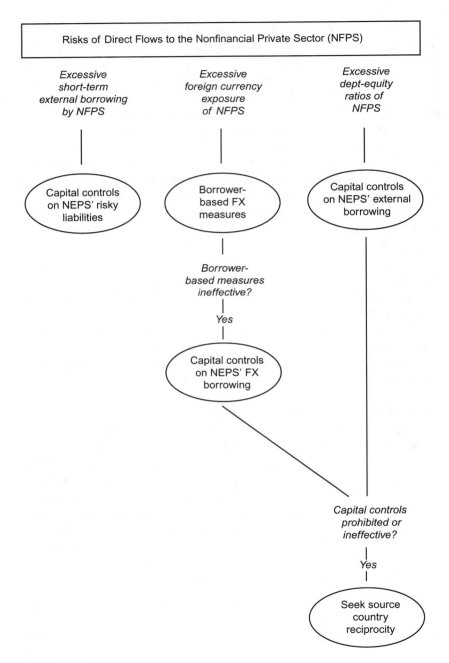

**Figure 11.2(b)**
Responding to flows that bypass the domestic banking system.
*Source*: Authors' illustration.

1. *Nonfinancial entities (firms or households) take on an excessively risky external liability structure* (e.g., short-term debt). As discussed in chapter 7, atomistic agents may not fully internalize the risks associated with the liability structure of their borrowing. If the risk stems mainly from the external character of the liability (e.g., nonresident creditors being more likely to call loans and rush for the exit in times of stress), then a capital control would be the most appropriate instrument. This could take the form of a tax on foreign borrowing (perhaps calibrated to the maturity of the instrument), a quantitative limit (e.g., on corporate issuance), or an outright prohibition on certain types of liabilities.

2. *Private nonfinancial balance sheets have excessive currency risk.* Even if borrowing is not excessive in aggregate, lower interest rates may tempt borrowers to take on excessive FX risk. While the most appropriate instrument in this case would be a measure that discriminates on the basis of the transaction's currency, not the residency of the parties to that transaction, this would be difficult to apply in practice. Instead a capital control, albeit one that specifically penalizes FX borrowing, might be the best alternative. In a few instances, countries have imposed borrower-based FX measures, which operate regardless of whether the flows are intermediated by domestic banks or bypass them. (Article 318 of Brazil's Civil Code, for example, prohibits the writing of any financial contract denominated in foreign currency, including between residents and subsidiaries or branches of foreign banks. In August 2010, Hungary's legislature introduced a law that prohibited the registration of FX-denominated mortgages in the land registry, effectively banning such mortgages from all sources.[27]) If neither borrower-based measures nor capital controls can be applied, then the only recourse would be to seek reciprocity (as discussed in chapter 10), whereby the regulators in the source country would be requested to impose the same prudential measures on their banks operating in the recipient country as the recipient country regulators impose on their own banks in the domestic market.[28]

---

27. The Hungarian measure was removed in May 2011 as EU regulations made such a ban difficult, but FX loans were restricted to those who earned an income of at least fifteen times the Hungarian minimum wage as calculated in the foreign currency in which the loan was denominated. The European Commission, however, launched an infringement procedure against Hungary in June 2013 for this limitation on eligibility for FX-denominated mortgages on the grounds that it violated the EU principle of the free movement of capital.

28. This would not work if the nonfinancial corporate sector were raising funds directly in the capital markets, but such exposure may be of less concern as only multinational corporations are likely to be able to do so.

3. *Direct borrowing from abroad by nonfinancial entities fuels asset price infla-tion.* Since such borrowing bypasses the domestic banking system, neither monetary policy nor prudential regulation will likely have much traction, and capital controls on foreign borrowing (and complementary instru-ments) could be needed.[29] At the same time, if most of the lending is by foreign financial institutions, the recipient-country government may be less concerned about losses they incur—except inasmuch as defaults lead to fire sales that depress asset prices more generally and result in negative externalities. Again, if capital controls cannot be imposed, the recourse would be to seek reciprocity from source-country regulators.

The key takeaway is that for flows bypassing the regulated financial system, the case for using capital controls is inevitably stronger simply because the flows are outside the usual perimeter of prudential poli-cies. While it may be possible to extend that perimeter to cover other domestic financial entities (and thus apply prudential measures rather than capital controls), or to prevent borrowers themselves from engag-ing in risky financial behavior (e.g., by outlawing foreign currency bor-rowing altogether), the scope for doing so, especially in the short run, is likely to be limited. The main exception is when the country has inter-national obligations that prohibit the use of capital controls, in which case the authorities have little choice but to try to impose measures that do not discriminate explicitly on the basis of residency (though, depend-ing on the circumstances, the competent body may rule that even currency-based measures constitute de facto capital controls, violating treaty obligations). In some cases (e.g., within the EU), it may be possible to persuade the source-country regulators to act reciprocally and apply the same prudential measures on their banks' operations in the recipi-ent country as the recipient-country regulators are imposing on domes-tic banks.

### 11.4.3   Design of Capital Controls for Balance-sheet Vulnerabilities

As argued in the introduction, when it comes to balance-sheet concerns, it may make sense to have structural capital controls targeted at highly risky flows whose costs exceed their benefits. As also noted there, how-ever, the set of flows against which there should be permanent measures is likely to be small. Accordingly, there will be instances in which the

---

29. If information is available on the extent of direct borrowing abroad by nonfinancial entities, prudential regulations could discourage borrowing abroad by limiting access to local loans—for example, by setting higher reserve requirements on local bank loans to firms with large external indebtedness.

surge is widening balance-sheet vulnerabilities to the point that they threaten to overwhelm the normal regulatory framework, and capital controls need to be cyclically imposed or tightened. These measures should then be kept in place at least as long as the flows continue, and preferably until the mismatches on domestic balance sheets have returned to safer levels.

In terms of their scope, it is more logical for the controls to be narrow and targeted at the riskiest forms of liabilities. However, there is a trade-off in terms of effectiveness in applying controls narrowly because they can then be circumvented more easily through exempt transactions, relabeling, or derivative markets. For instance, foreign direct investment (FDI) is generally viewed as beneficial to the economy and is often exempt from controls, which gives an important avenue for avoidance by "relabeling" of flows. When controls have narrow coverage (e.g., they only apply to debt), foreign investors can try to enter the country in the form of tax-exempt equity inflows. Once inside, they can purchase the debt instruments through a local shell company, or sell the equity locally, and use the proceeds to purchase debt—thus avoiding the control.[30]

Another avenue for circumvention may be through the use of derivatives (in those countries with sufficiently developed derivatives markets). A foreign investor who wants a certain amount of exposure to domestic assets without paying the tax on the full amount could purchase a derivative instrument (so that the flows into the country are just the required margin, rather than the full desired exposure). While this would reduce the revenue collected, the capital control would achieve its purpose of reducing the aggregate inflow. However, to the extent that the local counterparty to the derivative transaction (such as a local bank) tries to hedge, this will require the same flow (but now between the local bank and, usually, another foreign party). If the latter transaction is not taxed, then use of derivatives essentially allows circumvention of the control on the inflow.[31] But if it is taxed at the same rate as the original inflow would have been, then the local bank must charge

---

30. Large institutional investors are, however, likely to be deterred from trying to evade controls as their recourse to the domestic legal system to enforce obligations may be limited.

31. Note that if bank borrowing (e.g., from a parent or subsidiary) is not taxed, this in itself provides a loophole to capital controls. But the bank's ability to exploit this loophole may be limited by regulation on its open FX position. In the example considered here, the bank closes its derivative FX position by borrowing abroad.

correspondingly more for the derivative transaction, and the foreign investor faces the same cost as if he had paid the tax on the original instrument rather than buying exposure in the derivatives market.[32]

In other words, by closing such loopholes, capital controls can be made (more) effective. But national authorities are sometimes reluctant to do so for fear of stifling the growth of the derivatives markets. Accordingly, capital controls may need broader coverage (than would otherwise be desirable) to reduce the scope for circumvention. Even then some circumvention is inevitable, especially in countries with sophisticated financial markets, as long as the incentives for doing so exceed the costs. Considerable administrative capacity (that may involve significant costs) will usually be required to ensure full effectiveness. Thus, it is important to weigh the benefits of limiting circumvention against the costs of such measures, which will be borne not only by the authorities but also by the banks, which may face compliance costs in implementing the controls.

When it comes to the choice between price- or quantity-based measures for addressing balance-sheet vulnerabilities, the former have certain advantages (as noted above), especially in terms of cyclically adjusting the measure. It is noteworthy, however, that most prudential regulations in the financial sector are quantity- rather than price-based (e.g., open FX limits; capital adequacy ratios). This is because when the authorities face information asymmetries and uncertainty about the private sector's response, it can be difficult to calibrate price-based measures appropriately (Weitzman 1974). Accordingly, quantitative limits may be more appropriate when capital controls are being imposed for balance-sheet vulnerabilities, provided that they can be designed in a transparent and rules-based manner.[33]

---

32. Brazil's experience with its foreign exchange transactions tax is instructive in this regard, suggesting that specific design features not inherent to a capital inflow tax indeed provided a significant loophole which undermined the effectiveness of the measure (Chamon and Garcia 2016). That said, many EMEs currently do not have such large derivatives markets, so at least the onshore markets may not give as much scope for circumvention.

33. Most domestic financial regulation is quantitative (e.g., rules that limit open FX position of banks in relation to capital) or a combination of price- and quantity-based (e.g., capital adequacy requirements), presumably because small misjudgments about the private sector's incentives and reaction can result in excessive risk, with adverse effects on financial stability. For example, large exchange rate movements can wipe out a bank's capital in the presence of sizable open FX positions, so it is understandable that the regulator would seek to cap the exposure rather than price that risk and charge it

## 11.5 Conclusion

Confronted by an inflow surge, national authorities may need to address growing macroeconomic imbalances and balance-sheet vulnerabilities. This chapter lays out a logical sequence of measures to adopt (beyond any structural capital controls and prudential measures that are already in place), though that need not coincide with the chronological sequence, depending upon the lead times to adopt and implement various policies. In sum, once the monetary authorities have allowed the exchange rate to appreciate to a level that is not undervalued from a multilaterally consistent medium-term perspective, they may want to start intervening in the FX market to prevent further appreciation, sterilizing the intervention if there are inflationary pressures.[34] If the economy shows signs of overheating, either in terms of goods prices or asset prices, monetary and (on a longer fuse) fiscal tightening might be necessary, together with macroprudential measures to contain excessive credit growth. To the extent these policies prove—or are likely to prove—insufficient, the authorities need to consider bolstering them by imposing or tightening capital controls, which may also help to increase the traction of both monetary policy and foreign exchange market intervention. At the same time, national authorities must be mindful of growing balance-sheet mismatches in the economy and should avail themselves of both prudential measures and capital controls to shift the composition of inflows toward less risky forms of liabilities. There is considerable scope for tailoring the design of capital controls to their intended objective—as a backstop to macro policies to address macroeconomic imbalances, or as a primary instrument to target specific balance-sheet mismatches, or some combination of both.

Of course, in reality, the policy-making process is likely to be much more complicated. Coordinating the agencies responsible for different policies—the central bank, ministry of finance, macroprudential regulator—will be challenge enough for most governments. Each measure has its own decision and implementation lag—monetary policy and FX intervention generally being the shortest, capital controls or macroprudential measures (together with fiscal policy) usually being

---

against the bank's capital. Some forms of lending are so risky that the regulator may decide to outright ban them (e.g., high-LTV loans, or FX lending to households).

34. As noted earlier, ideally the calculation of the equilibrium real exchange rate would take into account any domestic distortions or externalities.

the longest. Some measures—fiscal, and certain capital controls—need legislative approval; others require compliance by the private sector. Given uncertainties about the effects of measures, moreover, policy makers will normally want to adopt a portfolio approach, trying a variety of measures, rather than relying on any single instrument. Nevertheless, the framework presented here helps anchor the policy response, always recognizing that in practice policy making is usually more of an art than a science.

# 12 Concluding Thoughts

*If economists could manage to get themselves thought of as humble, competent people on a level with dentists, that would be splendid.*

—Keynes (1930, 98)

Attitudes toward capital account regulation have waxed and waned over the years. But the global financial crisis and its aftermath have been rude reminders that not all borrowing and lending decisions are rational, that markets can and often do misprice risk, and that volatile capital flows can wreak economic and financial havoc. One solution would be to retreat into financial autarky, barring most capital flows or at least subjecting them to heavy regulation and control. Yet that might mean forgoing the benefits that foreign flows can bring, including financing of productive investments and of much-needed public infrastructure. An alternative solution is to try to manage capital inflows. This might mean having in place structural measures to discourage especially risky types of liabilities or transactions, as well as cyclical responses to inflow surges by means of macroeconomic policies, prudential measures, and capital controls. This is the tack we have taken in this book.

The management of capital flows is not a new phenomenon. As discussed in chapter 2, while cross-border capital flows flourished in the late nineteenth and early twentieth centuries, and official attitudes continued to frown on capital controls in the interwar period at least in some influential quarters, the consequences—in the form of capital flight, hot-money flows, competitive devaluations, and protectionism— were far from benign. As the Great Depression drew to a close, attitudes began to change with the realization that free-flowing capital was actually an impediment to sustaining prosperity and stability. The new monetary order that was crafted at Bretton Woods reflected the conviction that unfettered capital movements were fundamentally at odds with the objectives of macroeconomic management and the growth of world trade. Keynes and White believed that capital controls should be a structural element of the global monetary system, and they clearly believed that global cooperation was needed to make such measures effective; we believe their views are as salient today as they were then.

Capital account regulations were an important part of the global monetary order during the Bretton Woods years, though cooperation—managing flows at both ends—proved elusive because the United States (notably its banking interests) wanted no part of it. An ideological drive toward freely flowing global flows nevertheless led industrialized nations to gradually dismantle controls, although during that process they often resorted to temporary controls, both on outflows and on inflows, to manage hot-money flows.

By the late 1970s, when the amendment to the IMF's articles was being negotiated, the United States managed to insert "exchange of capital among countries" as an essential goal of the international monetary system (alongside the exchange of goods and services). The 1980s and 1990s thus saw a push toward greater financial openness in emerging market countries. Open capital accounts, while not explicit in the Washington Consensus, became very much part of the ideology that countries should follow, together with floating exchange rates, deregulation, fiscal discipline, and inflation targeting—all of which would provide a mutually reinforcing backdrop for all manner of economic policy discipline. It was in such an economic policy environment that the IMF advocated a mandate for itself to promote capital account liberalization in all member countries: capital controls only made sense in extremis and even then were to be dismantled expeditiously given their tendency to leak or do lasting damage.

Some two decades later, empirical evidence that a fully open capital account yields benefits that outweigh costs is mixed at best. Meanwhile, the insight of Keynes and White that freely flowing cross-border flows can be fundamentally at odds with the ability of policy makers to chart desirable economic outcomes resonates as much today as it did on the eve of Bretton Woods. Yet even today, notwithstanding the experience of waves of capital flow–induced crises in Latin America, Asia, and Europe, most emerging markets remain fairly open, and it is not far-fetched to argue that the direction of any future reform of the international monetary system is more likely to be in line with what was advocated on the eve of the Asian crisis than what Keynes and White had hoped for at Bretton Woods. Against this backdrop, our purpose in this book has been to take a step back and to chart a course for policy action that we believe is both feasible and desirable for countries seeking to mitigate the risks associated with volatile capital flows, while still benefitting from foreign finance.

Our analysis of capital flow surges and their consequences in chapters 3 and 4 yields three salient facts. First, capital surges into emerging markets—and stops surging—largely because of global factors outside the countries' control, with US monetary conditions notable among them. Second, capital inflows can bring important benefits, but they are also prone to generating macroeconomic and financial imbalances that often result in financial crises. An emerging market is thus three to five times more likely to suffer a financial crisis *following* an inflow surge than in normal times. Third, the nature of flows—foreign direct investment, portfolio debt or equity, banking flows—has profound implications for the risks from engaging in intertemporal asset trade. Some flows are more stable even in a world of flighty global push factors and produce net benefits to the recipient country; others provide fickle financing and leave domestic balance sheets dangerously exposed to currency, maturity, and collateral revaluation risks.

Fortunately, push factors do not seal the destiny of countries, which can deploy tools to improve the *structural* mix of flows as well as dampen the effects of capital flow *cycles*. Far from detracting from longer-term growth and development objectives, dampening the boom-bust cycle in capital flows could underpin such objectives by fostering economic stability, which is a sine qua non for sustained investment and growth. Although it is not a foregone conclusion that preventing crises is better than trying to pick up the pieces afterwards (as Alan Greenspan famously claimed prior to the US financial crisis), in our view if emerging market policy makers can successfully manage inflows—in the sense that their country reaps most of the benefits while avoiding the costs—that is surely better than either financial autarky or complete laissez-faire. The call for effective management is thus likely to involve both structural measures (to improve the mix of flows) and cyclically varying macroeconomic policies, prudential measures, and capital controls.

To provide a framework for thinking how policy makers might respond, in chapter 5 we proposed a logical mapping between the various possible macroeconomic imbalances (economic overheating, currency overvaluation, excessive credit growth) and macroeconomic policies (the policy interest rate, foreign exchange (FX) intervention, and macroprudential measures), with cyclical capital controls acting as a backstop when the macro tools are unlikely to be able to deal with the consequences at reasonable cost. While this mapping is hardly earth-shattering, it is quite at odds with much of the conventional policy advice given to emerging markets—for example, that inflation-targeting central banks should not intervene in the FX markets (except during periods of disorderly market conditions) for fear of undermining their credibility. In chapter 6 not only did we show that FX intervention is fully compatible with inflation targeting, we also established that having the additional instrument can increase the range of parameters over which inflation targeting (IT) is preferable to discretionary monetary policy, and therefore enhance the credibility of the IT framework. Although we make this point in specific reference to FX intervention (in part, because, alongside the policy interest rate, sterilized intervention is the most flexible and commonly used tool in emerging markets), we believe that the principle holds more generally: central banks should not shy away from using all the instruments at their disposal, depending, of course, on the tools' relative costs and effectiveness.

Beyond macroeconomic imbalances, capital inflows can contribute to balance-sheet vulnerabilities. The key insight from chapter 7 is that the riskiness of a liability depends upon the magnitude of the real transfer the debtor needs to make during times of stress (such as a sudden stop or a capital outflow episode)—making short-term, foreign currency–denominated debt owed to nonresidents the riskiest type of liability. Inasmuch as the private sector does not fully internalize these risks, there is a role for the government to try to tilt the composition of inflows toward less risky forms of liabilities (foreign direct investment, equity, local currency–denominated debt). At least the theoretically optimal intervention will involve the use of capital controls because, in general, a liability to a nonresident creditor will be riskier than the corresponding liability to a resident.

Theory is all very well, but what is of relevance to policy makers is that they achieve their intended results. Here the analysis of chapter 8 suggests that emerging markets do deploy a variety of policy instruments in the face of capital inflows (the one instrument that is almost never used—tightening discretionary fiscal policy—is the sole policy response that conventional wisdom prescribes), while the evidence on their effectiveness in chapter 9 is encouraging. Sterilized intervention does seem to have some impact on currency appreciation and on banking system credit growth; macroprudential policies affect the latter also. In terms of a backstop to macroeconomic policies, the introduction or tightening of capital controls results in a sharp drop of currency-appreciation pressures, though the effects on curbing domestic credit growth seem to be weaker. There is quite compelling evidence that capital controls and currency-based prudential measures are able to shift the composition of inflows toward safer types of liabilities or otherwise reduce financial sector risks. It is striking that emerging markets that had inflow controls and currency-based prudential measures in place during the run-up to the global financial crisis fared much better than those that had allowed fully unfettered capital inflows and the resulting macro imbalances and balance-sheet vulnerabilities. While each country's circumstances are unique, emerging market policy makers appear to have a relatively effective tool kit at their disposal and they should make full use of it.

In considering policy responses, we have mostly concentrated on the unilateral response of emerging market countries, given the reality that they are mostly on their own. We touch upon multilateral considerations in two contexts: the interaction of recipient countries taking measures to stem flows into their countries, and possible cooperation between source countries and recipient countries in controlling cross-border flows (chapter 10); and the "exchange rate test" (chapter 11) whereby, in the face of inflows, countries are expected to allow the currency to appreciate to its multilaterally consistent equilibrium value before implementing measures (FX intervention or capital controls) that would curb the appreciation. The latter stricture stems from IMF member countries' obligations (under Article IV of its Articles of Agreement) to avoid "manipulating exchange rates or the international monetary system in order to prevent effective balance of payments adjustment or to gain an unfair competitive advantage over other members." Because the IMF does not have jurisdiction over the capital account, it cannot mandate that source countries cooperate with recipient countries in managing cross-border capital flows (and, as recounted in chapter 2, even Keynes and White's original proposal, which would have required cooperation in enforcing capital controls, got watered down by New York banking interests). Yet surely the willingness of emerging markets to act as good citizens of the international monetary system and ensure that they indeed pass the exchange rate test (i.e., allow the currency to appreciate to its multilaterally consistent equilibrium level) would be much enhanced if they could be confident that source countries would cooperate in managing excessive or disruptive capital flows. A good starting point would be cooperation in managing cross-border banking flows, and mutual recognition of reciprocity in financial sector regulation (beyond the exhortation in the IMF's *Institutional View on the Liberalization and Management of Capital Flows*, and the limited countercyclical capital charge reciprocity under Basel III).

The policy makers' vade mecum that we have laid out raises broader issues for the global monetary system. Notwithstanding the fact that some of the emerging markets may have liberalized their capital accounts prematurely, it questions whether emerging markets—and, a fortiori, frontier markets and low-income countries—have further to gain from opening up, or indeed whether they would not be better off retaining restrictions on at least the riskiest forms of foreign liabilities and transactions. This is particularly pertinent since most of these countries, unlike advanced economies, do not enjoy the liquidity insurance provided by swap facilities let alone the reserve currency status. Left out in the cold, they are forced to self-insure through reserve accumulation, which is costly both to the country and to the international monetary system. Alternative forms of insurance—especially structural capital controls or even rollbacks to earlier liberalization—could arguably yield favorable benefit-cost trade-offs, particularly if they result in a safer mix of flows that makes economies less prone to risks from changes in global push factors.

As the quotation by Keynes at the start of the chapter indicates, the goal of economists should be to solve practical problems. Emerging market countries' episodic access to global capital markets is a clear and present practical problem for which advice is sorely needed. This book is an effort to provide such advice, a manual for how different elements of the policy tool kit might fit together and be deployed. The solutions are sometimes unconventional. Keynes, in his *General Theory*, warned that "worldly wisdom teaches that it is better for reputation to fail conventionally than to succeed unconventionally," but we are happy to defy worldly wisdom. We hope that this book has equipped emerging market policy makers with a framework to chart their own course for managing capital flows—to reap the benefits while avoiding the costs—without worrying too much about conforming to convention. If we have succeeded in that, we have succeeded.

# Data Appendix

| Variable | Description | Source | Chapter |
|----------|-------------|--------|---------|
| *Capital flows (1970–2013)* | | | |
| Net capital flows | Net financial flows excluding financing items and other investment liabilities of the general government; i.e., the difference between International Financial Statistics database series codes "...4995W.9" and "...4753ZB9" (in terms of *Balance of Payments Manual*, fifth edition presentation) | IMF's International Financial Statistics (IFS) and World Economic Outlook (WEO) databases | Chapter 1, chapter 2 (figures 2.8–2.9), chapter 3, chapter 8, chapter 9 |
| Asset flows | Net asset flows excluding reserve assets (in terms of *Balance of Payments Manual*, fifth edition presentation). Sum of direct investment abroad flows, portfolio investment assets flows, financial derivative assets flows, and other investment assets flows (i.e., sum of IFS series codes: ...4505..9...; ...4602..9...; ...4900..9...; ...4703..9... | IMF's IFS and WEO databases | Chapter 1, chapter 3, chapter 8, chapter 9 |

(continued)

(continued)

| Variable | Description | Source | Chapter |
|---|---|---|---|
| Liability flows | Net liability flows excluding other investment liabilities of the general government (in terms of *Balance of Payments Manual*, fifth edition presentation). Sum of direct investment in reporting country, portfolio investment liability flows, financial derivative liability flows, other investment liability flows minus other investment liability flows of general government (i.e., IFS series codes: sum ( . . . 4555Z.9 . . . ; . . . 4652Z.9 . . . ; . . . 4905..9 . . . ; . . . 4753W.9 . . . ) minus . . . 4753ZB9 . . . ) | IMF's IFS and WEO databases | Chapter 1, Chapter 3, chapter 8, chapter 9, chapter 10 |
| Bank asset flows | Exchange rate–adjusted changes in the gross international financial claims of resident banks in the reporting country on bank/nonbank sectors of recipient countries (i.e., changes in total stock, amount outstanding, of reporting-country banks' foreign assets, accounting for repayments and exchange rate effects) | Bank for International Settlements (BIS) Locational Statistics by Residence | Chapter 10 |

*Capital flows and stock (historical data)*

| Variable | Description | Source | Chapter |
|---|---|---|---|
| Net capital exports (1860–1913) | Net financial outflows (in local currency) | Bloomfield 1968 | Chapter 2 (figure 2.1) |
| Net capital imports (1860–1913) | Net financial inflows (in local currency) | Bloomfield 1968 | Chapter 2 (figure 2.1) |

| Variable | Description | Source | Chapter |
|---|---|---|---|
| Net capital flows (1923–1944) | Net capital flows (i.e., the difference between inward and outward flows) including errors and omissions | League of Nations 1931, 1932, 1938, 1939, 1948 | Chapter 2 (figures 2.3, 2.5) |
| Net capital flows (1950–1973) | Net capital flows (i.e., difference between inward and outward flows) including errors and omissions, but excluding reserve assets and related items | IMF's *Balance of Payments Yearbook* (various issues) | Chapter 2 (figure 2.7) |
| Long-term capital stock (1914) | External assets, total and by destination (in USD) | Feis 1965 | Chapter 2 (table 2.1) |
| *Capital controls* | | | |
| Bond inflow controls | Average of two binary variables: presence of restrictions on purchase of bonds and other debt securities by nonresidents, and their sale abroad by residents (1 = presence of restrictions) | Authors' calculations based on the IMF's *Annual Report on Exchange Arrangements and Exchange Restrictions* (*AREAER*) | Chapter 9, chapter 10 |
| Bond outflow controls | Average of two binary variables: presence of restrictions on sale of bonds and other debt securities by nonresidents, and their purchase abroad by residents (1 = presence of restrictions) | Authors' calculations based on the IMF's *AREAER* | Chapter 10 |
| Equity inflow controls | Average of two binary variables: presence of restrictions on purchase of shares or other securities of a participating nature by nonresidents, and their sale abroad by residents (1 = presence of restrictions) | Authors' calculations based on the IMF's *AREAER* | Chapter 9, chapter 10 |

(continued)

(continued)

| Variable | Description | Source | Chapter |
|---|---|---|---|
| Equity outflow controls | Average of two binary variables: presence of restrictions on sale of shares or other securities of a participating nature by nonresidents, and their purchase abroad by residents (1 = presence of restrictions) | Authors' calculations based on the IMF's *AREAER* | Chapter 10 |
| Financial credit inflow controls | Binary variable with 1 indicating restrictions on financial credits by nonresidents to residents | Authors' calculations based on the IMF's *AREAER* | Chapter 9, chapter 10 |
| Financial credit outflow controls | Binary variable with 1 indicating restrictions on financial credits by residents to nonresidents | Authors' calculations based on the IMF's *AREAER* | Chapter 10 |
| Inward direct investment controls | Binary variable with 1 indicating presence of restrictions on inward direct investment (or liquidation of direct investment) | Authors' calculations based on the IMF's *AREAER* | Chapter 9, chapter 10 |
| Outward direct investment controls | Binary variable with 1 indicating presence of restrictions on outward direct investment | Authors' calculations based on the IMF's *AREAER* | Chapter 10 |
| Money-market inflow controls | Average of two binary variables: presence of restrictions on purchase of money-market instruments by nonresidents, and their sale abroad by residents (1 = presence of restrictions) | Authors' calculations based on the IMF's *AREAER* | Chapter 9, chapter 10 |

| Variable | Description | Source | Chapter |
|---|---|---|---|
| Money-market outflow controls | Average of two binary variables: presence of restrictions on sale of money-market instruments by nonresidents, and their purchase abroad by residents (1 = presence of restrictions) | Authors' calculations based on the IMF's *AREAER* | Chapter 10 |
| Collective investment inflow controls | Average of two binary variables: presence of restrictions on purchase of collective investment securities by nonresidents, and their sale abroad by residents (1 = presence of restrictions) | Authors' calculations based on the IMF's *AREAER* | Chapter 9, chapter 10 |
| Collective investment outflow controls | Average of two binary variables: presence of restrictions on sale or local issuance of foreign collective investment securities, and their purchase abroad by residents (1 = presence of restrictions) | Authors' calculations based on the IMF's *AREAER* | Chapter 10 |
| Overall capital inflow controls | Average of bond, equity, inward direct investment, money market, financial credit, and collective investment inflow controls indices | Authors' calculations based on the IMF's *AREAER* | Chapter 1 (figure 1.7), chapter 9 (figure 9.3, tables 9.8–9.12), chapter 10 |
| Overall capital outflow controls | Average of bond, equity, outward direct investment, money market, financial credit, and collective investment outflow controls indices | Authors' calculations based on the IMF's *AREAER* | Chapter 1, chapter 10 |
| Overall capital account openness | Index (high = liberalized; low = not liberalized) | Chinn and Ito 2008 | Chapter 3, chapter 4, chapter 8 |

(continued)

(continued)

| Variable | Description | Source | Chapter |
|---|---|---|---|
| Changes in capital inflow controls | Changes in restrictions on equity, bond, and banking sector inflows | Ahmed et al. 2015 | Chapter 8, chapter 9 (figure 9.2, table 9.7) |
| *Capital controls (historical data)* | | | |
| Exchange restrictions | Number of major economies with exchange restrictions | League of Nations World Economic Survey (1931–1932) | Chapter 2 (figure 2.4) |
| Inflow controls (1950–2010) | Overall capital inflow restrictiveness index based on the severity of restrictions on inflow transactions of all asset types (0 = none; 0.25 = mild; 0.75 = significant; 1 = extreme) | Authors' calculations based on the IMF's *AREAER* | Chapter 2 (figure 2.10) |
| Outflow controls (1950–2010) | Overall capital outflow restrictiveness index based on the severity of restrictions on outflow transactions of all asset types (0 = none; 0.25 = mild; 0.75 = significant; 1 = extreme) | Authors' calculations based on the IMF's *AREAER* | Chapter 2 (figure 2.10) |
| *Prudential measures* | | | |
| Lending locally in foreign exchange (FX) | Binary variable with 1 indicating restrictions on the financial sector to lend domestically in FX | Authors' calculations based on the IMF's *AREAER* | Chapter 1 (figure 1.6), chapter 9, chapter 10 |
| Purchase of locally issued FX securities | Binary variable with 1 indicating restrictions on the financial sector on the purchase of locally issued securities denominated in FX | Authors' calculations based on the IMF's *AREAER* | Chapter 1 (figure 1.6), chapter 9, chapter 10 |

| Variable | Description | Source | Chapter |
|---|---|---|---|
| Open FX position limits | Binary variable with 1 indicating the existence of limits on banks' open FX positions (countries with fixed exchange rate regimes where an open FX position limit exists, but the anchor currency is excluded from the computation of the FX position are coded as not having the restriction in place) | Authors' calculations based on the IMF's *AREAER* | Chapter 1 (figure 1.6), chapter 9, chapter 10 |
| FX reg1 | Average of restrictions on lending locally in FX, and the presence of open FX position limits | Authors' calculations | Chapter 9 |
| FX reg2 | Average of restrictions on lending locally in FX, purchase of local securities denominated in FX, and the presence of open FX position limits | Authors' calculations | Chapter 9 |
| Accounts abroad | Binary variable with 1 indicating the existence of restrictions on the financial sector on maintaining accounts abroad | Authors' calculations based on the IMF's *AREAER* | Chapter 10 |
| Lending to nonresidents | Binary variable with 1 indicating the existence of restrictions on the financial sector on lending to nonresidents | Authors' calculations based on the IMF's *AREAER* | Chapter 10 |
| Reserve requirement (RR) on FX deposits | Reserve requirement on foreign currency deposits in banks | Federico, Vegh, and Vulletin 2014 | Chapter 1 (figure 1.6) |
| RR on local currency deposits | Average reserve requirement on local currency deposits in banks | Federico, Vegh, and Vulletin 2014 | Chapter 1 (figure 1.6), chapter 8, chapter 9 |

(continued)

(continued)

| Variable | Description | Source | Chapter |
|---|---|---|---|
| Domestic macroprudential measures | Changes in countercyclical capital requirements, dynamic loan loss provisioning, caps on loan-to-value and debt-to-income ratios, limits on credit growth and consumer loans, and other housing sector–related measures | Authors' calculations based on Akini and Olmstead-Rumsey (2015) | Chapter 8, chapter 9 |
| *Gross domestic product (1970–2013)* | | | |
| Nominal gross domestic product (GDP) | GDP, current prices (in local currency and USD) | IMF's IFS and WEO databases | Chapter 3, chapter 4, chapter 8, chapter 9, chapter 10 |
| Real GDP | GDP, constant prices | IMF's WEO database | Chapter 3, chapter 4, chapter 8, chapter 9, chapter 10 |
| Real GDP growth rate | Percentage change in real GDP | Authors' calculations | Chapter 3, chapter 4, chapter 8, chapter 9, chapter 10 |
| Real GDP per capita | GDP per capita, in constant 2005 USD (log) | World Bank's World Development Indicators | Chapter 3, chapter 4, chapter 9, chapter 10 |
| Output gap | Log difference between actual and trend real GDP (in percent of trend real GDP), where the trend is obtained from Hodrick-Prescott filter | Authors' calculations | Chapter 4, chapter 8 |
| *Gross domestic product (historical data)* | | | |
| GDP (1860–1913) | GDP, current prices (in local currency) | Mitchell 2013 | Chapter 2 |

| Variable | Description | Source | Chapter |
|---|---|---|---|
| *Exchange rate regime* | | | |
| Gold standard (1919–1937) | Number of countries on gold/gold exchange standard out of a sample of 54 countries | Authors' calculations based on Eichengreen (1992) | Chapter 2 (figure 2.2) |
| Gold standard abandonment (1931–1932) | Number of major economies abandoning gold standard | League of Nations World Economic Survey (1931–1932) | Chapter 2 (figure 2.4) |
| Exchange rate regime (de facto) | Fixed or intermediate exchange rate regime = 1; Floating regime = 0 | Ghosh, Ostry and Qureshi 2015 | Chapter 3, chapter 4, chapter 9, chapter 10 |
| *Exchange rate* | | | |
| Real effective exchange rate (REER) change | Percentage change in REER index | Authors' calculations based on REER data obtained from the IMF's Information Notice System (INS) database | Chapter 4, chapter 8, chapter 9 |
| REER deviation from trend/overvaluation | Log difference between actual and trend REER (in percent of trend REER), where the trend is obtained from Hodrick-Prescott filter | Authors' calculations | Chapter 3, chapter 4 |
| *Interest rates* | | | |
| Domestic interest rate | Central bank policy/ discount rate | IMF's IFS database | Chapter 3, chapter 8, chapter 9 |

(continued)

(continued)

| Variable | Description | Source | Chapter |
|---|---|---|---|
| Real domestic interest rate | [(1 + domestic nominal interest rate)/ (1 + expected inflation)]–1, where expected inflation is defined as one-period ahead (observed) CPI inflation | Authors' calculations | Chapter 3, chapter 10 |
| US 3-month Treasury Bill rate | US 3-month T-bill rate, constant maturity | IMF's IFS database | Chapter 3, chapter 4, chapter 8, chapter 9 |
| US 10-year government bond yield | US 10-year government bond yield | IMF's IFS database | Chapter 3 |
| Real US interest rate | [(1 + US nominal (T-bill or bond yield) interest rate)/ (1 + expected inflation)]–1, where expected inflation is defined as one-period ahead (observed) US CPI inflation | Authors' calculations | Chapter 3, chapter 4, chapter 8, chapter 9 |
| *Other macroeconomic variables* | | | |
| Bank foreign liabilities | Foreign liabilities of the banking system | IMF's IFS database | Chapter 4, chapter 9 |
| Commodity price index | Log difference between actual and trend commodity price index (in percent of trend commodity price index), where the trend is obtained from Hodrick-Prescott filter. (Commodity prices in logs used in chapter 8) | IMF's WEO database and authors' calculations | Chapter 3, chapter 8 |
| Common lender effects | External position of reporting banks in source country vis-à-vis crisis country, as a percent of total external position of reporting banks in source country. Crisis countries are as follows: Mexico | Authors' calculations based on BIS data | Chapter 10 |

| Variable | Description | Source | Chapter |
|---|---|---|---|
| | (1994–1995); Indonesia, Korea, Malaysia and Thailand (1997–1998); USA (2007–2008); Greece, Ireland, Portugal and Spain (2010–2011) | | |
| Consumer price index (CPI) | Index, year average | IMF's INS database | Chapter 3 |
| CPI inflation | Percentage change in CPI | Authors' calculations | Chapter 3, chapter 4, chapter 8 |
| Crisis (banking and currency) | Binary variable with one indicating a crisis | Laeven and Valencia 2013 | Chapter 4 |
| Current account balance | Balance on the current account | IMF's WEO database | Chapter 3, chapter 10 |
| Debt liabilities to total liabilities | Total external debt liabilities to total external liabilities | Authors' calculations based on Lane and Milesi-Ferretti (2007) | Chapter 9 |
| Domestic private sector credit | Credit by banks to the domestic private sector (in local currency) | IMF's IFS database | Chapter 3 |
| Domestic private sector credit growth | Percentage change in domestic private sector credit | Authors' calculations | Chapter 9 |
| External debt to GDP | Total external debt to GDP | IMF's WEO database | Chapter 4 |
| Financial development | Domestic credit to GDP | Authors' calculations | Chapter 3, chapter 8, chapter 9, chapter 10 |
| Fiscal balance to GDP | General government fiscal balance to GDP | IMF's WEO database | Chapter 4, chapter 10 |
| Foreign exchange lending | Loans by domestic banks in foreign currency (to total loans by banks) | IMF's Vulnerability Exercise database | Chapter 4, chapter 9 |
| Foreign exchange reserve flows | Flows of foreign exchange reserve assets (excluding valuation changes; in USD) | IMF's IFS database | Chapter 8, chapter 9 |

(continued)

(continued)

| Variable | Description | Source | Chapter |
|---|---|---|---|
| Foreign exchange intervention | Foreign exchange reserve flows to GDP | Authors' calculations based on the IMF's IFS database | Chapter 8, chapter 9 |
| Global financial crisis (GFC) | Binary variable with one indicating the global financial crisis (2008Q4–2009Q1 = 1) | Authors' calculations | Chapter 8, chapter 9 |
| Government expenditure to GDP | General government spending to GDP | IMF's WEO database | Chapter 8 |
| Institutional quality index | Average of ICRG's 12 political risk components | Political risk group | Chapter 3, chapter 8, chapter 9 |
| Left-wing government | Binary variable with one indicating the presence of a left-wing government | Updated database of political institutions by Beck et al. (2001) | Chapter 9, chapter 10 |
| Loan to deposit ratio | Loan-to-deposit ratio of the domestic financial system | IMF's IFS database | Chapter 4 |
| M2 | Money and quasi-money (in local currency) | IMF's IFS database | Chapter 9 |
| Optimal current account ("external financing need") | Obtained from the intertemporal optimizing model of the current account following Ghosh (1995) | Authors' calculations | Chapter 3 |
| Regional contagion | Proportion of countries in the region with a surge (in surge occurrence regressions). Average net capital flow to GDP in countries with a surge in the region (in surge magnitude regressions) | | Chapter 3 |
| Return on equity | In percent | Global Development Finance Report | Chapter 10 |

| Variable | Description | Source | Chapter |
|---|---|---|---|
| S&P 500 index volatility | Annual average of 12-month rolling standard deviation of (year-on-year) S&P 500 index returns | Authors' calculations based on Bloomberg | Chapter 3, chapter 4 |
| Stock of foreign exchange reserves | Stock of foreign exchange reserve assets (in USD) | IMF's IFS database | Chapter 3, chapter 4 |
| Stock market capitalization | In percent of GDP | Global Development Finance Report | Chapter 10 |
| Terms of trade change | Percentage change in terms of trade | IMF's WEO database | Chapter 4, chapter 9 |
| Trade openness | Total exports and imports to GDP | Authors' calculations based on the IMF's WEO database | Chapter 3, chapter 4, chapter 8, chapter 9, chapter 10 |
| Trading partner growth | Export-share weighted average of real GDP growth of top trading partners | IMF's WEO database | Chapter 4, chapter 9 |
| VIX/VXO index | Chicago Board Options Exchange Market Volatility Index (high values indicate greater volatility of S&P 500 index options) | Bloomberg | Chapter 3, chapter 8, chapter 9, chapter 10 |
| *Firm-level variables* | | | |
| Firm size | Total assets in USD (in log) | Worldscope database | Chapter 4 (box 4.1) |
| Firm investment | Capital expenditure to total assets | Worldscope database | Chapter 4 (box 4.1) |
| Real export growth | Percentage change in real exports (i.e., nominal exports divided by CPI) | Authors' calculations based on Worldscope database | Chapter 4 (box 4.1) |

# Glossary

*AREAER*   IMF *Annual Report on Exchange Arrangements and Exchange Restrictions*

**BIS**   Bank for International Settlements

**BIT**   Bilateral investment treaty

**BOP**   Balance of payments

**DTI**   Debt-to-income ratio

**EC**   European Community

**EEC**   European Economic Community

**EMEs**   Emerging market economies

**EU**   European Union

**FDI**   Foreign direct investment

**FTA**   Free trade agreement

**FX**   Foreign exchange/currency

**GDP**   Gross domestic product

**GNP**   Gross national product

**IMF**   International Monetary Fund

**IS**   Investment-saving

**IT**   Inflation-targeting

**IV-2SLS**   Instrumental variable two-stage least squares

**LM**   Liquidity preference-money supply

**LTV**   Loan-to-value ratio

**OECD**   Organisation for Economic Co-operation and Development

**OLS**   Ordinary least squares

**REER**   Real effective exchange rate

**RR**  Reserve requirement

**SME**  Small and medium-size enterprises

**URR**  Unremunerated reserve requirement

**VIX/VXO**  Chicago Board Options Exchange (CBOE) Volatility Index

# References

Abdelal, Rawi. 2006. "Writing the Rules of Global Finance: France, Europe, and Capital Liberalization." *Review of International Political Economy* 13 (1): 1–27.

Abdelal, Rawi. 2007. *Capital Rules*. Cambridge, MA: Harvard University Press.

Abenoja, Zeno. 2003. "Foreign Exchange Market Intervention: A Short Review of Transmission Channels and Practices." *Bangko Sentral Review* 5:1–25.

Acharya, Viral. 2009. "A Theory of Systemic Risk and Design of Prudential Bank Regulation." *Journal of Financial Stability* 5 (3): 224–255.

Acosta-Ormaechea, Santiago, and David Coble. 2011. "Monetary Transmission in Dollarized and Non-Dollarized Economies: The Cases of Chile, New Zealand, Peru and Uruguay." IMF Working Paper WP/11/87. Washington, DC: International Monetary Fund.

Adam, Michal, Witold Koziński, and Janusz Zieliński. 2013. "To What Extent Can Central Banks Influence Exchange Rates with Foreign Exchange Interventions? The Case of Poland." In *Market Volatility and Foreign Exchange Intervention in EMEs: What Has Changed?* BIS Papers No. 273: 279–291.

Adler, Gustavo, Noemie Lisack, and Rui Mano. 2015. "Unveiling the Effects of Foreign Exchange Intervention: A Panel Approach." IMF Working Paper WP/15/130. Washington, DC: International Monetary Fund.

Adler, Gustavo, and Camilo E. Tovar. 2011. "Foreign Exchange Intervention: A Shield against Appreciation Winds?" IMF Working Paper WP/11/165. Washington, DC: International Monetary Fund.

Afanasieff, Tarsila, Fabiana Carvalho, Eduardo de Castro, Rodrigo Coelho, and Jaime Gregório. 2015. "Implementing Loan-to-Value Ratios: The Case of Auto Loans in Brazil (2010–11)." Banco Central Do Brasil Working Paper No. 380. Brasilia: Banco Central Do Brasil.

Ahmed, Shaghil, Stephanie Curcuru, Frank Warnock, and Andrei Zlate. 2015. "The Two Components of International Capital Flows." Mimeo. University of Virginia.

Ahmed, Shaghil, and Andrei Zlate. 2014. "Capital Flows to Emerging Market Economies: A Brave New World?" *Journal of International Money and Finance* 48:221–248.

Aizenman, Joshua, Brian Pinto, and Artur Radziwill. 2007. "Sources for Financing Domestic Capital—Is Foreign Saving a Viable Option for Developing Countries?" *Journal of International Money and Finance* 26 (5): 682–702.

Akerlof, George A., Olivier Blanchard, David Romer, and Joseph E. Stiglitz. 2014. *What Have We Learned? Macroeconomic Policy after the Crisis.* Cambridge, MA: MIT Press.

Akinci, Ozge, and Jane Olmstead-Rumsey. 2015. "How Effective Are Macroprudential Policies? An Empirical Investigation." International Finance Discussion Papers No. 1136. Washington, DC: Federal Reserve Board.

Alesina, Alberto, Vittorio Grilli, and Gian Maria Milesi-Ferretti. 1993. *The Political Economy of Capital Controls.* NBER Working Paper No. 4353. Cambridge, MA: NBER.

Alfaro, Laura, Anusha Chari, and Fabio Kanczuk. 2014. "The Real Effects of Capital Controls: Financial Constraints, Exporters, and Firm Investment." Harvard Business School WP 15–016.

Alfaro, Laura, Sebnem Kalemli-Ozcan, and Vadym Volosovych. 2008. "Why Doesn't Capital Flow from Rich to Poor Countries? An Empirical Investigation." *Review of Economics and Statistics* 90 (2): 347–368.

Alla, Zineddine, Raphael Espinoza, and Atish R. Ghosh. 2015. "A Micro-Founded Model of Intervention in the Foreign Exchange Market." Mimeo. Washington, DC: International Monetary Fund.

Ariyoshi, Akira, Karl Habermeier, Bernard Laurens, Inci Ötker-Robe, Jorge Iván Canales-Kriljenko, and Andrei Kirilenko. 2000. "Capital Controls: Country Experiences with Their Use and Liberalization." IMF Occasional Paper 190. Washington, DC: International Monetary Fund.

Arteta, Carlos, Barry Eichengreen, and Charles Wyplosz. 2001. "When Does Capital Account Liberalization Help More Than It Hurts?" NBER Working Paper No. 8414. Cambridge, MA: NBER.

Artis, Michael, and Mathias Hoffman. 2006. "The Home Bias and Capital Income Flows between Countries and Regions." CEPR Discussion Papers 5691. London: CEPR.

Artis, Michael, and Mathias Hoffman. 2007. "Declining Home Bias and the Increase in International Risk Sharing: Lessons from European Integration." CEPR Discussion Papers 6617. London: CEPR.

Athanasoulis, Stefano, and Eric van Wincoop. 2000. "Growth Uncertainty and Risk Sharing." *Journal of Monetary Economics* 45 (3): 477–505.

Australian Treasury. 1999. "Australia's Experience with the Variable Deposit Requirement." *Economic Roundup*, Winter, 45–56. Available online at http://archive.treasury.gov.au/documents/193/HTML/docshell.asp?URL=round5.asp.

Avdjiev, Stefan, Robert N. McCauley, and Hyun Song Shin. 2015. "Breaking Free of the Triple Coincidence in International Finance." BIS Working Papers No. 524. Basel: Bank for International Settlements.

Baba, Chikako, and Annamaria Kokenyne. 2011. "Effectiveness of Capital Controls in Selected Emerging Markets in the 2000s." IMF Working Paper WP/11/281. Washington, DC: International Monetary Fund.

Bakker, Age, and Bryan Chapple. 2002. "Advanced Country Experiences with Capital Account Liberalization." IMF Occasional Paper 214. Washington, DC: International Monetary Fund.

Balassa, Béla. 1978. "Exports and Economic Growth: Further Evidence." *Journal of Development Economics* 5 (2): 181–189.

Baldwin, Richard. 1988. "Hysteresis in Import Prices: The Beachhead Effect." *American Economic Review* 78 (4): 773–785.

Baldwin, Richard, and Paul Krugman. 1989. "Persistent Trade Effects of Large Exchange Rate Shocks." *Quarterly Journal of Economics* 104 (4): 635–654.

Bank of England. 1967. "The U.K. Exchange Control: A Short History." *Quarterly Bulletin* 7 (3): 245–260.

Barabás, Gyula. 2003. "Coping with the Speculative Attack against the Forint's Band." MNB Background Studies, 2003/3. Budapest: Magyar Nemzeti Bank.

Barro, Robert J. 1991. "Economic Growth in a Cross Section of Countries." *Quarterly Journal of Economics* 106 (2): 407–443.

Barro, Robert J., and David B. Gordon. 1983. "Rules, Discretion and Reputation in a Model of Monetary Policy." *Journal of Monetary Economics* 12 (1): 101–121.

Bazdarich, Michael. 1978. "Optimal Growth and Stages in the Balance of Payments." *Journal of International Economics* 8 (3): 425–443.

Beck, Thorsten, George Clarke, Alberto Groff, Philip Keefer, and Patrick Walsh. 2001. "New Tools in Comparative Political Economy: The Database of Political Institutions." *World Bank Economic Review* 15 (1): 165–176.

Becker, Törbjörn I., Olivier Jeanne, Paolo Mauro, Jonathan D. Ostry, and Romain Ranciere. 2007. "Country Insurance: The Role of Domestic Policies." IMF Occasional Paper No. 254. Washington, DC: International Monetary Fund.

Bekaert, Geert, Campbell Harvey, and Christian Lundblad. 2001. "Emerging Equity Markets and Economic Development." *Journal of Development Economics* 66 (2): 465–504.

Bhagwati, Jagdish. 1998. "The Capital Myth: The Difference between Trade in Widgets and Dollars." *Foreign Affairs* 77 (3): 7–12.

Bianchi, Javier. 2011. "Overborrowing and Systemic Externalities in the Business Cycle." *American Economic Review* 101 (7): 3400–3426.

Binici, Mahir, Michael Hutchison, and M. Schindler. 2010. "Controlling Capital? Legal Restrictions and the Asset Composition of International Financial Flows." *Journal of International Money and Finance* 29 (4): 666–684.

Blanchard, Olivier, Gustavo Adler, and Irineu de Carvalho Filho. 2015. "Can Foreign Exchange Intervention Stem Exchange Rate Pressures from Global Capital Flow Shocks?" IMF Working Paper WP/15/159. Washington, DC: International Monetary Fund.

Blanchard, Olivier, Marcos Chamon, Atish R. Ghosh, and Jonathan D. Ostry. 2015. "Are Capital Inflows Expansionary or Contractionary?" IMF Working Paper WP/15/226. Washington, DC: International Monetary Fund.

Blanchard, Olivier, David Romer, Michael Spence, and Joseph Stiglitz. 2012. *In the Wake of the Crisis: Leading Economists Reassess Economic Policy*. Cambridge, MA: MIT Press.

Bloomfield, Arthur. 1938. "The Foreign Trade Doctrines of the Physiocrats." *American Economic Review* 28 (4): 716–735.

Bloomfield, Arthur. 1950. *Capital Imports and the American Balance of Payments 1934–1939.* Chicago: University of Chicago Press.

Bloomfield, Arthur. 1968. *Patterns of Fluctuation in International Investment before 1914.* Princeton Studies in International Finance, No. 21. Princeton, NJ: International Finance Section, Department of Economics.

Bonfiglioli, Alessandra. 2008. "Financial Integration, Productivity and Capital Accumulation." *Journal of International Economics* 76 (2): 337–355.

Borensztein, Eduardo, José De Gregorio, and Jong-Wha Lee. 1998. "How Does Foreign Direct Investment Affect Economic Growth?" *Journal of International Economics* 45 (1): 115–135.

Borio, Claudio, and Piti Disyatat. 2011. "Global Imbalances and the Financial Crisis: Link or No Link?" BIS Working Papers No. 346. Basel: Bank for International Settlements.

Borio, Claudio, Harold James, and Hyun Song Shin. 2014. "The International Monetary and Financial System: A Capital Account Historical Perspective." BIS Working Papers No. 457. Basel: Bank for International Settlements.

Boughton, James. 2002. "Why White, Not Keynes? Inventing the Post-War International Monetary System." IMF Working Paper WP/02/52. Washington, DC: International Monetary Fund.

Brainard, William. C., 1967. "Uncertainty and the Effectiveness of Policy." *American Economic Review* 57 (2): 411–425.

Brocard, Lucien. 1902. *Les doctrines economiques et sociales du Marquis de Mirabeau dans L'ami des hommes.* Paris: V. Giard et E. Briere.

Broto, Carmen. 2013. "The Effectiveness of Forex Interventions in Four Latin American Countries." *Emerging Markets Review* 17:224–240.

Brown, Brendan. 1987. *The Flight of International Capital: A Contemporary History.* London: Croom Helm.

Brune, Nancy, and Alexandra Guisinger. 2007. "Myth or Reality? The Diffusion of Financial Liberalization in Developing Countries." Yale University MacMillan Center Working Paper. New Haven, CT: Yale University.

Brunnermeier, Markus, José De Gregorio, Barry Eichengreen, Mohamed El-Erian, Armino Fraga, Takatoshi Ito, Philip R. Lane, Jean Pisani-Ferry, Eswar Prasad, Raghuram Rajan, Maria Ramos, Hélène Rey, Dani Rodrik, Kenneth Rogoff, Hyun Song Shin, Andrés Velasco, Beatrice Weder di Mauro, and Yongding Yu. 2012. "Banks and Cross-Border Capital Flows: Policy Challenges and Regulatory Responses." Washington, DC: Brookings Institution.

Bruno, Valentina, Ilhyock Shim, and Hyun Song Shin. 2015. "Comparative Assessment of Macroprudential Policies." BIS Working Papers 502. Basel: Bank for International Settlements.

Bruno, Valentina, and Hyun Song Shin. 2014. "Assessing Macroprudential Policies: Case of South Korea." *Scandinavian Journal of Economics* 116 (1): 128–157.

Bruno, Valentina, and Hyun Song Shin. 2015. "Capital Flows, Cross-Border Banking and Global Liquidity." *Review of Economic Studies* 82 (2): 535–564.

Caballero, Julián. 2016. "Do Surges in International Capital Inflows Influence the Likelihood of Banking Crises?" *Economic Journal* 126 (591): 281–316.

Calderon, Cesar, and Megumi Kubota. 2012. "Gross Inflows Gone Wild: Gross Capital Inflows, Credit Booms, and Crises." World Bank Policy Research Working Paper 6270. Washington, DC: World Bank.

Calvo, Guillermo A., 1988. "Costly Trade Liberalizations: Durable Goods and Capital Mobility." *IMF Staff Papers* 35 (3): 461–473.

Calvo, Guillermo A., Leonardo Leiderman, and Carmen M. Reinhart. 1993. "Capital Inflows and Real Exchange Rate Appreciation in Latin America: The Role of External Factors." *IMF Staff Papers* 40 (1): 108–151.

Camors, Dassatti, and José-Luis Peydró. 2014. "Macroprudential and Monetary Policy: Loan-Level Evidence from Reserve Requirements." Mimeo. Universitat Pompeu Fabra.

Campa, José. 2004. "Exchange Rates and Trade: How Important Is Hysteresis in Trade?" *European Economic Review* 48 (3): 527–548.

Cardarelli, Roberto, Selim Elekdag, and Ayhan Kose. 2009. "Capital Inflows: Macroeconomic Implications and Policy Responses." IMF Working Paper WP/09/40. Washington, DC: International Monetary Fund.

Cardenas, Mauricio. 2007. "Controle de Capitales en Colombia Funcionan o No?" *Debate de Coyuntura Económica*, December. Bogotá, Colombia, Fedesarollo.

Cardenas, Mauricio, and Felipe Barrera. 1997. "On the Effectiveness of Capital Controls: The Experience of Colombia during the 1990s." *Journal of Development Economics* 54 (1): 27–57.

Cardoso, Eliana, and Ilan Goldfajn. 1998. "Capital Flows to Brazil: The Endogeneity of Capital Controls." *IMF Staff Papers* 45 (1): 161–202.

Cardoso, Jaime, and Bernard Laurens. 1998. "Managing Capital Flows: Lessons from the Experience of Chile." IMF Working Paper WP/98/168. Washington, DC: International Monetary Fund.

Carvalho, Bernardo, and Márcio Garcia. 2008. "Ineffective Controls on Capital Inflows under Sophisticated Financial Markets: Brazil in the Nineties." In *Financial Markets Volatility and Performance in Emerging Markets*, edited by S. Edwards and M. Garcia, 29–96. Cambridge, MA: NBER.

Cerra, Valerie, and Sweta Saxena. 2008. "Growth Dynamics: The Myth of Economic Recovery." *American Economic Review* 98 (1): 439–457.

Cerutti, Eugenio, Stijn Claessens, and Luc Laeven. 2015. "The Use and Effectiveness of Macroprudential Policies: New Evidence." IMF Working Paper WP/15/61. Washington, DC: International Monetary Fund.

Chamon, Marcos, and Márcio Garcia. 2016. "Capital Controls in Brazil: Effective?" *Journal of International Money and Finance* 61 (C): 163–187.

Chamon, Marcos, Márcio Garcia, and Laura Souza. 2015. "FX Interventions in Brazil: A Synthetic Control Approach." Discussion Paper No. 630. Department of Economics PUC-Rio, Brazil.

Chamon, Marcos, Atish R. Ghosh, and Jun Il Kim. 2012. "Are All EME Crises Alike?" In *Global Economic Crisis: Impacts, Transmission, and Recovery*, edited by M. Obstfeld, D. Cho, and A. Mason, 228–249. Cheltenham: Edward Elgar Press.

Chinn, Menzie D., and Hiro Ito. 2006. "What Matters for Financial Development? Capital Controls, Institutions, and Interactions." *Journal of Development Economics* 81 (1): 163–192.

Chinn, Menzie D., and Hiro Ito. 2008. "A New Measure of Financial Openness." *Journal of Comparative Policy Analysis* 10 (3): 309–322.

Chuhan, Punam, Stijn Claessens, and Nlandu Mamingi. 1993. "Equity and Bond Flows to Latin America and Asia: The Role of Global and Country Factors." World Bank Policy Research Working Paper 1160. Washington, DC: World Bank.

Chwieroth, Jeffrey. 2010. *Capital Ideas: The IMF and the Rise of Financial Liberalization.* Princeton, NJ: Princeton University Press.

Claessens, Stijn, Swati R. Ghosh, and Roxana Mihet. 2013. "Macroprudential Policies to Mitigate Financial System Vulnerabilities." *Journal of International Money and Finance* 39 (C): 153–185.

Clements, Benedict, and Herman Kamil. 2009. "Are Capital Controls Effective in the 21st Century? The Recent Experience of Colombia." IMF Working Paper WP/09/30. Washington, DC: International Monetary Fund.

Cline, William. 2010. *Financial Globalization, Economic Growth, and the Crisis of 2007–09.* Washington, DC: Peterson Institute for International Economics.

Combes, Jean-Louis, Tidiane Kinda, and Patrick Plane. 2012. "Capital Flows, Exchange Rate Flexibility, and the Real Exchange Rate." *Journal of Macroeconomics* 34 (4): 1034–1043.

Concha, Alvaro, Arturo J. Galindo, and Diego Vasquez. 2011. "An Assessment of Another Decade of Capital Controls in Colombia: 1998–2008." *Quarterly Review of Economics and Finance* 51 (4): 319–338.

Cooper, Richard. 1998. "Should Capital-Account Convertibility Be a World Objective?" In *Should the IMF Pursue Capital-Account Convertibility?* Essays in International Finance No. 207. Princeton NJ: Princeton University.

Cordella, Tito. 2003. "Can Short-Term Capital Controls Promote Capital Inflows? *Journal of International Money and Finance* 22 (5): 737–745.

Cordella, Tito, Pablo Federico, Carlos Vegh, and Guillermo Vuletin. 2014. "Reserve Requirements in the Brave New Macroprudential World." Policy Research Working Paper 6793. Washington, DC: World Bank.

Costinot, Arnaud, Guido Lorenzoni, and Iván Werning. 2011. "A Theory of Capital Controls as Dynamic Terms-of-Trade Manipulation." NBER Working Paper No. 17680. Cambridge, MA: NBER.

Crabbe, Leland. 1989. "The International Gold Standard and U.S. Monetary Policy from World War I to the New Deal." *Federal Reserve Bulletin* 75 (6): 423–440.

Das, Sanghamitra, Mark Roberts, and James Tybout. 2007. "Market Entry Costs, Producer Heterogeneity, and Export Dynamics." *Econometrica* 75 (3): 837–873.

Daude, Christian, Eduardo Levy-Yeyati, and Arne Nagengast. 2014. "On the Effectiveness of Exchange Rate Interventions in Emerging Markets." Working Papers, Center for International Development at Harvard University.

De Gregorio, José, Sebastian Edwards, and Rodrigo O. Valdés. 2000. "Controls on Capital Inflows: Do They Work?" *Journal of Development Economics* 63 (1): 59–83.

De Nicolò, Gianni De, Giovanni Favara, and Lev Ratnovski. 2012. "Externalities and Macroprudential Policy." IMF Staff Discussion Note SDN/12/05. Washington, DC: International Monetary Fund.

Dekle, Robert, Hyeok Jeong, and Heajin Ryoo. 2005. "A Re-Examination of the Exchange Rate Disconnect Puzzle: Evidence from Japanese Firm Level Data." Institute of Economic Policy Research Working Paper 06.46. University of Southern California.

Dell'Ariccia, Giovanni, Julian di Giovanni, André Faria, Ayhan Kose, Paolo Mauro, Jonathan D. Ostry, Martin Schindler, and Marco Terrones. 2008. "Reaping the Benefits of Financial Globalization." IMF Occasional Paper No. 264. Washington, DC: International Monetary Fund.

Dell'Ariccia, Giovanni, Deniz Igan, Luc Laeven, Hui Tong, Bas Bakker, and Jérôme Vandenbussche. 2012. "Policies for Macrofinancial Stability: How to Deal with Credit Booms." IMF Staff Discussion Note SDN/12/06. Washington, DC: International Monetary Fund.

Demirgüç-Kunt, Asli, and Enrica Detragiache. 1998. "Financial Liberalization and Financial Fragility." IMF Working Paper WP/98/83. Washington, DC: International Monetary Fund.

Devereux, Michael, and Gregor Smith. 1994. "International Risk Sharing and Economic Growth." *International Economic Review* 35 (3): 535–550.

Diaz-Alejandro, Carlos. 1985. "Good-Bye Financial Repression, Hello Financial Crash." *Journal of Development Economics* 19 (1–2): 1–24.

Disyatat, Piti, and Gabriele Galati. 2005. "The Effectiveness of Foreign Exchange Intervention in Emerging Market Countries: Evidence from the Czech Koruna." BIS Paper No. 172. Basel: Bank for International Settlements.

Dixit, Avinash. 1989a. "Entry and Exit Decisions under Uncertainty." *Journal of Political Economy* 97 (3): 620–638.

Dixit, Avinash. 1989b. "Hysteresis, Import Penetration, and Exchange Rate Pass-Through." *Quarterly Journal of Economics* 104 (2): 205–228.

Domaç, Ilker, and Alfonso Mendoza. 2004. "Is There Room for Foreign Exchange Interventions under an Inflation Targeting Framework? Evidence from Mexico and Turkey." World Bank Policy Research Working Paper No. 3288. Washington, DC: International Monetary Fund.

Dominguez, Kathryn. 1990. "Market Responses to Coordinated Central Bank Intervention." *Carnegie-Rochester Conference Series on Public Policy* 32:121–163.

Dominguez, Kathryn. 1998. "Central Bank Intervention and Exchange Rate Volatility." *Journal of International Money and Finance* 17 (1): 161–190.

Dominguez, Kathryn, Rasmus Fatum, and Pavel Vacek. 2013. "Do Sales of Foreign Exchange Reserves Lead to Currency Appreciation?" *Journal of Money, Credit and Banking* 45 (5): 867–890.

Dominguez, Kathryn, and Jeffrey Frankel. 1993. "Does Foreign Exchange Intervention Matter? The Portfolio Effect." *American Economic Review* 83 (5): 1356–1369.

Dooley, Michael. 1996. "A Survey of Literature on Controls over International Capital Transactions." *IMF Staff Papers* 43 (4): 639–687.

Dorrance Graeme, and E. Brehmer. 1961. "Controls on Capital Inflow: Recent Experience of Germany and Switzerland." *IMF Staff Papers* 8:427–438.

Edison, Hali, Ross Levine, Luca Ricci, and Torsten Sløk. 2002. "International Financial Integration and Economic Growth." *Journal of International Money and Finance* 21 (6): 749–776.

Edison, Hali, and Carmen M. Reinhart. 2001. "Stopping Hot Money." *Journal of Development Economics* 66 (2): 533–553.

Edwards, Sebastian. 1999. "How Effective Are Capital Controls?" *Journal of Economic Perspectives* 13 (4): 65–84.

Edwards, Sebastian. 2001. "Capital Flows and Economic Performance: Are Emerging Economies Different?" NBER Working Paper No. 8076. Cambridge, MA: NBER.

Edwards, Sebastian. 2005. "Capital Controls, Sudden Stops, and Current Account Reversals." NBER Working Paper No. 11170. Cambridge, MA: NBER.

Edwards, Sebastian, and Roberto Rigobon. 2009. "Capital Controls on Inflows, Exchange Rate Volatility and External Vulnerability." *Journal of International Economics* 78 (2): 256–267.

Eichengreen, Barry. 1992. *Golden Fetters*. New York: Oxford University Press.

Eichengreen, Barry, and Andrew Rose. 2014. "Capital Controls in the 21st Century." CEPR Policy Insight No. 72. London: Centre for Economic Policy Research.

Einzig, Paul. 1934. *Exchange Control*. London: Macmillan.

Einzig, Paul. 1970. *History of Foreign Exchange*. London: Macmillan St Martin's Press.

Elekdag, Selim, and Yiqun Wu. 2013. "Rapid Credit Growth in Emerging Markets: Boon or Boom-Bust?" *Emerging Markets Finance and Trade* 49 (5): 45–62.

Epstein, Gerald, and Juliet Schor. 1992. "Structural Determinants and Economic Effects of Capital Controls in OECD Countries." In *Financial Openness and National Autonomy*, edited by T. Banuri and J. B. Schor, 136–161. Oxford: Clarendon Press.

European Systemic Risk Board. 2014. *The ESRB Handbook on Operationalising Macroprudential Policy in the Banking Sector*. Frankfurt: ESRB.

Falvey, Rod, and Cha Dong Kim. 1992. "Timing and Sequencing Issues in Trade Liberalisation." *Economic Journal* 102 (413): 908–924.

Fanno, Marco. 1939. *Normal and Abnormal International Capital Transfers*. Minneapolis: University of Minnesota Press.

Farhi, Emmanuel, and Iván Werning. 2013. "A Theory of Macroprudential Policies in the Presence of Nominal Rigidities." NBER Working Paper No. 19313. Cambridge, MA: NBER.

Feder, Gershon. 1983. "On Exports and Economic Growth." *Journal of Development Economics* 12 (1–2): 59–73.

Federico, Pablo, Carlos Vegh, and Guillermo Vuletin. 2014. "Reserve Requirement Policy over the Business Cycle." NBER Working Paper No. 20612. Cambridge, MA: NBER.

Feis, Herbert. 1965. *Europe: The World's Banker.* New York: Norton.

Fernández, Andrés, Michael Klein, Alessandro Rebucci, Martin Schindler, and Martín Uribe. 2015. "Capital Control Measures: A New Dataset." NBER Working Paper No. 20970. Cambridge, MA: NBER.

Fernández, Andrés, Alessandro Rebucci, and Martín Uribe. 2015. "Are Capital Controls Countercyclical?" *Journal of Monetary Economics* 76 (November): 1–14.

Fernandez-Arias, Eduardo. 1996. "The New Wave of Private Capital Inflows: Push or Pull?" *Journal of Development Economics* 38 (2): 389–418.

Fernandez-Arias, Eduardo, and Peter Montiel. 1996. "The Surge in Capital Inflows to Developing Countries: An Analytical Overview." *World Bank Economic Review* 10 (1): 51–77.

Fischer, Stanley. 2015. "Macroprudential Policy in the US Economy." Address to the fifty-ninth Economic Conference of the Federal Reserve Bank of Boston, Boston, MA: October 2, 2015. Available online at http://www.federalreserve.gov/newsevents/speech/fischer20151002a.htm#f12.

Fleming, J. Marcus. 1962. "Domestic Financial Policies under Fixed and Floating Exchange Rates." *IMF Staff Papers* 9 (3): 369–379.

Forbes, Kristin J. 2007. "One Cost of the Chilean Capital Controls: Increased Financial Constraints for Smaller Traded Firms." *Journal of International Economics* 71 (2): 294–323.

Forbes, Kristin J., Marcel Fratzscher, Thomas Kostka, and Roland Straub. 2012. "Bubble Thy Neighbor: Portfolio Effects and Externalities from Capital Controls." NBER Working Paper No. 18052. Cambridge, MA: NBER.

Forbes, Kristin J., Marcel Fratzscher, and Roland Straub. 2015. "Capital Flow Management Measures: What Are They Good For?" NBER Working Paper No. 20860. Cambridge, MA: NBER.

Forbes, Kristin J., and Francis E. Warnock. 2012. "Capital Flow Waves: Surges, Stops, Flight and Retrenchment." *Journal of International Economics* 88 (2): 235–251.

Frankel, Jeffrey, and David Romer. 1999. "Does Trade Cause Growth?" *American Economic Review* 89 (3): 379–399.

Frankel, Jeffrey, and Andrew Rose. 1996. "Currency Crashes in Emerging Markets: An Empirical Treatment." *Journal of International Economics* 41(3/4): 351–366.

Fratzscher, Marcel. 2011. "Capital Flows, Push versus Pull Factors and the Global Financial Crisis." NBER Working Paper No. 17357. Cambridge, MA: NBER.

Freedman, Charles, and Inci Ötker-Robe. 2010. "Important Elements for Inflation Targeting for Emerging Economies." IMF Working Paper WP/10/113. Washington, DC: International Monetary Fund.

Friedman, Milton. 1953. *Essays in Positive Economics*. Chicago: University of Chicago Press.

Furceri, Davide, Stéphanie Guichard, and Elena Rusticelli. 2012a. "The Effect of Episodes of Large Capital Inflows on Domestic Credit." *North American Journal of Economics and Finance* 23 (3): 325–344.

Furceri, Davide, Stéphanie Guichard, and Elena Rusticelli. 2012b. "Episodes of Large Capital Inflows, Banking and Currency Crises, and Sudden Stops." *International Finance* 15 (1): 1–35.

Galati, Gabriele, and Richhild Moessner. 2012. "Macroprudential Policy—A Literature Review." *Journal of Economic Surveys* 27 (5): 846–878.

Gallagher, Kevin. 2010. "Policy Space to Prevent and Mitigate Financial Crises in Trade and Investment Agreements." G-24 Discussion Paper Series No. 58. Geneva: United Nations Conference on Trade and Development.

Gallagher, Kevin. 2013. "Safeguarding United States' Trade and Investment Treaties for Financial Stability." Global Economic Governance Initiative Policy Brief Issue 1. Boston: Boston University.

Gallagher, Kevin. 2014. *Capital Rules: Emerging Markets and the Regulation of Cross border Capital*. Ithaca: Cornell University Press.

Gallego, Francisco, Leonardo Hernández, and Klaus Schmidt-Hebbel. 1999. "Capital Controls in Chile: Effective? Efficient?" Central Bank of Chile Working Paper No. 59. Santiago: Banco Central de Chile.

Gersl, Adam, and Tomas Holub. 2006. "Foreign Exchange Interventions under Inflation Targeting: The Czech Experience." *Contemporary Economic Policy* 24 (4): 475–491.

Gertler, Mark, and Kenneth Rogoff. 1990. "North-South Lending and Endogenous Capital Market Inefficiencies." *Journal of Monetary Economics* 26 (2): 245–266.

Ghosh, Atish R. 1991. "Strategic Aspects of Public Finance in a World with High Capital Mobility." *Journal of International Economics* 30 (3–4): 229–247.

Ghosh, Atish R. 1992. "Is It Signaling? Exchange Intervention and the Dollar-Deutschemark Rate." *Journal of International Economics* 32 (3–4): 201–220.

Ghosh, Atish R. 1995. "International Capital Mobility amongst the Major Industrialised Countries: Too Little or Too Much?" *Economic Journal* 105 (428): 107–128.

Ghosh, Atish R. 2002. "Central Bank Secrecy in the Foreign Exchange Market." *European Economic Review* 46 (2): 253–272.

Ghosh, Atish R., and Jun Il Kim. 2008. "Export Subsidies, Undervalued Exchange Rates, and Consumption Taxes—Some Equivalence Results of Relevance to Bretton Woods II." Mimeo. Washington, DC: International Monetary Fund.

Ghosh, Atish R., and Paul R. Masson. 1994. *Economic Cooperation in an Uncertain World*. Oxford: Blackwell Press.

Ghosh, Atish R., and Jonathan D. Ostry. 1995. "The Current Account in Developing Countries: A Perspective from the Consumption-Smoothing Approach." *World Bank Economic Review* 9 (2): 305–333.

Ghosh, Atish R., Jonathan D. Ostry, and Marcos Chamon. 2016. "Two Targets, Two Instruments: Monetary and Exchange Rate Policies in Emerging Market Economies." *Journal of International Money and Finance* 60:172–196.

Ghosh, Atish R., Jonathan D. Ostry, and Mahvash S. Qureshi. 2015. "Exchange Rate Management and Crisis Susceptibility: A Reassessment." *IMF Economic Review* 63 (1): 238–276.

Ghosh, Atish R., Jonathan D. Ostry, and Mahvash S. Qureshi. 2017. "Managing the Tide: How Do Emerging Markets. Respond to Capital Flows?" IMF Working Paper WP/17/69. Washington DC: International Monetary Fund.

Ghosh, Atish R., and Mahvash S. Qureshi. 2016. "What's in a Name? That Which We Call Capital Controls." IMF Working Paper WP/16/25. Washington, DC: International Monetary Fund.

Ghosh, Atish R., Mahvash S. Qureshi, Jun Il Kim, and Juan Zalduendo. 2014. "Surges." *Journal of International Economics* 92 (2): 266–285.

Ghosh, Atish R., Mahvash S. Qureshi, and Naotaka Sugawara. 2014. "Regulating Capital Flows at Both Ends: Does It Work?" IMF Working Paper WP/14/188. Washington, DC: International Monetary Fund.

Glick, Reuven, Xueyan Guo, and Michael Hutchison. 2006. "Currency Crises, Capital Account Liberalization and Selection Bias." *Review of Economics and Statistics* 88 (2): 698–714.

Glocker, Christian, and Pascal Towbin. 2012. "The Macroeconomic Effects of Reserve Requirements." Banque de France Working Paper No. 374. Paris: Banque de France.

Goh, Soo Khoon. 2005. "New Empirical Evidence on the Effects of Capital Controls on Composition of Capital Flows in Malaysia." *Applied Economics* 37 (13): 1491–1503.

Goode, Richard, and Richard S. Thorn. 1959. "Variable Reserve Requirements against Commercial Bank Deposits." *IMF Staff Papers* 7 (1): 9–45.

Goodhart, Charles. 2008. "The Boundary Problem in Financial Regulation." *National Institute Economic Review* 206 (1): 48–55.

Goodhart, Charles, Anil Kashyap, Dimitrios Tsomocos, and Alexandros Vardoulakis. 2012. "Financial Regulation in General Equilibrium." NBER Working Paper No. 17909. Cambridge, MA: NBER.

Gordon, Roger, and A. Lans Bovenberg. 1996. "Why Is Capital So Immobile Internationally? Possible Explanations and Implications for Capital Income Taxation." *American Economic Review* 86 (5): 1057–1075.

Gourinchas, Pierre-Olivier, and Olivier Jeanne. 2006. "The Elusive Gains from International Financial Integration." *Review of Economic Studies* 73 (3): 715–741.

Gourinchas, Pierre-Olivier, and Maurice Obstfeld. 2012. "Stories of the Twentieth Century for the Twenty-First." *American Economic Journal: Macroeconomics* 4 (1): 226–265.

Greenspan, Alan. 2002. "Economic Volatility." Remarks at the Federal Reserve Bank of Kansas City Annual Conference; Jackson Hole, Wyoming; August 30, 2002. Available online at http://www.federalreserve.gov/boarddocs/speeches/2002/20020830/.

Grilli, Vittorio, and Gian Maria Milesi-Ferretti. 1995. "Economic Effects and Structural Determinants of Capital Controls." *IMF Staff Papers* 42 (3): 517–551.

Gronn, Adun, and Maria Wallin Fredholm. 2013. "Baltic and Icelandic Experiences of Capital Flows and Capital Flow Measures." IMF Working Paper WP/13/242. Washington, DC: International Monetary Fund.

Grubel, Herbert G., 1968. "Internationally Diversified Portfolios: Welfare Gains and Capital Flows." *American Economic Review* 58 (5): 1299–1314.

Guimarães, Roberto F., and Cem Karacadag. 2004. "The Empirics of Foreign Exchange Intervention in Emerging Market Countries: The Cases of Mexico and Turkey." IMF Working Paper WP/04/123. Washington, DC: International Monetary Fund.

Guinigundo, Diwa. 2013. "A Note on the Effectiveness of Intervention in the Foreign Exchange Market: The Case of the Philippines." In *Market Volatility and Foreign Exchange Intervention in EMEs: What Has Changed?* BIS Papers No. 273: 263–277.

Gupta, Poonam, Deepak Mishra, and Ratna Sahay. 2007. "Behavior of Output during Currency Crises." *Journal of International Economics* 72 (2): 428–50.

Hahm, Joon-Ho, Frederic Mishkin, Hyun Shin, and Kwanho Shin. 2012. "Macroprudential Policies in Open Emerging Economies." NBER Working Paper No. 17780. Cambridge, MA: NBER.

Hanson, Samuel, Anil Kashyap, and Jeremy Stein. 2011. "A Macroprudential Approach to Financial Regulation." *Journal of Economic Perspectives* 25 (1): 3–28.

Harrison, Anne, Inessa Love, and Margaret McMillian. 2004. "Global Capital Flows and Financing Constraints." *Journal of Development Economics* 75 (1): 269–301.

Helleiner, Eric. 1994. *States and the Re-emergence of International Finance: From Bretton Woods to the 1990s.* Ithaca, NY: Cornell University Press.

Helleiner, Eric. 2015. "Controlling Capital Flows 'At Both Ends': A Neglected (But Newly Relevant) Keynesian Innovation from Bretton Woods." *Challenge* 58 (5): 413–427.

Henry, Peter. 2007. "Capital Account Liberalization: Theory, Evidence, and Speculation." *Journal of Economic Literature* 45 (4): 887–935.

Herrmann, Sabine, and Dubravko Mihaljek. 2010. "The Determinants of Cross-Border Bank Flows to Emerging Markets: New Empirical Evidence on the Spread of Financial Crises." BIS Working Paper No. 315. Basel: Bank for International Settlements.

Hobson, Charles K. 1914. *The Export of Capital.* London: Constable & Co.

Hooper, Peter, Karen Johnson, and Jaime Marquez. 1998. "Trade Elasticities for G-7 Countries." International Finance Discussion Papers No. 609. Washington, DC: Federal Reserve Board.

Horsefield, J. Keith. 1969. *The International Monetary Fund, 1945–1965, Volume I: Chronicle.* Washington, DC: International Monetary Fund.

Igan, Deniz, and Heedon Kang. 2011. "Do Loan-to-Value and Debt-to-Income Limits Work? Evidence from Korea." IMF Working Paper WP/11/297. Washington, DC: International Monetary Fund.

International Monetary Fund. 2005a. "Aide-Memoire: IMF Staff Visit to the Republic of Latvia, November 30–December 2, 2005." Washington, DC: International Monetary Fund. Available online at https://www.imf.org/external/np/ms/2005/120205a.htm.

International Monetary Fund. 2005b. "Evaluation Report: The IMF's Approach to Capital Account Liberalization." Washington, DC: International Monetary Fund.

International Monetary Fund. 2010a. "The Fund's Mandate—The Legal Framework." Washington, DC: International Monetary Fund.

International Monetary Fund. 2010b. "The Fund's Role Regarding Cross-Border Capital Flows." Washington, DC: International Monetary Fund.

International Monetary Fund. 2011a. "Assessing Reserve Adequacy." Available online at https://www.imf.org/external/np/pp/eng/2011/021411b.pdf.

International Monetary Fund. 2011b. "The Multilateral Aspects of Policies Affecting Capital Flows." Washington, DC: International Monetary Fund.

International Monetary Fund. 2011c. "Recent Themes in Managing Capital Inflows—Cross-Cutting Themes and Possible Guidelines." Washington, DC: International Monetary Fund.

International Monetary Fund. 2011d. "Recent Themes in Managing Capital Inflows—Cross-Cutting Themes and Possible Guidelines—Supplementary Information." Washington, DC: International Monetary Fund.

International Monetary Fund. 2012a. "The Liberalization and Management of Capital Flows: An Institutional View." Washington, DC: International Monetary Fund.

International Monetary Fund. 2012b. "Liberalizing Capital Flows and Managing Capital Outflows." Washington, DC: International Monetary Fund.

International Monetary Fund. 2013a. "Assessing Reserve Adequacy—Further Considerations." Available online at http://www.imf.org/external/np/sec/pr/2014/pr1496.htm.

International Monetary Fund. 2013b. "Key Aspects of Macroprudential Policy." Washington DC: International Monetary Fund.

International Monetary Fund. 2014. "Assessing Reserve Adequacy—Specific Proposals." Washington, DC: International Monetary Fund.

International Monetary Fund. 2015. "Monetary Policy and Financial Stability." Washington, DC: International Monetary Fund.

Ishii, Shogo, and Karl Habermeier. 2002. "Capital Account Liberalization and Financial Sector Stability." IMF Occasional Paper 211. Washington, DC: International Monetary Fund.

Jankov, Ljubinko. 2009. "Spillovers of the Crisis: How Different Is Croatia?" In Proceedings of OeNB Workshops No. 15, edited by P. Mooslechner and E. Gnan, 126–134. Vienna: Oesterreichische Nationalbank.

Jeanne, Olivier, and Anton Korinek. 2010. "Excessive Volatility in Capital Flows: A Pigouvian Taxation Approach." *American Economic Review* 100 (2): 403–407.

Jeanne, Olivier, Arvind Subramanian, and John Williamson. 2012. *Who Needs to Open the Capital Account?* Washington, DC: Peterson Institute for International Economics.

Johnson, Elizabeth, and Donald Moggridge. 1980. *Collected Writings of John Maynard Keynes.* Vol. XXV. Cambridge: Cambridge University Press.

Johnston, R. Barry, Salim M. Darbar, and Claudia Echeverria. 1997. "Sequencing Capital Account Liberalization: Lessons from the Experiences in Chile, Indonesia, Korea, and Thailand." IMF Working Paper WP/97/157. Washington, DC: International Monetary Fund.

Johnston, R. Barry, and Natalia Tamirisa. 1998. "Why Do Countries Use Capital Controls?" IMF Working Paper WP/98/181. Washington, DC: International Monetary Fund.

Judson, Ruth, and Ann Owen. 1999. "Estimating Dynamic Panel Data Models: A Guide for macroeconomists." *Economic Letters* 65 (1): 9–15.

Kamil, Herman. 2008. "Is Central Bank Intervention Effective Under Inflation Targeting Regimes? The Case of Colombia." IMF Working Paper WP/08/88. Washington, DC: International Monetary Fund.

Kaminsky, Graciela L., and Karen Lewis. 1996. "Does Foreign Exchange Intervention Signal Future Monetary Policy?" *Journal of Monetary Economics* 37 (2): 285–312.

Kaminsky, Graciela L., Richard Lyons, and Sergio Schmukler. 2001. "Mutual Fund Investment in Emerging Markets: An Overview." Policy Research Paper 2529. Washington, DC: World Bank.

Kaminsky, Graciela L., and Carmen M. Reinhart. 1999. "The Twin Crises: The Causes of Banking and Balance-of-Payments Problems." *American Economic Review* 89 (3): 473–500.

Kaminsky, Graciela L., and Sergio L. Schmukler. 2008. "Short-Run Pain, Long-Run Gain: Financial Liberalization and Stock Market Cycles." *Review of Finance* 12 (2): 253–292.

Keynes, John M. 1930. "Economic Possibilities for our Grandchildren." *The Nation and Athenaeum* 48 (3): 96–98.

Keynes, John M. 1936. *The General Theory of Employment, Interest and Money.* New York: Harcourt Brace and Co.

Kim, Choongsoo. 2013. "Macroprudential Policies: Korea's Experiences." Paper presented at the Rethinking Macro Policy II Conference: First Steps and Early Lessons, April 16–17, 2015. Washington, DC.

Klein, Michael. 2012. "Capital Controls: Gates versus Walls." *Brookings Papers on Economic Activity* 45 (2): 317–367.

Klein, Michael, and Giovanni Olivei. 2008. "Capital Account Liberalization, Financial Depth, and Economic Growth." *Journal of International Money and Finance* 27 (6): 861–875.

Korinek, Anton. 2011. "The New Economics of Prudential Capital Controls." *IMF Economic Review* 59 (3): 523–561.

Kose, Ayhan, Eswar Prasad, Kenneth Rogoff, and Shang-Jin Wei. 2009. "Financial Globalization: A Reappraisal." *IMF Staff Papers* 56 (1): 8–62.

Kose, Ayhan, Eswar Prasad, Ashley Taylor. 2010. "Thresholds in the Process of International Financial Integration." *Journal of International Money and Finance* 30 (1): 147–179.

Kose, Ayhan, Eswar Prasad, and Marco Terrones. 2009. "Does Financial Globalization Promote Risk Sharing?" *Journal of Development Economics* 89 (2): 258–270.

Kraft, Evan, and Tomislav Galac. 2011. "Macroprudential Regulation of Credit Booms and Busts–The Case of Croatia." World Bank Policy Research Working Paper No. 5772. Washington, DC: International Monetary Fund.

Kuttner, Kenneth, and Ilhyock Shim. 2013. "Can Non-Interest Rate Policies Stabilise Housing Markets? Evidence from a Panel of 57 Economies." BIS Working Paper No. 433. Basel: Bank for International Settlements.

Laeven, Luc, and Fabián Valencia. 2013. "Systemic Banking Crises Database. *IMF Economic Review* 61 (2): 225–270.

Lahura, Erick, and Marco Vega. 2013. "Asymmetric Effects of FOREX Intervention Using Intraday Data: Evidence from Peru." BIS Working Papers No. 430. Basel: Bank for International Settlements.

Lambert, Frederic, Julia Ramos-Tallada, and Cyril Rebillard. 2011. "Capital Controls and Spillover Effects: Evidence from Latin American Countries." Banque de France Working Paper No. 357. Paris: Banque de France.

Lane, Philip, and Gian Maria Milesi-Ferretti. 2001. "The External Wealth of Nations: Measures of Foreign Assets and Liabilities for Industrial and Developing Countries." *Journal of International Economics* 55 (2): 263–294.

Larraín, Felipe, Raúl Laban, and Rómulo Chumacero. 1997. "What Determines Capital Inflows? An Empirical Analysis for Chile." John F. Kennedy School of Government Faculty Research Working Paper Series R97–09. Cambridge, MA: Harvard University.

Le Fort, Guillermo, and Carlos Budnevich. 1997. "Capital Account Regulations and Macroeconomic Policy: Two Latin Experiences." Central Bank of Chile WP 06, Santiago.

League of Nations. 1932. *World Economic Survey, 1932.* Geneva: League of Nations.

League of Nations. 1938. *Report on Exchange Control.* Geneva: League of Nations.

League of Nations. 1944. *International Currency Experience: Lessons from the Interwar Period.* Princeton, NJ: Princeton University Press.

Lee, Jaewoo, Gian-Maria Milesi-Ferretti, Jonathan D. Ostry, Alessandro Prati, and Luca A. Ricci. 2008. "Exchange Rate Assessments: CGER Methodologies." IMF Occasional Paper 261. Washington, DC: International Monetary Fund.

Lee, Jong Kyu. 2013. "The Operation of Macroprudential Policy Measures: The Case of Korea in the 2000s." BOK Working Paper No. 2013–1. Seoul: Bank of Korea.

Leiderman, Leonardo, Rodolfo Maino, and Eric Parrado. 2006. "Inflation Targeting in Dollarized Economies." IMF Working Paper WP/06/157. Washington, DC: International Monetary Fund.

Levine, Ross. 2001. "International Financial Liberalization and Economic Growth." *Review of International Economics* 9 (4): 688–702.

Lim, Cheng Hoon, Francesco Columba, Alejo Costa, Piyabha Kongsamut, Akira Otani, Mustafa Saiyid, Torsten Wezel, and Xiaoyong Wu. 2011. "Macroprudential Policy: What Instruments and How to Use Them? Lessons from Country Experiences." IMF Working Paper WP/11/238. Washington, DC: International Monetary Fund.

Lipton, David, and Jeffrey Sachs. 1983. "Accumulation and Growth in a Two-Country Model: A Simulation Approach." *Journal of International Economics* 15 (1–2): 135–159.

Lucas, Robert. 1990. "Why Doesn't Capital Flow from Rich to Poor Countries?" *American Economic Review Papers and Proceedings* 80 (2): 92–96.

Magud, Nicolas, and Carmen M. Reinhart. 2007. "Capital Controls: An Evaluation." NBER Chapters, in *Capital Controls and Capital Flows in Emerging Economies: Policies, Practices and Consequences*, 645–674. Cambridge, MA: NBER.

Mandeng, Ousmène. 2003. "Central Bank Foreign Exchange Market Intervention and Option Contract Specification: The Case of Colombia." IMF Working Paper WP/03/135. Washington, DC: International Monetary Fund.

Masson, Paul R., Miguel A. Savastano, and Sunil Sharma. 1997. "The Scope for Inflation Targeting in Developing Countries." IMF Working Paper WP/97/130. Washington, DC: International Monetary Fund.

McGuire, Patrick, and Goetz von Peter. 2012. "The Dollar Shortage in Global Banking and the International Policy Response." *International Finance* 15 (2): 155–178.

McKinnon, Ronald I. 1973. *Money and Capital in Economic Development*. Washington, DC: Brookings Institution.

McKinnon, Ronald I., and Huw Pill. 1997. "Credible Economic Liberalizations and Overborrowing." *American Economic Review Papers and Proceedings* 87 (2): 189–193.

Meade, James. 1951. *The Balance of Payments*. London: Oxford University Press.

Mendoza, Enrique. 2002. "Credit, Prices, and Crashes: Business Cycles with a Sudden Stop." In *Preventing Currency Crises in Emerging Markets*, edited by S. Edwards and J. A. Frankel, 335–392. Chicago: University of Chicago Press.

Mendoza, Enrique, and Marco Terrones. 2012. "An Anatomy of Credits Booms and Their Demise." NBER Working Paper WP1837. Cambridge, MA: NBER.

Mihaljek, Dubravko. 2005. "Survey of Central Banks' Views on Effects of Intervention." BIS Papers No. 24; 82–96. Brussels: Bank for International Settlement.

Milesi-Ferretti, Gian Maria, and Cédric Tille. 2011. "The Great Retrenchment: International Capital Flows During the Global Financial Crisis." *Economic Policy* 26 (66): 285–342.

Mills, J. Saxon. 1922. *The Genoa Conference*. London: Hutchinson & Co.

Mishkin, Frederic. 2000. "Inflation-Targeting in Emerging Market Countries." NBER Working Paper No. 7618. Cambridge, MA: NBER.

Mishkin, Frederic. 2008. "How Should We Respond to Asset Price Bubbles?" Remarks at the Wharton Financial Institutions Center and Oliver Wyman Institute's Annual Financial Risk Roundtable; Philadelphia; May 15, 2008. Available online at http://www.federal reserve.gov/newsevents/speech/mishkin20080515a.htm.

Mishkin, Frederic, and Miguel A. Savastano. 2001. "Monetary Policy Strategies for Latin America." *Journal of Development Economics* 66 (2): 415–444.

Mitchell, Brian. 2013. *International Historical Statistics 1750–2010*. Basingstoke: Palgrave Macmillan.

Mohanty, Madhusudan, and Bat-el Berger. 2013. "Central Bank Views on Foreign Exchange Intervention." BIS Papers No. 73; 55–74. Brussels: Bank for International Settlement.

Montiel, Peter, and Carmen Reinhart. 1999. "Do Capital Controls and Macroeconomic Policies Influence the Volume and Composition of Capital Flows? Evidence from the 1990's." *Journal of International Money and Finance* 18 (4): 619–635.

Mundell, Robert. A. 1963. "Capital Mobility and Stabilization Policy under Fixed and Flexible Exchange Rates." *Canadian Journal of Economic and Political Science* 29 (4): 475–485.

Nordstrom, Anna, Scott Roger, Mark R. Stone, Seiichi Shimizu, Turgut Kisinbay, and Jorge Restrepo. 2009. "The Role of the Exchange Rate in Inflation-Targeting Emerging Economies." IMF Occasional Paper 267. Washington, DC: International Monetary Fund.

Obstfeld, Maurice. 1995. "Risk-Taking, Global Diversification, and Growth." *American Economic Review* 84 (5): 1310–1329.

Obstfeld, Maurice. 2010. "Expanding Gross Asset Positions and the International Monetary System." Remarks at the Federal Reserve Bank of Kansas City symposium on "Macroeconomic Challenges: The Decade Ahead"; Jackson Hole, Wyoming; August 26–28, 2010.

Obstfeld, Maurice. 2012. "Does the Current Account Still Matter?" *American Economic Review Papers and Proceedings* 102 (3): 1–23.

Ostry, Jonathan D., Atish R. Ghosh, Marcos Chamon, and Mahvash S. Qureshi. 2011. "Capital Controls: When and Why?" *IMF Economic Review* 59 (3): 562–580.

Ostry, Jonathan D., Atish R. Ghosh, Marcos Chamon, and Mahvash S. Qureshi. 2012. "Tools for Managing Financial-Stability Risks from Capital Inflows." *Journal of International Economics* 88 (2): 407–421.

Ostry, Jonathan D., Atish R. Ghosh, Karl Habermeier, Marcos Chamon, Mahvash S. Qureshi, Luc Laeven, and Annamaria Kokenyne. 2011. "Managing Capital Inflows: What Tools to Use?" IMF Staff Discussion Note 11/06. Washington, DC: International Monetary Fund.

Ostry, Jonathan D., Atish R. Ghosh, Karl Habermeier, Marcos Chamon, Mahvash S. Qureshi, and Dennis B. S. Reinhardt. 2010. "Capital Inflows: The Role of Controls." IMF Staff Position Note 10/04. Washington, DC: International Monetary Fund.

Papaioannou, Elias. 2009. "What Drives International Financial Flows? Politics, Institutions and Other Determinants." *Journal of Development Economics* 88 (2): 269–281.

Pattanaik, Sitikantha, and Satyananda Sahoo. 2003. "The Effectiveness of Intervention in India: An Empirical Assessment." Reserve Bank of India Occasional Papers, Vol. 22.

Pérez-Forero, Fernando, and Marco Vega. 2014. "The Dynamic Effects of Interest Rates and Reserve Requirements." Banco Central de Reserva del Perú Working Paper 2014–018. Lima: Banco Central de Reserva del Perú.

Phillips, Steven, Luis Catão, Luca Ricci, Rudolfs Bems, Mitali Das, Julian Di Giovanni, D. Filiz Unsal, Marola Castillo, Jungjin Lee, Jair Rodriguez, and Mauricio Vargas. 2013. "The External Balance Assessment (EBA) Methodology." IMF Working Paper WP/13/272. Washington, DC: International Monetary Fund.

Prasad, Eswar, Raghuram Rajan, and Arvind Subramanian. 2007. "Foreign Capital and Economic Growth." *Brookings Papers on Economic Activity* 38 (2007–1): 153–230.

Prasad, Eswar, Kenneth Rogoff, Shang-Jin Wei, and Ayhan Kose. 2003. "Effects on Financial Globalization on Developing Countries: Some Empirical Evidence." IMF Occasional Paper 220. Washington, DC: International Monetary Fund.

Quinn, Dennis P. 1997. "The Correlates of Change in International Financial Regulation." *American Political Science Review* 91:531–551.

Quinn, Dennis P., and A. Maria Toyoda. 2008. "Does Capital Account Liberalization Lead to Economic Growth?" *Review of Financial Studies* 21 (3): 1403–1449.

Ranciere, Romain, Aaron Tornell, and Athanasio Vamvakidis. 2010. "Currency Mismatch and Systemic Risk in Eastern Europe." *Economic Policy* 84 (1): 599–658.

Ranciere, Romain, Aaron Tornell, and Frank Westermann. 2006. "Decomposing the Effects of Financial Liberalization: Crises vs. Growth." *Journal of Banking and Finance* 30 (12): 3331–3348.

Razin, Assaf, Efraim Sadka, and Chi-Wa Yuen. 1998. "A Pecking Order of Capital Inflows and International Tax Principles." *Journal of International Economics* 44 (1): 45–68.

Razin, Assaf, Efraim Sadka, and Chi-Wa Yuen. 2000. "Do Debt Flows Crowd Out Equity Flows or the Other Way Round?" *Annals of Economics and Finance* 1 (1): 33–47.

Ree, Jack, Kyoungsoo Yoon, and Hail Park. 2012. "FX Funding Risks and Exchange Rate Volatility–Korea's Case." IMF Working Paper WP/12/268. Washington, DC: International Monetary Fund.

Reinhardt, Dennis, and Salvatore Dell'Erba. 2013. "Not All Capital Waves Are Alike: A Sector-Level Examination of Surges in FDI Inflows." Bank of England Working Paper 474.

Reinhardt, Dennis, and Rhiannon Sowerbutts. 2015. "Regulatory Arbitrage in Action: Evidence from Cross-Border Lending." Available online at http://www.voxeu.org /article/regulatory-arbitrage-action-evidence-cross-border-lending.

Reinhart, Carmen M., and Vincent R. Reinhart. 2008. "Capital Flow Bonanzas: An Encompassing View of the Past and Present." NBER Working Paper No. 14321. Cambridge, MA: NBER.

Reinhart, Carmen M., and Kenneth Rogoff. 2009. "The Aftermath of Financial Crises." *American Economic Review* 99 (2): 466–472.

Reinhart, Carmen M., and R. Todd Smith. 1998. "Too Much of a Good Thing: The Macroeconomic Effects of Taxing Capital Inflows." In *Managing Capital Flows and Exchange Rates: Perspectives from the Pacific Basin*, edited by R. Glick, 436–464. Cambridge: Cambridge University Press.

Reinhart, Carmen M., and R. Todd Smith. 2002. "Temporary Controls on Capital Inflows." *Journal of International Economics* 57 (2): 327–351.

Rey, Hélène. 2013. "Dilemma not Trilemma: The Global Financial Cycle and Monetary Policy Independence." Paper presented at the Jackson Hole Symposium; Jackson Hole, Wyoming, August 24, 2013. Available online at http://www.kansascityfed.org/publicat /sympos/2013/2013Rey.pdf.

Rhee, Yung, and C.-Y. Song. 1999. "Exchange Rate Policy and Effectiveness of Intervention: The Case of South Korea." In *Exchange Rate Policies in Emerging Asian Countries*, edited by S. Collignon, Yung C. Park, and Jean Pisani-Ferry, 66–99. London: Routledge.

Rincón, Hernan, and Jorge Toro. 2010. "Are Capital Controls and Central Bank Intervention Effective?" Banco de la República Working Paper No. 625. Bogota: Banco de la República.

Rodrik, Dani. 1987. "Trade and Capital-Account Liberalization in a Keynesian Economy." *Journal of International Economics* 23 (1–2): 113–129.

Rodrik, Dani. 1998. "Who Needs Capital-Account Convertibility?" In *Should the IMF Pursue Capital-Account Convertibility*. Essays in International Finance No. 207. Princeton NJ: Princeton University.

Rodrik, Dani. 2008. "The Real Exchange Rate and Growth." *Brookings Papers on Economic Activity* 39 (2): 365–439.

Rodrik, Dani, and Arvind Subramanian. 2009. "Why Did Financial Globalization Disappoint?" *IMF Staff Papers* 56 (1): 112–138.

Rogoff, Kenneth. 1985. "Can International Policy Coordination Be Counterproductive?" *Journal of International Economics* 18 (3–4): 199–217.

Sachs, Jeffrey. 1981. "The Current Account in the Macroeconomic Adjustment Process." NBER Working Paper No. 796. Cambridge, MA: NBER.

Saizar, Ana, and Nigel Chalk. 2008. "Is Monetary Policy Effective When Credit Is Low?" IMF Working Paper WP/08/288. Washington, DC: International Monetary Fund.

Sangmanee, Amporn. 2001. "Central Bank Intervention and Market Expectations of Exchange Rate Regime Shift: The Case of the Thai Baht at the Onset of the Asian Crisis." Mimeo. Basel: Bank for International Settlements.

Schindler, Martin. 2009. "Measuring Financial Integration: A New Data Set." *IMF Staff Papers* 56 (1): 222–238.

Schuknecht, Ludger. 1999. "A Simple Trade Policy Perspective on Capital Controls." *Finance and Development*. Washington, DC: International Monetary Fund.

Schularick, Moritz, and Alan M. Taylor. 2012. "Credit Booms Gone Bust: Monetary Policy, Leverage Cycles, and Financial Crises, 1870–2008." *American Economic Review* 102 (2): 1029–1061.

Shin, Hyun Song. 2010. "Non-Core Liabilities Tax as a Tool for Prudential Regulation." Mimeo. Princeton University. Available online at http://www.princeton.edu/~hsshin/www/NonCoreLiabilitiesTax.pdf.

Shin, Hyun Song. 2013. "Adapting Macroprudential Approaches to Emerging and Developing Economies." In *Dealing with the Challenges of Macro Financial Linkages in Emerging Markets*, edited by O. Canuto and S. Ghosh, 17–55. Washington, DC: World Bank.

Simon, Matthew. 1968. "The Pattern of New British Portfolio Foreign Investment, 1865–1914." In *The Export of Capital from Britain, 1970–1914*, edited by A. R. Hall, 15–44. London: Methuen & Co.

Solomon, Robert. 1982. *The International Monetary System, 1945–1981*. New York: Harper & Row.

Solow, Robert. 1957. "Technical Change and the Aggregate Production Function." *Review of Economics and Statistics* 39 (3): 312–320.

Staley, Eugene. 1935. *War and the Private Investor*. New York: Double, Doran & Co.

Steil, Benn. 2013. *The Battle of Bretton Woods: John Maynard Keynes, Harry Dexter White, and the Making of a New World Order*. Princeton, NJ: Princeton University Press.

Stiglitz, Joseph. 2000. "Capital Market Liberalization, Economic Growth, and Instability." *World Development* 28 (6): 1075–1086.

Stockman, Alan, and Alejandro Hernández D. 1988. "Exchange Controls, Capital Controls, and International Financial Markets." *American Economic Review* 78 (3): 362–374.

Stone, Mark, W. Christopher Walker, and Yosuke Yasui. 2009. "From Lombard Street to Avenida Paulista: Foreign Exchange Liquidity Easing in Brazil in Response to the Global Shock of 2008–09." IMF Working Paper WP/09/259. Washington, DC: International Monetary Fund.

Summers, Lawrence H. 1998. "Building an International Financial Architecture for the 21st Century." Remarks at the Cato Institute, sixteenth Annual Monetary Conference; Washington, DC; October 22, 1998.

Svensson, Lars. 2015. "Cost-Benefit Analysis of Leaning against the Wind." Presentation delivered at the AQR Institute of Asset Management event "Perspectives: Unprecedented Monetary Policy Intervention." London Business School; London; June 25, 2015. Available online at http://larseosvensson.se/2015/06/25/cost-benefit-analysis-of-leaning -against-the-wind-2/.

Tamirisa, Natalia. 2004. "Do Macroeconomic Effects of Capital Controls Vary by Their Type? Evidence from Malaysia." IMF Working Paper WP/04/3. Washington, DC: International Monetary Fund.

Tapia, Matías, and Andrea Tokman. 2004. "Effects of Foreign Exchange Intervention Under Public Information: The Chilean Case." Economia, LACEA 4: 1–42.

Tashu, Melesse. 2014. "Motives and Effectiveness of Forex Interventions: Evidence from Peru." IMF Working Paper WP/14/217. Washington, DC: International Monetary Fund.

Taussig, Frank. 1928. International Trade. New York: MacMillan.

Taylor, Mark P., and Lucio Sarno. 1997. "Capital Flows to Developing Countries: Long- and Short-Term Determinants." World Bank Economic Review 11 (3): 451–470.

Terrier, Gilbert, Rodrigo Valdés, Camilo Tovar, Jorge Chan-Lau, Carlos Fernández-Valdovinos, Mercedes García-Escribano, Carlos Medeiros, Man-Keung Tang, Mercedes Vera Martin, and Chris Walker. 2011. "Policy Instruments to Lean against the Wind in Latin America." IMF Working Paper WP/11/159. Washington, DC: International Monetary Fund.

Thursby, Jerry, and Marie Thursby. 1987. "Bilateral Trade Flows, the Linder Hypothesis, and Exchange Risk." Review of Economics and Statistics 69 (3): 488–495.

Tobin, James. 1978. "A Proposal for International Monetary Reform." Eastern Economic Journal 4 (3–4): 153–159.

Tobin, James. 1996. "A Currency Transactions Tax, Why and How." Open Economics Review 7 (1): 493–499.

Tornell, Aarón, and Andrés Velasco. 1992. "The Tragedy of the Commons and Economic Growth: Why Does Capital Flow from Poor to Rich Countries?" Journal of Political Economy 100 (6): 1208–1231.

Tovar, Camilo E., Mercedes Garcia-Escribano, and Mercedes Vera Martin. 2012. "Credit Growth and the Effectiveness of Reserve Requirements and Other Macroprudential Instruments in Latin America." IMF Working Paper WP/12/142. Washington, DC: International Monetary Fund.

Valdes-Prieto, Salvador, and Marcelo Soto. 1998. "The Effectiveness of Capital Controls: Theory and Evidence from Chile." Empirica 25 (2): 133–164.

Vandenbussche, Jérôme, Ursula Vogel, and Enrica Detragiache. 2012. "Macroprudential Policies and Housing Prices—A New Database and Empirical Evidence for Central, Eastern, and Southeastern Europe." IMF Working Paper WP/12/303. Washington, DC: International Monetary Fund.

Viner, Jacob. 1928. "Political Aspects of International Finance." *Journal of Business of the University of Chicago* 1 (April): 141–173.

Volcker, Paul, and Toyoo Gyohten. 1992. *Changing Fortunes: The World's Money and the Threat to American Leadership.* New York: Three Rivers Press.

Wei, Shang-Jin. 2001. "Domestic Crony Capitalism and International Fickle Capital: Is There a Connection?" *International Finance* 4 (1): 15–45.

Weitzman, Martin. 1974. "Prices versus Quantities." *Review of Economic Studies* 41 (4): 477–491.

Williamson, John. 1990. "Latin American Adjustment: How Much Has Happened?" Washington, DC: Institute for International Economics.

Williamson, John. 2009. "A Short History of the Washington Consensus." *Law and Business Review of the Americas* 15 (1): 7–23.

Zhang, Longmei, and Edda Zoli. 2014. "Leaning against the Wind: Macroprudential Policy in Asia." IMF Working Paper WP/14/22. Washington, DC: International Monetary Fund.

# Index

Note: Italicized page numbers indicate tables, figures and boxes.

overview of management options for,
161–163, 182–183
policy instrument interaction with,
394–396, *395*
during surges, 142–143, *143*, 148–149
unavailability of conventional policy
instruments to address, 176–182, *178, 180*
vade mecum on response to, 382,
392–399, *395, 397–398*, 405nn24–25,
411–412
Macroeconomic policies. *See* Foreign
exchange rate policies;
Macroprudential policies; Monetary
policies
Macroprudential policies
active capital flows policy management
using, 8, 17, 19–20, *21*
balance-sheet vulnerabilities addressed
via, 216, 221, 228–229, *230, 231,*
232–233, 234, 400, *401, 402–404,* 404–407
capital controls distinction from, 8n11,
18–20, 253
countries' policy responses using, 240,
*240,* 253–259, *255, 256, 258–259,*
265–267, *266,* 270–273, *275,* 416–417
currency-based (*see* Currency-based or
FX-related prudential measures)
definition and description of, 19–20
effectiveness of, 280, 287–294, *288–289,*
*291, 293–294,* 297, *298,* 300, 303–318,
*304, 306–307, 309–310, 312–313, 315–318*
history of capital flows policies on, 63,
64, 77–78
inflation-targeting frameworks *vs.,*
209–212, *210–211*
liability- *vs.* asset-side measures in, *231,*
232–233
macroeconomic imbalances addressed
via, 163, 164, 166, *174,* 174–175,
176–178, 179–181, *180,* 182–183, 382n4,
393–396, *395,* 416
multilateral considerations with, *349,*
349–354, *352–353,* 358–359, 374–375,
*376–377*
nondiscriminatory prudential measures
as, 20, 24, 164n2, 209, 229, 253, *255,*
405n24
structural *vs.* cyclical, 24
vade mecum addressing use of, 381–382,
385, 387–388, *389–390,* 391, 393–396,
*395,* 400, *401, 402–404,* 404–407, 411–412

Malaysia
effectiveness of policy instruments in,
*296*
history of capital flows policies in, *57,* 58
policy responses in, *243, 246, 249*
surges in, *89, 157*
Mantega, Guido, 6
Maturity mismatches
as consequence of capital flows, 128
definition and description of, 16
riskiness of, 219, 400
Mexico
effectiveness of policy instruments in,
282, *283*
history of capital flows policies in, 34,
51n37
inflation-targeting frameworks in, *187*
policy responses in, *244, 247, 248, 250,*
*270, 274*
surges in, *89, 157*
Mirabeau, Marquis de, 29
Mitterand, François, 53
Monetary policies
active capital flows policy management
using, 8, 17, 18
capital controls reemergence in response
to, 5–7
countries' policy responses using,
239–240, *240,* 241–248, *242, 243–244,*
*246–247,* 251–253, *252,* 265–267, *266,*
*269, 275*
discretionary, *vs.* inflation-targeting
frameworks, 188, 191–200, *201,*
202–206, *203–205,* 210–211, *211,* 416
effectiveness of, 279
gold standard and (*see* Gold standard)
history of capital flows policies and,
74–75
interest rate changes via (*see* Interest
rates)
macroeconomic imbalances addressed
via, 166, 171, *172,* 176–181, *178, 180,*
182–183, 393–396, *395,* 415
multilateral considerations with,
383n6
signaling channel identifying future,
281
simulations for, 202–206, *203–205*
vade mecum addressing use of, 382, 387,
391, 393–396, *395,* 411–412
Morgenthau, Henry, 42